MASTERPLOTS II

POETRY SERIES
REVISED EDITION

MASTERPLOTS II

POETRY SERIES
REVISED EDITION

7

Skipper Ireson's Ride–Translations

Editor, Revised Edition
PHILIP K. JASON

Project Editor, Revised Edition
TRACY IRONS-GEORGES

Editors, Supplement
JOHN WILSON   **PHILIP K. JASON**

Editor, First Edition
FRANK N. MAGILL

SALEM PRESS

Pasadena, California   Hackensack, New Jersey

Editor in Chief: Dawn P. Dawson
Project Editor: Tracy Irons-Georges   *Research Supervisor:* Jeffry Jensen
Production Editor: Cynthia Beres   *Research Assistant:* Jeff Stephens
Copy Editor: Lauren Mitchell   *Acquisitions Editor:* Mark Rehn

Some of the essays in this work originally appeared in *Masterplots II, Poetry Series*, edited by Frank N. Magill (Pasadena, Calif.: Salem Press, Inc., 1992), and in *Masterplots II, Poetry Series Supplement*, edited by John Wilson and Philip K. Jason (Pasadena, Calif.: Salem Press, Inc., 1998).

∞ The paper used in these volumes conforms to the American National Standard for Permanence of Paper for Printed Library Materials, Z39.48-1992 (R1997).

Library of Congress Cataloging-in-Publication Data
Masterplots II. Poetry series.— Rev. ed. / editor, Philip K. Jason ; project editor, Tracy Irons-Georges
    p. ; cm.
    Rev. ed.: Masterplots two / Frank Northen Magill, 1992-1998.
    Includes bibliographical references and indexes.
    ISBN 1-58765-037-1 (set : alk. paper) — ISBN 1-58765-044-4 (vol. 7 : alk. paper) —
    1. Poetry — Themes, motives. I. Title: Masterplots two. II. Title: Masterplots 2. III. Jason, Philip K., 1941-   . IV. Irons-Georges, Tracy.

PN1110.5 .M37 2002
809.1—dc21

                                                                    2001055059

Second Printing

PRINTED IN THE UNITED STATES OF AMERICA

TABLE OF CONTENTS

TABLE OF CONTENTS

TABLE OF CONTENTS

MASTERPLOTS II

POETRY SERIES
REVISED EDITION

SKIPPER IRESON'S RIDE

Author: John Greenleaf Whittier (1807-1892)
Type of poem: Ballad
First published: 1857; collected in *Home Ballads and Poems*, 1860

The Poem

"Skipper Ireson's Ride," a ballad in nine eleven-line stanzas, is a story told through a third-person narrator who reports on the words and actions of the poem's characters but does not take part in them. Typically, a ballad presents one dramatic or exciting episode, not a fully developed story. As the title suggests, "Skipper Ireson's Ride" focuses on one brief moment in the man's life: his ride out of the town of Marblehead, Massachusetts.

The poem opens by harkening back to strange rides from legends and fables that would have been familiar to Whittier's nineteenth century educated audience: Apuleius on a golden ass, the Tartar king Calendar's ride on a brass horse, and Muhammad's winged mule. The tone is at the same time grand and ridiculous. Soon Ireson takes his place among this strange company, for it is revealed that Skipper Ireson's ride is not on a swift horse or chariot, as might be expected. Instead, the refrain (repeated with slight variation at the end of each stanza) introduces

> Old Floyd Ireson, for his hard heart,
> Tarred and Feathered and carried in a cart
> By the women of Marblehead!

The next two stanzas take up the action *in medias res*, as the women struggle with the cart and hurl insults at Ireson. Whittier uses exaggerated comparisons to heighten the grim humor. Ireson appears as a "rained-on fowl" with "body of turkey, head of owl." The rioting women, on the other hand, are compared with the Maenads, female followers of Bacchus, as they might appear "wild-eyed, free-limbed," on an ancient vase.

In the fourth stanza the poet explains the reason for Ireson's punishment: When his ship was sinking, full of his own townspeople, he sailed away and left the crew to drown. No motive is given for this action; the poem is concerned only with the punishment itself, dealt out by women who have lost their men because of Ireson's actions. Stanza 5 mourns the wrecked ship that "shall lie forevermore" and the women who "looked for the coming that might not be." The tone of stanzas 4 and 5 is mournful, with no traces of humor.

The sixth stanza returns to the action as the cart passes through the town, and old women and men lean out of their homes cursing. Suddenly, with the seventh stanza, the tone changes again, to a peaceful and lyrical description of the beautiful Salem road. For the first time, the poet focuses on Ireson himself, who sits numbly, unaware of the beautiful flowers beside the road or of the voices shouting at him. In stanza 8,

Ireson speaks for the first and only time, crying out that he can bear this punishment from his neighbors, but he cannot bear to face God and his own guilt. The poem ends with the women deciding to leave further punishment to God. With "half scorn, half pity," they release him and leave him "alone with his shame and sin."

Forms and Devices

"Skipper Ireson's Ride" has often been considered the greatest American ballad of the nineteenth century. Part of its strength lies in Whittier's skillful juxtaposition of specific local elements—a common element in his most successful ballads—with references to the ancient world of classical poetry. The most obvious example of this juxtaposition occurs in the refrain. When the refrain is spoken by the narrator, it is in formal, educated language, but when the village women cry out the refrain, the poet presents their distinctive Marblehead dialect, and "Tarred and feathered and carried in a cart" becomes "Torr'd an' futherr'd an' corr'd in a corrt." No comment is made about the shift; the poet simply wants to reader to hear the poem told in two distinct voices.

Specific references to local geography, including the names of Marblehead, Chaleur Bay, and the Salem road, place the action of the poem firmly in the real world. At the same time, comparisons of Ireson to Apuleius or Muhammad, and of the women to conch-blowing followers of Bacchus, elevate the story to the realm of the fantastic. The women are both real-life residents of a real fishing village, surrounded by its fog and rain, hearing winds and seabirds, smelling apple blossoms and lilacs, and also mythical creatures, the stuff of story and song. Again, the narrator does not call attention to the contrasts. This matter-of-fact juxtaposition claims for the story of Skipper Ireson a place among the greats; the rustic citizens of old Marblehead are not only poor fishing folk but also representatives of the passionate emotions that define humanity.

Those passionate emotions do not exist one at a time in the human heart. Love, hate, anger, pity, and sorrow may appear in one person all at once, especially in a time of grief. As the critic John Pickard has ably demonstrated, Whittier's sudden shifts in the poem echo the shifting emotions experienced by the surviving townspeople. Thus the focus moves abruptly in and out, backward and forward, from a wide historical overview to a direct look (but from a distance) at the feathered Ireson, from a wide-angle crowd scene to a flashback of the sinking ship, back to the crowd, then to a serene look at beautiful scenery followed by a tightly focused look at Ireson. Similarly, the background noises in the story change from "shouting and singing" with "conch-shells blowing and fish-horns' twang" to the shouted conversation between the doomed fishermen and Ireson, to the silence of the wrecked ship with only "winds and sea-birds" for sound, to the hoarse and "treble" cursing of the older villagers, to the calm beauty of the Salem road, and finally to Ireson's pitiable outcry and the women's "soft relentings." This cacophony of sound and silence, along with the shifting visual focus, keeps the reader off balance, heightening the dramatic tension.

Themes and Meanings

The meaning of "Skipper Ireson's Ride" is encapsulated in the refrain, in the central figure's transformation from "Old Floyd Ireson" in the first stanza to "Poor Floyd Ireson" in the last. During the poem, Ireson changes, or his neighbors' perception of him changes, from a man to be hated and cursed to one to be treated with scorn yet pity. The theme of a person coming to a new understanding is as old as literature, and often this acquisition of new knowledge or insight involves a journey. The journey might be a protracted one through a long work such as Homer's *The Odyssey* or Dante's *The Divine Comedy*, or a brief visit from city to country or from country to city, or even a short ride out of town on a rail. The technique of echoing a psychological or moral journey by a literal journey through space is effectively employed here.

For the characters of Whittier's New England poems, the themes of transformation and redemption, and of error and correction, were best understood in a Christian religious context. The mob of women who have tarred and feathered Skipper Ireson act from the human emotions of grief and rage, and they seek human vengeance. Their method of punishment is to humiliate Ireson, to make him (or show him to be) less than a man. Yet they are not fully human in their own actions; with the exception of the brief mournful passage in stanza 5, they are seen only as a mob, never as individuals.

When Ireson at last cries out his confession, everything changes. Instantly, the shouting stops. With his first cry of "Hear me, neighbors" there is the possibility of seeing the characters not just as mob and victim—us and them—but as members of the same community. Ireson acknowledges his guilt and points out that his shame before his neighbors can never pain him as much as his pain before God. As the women are called to remember their own relationships with God, they too are transformed. They begin to step forward as individuals, "the wife of the skipper lost at sea" or "an old wife mourning her only son." When they become individuals again, standing themselves before God, their own hard hearts start to soften. They do not reach perfect grace or perfect forgiveness, but with "half scorn, half pity" they release Ireson and give him a cloak. It is left to the narrator, not the women, to refer to the captain now as "Poor Floyd Ireson."

The poem ends with Ireson alone and ashamed. There is no moral statement at the end. The narrator reveals nothing of Ireson's motive for his betrayal of the fishermen or of what happens to him after he acknowledges his sin. Perhaps he implies that these matters are not the reader's concern, that they should remain between Ireson and God.

Whittier based his poem on a fragment of a folk song he learned from a schoolmate, expanding on that fragment with a story of his own imagining. Years after the poem was published, he learned that Ireson actually had not been responsible for the abandoning of the ship but had been blamed for it by an unscrupulous crew.

Cynthia A. Bily

SKUNK HOUR

Author: Robert Lowell (1917-1977)
Type of poem: Lyric
First published: 1958; collected in *Life Studies*, 1959

The Poem

"Skunk Hour" is written in free verse, but with a formal pattern of eight six-line stanzas (sestets) with a loosely regular rhyme scheme. The title suggests a particular hour in the day—the hour when skunks are likely to come out—and implies that this hour occurs on a regular basis. The title hints that time will be an important element in the poem.

Set in Maine, where Robert Lowell had a summer home, the poem begins by showing a series of events that denote a decaying society: The elderly heiress has bought up the houses facing hers and let them go to ruin; the millionaire has lost his money and auctioned off his yacht; the homosexual decorator has used the tools of fishing (net, cork, and awl) to brighten his shop. These events suggest that the human order has somehow gone wrong. They are narrated as one tells a story, in the third person. Although they are recounted in the present tense, in each case the action has already occurred.

Beginning with the fifth stanza, exactly halfway through the poem, the poet enters in the first person. (Lowell's biography almost insists that the speaker and the poet be considered identical.) He remembers (in the past tense) "one dark night" when he drove his "Tudor Ford" up the hill to watch for lovers in their cars. In the only metaphor of the poem, he describes the cars as though they were boats, lying together "hull to hull." He concludes, "My mind's not right." From this point on, the poet speaks from immediate experience, and it becomes increasingly clear that the external circumstances of the first four stanzas reflect the poet's vision of himself.

From stanza 6 on, the reader "overhears" the poet's thoughts, as in a more conventional lyric. The poet listens to a love song on the radio and feels himself to be loveless, tormented: "I myself am hell," he says, in a phrase layered with reference. At the same time that the poet speaks it in the present, its reference is to John Milton's Satan in *Paradise Lost* (1667), which, in turn, refers to Dante's *La divina commedia* (c. 1320; *The Divine Comedy*). In this way, Lowell places himself in a literary history.

The actual present moment of this poem does not occur until the seventh stanza, when the skunks march down Main Street. The poet feels almost invisible, standing on the back steps, lonely and isolated, watching a mother skunk and her kittens march past the Trinitarian church, past him, to the garbage pail. He sees their glinting eyes in the moonlight and knows that they see him. The mother skunk, intent on a cup of sour cream, does not do what skunks can do when they are threatened; she simply looks back to the food and drops her tail.

The poem ends with the skunk's refusal to react, which seems important. She "will not scare." It is as if Lowell, by allowing time to flow around him, finds in the one present moment some answer to his sense of failure and alienation. The outside world had reflected the inner hell, but, in this moment of stillness, when the tail is lowered, there is affirmation. Whether it is an affirmation that resolves the problem of identity and relationship to others, the reader cannot know.

Forms and Devices

In *Life Studies*, 1959, Lowell broke from the formal verse for which he was already famous to write in free-verse lines. "Skunk Hour" is its final poem, unfolding in a pattern that exhibits Lowell's sure sense of rhyme. A quick examination of each stanza reveals its particular variation. "Skunk Hour" is more a study in sound, however; with its dense, packed language, it is very difficult to read aloud. There is often evidence of an iambic beat, as though that were the ghost rhythm on which the poem was built. Examples of this rhythm are the moments when the speaker says "My mind's not right" and the final line "and will not scare."

Sound seems, somehow, to mirror meaning. The shift from a continuous past to an active present is marked by a shift of consonants. The early use of *l* sounds—the soothing sound of the past—changes, in the later stanzas, into a harsh, intense present dominated by *r* and *k* sounds. In addition, an urgency of accented syllables, or stresses, alters the tone of the poem as it moves into the present. "They march on their soles up Main Street:/ white stripes, moonstruck eyes' red fire" (with its many spondees) slows the voice for emphasis.

Shortly after seeing Allen Ginsberg read his poetry in San Francisco in March, 1957, Lowell began to feel that his own poems were stiff and humorless. In *Life Studies*, published two years later, he worked to make them clearer and more colloquial. "Skunk Hour" is dedicated to the poet Elizabeth Bishop, whose work Lowell greatly admired. Her poem "The Armadillo" served as a model; Lowell admired its straightforward images and its use of fact. The images in "Skunk Hour" reveal a new directness of his own. Even such a strange and visually uncertain image as "A red fox stain covers Blue Hill" refers, in actuality, to a particular fall color in a specific place. There is also a hint of violence in the use of the word "stain," a foreshadowing of his mental state. The effect of these specific details is one of intimacy, but not necessarily of coherence. The reader sees things as the poet apprehends them. With equal ease, one sees into the mind of the poet as one experiences, with him, a moment of extreme pain. Nothing is cushioned through metaphor; the poem is harsh in its honesty.

There are layers of time working within "Skunk Hour." "Century," "season," "now," "night," "hour"—time seems to condense as though it were working toward the final moment on the steps. Yet the hour occurs nightly, so it expands in the form of recurrence—the recurrence of a natural order suggested by the skunks themselves. Time is, in some sense, the very subject of the poem. In this way, the poem could be said to work on a metaphorical level, but it is clearly left up to the reader to decide the meaning.

Themes and Meanings

Robert Lowell's poems demonstrate the fusion of a personal and historical past. Time blurs, yet the stasis achieved only emphasizes loss and a sense of an irretrievable past. The poems move inward, deepening their colors. Each successive layer of time adds texture and insight.

As the culminating poem of *Life Studies*, "Skunk Hour" ends a book that traces the deterioration of Western civilization, the demise of Lowell's prominent American family, and the disintegration of the poet's sense of self. Questioning his own sanity, Lowell exhibits what has come to be known as the "confessional" stance. He allows the reader to act as the priest, hearing the confession. It must be cautioned that the reader is priest, not psychiatrist. The object of confession is absolution and a state of grace. In Lowell, there is a sense of the life examined, over and over, in search of salvation. Other confessional poets, such as John Berryman and Sylvia Plath, do not necessarily reveal such a desire for redemption, but Lowell's poems always seem to be striving for a moment of grace.

Seen in this light, the "chalk dry and spar spire" of the Trinitarian church can be seen to represent the failure of religion to offer twentieth century answers. In his essay "On 'Skunk Hour,'" in *The Collected Prose* (1987), Lowell himself declared, "My night is not gracious, but secular, puritan, and agnostic. An existentialist night." In this personal wasteland, Lowell laments that the social order has failed him, that he has failed himself. His own narrowed circumstances have been placed in history, set against the backdrop of the town and against the living memory of the dark night that occasioned the poet's malaise.

"Skunk Hour" might be simply another poem about humankind's inability to live within its own history, an alien creature on the earth. There is a moment, however, when the poem literally stops and holds its pose for a moment before going on. The speaker holds his breath. The mother skunk drops her tail. This is the moment when she decides to live and let live, disdaining an entry into the human world. The skunks are seen with a mixture of awe and amusement. Lowell refuses to end the poem on a note of transcendence; a flat statement of fact will have to suffice. The affirmation is ambiguous at best.

"Skunk Hour" is a combination of two modes of perception—memory and attention. It is rooted in attention, in the perception of the moment, yet memory is the medium through which the present is seen. Thus it carries the present and past simultaneously. The poem's cumulative effect is a meshing of time; it comes back into phase with itself. The final synthesis comes from a fullness and complexity surrounding the lyric moment. The present hell is only understood through the past—the "dark night" that allowed the poet, and therefore the reader, to find a source of hope in the skunk's active presence in the night.

Judith Kitchen

THE SLATE ODE

Author: Osip Mandelstam (1891-1938)
Type of poem: Ode
First published: 1928, as "Grifel'naia oda," in *Stikhotvoreniya*; English translation collected in *Poems*, 1973

The Poem

"The Slate Ode," written in 1923, is one of Osip Mandelstam's longer poems, consisting of nine stanzas of regular iambic tetrameter. That is the traditional Russian odic meter, although Mandelstam chooses an eight-line stanza over the more typical ten-line stanza. Calling his work an ode, Mandelstam is associating himself with the archaizing drive among Russian post-Symbolists, since the use of generic labels such as "ode" or "elegy" as a way of marking meaningful distinctions had been in decline since the 1830's, along with the hierarchy of poetic forms which held for the eighteenth century.

The modernist revival of such forms as the ode is part of an attempt to model a continuous history in an age of war and revolution, an age in which, as Mandelstam once wrote, "the contemporary European has been evicted from his own biography." "The Slate Ode" not only revives an archaic genre but also alludes to a specific predecessor poem, "Reka vremen" ("The River of Time"), composed on a slate tablet by the great eighteenth century poet Gavrila Derzhavin just before his death in 1816.

Mandelstam's poem seems to take as its setting a starry night landscape, in which stone and water (the elements of "The Slate Ode" and "The River of Time") predominate. For several reasons, however, this landscape will not stabilize. First, one of its elements, a flinty path, is said to come from an old song, and "song," in Russian verse, is a synonym for "poem." Second, there are no identifiable references to location; instead, the linguistic quality of the setting is emphasized in this poem which speaks of "the speech of slate and air." Third, the components that might suggest a specific setting will not stay in their expected places: If the poem locates a slate-pencil drawing on the "layered rock of the clouds," the landscape motifs must be primarily figurative. In other words, the details are not occasioned by a particular place but point instead to the movement of the poet's consciousness.

The poet appears in the second stanza, contained within a "we" that is characterized by a sheepish somnolence. By contrast, nature, represented by geological motifs, is an active writer, whose rough draft, written with water on the earth's surface, is ripening. In the third stanza, this draft is figured as a precipitous, deeply etched, stony landscape, rendered metaphorically as a vision of steeply vertical cities.

The fourth and fifth stanzas emphasize time rather than space. It is night, the time of poetic creativity, and the transient impressions of the day are fading. The fifth stanza—the "hinge" of the poem—announces a condition of ripeness, which in the following two stanzas will be transfered from nature to the materials in the poetic imagination; that is, the fruit ripened to bursting is the poem ready to take shape. Only now, having achieved access to his creative resources, does the poet speak as an "I," the first-person singular appearing in stanza 6. In stanza 7, the voice of memory and of the poetic tradition brings understanding and directs the poet's hand in a transcription that is at once instantaneous and firm. (For Mandelstam, the poetic legacy is carried by the voice, because he believed that a poet's verses preserved his actual voice.)

As is typical for Mandelstam, the triumph of the creative process triggers reflections on the poet's self-definition, which is the theme of the eighth stanza. In the final stanza, which closely echoes the first, the poet claims his place within Russian poetry, declaring his intention to effect a junction between his own verse and the verse of his great predecessors.

Forms and Devices

One of the characteristic features of Mandelstam's writings is his refusal to accept the modern opposition between nature and culture. Instead, he sees them as continuous with each other; as he put it in the opening line of "Priroda—tot zhe Rim," a 1914 lyric (the first clause is also the title), "Nature is the same as Rome, and was reflected in it." All of "The Slate Ode" is built on a master metaphor that equates nature and culture, or the physical processes of nature and the work of the poet. All that is already contained in the poem's key word, "slate."

Besides being a synecdoche for Derzhavin's last poem, the motif of slate triggers the whole string of geological images on the one hand and the image of the writer's slate pencil, the emblem of his poetic activity, on the other. In an illustrative example of the fusion of culture and nature, the scratching of the poet's pencil becomes the "slate screech," and the pencil points mutate into the beaks of fledgling birds.

More generally, geological history, pictured as writing, is imbued with conscious intention, while poetry becomes a form of natural history, of attending to nature's writing. On an even more abstract plane, mind and earth become each other's analogues. For example, water flowing back to its underground sources is a metaphor for poetic resources which are not yet ready to emerge from the unconscious. By the same token, a vertiginous landscape prefigures the soaring of the poet's imagination.

Finally, the equation of geology with poetry in the poem's ruling metaphor is implicated in Mandelstam's revision of Derzhavin. "The River of Time" is a deeply pessimistic meditation, which asserts that historical memory and poetry alike are doomed to oblivion. By contrast, "The Slate Ode" implies that although the cultural record must contain its terrors and violent shifts, poetry, like the geological record, can preserve everything. For Mandelstam, the water does not destroy but rather writes.

Themes and Meanings

When it first appeared, Mandelstam's "Slate Ode" was attacked for its obscurity; in subsequent years, however, it has been considered one of his masterpieces. It dates from a time of transition, a period of intense poetic creativity that would be succeeded by five years in which Mandelstam would write no verse. The poem is part of a prolonged attempt at stocktaking, in which the poet must decide what legacy he will bring from his prerevolutionary Russian-Jewish past into his postrevolutionary identity as a contributor to Soviet Russian literature. Hence his acceptance (in stanza 8) of the synthetic identity of the "double-dealer, with a double soul" and his refusal of the organic identity, suggested by such traditional trades as that of the "mason," "roofer," or "boatman" (the Russian more commonly means "shipbuilder").

Mandelstam's list of trades is full of suggestiveness for the Russian reader; the young Peter the Great, for example, worked in a Dutch shipyard and became the "shipbuilder" of the Russian Navy. The term "mason," however, is more likely to trigger associations for the English-speaking reader, who may be aware of the conspiracy theories, which antidemocractic and anti-Semitic forces have revived, linking the Masonic movement and the Jews. In Mandelstam's Russian, the dual reference to the mason's trade and to freemasonry is stronger. Hence, one implication of the poet's self-definition is a rejection of anti-Semitic stereotypes.

Mandelstam's prose and verse alike in the early and mid-1920's are filled with eschatological forebodings. While Mandelstam never conclusively abandoned the faith in revolution acquired in his formative years, he was only too aware of the antihuman values which were taking shape in the Soviet Union. Generally contemptuous of the past, the emerging Soviet worldview seemed to threaten the highest values transmitted by Russian culture with annihilation. If he makes of his ode a dialogue with Derzhavin's deathbed verses, it is because Mandelstam feels the attraction of Derzhavin's final judgment on human effort.

For the rest of his career, Mandelstam's verse will struggle against the threat of being separated from its own wellsprings. In "The Slate Ode," as in much of Mandelstam's verse from this period on, a frequently elliptical poetic language will encrypt the past to preserve it for the future. Humble, everyday objects will become the cryptograms for encoding the cultural text. Whereas the young Mandelstam had confidently measured his own ambitions against the glory of a Gothic cathedral ("Notre Dame," 1912), in "The Slate Ode" he makes the fragile pencil, scratching away at its indelible record, the emblem of his poetic mission.

Charles Isenberg

THE SLEEPERS

Author: Walt Whitman (1819-1892)

Type of poem: Lyric

First published: 1855, untitled, in *Leaves of Grass*; as "Night Poem," in *Leaves of Grass*, 1856; as "Sleep-Chasings," in *Leaves of Grass*, 1860; as "The Sleepers," in *Leaves of Grass*, 1871

The Poem

In its final version, "The Sleepers" contains 184 lines, in free verse, divided into eight sections with varying numbers of lines. In the first section, the speaker overcomes initial disorientation by fixing his attention on the ordered arrangement of sleepers, from children in their cradles to a mother sleeping with her child "carefully wrapt." The poet embraces all in his vision, arranging them in pairs of opposites. He pauses to comfort the restless. He lies down with others, to become each and all; he enters their dreams and becomes "a dance" of vitality. He encounters strange, delightful companions who move with him, "a gay gang of blackguards." The poet-speaker becomes both beloved and lover at the end of the first section: He is the woman waiting in the dark, and he is the man who arrives to love; then he is confused between them, as he becomes the dark itself. Finally, he fades away with the dark.

The second section is a descent toward death. Here the speaker is first an old woman, then a "sleepless widow," and finally a shroud covering a corpse in its coffin, in its grave.

In the third section, the speaker bursts from the grave to watch a swimmer battling "swift-running eddies" of the sea. The poet helplessly calls out for the sea to cease its assault on the swimming man, but the scene ends with the drowning of the swimmer, whose body is dashed until his corpse is driven out of sight.

As if from the same beach as in section 3, the next section reports an account of a shipwreck. Here, the poet hears sounds of distress and cries of fear that diminish into nothingness. Again, the speaker feels the nightmare experience of helplessness as he runs back and forth on the beach in a futile effort to prevent the wreck. Bodies are washed ashore, and the poet helps carry them to a barn, where they are laid out in rows, like all the other sleepers of the vision.

The fifth section retains the beach location as the speaker assumes the posture of George Washington at the Battle of Brooklyn Heights, in which the general suffers for his dying soldiers. This dissolves into a later scene of Washington bidding his soldiers farewell at the end of the war.

Section 6 continues the historical retrospective, though here it is more personal; the poet identifies with his mother in one of her memories. The object of vision here is a beautiful "red squaw" who visited the homestead of the poet's mother; that woman, seen only once, has remained in the memory of the mother to become the vision of the poet.

Section 7 initiates a series of "returns." The sleepers dream of their homes. In a context of autumnal harvest, the poet gathers in the dreams of his sleepers: Sailors dream of sailing home; exiles, of returning to their native lands; emigrants from Ireland, Holland, and numerous other European countries dream of returning whence they came. In the poet's vision, however, there is no difference between going out and coming in. All "are averaged now," with differences and degrees dissolved by "night and sleep" into the beauty of "peace." In this condition, the soul is released to "enclose the world" in an order promising perfection to all. Grotesque distortions of human form "wait" for the beauty promised by spirit: "the twisted skull waits, the watery or rotten blood waits."

The poem concludes with a grand procession of humanity, as the sleepers "flow hand in hand" even as they lie prone in sleep. Here, the poet envisions a spiritual transfiguration of individuals into a universal brotherhood, awakening to a new reality in their sleeping dreams. Men and women join hands forever, as do fathers and sons, mothers and daughters, old and young, masters and slaves. Bodies are transformed by spiritual awakening, as the poet himself returns, entrusting himself to the night, every night, to be its lover as well as its child.

Forms and Devices

Each section of "The Sleepers" contains a varying number of stanzas, or verse paragraphs, with varying numbers of lines of free verse. Each stanzaic unit is also a grammatical whole, a statement complete in itself, whose form generally extends a first line into longer and longer lines. This creates an impression of energetic progress, from line to line, stanza to stanza, section to section.

Although each line of verse is "free" (that is, unmeasured), it is not without form. The devices that give form to the poem are parallelism, repetition, and controlled point of view. The most emphatic is parallelism. There is a balancing of grammatical units, usually at the beginnings of lines, to create a "rhetorical rhyme." For example, in the first stanza of section 1, lines 2 through 5 are introduced with present participles: "Stepping," "Bending," "Wandering," and "Pausing." These create continuous action, present process. The second stanza of section 1 consists of two lines, each beginning with the same word, "How": a couplet of initial, exact rhyme. Stanzas 3 through 5 in section 1 are a series (a catalog) of phrases and clauses introduced by "The." These lines of noun phrases (third-person objects) are countered in later stanzas with parallel first-person openings: "I stand," "I pass," "I go," and so on. Parallelism occurs at the ends as well as at the beginnings of lines, through repetition of the same grammatical forms and, sometimes, the same word: "sleep" or "sleeps" ends eight lines between lines 15 and 25.

Images of movement abound in the poem, outward balancing inward movement: The speaker "steps" out to start the poem, "pierces the darkness," "descends," "turns," and finally "returns." This movement is governed by a controlling "I" as a central point of view, outside the vision at the same time it enters and moves through the vision. The final three stanzas of the poem appropriately turn around initial, parallel line openings on the word "I"; seven of the last eight lines begin this way, as if each line were a radius emanating from a central "I." The subject "I," however, does not finally dominate, and a sense of great egotism is avoided since the final word of the poem is "you."

Themes and Meanings

Although the poem took different titles over the years of its revisions (indicating that it resisted the final formulation that a title can impose), its settled title focuses upon the figures asleep in a night of the poet's dreaming. The poet-speaker is one of the sleepers, but he is also all of them at once in his "vision" of them asleep, of them awake, and of them dead and dying. He enters the dreams of sleepers to become the figures of their dreams, just as they are the figures of his dreams.

There are three points of view, perhaps four, in "The Sleepers." The subject of sleeping becomes a theme of interest because of these shifting points of view, as sleeping is turned from a literal into a metaphorical term: physical sleep (as death-in-life), with its resting physical energy, is transformed into the spiritual energy of life-in-death. The mode of this transformation is poetic vision, a power of imagination capable of penetrating all objects; it reshapes the grotesque, shapes the shapeless, and restores life to the lifeless.

The most self-conscious point of view is that of the poet-speaker, who announces his movements of consciousness; he is aware that he sleeps and dreams in his sleep. This speaking subject is like the subject of psychoanalysis, the one who reports a dream as a memory recollected from sleep. There is another, more constricted, speaker *within* the poet-as-speaker: one who moves within the dream, the representative of the dreamer. The poem presents a double subject, waking and dreaming speakers. The dreaming speaker also divides, first into two, and then into several others. The first division produces a dream figure who can move as a sleeping companion with all other sleepers in the dream; the second division occurs when the representative of the dreamer enters the dreams of others, to become an "other" and many "others." The outermost limit is reached in the blankness of death. Rebelling against this blankness, the multiple points of view reorganize to become one again at the end, and the cycle is poised to repeat itself.

The meaning that emerges from this plurality of points of view is that life is various but unified. The poet's vision comprehends differences as spiritual communion, and sleep is the vehicle for the visionary experience born of "mother" night. Capable of healing and renewal, the poet is godlike, and his poem is creative.

Richard D. McGhee

SLEEPING IN THE WOODS

Author: David Wagoner (1926-   )
Type of poem: Lyric
First published: 1973; collected in *Sleeping in the Woods*, 1974

The Poem

"Sleeping in the Woods" is a poem composed of forty-eight lines of free verse that seems to ebb and flow on the page. The gerund in the title (sleeping), along with other verbals (participles and gerunds usually ending "-ing"), is common in David Wagoner's poems and notably in their titles. The first poem in the collection *Sleeping in the Woods* is "The Singing Lesson," and other titles in that book include "Talking to Barr Creek," "Beginning," "Living in the Ruins," "An Offering for Dungeness Bay," and "Raging." Discounting such nouns and pronouns as "ceiling," "morning," and "anything" that end in "-ing," Wagoner includes some forty verbals in this poem, which leaves readers with a sense of flow that may suggest progression, abundance, or change. Certainly the use of verbals keeps the poem in motion and does not allow either stability or rest, despite what the title might imply.

Wagoner is fond of confronting an undesignated character in his poems by using the second-person "you," which tends to lure readers into identifying themselves with that character while the poet remains somewhat distant as a teacher or adviser. The voice of the poet, which can even be godlike at times, may be compassionate and genuinely helpful, or it may be sinisterly ironic. Many of Wagoner's best poems (including this one) are meditative in nature, but the tone is conversational. He enjoys moving between the profound and the playful, with much of the playfulness dependent on the ambiguous nature of language. Readers must always be prepared for puns, sometimes very serious ones, almost none of which are accidental in Wagoner's poems.

In the opening lines of the poem, the speaker indicates that "you" are lost in the woods and must bed down for the night. In the third line he writes, "you have nothing," and for an instant the reader is confronted with annihilation; however, that instant lasts for only as long as it takes to read the next line: "you have nothing/ But part of yourself to lie on." Wagoner depicts the character in the poem "standing," "kneeling," "crouching," "turning over old leaves," and "going under" in the process of bedding down. The play on "going under" suggests simply crawling in under the leaves but also being ruined or overwhelmed. In this process, the person (or persona) in the poem becomes "like any animal" entering "the charmed circle/ Of the night," but the human body is awkward and not readily adaptable for such a purpose. The speaker represents the persona as stiff-necked, "One ear-flap at a time knuckling your skull."

The phrase "But now" that opens the fifteenth line indicates a second movement in the poem, in which the persona is "lying still," watching the shadows, and going to sleep ("not *falling* asleep," the speaker advises, not losing anything to the earth beneath) without a ceiling or walls. The persona is now settled down at "the place where it is always/ Light"; that is, the persona is entering a dream state, and dreams may reveal deep truths. The dream, however, may be "sunk in blood," and all night the mind might plague the sleeper with fear of being food for wild animals. The speaker teases the persona by suggesting that the persona's body ("hidebound substance") might provide food for the very low ("mites") or the very high ("angels").

Near the end of line 37, the speaker quite casually advises, "Turn up/ In time, at the first faint stretch of dawn, and you'll see/ A world pale-green as hazel." The awakening is lyrical and rejuvenating as the persona's "cupped hand" is "lying open/ . . . in the morning like a flower." It is not at all unusual for Wagoner to resort to a pun as he ends a poem: "Making light of it,/ You have forgotten why you came, have served your purpose, and simply/ By being here have found the right way out./ Now, you may waken." Whatever it was that drew the persona into the woods has been rendered trivial by the experience of having come to terms with it.

Forms and Devices

Wagoner has compared the undulating lines in this and several other of his poems to a sine wave or an expansion-contraction pulsation. Typically, readers encounter a long line with five or six heavily stressed syllables, then a shorter one of four or five stresses, and then an even shorter one of just two or three stressed syllables. On the page, these lines look almost like tercets (three-line stanzas), but they are not self-contained units; that is, the loosely constructed sentences flow over the line endings, prompting readers to anticipate one thing at the end of a line only to be surprised by the first word or phrase in the next line. Most of Wagoner's lines end without punctuation marks (enjambment), and the sentences are often quite lengthy (one of them in this poem is nearly 170 words long and rambles over twenty-three lines). The effect of this kind of syntax and line play is to keep readers alert, but the result of being an attentive reader of a poem by Wagoner is not so often clarity as it is an awareness of the multiple meanings of words and of the events they define. The ambiguity is intentional.

The greatest risk Wagoner takes in the poem is that of the verbals themselves and the possibility that readers will be annoyed by the repetitive use of the "-ing" ending. However, he often uses such rhetorical devices as parallelism to create a sense of balance and poise, as in these lines near the middle of the poem: "The ground beneath you neither rising nor falling,/ Neither giving nor taking." Wagoner's ear is attuned to the subtleties of sound, and a careful reading aloud of certain passages will reveal patterns of alliteration and assonance that account for the lyrical or musical impact common to the best unrhymed, free-verse poems: "Whoever stumbles across you in the dark may borrow/ Your hidebound substance for encouragement/ Of mites or angels." The soft *m*'s and *b*'s and the prevailing short vowel sounds become the major key. Later, near the end of the poem, the reader becomes especially conscious of long *e* and *i* sounds: "The chalk-green convolute lichen by your hand like sea fog,/ The fallen tree beside you in half-light/ Dreaming a greener sapling." Wagoner closes his poem with an assonantal triangle featuring the long *a:* "By being here have found the right way out./ Now you may waken."

Themes and Meanings

This poem opens with a dependent clause: "Not having found your way out." The speaker then uses the imperative mode: "begin/ Looking for somewhere to bed down at nightfall." In pointing out that the persona in the poem has "nothing/ But part of yourself to lie on," the speaker implies that the persona must now lie on the bare ground and that the persona has only the self on whom to rely. In the "charmed circle/ Of the night," the persona will discover the way out of the woods, presumably out of confusion and uncertainty. In effect, as the penultimate line declares, the experience of being lost will lead the persona to find "the right way out." One runs into such circumstances frequently in literature and life. Dante Alighieri's persona in *La Divina commedia* (c. 1320; *The Divine Comedy*) is lost "in a dark woods," where he is confronted by wild beasts. A common, paradoxical motif of mysticism holds that light breaks forth out of darkness or that one must become aware of being lost in order to find one's way, and the result is a spiritual awakening or "enlightenment." Essentially, that is what happens in this poem.

The key to the enlightenment of the persona may be found about midway through the poem, where the persona is described as sleeping without ceiling or walls for the first time. In direct contact with the "imponderable" earth, the threshold between the ordinary and the extraordinary, between the conscious and the unconscious, and between sight and insight is depicted as "slackening." The "place where it is always/ Light" is the dream world of the unconscious where the stars that are concealed by leaves and branches in ordinary forests "burn/ At the mattering source/ Forever." Although the playfully sinister speaker teases the persona with the possibility of being reduced to physical food for mites and spiritual sustenance for angels, the persona is assured that "whatever they can't keep is yours for the asking." The persona then promptly "sees" the beauties of the green world and light, and whatever problems led that person into the woods are forgotten. It is at that point, only in the last line of the poem, that the speaker informs the persona, "Now, you may waken." The theme of spiritual awakening, of regeneration and enlightenment through the medium of solitude in nature, is fundamental to this poem.

Ron McFarland

SMALL TOWN WITH ONE ROAD

Author: Gary Soto (1952-   )
Type of poem: Lyric
First published: 1985; collected in *Who Will Know Us*, 1990

The Poem

"Small Town with One Road" is a short poem in free verse, its thirty-three lines forming one stanza. The title suggests a quiet poem, and it is, presenting a reflective commentary on life within the valley as compared with a life beyond. The poem is written in the first person. The speaker is a father, and he and his daughter are contemplating their view of the valley, but the speaker is primarily addressing the reader.

The first section of the poem is primarily descriptive, as Soto depicts the lives of Mexican American farm workers and their families in a hot, dry valley in central California. A road of black asphalt runs through the valley, a road that Soto later uses symbolically as a dividing line between the hard life in the valley and life beyond. "Kids could make it" across, he says, literally meaning that they could "leap barefoot" to the little store where they buy candy and snowcones. Before describing what could be considered the children's bleak future, Soto reminds the reader that these children are like all children, eager to taste the sweetness of candy on their tongues. The lives of the children in the valley include "a dog for each hand,/ Cats, chickens in the yard." At home, the children hear cooking in the kitchen and know they will be having beans for dinner, as they usually do: "Brown soup that's muscle for field work." The universality of the life of manual labor is underscored by the next two lines, "Okie or Mexican, Jew that got lost,/ It's a hard life where the sun looks." The poem is about all migrant workers, no matter what their heritage.

The poem shifts when the view changes from the fields to a life just beyond, one where the "cotton gin stands tall in the money dream." The mill represents a more substantial amount of money, a true "paycheck for the wife." The poem then shifts again; the last section of the poem is contemplative and personal. "We could go back," the poet thinks. The phrase echoes the first words of the poem, "We could be here," the full meaning of which now becomes clear: The poet has lived here before and is speaking of a life he knows personally. He muses, "I could lose my job,/ This easy one that's only words": He could then be working in the fields or performing other manual labor. As he and his daughter eat their snowcones along the roadside, he sees a young boy crossing the road, " He's like me,'/ I tell my daughter." The poem ends on a hopeful note as the boy leaps "Across the road where riches/ Happen on a red tongue."

Forms and Devices

Soto is a noted author who grew up in California, the son of working-class Mexican American parents; he experienced the rigors of working as a migrant laborer. Knowing two worlds as he does, his sparse language mirrors the world in which he grew up.

The poem's sentence structure is powerful because it is direct. "We could be here," Soto begins. Later, in parallel language, he thinks, "We could go back." In between he explains and describes, using few poetic devices. The poem contains only one simile, an ironic one. Papa's field "wavered like a mirage"—not like the oasis which might be envisioned by a straggler in the desert, but a world so intense that a fieldworker's vision of it shimmers in the heat. The blur of the field becomes the blur of life, a kind of blindness that occurs when sights must be set on little beyond day-by-day existence.

Personification reinforces the connection that Soto feels with those on both sides of the highway. The highway is "big-eyed/ With rabbits that won't get across," an image of anyone trying to escape from the valley without "look[ing] both ways," something the "brown kid" knows how to do at the end of the poem. He knows how to leave the "hard life where the sun looks." The sun is personified; it does not merely shine but "looks" fiercely, the strength of the "look" making work in the field that much more tiresome and difficult. Soto writes of the cotton gin's appeal, a means beyond the field to earn more money to change one's life circumstances. "The cotton gin stands tall," prompting the reader to envision someone with head erect, chin out, shoulders back— an image resonant with being proud of one's industry and accomplishment.

It is noteworthy how this image contrasts with that of the fieldworkers, of the bean pickers as they bend over, day after day, to harvest. Nor is it like the image of the fruit pickers whose heads and shoulders are lost amid the branches of the fruit trees. For the fieldworker, gone is the clarity of figure and accomplishment that one may acquire by working in the mill.

Soto's words are sparse because there is little in the valley that would inspire one to "wax poetic" about. Elaborate, extended metaphors comparing this limiting, physical world to a more complicated one would not work; this poem is about an uncomplicated lifestyle and people who strive to survive. Soto portrays life in the valley as one which is a struggle simply to endure from one day to the next. Yet with a single, one-syllable word Soto provides hope for all those in the valley, and especially for the children, who in their innocence "leap" across the road. The responsibilities and burdens of adulthood are not yet ones which they must shoulder, and Soto knows—from his own experience—that it is possible for children to leave the backbreaking life of their parents and "leap" to another kind of life.

Themes and Meanings

Soto uses children to represent the hope for all people. At the beginning of the poem, the children "leap"—a joyful word, and one that describes well the buoyancy and resiliency of childhood—to the store, just as the "brown kid" leaps across the road at the end. In a larger sense, life beyond the fields is worth leaping for. While money is not the singular criterion for a satisfying life (and while oftentimes in literature money, or the pursuit of it, is equated with corruption), Soto's poem reminds the reader of the effects of poverty. Too much money may corrupt, but sufficient funds are needed to buy the necessities of life: food, shelter, clothing, medical care, and even the ability to send children to school. Once children of migrant workers are seven or eight years old, and sometimes even earlier, they are typically no longer sent to school but are expected to work in the fields. Thus they work to earn their keep.

The speaker has escaped life in the valley, and he and his daughter "suck roadside/ Snowcones" as they "look about." They do not "eat," "nibble," or "lick" the snowcones, but "suck" them, a much more aggressive word that reflects Soto's statement, "Worry is my daughter's story." Given that he, too, is eagerly consuming his snowcone, the reader notes that it remains Soto's story as well. The family could conceivably have to go back to that way of life some day; life's twists leave no one immune to situations that might diminish material possessions and force each person to survive rather than thrive. Thriving in the world beyond the valley means working at careers that not only meet physical needs but also nurture spiritual or intellectual needs. His daughter touches his hand, wanting the reassurance that her father, while acknowledging such a possibility, will protect her from it. She is counting on that human connection for comfort and optimism.

While the poem is autobiographical, its appeal is universal. Soto suggests others besides Hispanics who may find themselves "in the valley." He includes the "Okies," a reference to people from Oklahoma who were displaced by the dust storms of the 1930's and came to California to work in the fields in hope of a better life, a plight immortalized by John Steinbeck in *The Grapes of Wrath* (1939). He includes the Jews who "got lost," a reference to the wandering tribes of Israel, perhaps when they were lost in the wilderness for forty years under Moses's leadership, or perhaps the timeless struggle of Jews around the world to find a home.

Soto paints a contemporary picture for all people. In uncertain economic times, anyone—not only Hispanics, Okies, or Jews—"could be here." Yet all people have the possibility to attain the "Riches" that can "Happen on a red tongue," for no matter what heritage, all people have the opportunity to savor "Sweetness," the "red stain of laughter," the essence of life.

Alexa L. Sandmann

A SMELL OF CORDWOOD

Author: Pablo Neruda (Neftalí Ricardo Reyes Basoalto, 1904-1973)
Type of poem: Ode
First published: 1956, as "Oda al olor de la leña," in *Nuevas odas elementales*; English translation collected in *Selected Poems of Pablo Neruda*, 1961

The Poem

"A Smell of Cordwood" is an ode (a song of praise) in seven stanzas; it is written in free verse. The title is significant in that it states the rather unusual subject matter being praised: the smell of ordinary wood.

The opening stanza begins abruptly, *in medias res* (in the middle of things). The speaker of the poem describes the feeling of the cold and starry night as it rushes in through the door of his home "on an ocean/ of galloping hooves." Night is personified as an invading presence.

In the next brief stanza, out of the darkness, "like a hand," comes "the savage/ aroma/ of wood on the woodpile." Like the night that invaded the speaker's domicile, the aroma of wood is humanized; it savagely assaults and overwhelms the speaker's senses.

The third stanza infuses the odor of the wood with life and form; it "lives/ like a tree." The odor is so palpable, so intense, in fact, that the poet, deliberately confusing the senses, calls it "visible." The stanza ends with another metaphor. The wood becomes so "alive" that it is as if it "pulsed like a tree."

When the speaker describes the odor as "Vesture/ made visible" in the next stanza (two lines), the metaphor in the preceding stanza is continued. This line is a play on the biblical phrase "and the Word was made flesh." Instead of the Word, however, the odor is made flesh. Moreover, the word "vesture" has a religious connotation of its own; it recalls the vestments of a priest. The next stanza is also two lines long: "A visible/ breaking of branches." The odor of the wood, then, becomes as "visible" a vestment of the tree as a broken branch.

In the sixth stanza, the speaker of the poem turns back and reenters the house. He notices in the distance the sparkle of particles in the sky. Yet the smell of wood overpowers all other senses and takes hold of the speaker's heart. The metaphors used to compare the seizure of the heart by the smell are that of a hand grasping at the heart, jasmine assaulting the senses, and, finally, "a memory cherished."

In the last stanza, the lengthiest, the speaker tries to describe the scent of the wood in negative terms. It is not, for example, "harrowing/ pine odor," or "slashed/ eucalyptus," or "like/ the green/ exhalation/ of arbors." It is something more obscure, more subtle. The speaker says that it is a fragrance that offers itself only once. It awaited the speaker there, that night, and "struck like a wave," then it disappeared into the speaker's blood or became part of him as he opened the door to the night.

Forms and Devices

Pablo Neruda's poetics in "A Smell of Cordwood," as well as throughout the three volumes translated as *The Elementary Odes of Pablo Neruda* (1961), strongly based on clarity and simplicity, is effectively portrayed by, and revealed through, the typographical medium employed. In the typographical arrangement of "A Smell of Cordwood," the separation of lines and the white spaces between words, as well as between stanzas, influence the meaning of the poem in the same way that silences and pauses form an integral part of a musical composition.

Neruda makes use of numerous lines in which only one word appears. This line division is clearly a great help to the unsophisticated reader of poetry, allowing him or her to concentrate on one or two words at a time, to grasp their meaning before continuing further. The simplified syntax of the Elementary Odes is particularly effective when Neruda's subject matter is a description of nature, as in this poem. In this case, the description, proceeding step by step and sense by sense, is reflected in the typography, in which each aspect of the scent of cordwood is expressed in isolation, as a single unit. Every line is a separate brushstroke contributing to the total effect, yet every line is also capable of existing as a discrete unit. Neruda's method in the odes has been likened to that of the finest nature artists. Vincent van Gogh, for example, used such simple brushstrokes and colors in his paintings.

In several of the Elementary Odes, the short line also functions in a way that makes it suggestive of the subject matter. In this poem about odor, for example, Neruda uses lines as short and concise as gusts of night air. The typography of the poem very simply creates a perfect blend of intention, form, and content. As a result of employing the short line, as well as the consequent break with the traditional effects of metrics, Neruda's odes are not only among his most easily accessible works but are also among his most translatable works.

Besides the language and syntax, the imagery of the poem is nearly always clear and unequivocal. Meaning is often literal. In the poem, Neruda sings the essential themes of humankind and exalts one element that makes up the material world in its individual form: the sense of smell. The poem is joyful, optimistic, and clear; the world represented is coherent, rational, and structured—in a word, realistic.

Themes and Meanings

An almost blind faith in the truth of the senses is one of the major themes of Neruda's poem. As is the case with most of the Elementary Odes, "A Smell of Cordwood" is a canticle of material passion to a simple sensuous experience in this world. In Neruda's instinctive materialism and ardent surrender to nature, the poet exhibits a new romanticism, intuitional and primitive, a weapon aimed at the idealism and intellectualism of the modernists. In this poem he sought above all things to communicate, to abandon whatever might obscure the understanding of his reader.

The truth of the senses, in the poem, is self-evident and needs no complex analysis or interpretation. The point of departure for the speaker's experience appears small, insignificant, and not fully poetic. Neruda, however, quickly establishes an emotional link with the scent of cordwood. The speaker sees each aspect of that night as a gift; Neruda's poetry is also a gift to a world that offers him beauty and life. Poetry, like the scent of pine, is a vehicle through which to give back to the world some of the beauty first given by the world to the poet's senses.

The emotional link that the poet establishes with the fragrance in "A Smell of Cordwood" is accomplished by reminding the reader what the speaker's impression was when he smelled the scent for the first time: "a fragrance/ that gives itself/ once, and once/ only." By indirectly likening the scent offered by the wood to the sensuality a woman might offer, Neruda adds a human dimension to a basic property of nature that it did not have before. Consequently, the reader is reminded of the link between the natural scent and nature of humankind. Linking that natural world with the human world, particularly at the end of the poem, when the speaker states that the fragrance became "lost" in his blood, Neruda underscores the fact that not only the fragrance but also the memory of the fragrance will live on in the speaker as well as in the reader of the poem.

Genevieve Slomski

SMOKEY THE BEAR SUTRA

Author: Gary Snyder (1930-   )
Type of poem: Narrative
First published: 1969; collected in *A Place in Space: Ethics, Aesthetics, and Water-sheds*, 1995

The Poem

Gary Snyder's "Smokey the Bear Sutra" instructs readers about how humankind may live harmoniously in the natural environment with fellow living things. The characteristics of the ancient Buddha are attributed to Smokey the Bear, a character created by the United States Forest Service, as Snyder playfully explains that Smokey the Bear will enlighten those dedicated to protection of woodlands and waterways and punish those who mock Smokey or oppose his efforts to preserve the environment.

The poem begins 150 million years ago as the Great Sun Buddha addresses all life forms on the subject of bringing enlightenment to earth. This Buddha prophesies that the American continent will one day exist and will be blessed with numerous wondrous natural phenomena, but will also be endangered (though not irretrievably) by humankind. The Buddha announces that this dangerous situation will occasion the Buddha's return in the form of Smokey the Bear so that nature's harmony may endure.

The poem proceeds to a description of Buddha's manifestation as Smokey the Bear, with each characteristic of the Forest Service figure aligned to the purposes of Buddhist enlightenment. Smokey is "standing on his hind legs" because he is "aroused and watchful." He bears a shovel because he "digs to the truth." His left paw makes a gesture—the "Mudra of Comradely Display." Smokey wears "blue work overalls" to denote his affiliation with "slaves and laborers"; his "broad-brimmed hat of the West" connects him to the "forces that guard the Wilderness." Because his belly is round and full, one easily associates him with kindness and plenitude.

The concluding section certifies that those who recite the Smokey the Bear Sutra and enact its ideas will save the planet, promote harmony, and achieve "HIGHEST PERFECT ENLIGHTENMENT." In a parenthetical note, Snyder adds that the poem "may be reproduced free forever," demonstrating that the intent of the poem is not to garner notoriety or profit for the author, but to create an endless chain of free communication, which will assist in the creation of world enlightenment and the protection of the environment. In the same spirit, Snyder leaves the poem unsigned, leaving the focus on the message rather than the author.

Forms and Devices

At first inspection, "Smokey the Bear Sutra" seems to embody few characteristics associated with poetry. The work is set in paragraphs, not stanzas with line breaks. No rhyme or metrical pattern is evident. Although Smokey the Bear is a representative figure for the Buddha, the work does not exploit figurative language, such as metaphors or similes. One might declare that the work is written in the free-verse form made popular by Walt Whitman, but "Smokey the Bear Sutra" does not incorporate Whitman's extensive catalogs or the rush and exuberance of his language. One might declare that "Smokey the Bear Sutra" is a prose poem because of its compressed expression, its natural cadences, and its sonority, but the distinction from conventional prose remains unconvincing.

A key factor lifting Snyder's work above ordinary language is that Snyder views himself not as the author of "Smokey the Bear Sutra" but as a channel through which the Buddha delivers his message. Snyder said that one day in February, 1969, he became aware that the Sierra Club, which is dedicated to preserving the environment, was to meet the following day, and he sat down to write. According to Snyder, "the sutra seemed to write itself"; that is, the spirit of the Buddha governed the writing experience, and the resulting sutra was the work of the Buddha, not the human who set down the words. With this spontaneous and inspired composition in mind, one may view the language as a divine creation, just as one may take the language of the Bible to be divine. Snyder went to the meeting of the Sierra Club the next day to distribute copies of the Buddha's sutra.

The intensity of the message is created through the joining of opposing forces. The poem begins in seriousness and solemnity, with the Great Sun Buddha delivering "a great Discourse to all the assembled elements and energies," proclaiming the majesty of geographical features such as Mount Rainier, Big Sur, the Mississippi River, and the Grand Canyon. However, the poem makes a dramatic leap as Smokey the Bear, a cartoon character from a publicity campaign of the Forest Service, is designated as the next manifestation of the Buddha. The effect of the connection between the Buddha and Smokey is charming humor, especially as the connection is cleverly sustained through each component of Smokey's image.

In addition to this pleasingly unexpected connection, the poem embodies other opposing ideas. The Great Sun Buddha reveals his complexity by referring to his "obstinate compassion." Humankind pursues "loveless knowledge." These oxymorons are enhanced by the contradictory ideas applied to characters. Smokey is capable of rage and power, but he is also compassionate. Humankind has "its own strong intelligent Buddha-nature" but is also destructive.

The language of the poem is also heightened through the use of aphorisms. A sutra is a collection of aphorisms, and these pithy expressions of truth recur in "Smokey the Bear Sutra." The poem declares that "all creatures have the full right to live to their limits" and "all true paths lead through mountains." Although some humans may believe that wealth can be taken from others and selfishly accumulated, the truth is that "all is contained vast and free in the Blue Sky and Green Earth of One Mind." Happy in its abundance, "the great Earth has food enough for everyone who loves her and trusts her."

Humor sweetens the lessons of the poem, and as stated above, the connection between Buddha and Smokey combines playfulness with the serious message. This playful spirit is made evident also in wordplay, in which the meaning of the words of the Forest Service's Smokey is altered to suit the poem's purposes. Concerned about forest fires caused by careless smokers, the Forest Service calls for smokers to "put out" their cigarettes, or "butts," by drowning them with water or by crushing them underfoot. The poem converts the meaning of "to put out" to "to cast into exile," declaring that Smokey will "put out" people who "hinder or slander him." If force is necessary to control those who threaten the world's harmony, then Smokey can be summoned with his "WAR SPELL," which converts "butts" (cigarettes) to "butts" (the rear ends of destructive humans): "DROWN THEIR BUTTS/ CRUSH THEIR BUTTS/ DROWN THEIR BUTTS/ CRUSH THEIR BUTTS."

The rewards that follow from Smokey's enlightened enforcement are also humorously idyllic: Those dedicated to Smokey's cause are guaranteed "ripe blackberries to eat and a sunny spot under a pine tree to sit at." Indeed, Smokey's allies will enjoy "tender love and caresses of men, women, and beasts."

Themes and Meanings

At the center of the poem's meaning is Smokey's "great Mantra," which is a vow of loyalty to the environment and against those who would destroy it: "I DEDICATE MYSELF TO THE UNIVERSAL DIAMOND—/ BE THIS RAGING FURY DESTROYED." The sky, mountains, wilderness, rivers, and wildlife all must be protected. Under this protection are also "Gods and animals, hoboes and madmen, prisoners and sick people, musicians, playful women, and hopeful children." To be opposed are "wasteful freeways and needless suburbs." The threat of "advertising, air pollution, or the police," the blight of "cars, houses, canned food, universities, and shoes" must also be counteracted. "Smokey the Bear Sutra" is a declaration of opposition between the high-minded people believing in enlightened, harmonious inhabitation of the planet and "the worms of capitalism and totalitarianism." Nevertheless, the opposition is not vicious or mean-spirited. The humor of the poem suggests the buoyant good spirit that can prevail in the protection of the environment.

Beyond this theme about the defense of the planet and an enlightened way of life, Snyder also makes several artistic statements in "Smokey the Bear Sutra." By writing in an open form that resembles prose, he challenges the idea that poems must include standard poetic features, such as rhyme, meter, and figurative language. He further questions the doctrine that a poem should stand only as an aesthetic object to be admired for its beauty; Snyder presents his poem as an instrument for social change and urges that the poem's truths be put into practice. Finally, Snyder offers a commentary on authorship. Do authors write because of their dedication to the combination of form and theme, or do authors seek out personal recognition and gratification? Since the Buddha is the real author of "Smokey the Bear Sutra" and Snyder assumes anonymity and renounces profit, the poem has independence and integrity not possible in signed and copyrighted poems.

The importance of "Smokey the Bear Sutra" is partly that it corresponds strongly to the central ideas of Snyder's literary career and partly that it presents themes that become more urgent with each passing decade. Ecology, Buddhism, and open form are central concerns in "Smokey the Bear Sutra," as they are in Snyder's other works, especially *Turtle Island* (1974), which won the Pulitzer Prize in 1975. As society confronts the problems of pollution, overpopulation, and restrictions on artistic expression, Snyder's work must be acknowledged as an important part of the ongoing debate.

William T. Lawlor

SNAKE

Author: D. H. Lawrence (1885-1930)
Type of poem: Lyric
First published: 1921; collected in *Birds, Beasts, and Flowers*, 1923

The Poem

"Snake" is a seventy-four-line free-verse poem divided into nineteen verse paragraphs (stanzas of unequal length). Like many modern lyrics, it incorporates a narrative element, recording the poet's encounter with a snake at his water-trough. Through this structure and carefully mobilized imagery, the poet reveals his conflicted, deepening consciousness, which moves from casual description to epiphanic confession. Written when D. H. Lawrence and his wife Frieda were living in Taormina, Sicily, in 1920-1921, the poem is derived from Lawrence's actual experience there. Its imagery and themes, however, are anticipated in the second section of his 1917 essay "The Reality of Peace."

The setting is a hot July day upon which the poet takes his pitcher to the water-trough, where a snake is drinking. The first five verse paragraphs establish the scene and provide the occasion for the poet's initial, sensual description of the snake. Domestic and exotic images are combined as the pajama-clad poet observes the snake "In the deep, strange-scented shade of the great dark carob-tree." Light and dark are contrasted in the snake's golden color and the surrounding gloom. The poet conjures the creature's snakiness with emphasis on his "straight mouth," "slack long body," and flickering, "two-forked tongue." He also compares the snake to domesticated farm animals ("drinking cattle") and to a human by referring to the snake as "someone" and describing him as musing. This imagery, which suggests an ascending hierarchy, anticipates the symbolic leaps later in the poem, when the poet compares the snake to a god, a king, and, finally, "one of the lords/ Of life."

The sixth verse paragraph introduces the poet's inner conflict, arising from his voice of education that instructs him to kill the "venomous" snake. The five ensuing ones trace the poet's intensifying crisis as voices challenge his manhood and courage as well as his instinctive admiration for the animal, which he feels has honored him by seeking his hospitality at the trough. He includes the reader in his dialectical self-scrutiny:

> Was it cowardice, that I dared not kill him?
> Was it perversity, that I longed to talk to him?
> Was it humility, to feel so honoured?

In verse paragraphs 12 through 14, the conflict is transposed outside the poet, when the speaker hurls a log in protest at the withdrawing snake. The concluding stanzas record the poet's fascination, regret, guilt, admiration, and pettiness, respectively. Lawrence's invocation of the albatross from Samuel Taylor Coleridge's "The Rime of the Ancient Mariner" underscores the poet's sense of sin and need for atonement. His use of the possessive "my" to refer to the otherworldly snake suggests that a profound transformation has occurred. Though banishing the creature by his "mean act," he claims it as his own. The implication is that were the snake to return, the poet would submit to its presence, its coming and going alike.

Forms and Devices

The free-verse form of "Snake," a form Lawrence champions in his essay "Poetry of the Present" (1918), facilitates his drive for knowledge through meditation and emotional perception. The long, unrhymed lines are written in straightforward, collo-quial diction, inviting the reader to participate in the poet's experience. Divided into verse paragraphs, they approximate the quality of prose and, like the essays Lawrence was writing at about the same time, track a process of argument and self-discovery.

The lines conform at once to the physical and emotional experience of the poem, to the object of the long, slithering snake, and to the poet's fluid mind, which travels over experience, comprehending itself in the light of what it finds. Many free-verse con-ventions derived from Walt Whitman's poetry appear in Lawrence's po... organic rhythm, parallel structure, and repetition. Yet the tone of the poem is personal in a way Whitman's poems are often not, and Lawrence deploys imagery more in the vein of the imagists and the English Romantic poets.

In focusing on the snake, Lawrence recalls past literary texts, from Genesis to John Milton's *Paradise Lost* (1667, 1674), but Lawrence uses traditional imagery for his own ends. The serpent of eternity, the phallic god, the snake, usually a figure of evil, is a positive force here, while the poet has "something to expiate." Images of light and dark, often associated with virtue and sin respectively, are upended: "For in Sicily the black, black snakes are innocent, the gold are venomous." Even the black hole into which the snake retreats appears as an entrance to some desirable mystery. It is "the dark door of the secret earth," while the poet's "intense still noon" is, by contrast, a flood of missed opportunity and failure. In Lawrence's poem, the snake is a symbol for those elements associated with it: darkness, death, the underworld, and the erotic; the poet's ambivalent feelings are directed at those things as well.

Through Lawrence's particular turn of figures, he presents a central paradox in the poem. Contrary to what education dictates, the poisonous yellow snake is appealing. For all its reptilian features, it appears lordly, superior to man, not (as the customary view would have it) beneath him. Description becomes a means of perception as Lawrence transforms the snake from a creature that is obviously not human to one that is divine.

While the snake is clearly a metaphor, Lawrence attempts to depict the animal as it really is. He focuses on its concrete characteristics. In doing so, he manages to be per-sonal, while keeping emotion in check, refuting the critic R. P. Blackmur's claim that Lawrence's use of expressive form excludes craft and control of imagery. The poi-gnancy of the last four lines derives precisely from Lawrence's control throughout the poem and his ability to find imagery that does the emotional work of the poem—that presents, borrowing T. S. Eliot's phrase, an "objective correlative" for the feelings ex-pressed.

Themes and Meanings

In "Snake," as in many of the poems in the collection *Birds, Beasts, and Flowers* (1923), Lawrence explores the otherness of the creature world, defined chiefly by its purity and innocence in contrast to the corrupt human world. The poem is a subtle celebration of nature in the Wordsworthian tradition of nature poetry, wherein the ordinary becomes an occasion for celebration and revelation.

Lawrence's intense contemplation reveals what he shares with the snake (that creature state within himself) and what divides him from it—human consciousness. His imagery reflects the distinction he often makes between two modes of consciousness, that of intuition or instinct (the blood self) represented by the snake and that of intellect (the nerve/brain self) evident in humans. As he asserts in "Fantasia of the Unconscious" (1922), the snake's consciousness "is *only* dynamic, and non-cerebral," while a person is composed of warring elements of instinct and willful intellect. In the poem, this conflict is dramatized first in the poet's instinctive attraction to the snake and the educated voice which tells him to destroy it, and again in his banishment of the snake and subsequent longing for its return.

The liabilities of human education is a recurring theme in Lawrence's work. In "Fantasia of the Unconscious," he argues that established ideas that do not square with a human being's "dynamic nature" arrest his individuality and damage his psyche. Clearly, in "Snake," the ideas fostered by education outside the poet impede his submission to the creature he admires.

Rather than deny instinct, Lawrence would strive for an acceptance of duality and polarity in the world as well as in himself. In "Snake," polarity and struggle are reflected in the contrasting juxtaposed imagery, the flux of conflicting feelings, and the ordinary diction with its mythic overtones. They find balance or resolution in the closing epiphany, in which Lawrence realizes artistically a need expressed philosophically in "The Reality of Peace": "I must humble myself before the abhorred serpent and give him his dues as he lifts his flattened head from the secret grass of my soul."

In the wake of Harold Bloom's *The Anxiety of Influence* (1973), it is tempting to read "Snake" as an expression of Lawrence's ambivalence toward his literary precursors (Thomas Hardy, William Wordsworth, and Milton, among others) and his anxiety over the problem of originality. How can any poet writing after William Shakespeare and Milton escape being derivative?

Such a reading is inspired by Lawrence's imagery, which posits the poet as a "second comer" to the trough, the snake which figures throughout literature, and the allusion to Coleridge at the end of a poem wherein the poet ostensibly disavows his education. Such a reading is valuable and justified inasmuch as Lawrence was steeped in literature of the past, and it adds a provocative dimension to the other themes and meanings of the poem.

Gardner McFall

SNAPSHOTS OF A DAUGHTER-IN-LAW

Author: Adrienne Rich (1929-   )
Type of poem: Dramatic monologue
First published: 1963, in *Snapshots of a Daughter-in-Law*

The Poem

"Snapshots of a Daughter-in-Law" is a ten-part poem, with each part composed of an uneven number of lines and stanzas. The speaker appears at first to address an older woman, probably the mother-in-law of the other, younger woman in the poem, a daughter-in-law. The two women are respectively "you" and "she," but neither of the two women "converses" with the speaker in the poem.

In each part, the speaker refers or alludes to a literary passage or phrase. The references provide her with a foundation for a philosophical discussion with the two women. Italicized phrases in the poem indicate the speaker's reference to another source, and at times she alters the original quotation. In part 3, for example, "*ma semblable, ma soeur*" is a variation of the phrase by the French poet Charles Baudelaire that reads, "mon semblable, mon frère." By changing *frère* (brother) to *soeur* (sister), the speaker emphasizes her discussion of womanhood.

Although the parts are numbered, the poem as a whole does not develop into a chronological narrative. The speaker structures her thoughts according to emotions or experiences. The first four parts of the poem set up the strained relationship between the two women in a series of "snapshots." The older woman, "once a belle in Shreveport," still dresses and plays the part of a Southern debutante. The speaker is critical of her fineries and accuses the older woman of a terrible sacrifice. The mother-in-law is now in the prime of her life, but because she chose superficial beauty over developing her intellectual skills, her mind is now "heavy with useless experience, rich/ with suspicion, rumor, fantasy."

In the third stanza of part 1, the daughter-in-law is characterized as "Nervy" and "glowering." She considers her mother-in-law's uselessness and, in the second part, the younger woman is caught in vignettes which reveal her dissatisfaction with domestic life. She hears voices or remembers something she had previously read; clearly she is struggling with what she thinks set against what she does as a dutiful daughter-in-law. In the next two parts, the speaker uses a kind of verbal camera to capture the two in snapshots which depict their conflict.

The next six parts are devoted to the thoughts roaring in the younger woman's mind. As the poem progresses, the reader begins to sense that the speaker and the young woman share an uncanny resemblance. In fact, toward the end of the poem, "you" and "I" become "we," and it is then obvious that all along the speaker has been criticizing her self.

Forms and Devices

The profusion of literary voices and the shifts in address between the speaker and the two women are confusing until the reader realizes that the speaker's perspectives are those of the daughter-in-law. The relationship that the speaker/daughter-in-law has with the older woman is riddled with their differences in attitude, values, and expectations.

The speaker is more comfortable speaking of the daughter-in-law—indeed, of herself—as a "she" rather than as "I" to gain psychological distance from the older woman, whose values she rejects. The younger woman's mind is fertile, though unexpressed, given the constraints of everyday life. Rather than have time to develop or write down her thoughts, she is seen making coffee or "dusting everything on the whatnot every day of life." The apparent frustration is revealed in the snapshots of her "Banging the coffee-pot into the sink" and sneaking moments to read while "waiting/ for the iron to heat," or "while the jellies boil and scum."

The poem is interspersed with the voices of learned men and women which the daughter-in-law might have encountered in those precious stolen moments of reading. The voices challenge the conventions—"*tempora and mores*" (times and customs)— of being a woman. The wisdom of thinkers such as the feminists Mary Wollstonecraft (part 7) and Simone de Beauvoir (part 10) as well as the poets Baudelaire (part 3) and Emily Dickinson (part 4) augment the speaker's own thoughts.

The literary allusions provide the speaker with authority as she criticizes the kind of lives women such as the mother-in-law lead. At the same time, the speaker does not yet know how to transform her knowledge into action. In part 5, she is seen shaving her legs as she ironically considers this female beauty ritual with others—"*Dulce ridens, dulce loquens*" (sweet laughter, sweet chatter).

The allusions authorize and justify the speaker's dissatisfaction, and they allow her to think beyond the everyday facts of existence. With them, she makes metaphors for her perceived entrapment, such as the image of the caged bird in parts 3, 4, and 6. By part 10, the speaker offers a snapshot of freedom: "Her mind full to the wind, I see her plunge/ breasted and glancing through the currents,/ taking the light upon her." Although the daughter-in-law's burden, or "her cargo," is never lightened, it has—through the inspiration of other voices—been "delivered/ [made] palpable/ ours."

Throughout the poem, the reader is led through the speaker's emotions and intellect. Because the speaker is actually addressing her own self in the role of a daughter-in-law, the poem's dramatic monologue is a kind of self-education as well. The poem is thus highly personal in the way it develops and in the choice of literary voices presented.

The poem's difficulty arises from the speaker's use of unfamiliar words and phrases. This strategy, however, is essential to the poem because it expresses and heightens the speaker's situation: She is an educated woman whose "*fertilisante douleur*" (enriching pain) is confinement to household chores. She will not simply accept the limitations of this domain; unfortunately, neither is she shown actively rebelling against her present condition. The voices painfully remind her that her life is unsatisfactory, but they stop short of prescribing a cure.

Nevertheless, while the poem seems to end on this discouraging note, the self-criticisms have been an educational process. The speaker has carefully scrutinized snapshots of herself. As she identifies the moments and causes of her dissatisfaction, the voices help her to enact a drama that makes it possible for the speaker to tell herself in the monologue that she must take action.

Themes and Meanings

Adrienne Rich wrote the poem over a period of two years when she herself was married to a Harvard economist and was a young mother with three children. Like the daughter-in-law in the poem, Rich lived within patriarchal structures that constrain a woman's intellect. In the early 1960's, white, middle-class, and educated women were expected to find men to marry and then be in the service of the American family. The speaker in the poem sees herself as a daughter-in-law, or as a person who exists in relation to other people and structures.

The conflict between the mother-in-law and the younger woman in the early part of the poem expresses the latter's desire to break from the confining conventions. They are "two handsome women, gripped in argument,/ each proud, acute, subtle," and "knowing themselves too well in one another" they provide the other with impetus to perceive differences in their entrapments: The mother-in-law's outworn beauty and the daughter-in-law's fertile intelligence are the main sources of their differences.

In part 6, the mother-in-law asks, "has Nature shown/ her household books to you, daughter-in-law,/ that her sons never saw?" The tone is contentious, but at heart, the older woman seems also to goad the younger woman onward in the latter's intellectual quest, as though to say, it may be too late for me, but not yet for you. By part 9, the speaker is aware that the disagreements between women are finally harmful to all women: "The argument *ad feminam*, all the old knives/ that have rusted in my back, I drive in yours" (from part 3) becomes a realization in part 9 that "Our blight has been our sinecure." The "our" is significant, since it signifies union rather than division. The "martyred ambition" of all women, then, becomes an important theme for the entire poem.

Significantly, the mother-in-law appears only in the first half of the poem, even though the break between the two remains ambiguous. Because the younger woman starts contemplating the literary voices rather than expending energy fighting with the mother-in-law, she embarks on a truly individual project. She demonstrates her emancipation in the second half of the poem by reflecting upon and questioning the value of the voices.

In this early poem, Rich was discovering the ways that women speak to each other and, most important, to themselves. "Snapshots of a Daughter-in-Law," with its suggestions of camera shots and shifts in focus, is mostly a poem of the young woman's mind. The speaker refers to herself as "she" to indicate the difficulty of perceiving herself as an autonomous individual.

The poem's tone is self-admonishing at times and, especially in the domestic snapshots of herself, the speaker is extremely critical. The portrait of the physical woman confined at home is not flattering: She is sullen, even vehement in her actions. The woman's strength resides in her mind and thoughts, where she rebukes the conventions and hears the orchestration of voices that signify a real need to further her intellectual growth.

Cynthia Wong

THE SNOW MAN

Author: Wallace Stevens (1879-1955)
Type of poem: Lyric
First published: 1923, in *Harmonium*

The Poem

"The Snow Man" is a short fifteen-line poem divided into five tercets. The title conjures up an image of a human artifact. The resemblance between a real human figure and a snowman, however, is hardly exact, for a high degree of conventional stylization goes into the making of a snowman—differently sized balls for head, torso, and limbs, coals for eyes, carrot for nose, and so on. Nevertheless, the snowman is a strategically apt image, for Stevens's poem deals with the attempt of the speaker to resist succumbing to the temptation to anthropomorphize or to personify—that is, to impose human form on nature or to impute human qualities to inanimate things or forces. As the opening line indicates, "One must have a mind of winter" to approach a frigid January landscape on its own terms, to see it as it really is, and thus to keep the snow and the man separate, as Stevens's deliberate separation of the two words in his title suggests.

In spite of this desire for separation, the snow and the man cannot really be kept apart, for any attempt to approach winter on its own inhuman terms is foredoomed to failure insofar as one must use as one's medium the human terms of a shared cultural vocabulary. A scene of winter, verbally rendered, is necessarily an approximation, for word-using animals, by definition, have no nonlinguistic or nonsymbolic access to the structure of the real and thus can only more or less encompass things as they are. The speaker is acutely aware of how difficult it is "not to think/ Of any misery in the sound of the wind,/ In the sound of a few leaves." He concedes that one must "have been cold a long time" to avoid humanizing the scene by personifying it, to avoid seeing it as a reflection of misery or some other negative human feeling. To behold "Nothing that is not there and the nothing that is," one must be nothing oneself. Yet as Stevens reflects in his poem "The Plain Sense of Things" (1952), "the absence of imagination [has]/ Itself to be imagined." The inhuman reality of wordless nature can only be approached through the word-soaked world of human imagination. The poem itself is an enactment of this paradox.

Forms and Devices

To portray the relationship between the mind of winter and the landscape of winter, Stevens uses predominantly visual images: "the boughs/ Of the pine-trees crusted with snow," "the junipers shagged with ice," and "The spruces rough in the distant glitter/ Of the January sun." For Stevens, the seasons are analogues not only for the cycle of human life but also for the cyclical nature of the human imagination. Winter is as close as one comes to an unadulterated reality purged clean of humanizing additions such as personification and anthropomorphism, as close as one comes to an inhuman landscape in which one can find no human meaning. Spring is an analogue for the mind's finding what will suffice by giving reality some measure of human shape. Summer is an analogue for the time of physical paradise, an imagined world wholly bearable and wholly hospitable to human beings. Fall, finally, is an analogue for the overripeness that leads to rottenness and that initiates the slow decay into winter.

It is fitting, therefore, that this poem about the mind of winter visually abounds in wintry images and auditorially attunes itself to "the sound of the wind/ . . . That is blowing in the same bare place/ For the listener." The poem itself for the most part is also a bare place in that the speaker studiously avoids thinking of "any misery in the sound of the wind" by avoiding anthropomorphic figures of speech. The forms and devices that are *not* there make possible the beholding of "Nothing that is not there and the nothing that is." The imagination, Stevens maintains, adds nothing to the world except itself. Save for the paradox inscribed in the final two lines, the poem is virtually devoid of figurative language. Though words such as "crusted," "shagged," and their cognates have connotative value, their evocative function is strictly subservient to their descriptive function.

Themes and Meanings

For Stevens, the imagination is not merely a way of creating but also a way of knowing, and "The Snow Man" is a self-consciously paradoxical attempt to imagine the absence of imagination by trying to capture in words a reality that is in essence wordless and by trying to put into human terms a nature that is in essence inhuman. It is significant that the speaker refers to "a mind of winter," for the one thing he cannot deliver is winter in itself. However much he tries to avoid the pitfalls of personification and anthropomorphism, however much he tries "not to think/ Of any misery in the sound of the wind," he cannot help but posit some connection between the poverty that resides within a mind of winter and the poverty that resides within a landscape of winter. Insofar as "the listener" lives in the prison house of language and is thereby shaped and determined by the preconceptions and values of a given vocabulary, he cannot in reality become nothing himself and cannot behold "Nothing that is not there and the nothing that is." He and his audience are relegated to imagining themselves occupying an absolute vantage point from which they are able to see things as they are and thus to see "Nothing that is not there." Nevertheless, the minute they posit "the nothing that is" and impose philosophical meaning on it (or draw meaning from it), they have entered a realm of imaginative abstraction from which there is no escape. The limits of their language are the limits of their world. Language always adds something that is not there to the nothing that is, and the poem itself is an eloquent demonstration of this insurmountable paradox.

It is no exaggeration to say that the entirety of Wallace Stevens's corpus is about the mutually dependent and perpetually unstable relationship between imagination and reality. As he reflects in *The Necessary Angel* (1965), "[T]he imagination loses vitality when it ceases to adhere to what is real. When it adheres to the unreal and intensifies what is unreal, while its first effect may be extraordinary, that effect is the maximum effect that it will ever have." When language fails to adhere to reality, the result is myth—the deceptive and spurious consolations of religion, romanticism, supernaturalism, and the like. When language adheres too closely to reality, the result is naturalism—the dreary determinism and impoverished reductivism of science, materialism, realism, and so on. For Stevens, imagination and reality are interdependent. By providing ideas of order and explanatory fictions, poetry gives a coherence and meaning to the chaos and poverty of human life, lending to it a sense and savour that "the gaunt world of reason" cannot proffer. Creating fictions, Stevens maintains, is the essential gift of the human mind; believing them is its curse. In a sceptical age, poetry must take the place of empty heaven and its hymns, but the material of poetry must be reality, not myth. Poetry, for Stevens, is life's redemption.

In "Notes Toward a Supreme Fiction" (1942), Stevens maintains that a fiction must have three attributes: It must be abstract, it must change, and it must give pleasure. Humankind makes the world manageable by abstraction, a device of economy that prevents one from being overwhelmed by an excess of sensory data. Such simplifications or even falsifications of intellect have obvious survival value and cannot be permanently discarded. Stevens, however, wants to go beyond intellectual abstractions, beyond the dead formulae and prefabricated notions that the gaunt world of fact and reason enshrines. He wants to fabricate his own imaginative abstractions, fictions that will deautomatize ordinary perception and reveal novel and unexpected configurations of experience, configurations that are obscured by stultifying conventions of common sense. Such fictions must change because the world must be continually defamiliarized and reinvented lest these fresh fictions degenerate into stale myths. Moreover, for the poverty of the human condition to be mitigated, such fictions must give pleasure. What Stevens calls the gaiety of language, with its exaltations of the present and its fortuitous integrations, is the only believable substitute for the obsolete joys of heaven.

Greig Henderson

SNOW WHITE AND THE SEVEN DWARFS

Author: Anne Sexton (1928-1974)
Type of poem: Narrative
First published: 1971, in *Transformations*

The Poem

Like Anne Sexton's other fairy-tale poems collected under the title *Transforma-tions*, "Snow White and the Seven Dwarfs" is a long (164 lines), free-verse narrative based on the version of the Snow White tale collected by Jacob and Wilhelm Grimm in Germany in the nineteenth century. The darkness and violence of this version may surprise readers who are accustomed to fairy tales that have been sanitized to make them suitable for children, but although Sexton has established a very modern voice in this and the other *Transformations* poems, she remains faithful to the action that the Grimm brothers recorded.

In "The Gold Key," the comparatively short poem that introduces the collection, the poet speaks of herself as a "middle-aged witch" with her "mouth wide," ready to tell readers "a story or two." The "witch" then imagines a sixteen-year-old boy who "wants some answers." He is really each of the readers, the witch says, suggesting that the answers are to be found in the tales of transformation recorded by the Grimm brothers. In that introduction, Sexton is explaining why adult readers should pay attention to the sort of story usually considered to be children's entertainment; she implies that these stories have important meanings.

In "Snow White and the Seven Dwarfs," Sexton begins with a verse paragraph that describes the character of the virgin in fairy tales; the virgin is not only pure but also doll-like. Only in the next paragraph does Sexton identify this particular virgin as Snow White. She also introduces the beautiful but vain stepmother queen and the magic mirror that tells her that Snow White is more beautiful than she is. The story progresses through its familiar events: The queen orders her huntsman to kill Snow White and to bring the queen her heart. Instead, he frees her and brings the queen a boar's heart, which she eats. Snow White wanders through dangerous forests for seven weeks and at last comes to the cottage of the seven dwarfs for whom she agrees to keep house. They warn her against opening the door while they are off at their mines, but Snow White is tricked by the disguised queen, who offers her a piece of lacing. The dwarfs rescue Snow White from the deathlike swoon caused by her tightly laced bodice. A second time they rescue her when she is tricked with a poisoned comb. When she succumbs to the queen's offer of a poisoned apple, however, they can do nothing. Sadly they display Snow White's body in a glass coffin. That is how a prince sees her and falls in love with her. When the dwarfs allow him to carry her body to his castle, the poisoned apple is dislodged and Snow White revives and marries her prince. The evil queen is invited to the wedding, where she is given "red-hot iron shoes" in which she dances until she dies. Readers are not told that Snow White and the prince live happily ever after, however; instead, Sexton's final image is of Snow White holding court and looking into her own mirror.

Forms and Devices

As she does with all the *Transformations* poems, Sexton adds her own voice to the plot elements of the story. It is a voice that is sometimes comic and sometimes admonitory. One source of its comedy rises from the introduction of contemporary items into the traditional tale. When the wicked queen eats what she thinks is Snow White's heart, for instance, she chews it "like a cube steak." The queen's gift of lacing binds Snow White "tight as an Ace bandage." When she revives, she is "as full of life as soda pop." When Snow White opens the cottage door to evil a second time, Sexton calls her a "dumb bunny," and the prince lingers at Snow White's coffin so long, Sexton says, that his hair turns green.

Although the cube steak and the Ace bandage show Sexton's gift for the comic simile, her figurative language can also make her story more vivid and underscore the themes that emerge in the tale. During Snow White's trek through the forest, she meets hungry wolves, each with "his tongue lolling out like a worm." The forest's nightmare birds call out "lewdly,/ talking like pink parrots." The poisoned comb is "a curved eight-inch scorpion." Sexton compares the red-hot iron shoes in which the wicked queen dances to her death to a pair of red-hot roller skates, uniting the comic with the darkly grotesque.

In this poem, as in many Sexton poems, the reader is also aware of another element in the speaker's voice, an admonitory voice that sometimes breaks into the narrative to direct the reader's attention to an important event or to explain how to interpret a motive or theme. Although editorial intrusion seems more characteristic of nineteenth century literature than of work from the latter half of the twentieth century, Sexton's ironic tone makes it seem both modern and appropriate. After introducing the stepmother's beauty, for example, Sexton addresses the reader directly: "Beauty is a simple passion,/ but, oh my friends, in the end/ you will dance the fire dance in iron shoes." The iron shoes foreshadow the end of the poem. Sexton also uses modern details such as the roller skates to unite parts of the story, as she does with references to the mirror.

Themes and Meanings

In the versions of "Snow White and the Seven Dwarfs" that have been sanitized for children, the action of the poem usually seems to concentrate on the possibility of violence aimed at the innocent young. In those stories, although the reader assumes the queen to be motivated by her envy of Snow White's youth and beauty, her motives seem to be subsidiary to the theme of violence itself. In Sexton's version, the queen's pride, which "pumped in her like a poison," is diagnosed directly as motivation. Indeed, Sexton says that before the mirror labels Snow White as the most beautiful woman in the land, the girl has been "no more important" to the queen than "a dust mouse under the bed." The mirror's announcement makes the queen suddenly aware of encroaching age and makes her determined to kill Snow White. At the end, the queen is punished for her pride by dancing to death in the red-hot shoes.

Sexton goes beyond simply making the queen a villain, however. In the poem's second verse paragraph, Sexton uses the second-person "you" to suggest to the reader that everyone is subject to the corrupting effects of pride and may be subject to its rewards: "Oh my friends, in the end/ you will dance the fire dance." At the end, Sexton describes the queen's punishment. After describing the shoes that await the queen, Sexton suddenly returns to the second person as someone warns the queen: "First your toes will smoke/ and then your heels will turn black/ and you will fry upward like a frog,/ she was told." Although the "you" in this second passage refers to the queen, the words "she was told" follow the vivid description and invite the reader to recall the earlier warning. Indeed, at the poem's very end, the last picture is of Snow White consulting her own mirror "as women do." Sexton suggests that even Snow White can be infected by the "simple passion" of beauty and the poison of pride that may accompany it.

Another image at the poem's end suggests a second theme: Snow White's "china-blue doll eyes," which "open and shut" like the eyes of a child's doll. The phrases recall the description of the virgin, that "lovely number" introduced in the poem's first verse paragraph. The virgin is the innocent heroine of this tale and many other fairy tales, but Sexton's imagery suggests that she is as empty and artificial as a toy. The opening paragraph introduces another theme as well. The virgin's eyes "Open to say,/ Good Day Mama,/ and shut for the thrust/ of the unicorn." The reference to the unicorn recalls the ancient folktale that a unicorn can be captured only by a virgin; the animal will willingly give itself up to her. Here, however, the "thrust" of the unicorn underscores its sexual symbolism. The virgin's apparent purity, Sexton suggests, may be a ploy by which she captures and marries the prince. Sexton also hints at Snow White's sexual nature in the description of her wandering through the forests of wolves with phallic tongues and lewdly calling birds until she takes refuge in the dwarfs' "honeymoon cottage." Like the virginal heroines of several of Sexton's Grimm poems, Snow White's purity is mostly appearance, and she carries in her the potential for the same sort of evil as her persecutor, the same evil that may put all readers in the iron shoes.

Ann D. Garbett

THE SNOWSTORM

Author: Marina Tsvetayeva (1892-1941)
Type of poem: Verse drama
First published: 1923, as *Metel*; in *Izbrannye proizvedeniya*, 1965

The Poem

The Snowstorm is a short play that Marina Tsvetayeva subtitled "dramatic scenes in verse." It is the first of Tsvetayeva's dramatic works and was written in Moscow in December, 1918. Tsvetayeva's early dramatic works are written in a neoromantic style. Although Tsvetayeva is not generally considered as one of the Russian Symbolist writers, or as a member of any group of poets writing during what is known as the Silver Age of Russian poetry, this play is noticeably influenced by the Symbolists.

The play takes place at an inn in Bohemia on New Year's Eve. A group of travelers is caught in a snowstorm. As is typical of a Symbolist play, the characters are types. They do not have individual identities, but instead represent a certain group of characteristics. An Innkeeper, a Huntsman, a Trader, an Old Woman, and a Lady in a Cape are gathered. The Old Woman is described as representing the essence of the eighteenth century. The Lady in the Cape remains aloof from the rest of the group, and her identity remains a mystery until near the end of the play. The three men seem merely to provide a backdrop of vulgarity to contrast with the action in the final scene. In that respect, they function as a chorus.

After defending the Lady from the sarcastic comments of the three men, the Old Woman gives the Lady a diamond ring that was once given to her by the king. It is understood that she must have the ring, but no explanation is offered. When the ring is given, sleigh bells are heard. A Gentleman in a Cape appears who introduces himself as Prince of the Moon, Chevalier of the Rotonde, and Knight of the Rose.

The Lady in the Cape turns out to be the Countess Lanska, who has suddenly realized that she no longer loves her husband and has set out in the snowstorm, not knowing quite why she did so. She talks to the Gentleman with great intimacy, feeling sure that she has met him before. The dialogue grows increasingly fantastic as the Gentleman confesses that they knew each other in a previous existence and that theirs is a preordained encounter. He puts a spell on her, forcing her to forget the encounter, and departs while she sleeps. He then disappears at the stroke of midnight, accompanied, once again, by the ringing of sleigh bells.

This drama in verse is not formally divided into acts, probably as a result of its brevity, but three scenes can be easily distinguished. The first scene consists of the arrival of the travelers at the inn and the ensuing conversation of the Trader, the Huntsman, and the Innkeeper. The second scene includes the soliloquy of the Old Woman and the cryptic exchange between the Old Woman and the Lady. The final scene is the mystical conversation that occurs between the Lady in the Cape and the mysterious Gentleman.

While the play does preserve the the the unities of time, place, and action thought to be essential to classical dramatic works, the plot, in the neoromantic vein of the Symbolists, is minimal. The action of the play gradually ascends from the vulgarity of the three men to the archaic speech of the Old Woman and finally to the mystical meeting of the Gentleman and the Lady. The action progresses from the real world to a world of higher forms.

Forms and Devices

In this drama, Tsvetayeva experiments with the elliptical style that is characteristic of her later verse. As in her lyrics, the verses begin in a regular metrical pattern and then gradually vary in rhythm. Tsvetayeva varies her style according to each character, although the style of writing remains essentially her own. In fact, Tsvetayeva is often noted for her ability to sustain different tones within the same collection of verse. In the first section of the play, the elliptical style lends a quality of colloquial speech to the opening conversation of the three men.

The exchange between the Lady and the Gentleman in the last section is modeled on Aleksandr Blok's style, as is Tsvetayeva's later "Verses to Blok." Repetition of the first word of the stanza is prominent in this section, lending an incantatory quality to the conversation. It is reminiscent of the singsong quality of a prayer. The speech of the Old Woman and the Gentleman is marked by archaisms and the longer lines characteristic of eighteenth century Russian versification. Although the repetitive patterning and archaisms are reminiscent of Blok, they are successfully assimilated into Tsvetayeva's lyric poetry. Tsvetayeva's later poetry is characterized by a mixture of colloquial and archaic diction. She also experimented with the repetition of sounds and roots of words in her mature verse as well as simply the repetition of certain words.

The similarities in the characterization of the Gentleman in the Cape and the Lady in the Cape are another significant aspect of Tsvetayeva's work as a whole. The main characters in her longer, epic poems often have qualities associated with the opposite sex; she often pairs male and female characters to represent two halves of the whole. This seems to be true of the Lady and Gentleman in *The Snowstorm*.

The play is couched in imagery typically found in Symbolist poetry. The most important of these images is the snowstorm itself. In the romantic tradition, the poet was considered to have a special bond with nature. Nature often reflected the inner world of the poet. In Symbolist verse, nature has a mystical function. It often creates a passageway to a spiritual realm. For the Russian Symbolists, this higher world was embodied in the form of a woman, the Divine Sophia.

Tsvetayeva, in her mature verse, tends to transform the external world into an inner reality. Images of nature are not very prominent in most of her poetry. In this particular work, however, she uses the image of the snowstorm in a way that is similar to that of the Symbolists. The snowstorm obscures everyday reality. By obscuring this world, it allows passage to a higher, but still mysterious, form of reality. Only a chosen few are able to catch a glimpse of it. The Lady in the Cape leaves the world of everyday reality—and her husband—in the storm and then passes into the magical world of the Gentleman in the Cape.

Themes and Meanings

The basic situation of the play is taken from the work of the Russian Symbolist poet Aleksandr Blok, whom Tsvetayeva greatly admired. In Blok's play *Neznakomka* (1906; mysterious woman), as in *The Snowstorm*, there is a mysterious bond between an astral being and a chosen mortal. The main character in Blok's play, however, is a poet who almost meets the embodiment of his own philosophical construction. Blok's play takes on a rather satirical tone. He pokes fun at images from his own poetry and ideas associated with the Symbolists.

Tsvetayeva's play, on the other hand, cannot be perceived as satirical in any way. Another significant difference lies in the fact that the genders of the protagonists are reversed in Tsvetayeva's play. The woman is mortal while the man is the being from another plane.

The play as a whole is a work in the tradition of Russian Symbolism. The concept of escaping from an unbearable present into the world of imagination is an idea taken from the Symbolist tradition. This concept is, however, central to Tsvetayeva's work. It seems that Tsvetayeva had a natural affinity for many of the concerns of the Russian Symbolists. Her feeling of alienation from Russian society and from the émigré society of Berlin and Paris bred a desire to escape from this world. Tsvetayeva escaped into the world of her poetic imagination.

The escapist tendency of the settings and treatments in her plays is prominent in her lyric output as well. In Tsvetayeva's work, there is an impulse toward a fixed world of peace and transcendence. *The Snowstorm* exhibits a fairy-tale quality with its fantastic plot and two-dimensional characters. Tsvetayeva was a master of transforming everyday reality into myth. In other poems, she often cast herself in the roles of literary or mythic personae, such as Phaedra or Ophelia.

There has been no known attempt to produce any of Tsvetayeva's verse dramas on stage. Tsvetayeva's dramatic works should really be considered poems in dramatic form rather than plays. Tsvetayeva had matured as a lyric poet at the time this first drama was written, but was just beginning to experiment in dramatic forms. While this short drama in verse is not a striking contribution to the development of Russian literature of the period, it remains a significant part of Marina Tsvetayeva's literary achievement.

Pamela Pavliscak

THE SOLDIER

Author: Rupert Brooke (1887-1915)
Type of poem: Sonnet
First published: 1915, in *1914 and Other Poems*

The Poem

"The Soldier" is a sonnet of two stanzas: an octet of eight lines and a sestet of six lines. It is the last in a series of five sonnets composed shortly after the outbreak of World War I. The poems are linked by theme as well as form; all reflect idealism and optimism in the face of war, expressing the idea of release through self-sacrifice that many experienced with the coming of that war. "The Soldier" is about the probable death of a soldier, but the poem has little to do with dying.

The first stanza establishes the situation. The first-person speaker requests that "If I should die, think only this of me:/ That there's some corner of a foreign field/ That is for ever England." Even in the war's earliest stages there was the realization that the battles would result in death for at least some of the combatants. The pain of dying or the physi-cal degradation of death are totally absent, however; the references that follow are all to life. Brooke asserts that where his body is eventually buried, "a richer dust [will be] con-cealed." The dust of his body is richer than that surrounding it because he was a part of his country. The England that Brooke describes exhibits the characteristics of the rural countryside—in particular, a tranquil landscape like that of his native Cambridgeshire. The "English air," the flowers, rivers, roads, paths, and "suns of home" all define what the narrator claims that his country gave to and forged in him.

The second stanza assumes the speaker's death; however, death itself is absent: The conditional "if" of the first stanza has simply happened. As a result, the speaker has become transfigured: "this heart, all evil shed away,/ A pulse in the eternal mind." In his death, the narrator returns something of what England gave to him as he "gives somewhere back the thoughts by England given." The references are again to life, not death: "dreams happy as her day," "laughter," and "hearts at peace, under an English heaven."

The poem celebrates an idealized vision of pastoral England and the noble qualities of her inhabitants. Brooke's language emphasizes the universal, so that the England of the poem becomes every soldier's home, and the dead soldier is every Englishman. The tone is uplifting and idealistic but also self-sacrificial. There is a sense of roman-tic inevitability about the privilege and duty of dying for one's country. Feelings of pa-triotism and nationalism give nobility to that sacrifice, a sacrifice willingly crowned by death.

Forms and Devices

In "The Soldier," Brooke demonstrates his mastery of the sonnet, using the classic form to heighten the decorum and idealization conveyed by the poem. The long iambic pentameter lines and disciplined rhyme scheme enhance the poem's formal tone. Interestingly, Brooke uses the form originally borrowed from the Italian Renaissance poet Petrarch rather than the modified one popularized by William Shakespeare, who converted the octet and sestet of the Petrarchan sonnet into the three quatrains and couplet of the English sonnet. The advantage is that the Italian sonnet's sestet allows a more leisurely, fully developed concluding statement.

The imagery of the poem revolves around the generalities of the idealized English countryside. Brooke, in the first stanza, makes use of a litany of scenes from nature: "her flowers to love, her ways to roam,/ . . . breathing English air,/ Washed by the rivers, blest by suns of home." The images are almost placid in feeling, conveying a sense of Edenic escape. Brooke and many of his generation in the years before the war attempted to distance themselves from what they perceived as the corrupting influences of the too urban, modern world of early twentieth century Britain.

Brooke's rural images might also be seen as an intentional contrast to the horrors of modern warfare. Brooke had no experience in battle, but as a member of the upper-middle classes, acquainted with such politicians as Winston Churchill (then head of the Admiralty), he must have known the destruction that industry and technology would bring to the war. The rural images of a preindustrial England evoked in the poem may represent a deliberate denial of the barbed wire and machine guns of no-man's-land.

Brooke uses the melodic effects of assonance and alliteration throughout "The Soldier." He repeats the long *i* sound in "I" and "die" in the first line and the short *e* in "for ever England" in the third. Examples of alliteration are even more abundant, among them the repeated *f* in "foreign field," the play on "rich" and "richer" in the fourth line, the sonorous *b*, *s*, and *r* sounds of the seventh and eighth lines, and the *s*, *d*, *l*, and *h* sounds in the last three lines. He also reinforces his patriotic theme by repeating the words "England" and "English" on six occasions in the poem's fourteen lines.

Critics have also noted the use of what is sometimes called "high" diction by many writers in the late nineteenth and early twentieth centuries. Brooke's "The Soldier" exemplifies this choice of language. Rather than discussing dead bodies, he uses the word "dust"; instead of the battlefield or the front, "field" suffices; "heaven" is preferred to sky. Perhaps his most famous use of such diction comes from another of his poems, "The Dead," also printed in *1914 and Other Poems*: "the red/ Sweet wine of youth" becomes a euphemism for blood. This selection of alternative words reflects the revived interest in the chivalry of the Middle Ages which had become so common among the educated classes, again in reaction to the wrenching transformation caused by the industrial revolution.

Themes and Meanings

Brooke's "The Soldier" is one of the most often quoted of the many poems which were written during World War I, a war that affected a significant number of poets, particularly from Great Britain. Brooke's poems were among the first, but he was later joined by Edmund Blunden, Robert Graves, Siegfried Sassoon, Isaac Rosenberg, and

Wilfred Owen. All responded to the challenge and trauma engendered by the "Great War," though in disparate ways.

"The Soldier" is less a war poem than an elegy on sacrifice. The subject is ostensibly war, and the speaker is a soldier, but there is nothing in the poem that suggests warfare as such. Instead, the poem justifies the soldier's willing sacrifice on "a foreign field," an explanation that has more to do with idealized concepts about oneself and one's country than the causes of war. There is nothing about the enemy or fighting, and only one direct reference to death, at the very beginning of the poem. Even this reference is softened by the qualifying "if," although the rest of the poem assumes that the speaker will indeed die.

What one should sacrifice himself for is his country, underscored by the constant use of "England" or "English" throughout the poem. This reflects the strong sense of nationalism endemic throughout Western civilization in the early twentieth century. As traditional religious feelings lost their impact upon some sections of society, nationalism became, for many, a new religion worthy of worship and commitment.

Yet "The Soldier" is a paean not to the England of Brooke's day so much as to the ideal of a pastoral England. This nostalgic vision excluded the present, in which factories and cities had become the norm. Brooke's poem is an elegy on nature and the transcendent values of the natural world, as manifested in the English landscape.

The poem is also about escape—not only from the ugly industrialism and urbanization which disgusted Brooke, but also from the frustrations of personal life. To die can be a release, and to die in a noble cause justifies the self's sacrifice. Brooke was not unique: Many in 1914 saw the war as a release from lives stultified by personal and societal obstacles.

Brooke's idealism did not long survive him. He enlisted in the military, but before he could see action in battle he died of infection in the spring of 1915. The war went on, and the number of deaths multiplied—there were sixty thousand British casualties, for example, at the first day of the Battle of the Somme in 1916. For other poets, the war lost its allure and death its nobility; in Wilfred Owen's "Dulce et Decorum Est," to die for one's country became an obscenity. In that context, Brooke's "The Soldier" appeared only naïve. His idealism was replaced by a world without ideals; his love of his English countryside gave way to a lost generation. Nevertheless, the search for transcendent meaning in life and the commitment to a noble cause have been recurring themes throughout human history; perhaps ultimately "The Soldier" is less a poem praising war and patriotism than it is a quest for personal identity.

Eugene Larson

SOLILOQUY OF THE SPANISH CLOISTER

Author: Robert Browning (1812-1889)
Type of poem: Dramatic soliloquy
First published: 1842, in *Dramatic Lyrics*

The Poem

Robert Browning's "Soliloquy of the Spanish Cloister," in nine stanzas of seventy-two lines, consists of the under-the-breath mutterings of a cloistered monk as he observes with hatred Brother Lawrence watering his myrtle-bushes in the convent garden. Everything about Brother Lawrence irritates the speaker deeply. He cannot stand the way that the monk spends refection talking about the weather and his beloved plants, the way he eats and drinks hardily while the speaker is always careful to demonstrate his own piety by laying his knife and fork crosswise and by drinking his "watered orange pulp" in three sips to represent the Trinity.

He imagines how Brother Lawrence must lust deeply, if only he would show it, after "brown Dolores," who often sits outside the convent wall combing her long, black, lustrous hair. Even as the speaker observes Brother Lawrence trimming his flowers, he takes great pleasure when one snaps, and he gleefully admits keeping the plants "close-nipped on the sly."

Thus the speaker contemplates how most effectively to destroy the soul of the hated brother. Perhaps he could trap him in one of the twenty-nine sins listed in a passage in Galatians just as he was at the point of death and send him off to Hell, or turn down the most lurid page of all in his pornographic novel and slip it in among the garden tools. That certainly would cause the despised brother to grovel in the hands of "Belial," the devil.

He even fantasizes selling his soul to the devil (but being sure to leave a loophole in the contract) when the vesper bells ring calling the brothers to prayer. The poem closes as the speaker curses Brother Lawrence—"you swine!"—before they have to enter into prayers together.

Forms and Devices

Browning's appeal has often come from the dramatic presentation of inner psychological character, frequently of figures out of the mainstream of normal experience. In "Soliloquy of the Spanish Cloister," Browning uses the technique of soliloquy taken from the stage. Whereas the speaker actually voices his thoughts, unlike in dramatic monologues, nobody in the poem hears him. As a result of this technique, the poem achieves immediacy—everything happens within the time frame of the actual reading of the poem, just as it would if this soliloquy were spoken on stage.

Furthermore, the dramatic nature of the form allows Browning to avoid stilted poetic diction and instead to demonstrate the forceful language of the speaker in a variety of forms:

> If hate killed men, Brother Lawrence,
> God's blood, would not mine kill you!

This allows Browning to show the reader a speaker who sometimes voices his own opinions, sometimes quotes from the Bible, and sometimes mocks or parodies Brother Lawrence's hated affectations. At times the reader may even sympathize with the speaker in his disdain for the boring Brother Lawrence. In short, the dramatic nature of this poem allows the full display of the speaker's ambiguous personality.

Remarkably, while the poem sounds so dramatically real, Browning reveals his true virtuosity through the poetic forms he uses. Each stanza consists of eight variously trochaic and iambic tetrameter lines. Tetrameter often is used for fast movement in a poem, as in stanzas 7 and 8, but speed and natural speech cadences are achieved also by the use of irregular rhymes and frequent double rhymes, for example in the last lines of the poem, in which every line ends with a double rhyme:

> Blasted lay that rose-acacia
> We're so proud of! *Hy, Zy, Hine* . . .
> St, there's Vespers! Plena gratiâ
> *Ave, Virgo!* Gr-r-r—you swine!

The phrase "*Hy, Zy, Hine*" represents the ringing of the vesper bells but also signals the beginning of the final curse on Brother Lawrence.

Themes and Meanings

"Soliloquy of the Spanish Cloister" ostensibly deals with the lives of only two monks, but Browning intends to give a glimpse into the whole monastic system while unintentionally revealing his own Protestant prejudices against asceticism. No historic basis serves as a source for the poem; instead, Browning treats the cloister as a breeding ground for extremely narrow-minded thinking and gross jealousy of all that does not satisfy powerful egos. This poem gives the sour-natured attitude of mind of a monk jealous of a brother, whom he hates merely because of his genial nature and goodness. Brother Lawrence does come off like a terrible bore, however, and perhaps his dullness lends to the humorous counterpoint of the speaker's lust for physical enjoyment in life. In stanza 1, Brother Lawrence's simple caring for his garden galls the speaker utterly:

> What? your myrtle-bush wants trimming?
> Oh, that rose has prior claims—
> Needs its leaden vase filled brimming?
> Hell dry you up with its flames!

The speaker further despises Brother Lawrence for his simple interest in spiritual life and his neglect of those petty superstitious forms, the observance of which the ill-natured monk congratulates himself.

> When he finishes refection,
>   Knife and fork he never lays
> Cross-wise, to my recollection,
>   As do I, in Jesu's praise.
> I the Trinity illustrate,
>   Drinking watered orange pulp—
> In three sips the Arian frustrate;
>   While he drains his at one gulp.

The reader must delight in this at-times humorous portrait of the monk, all the while disapproving of his attitude, but all the same enjoy his shocking exuberance, his demonic intensity, his zest for earthly pleasure. Yet when everything is finally considered, "Soliloquy of the Spanish Cloister" is a serious analysis of emotional hatred that too close and too long association might develop in an uncharitable person.

Paul Varner

THE SOLITARY REAPER

Author: William Wordsworth (1770-1850)
Type of poem: Pastoral
First published: 1807, in *Poems in Two Vols.*

The Poem

"The Solitary Reaper" is a short lyrical ballad, composed of thirty-two lines and divided into four stanzas. As the title suggests, the poem is dominated by one main figure, a Highland girl standing alone in a field harvesting grain. The poem is written in the first person and can be classified as a pastoral, or a literary work describing a scene from country life. The eyewitness narration conveys the immediacy of personal experience, giving the reader the impression that the poet did not merely imagine the scene but actually lived it. However, Wordsworth's sister, Dorothy, writes in her *Recollections of a Tour in Scotland* that the idea for "The Solitary Reaper" was suggested to William by an excerpt from Thomas Wilkinson's *Tour in Scotland*. Since Wordsworth's poem is not autobiographical, one can assume that the poet is adopting a persona, or taking on a fictional identity (usually referred to as the "speaker" of the poem).

"The Solitary Reaper" begins with the speaker asking the reader to "behold" the girl as she works in the field. The first stanza is a straightforward description of the scene. The girl is standing alone in the field, cutting grain, and singing a "melancholy strain." Wordsworth emphasizes the girl's solitude by using words such as "single," "solitary," "by herself," and "alone." Solitaries are common figures in Wordsworth's poetry and are usually surrounded by a natural environment. The act of reaping alone in the field binds the girl intimately to the earth. Also, as the girl sings and the melody fills the lonely valley, she becomes almost completely merged with nature.

The next two stanzas describe the speaker's reaction to the maiden's song. The words of the song are in a language unknown to him, but he remains transfixed by the melody, which seems to stretch the limits of time and space. He associates the sweetness of the reaper's song with the beautiful cries of the nightingale and the cuckoo, both familiar images of transcendence in Romantic poetry. As he allows the song to engulf his consciousness, he envisions far-off places and times of long ago. His imagination transports him from the field in which he stands to the edge of infinity.

In the fourth stanza, the speaker abruptly shifts his attention from his musings to the scene before him. He continues to listen, but the transcendent moment is past. He again calls attention to the reaper, who is unaware of the speaker's presence or the effect her song has had on him. As the speaker walks away from the field, the song fades from his hearing, but its plaintive melody echoes in his heart and his imagination.

Forms and Devices

Wordsworth uses several poetic devices in "The Solitary Reaper." Among them is apostrophe, which is defined as a figure of speech where the speaker of the poem addresses a dead or absent person, an abstraction, or an inanimate object. At the beginning of the poem the speaker invites the reader to "Behold, her single in the field,/ Yon solitary Highland Lass!" He further cautions the reader to "Stop here, or gently pass!" Although the reader is not present, the speaker's imperative to "behold" the girl at her work puts the reader vicariously in the company of the speaker, as if they were walking the Highlands together. After the first four lines, the speaker shifts his attention away from the implied presence of the reader and does not allude to it again.

Metaphor, another common poetic device, is also found in "The Solitary Reaper." The poet uses metaphor to compare two images without explicitly stating the comparison. For example, in the second stanza the speaker compares the song of the reaper to those of the nightingale and cuckoo. Although the three songs are fundamentally different from one another, they become metaphors for transcendence as they suggest to the speaker distant times and places. Because the maiden's song is in a language unknown to the speaker, he is freed from trying to understand the words and is able to give his imagination full rein. The bird-songs and the girl's song are thus intertwined, a further link of the maiden to nature.

Suggestion through imagery is also used in connection with the reaper herself. The poet offers little description of her beyond the bare essentials given in stanzas 1 and 4. All the reader knows is that the reaper is a simple peasant girl singing a rather sad song while harvesting grain in a field. However, the speaker's imaginative associations make her much more. He connects her with shady haunts of Arabian sands, the cuckoo and the nightingale, the seas beyond the Hebrides, epic battles, and the common human experiences of sorrow and pain. From his perspective, she becomes the center of the universe, if only for a moment. Like her song, she dwarfs time and space, to become a metaphor for the eternal.

Music is also a dominant image in the poem. It is reinforced by the ballad form whose tones, rhythms, and rhymes emphasize the lyrical feeling. The musical image is further underscored by the use of alliteration. The repetition of *s* sounds, which are threaded throughout the poem, lends a tonal unity to the piece. For example, in the first four lines of the first stanza, fourteen words contain *s*. This pattern is repeated in the other stanzas but decreases toward the end of the poem as the reaper's song releases its grip on the consciousness of the speaker.

Themes and Meanings

"The Solitary Reaper" is about the power of the imagination to transform common, everyday events into representations of a larger reality. To the Romantic poets, imagination was not a synonym for fantasy. Instead they saw it as closely allied with intuition and emotion. This faculty enabled the poet to see familiar things in a radically different way. Samuel Taylor Coleridge, a Romantic poet himself and a friend of Wordsworth, noted that "the grandest efforts of poetry are when the imagination is called forth, not to produce a distinct form, but a strong working of the mind . . . the result being what the poet wishes to impress, namely, the substitution of a sublime feeling of the unimaginable for a mere image." The aim of the Romantics was to express an abstract idea using concrete images that were usually drawn from nature.

The poem is an example of the commonplace pointing the sensitive observer toward an ideal of unity or completeness of being. Although the reaper is a flesh-and-blood person, she becomes a spiritual gateway for the speaker of the poem. The natural environment that surrounds her only heightens her mystery. Her simple song is an expression of her own heritage and background, yet the speaker imagines it to be an articulation of the eternal, the boundless, the ultimate reality. This intuitive impression of the infinite leaves the speaker a different person than when he first encountered the girl. The wonder of her song permeates his intellect and lingers in his heart long after he hears the last notes.

Wordsworth's conviction that the infinite can be encountered in the finite emerges from his own personal experience. Frequently when he walked alone in nature, he detected a pervading presence, a consciousness that would break into the ordinary moments of his life and turn them into flashes of revelation. In addition to "The Solitary Reaper," Wordsworth's *The Prelude* and "Lines: Composed a Few Miles Above Tinturn Abbey" offer examples of poems that reflect intense instances of mystical insight as well as the sometimes uneasy, sometimes joyous response the poet had toward these visionary experiences. In "The Solitary Reaper" Wordsworth celebrates such illuminating moments. The girl, her song, and her natural surroundings combine in a unified whole and contribute to the speaker's expanded vision of reality.

For modern readers, whose lives overflow with activity, the theme of encountering the transcendent in nature or through everyday events may at first seem strange. Since many people have little chance to walk in the woods or stroll through farmland, readers might be tempted to dismiss Wordsworth's poem because the setting and situation do not reflect their own experiences. Although the values, concerns, and lifestyle of Wordsworth's time were different, the yearning of the human spirit to feel connected to something larger than itself remains as strong today as it was during the nineteenth century. Modern people long for a quiet place to recollect themselves, a place where they can catch a glimpse of the eternal in the details of their lives. Thus the theme of transcendence in "The Solitary Reaper" is timeless, as it speaks to the needs of the human spirit.

Pegge Bochynski

SOMEWHERE I HAVE NEVER TRAVELLED, GLADLY BEYOND

Author: E. E. Cummings (1894-1962)
Type of poem: Lyric
First published: 1931, in *W: Seventy New Poems*

The Poem

The poem "somewhere i have never travelled, gladly beyond" first appeared in E. E. Cummings's *W: Seventy New Poems*, a collection of seventy poems. It is poem 57 in a section often labeled "Poems in Praise of Love and Lovers." While the first thirty-five poems in the collection emphasize the author's low estimate of humans as social animals, the final half stresses a positive view of humankind based on individual love and on the bonding created by relationships.

The poem is an interior monologue using Cummings's lyric and mythic style. Using the Renaissance archetypes of gardens, flowers, and nature as symbols for his mistress and her laudable qualities, Cummings explores the essential rhythms and cycles of the natural world while drawing parallels to idyllic love.

The woman in the poem is thought to be Anne Barton, a witty, vivacious socialite who began an affair with Cummings in 1925. She was his second love, and she restored his liveliness of spirit after his disastrous affair with a married woman who bore Cummings's first child. The poem begins with a travel/discovery image, as Cummings tries to explore the nature of his relationship with the woman. He is captivated by her but finds her very nearness disconcerting; it reveals what he is missing without her. Stanzas 2 and 3 picture Cummings as a flower, a reversal of the typical comparison of women to flowers; it also portrays the woman as spring and snow, natural and opposing elements. The opening and closing of the flower signify the power of the woman to control Cummings; her very touch opens his petals or closes the heart of his flower.

The woman's frailty, mentioned in stanza 1, is reiterated in stanza 4; paradoxically, it is the source of her power. This power is intense and compelling; it has the power to "render death and forever with each breathing" (line 16). Cummings's effort to understand the incomprehensible is stressed in the final stanza, but he is only able to say that the inexplicable exists in such depth that words cannot do it justice.

Though the poem is basically positive and consists of unabashed praise, several paradoxes seem to capture the problems of love as well. This portrait is at times disconcerting, for "beyond any experience" may suggest an inner stillness beyond reach that the poet cannot obtain. A "remote voice" also implies the unpleasant possibility of loss; the "silence" may suggest either muffled suppression or quiet peace.

Finally, the touch imagery suggests not only physical contact but also an inability to comprehend or come to grips with a situation. Such a picture accurately paints the textures and color of love—it is both bane and blessing.

Forms and Devices

Cummings's "somewhere i have never travelled, gladly beyond" utilizes several experimental forms in order to transport the reader beyond the seen world into the unseen. The poem's synesthetic style is the most important innovation here; Cummings linguistically merges each of the five senses with traits that belong to another sense. The poem begins with sight (eyes) but also emphasizes sound (silence). The second, third, and fourth stanzas deal with the sense of touch and revolve around variations based on the words "closed" and "open." Yet the ability to feel is also strangely joined with the sight image of stanza 1 as the words "look," "colour," "petal," and "rose" in the middle stanza imply the necessity of vision.

The synesthesia repeats in stanza 5 as Cummings joins sound and sight in the words "the voice of your eyes." Smell is also implied in "deeper than all roses." The images culminate in touch, smell, sound, a visual image (having small hands), and the personification of rain.

Experiments with punctuation, capitalization, ellipsis, and fragmentation are also part of the uniqueness of the poem. For example, commas, semicolons, colons, and parentheses are present, while no periods are used. As a result, the reader slides effortlessly from idea to idea, and a simultaneousness of imagery is created.

Other poetic techniques employed by Cummings in the poem include oxymoron and simile. Oxymoron, the joining of opposites, is evident in "the power of your intense fragility" and "rendering death and forever with each breathing." Similes, comparisons using "like" or "as," are evident in the reference to the beloved as "Spring" or to himself as the heart of a flower. Personification is also used when Cummings gives human qualities to texture, flowers, and rain.

Another factor is Cummings's word choices, which suggest a linguistic joining of form and meaning. The complexity of the love relationship is expressed in monosyllabic words with ordinary suffixes. This joining is also evident in the meter of the poem, which appears to be a type of sprung-rhythm pentameter and suggests the flexibility of opening and closing stressed in stanzas 1 through 3. The perfect rhyme of the final stanza ("understands" and "hands") also seems to suggest the perfection of the relationship, a perfection that cannot be expressed in word meaning but may be captured in the word appearance, sound, and pacing provided by the author. As the imagery moves from spring to winter to spring again, it is evident that the author has utilized the seasons and the garden to integrate growth, birth, and dying as manifestations of love.

Themes and Meanings

The narrator of this love poem tries to express the inexpressible, to describe the intensity of his emotions. He finds himself unable to meet the challenge except in paradoxical words that simultaneously express his surprise and wonder at the mystery of love.

The narrator describes the love as similar to a foreign territory, an area never before explored; the effect of the journey is stunning, evoking a disorientation which causes the senses to overlap. Yet at the same time he finds himself unable to delineate the specific elements which attract him; instead, he explores the inexpressible by saying that the sense of touch fails when objects are too near. Love can also bring about a beautiful and sudden seclusion, with the individual shutting out other demands in favor of love; the speaker depicts such a closing by using the image of a flower as it begins to close when it senses falling snow.

Cummings's descriptions of his beloved as having texture and color indicate her depth of character, but they also, when combined with the word "countries" at the end of line 15, suggest mapmaking and tie in with the poem's initial image of traveling. Just as explorers of new lands are awed by their initial discoveries, so the narrator reacts with surprise at the variety he finds in his lover, a woman who with her very breathing destroys or breaks down the fear of death and eternity.

The narrator reiterates his inability to understand exactly what it is about the beloved that possesses the power to open and close him. The image of the garden is repeated, as the flower (rose) symbolizes both the narrator and his beloved, and the powerful final line states the incomparable quality of love. No body and no thing (lines 13 and 20) can truly attain the level of the narrator and his beloved. The rain, nurturer of the symbolic garden, though it is important, pales in importance to the small hands of the beloved, whose touch has moved the narrator to ecstasy, to a height of emotion never before experienced.

The five senses, emphasized and raised by the association with love, are combined with the traditional and archetypal symbols of a garden and flowers to serve as symbols for wordlessness, for the inexpressible expressed and given life by the poet's effort.

Michael J. Meyer

SOMNAMBULE BALLAD

Author: Federico García Lorca (1898-1936)
Type of poem: Lyric/ballad
First published: 1928, as "Romance sonámbulo," in *Romancero gitano*; English
translation collected in *Gypsy Ballads*, 1990

The Poem

Despite the poet's declaration that he himself did not know what was going on in
the poem, "Somnambule Ballad," Federico García Lorca's supreme dream poem,
readily yields most of its secrets to the patient reader. It narrates the plight of a
wounded gypsy smuggler seeking refuge from the Guardia Civil (Civil Guards, the
rural Spanish police force, at one time noted for its harshness) in the house where his
sweetheart lived. Incantatory phrases, haunting images, and a confusion of the real
and dream worlds form the background against which this ballad's action takes place.

A strong sense of Andalusia, a province in southern Spain, pervades the poem.
Country houses there typically have verandas on their roofs to allow the inhabitants to
appreciate the cool evening breezes, and a cistern or water tank can be found in most
Andalusian patios.

The poem opens by invoking the allure of the color green, makes a reference to the
smuggler's means of transport (ship and horse), and then describes a mysterious girl
transfixed on a veranda. Her hair and eyes reflect the moonlight; while under its spell,
she is surrounded by things that see her but that she herself cannot see. This is the first
of many instances in which the characters in this dream ballad seem impotent, unable
to move and to answer for themselves.

The narrator hears someone coming, and a dialogue occurs between two men—one
of them the smuggler, the other his "compadre," who is possibly also the father of the
bewitched girl on the veranda. The young and wounded smuggler wants to exchange
his horse, saddle, and dagger for the domestic comforts of the compadre's house in order to die decently in a bed with fine linen instead of ignominiously by the side of the
road. His friend, however, with the impotence common to dreams, and perhaps under
the same spell as the green-haired girl on the veranda, says that he is no longer master
of himself nor of his house; despite the smuggler's gaping wound, he cannot help.

The young man begs permission at least to climb to the veranda to see the girl.
Leaving a trail of blood and tears, the two friends make their way to the roof. The
smuggler cries out for the girl, and his friend retorts that for many a night, free of the
moon's spell, with fresh face and black hair she waited for the young man.

In a sudden shift of scene, the narrator describes the girl as sustained on a shaft of
moonlight as she rocks back and forth on the top of the cistern. The sound of the
drunken Civil Guards beating on the door seals the young man's fate, and the poem
closes with the lines with which it began.

Forms and Devices

García Lorca closely copied the classical Spanish ballad in both form and technique as he composed his modern versions. An indeterminate number of eight-syllable lines rhyming in assonance (vowels) in even-numbered lines is the set pattern for these lyrics. They also make use of dramatic dialogue and are given to exaggeration. Three hundred ladies-in-waiting accompany Roland's wife in the sixteenth century ballad "Doña Alda," and three hundred roses (splotches of blood) stain the smuggler's shirt in García Lorca's ballad. Spanish ballads frequently close on a note of impending doom: an unanswered question, an intruder knocking at the door. The listener or reader must supply the ominous details. García Lorca uses this device when he has the narrative line of the poem cease as the drunken Civil Guards pound on the door of the house where the smuggler has taken refuge. Part of the attraction of García Lorca's gypsy ballads is in their blend of a very traditional and popular form of literature with modernism.

The same mysterious, singsong lines open and close the poem. Green suggests nature, growth, and vegetation; it also introduces the color of the moon (the moon is made of green cheese, goes an old children's sayi∩   English) that tinges the face of the gypsy girl. In Spanish, *verde* has an additional connotation of "off-color, dirty," a sexual association that no English translation can bring out. After the first two lines chant about the magic of the color green, they are followed by two lines that state simply the existence of objects of reality in their logical and natural surroundings: the ship on the sea, the horse on the mountain. Thus the poem at once establishes its characteristic play between dreams and reality.

García Lorca also makes use of images that have more prescribed meanings. Wounded in the mountain pass of Cabra and losing a considerable amount of blood, the smuggler speaks in metonymies. Horse, saddle, and dagger represent the active, adventurous, masculine life of the smuggler; house, mirror, blanket stand for the safe, domestic, and feminine aspects of shelter.

García Lorca is celebrated for his flair for metaphor, and this poem has many examples. When he writes that the fig tree rubs the wind with the sandpaper of its branches, he is employing one of his favorite devices: the reversal of normal roles. It would be natural for the wind to rustle against the harsh branches of the fig tree, not for the leaves to sand the wind. The metaphors often make extravagant or unusual associations. The outline of a mountain against the sky can be compared to the arched back of a cat, whose hairs stand on end like the century plant (agave). From the veranda, the tin plate lanterns turn into glass tambourines, whose sound (glare) clashes with the light of dawn.

Most of the metaphors present startling ways to look at the reality of nature. They are not only for decoration, however; they contribute to the theme. The gypsies are pursued by the forces of society (the Civil Guards), and whenever this takes place, elements of nature react in consternation: the wind blows, the mountain bristles, the moon intrudes.

Themes and Meanings

The gypsy population of Spain is concentrated in Andalusia. García Lorca grew up in Granada and knew well flamenco, the flamboyant music and dance of the gypsies. Living on the margin of Spanish society and often outside the law, the gypsies were looked upon with suspicion by the middle class and were persecuted by the infamous Civil Guards. In his earliest poetry (much of it still unpublished), García Lorca displayed a ready sympathy for the underdog. He found it easy to champion the gypsies in Spain and later the blacks in New York, and the enduring theme of his work is the evil of oppression in both its private and public forms.

From this web of social facts and personal interests grew the *Gypsy Ballads* (*Romancero gitano*). García Lorca proposed mythologizing the gypsies, turning them into subjects of poetry. In the ballads, he puts the gypsies on an equal footing with the forces of nature. They interact with the moon, wind, sun, stars, and ocean in one enlarged magical community. As in any community, friends and enemies vary. The sea can frown and olive trees grow pale as the gypsy girl Preciosa is pursued by the satyr wind in one of the famous ballads. Nearly all the gypsy ballads tell of an encounter between the idealized "natural" gypsies and the fierce forces of law and order. Such is clearly the case in "Somnambule Ballad," for in García Lorca's time, gypsies were often smugglers and it was the Civil Guard's business to catch them.

Much of the attraction of the "Somnambule Ballad" derives from its skillful handling of the dream atmosphere. Sigmund Freud said there are basically two kinds of dreams, wish-fulfillment dreams and anxiety dreams, and García Lorca has managed to present both in a single poem. The opening lines sing of the desire for green, or for some kind of elemental force that can be love, sex, or nature and can permeate the world (the wind becomes green). The poem is framed by the narrator's deep desires. Within the body of the ballad, anxiety centers on the fate of the young man, his sweetheart (how did she die? did she throw herself into the cistern?), and the identity of the old man, all dramatized by the omnipotent and drunken Civil Guards.

Salvador Dalí, when he first heard García Lorca read the poem, is said to have remarked that there seemed to be a plot and yet there was not. In capturing so well this paradox of the dream state, García Lorca created an arresting poem.

Howard Young

A SONG FOR ST. CECILIA'S DAY

Author: John Dryden (1631-1700)
Type of poem: Ode
First published: 1687; collected in *Examen Poeticum*, 1693

The Poem

The first of John Dryden's two Saint Cecilia's Day odes, "A Song for St. Cecilia's Day," was written to commemorate November 22 as the day devoted to the patron saint of music. His second, *Alexander's Feast* (1697), a longer and more elaborate composition, appeared ten years later, near the end of Dryden's career. The practice of writing odes to commemorate St. Cecilia began in England in 1683, and Dryden was among the first poets to write at the invitation of a London musical society. Giovanni Battista Draghi's musical adaptation, the first of several for the poem, accompanied the initial publication. In form, it is an ode, consisting of seven stanzas and a grand concluding chorus, sixty-three lines in all.

The structure resembles the Horatian or Roman ode in its linear and logical development. Two general introductory stanzas are followed by five others, which identify and trace the effects of musical instruments, plus a concluding chorus. Yet the stanzas, unlike those of the Horatian ode, are irregular, employing a variety of meters and ranging in length from four to fifteen lines. Writing at a time when the classical ode was little understood, Dryden may have adapted this stanzaic irregularity from Pindar, whose Greek odes were highly esteemed.

The initial stanza opens the poem with the statement that creation, bringing order and harmony to chaotic matter, was accompanied by music. This vision of creation derives from Lucretius and Ovid, classical Roman poets whose works Dryden knew well. To stress the power of music, Dryden emphasizes the role of musical harmony in imparting order to the universe. The second stanza narrows the theme to the power of music in arousing human emotion, the poem's major theme. In the biblical account of the origin of music (Genesis 4:21), in which Jubal excited his hearers to wonder by blowing upon a sea shell, Dryden finds confirmation of the power of music over the emotions.

In stanzas 3 through 7, Dryden governs the structure by showing that each instrument arouses a particular human emotion in the hearer. These five stanzas, dealing with seven instruments, offer a basically chronological arrangement of instruments invented by man. Trumpets and drums arouse emotions associated with warfare, such as anger and courage. The flute and lute appeal to the soft emotions associated with romantic love, both its tenderness and its complaints of woe. Violins' sharp tones suggest the jealousy and pain of discordant love. Finally the organ, traditionally credited to St. Cecilia's invention, creates the sustained, majestic tones that inspire religious devotion.

Contrasting St. Cecilia with Orpheus, the legendary classical musician whose lyre moved trees to abandon their roots, the poem confers the greater power upon St. Cecilia. For, while she played her organ, an angel appeared, thinking that the sounds came from heaven. She thus produced the closest approximation on earth to the heavenly music that Dryden celebrated in the first stanza.

In the final stanza, a "Grand Chorus," the poem envisions future heavenly music, when at the sound of the trumpet all shall gather on the final day. As music began the creation and sustained its harmony through the music of the moving spheres, so it will end it, and music will "untune the sky."

Forms and Devices

The ode form, permitting verses of varying lengths, enables Dryden to achieve a rich diversity of poetic effects. Varied rhyme schemes and intricate sound effects create the beat and cadence of musical passages. In the ode, he relies less heavily on schemes of repetition that are prominent in his heroic couplets, although, along with figures of speech, they do contribute as well to the poem's effects.

Just as the stanzas in the ode vary from four to fifteen lines, the lines vary from iambic trimeter to iambic pentameter, with a larger number of iambic tetrameter verses, permitting a complexity of metrical effects. The rhymes are similarly irregular and, therefore, form no pattern of inner consistency from stanza to stanza.

By the time he wrote the ode, Dryden was a master of sound effects beyond onomatopoeia, and the ode reflects his exquisite ear for poetic sounds. Onomatopoeic words such as "whisper'd," "clangor," and "thund'ring" have their texture enhanced by accompanying echoes and vigorous, direct meters: "The Trumpet's loud clangor/ Excites us to arms/ With shrill notes of anger,/ And mortal alarms." Short lines, forceful syllables—the final line shortened to five syllables—and a heavy reliance on the *s* sound heighten intensity. In stanza 7, contrasting Orpheus and St. Cecilia, the poem demonstrates how altering metrical form can create emphasis:

> Orpheus could lead the savage race;
> And trees unrooted left their place,
>> Sequacious of the lyre;
> But bright Cecilia rais'd the wonder high'r:
> When to her Organ vocal breath was giv'n,
> An angel heard, and straight appear'd,
>> Mistaking earth for heav'n.

Orpheus is accorded an iambic tetrameter line, largely regular and direct, but Dryden significantly emphasizes St. Cecilia by introducing her with an iambic pentameter line, made even more emphatic because it rhymes with a preceding trimeter.

The range of poetic sound effects can be studied by contrasting the abrupt staccato depiction of the drum, "The double double double beat/ Of the thund'ring Drum," to the extended majestic sounds used to describe the organ: "What human voice can reach,/ The sacred Organ's praise?/ Notes inspiring holy love."

In the first passage, alliteration, short vowels, onomatopoeia, and assonance create echoes of drumbeats. In the second, sonorants, long vowels, and assonance lengthen the sounds to mimic the elongated tones of the organ.

Although Dryden makes extensive use of simple repetition for rhythmic effects, he relies little on complex schemes of repetition, except for sound effects achieved through assonance, alliteration, and onomatopoeia. A notable exception occurs in the climactic conclusion: "The dead shall live, the living die,/ And Music shall untune the sky." In this passage, balance and alliteration combine with polyptoton (a type of word repetition) and paradox to produce highly memorable poetry. Figures of speech are also used sparingly in what is essentially a tour de force of sounds. Yet the metaphor "crumbling pageant" for the world in the chorus, and the personifications of instruments, endowing them with human power, enrich the imaginative texture of the ode.

Themes and Meanings

"A Song for St. Cecilia's Day" celebrates the power of music by drawing upon classical myths and Christian and Jewish sources and legends. The dominant theme is directly expressed in the line "What passion cannot Music raise and quell!" Its development associates specific passions with specific instruments. This theme is developed, however, within the larger context of the hexameral tradition which associates music with the creation and of the Christian eschatological tradition which associates the trumpet with Judgment Day and the crumbling of creation. The power of music to raise passions is developed in the middle five stanzas about how music from individual instruments raises emotions; only in the eschatological Grand Chorus does Dryden explore how music quells emotions.

The mythic figures mentioned in the poem contribute to the idea of music developing from humble origins after the fall of man. The sublime music of creation of the first stanza that regulates the spheres remains unheard by men after the Fall in the Garden of Eden. Instead, Jubal creates the first musical sounds by blowing upon a sea shell and, as Dryden's description indicates, fills his hearers with wonder. Orpheus, from Greek mythology, confirms the power of music by his appeal to the plant and animal kingdoms. Thereafter, music increases its power over human emotions, as more complex instruments are fashioned. Dryden's descriptions of drums and trumpets exciting war's valor and anger and of flutes, lutes, and violins exciting the pleasures and pains of love (stanzas 3 to 5) suggest the conflict between love and honor that wracks the heroes of his heroic plays. By giving the organ the final place in the development of the instruments he names, Dryden accords it—and its emotion, religious devotion—greatest power and dignity. The intimation that the organ was invented after the violin is incorrect, yet Dryden never questions the legend that St. Cecilia invented the instrument.

Contrasting Orpheus, whose lyre gave trees the ability to separate from their roots and to move to music, with St. Cecilia, who drew an angel to her sounding organ, takes Dryden to the origins of music. In Dryden's hierarchical arrangement of levels of being, the appeal to an angel's passion surpasses any appeal to elemental or human emotions.

Dryden's climactic sequence of instruments leads almost inexorably to the final eschatological vision of the trumpet that ends all creation and quells normal human emotion. The mythical music of the spheres, heard since creation only by the inhabitants of heaven and ever since denied to man, gives way to the sound of the trumpet. The sky itself is untuned by the final cataclysmic event, and afterward only heaven itself retains the harmony that had previously informed and regulated the creation.

Stanley Archer

SONG OF MYSELF

Author: Walt Whitman (1819-1892)
Type of poem: Epic
First published: 1855, untitled, in *Leaves of Grass*

The Poem

Begun as early as 1847, "Song of Myself" first appeared as one of the twelve untitled poems of the first edition of *Leaves of Grass* (1855). Regularly revised, it became "Poem of Walt Whitman, an American" in the second edition (1856) and "Walt Whitman" in the third through sixth editions (1860, 1867, 1871, and 1876). Not until the seventh edition of *Leaves of Grass*, published in 1881, did the poem undergo its final metamorphosis in name as well as form. The first and final versions of "Song of Myself" are virtually identical in subject, style, and even length (1,336 and 1,346 lines respectively). Phrasings occasionally differ, but never crucially so. ("I celebrate myself," the 1855 edition begins; "and sing myself," Whitman later added). The division of the free-flowing untitled poem into fifty-two numbered sections, like the addition and subsequent revision of the title, proves more significant, for this overt structuring appears to add a sense of order and progression that the poem originally seemed to lack. This is not to say that the 1855 text was formless, or that structure is something Whitman arbitrarily imposed. The numbering merely accents the organic principle from which the poem develops, for the poem's unity derives less from the numbering of its sections according to the yearly cycle of weeks than from the fusion of song and self.

Not identifying himself by name until section 24—and even then in half-biblical, half-comical fashion, as "Walt Whitman, a kosmos, of Manhattan the son" (in the 1855 edition, "Walt Whitman, an American, one of the roughs, a kosmos")—the thirty-seven-year-old narrator strikes a decidedly proud and personal pose and addresses the reader in a doubly direct manner. From the outset, he incorporates his listener/reader into the poem (as "you") and permits "nature" to speak "without check, with original energy," which is to say, free of the constraints of either poetic convention or social decorum. The freedom Whitman takes evidences itself not only in his language and intimate mode of address, but in his very posture as well. The poem presents not merely a mind thinking or a voice speaking, but an entire body reclining on the ground, leaning and loafing, "observing a spear of summer grass." Like Henry David Thoreau in *Walden: Or, Life in the Woods* (1854), Whitman situates himself and his poem outdoors and therefore outside convention and tradition; and, like Ralph Waldo Emerson in his essay *Nature* (1836), Whitman deliberately conflates natural world and poetical word, leaf of grass and *Leaves of Grass*. Radically democratic and explicitly (as well as metaphorically) sexual, "Song of Myself" goes well beyond even the extended bounds of Transcendentalist thought in its celebration of the relation between physical and spiritual, individual and universal.

The middle third of the poem extends still further the sexual union of self and other, body and soul. As earlier he had claimed to be able to "resist anything better than my own diversity," now it is sensuous contact of any kind that Whitman's "hankering, gross, mystical, nude" figure cannot resist. Taking Emerson's symbol of the "transparent eyeball" (from *Nature*) to the very frontiers of poetic expression, Whitman indulges in an orgy of seeing, hearing, and feeling (sections 25-28). The scene culminates in orgasmic release (section 29), and is in turn followed (section 30) by a postcoital peace that passeth understanding. The knowledge that "All truths wait in all things" leads to the poem's longest and most exuberant catalog (section 33). Paradoxically "afoot with my vision" and flying "those flights of the fluid and swallowing soul" (while rooted to the very spot where his song began, still leaning and loafing, still observing the same multi-meaninged leaf of grass), Whitman continues his transgression of all social, temporal, and spatial boundaries.

By line 798, however, the pace begins to slacken as Whitman identifies closely and narrowly with one segment of society only: the injured, the imprisoned, the enslaved, the despised. Whitman has become one of the "trippers and askers" that surrounded him earlier. Finding himself "on the verge of a usual mistake," he pulls back barely in time, resuming "the overstaid fraction," the individual I. Saved from torpor and despair, he rises from the dead, an American Christ, and rises from the recumbent position he has maintained, appearances to the contrary, throughout the poem, to proclaim his faith in himself and in all others, equally divine, and in a vaguely defined but enthusiastically embraced cosmic plan.

Declaring an end to his loitering and talking, he prepares to resume the role or guise he left off to become the chanter of this "Song of Myself." The poem's last eight sections are marked by the urgency of his departure: by last-minute preparations, last words of advice, and reluctance to leave at all until his listener, who is also his student and comrade, brother and sister, speaks his or her own word in response. Standing accused by the free-flying hawk, Whitman reluctantly but also joyously and certainly garrulously sounds the last words of his "barbaric yawp," continuing his "perpetual tramp," not so much departing the scene as dispersing himself into the elements themselves.

Forms and Devices

"Who troubles himself about his ornaments or fluency is lost," Whitman warned in the preface to the 1855 edition to *Leaves of Grass*. His admonition is, however, in a way misleading. While it accurately measures the great distance between his "barbaric yawp" and the conventionality that characterized the standard poetry of his day, Whitman's remark may lead readers to assume that "Song of Myself," or any Whitman poem, is somehow artless. Whitman divested himself of the "ornaments" and "fluency" of conventional verse in order to craft a poetry more natively American, not only in subject but also in style. He took upon himself the task of discovering a poetic form as raw, as free, as unfinished, as expansive, as experimental, and as full of promise as his Transcendentalist conception of his country. Unlike Henry Wadsworth

Longfellow, he did not, except briefly, look back to the American past; he looked instead to the present moment and to a projected future. Unlike his fellow Transcendentalist Thoreau, one of his earliest supporters, Whitman did not count a man rich in relation to the number of things he could do without. Whitman's "omnivorous lines" give the illusion of leaving nothing out, of being democratically all-inclusive, a strange mixture (as Emerson himself noted) of the *Bhagavad Gītā* and the *New York Herald*. The poem's democratic thrust is most obviously at work in Whitman's lengthy catalogs, and more subtly in the combining of these catalogs with passages of considerable narrative power and others of great lyrical intensity.

Free in form and epic in reach, "Song of Myself" creates a structure all its own based upon repetition of words, phrases, and parallel syntactical structures. At both the micro and macro levels, the poem develops its own cumulatively powerful rhythm of ebb and flow, absorption and release, stasis and motion, or, to borrow Whitman's own operatic conceit, aria and recitative. Singing, however, serves as only one of a multiplicity of metaphors at work in "Song of Myself," no more but also no less important than building, weaving, and sexual union. Each plays its pervasive but ultimately partial role in Whitman's drama of the emerging self.

The merging of self and other in terms of sympathetic identification serves to hold the poem's varied materials together in one organic, evolving whole. As important as this metaphorical merging is the emphasis the poem places on the "I" that emerges from the speaker's self-generating, self-projecting performance. The Whitmanian persona comes to embody the paradoxical process of becoming what he has always been and must be. Freeing himself from all poetic and social constraints, he becomes his own transgressive self: an Emersonian representative man, a Transcendentalist version of the typically American tall-tale hero, bragging for all mankind.

Themes and Meanings

Early in the poem, a child asks, "What is the grass?" Although he claims, or pretends, not to know the answer, the Whitmanian persona goes on to offer a number of surmises, each plausible, each partial. "Song of Myself" constitutes one such seemingly simple yet punningly enigmatic leaf of grass: a poem in a book, *Leaves of Grass*, that expands and changes shape over nine separate editions even as it remains in essence always the same. The poem is for the reader what the grass is for the child: a "uniform hieroglyphic" for which there is no single Rosetta Stone by which it may be deciphered, other than the faith that Whitman cheerfully and insistently proclaims. Its "barbaric yawp" opens itself to a variety of interpretative strategies but chiefly attests its own capacity to outstrip them all: "Do I contradict myself?/ Very well then I contradict myself,/ (I am large, I contain multitudes.)"

The self that Whitman sings and celebrates proves as much a "uniform hieroglyphic" as the grass: equally evocative, multiform, and full of contradictions. It is as much a physical presence as a projected (spiritual) possibility. It is Emerson's self-engendered, self-reliant man, one who exists not in Thoreauvian isolation but in "ensemble," speaking the word "en-masse." As self-appointed bard of democracy, Whitman projects an "I" as expansive and diverse as the country itself, in a poetic form and language as experimental and new as the nation and its democratic political system.

Even as it overtly and enthusiastically expresses Whitman's faith in cosmic evolution and therefore in the essential indivisibility of Emersonian self-reliance and Over-Soul, "Song of Myself" also expresses in the very stridency of its affirmation a division deep within the poem's prototypical "self," within the poet himself (psychologically considered), and within the country (both socially and politically). It offers a Transcendentalist solution to the crisis of union that, only five years after the poem made its first appearance, would lead to civil war. "Song of Myself" presents, therefore, a complex set of variations on the theme sounded in more narrowly political terms in Abraham Lincoln's famous 1858 "A House Divided" speech. The poem did not resolve the national debate, nor did it bring about the Transcendentalist democracy Whitman envisioned—nor, apparently, did it ease the psychosexual divisions within Whitman's own psyche. Those failures, however, must be measured against the greatness of a work generally regarded not only as its author's most ambitious but also as one of American literature's most representative.

Robert A. Morace

SONG OF NAPALM

Author: Bruce Weigl (1949-   )
Type of poem: Lyric
First published: 1982; collected in *The Monkey Wars*, 1985

The Poem

"Song of Napalm" is a free-verse poem of forty-five lines divided into five stanzas. The title is ironic: "Song" suggests something lovely and lyric, while napalm, on the other hand, is a deadly, incendiary jelly that the United States military dropped on villages during the Vietnam War. When dropped as a bomb, napalm ignites, and the burning jelly sticks to its victims and burns them to death. Because of the title, the reader knows that Bruce Weigl will once again be exploring the Vietnam War, a subject he treats frequently.

The opening stanza presents an idyllic scene of a pasture after a storm told in the past tense. Because the poem is dedicated to the poet's wife, it is easy to assume that the two people watching as horses "walk off lazily across the pasture's hill" are the poet and his wife. However, the image, although pastoral, also contains the germ of foreboding: The narrator stares through a "black screen," he describes the grass as "scarlet," and he associates tree branches with barbed wire. The image of the barbed wire seems to propel the poet into the flux of past and present in the next stanza. The storm has passed, and he asserts that he has "turned [his] back on the old curses." However, his belief is mistaken; in the first line of the third stanza, he shifts to the present tense although he describes a scene from the distant past. The thunder from the storm becomes a "pounding mortar" in his flashback, and, when he closes his eyes, he sees a "girl/ running from her village, napalm/ stuck to her dress like jelly."

In the fourth stanza, the poet tries to imagine that the girl somehow escapes the burning napalm. He does this so that he "can keep on living." Yet he acknowledges the lie and once again returns to the vision of the burning girl. She not only burns to death in the flashback but also is permanently "burned behind" the poet's eyes. This vision from the past continues to haunt the poet. In the last lines of the poem, Weigl connects the pasture and Vietnam by describing the pasture as "jungle-green." This connection between home and Vietnam acknowledges the burning girl's presence in the present, an indication that the experience of the Vietnam War is not something that can remain hidden in the past.

Forms and Devices

Weigl uses a variety of sensory images and metaphors to take the reader on a round trip from a rain-swept pasture to the horrors of the Vietnam War and back again. The poem opens with an image of a storm replete with pounding rain and thunder. Although the storm has passed, its aftereffects can still be seen in the pasture, in the color of the grass, and in the moisture that the retreating horses kick up with their hooves.

Likewise, as the poem moves forward, readers realize that the "storm" of Weigl's Vietnam War experience continues to make its effects felt in the present. Thus, the pounding rain and the thunder become the pounding of a mortar in an auditory image that links the pasture and the Vietnam War.

A second powerful metaphoric image occurs in lines 4 and 5: "We stared through the black screen/ our vision altered by the distance." Literally, the black screen is no more than the screen door of the poet's home. However, readers are reminded of what looking through a screen door is like: People ignore the mesh as they view a scene beyond, yet their vision is subtly shifted by the presence of the screen. Metaphorically, the screen serves two purposes: First, the "black screen" is the canvas on which Weigl's memory plays out its visions of the Vietnam War; second, the black screen serves as a filter or a mesh that screens the memory of the burning girl in a particular way. Thus, Weigl's vision of the horses in the pasture is "altered by the distance" in much the same way that his vision of the past is altered by the distance of time.

In stanza 3, Weigl uses visual, auditory, tactile, and kinesthetic images as the scene from the present melts into the scene from the past. Even with his eyes closed, Weigl sees the burning girl "running from her village, napalm/ stuck to her dress like jelly,/ her hands reaching for the no one/ who waits in waves of heat before her." Readers can feel the heat on their skins as they too watch the girl burn, the mortar pounding in the background. Furthermore, Weigl emphasizes that the past continues into the present by his choice of the present participles "running" and "reaching" to form a kinesthetic image describing the girl's actions. In the final stanza, Weigl presents the ghastly image of the child burning to death:

> and the girl runs only as far
> as the napalm allows
> until her burning tendons and crackling
> muscles draw her up
> into that final position
> burning bodies so perfectly assume. . . .

Again, Weigl has chosen to use the present participles "burning" and "crackling" as kinesthetic images. Used as adjectives, the present participles inject gruesome movement into the poem. Furthermore, the word "crackling" is also an auditory image: Readers not only see the girl burn, but they hear it as well. Ironically, the "final position" the burning body assumes is also the fetal position, the posture of the body in birth as well as death. With his final image, Weigl returns the reader to the opening scene with one important difference: At the very end of the poem he folds home and Vietnam together in the "jungle-green pasture."

Themes and Meanings

Throughout the body of Weigl's work, and most particularly in the poems found in the volume *Song of Napalm* (1988), the poet's experiences in the Vietnam War erupt into the heart of his poetry. Regardless of the intensity of his subject matter, however,

Weigl never tries to substitute content for craft. His poetry is lean, spare, and carefully crafted, and he displays an acute awareness of the role art plays in the production of truth. "Song of Napalm," widely anthologized and considered by many critics to be one of the best poems to come out of the Vietnam War experience, is just such a poem, careful in its craft and brutal in its message. Like Yusef Komunyakaa in "You and I Are Disappearing" from the poetry collection *Dien Cai Dao* (1988), Weigl conjures the image of a burning girl to remind readers of the terrible cost of the Vietnam War. At the same time, Weigl questions the possibility of life after the war: How does someone continue to live with the image of a burning girl permanently etched behind the eyes? In "Song of Napalm," as in many of Weigl's Vietnam War poems, home and Vietnam do not exist as separate entities but rather coexist as contiguous realities; that is, even when he is contemplating an American scene, images of Vietnam intrude, changing the scene before him. The two locations, war and home, fuse and become the unit of Weigl's life. Just as in John Balaban's poem "After Our War," collected in *Blue Mountain* (1982), images of the war follow the poet home, raising questions about life after war.

"Song of Napalm" is a poem with three characters: the speaker, his wife, and the burning girl. By opening the poem with a dedication to his wife and returning to the plural pronoun "us" in the final line, Weigl starts and ends in the present, which includes life with his wife. The present, however, encapsulates the memories of the past. Furthermore, the use of the present tense to describe the scenes from Vietnam suggests that the past may exist more immediately for the poet than does his present reality. Yet the past that Weigl remembers is "altered by the distance" of years and miles. Likewise, his vision of the present is altered by the past. A simple meditation on a pasture with horses after the rain turns into a memory of a charred, dead girl.

The central question of the poem, then, is: How can one live with the double vision of home and war? Weigl suggests that his ability to live in the present somehow depends on his ability to either reimagine the past through lies or confront the past's intrusion into the present through art. In "Song of Napalm," Weigl briefly attempts the first: He tries to reconstruct his memory of the burning girl in order to ease her pain, his pain, and the pain of his wife. Yet this attempt fails as "the lie swings back again." Without a solution, he admits that he cannot change the past or deny it. What he does, however, is resurrect the child as art, the image of her charred body serving to remind readers that although their vision is "altered by the distance," the war really happened, and home can never be the same again.

Diane Andrews Henningfeld

SONG OF THE CHATTAHOOCHEE

Author: Sidney Lanier (1842-1881)
Type of poem: Lyric
First published: 1884, in *Poems of Sidney Lanier*

The Poem

Within the framework of five stanzas of ten lines each, Sidney Lanier's "Song of the Chattahoochee" takes the reader on a river journey from the mountains to the sea. Essentially, the poem foretells the 436-mile route of the Chattahoochee River as it rises in Habersham County in northeast Georgia to flow southwest diagonally across the state to form Georgia's western boundary with Alabama before crossing into Florida and eventually spilling into the Gulf of Mexico. The poem draws parallels between the gravitational momentum of the river and the social, creative, and spiritual responsibilities of humankind.

Told from the perspective of the river itself, the poem begins in the higher elevations of Habersham and Hall, both counties in northeast Georgia. It is here that the river's source can be traced and here that the river acquires its impetus "to reach the plain." Already in the first stanza, however, there are topographical impediments to the river's motion: steep heights, rock-strewn beds, and narrow banks.

The middle three stanzas serve to add to these topographical obstructions a host of organic distractions, all aimed at inducing the river to delay its journey. The second stanza, for example, is populated by water vegetation such as rushes, reeds, and "willful waterweeds" as well as shoreside vegetation like the "laving laurel" and "fondling grass." All combine forces to convince the river to *"Abide, abide"* and not continue on its course.

These humble plants are joined, in the third stanza, by majestic, "overleaning" trees that hope to slow the river's progress by offering the comfort of shade. This is surely a strong inducement when one considers the vibrant heat of the American South. Here, Lanier, a Georgian by birth, offers a catalog of his state's native trees: hickory, poplar, chestnut, oak, walnut, and pine. With "flickering meaning and sign," a language of dappled sun and shadow, the trees add their message to "pass not" the hills and valleys of northern Georgia.

To the voices of the plant life in the second and third stanzas, Lanier, in turn, adds a further distraction in the fourth stanza: the river stones that serve not only to "bar" the river's passage but also to act as "lures" because of their light-reflecting surfaces. Among these "luminous" precious stones in the watery depths are white quartz, ruby, garnet, and amethyst.

The sea calls to the river more loudly than the voices of Habersham and Hall Counties, and it reminds the river of its ultimate goal, which is outlined in the fifth and final stanza. The sea's voice is the voice of duty. This obligation to reach the state's lower elevations apparently has four objectives: providing irrigation to parched crops, turning waterwheels as a power source for gristmills or factories, nourishing flowers, and eventually joining the sea.

Forms and Devices

As evidenced by his 1880 volume *The Science of English Verse*, Lanier was long interested in the relationship between music and poetry. This is not surprising, since he made a living as a professional musician (first flutist of the Peabody Orchestra in Baltimore, Maryland) and composer before he published his first poem. Once he took up the pen, as both theorist and practitioner, he experimented with verbal materials in order to achieve the auditory effect of music in his writing.

In its basic form, "Song of the Chattahoochee" is lyrical. All five stanzas of ten lines each follow the same scheme of end rhyme: *abcbcddcab*. Furthermore, each stanza begins and ends with a two-line refrain.

Some critics have argued that the essence of Lanier's verse lies not in the sense but in the sound. Certainly "Song of the Chattahoochee" derives most of its interest from the poet's ability to mimic the sound of the river and its course. In this regard, there are two countervailing clusters of poetic devices. On the one hand, there are effects that are used to establish and maintain momentum; on the other hand, there are devices used to slow the rhythm of the poem.

In the first category are those devices that Lanier uses to mirror the river's fundamental propulsion. His use of internal and end rhyme, repetition, action verbs, long prepositional phrases, consonantal alliteration ("Run the rapid" in line 4 and "flee from folly" in line 7), and enjambment or run-on lines (lines 7 and 8) gives the poem a forward momentum.

These effects are subtly augmented by the poet's skillful manipulation of the refrain. Regardless of minor variations in each iteration, the first line, ending in "hills of Habersham," is always one word longer than the second line, ending in "valleys of Hall." This slight reduction in length from one line to the next in the refrain gives additional momentum to the poem as a whole. Furthermore, there are three instances, in the first, third, and fifth stanzas, when the eighth line of the stanza text overlaps the first line of the refrain, thus mirroring how the river flows into the sea.

In contrast to these elements that promote fluidity of line, Lanier employs a number of devices to imitate the impediments that the river must counter on its journey to the sea. These include caesuras or medial breaks, as in line 33 ("The white quartz shone, and the smooth brook-stone") and the use of long vowels as in the two-word plea of the rushes and reeds in the second stanza: "*Abide, abide.*" The end result of all of Lanier's effort is a poem created for the ears, one that is meant to be read aloud.

Themes and Meanings

In his "Confederate Memorial Address" delivered at a cemetery in Macon, Georgia, in 1870, Lanier first used the image of the river's acceptance of its responsibility to stay its course despite many impediments to represent the heroic survival of Southern manhood and womanhood during and after the Civil War. Himself a Confederate soldier and the survivor of a four-month stay in a series of Union prison camps after his capture on a blockade runner in 1864, Lanier had firsthand knowledge about the significant challenges that faced his native region, and he became an important spokesperson for what came to be known as the New South.

"Song of the Chattahoochee" echoes some of the practical advice that Lanier offered his fellow Southerners on how they might rebuild their lives after the devastation of the war years. Just as the river seeks to "toil" and to bring relief to "dry fields," so Lanier advocated, most vividly in his poem "Corn" (1875), that the South needed to abandon its dependence on cotton in favor of crops less abusive to the soil and less dependent on the vagaries of trade. Just as river water turns the mill wheel, so Lanier advocated homegrown industry, an argument most fully explored in his 1880 essay "The New South."

In addition to its place in his larger philosophy of regional reconstruction, the poem seems consistent with other Lanier works dealing with the theme of union with some spiritual force larger than the individual self. In Lanier's poem "Sunrise" (1884), for instance, the poet experiences a final synthesis with "my lord the Sun"; likewise, in "Song of the Chattahoochee," the river answers the call of the "lordly main." Certain critics have interpreted the river's duty as representative of the individual's irresistible urge to be reunited with the source of one's spiritual power and identity.

Finally, "Song of the Chattahoochee" clearly belongs to a literary tradition of onomatopoeic verse, a type of poetry that signifies meaning through the use of sound effects. In this regard, some critics have remarked on how much the poem resembles British poet Alfred, Lord Tennyson's "The Brook" (1855), a work with which Lanier was familiar. Tennyson's poem is comprised of a small stream's first-person account of its journey past hills, through lowland vegetation, under the cover of trees, and over stony beds to reach a large river. Along the way, the brook chatters and babbles and murmurs. In addition to the inspiration to be derived from "The Brook," Lanier set three of Tennyson's other poems to music. For his song "Flow Down, Cold Rivulet" (1871), based on Tennyson's poem "A Farewell" (1842), Lanier created an undulating bass line in the piano accompaniment to replicate the movement of water. In Tennyson's "A Farewell," the speaker bids goodbye to the rivulet as it flows onward to merge with the sea.

Like other poems that rely more on sound than on sense, "Song of the Chattahoochee," which some critics claim is the most popular of Lanier's poems, will continue to attract a readership primarily because of its appeal to the auditory imagination.

S. Thomas Mack

THE SONG OF THE HAPPY SHEPHERD

Author: William Butler Yeats (1865-1939)
Type of poem: Pastoral/meditation
First published: 1885, as "An Epilogue to 'The Island of Statues' and 'The Seeker'"

The Poem

"The Song of the Happy Shepherd" is actually a theme poem, a declaration of poetic independence. It appears at the beginning of his first volume, and William Butler Yeats intended it as a manifesto—a statement of his poetic creed and a guide to the kind of poetry he was writing and would write. In it, he established his relationship to the poetry of the past and asserted that the role of poetry would have to change in the modern world. He stated that poetry would have to become more divorced from the things of the world, closer to the truths of the heart, more a law to itself.

The poem is divided into three unequal parts. Yeats begins by establishing the persona of the happy shepherd, following the ancient convention of the pastoral, centered on the country singer who comments from his innocent vantage point on the ways of the world. Yet almost at once he breaks from that convention by chanting, "The woods of Arcady are dead,/ And over is their antique joy." Arcady was the classical location of the pastoral. This shepherd is asserting that the old vision no longer holds, that the old kind of poetry has failed. Having given up on dreams, the world now demands "Grey Truth"—the dingy matter of the daily newspaper. The shepherd derides the attention given to "the many changing things," concluding instead that only words can confer value and permanence. Even the kings of the past now litter the trash containers of history, lucky to be recalled by words. Moreover, the discoveries of science suggest that all the things of this world may be little more than temporary accidents.

The second section begins by repeating this conclusion: History records only "dusty deeds"; truth is an illusion. Pursuit of truth can only force one to escape in dreams. The only real truths are personal. Scientists, for example, have deadened themselves to produce "cold star-bane"—dead figures and facts about dead things. It would be far better to fashion lovely bodies out of words, as singing into an echoing shell may recombine the original sounds into a higher music. Songs also fade away, but they die in beauty and remain beautiful in death.

In the third section, the shepherd takes his leave to follow on his singing way. He is called to tread the wood region of fable and romance, never far off for an Irish poet. This region of the old earth is still haunted by creatures of fancy, the forces he must immortalize in song. These are the "songs of old earth's dreamy youth," now inaccessible from routine daily life. That proves the necessity of poetry today, for it alone preserves the way into faerie, more important now than ever before.

Forms and Devices

"The Song of the Happy Shepherd" is composed in three sections of alternately rhymed iambic tetrameter—a somewhat flexible pattern first used in English by John Milton and freely imitated thereafter. Yeats develops his topics in a relatively straightforward way, employing few exotic or difficult figures, although some of the diction is ambiguous and some syntax gnarled. The principal device is simple: repetition of phrase and verbal pattern.

The first section, of twenty-one lines, establishes the situation and background by means of allusion. "Woods of Arcady" refers to the groves of Attic Greece, supposedly frequented by the first generations of poets in Western civilization. Then appear two lines that work on several levels simultaneously: "Of old the world on dreaming fed;/ Grey Truth is now her painted toy." The persona states that dreams sustained the world formerly, implying that they can do so no longer; the world has grown estranged from dreams. Now, in place of that wholesome food, she diverts herself with painted toys—baubles so empty in themselves that they have to be tricked out with paint to attract any interest. The best that can be done with current truth is to daub it with gray; it is too ambiguous to be either black or white. This kind of degeneration exhibits itself in all aspects of modern life: the restlessness and inattentiveness, the sickness of the children, even the dreariness of the dancing. Chronos—the spirit of time—sings now a "cracked tune," suggesting the corruption of civilization, the running down of time. In this context, only words—paradoxically—have substance, though on an earth that itself may be only "a sudden flaming word" that substance may be slight.

The second section of twenty-three lines weaves itself around the recurrent phrase "this is also sooth." By "sooth," Yeats means more than an old poetic synonym for truth, which in any case he has just discarded as a norm. As in the compound "soothsayer," "sooth" connotes the kind of truth hidden to most observers but of enduring moment—perhaps what he refers to later as the truth of the heart. The word also homonymically conjures up "soothe"—suggesting the kind of truth that alone consoles, that eases the pain otherwise generated by life. This section contains the key to the only solace now viable, something more also than the mere dreams to which that relentless pursuit of facile, mechanical truth will drive human beings.

Two specific images form the poles of this section. One is the "cold star-bane" of the "starry men." This difficult phrase is a Yeats coinage. By analogy with wolfbane, it is the kind of lore that can be used to banish the stars. Thus it is the kind of knowledge that becomes a substitute for the thing itself, that drives the real presence away. It is star-bane because it diminishes the wonder of the stars by dwindling them to gray facts. The second image is of the "twisted, echo-harboring shell" which replaces the words of a simple story and transfixes them in beauty. That is the material instrument which makes music of human speech, the song which preserves the truths of the heart and soothes the soul.

The final section recapitulates the first two, again ending with the refrain on "sooth," but the techniques of this section are different. Here, Yeats arranges a cascade of images to illustrate heart truths: "a grave/ Where daffodil and lily wave"; a "hapless fawn/ Buried under the sleepy ground." These ingredients are those of the faerie land of the imagination, accessible only by turning one's back on the world of fact. In this way, man can keep in touch with the essential world of "earth's dreamy youth."

Themes and Meanings

Though called a "song," this poem is far from lyrical, and this discrepancy marks its first break with the past. The implication is that the old kind of song no longer works; it lacks currency. The poem's title also establishes the persona of the happy shepherd, suggesting with apparent inconsistency a link with the ancient tradition of pastoral poetry, which was centered in the fictitious invention of a timeless landscape populated with innocent sheep and blissful shepherds whose simple singing became poetry. Curiously, in both the original Greek and Roman versions of this convention, and in its Renaissance revival, the pastoral world is considered a refuge from and an antitype to the political world of influence and inside trading. Thus it can be used as a basis for social critique. By similarly withdrawing his happy shepherd, Yeats creates a persona removed from the world and privileged to comment on it.

That is exactly what his happy shepherd does. He begins by lamenting the fate of the woods of Arcady, because that is an image not only of his real home but also of a parallel universe necessary for the spiritual health of modern man. Having rejected that parallel universe, man today has nothing with which to nourish his soul in this world of gray fact. Mankind diverts itself with illusions, but evidences of spiritual decay abound in so-called civilization. The shepherd proclaims that in this materialistic jungle, only words offer certitude and value, for they alone provide access to the eternally green and eternally fertile world of "earth's dreamy youth." Words alone open gates to dreams.

The shepherd also announces a counter theme: However seductive the world of fact, recorded in history and analyzed by science, it is ultimately empty, because it does not sustain the spirit. The greatest of kings, including those who derided words—as Pontius Pilate joked about truth—are now reduced to words fumbled by schoolboys. Moreover, the earth and its fabled history occupy but a moment on a cosmic timetable. The old theory of auromancy, or sound magic, held that words preceded and created things, which means that even the world was once only a momentary word in the mouth of the Creator: In the beginning was the Word, as the Gospel of John presents it.

In such a situation only eternal words, the words that attach to dreams, are worth cherishing and preserving. That becomes the shepherd's third theme. These words are those of life, which connect modern imaginative consciousness with the mythic past of the planet and early man. The spirit of man cannot survive, the shepherd argues, without the solace provided by song, by words turning themselves to music through the agency of the poet. The kind of instinctive faith possible in the past is no longer available. Lacking that, people find refuge increasingly rare. The shepherd offers the help of dreamsong.

The final theme offers the possibility even of transcending or accepting death. The last stanza resembles John Milton's elegy "Lycidas" (1637) closely enough to constitute an allusion. In both, the shepherd leaves the scene, vowing to keep alive the memory of one untimely dead. In both cases, the song helps conjure up again the image of the departed, depicting him as once more transfigured by and enshrined in the song of the dream.

James Livingston

THE SONG OF THE INDIAN WARS

Author: John G. Neihardt (1881-1973)
Type of poem: Epic
First published: 1925; collected in *A Cycle of the West,* 1949

The Poem

   The Song of the Indian Wars is an epic poem in fourteen sections written in rhymed couplets and iambic pentameter. It is the fourth of a series of poems ("songs") that form a larger epic, *A Cycle of the West,* which deals with a period of discovery, exploration, and settlement in American history (1822 to 1890). It was a period when American Indian cultures were being overcome by the migration of a powerful people (the Europeans) driven by their own needs and their dreams of a waiting paradise. This "song" deals with the period after the Civil War, a period of movement into Indian territory by whites and of resistance by the Plains Indians such as the Sioux, Cheyenne, and Arapahoe. It ends with the death of its main character, Crazy Horse. The events were real events, and the poem's central characters were real historical individuals.

   The song opens with "The Sowing of the Dragon," four years after Appomattox, as whites are looking westward to a land "clad with grains and jeweled with orchard." Up along the bottoms of the Kaw, Republican, Platte, and Solomon Rivers come the sounds of wheel and hoof; "ten thousand wagons scar the sandy flat." Ancestral pastures are gutted by the plow, and towns suddenly roar where there had been only space as wide as air. These "takers of the world" are of the "Cadmian brood," sowing the dragon seeds of war. The Indians see the end of their sacred things and dread the dwindling of their holy places, so war sweeps down the rivers. Ox-driven caravans are plundered, and settlers are slaughtered.

   In the next section, members of different tribes meet, torn between those who trust the treaties with the whites and those who remember only the broken promises. Spotted Tail, the voice of peace (now and later in the poem), urges conciliation; Red Cloud, the voice of war, urges resistance and carries the day. In the next section, a Cheyenne, Black Horse, comes to the Sioux and urges conciliation but is driven away by an angry mob. Red Cloud speaks again for war, supported by Sitting Bull. In the fourth section warfare begins when Indians attack a log train and soldiers from Fort Kearney scatter the Indians. The Army commander at Fort Kearney hears of a gathering of Sioux on the Powder River. Captain Fetterman boasts that he can easily destroy them, vows to wipe them out, and rides out to find them. He is ambushed, and he and his men are massacred. After the winter lull, Indians attack a wagon train near the fort. The soldiers escorting it crouch behind bales of hay, which the Indians set afire with flaming arrows; they then withdraw.

   When summer comes, the Great White Father in Washington intervenes, closing the country to whites between the Missouri River and the Big Horn. Red Cloud is not convinced, however, and the next spring brings news from Kansas of women captured, men slaughtered, and trains burned along the Santa Fe Trail. A contingent of cavalry pursues the Indians, who stop their withdrawal, then turn at Beecher's Island and attack. Beecher is killed, and the soldiers are surrounded for five days until rescued by reinforcements.

In the eighth section, after his victory at the Battle of Washita, the reputation of General George Armstrong Custer, "The Yellow God," spreads throughout the West, and for four years there is peace. Then Custer leads his army into the Black Hills of the Dakotas, an area which they discover is a "paradise of deer and singing streams." Their reports spread back east and bring a stream of whites with dreams of wealth to be exploited. Alarmed, the young Sioux gather and chant their war songs to the drums. Many of them join Sitting Bull at the Tongue and Powder Rivers. The government in Washington orders all Indians to go to reservations or be declared hostile, but Crazy Horse's people stay where they are. The cavalry rides into their camp and sets fire to the lodges where the Indians lie asleep; they leave a trail of blood. The surviving Sioux flee in panic up the slopes of the mountains, later returning to find a destroyed village; the village settles down, now only a "miracle of patches."

When the news of the massacre spreads among the Sioux, the young braves are aroused. The whole white world seems to be sweeping the prairies. The braves set out on a series of raids, but the whites are joined by many from the traditional enemies of the Sioux—the Roos and Crows. The Sioux turn to the Great Spirit for help, raising a pole in the center of their village and performing the Sun Dance. The white army gathers its forces to clear a path for Custer, who then proceeds recklessly, not waiting for the reinforcements. The Indians attack. After the dust settles, there is nothing but bodies "gleaming white the whole way to the summit of the hill." A brooding silence reigns. Reinforcements arrive, but too late. Reno scatters the Sioux, who flee to Big Horn Mountain.

In section 13, despite their victory, the Sioux lose heart. The people are listless. Their only hope is flight, but they are uncertain as to where they should flee. They turn eastward. General Crook follows their diverging trails, which reveal that they are "like quails before the hunter." Crazy Horse and Gall, with their people, have vanished. Crazy Horse turns westward instead and reaches the valley of the Powder River, where he hopes they will find peace. In January, however, news arrives of approaching soldiers. Crazy Horse's people flee to the head of the Little Powder River. Spotted Tail, still the advocate of peace, comes and urges compliance with the whites, and Crazy Horse finally brings his people in. As the last Sioux comes into the reservation, Crazy Horse says, "Now let my people eat."

After a while, news comes how Nez Perce leader Joseph, undaunted, has fought the whites and reappeared down the Yellowstone River. Hearing this, the whites now fear what Crazy Horse might be thinking, since he has left the reservation and gone to the camp of Spotted Tail, his uncle and the advocate of peace, to be with his people there. The white officer asks him to return to Camp Robinson for talks, in all sincerity promising him that no harm will come to him. Crazy Horse believes him and comes to the fort, but when he arrives he is hustled among bayonets to a barred room. Frightened, he struggles. A soldier, now also frightened, panics and stabs him. Lying on the floor, Crazy Horse sings his death chant, "I had my village and my pony herds/ On Powder where the land was all my own./ I only wanted to be left alone./ I did not want to fight," and dies. Crazy Horse's mother and father come to get the body, and they bear it away on a pony-drag to lie somewhere among the Badlands: "Who knows the crumbling summit where he lies/ Alone among the badlands?"

Forms and Devices

   The Song of the Indian Wars is an epic, one of five in Neihardt's *Cycle of the West*. As an epic it has the traditional epic's battle scenes. Each represents a different facet of warfare: the tense attack on the Wagon Boxes, the battle of Beecher's Island, the massacre of Crazy Horse's village; the ambush of Custer. The sympathy of the epic shifts in each scene between the white troops and the Indians. In each scene the intense battle action is interspersed with human details. At the Wagon Boxes, Old Robertson unlaces a boot and nooses the leather lace to reach between a trigger and a toe; another trooper sits cross-legged calmly picking jammed bullets out of a gun. At Beecher's Island, Condon dashes out from behind a barrel of beans waving his rifle and shouting, "Come on! ye dairty blatherskites. We kin lick yez all," before he falls bene.. ˑ shower of arrows.

   The epic hero is Crazy Horse, Neihardt's "ideal epic hero," always portrayed as possessing courage in the face of overwhelming odds, always maintaining a certain dignity, even in death. Of the battle with Custer, Crazy Horse says, "I fought him and I whipped him. Was it wrong/ To drive him back? That country was my own.// I did not want to see my people die.// His soldiers came to kill us and they died." The brother-in-law of Red Cloud, the advocate of warfare in the Sioux council, Crazy Horse was one of the principal chiefs of that tribe and one of the main leaders of those Indians who defied the authority of the United States for several years. Although a relatively young man, he was the most respected man in the tribe. The name "crazy" is a poor translation of the Sioux word *witko*, which means "magic" or "enchanted," referring to his supposed special and sacred vision. Neihardt places him in juxtaposition with the whites' idea of a great general, Custer, who possesses their ideal kind of courage. Crazy Horse is heroic like a lonely man bravely fighting the sea.

   The Song of the Indian Wars, like all true epics, is the mirror of a society—in this case, that of the Plains Indian. It reveals its structure in peace and in war, along with details of daily life and tribal mores. It focuses on the several tribal chiefs, on tribal and intertribal councils for decision making, and on the details of ceremonial procedure. It records the great orations before the councils, most of them accounts garnered from the memories of someone present. The nomadic life is portrayed, as the tribes from time to time fold their tepees and wander up the rivers. As war looms, the young men chant to the drums, and a sacred pole is raised in the center of the village, where the men perform the Sun Dance. Indian strategies in warfare are described: the flaming arrows, the surprise raids, the dissolving of the trails they leave behind, and the fading away after defeats—and sometimes after victories. There is the ceremony in donning the war bonnet and the death-paint. There are the prayers to the Great Spirit, the body-drag for the dead.

Neihardt's method of composition was unique. He believed in a prodding demon as the motivating force behind his poetry, compelling him to preserve a "great heroic race-mood that might otherwise be lost." As Lucile Aly tells it in her *John G. Neihardt* (a 1976 monograph in Boise State University's Western Writers Series), "To recreate the mood, he began each session by . . . immersing himself in the atmosphere until he reached a near trance state," working and reworking each line. Indian language, for which Neihardt had a well-tuned ear, translates into elevated speech appropriate for an epic—straightforward, dignified, and poetic. The poem often achieves a special, emotionally elevating cadence, especially in the orations before the councils.

Themes and Meanings

The Song of the Indian Wars is an epic of westward expansion and the displacement of Native Americans after the end of the American Civil War—one of the great archetypal movements in the history of the world. White people with their dreams are migrating into the vast expanses of a land that is new to them but ancient and holy to Indians. The poem is a record of a confrontation with tragic overtones for both parties.

The story is told impersonally but with an overriding compassion for both sides. It avoids stereotypes and alternates between the viewpoints of Indians and whites, both involved in a struggle neither fully understands. For the Indians it is the end of sacred things and the dwindling of holy places; for the whites it is the promise of a land "clad with grains,/ Jewelled with orchard." For Indians it involves displacement from their homeland, for whites an unexplored frontier to be conquered and settled. Neihardt saw the Indian Wars as a confrontation between the old and the new, a "watershed of history." It is a struggle fraught with tragedy: the wounded and dead in the massacre of Crazy Horse's village and the vast expanse of white bodies strewn across the valley at the Little Big Horn.

Blair Whitney, in *John G. Neihardt* (1976), sees in this epic the fulfillment of the destiny of a race (whites of European descent) and the triumph—for good or ill— of Western civilization. The struggle brings out the best qualities of the immigrants— intelligence, strength, heroism, and faith. Yet it also involves the demise of a radically different culture of equal value. One, the European, is a logical, rational, acquisitive culture; whites are the masters of technology. The other, the Indian, is a spiritual culture with very simple technology that uses the land for hunting. Praying is an integral part of the Indian faith. Neihardt's theme, Whitney continues, is selfishness versus unselfishness. In the section entitled "The Yellow God," the heading has a double meaning: the debasing greed for gold sought by the invading prospectors, and the blond "yellow god" Custer, who has come to the Black Hills to protect them. The irony shows in Neihardt's lines describing this "errant Galahad" searching for an unworthy grail and mistaking "the color of the gleam." The Indian Wars were more than a fight over territory; they were also contests between two ways of life. The Indian cannot understand the white drive to conquer the earth, to acquire more and more land. Neihardt symbolically portrays a confrontation between buffalo and train.

This epic is also about a sometimes hostile nature. At times it seems as though the elements had cursed the plains. Burning August gives way to the sudden, chill monotony of rains, and horses must struggle against the suck of gumbo flats and hills of clay. Crows and buzzards hover overhead. In the wagon train, women and children sometimes sicken and even die. The dead must be buried along the trail. *The Song of the Indian Wars*, as Aly observes, is about ordinary men who are transformed into heroes by events, who are struggling against impossible odds to preserve values they cherish. It "represents the universal striving to sustain life, and the pathos of a world where brave and noble men must attack each other in a mistaken attempt to satisfy the same human needs."

Thomas Amherst Perry

SONG OF THE OPEN ROAD

Author: Walt Whitman (1819-1892)
Type of poem: Dramatic monologue
First published: 1856, as "Poem of the Road," in *Leaves of Grass*; as "Song of the Open Road" in *Leaves of Grass*, 1867

The Poem

"Song of the Open Road" by Walt Whitman is familiar, widely admired, and often alluded to by later readers and writers. In certain respects, the poem is iconic, for it speaks symbolically of American mobility, restlessness, and love of freedom and open spaces. The poem's 224 lines, which in 1881 Whitman arranged in fifteen sections, are divisible into two parts: sections 1-8, the persona's exuberant description of the healthful lessons and benefits of open-air living on the road, and sections 9-15, the persona's impassioned invitation to companions to join him in his liberating and ultimately spiritual journey.

The poem begins with the first-person narrator setting out on a "long brown path." The journeyer is "Afoot and light-hearted," for he is done with the routines, customs, and safe behaviors of his previous life, "done with indoor complaints, libraries, querulous criticisms." He renounces a life devoted to the conventional pursuit of material success: "Henceforth I ask not good-fortune, I myself am good-fortune."

Early in section 2 the journeyer acquires an egalitarian ethos; he learns "the profound lesson of reception, nor preference nor denial" of any man or woman. Even nature, it appears, is governed by a democratic principle, as the persona observes the "light that wraps [him] and all things in delicate equable showers!" In section 5, in a moment of quasi-mystical dilation, the journeyer declares his spiritual independence: "From this hour I ordain myself loos'd of limits and imaginary lines,/ Going where I list, my own master total and absolute."

The first half of the poem concludes with reflections on wisdom, which is not to be found in schools, philosophies, or religions: "Wisdom is of the soul, is not susceptible of proof, is its own proof." To understand the nature of wisdom is to discover the source of happiness.

Beginning in section 9 of "Song of the Open Road" and extending through the fifteenth and last section, the persona speaks directly and insistently to the reader: "Allons! whoever you are come travel with me!" The word *allons*, French for "let us go!" or "come on!," introduces all but one of the poem's final seven sections. Rising to a fever pitch, the persona urges his reader to reject the established and formulaic: "Allons! from all formules!/ From your formules, O bat-eyed and materialistic priests." He exhorts all men and women "to know the universe itself as a road, as many roads, as roads for traveling souls." He warns that to journey on the open road is to endure a struggle, a battle. He says he must be honest: "I do not offer the old smooth prizes, but offer rough new prizes,/ These are the days that must happen to you." The poem ends with the persona awaiting an affirmative response from his reader, his would-be "Camerado."

Forms and Devices

Like nearly all the poems Whitman included in the final edition of *Leaves of Grass*, "Song of the Open Road" is written not in traditional accentual-syllabic meters but in free verse. Whitman did not invent this poetic technique but remains one of its most celebrated practitioners. His distinctive use of free verse is indebted to the prosody of the English Bible and is notable for its long line. Sometimes, as in section 13 of "Song of the Open Road," one of his lines is so long that it threatens to exceed the very boundaries of the page and has to be broken up into indented units:

> All religion, all solid things, arts, governments—all that was
>   or is apparent upon this globe or any globe, falls into
>   niches and corners before the procession of souls along
>   the grand roads of the universe.

Thirty-six words appear in this line.

Other prominent characteristics of Whitman's free verse include syntactic parallelism (a sequence of coordinate phrases or clauses), repetition (especially anaphora, which involves repeating the same word or words at the beginning of lines), and cataloguing (a list or inventory of persons, places, objects, occupations, or ideas). The first two techniques are related devices essentially designed to create prosodic regularity and are illustrated by a passage in section 4:

> I think heroic deeds were all conceiv'd in the open air, and
>   all free poems also,
> I think I could stop here myself and do miracles,
> I think whatever I shall meet on the road I shall like, and
>   whoever beholds me shall like me,
> I think whoever I see must be happy.

Cataloguing or list-structure can be found in various parts of the poem but the best example, even if only a few of its lines can be quoted here, occurs in section 12:

> Allons! after the great Companions, and to belong to them!
> They too are on the road—they are the swift and majestic
>   men—they are the greatest women,
> Enjoyers of calms of seas and storms of seas,
> Sailors of many a ship, walkers of many a mile of land,
> Habituès of many distant countries, habituès of far-distant dwellings.

At first one is inclined to call the form of "Song of the Open Road" a lyric, but closer inspection reveals it is more accurately described as a dramatic monologue, a type of poem in which a single narrator makes a sustained speech to a silent audience.

In the first half of the poem the persona often directly addresses the road or highway. In the last half he addresses men and women who might be recruited as fellow travelers. From no addressee does the persona receive a response.

Themes and Meanings

Whitman expresses his main theme in the poem through the first-person narrator, or the "I." This persona or dramatic personality dominates "Song of the Open Road" and connects its diverse subjects and argument. The role of this dramatic personality and the ideology it has to offer are inseparable, for the personality is emblematic of the joyous journeyer, the individual who has broken away from the herd and achieved autonomy, the spiritual wayfarer traveling light and footloose. Just as important as the "I" are Whitman's many uses of "you," which refer not only to the road or to would-be male and female "companions" but also to the reader. Ultimately, the dialogic relationship between persona and reader is at the heart of the poem's meaning. Other important themes include the necessity of a profoundly democratic receptivity, of diverse experience, of "adhesiveness" or comradeship, and of contact with nature. Regarding life in the open air, the persona declares that "The earth never tires,/ . . . there are divine things well envelop'd."

One finds in "Song of the Open Road" that the persona has enacted or is in the process of enacting various "movements": from the social world to the world of nature, from the realm of constraints and restrictions to the realm of limitless possibilities, from the literal to the symbolic, from an enervating rationality to intuition, from the static to the dynamic, and from the physical or material to the spiritual or mystical. This striking motility is in keeping with the poem's overriding messages. It is also in keeping with the work's expansiveness and sense of adventure.

"Song of the Open Road" is not a poem that summarizes all or even most of Whitman's themes but it does contain several ideas that figure prominently throughout his work. The poem can be usefully compared to other pieces in the poet's canon. It shares with "There Was a Child Went Forth" a fascination with the way in which an individual absorbs what he or she experiences and with how that individual's self evolves and matures. It shares with "Passage to India" an urge to "sail pathless and wild seas," that is, an urge to embark on a transcendental voyage to the soul. It perhaps resembles most closely the epic "Song of Myself," a poem with which it shares a tutorial persona; oratorical appeals to the reader; an affirmation of traveling, spacious catalogs, and sweeping vistas; and a buoyant tone. "Song of the Open Road" finally falls short of the animation, color, zest for life, and sharp imagery of "Song of Myself," but it doubtless surpasses the longer poem in focus, compactness, and singleness of tone.

Walt Whitman's "Song of the Open Road" reminds many of its readers just how central the road has been in the American imagination. The poem is quite possibly the most important of the country's early examples of "road literature." Consider just a handful of the American road writings that have been published since the middle of the nineteenth century: *Roughing It* (1872) by Mark Twain, *On the Road* (1957) and

The Dharma Bums (1958) by Jack Kerouac, and *Travels with Charley: In Search of America* (1962) by John Steinbeck. Anyone who contemplates the road as presented in these diverse novels and autobiographies will without question gain valuable insights into the history of American culture.

Donald D. Kummings

THE SONG OF THE POORLY LOVED

Author: Guillaume Apollinaire (Guillaume Albert Wladimir Alexandre Apollinaire
de Kostrowitzky, 1880-1918)
Type of poem: Lyric
First published: 1909, as "La Chanson du Mal-Aimé"; revised in *Alcools*, 1913; English translation collected in *Selected Writings*, 1950

The Poem

"The Song of the Poorly Loved" consists of fifty-nine stanzas, each five lines long.
It is divided into seven sections, three of which have their own titles. Guillaume
Apollinaire assembled it, probably in 1904, from poems and fragments he had written
at various times over the previous few years.

The initial motivation for the poem came from Apollinaire's own life: In Germany,
he had met and fallen in love with a young Englishwoman named Annie Playden. He
visited her twice in London with intentions to marry her, but she emigrated to America. The poem opens in misty London, where Apollinaire was rebuffed by Annie in
November, 1903, and closes the following June in Paris, where he returned with all
hope lost in May, 1904. As the comparison between his love and the phoenix in the
five-line epigraph indicates, the poem revolves around Apollinaire's efforts to resurrect his life after this unhappy love affair.

The long first section begins with a nightmarish episode in London. The poet is
confronted by two figures who resemble his beloved and remind him of the transitory
nature of love. He compares the mistreatment he has suffered to various fictional and
historical examples of fidelity. Contemplation of his memories and regrets brings him
to the nostalgic recollection of the heyday of his love. This he depicts in the three-
stanza second section, which he calls an "Aubade" (a traditional form of morning love
song).

In the third section, the poet is in Paris, reflecting on the death of love and on his inability to put his unhappy experience behind him. In pondering his faithfulness, he
once again compares himself to a legendary paradigm of fidelity, this time the Za-
porogian Cossacks of the Ukraine. Asked by the Turkish sultan to join his army, these
Christian warriors of the seventeenth century are said to have rejected the invitation to
betray their faith in a violently worded letter. In the three-stanza fourth section, the
poet composes his version of the Cossacks' insulting and obscene reply.

In the first stanzas of the long fifth section, the poet returns to his own very mixed
feelings about his beloved, expressing bitter disdain, then enduring commitment.
Wondering what it will take to make him happy, the poet examines grief and unhappiness, both in relation to his own experience and in general. In thinking about his memories, he addresses his shadow—an image of his past, which will always follow him.
Then he describes the transition from winter to spring, and this change signals the beginning of a more positive and productive attitude toward his past.

It seems as if the poet cannot completely come to terms with the pain of his unhappy love affair until he has somehow exorcised his melancholy, and this is apparently what he accomplishes in the sixth section. "The Seven Swords" is the most obscure part of this difficult poem: It has been interpreted in many different ways, none of which can claim to be definitive. Most significant, however, is the conclusion, namely the poet's claim that he never knew the beloved.

Consequently, in the eleven-stanza seventh section, the poet writes about fortune and fate with a new detachment. He tells of the mad Bavarian king, Ludwig II, who committed suicide—a reaction to unhappiness that the poet no longer feels inclined to emulate. Instead, he turns to Paris, seeing the modern city with a new responsiveness. The poem closes with a confident assertion of the poet's creative ability: Rather than feeling alienated from the city around him as he mourns his lost love, he is now sure that he can draw inspiration from both the present and the past.

Forms and Devices

Probably the most striking formal feature of "The Song of the Poorly Loved" is the enormous variety of tone and mood. Apollinaire borrows techniques from the poetic practice of both the recent and the distant past and adds his own inventions to create an original and quintessentially modern work.

In many passages, Apollinaire's writing owes much to the French Symbolist poets who were his illustrious predecessors. The description of the poet's melancholic state of mind in stanzas 9 through 11 employs images and formulations similar to those used by Charles Baudelaire in his "Spleen" poems. The complex syntax of stanza 13 is reminiscent of the work of Stéphane Mallarmé. Yet Apollinaire constantly disrupts this Symbolist tone by employing surprisingly crude language; the lyrical evocation of spring in stanzas 38 and 39, for example, is followed by the use of *cul* ("ass") as a simile.

The range of language in "The Song of the Poorly Loved" is such that scatological words rub shoulders with extremely erudite allusions. Most readers will need to research such esoteric terms as "argyraspids"; and they may look in vain, since Apollinaire liked to coin his own neologisms.

Another aspect of the poem's variety is the constantly shifting perspective. Even within a single section, the poet's point of view may change from impassioned lover to dispassionate narrator to reflective commentator. All of the wide-ranging stylistic variation is carried out with great panache and considerable humor.

"The Song of the Poorly Loved" has earned a reputation as a breathtakingly ambitious yet brilliantly executed poem because Apollinaire succeeds in uniting all these elements. He does so partly by means of the narrative of the poet's quest, to which the poem always returns in spite of the long detours it takes. Additonally, the whole poem is written in stanzas of five eight-syllable lines, and in French the same rhyme scheme is retained throughout. This meter not only provides consistency, but also invests the poem with a compelling rhythm that, like the narrative thread, drives the poem forward.

Finally, Apollinaire uses two recurring stanzas to bind the poem together further. Stanza 13, which expresses the poet's aspirations toward something higher, symbolized by the Milky Way, is repeated as stanzas 27 and 49. The insertion of these five lines at three different turning points means that they serve as a measure of the poet's progress toward that higher realm. The final stanza of the poem first occurs in the third section, and this repetition also highlights the development of the poet's state of mind. The first time, it reads as a despondent expression of regret, but at the end it resounds as a triumphant assertion of confidence.

The modernity of the poem resides in Apollinaire's synthesis of so many disparate elements. Modernist literature is characterized by the lack of a stable center, of any reliable continuity; here the poet repeatedly disorients the reader by jumping from one mood and from one story to another. The order in which the poem proceeds is not dictated by conventional notions of time or logic. The technique of depicting the same event from several angles is related directly to the innovations of cubist painting (Apollinaire was an influential supporter of such contemporary artists as Pablo Picasso and Georges Braque). While the whole poem is unified by the voice of the "poorly loved," that aspect also reflects a very modern outlook: The poet's self is not depicted as a single, coherent entity, but rather as a succession of states of mind.

Themes and Meanings

While "The Song of the Poorly Loved" began as the expression of a young man's unhappy experience as a lover, the poem it grew into is primarily about a young man's sense of vocation as a poet. This is Apollinaire's main concern in this poem: how to turn one's past and present life into a source of creativity.

The past upon which the poet draws consists of his own personal experience, the literary forms and techniques of the centuries of poets who preceded him, and the vast range of his historical and cultural heritage. At first, the poet employs examples from the past to illuminate his own experience, but in doing so he remains too immersed in personal emotions. What he strives for and eventually finds is a way to use all of the past, including his own, as material for creative expression.

Apollinaire invests the poet with an analogous relationship with the present. Initially, the modern urban environment oppresses him, whereas what he seeks is a means to take advantage of it artistically. The poet demonstrates his progress toward this goal through the contrast between the London of the opening and the Paris of the close; by the end he is able to look Paris in the face and recognize both its sadness and its beauty.

A key metaphor for poetic creativity, established immediately by the title and epigraph, is the act of singing. At first it appears as if the poet will be singing about love, but in fact he will ultimately be singing about singing, that is, about the creative process. The "Aubade" is an example of simply singing about love, and the gently self-mocking tone in which the poet writes reflects his dissatisfaction with such modesty. The final stanza describes the true poet, one gifted and ambitious enough to make poetry out of any kind of experience.

"The Song of the Poorly Loved" also embodies a particular approach toward language and its possibilities. The linguistic variety that characterizes the poem in general, and especially the range of the language, constitutes a statement on Apollinaire's part about how poets may use words. By combining the most familiar and the most strange, the oldest and the newest, the poet can reenliven language, recognizing its past without being restricted by it.

Overall, the poem is about the quest for a means to transform experience into art, and it represents Apollinaire's own fulfillment of that quest. All seven sections are about experience turned into artistic form, but the final parts are the most original, because the poet has discovered his own voice. However one chooses to interpret "The Seven Swords," it is, like the closing stanzas about Paris, an emphatic statement of the poet's individualistic response to the inspiration of his past and his present.

Neil Blackadder

A SONG ON THE END OF THE WORLD

Author: Czesław Miłosz (1911-   )
Type of poem: Meditation
First published: 1945, as "Piosenka o Końcu świata," in *Ocalenie*; English translation
   collected in *The Collected Poems, 1931-1987*, 1988

The Poem

Divided into four stanzas, this twenty-six-line poem with its portentous title turns
out to be wryly quiet, an ironic contrast to the dramatic events some have expected
would accompany the end of the world. Concentrating on a description of vivid yet
commonplace, daily realities, Czesław Miłosz fashions a deliberately simple, naive
narrative of events.

The first stanza is devoted to descriptions of what might be called miniature worlds:
"a bee circles a clover," describing quite literally the circumference of its world. Similarly, the fisherman mending a "glimmering net," "happy porpoises" jumping in the
sea, the young sparrows playing about the rainspout, and the "gold-skinned" snake
each express a world or a dimension of the world "on the day the world ends." There is
a willed quality to this catalog of activities, a denial of change that is most explicit in
the poet's insistence on the snake's color, which is "as it should always be."

The second stanza shifts to an emphasis on collective and individual human activity—women walking through the fields "under their umbrellas," a drunk growing
sleepy "at the edge of a lawn," vegetable peddlers shouting in the street—while off in
the distance can be seen a "yellow-sailed boat." Rather than the end of the world,
again announced in the first line of the stanza, the descriptions seem to emphasize its
continuity—like the "voice of a violin lasts in the air."

The third stanza takes up the disappointment of those who had assumed the world
would end violently, with "signs and archangels' trumps." There is no unusual noise,
no disruption of the common pattern of the earth. As long as nature and the elements
continue in their course, as long as rosy babies are born, it is hard to believe that the
world is ending now.

In the fourth stanza, a single witness, busy at his work but with the insight of a prophet,
"binds his tomatoes" and repeats to himself twice that "there will be no other end of
the world." The implication seems to be that the world will not end in some remarkable
event but will complete itself in the same manner as the old man who is busy binding
the tomatoes, or the bee circling the flower, or the fisherman mending his net. And again,
the repetition of the last lines suggests a determination to celebrate the rudimentary values
of labor and persistence that has no time for profound thoughts on the end of the world.

Forms and Devices

The strength of the poem inheres in the unity and pattern of its imagery. Images of
light, for example, suffuse the poem with radiance. Often associated with a feeling of

hopefulness, these images seem to contradict the announced subject of the poem. The fisherman's "glimmering net," the "gold-skinned snake," the "yellow-sailed boat," and references to the sun and moon, to lightning and "a starry night," give the poem a strong tension, a counterforce to the gloomy announcement that this is the day the world will end.

At the same time, the evocation of sounds accompanies the light imagery, especially in the second stanza's description of the vegetable peddlers shouting in the street and violin's voice lasting in the air. These are sounds that have an end, no matter what their length, and lead into "a starry night," or the end of day.

The poet's use of imagery and sound, then, seems paradoxical, evocative of both the beginning and end of the natural and human cycles. The cycle of day and night, of sounds and sights, seems reassuring and yet leads to the figure of the "white-haired old man" and to his enigmatic statement that "There will be no other end of the world," implying that the world is already at an end. Does his white hair imply he is wise? Certainly the suggestion that he "would be a prophet" adds support to the idea that his point of view speaks for the poet's.

The old man's words provoke questions: Are the things of the world the very "signs" of its end? Is this how the old man interprets things, suggesting that the world ends in the very process of renewing itself, of binding itself up, of completing a cycle? The repetitiveness of his statement seems to mirror the repetitiveness of the world that must come to its own conclusion, as he comes to his own.

The poet's aim apparently is to make one see every day as a portent of the world's ending, as the old man does, and see it only in the images, in the scenes described, not in arguments or spectacles of the world's end, or in some special announcement, a trumpeting of the end. The shift to the present tense in the poem's last two lines emphasizes that there can be no more ending to the world than there is in the poem's present.

Themes and Meanings

At the end of the poem, Miłosz appends a place and date: "Warsaw, 1944." At this time, the Nazis were destroying the Polish city—literally leveling it to the ground, so that it might have seemed as though the world were coming to an end. The poem contains no direct reference to this event or to the war. Indeed, it is astonishingly tranquil, and its evocation of nature is beautiful. The closing lines have a remarkable force considering how Warsaw was coming to its end.

It is as if the poet took the major event of his time, the devastation of Poland and of much of Europe, and decided to dwell on the universal patterns of nature and of human labor and not on the immediate evidence before his eyes. He does not forget his time and place—indeed, he carefully notes them at the end of the poem—but he superimposes on his present a vision of the nature of things, of the old man's steady work and the knowledge of the world he repeats to himself, of the bees, porpoises, sparrows, vegetable peddlers, and so on that bring the world to quite a different end from the one the Nazis believed they were achieving.

In an interview, the poet has acknowledged that he was describing an ideal world, that his poem was a deliberate exercise in naïveté akin to William Blake's great poem "Song of Innocence." Miłosz wanted to capture in poetry an undefiled world as a counterweight to the horror of war. Even though his conception was artificial, it had a therapeutic value and an ironic thrust, showing that the poet could still imagine an ordered, aesthetically pleasing existence no matter how grim the reality of Warsaw's destruction actually became.

Very much a poem about how to relate to the world, it is, paradoxically, an expression of hope, for the world does not end in bombing and killing, or in "lightning and thunder," but in an old man's words, indefatigable and indomitable, as he tends his plants and finds his rootedness in the world. There is no other way to conceive of the ending of the world, in other words, except in his terms, and in the poem's attentiveness to the world's life, which is honored in and for itself, and as an extension of the poet's imagination.

There is no forcing of a point, no world order or philosophy imposed on the structure of the poem. Indeed, the poem rejects people's preconceptions of the way the world will end; it rejects, in total, any interpretation imposed on the evidence of the world it presents. In this respect, the old man's words are the wisdom of age, of the absence of ideology; his thoughts seem to arise out of the imagery of the world and prompt a return to a reading of that imagery and an enjoyment of the poem that is an end in itself.

Carl Rollyson

SONG: TO CELIA

Author: Ben Jonson (1573-1637)
Type of poem: Lyric
First published: 1616, in *The Forest*, part of *The Workes of Benjamin Jonson*

The Poem

"Song: To Celia" is a sixteen-line iambic poem written in four quatrains. The content of the poem divides after the second quatrain to form two octets representing two distinct scenes. The poem is the third of three songs addressed to Celia that are collected in *The Forest*. The other two, "Come my Celia" and "Kiss me, sweet," first appeared in Ben Jonson's play *Volpone* (1605).

"Song: To Celia" is Jonson's reworking of five different passages of prose from the Greek sophist writer Philostratus (third century C.E.). The lyric exists in several manuscript versions; Jonson reworked it until he hit upon what is generally considered his finest lyric, indeed one of the finest lyrics of the English Renaissance. In the eighteenth century, an anonymous composer set the poem to music, and it became a popular song.

The first half of the poem is a witty series of variations on the lover's pledge. Traditionally, a lover would toast his or her love and drink a glass of wine; here, the poet asks only for a pledge from Celia's eyes—a loving look—that he promises to return in kind. Even better, if she will "leave a kiss but in the cup" (that is, pledge a kiss), he will forget about wine. The pleasures of Celia's love are a more profound intoxication, a greater sensual delight, than alcohol.

The second quatrain starts more seriously. The poet claims his thirst is not physical, but that it arises from the soul, and that it can only be quenched with a "drink divine." This image flirts with the Christian concept of the "water of life" found in John 4:8-15, and it seems inappropriate in a sensual love lyric. The Christian sentiment, however, is undercut by the following reference to "Jove's nectar." Jove may be divine, but he is a pagan god who is known for his sensual, and specifically sexual, self-indulgence. Jonson claims that he would reject Jove's cup if he could drink from Celia's.

The second octet is a flashback. The poet had sent Celia a "rosy wreath" as a lover's token. He claims that he sent it not to honor her (obviously such a paltry, mortal token could not do justice to Celia's beauty), but in the hopes that the wreath would live forever in Celia's presence—she being a font of life, light, and joy.

The last quatrain tells of the poet's rejection. Celia sent the token back. The poet believes that she has breathed on the wreath and that her sweet smell still clings to it, but this is his fancy, his attempt to wring a compliment, and perhaps hope, out of his rejection. The poem ends on a slightly sad note as the poet tries to console himself, and perhaps even delude himself, regarding his rejection.

Forms and Devices

The lyric is dominated by two images: wine and the rosy wreath. The first octet offers a series of possible substitutions—love favors—that the poet is willing to accept in lieu of the traditional wine. Wine implies intoxication, the delirium of love, but also sensual gratification. The substitutes that the poet is willing to accept seem more ethereal: the glance, the kiss in a cup. Indeed, the wine itself becomes rarefied into Jove's nectar, a divine drink that reputedly had a rejuvenating effect—the same effect that Celia has on the poet.

The wreath dominates the second octet. It is a more concrete pledge than those requested in the first part of the poem, but it is rejected. The rose is the archetypal symbol of love in the English tradition. The wreath consists of a number of roses woven into a circle, which is itself a symbol of eternity. The eternal devotion that was the hallmark of the more spiritual love popularized by Petrarch is combined, then, with the sensual. While the circle may imply eternal love, the wreath's nonstatic quality is emphasized: "it grows, and smells." These flowers are still alive, growing as does the poet's love.

Finally, the wreath, an interweaving of flowers, stands for this poem itself, which is an ingenious interweaving of excerpts from the classical source. The weaving finds its analogue in the rhyme scheme of the poem. The short lines of both octets revolve on single rhymes and thus bind the poem together. The wreath itself has passed from the poet to the lover and back to the poet, describing in its movement a circle. It is the only physical thing that links the two, besides the poem itself.

This poem has a remarkably regular iambic meter that produces its lyrical quality. The only significant break in the rhythm is a caesura in the final line between "itself" and "but." This pause draws attention to the final qualification in the poem. While the other qualifications undercut the ideal and metaphoric, this final qualification asserts the lover as an ideal who changes reality—she has altered the wreath. The caesura also lends emphasis to the concluding "but thee." The poem ends with the lover, a marked contrast from the beginning of the poem, which emphasizes the poet.

Themes and Meanings

In this poem, as in most of his love poetry, Jonson reacts against the idealization of love, an idealization manifest in the imitation of Petrarchan conventions throughout Renaissance literature. This poem highlights the realistic by juxtaposing it with the ideal, an ideal that is maintained by the poet's persona even as it is contradicted by his own words.

The qualification process takes several forms. First there is the juxtaposition of long and short lines. In the first stanza especially, the long lines tend to be metaphorical and ideal, while the short lines, which usually start with a qualifying term such as "and," are more direct and concrete. The poem oscillates, then, between the ideal, or imagined, and the real.

This dialectic tension is manifested in the greater scale of the poem by the contrast between the first and second octet. The first octet depicts a scene set in the present.

The poet is with his lover, and he begs a pledge that is both physical and spiritual. It is an ideal, if unconsummated, moment of love. The second octet, however, is set in the past. The poet is physically separated from his love, and his love token is rejected by her. The events that preceded the opening octet then were less than hopeful, but the poet persists in his idealization despite the rejection. The poem itself becomes an emblem of this fruitless drive toward the ideal; with its perfect iambs, it encapsulates and elevates what may be a failed relationship.

Finally, the poem contrasts the ideal and real by juxtaposing the physical and the spiritual. The poet's first request is for a loving glance. His second is for a kiss in a cup. He has moved from the realistic to the metaphoric. From here, the poet leaps to the thirst of the soul, the divine, the classical, and the impractical.

In the second octet when a physical token (a wreath) is sent to the lover, the poet assumes that she will have a supernatural effect on the object: It will live forever in her presence. The token, however, is returned, and so the poet is brought back to the realm of the physical. The poet, though, believes the wreath is now miraculously endowed. The physical and realistic—the wreath—combines with the spiritual and ideal—the infinite circle that it describes. So love continually combines the real and the ideal, the actual event and its glorification in art.

Paul Budra

SONNET 1

Author: Elizabeth Barrett Browning (1806-1861)
Type of poem: Sonnet
First published: 1850, in *Sonnets from the Portuguese*, part of *Poems*

The Poem

Although Elizabeth Barrett Browning called her famous sonnet sequence *Sonnets from the Portuguese*, in order to suggest that the poems were translations, in actuality she wrote them all herself. The forty-four poems describe the development of the love between Elizabeth Barrett, an invalid almost forty years of age, and the vital, energetic poet Robert Browning, who was six years younger than she. Written during their courtship, the collection was not published until after Elizabeth and Robert had eloped, been married, and had a son.

All the *Sonnets from the Portuguese* are written in the form of a conventional Italian, or Petrarchan, sonnet—that is, a fourteen-line iambic pentameter poem with a prescribed rhyme scheme. Italian sonnets fall into two parts, an eight-line octave followed by a six-line sestet. This first sonnet varies from the pattern only slightly: The octave has been slightly expanded to eight and one-half lines, while the sestet, necessarily, is only five and one-half. The differentiation between octave and sestet is important, because generally in an Italian sonnet the movement to the second part of the poem is marked by a distinct shift or development in thought.

In this poem, the octave itself is based on a contrast. At one time, the poet says, she had thought about the way in which the Greek poet Theocritus had described life. To him, each year was precious, with its own gift; however, at the time when she was musing about Theocritus, the poet herself saw life very differently. To her, it was uniformly sad. Her years had been dark, not bright, and the recollection of them brought her only tears.

At that point, the poet recalls, she became aware of a presence behind her. This spirit seized her by the hair, taking control of her. In accordance with her melancholy view of life, she thought that it was Death which had come for her. To her amazement, however, the spirit identified itself as Love.

Thus the poem concludes with the word which states the theme of the entire sonnet sequence. It is the love of Robert Browning for her, and her love for him, which is to transform Elizabeth Barrett's life, which is to make her sing as rhapsodically as Theocritus.

Forms and Devices

Elizabeth Barrett Browning writes in a fairly simple, straightforward style. Yet the simplicity is as deceptive as that of the American poets Emily Dickinson and Robert Frost; through the skillful use of various poetic devices, Barrett Browning achieves her artistic purposes.

One of these devices, which is important in this first sonnet of the sequence, is that of repetition, which can be used to emphasize and to amplify physical or psychological description. In this sonnet, for example, "the sweet years" of which Theocritus wrote are further defined in the parenthetical phrase that follows, "the dear and wished-for years." By repeating the word "years" and altering the adjectives, that second phrase not only emphasizes the delight Theocritus found in life but also adds further meaning: Instead of merely bringing momentary pleasure, every period in the present creates the expectation of future pleasure.

That amplification is even more important as the octave proceeds into the description of the poet's own contrasting view of life. The seventh line closely parallels the second in form; it also begins with "sweet," as applied to years. In this case, however, "sweet" is united with "sad"; the implication is that the years were filled with disappointments and losses, with frustrated yearnings for a joy which could only be imagined, indeed, with the kinds of emotions the poet herself experienced after the deaths of her brothers and after her own seemingly permanent confinement to her couch and her bed. The simple combination of "sweet" and "sad" thus has an important effect. Still paralleling the second line, the seventh proceeds to a phrase that further explains the poet's viewpoint, "the melancholy years." Although there is no explicit statement as to the future, no "dreaded years" to match the earlier "wished-for years," the principle established in the first quatrain must still apply in the second. The nature of the present suggests the shape of the future, and if each year in the future is to be as unhappy as each year in the present, there is certainly nothing to look forward to, nothing to wish for. In the octave the contrast between the two viewpoints has been stressed both by repetition within each of these lines and by the similarity between the lines.

At the end of the octave, Barrett Browning uses repetition to establish her own hopelessness and to prepare for the unexpectedness of the event which she describes in the sestet. This segment of the poem is dominated by another poetic device, personification, a device already used effectively in the octave. The years are personified in the octave, probably as some kind of Greek supernatural beings. They have presents in their hands, at least for Theocritus. The personification continues into the description of the poet's life. Each of her years has cast "a shadow" on her; since only a substantial being can produce a shadow, once again the poet is personifying an abstraction.

While personification is important as ornamentation in the octave, it is crucial in the sestet. Although they were inexorable, the years had not used physical compulsion but had operated at some distance; however, Love is personified as something forceful and compelling. The spirit materializes, pulls the poet by the hair, questions her, and identifies itself. The voice speaks "in mastery"; there can be no argument with Love, only acquiescence. The joy that came from acquiescence will be described in the sonnets that follow.

Themes and Meanings

There are several levels of meaning in the first of the *Sonnets from the Portuguese*. First, the conflict that was settled with the writing of this sonnet is that between death and life. The sad, hopeless existence of the poet, a kind of death that evidently made her willing to submit to actual physical death, was defeated when she was happily conquered by love.

A second theme is that of time. If one is happy, the human power of recollecting and anticipating produces a triple pleasure; while enjoying the present, one recalls past happiness and looks for more happiness in the future. For the poet, however, both past and present are unhappy, and therefore the future can only be dreaded. This theme fuses with the first, for with such expectations, most people would indeed welcome death, as the poet seems to do.

A third theme is suggested in this important introductory sonnet, a theme that will be further developed as the sequence continues. This is the issue of sovereignty, implied in the forceful posture of personified Love and stated explicitly with the words "in mastery." It might appear that in the final lines, the figure that seizes the poet is in fact Robert Browning, capturing his beloved in the time-tested masculine fashion. Certainly Robert would never literally have seized the delicate Elizabeth by the hair, but the lines could be interpreted as implying that he imposed his will upon hers.

Such an interpretation would not be consistent with what is known about the relationship between the two poets. It was Elizabeth Barrett's poetry that first interested Robert Browning in her, and throughout their courtship and their marriage, both poets continued to work on their writing, encouraging each other in a very modern kind of partnership. As the critic Helen Cooper points out, the allusion in these lines is to the *Iliad* (c. 800 B.C.E.), where the goddess Athena pulls back Achilles, holding him by the hair so that he will not get into a fight. Certainly in Barrett Browning's poem, it is a divinity, not a human being, that has intervened in her life. The happy result, indicated by the description of the divinity's reply as "silver," is made clear in the rest of this sequence of love poems.

Rosemary M. Canfield Reisman

SONNET 6

Author: Elizabeth Barrett Browning (1806-1861)
Type of poem: Sonnet
First published: 1850, in *Sonnets from the Portuguese*, part of *Poems*

The Poem

Although the speaker in the poem is not identified as a woman, the poem reads better if one assumes that a woman is speaking. The conflict expressed in the opening two lines gains power if the speaker is seen as a woman fighting for her independence from a man, as well as a lover struggling to be free of her lover's dominating influence. It also helps to remember that in the background are two real-life lovers: An invalid (Elizabeth Barrett) is writing a series of sonnets to a lover (Robert Browning) whom her tyrannical father has forbidden her to see. This much biographical information, if not essential to an understanding of the poem, greatly enhances one's appreciation of it and makes the beginning of the sonnet clearer and the poet's conflict more poignant.

The poem opens abruptly with a command—"Go from me"—followed by a seeming retraction ("Yet I feel . . . ") that introduces the poet's conflict. She appears not to want her lover to go, but he must, for reasons left unexplained. The peremptory nature of the command makes his leaving seem imperative and the fact of his going final. His going will give her strength to "stand"—or will she rise because she is alarmed by his leaving, as if to stop him? The second line takes back the suggestion in the first line that his leaving will make her somehow strong and independent—when he is gone, she will live in his shadow.

Continuing into line 3 and further, the poet reveals an even closer bond between herself and her lover: She will never again direct the "uses" of her soul without an awareness of him. His influence will be felt as far within her own being as she herself can go. Inwardly in this way and outwardly ("nor lift my hand . . . in the sunshine"), she will always have a "sense" of his intimate presence, evident in a "touch upon the palm." Broadening her vision to include the great distance "Doom" places between them, she asserts that even then they will share the same heart. In line 10 she returns to her own inner and outer life, saying that both her actions and her dreams will include him. The two lovers will be as indistinguishable as the taste of the wine is from that of the grapes (lines 10-12). Finally, when the poet seeks God's assistance for herself, the lover's name is heard, and God sees in the poet's eyes the tears of both lovers. Her poem begins with an imperative, the necessary parting of two lovers; it then explains the extent to which their lives shall henceforth be intertwined, touching on the serenity of their union. It ends on an expression of grief mingled with a sublime sense that their union shall be seen by God himself.

Forms and Devices

The poem employs the rhyme scheme of the Petrarchan (or Italian) sonnet, rhyming *abba, abba, cdc, cdc*, and uses the conventional iambic pentameter line, varying the placement of the stresses in some of the lines. Line 1, for example, begins on a stressed syllable ("Go") instead of an unstressed syllable, as the regular lines do. Instead of pausing where the rhyme pattern marks a quatrain, octave, or tercet, as in the Petrarchan sonnet structure, Barrett Browning pauses within the lines. The first heavy pause occurs not half way into line 1 (after "me"). The argument continues without a heavy pause to the end of line 7 ("forbore—"), and comes to an end-stop just after the midpoint in line 8 ("palm."). Another end-stop occurs after "double" (line 10) and another after "grapes" (line 12). The effect of this patterning is to draw attention subtly away from the conventional rhyme pattern and pauses. By continuing her thought through the conventional pause points, she erases the seams of the sonnet structure in favor of the continuity of thought.

In line 1, enjambment—running the meaning from one line to the next around the line end—is used to reinforce thought. The reader comes to "stand," turns to line 2, and reads "Henceforward," reinforcing the image conveyed by "stand." In line 2, the poet's forceful response to her lover's departure is heavily qualified by "in thy shadow," which seems to reduce the poet to her lover's influence ("shadow"). The pause is followed immediately by "Nevermore," which is stressed twice (on "Never" and on "more") and is further emphasized by being placed at the end of the line. "Henceforward," at the beginning of line 2, is subtly contradicted by "Nevermore" at the end of the line.

In line 3, enjambment makes "Nevermore/ Alone" read almost like a single phrase, "Nevermore Alone," but because a slight pause occurs at the end of every line, the two words are actually read as two separate words, both individually qualifying Barrett Browning's assertion that she shall "Henceforward" be in her lover's shadow. The poet's conflict is thus emphasized by punctuation, placement, and metric peculiarities.

This way of proceeding, first suggesting an independent and solitary existence without her lover, then qualifying it with expressions of dependence and helplessness, comes to a major turning point in lines 7 and 8, which conclude just short of the sonnet's conventional octave. These two lines serve as a fulcrum in the poet's argument, giving the sonnet a balance dictated by the poet's feelings and ideas rather than by convention. Significantly, from line 8 to the end of the poem, the tone shifts from an inner conflict to self-confidence, culminating in line 12, where the poet declares an intention to "sue/ God for myself." At the same time, the yes-and-no conflict that characterizes the first eight lines subsides.

The imagery of the poem also reflects the poet's conflict. Images of strength are qualified by images that seem at first to weaken them but actually strengthen them. In line 1, "stand" suggests strength and independence, but it is qualified by "shadow," which suggests dependence. Addressing the "door" of her "individual life," the poet goes no further than the "threshold," suggesting hesitancy. Capable of action, she lifts her "hand," which might suggest an image of a feeble gesture were it not for "Serenely" (line 6) immediately following, which evokes the image of spiritual strength and grace. Even the tears in the final line suggest both grief and joy simultaneously.

Themes and Meanings

In this sonnet, the reader is in the world of profound feelings in the presence of spirit, although the physical world is not ignored. Indeed, it is used to convey the poet's feelings and inner states. She sees aspects of the physical world as an expression of the spiritual or abstract realm within her own being. The "threshold" of her "individual life" is a metaphorical expression of her inner state, though "sunshine" (line 6) moves thought into the physical realm despite its symbolic value. In subsequent lines, "palm," "land," "heart," "grapes," "eyes," and "tears" all refer to physical things, but their meanings in the poem relate to and reflect spiritual and emotional qualities. In them, her thoughts and feelings are embodied. What they represent, in the poem, explains how the poet sees her condition, herself, and her feelings.

As early as line 2, Barrett Browning suggests that she will be incapacitated by her lover's departure—she cannot act "Without the sense of. . ./ Thy touch upon the palm." Rather than rendering her helpless, however, her denial of his presence ("that which I forbore") will leave a "sense" of him with her, his "touch upon the palm." This image deftly suggests a strengthening, but his presence—no more than a "sense" and "touch"—nevertheless increases her, both spiritually and physically. Separation has taught her that she is both weakened by her lover's absence and strengthened by it, but only if she can see beyond the merely physical aspects of her life—"The widest land/ Doom takes to part us," for example. Seeing no further than the "hand" or the "palm" is to miss the highest meaning of their existence, and the purer realm of spirit. The poet makes her metaphors transpose physical into spiritual reality, where "thy heart in mine" can be and where "pulses" can "beat double."

Ordinary union pales before the union she feels and envisions; it is as real yet as rarefied as the taste of the grape in the wine, and the lovers are so commingled that in speaking her own name, God "hears that name of thine." The final line of the poem illustrates the poem's underlying paradox. Tears in the poet's eyes suggest grief, doubled because God will see both the poet's tears and her lover's, but in that union of grief (over their necessary parting) they will be united, and the tears may be seen as tears of joy and triumph. From their parting comes their ultimate oneness.

Bernard E. Morris

SONNET 7

Author: Elizabeth Barrett Browning (1806-1861)
Type of poem: Sonnet
First published: 1850, in *Sonnets from the Portuguese*, part of *Poems*

The Poem

Elizabeth Barrett Browning's audience probably understood the author of her sonnets to be a woman and probably read them as an expression of love from a woman to a man. It is known that before Elizabeth Barrett met her future husband, her health was very delicate and that it improved after their marriage. This much biographical information is useful, for it heightens the experience of the poem, especially since the sonnet deals with the poet herself nearly having died; knowing that two real-life lovers stand behind the poem increases its emotional impact.

The poem opens with the poet declaring that she sees the world differently since she "heard the footsteps" of her lover's "soul" beside her. Adding "I think" (line 1) to this declaration, however, suggests uncertainty as to the world-encompassing nature of the change. Her lover's footsteps moved between her and death (lines 3-7). She implies that her lover somehow saved her from "obvious death" and, in addition, taught her "the whole/ Of life in a new rhythm" (lines 6-7). Her recovery has given her new life and enough spirit to be glad ("fain") to drink the cup of sorrow or destiny ("dole"), which God "gave for baptism." She would even praise its sweetness, she says, addressing her lover, with him nearby.

The first six-and-a-half lines of the poem explain Barrett Browning's recovery from near death, a recovery of both life and spirit, because her lover brought love into her life. In line 7, the poet shifts from the past to the present—now she is ready to face life with him. The last five lines of the poem look around and ahead, explaining that further changes have followed from this revelation: "The names of country, heaven" are now changed. By implication, heaven is where her lover is or will be, "there or here." The "lute and song" the poet hears and "loved yesterday" are now valued only because her lover's name is in harmony with them.

Though addressed directly in line 9 ("Sweet"), the lover remains little more than a hidden reference, "footsteps" in line 2 and a "name" in the last line. Nevertheless, his presence has profoundly transformed her life—"all the world" and "the whole of life" have been affected by him, as well as her outlook and spirit, even her musical preferences. Still, he remains a shadowy figure, one who provided or inspired the "love" (line 6) that snatched the poet from the brink of death and taught her a new vision of life. The purpose of the poem, it seems, is to acknowledge the lover's influence and to indicate its extent, which has saved her life and changed the way she sees the world and "life."

Forms and Devices

The poem follows the structure of the Petrarchan (or Italian) sonnet by rhyming *abba, abba, cdc, cdc*, and it uses the conventional iambic pentameter line, varying the placement of the stresses in lines 6 through 8 and again in line 10. More important, Barrett Browning does not follow the conventional pattern of pauses—at the end of the first and second quatrains, for example (to establish the octave). Nor does the poem use pauses to divide the last six lines into the conventional set of two tercets. Instead, the pauses occur within the lines and are indicated by commas, ellipses (line 12), and the period (line 7). Only lines 9, 11, and 14 end with a heavy pause (a semicolon or period).

The effect of this pause patterning is to pace the argument unconventionally, using light pauses (the comma and line ends) to give emphasis and structure to the argument. Enjambment—running the meaning from one line to the next around the line end—is used to de-emphasize the rhymes in favor of the continuity of thought. Though the poem, with few heavy pauses, has a light touch, it tends to break up its argument into discrete parcels, as though the poet were not entirely sure of herself. Diffidence is hinted at in the "I think" of the first line, and line 3 (which contains four commas) breaks into a tripping rhythm, as if to convey how the "footsteps" moved "as they stole."

The use of commas enables the poet to give some of her words double meanings. In lines 9 and 10, for example, placing commas around "Sweet" and "heaven" respectively suggests more than one reading. Though obviously an address, "Sweet" could be read as a complement of "sweetness," reinforcing that sentiment. In line 10, however, the commas render "country" and "heaven" both apposite and complementary, though the sense of the line makes them coordinate ideas. Indeed, coordination plays a large role in the last six lines of the sonnet, whereas subordination dominates the first eight lines. This structural peculiarity corresponds to a shift in the argument from an emphasis on the past to the present and future and suggests that the poet regards the past in terms of unequal measures and the present and future in terms of spiritual and emotional equality.

Barrett Browning makes some use of repetition and wordplay to reinforce her sentiments and subtly to lighten the subject of the poem. Opening with a reference to the "face" of the world and imaging "footsteps" stealing ("as they stole") in the shadowy world of the spirit and death soften the impact of the subject on the reader. When the poet says that she "thought to sink," one might remember the hesitancy of "I think" in line 1 and not feel directly confronted by the "dreadful" (line 4) subject being reviewed. The poet seems to want to move still further from this dolorous realm by repeating "sweetness, Sweet," mentioning the "singing angels," and even using words such as "fain" and "anear" to reflect the "new rhythm" she has been taught. Although one is certainly not in fairy land, echoes of it pervade the poem.

Themes and Meanings

It may not be too farfetched to suggest that the poem's meaning includes a trip from the "brink of obvious death" to the brink of heaven, a trip more than hinted at in the final lines, with their "lute and song" and "singing angels." A change indeed has taken place, physically (the poet was apparently at death's door), emotionally (the entire sonnet, while acknowledging the grimmer aspects of existence, seems to want to leave those thoughts and celebrate the poet's recovery and rapturous new state), and spiritually. Though a physical recovery is suggested, the poem deals with events occurring in the soul or suggests the spiritual realm: the "outer brink," "love," "the whole of life in a new rhythm," "cup of dole," and so on. This dualism is clearly evident in line 10, where "country, heaven" are juxtaposed to suggest their interchangeability, at least in the poet's mind.

The poet's confidence with regard to her own physical and mental state seems to increase from the first line to the last. The focus certainly shifts from "The face of all the world" to a spiritual realm filled with angelic singing. Between those two realms, the poet declares that her love has taught her a "new rhythm" and a new way of hearing the music "loved yesterday." The poem develops an argument that mounts from earth to heaven, reflecting the poet's own rise from the brink of death to a place where she views "heaven" and hears the notes of an angelic song. Between these two realms— and on the way from the one to the other—the poet would drink. Her sonnet balances on that point midway between her start and her destination. At the center of the poem, the principal elements of the poet's vision blend metaphorically: Sorrow ("cup of dole") is turned by love into "sweetness." The drink, the act of drinking, and the sweetness that is discovered are all metaphorical embodiments that express the poet's spiritual salvation.

Appropriately, Barrett Browning follows her libation with song, as the second half of the poem indicates. Elevation of spirit is reflected in a shift not only from the physical to the heavenly realm but also in the meaning of "Move" (line 3) and "moves" (line 14). In the first reference, the lover is simply walking, "oh, still, beside me," stealing as he goes along. In the last line, however, the lover is moving in time with the "lute and song . . . loved yesterday." Deftly the poet has told her reader that love has saved her life and lifted her spirit into the heavenly realm; at the same time, it has made her lover's name musical as it "moves right in what they say." She has been caught up not only into love but into its music as well, a music that runs through all life.

Bernard E. Morris

SONNET 14

Author: Elizabeth Barrett Browning (1806-1861)
Type of poem: Sonnet
First published: 1850, in *Sonnets from the Portuguese*, part of *Poems*

The Poem

Elizabeth Barrett Browning did not title the forty-four individual poems in the *Sonnets from the Portuguese*; however, the first phrase of the first line of Sonnet 14, "If thou must love me," serves as a kind of title. As such, it indicates immediately that the sonnet will be framed as an argument, using an "if . . . then" structure. Moreover, the word "must" hints that the poem will be more complex than a straightforward question about whether the lover being addressed indeed loves the poem's speaker.

The sonnet begins with the poet talking directly to her lover. She says to him that if he must love her, he should love her only for the sake of love and for no other reason. She says "only" to emphasize that feeling to the utmost. She says not to love her for the cheer of her smile, nor for beauty or the singular nature of her countenance. He should not love her for her voice or for what she says, nor for a special frame of mind that "falls in well" with his. Do not love me for any of these reasons, she tells him, because they could all change over time—or his perceptions of them could change—and the love they have may therefore wither. She adds, do not love her because she needs to be loved and relies on the comfort and support he provides her. She says, love her for "love's sake." Love her because of love and because of the eternal quality of love on earth.

Taken out of the context of the other sonnets in *Sonnets from the Portuguese*, the idea of loving for only the idea of love itself seems to be confusingly circular. Yet the reader does come away with a strong sense of the fear of loss that underlies the poem. Barrett Browning married the dashing but somewhat footloose Robert Browning in 1846; for doing so, her father disowned her—for the rest of his life, he would not even communicate with his daughter. Furthermore, her brother had died in a boating accident in 1840. It is understandable that she would yearn for permanence and would worry about the loss of Browning's love after the losses and separations in her life.

Forms and Devices

What comes to mind immediately when reading Sonnet 14, "If thou must love me," is the point of view. Sonnets are traditionally given to a perspective of the poet addressing another person, a "you." The point of view is first-person singular, but its direction is entirely pointed at the other person—in this case, as in many, a lover. The reader is left out; that is, the speaker does not speak for the reader's emotions in particular, nor does the reader, in particular, feel something in common with the "you." Instead, one watches the psychological and emotional action unfold as one would watch a drama unfold. In *Sonnets from the Portuguese*, the drama is contained in a series or a sequence of sonnets that tells of the relationship between a man and a woman from the woman's point of view.

Sonnet sequences had traditionally been written by men, who placed their beloveds on a pedestal. The sonnets written by fourteenth century Italian poet Petrarch to Laura epitomize these works. Here the situation is reversed, and a reading of the entire sequence allows the reader to consider this issue more fully. The point of view is one to another, woman to man—and the reader is simply the audience, watching. The effect is to present the actors in their emotional pitches.

The principal device of the poem is the contrast between reasons people fall in love, stay in love, or fall out of love with the utmost reason for being in love—love itself. Barrett Browning arranges the poem in a structure that emphasizes this contrast. For example, the poem's frame is marked by the repetition of the phrase, "for love's sake." When one reads the phrase the second time, in the penultimate line of the poem, it is backed up by the argument Barrett Browning has made to her lover—an argument that readers have bought into by virtue of their role in the audience. The argument is, in a nutshell, that earthly desires for such things as beauty and lack of conflict should not override the eternal nature of love. She pleads with her lover to love her because love is eternal—hence, their love will be eternal.

Themes and Meanings

The main theme of Sonnet 14 is the eternal nature of love. It is not eternal, says the poet, if one lover loves the other for earthly, temporal reasons. These reasons she details in lines 3-12. Earthly reasons fade, as do human beings. Love itself does not fade and die, she states. Therefore, her lover should love her, if he must love her, for the sake of love only.

A crucial distinction here is the word "must." It is this word that casts the poem in the direction it ascends—toward "eternity." For example, if the poem had begun "If thou love me," one would find a different theme altogether. The poem would be about whether the lover truly loves. His love would be called into question, no doubt, even before the poet were to plead for a certain kind of love.

"Must," however, implies that the lover already loves the poet but that he does not have to. The "must" also suggests a different kind of vulnerability on the poet's part. Fate has a role here; she recognizes that if her lover "must" love her, if it is fated in the manner of a "must," then she wants him to love her for "love's sake only." She wants the love to be lifted out of the realm of human passion into the realm of eternal, heavenly passion. One thinks of the ending of the *Sonnets from the Portuguese*'s most famous poem, number 43 ("How do I love thee? Let me count the ways") that ends, "I shall but better love thee after death." The poet sees that if he must love her, it must be a love of eternal power.

This energy, then, becomes the power on which the love rests and through which it exists. To say the least, Barrett Browning has high expectations of her love. If she loses the love, she wants to lose for no less a reason than that the love could not attend to itself on its own course. It would fail because the lovers loved for less than ideal reasons—that is, for earthly and temporal reasons.

David Biespiel

SONNET 35

Author: Elizabeth Barrett Browning (1806-1861)
Type of poem: Sonnet
First published: 1850, in *Sonnets from the Portuguese*, part of *Poems*

The Poem

Sonnet 35, also known by its first six words, "If I leave all for thee," is written in rhymed iambic pentameter lines. The poem, written in the first person, is spoken not to the reader but to the poet's lover. The experience is universal: One lover addresses another. The energy of that address is also universal; it is fevered and intense. The reader watches, as an audience might watch a drama unfold. The sonnet is soliloquy-like, a monologue set apart from the action of stage and drama surrounding it.

The poem begins with the speaker, a woman, asking her lover whether he will make an equal "exchange." The items include nothing less than "all" of her love for all of his. There is a sense of extremes in this opening moment, and the reader senses a tone of desperation on the speaker's part. Something is awry. Her lover seems distant somehow, or she has lost something. The reader cannot be sure. Next she asks herself whether she would "miss" the quotidian of her life, whether the daily, temporal, and basically general talk, the "common" kiss, would be missed. She asks whether her lover could "fill that place" that she would have to give up for him.

The speaker has apparently lost something or someone, and she is deeply concerned about whether her lover can fill the absence. The poet is in grief, she says plainly: "I have grieved so I am hard to love." In this poem, unlike others in the *Sonnets from the Portuguese* sonnet sequence, the poet is preoccupied by something as earthly as death. Still, she wants the man to love her despite her grief. She asks him to open his heart to her, to provide his love for her (in exchange for her love for him) while she is mourning the loss she has suffered. In the final line, she compares herself to a dove who needs another to enfold her, to bring peace of mind to her.

In the summary of this sonnet, one sees that the poet is vulnerable and that the man, her lover, is beseeched to aid her, to bring her back into a less grieving state of mind. Knowing that to leave "all" for her lover is to be vulnerable, she began the poem by asking if he would do the same for her. At the end, she asks for him to take her anyway, so the question at the beginning becomes rhetorical.

It is almost impossible not to think of the courtship of Elizabeth Barrett and Robert Browning when reading the *Sonnets from the Portuguese*. The two poets met in 1845 and were married in September, 1846. Although they had fallen passionately in love, Barrett knew that if she were to marry Browning, her father would be upset, even furious (he suspected Robert Browning of planning to live on her money). The idea of leaving "all" for love was, therefore, a very real prospect. Indeed, her father did disinherit her. The Brownings traveled to Italy, and Elizabeth never saw her father again.

The grief she describes in the sonnet may also refer to (or at least have been inspired by) a particular event in her life. Her brother Edward had died in a boating accident for which she felt partially responsible. Barrett had gone to the English resort town of Torquay, in 1838, hoping that the climate would give some relief for the persistent cough she was suffering. Her brother visited her there but planned to return to London; she persuaded him to stay. When he drowned in the summer of 1840, she was overwhelmed by feelings of grief and guilt. One cannot help but wonder whether the sonnet's "dead eyes too tender to know change" were those of Edward.

Forms and Devices

The traditional sonnet structure is often called an argument. One often sees two or three variations or aspects of the argument, then a turn to a conclusion. For example, an unrequited love poem might run something like the following: Your eyes are dark as a river, your teeth are shiny as stones, your smile is like a waterfall; but you left me and I am drowning in the current of pain you have made. Three points are followed by a turn in emotion and direction.

Sonnet 35 presents an unusual argument. In fact, it is less an argument than an emotional imploring. The form follows the form described above, generally, but with these important differences. First, the poet addresses not only her lover but also herself. The effect of this device is to emphasize the indecisiveness the poet is experiencing. She wants to trade all of her love for all of her lover's love, but she is not so sure of her own end of the bargain. Second, she seems not entirely sure that her lover can fulfill his side of the bargain: "wilt thou fill that place. . . .?" The indecision increases; by line 8, the argument is plagued by doubt. What might have appeared to be a series of rock-solid points are thrown into disarray; emotion is overtaking reason.

Third, Barrett Browning introduces her own preoccupation: grief. These lines appear to be the most interesting, most startling, and most memorable of the poem. She reveals that because she herself has grieved, she is "hard to love." She recognizes that it is harder, perhaps, for him to exchange all of his love for her, since her love is more complex. Yet, she pleads, "love me—wilt thou?" Here is the turn in the emotional argument, if one can call it an argument. She seems to capitulate to him, saying that she will give all of her love regardless of what he may do.

Themes and Meanings

Elizabeth Barrett Browning, as the speaker of this poem, is troubled, and her indecision and her "grief" are the paths down which one might look to discover some of the meanings of the sonnet. She appears to be asking her lover not only to conquer love—hers and his—but also to conquer her grief, because she cannot rid herself of a sorrow. For her to have feelings of both grief—which is "love and grief beside"—and love is to complicate the emotion her lover may have for her: Does he want to try to win her love, which is complicated by the utmost sorrow in human emotion? Although she hopes that they might "exchange," she realizes that the deal is loaded and that she represents the worse end of the deal.

Thus, a theme of the sonnet is the complexity of human emotion. When one enters into a love relationship, one brings into it all of one's past experiences (all of one's baggage, as the saying goes) and one deposits them on the doorstep of the new lover. Even if one does not consciously bring the baggage to bear, it follows. One can never escape one's past—or, in the case of Sonnet 35, one's grief. The lover, if he or she chooses, may search through these bags for old bones and ghosts—and may find some. A lover may reveal what is inside and then ask: Can you love me anyway? Can you open your "heart wide"? One's past emotions become complicated in new ones; one begins to experience oneself and one's life as small and fleeting, like a dove, the final image of the poem.

Another theme in this poem is the nature of the relationship between man and woman, and it reflects the traditional view of the protecting nature of a man over his lover. The woman wants to have an emotionally equal relationship. She states this in the first two lines of the poem, but something intercedes. She begins to feel that she may have overstepped—that she is to blame. On the one hand, one may take this to mean that she recognizes her vulnerability. On the other, through a more feminist approach, one may see that she feels imprisoned by her past and believes that she has no alternative but to give herself over to her man. Readers will have to draw their own conclusions.

Nevertheless, the poet desires her lover to take her, baggage and all, and she is willing to give "all for thee" without hearing whether he will reciprocate. What the reader sees, then, is a poet in the throes of turmoil, in a poem that enacts the nature of that turmoil.

David Biespiel

SONNET 43

Author: Elizabeth Barrett Browning (1806-1861)
Type of poem: Sonnet
First published: 1850, in *Sonnets from the Portuguese*, part of *Poems*

The Poem

All the forty-four poems in Elizabeth Barrett Browning's sonnet sequence *Sonnets from the Portuguese* were written during the period of courtship that preceded her marriage to Robert Browning. As a whole, *Sonnets from the Portuguese* is considered one of the finest poetic sequences in literature. It is Sonnet 43, however, often titled "How do I love thee?" from its memorable first words, which is the best-known of the collection; indeed, it is one of the most-quoted love poems in English literature.

Sonnet 43 is an Italian sonnet, a fourteen-line iambic pentameter poem written in a specific rhyme scheme. The first line of the poem asks a question; the other thirteen lines answer it. The question is simply, "How do I love thee?" The answer involves seven different aspects of love, all of which are part of Elizabeth's feeling for Robert, and the projection of an eighth, eternal love in the future.

As the poem proceeds, each variation on the theme of love is introduced with the words "I love thee." In the octave (the first eight lines), the poem speaks of the spiritual side of her love, which aspires toward God; then she mentions its earthly aspect, the love that enriches daily life. More briefly, she mentions the fact that her love is given freely, almost as if it were prompted by the conscience, and that it is pure, in other words, selfless, like the action of a humble man unwilling to accept praise.

In the sestet (the final six lines), the poet looks at her love in three more ways. First, she explains that this love makes use of the emotions once spent on grief or on religious faith. From this mention of faith, she proceeds to a slightly different idea: that in loving Browning, she has rediscovered a love like that she once felt for the saints of religion. Finally, she explains that her love is all-encompassing, involving her entire life, including moments of unhappiness as well as happiness; that her love is as much a part of her as breathing, that is, the very act of living. In conclusion, the poet asserts that, God willing, this love can even transcend death and continue in the next world.

In most sonnets, there are eight or twelve lines stating a question, a conflict, a problem, or a possibility. In the final six lines, or sometimes in a final couplet, the question is answered, the conflict resolved, the problem solved, or the possibility denied or extended in some way. This sonnet is unusual in that the question is stated in the first line, and the rest of the poem is made up simply of various answers to that question. Even the last line and a half, which could be said to provide some kind of resolution, is really only another answer to the original question, which might be restated as "What are the various ways in which love affects the lover?"

Forms and Devices

It is a mark of Barrett Browning's skill that the repetition of the phrase "I love thee"—nine times in a poem only fourteen lines long—simply serves to make the poem more effective. The phrase is first used in the question; then, when the poet sets out to "count the ways," she keeps score by introducing each new idea with exactly the same words. Certainly the repeated phrase is more than a marker; it emphasizes the fact she is stating—that indeed she loves the man to whom the poem is addressed. The repetition is also realistic; at least in the early stages of the emotion, most people who are in love have a tendency to reiterate the declaration frequently. The fact that the poem is structured around the repetition of the phrase "I love thee" is, therefore, one source of its effectiveness.

In addition to carefully crafted phrases, most poems as popular as this sonnet have striking images. One thinks of the description of the snow, even the sound of the horse's bells, in Robert Frost's "Stopping by Woods on a Snowy Evening," or of the moonlit beach, the lights of the French shore, and the final dramatic reference to armed conflict in Matthew Arnold's "Dover Beach." In contrast, "How do I love thee?" has almost no descriptions. The only real images in the poem are the mention of light in the sixth line and the reference to "breath,/ Smiles, tears" in the thirteenth. One might include the rather vague stretching of the soul described at the beginning of the sonnet.

Instead of relying on sensuous imagery, Barrett Browning describes the abstraction, love, by means of other abstractions. For example, love is compared to that expansion of the soul in search of "the ends of Being" (or the meaning of the world) and of "ideal Grace" (evidently the grace of God). Similarly, the similes in lines 8 and 9 involve movement toward or away from two other abstractions, "Right" and "Praise." The later references to "griefs" and "faith," even to "lost saints," are all made without an imagistic context. Because of this lack of images, the almost incantatory repetition of the simple phrase "I love thee" becomes even more important; it helps the reader proceed through the abstractions, just as the word-pictures created by images do in other poems.

It also should be pointed out that metrically this poem is extremely regular. There are few variations from the iambic pattern. Instead, the sonnet proceeds in a quiet and stately manner that seems almost to deny, or at least to suggest a different definition of, the "passion" the poet stresses in the ninth line. Only with the three stressed syllables near the end of the sonnet, "breath,/ Smiles, tears" does the speaker reveal the depths of the emotion so reasonably described; immediately thereafter, she returns to her dignified iambics for the conclusion of the poem. In interpreting the poem, one must look carefully at the point where the metrical pattern breaks; it seems likely that it will be the thematic center of the sonnet.

Themes and Meanings

As a complete sequence, *Sonnets from the Portuguese* describes the development of Elizabeth Barrett's love for Robert Browning. As the forty-third poem in a sequence of forty-four, "How do I love thee?" describes a fully realized love. Earlier poems often had mentioned the past, when the poet did not dream that such happiness would ever be hers. In this poem, she defines her present happiness by explaining how her love incorporates and transcends her past spiritual and emotional experiences.

For example, Barrett Browning speaks of her love as being the striving of her soul for the divine, for the purposes of life and for that "Grace" that is the gift of God. Similarly, the seventh and eighth lines suggest that her love is like the spiritual quests for morality ("Right") and for humility ("Praise"). Her love has brought her back to the kind of innocent faith she knew in her childhood, but seemingly had lost. All these descriptions indicate that the kind of love Elizabeth now feels for Robert is akin to the love that enables a human being to love God and to experience God's love in return.

Earlier poems in the sequence had referred to the unhappiness and despair of the years before Elizabeth met Robert. In this sonnet, the poet triumphantly announces that her love has redeemed those years. For example, the capacity for intensity that she developed in past sorrows now can be utilized, instead, in the joy of her love. Similarly, the capacity for belief that she developed in her youth now can be exercised in the complete faith that provides the security of love.

Even though in Sonnet 43 many references stress the spiritual, the poet also makes it clear that the relationship is solidly based on earthly needs. In the temporal world, day alternates with night ("sun and candlelight"), happiness with unhappiness ("Smiles, tears"). Barrett Browning does not expect a heaven on Earth; all she needs is the presence of the beloved during the changes that define life in this world. Finally, she emphasizes her awareness of the final change: that from life to death. In the final lines, the heavenly and the earthly, the spiritual and the temporal are united. The rhyme words are significant. With the help of God, the lovers will proceed together from a last "breath" into a new life and an even more devoted love "after death."

Barrett Browning's description of a love that thus encompasses past, present, and future has appealed to both men and women for almost a century and a half. Recent feminist critics have pointed out another significance of the sequence, and especially of the later poems within it, such as this. From the Renaissance on, sonnets have been used by men for the expression of their own emotions, first for love-complaints and later for expressions of friendship, anger, and religious uncertainties. In *Sonnets from the Portuguese*, a woman poet expressed her love for a man in her own unmistakably feminine voice. Sonnet 43 focuses on Elizabeth, not on Robert; it is the revelation of a woman's own heart and soul, fortunately inspired by a man who was worthy of her.

Rosemary M. Canfield Reisman

SONNET LVI

Author: Fulke Greville (1554-1628)
Type of poem: Satire
First published: 1633, in *Caelica*

The Poem

"Sonnet LVI," reflecting Fulke Greville's peculiarly complex mind, is many things at once. As the title suggests, it is a lyrical "sonnet" (although that term had a much less rigid definition in Greville's day than it does now) on the subject of romantic, erotic love; in this way, it recalls some of the love poems in the sonnet sequence *Astrophil and Stella* (literally, "Star Lover and Star"), written by Sir Philip Sidney, Greville's contemporary and great friend. "Sonnet LVI" is also a satire, however, poking fun at certain key assumptions underlying courtly love poems, including many of Sidney's. Finally, Greville's poem is a kind of waking dream vision, one in which the philosophical, first-person narrator achieves an overblown, grandiose notion of his lover's beauty and of his own importance, only to have his illusions come crashing down around him, frustrating his romantic desires.

Indeed, the narrator is deluded from the very beginning. As the poem opens, he sees himself as a glittering knight, right out of the pages of King Arthur, setting forth on a noble, chivalric quest. This quest, however, turns out to involve sin, vanity, and hypocrisy more than nobility, in that the narrator seeks not for the Holy Grail but for "Cynthia," a married woman with whom the narrator is infatuated and longs to have an adulterous affair. Just at the point of achieving his questionable boon, the narrator is overcome by the lady's beauty and falls into a swooning, ultimately egotistical vision of mythic gods and goddesses, seeing himself as at one in their company, while totally ignoring the real, flesh-and-blood woman beneath him, "Naked on a bed of play." At this point, Cynthia has the good sense to leave him, no doubt in favor of a more sensible, earth-bound lover. Finding himself abruptly alone, the narrator bitterly rues his folly in confusing spiritual love with sexual delight.

As a poet, Greville was notorious for constantly tinkering with his verse, revising his body of work throughout his long, industrious life; accordingly, it is difficult to date any of his poems with precision. Further, the text of "Sonnet LVI" exists in at least two different manuscript versions, one of which, the so-called "Warwick MS," inserts a passage of some twenty-four additional lines (after line 24) into the only version of the poem commonly available today. However, scholar Richard Waswo argues persuasively that these twenty-four "missing" lines are helpful to a proper understanding of Greville's meaning. Therefore, students of "Sonnet LVI" might want to track down a printing of the poem in its longer form—perhaps in Waswo's influential study *The Fatal Mirror: Themes and Techniques in the Poetry of Fulke Greville* (1972).

Forms and Devices

Central to Greville's intentions in the poem is his use of situational irony: The poem is informed from first to last by a sense of the yawning gap between illusion and reality, between expectation and fulfillment. Greville's narrator is a megalomaniac, seeing all the universe as witnessing and applauding his erotic pursuits. Ravished by Cynthia's loveliness, he rashly calls himself "a God," variously identifying himself with Mars (the classical god of war), with Apollo (the patron god of poetry), and with Phaeton (a sun god who once nearly set all the world aflame).

He is none of these exalted figures; he is merely a quite ordinary man intent on conquering an ordinary, if attractive, woman. The narrator, like many people, insists upon elevating both his erotic impulses and his love object into the realm of the spiritual, the heavenly, the mythic. In doing so, he unconsciously reveals that his pursuit of the lady is actually no more than an exercise in exaggerated self-love, and she rightly abandons him. Here, then, lies the central irony of the poem's action: In mistaking earthly delights for spiritual ones and in looking up at the inaccessible heavens instead of down at the available woman, the narrator loses out on the lovemaking he has sought so arduously.

Also notable in the poem is Greville's facility with metaphor, a talent which has led critics to compare him favorably with the better-known John Donne (1572-1631). When the lady flees from him, for instance, the narrator successively compares himself to a riverbed deserted by its river, to the "Articke pole" abandoned by the sun, and finally to a condemned criminal confessing his sins at the site of his execution. These startling, unexpected metaphors have real power and contribute much to the disillusioned tone of the poem's conclusion.

Themes and Meanings

"I know the world, and believe in God," Greville once remarked, thereby revealing the deep fissure that ran through both his public and private lives. As a counselor to three successive English monarchs, the poet assuredly did "know the world," most notably the fractious, artificial world of the royal court. For many decades he was able to survive and even to flourish in this often treacherous environment. Greville was also a staunch Protestant of Calvinist persuasions, quick to pass flinty moral judgments on the same courtly life in which he participated so adroitly.

In the love poetry of the Renaissance English court—all aspiring courtiers sought to become adept at versifying—love is seen as an ennobling passion, the pursued lady as an object of extravagant worship, and the conventions of courtship as semireligious rituals. Furthermore, while the ultimate (and expected) object of the romantic chase is sexual consummation, the lady is nonetheless venerated not simply as an ideal of physical beauty but as an image or reflection of an ideal of spiritual beauty as well.

In some of its important aspects, this courtly love tradition owed much to the fourteenth century Italian poet Petrarch, many of whose sonnets lavishly praise his beloved "Laura" in this fashion. The Petrarchan mode was much imitated by sixteenth century Englishmen; indeed, the *Astrophil and Stella* sonnet sequence of Greville's friend Sidney (himself much imitated) is profoundly indebted to the Italian poet—to the point that Sidney was often referred to as "the English Petrarch" by his own contemporaries.

Greville was well aware of the philosophical underpinnings of such courtly love poetry, and he even toys with Petrarchan norms in the early poems of his *Caelica* collection. Given his Christian convictions, however, he must finally reject and mock these conventions, as he decidedly does in "Sonnet LVI." For the Calvinist Greville, the earth and the men and women who inhabit it are in a condition of steady moral decline, and they have been since humanity's fall from the Garden of Eden. In such a state, even an emotion as potentially noble as love has inevitably devolved into mere carnal lust. Accordingly, the Petrarchan lover, in mistaking his erotic impulse for something fine and spiritual, commits more than a blunder: He commits outright heresy.

The narrator of "Sonnet LVI" is clearly one such benighted courtly lover, intent on deifying both his love object and his own pursuit of her. Thus he likens the lady to the goddess Venus and sees in her earthly beauty a direct analogue to all things heavenly, including the Milky Way constellation. Similarly, he sees himself as godlike ("Surely I Apollo am") and, in a vision, seeks to ascend into the heavenly regions ("I stept forth to touch the skye"). However, at precisely this climactic moment his earthbound mistress, understandably irritated by the narrator's insistent, ego-ridden spiritualizing, deserts him ("Cynthia who did naked lye,/ Runnes away like silver streames"), thereby frustrating his erotic aims.

Deserted now, the narrator can only lament his loss and curse the romantic illusions that have thwarted his conquest. At no little cost, and quite to his surprise, he has learned that human love is a decidedly secular, not spiritual, matter. "Love is onely Natures art," he sorrowfully concludes, "Wonder hinders Love and Hate." In other words—in the words of Greville editor Geoffrey Bullough—human love "is a purely natural business, in which action is all and mute adoration a hindrance." Or as the poet and critic Yvor Winters bluntly puts it, this poem "states that love is physical and no more and that he who is distracted by spiritual concerns [in love's pursuit] is a fool." All that the narrator of "Sonnet LVI" ultimately has to show for his romantic quest is this hard-won, humiliating truth.

William Ryland Drennan

SONNET XVI

Author: John Milton (1608-1674)
Type of poem: Sonnet
First published: 1694, in *Letters of State . . .*

The Poem

Much of Sonnet XVI (subtitled *To the Lord General Cromwell*) is localized in time and place to England's seventeenth century. The allusions that make up the poem's primary content are to places and events that would have been immediately recognized by John Milton's contemporaries but are understood by a modern audience only if put into historical context. In the spring of 1652, the Parliament appointed a committee to consider the question of how much free religious discussion would be tolerated outside the official Puritan Church and its appointed clergy. This Committee for the Propagation of the Gospel was considering a proposal set before it by a group of fifteen Puritan ministers headed by John Owen, General Oliver Cromwell's personal chaplain. Milton believed that the proposals would place serious restrictions on freedom of conscience and feared that if passed, the new laws would be just the beginning of still greater prohibitions. One of the pamphlets being circulated that detailed the various proposals contained a recommendation that no one should be permitted to speak in public on any religious question without a certificate from two or more "godly and orthodox" ministers. Such a law would have placed unrestricted censorship into the hands of official clergy, who would be the sole arbiters of orthodoxy. Milton's contempt for these behind-the-scenes machinations is stated in no uncertain terms: ". . . new foes arise/ Threat'ning to bind our souls with secular chains."

Cromwell was already well established as a proponent of wide religious freedoms. When the proposals were under discussion in Parliament, Cromwell is reported to have said that he had "rather Mahometanism [Islam] were permitted among us than that one of God's children should be persecuted." Still, Cromwell was a realist and Milton may have feared that the politician might not go as far in the protection of free conscience as the poet's idealism would wish. Sonnet XVI repeats Milton's warnings to the Puritans contained in his prose masterpiece *Areopagitica* (1644) that the purported champions of liberty were soon to be guilty of imposing precisely the same bondage they had previously overthrown or, as Milton stated so succinctly in a previous sonnet, that "new Presbyter is but old Priest writ large."

The poem lends support to a head of state already engaged in a cause for which the poet cared deeply. Although Cromwell may well have been the most powerful person in England when Sonnet XVI was composed, the poem goes far beyond simple hagiography. It does not merely flatter or exalt a powerful man but rather urges his and Milton's agenda in a contentious political struggle—pushing the sonnet, a poetic form utilized primarily for praising some romantic ideal, into the realm of polemic. Furthermore, while Cromwell's achievements are indeed nobly versified in Sonnet XVI, it is too much to assume that the poem contains Milton's final estimation of the Lord Protector. The relationship between them was not as close, nor was Milton's adherence to the party line as total, as is sometimes assumed. His position as secretary for foreign tongues did not give him any real influence in the government or its councils. He was a secretary whose job was to translate state documents into Latin for publication on the Continent. So, while the poem may appear at first glance to be an attempt to curry favor and exalt the rich and famous, such was not its intention. It functions less as praise for Cromwell than a rallying cry for free-thinking Englishmen.

Forms and Devices

Sonnet XVI is modeled after the heroic sonnets of Torquato Tasso, one of Milton's favorite poets. It is arguably an apostrophe, the form of address that speaks to an absent or dead person, a thing, or an abstract idea as if it were present. While it is possible that Milton, a minor (though celebrated) functionary in Cromwell's Commonwealth government, had the opportunity to deliver the poem directly to the man he is addressing, no record of Cromwell's reception of or reaction to the sonnet is known to exist. Another legitimate way of reading the poem is to let the particulars give way to the general and to see Cromwell as the poetic ideal of people of good conscience who live in all places at all times. Thus the apostrophe's address would be not just to "the chief of men" but also to the best of what is human. The poem's subtitle, "On the proposals of certain ministers at the Committee for Propagation of the Gospel," clearly distances it from the Spenserian and Shakespearean tradition of reserving the sonnet for celebrating love and tender feelings.

Sonnet XVI employs the classic Italian octave-sestet division written in nearly uniform iambic pentameter. Throughout all his sonnets, Milton consistently utilized a rigorous Petrarchan rhyme scheme of *abba abba* for the octave, and Sonnet XVI is no exception. However, its concluding sestet of a *cddcee* scheme is unique for Milton and is his only sonnet to end in a couplet. This couplet is further isolated from Milton's usual pattern by the jarring fourteenth line, which introduces it. Line 14 contains twelve syllables, destroying the pentameter, and its word order is impossible to read with any regular scansion, destroying the iambic. The octave is devoted to praise and the sestet to admonition. Also unique to Sonnet XVI is the joining of the octave and the sestet by enjambment, a sentence or clause that carries its sense of meaning from one line to another: "yet much remains/ To conquer still." In this case, the enjambment not only unites two lines but also serves to bridge what are usually strictly separated poetic units.

Themes and Meanings

Milton has an unmatched ability to weave poetic structure with theme and meaning, making the way the poem is put together part of the meaning of the poem. For new readers, this may mean a frustrating bout of learning poetic terms and traditions. However, once a few of the basics are internalized, one begins to realize how the work of Milton has assumed its place, alone, at the top of the canon. He infused the new and unformed English language with a power and depth that his contemporary readers never dreamed it could possess and that poets of succeeding generations have continually aspired to equal.

In the octave, Milton praises Cromwell for his past achievements. With "matchless Fortitude," Cromwell, "our chief of men," has triumphantly led his country through war and political turmoil. Milton praises Cromwell's military victories at the Battle of Preston on the banks of "Darwen stream" at Dunbar and Worcester. Through every obstacle, Cromwell has plowed his way to "peace and truth." In these seemingly tossed-off lines, Milton alludes to commonly known context. According to Merritt Hughes, the figures of "Peace" and "Truth" were impressed on a commemorative coin issued by Parliament in honor of Cromwell's victories at Preston, Dunbar, and Worcester. Readers of Milton's time, upon first hearing the sonnet, could little anticipate that this lilting, seemingly innocent sonnet filled with happy thoughts could turn into a scathing condemnation of their most cherished institutions.

The enjambment that destroys the separation of the octave and sestet ("yet much remains/ To conquer still") also aborts the homily, cutting short its natural completion with a note of warning. The Puritans have won a kingdom, but will they lose their conscience? Milton urges Cromwell not to rest on his achievements: England has internal enemies of its soul more insidious than any of the external enemies that had threatened its borders. The challenges of wise government call for a valor equal to the battlefield: "peace hath her victories/ No less renown'd than war." Cromwell has an opportunity to rise up to a still greater glory by defending England's freedoms of religious tolerance from its homegrown predators.

The poem's final couplet conflates several well-known biblical references to wolves threatening sheep (for example, John 10:13, Matthew 7:15, and Acts 20:29) that could hardly have been misunderstood by the Puritan ministers targeted by the poet. The portrait of clergy as hireling wolves using the gospel for fangs to tear and rend the very flesh of England is introduced to the reader's ears by the dissonant line 14 that, of necessity, must be read with unnatural stress and emphasis. The final couplet, the only couplet to end any of Milton's sonnets, adds audible bestiality to the scenario with the ugly rhyme of "paw" and "maw." The poet had used the sheep and wolf images before. The ministers under condemnation in Sonnet XVI who were familiar with Milton's poetry might have recognized echoes from "Lycidas" and have been doubly incensed. In this earlier poem, Satan is the "prowling wolf" who leaps over the fence and into the fold. The sheep are successfully defended from external danger but subsequently die of an internal rot while their inattentive shepherds play loud and lively music.

Tony A. Markham

SONNET XVIII

Author: John Milton (1608-1674)
Type of poem: Sonnet
First published: 1673, in *Poems upon Several Occasions*

The Poem

John Milton's Sonnet XVIII—sometimes known as "On the Late Massacre in Piedmont"—was written against a background of religious dissent and persecution. While serving in Oliver Cromwell's Council of State as its secretary of foreign tongues, Milton received preliminary news of trouble between the French Catholic Duke of Savoy and a small, isolated sect of Protestants who lived in the French Alps. These Protestants were known as the Waldensians or Vaudois and were thought to have preserved a simple scriptural faith from earlier times.

The Waldensians were founded in the 1100's by a Lyonnais theologian and reformer named Peter Waldo. The Roman Catholic Church was disturbed by Waldo's lack of theological training and his translation of the Latin Bible into French. Waldensian views were based on a simplified reading of the Bible that emphasized moral rigor. They confessed, celebrated Communion, fasted, and preached poverty, but did not pray for the dead or venerate saints. The movement spread rapidly to Spain, northern France, Flanders, Germany, and southern Italy and into Poland and Hungary. Rome's responses ranged from excommunication to active persecution and execution. By the end of the thirteenth century persecution had virtually eliminated the sect in most of Europe, and by the end of the fifteenth century the members were confined by treaty to the French and Italian valleys of the Cottian Alps.

By Milton's time, the Waldensians had begun to intrude into the more fertile plains of Piedmont, Italy. Ordered by the Duke of Savoy to retreat, they had been pursued into the mountains and were massacred there by the Piedmontese soldiers on April 24, 1655. It is estimated that 1,712 men, women, and children were set upon and slaughtered with every kind of barbarity. A few fugitives escaped over the snow-covered Alps to carry word of the massacre to Paris and beg protection of the larger Protestant community.

In May of the same year, Milton, acting for Cromwell, wrote letters to various heads of state including Louis XIV of France, the kings of Denmark and Sweden, and the Dutch Republic and the Swiss Protestant cantons that strongly protested against the abrupt termination of freedom of worship for the Waldensians and its violent enforcement. Although these letters were necessarily couched in diplomatic language and were not the proper outlet for Milton's full expression of personal outrage, they nevertheless fully communicated his and England's ire and are adequate prose counterparts to the poem. Later in the year, after Sir Samuel Morland, Cromwell's special envoy to the Duke of Savoy, returned with his full report and the full degree of bloodshed was known, Milton was able to give free rein to his emotions and wrote this, his most impassioned sonnet. It was first published in 1673.

Forms and Devices

Sonnet XVIII is an apostrophe, a figure of speech that directly addresses either someone not present or an abstract quality. Apostrophes include prayers or other addresses to God and are associated with deep emotional expression. The apostrophe form is ideally suited to Sonnet XVIII, which not only is addressed to God but also is so passionate that one can almost hear it uttered between clenched teeth.

The poem breaks with conventional British sonnet technique in two basic ways: Its rhyme pattern is not the usual *abab cdcd efef gg* used by Edmund Spenser, William Shakespeare, and other earlier English poets. Instead it uses the enclosed *abba abba cdc dcd* of the first Italian sonneteers. Second, Milton's frequent use of enjambment marks a drastic departure with the British notion of the proper sonnet.

In a typical English sonnet, the statement of ideas coincides with the poem's division into quatrains, tercets, and couplets. Major themes finish and new ones begin in harmony with the divisions. Additionally, the verbal pauses required by normal speech patterns occur with almost perfect regularity at the ends of lines, and a complete sentence break anywhere inside the line of poetry is avoided. Yet the four major pauses of Sonnet XVIII all occur within the lines, and the octave is connected to the sestet by one of the poem's ten enjambments. By so doing, Milton was not so much breaking from tradition as returning to the patterns established by the original Italian sonneteers, primarily Giovanni della Casa, whose poetry treated the sonnet more as a whole unit, drawing the quatrains and tercets more closely together into a seamless fabric.

Whether deliberate or not, Milton's preference for earlier Italianate conventions over the later British modifications forms a rather elaborate conceit that pervades Sonnet XVIII. If the reader accepts a rough parallel between religious and literary orthodoxy, then Milton was doing the same thing in his poetry as the Waldensians in their faith. The sect believed it was living according to the original Christian edicts, breaking with the more recent innovations of the Roman Church, just as Milton was writing according to the original Italian masters, contrary to later British conventions.

Again, Milton may not have intended this particular twist of reasoning, but he had a particular genius for using the forms and conventions of poetry which would precisely mirror his themes. One could further conjecture that Sonnet XVIII's line-broken ideas and pause-broken lines litter the poem like bodies litter a field after a massacre. The jaggedness of Milton's composition mirrors for the reader the fractured limbs and shattered lives of the Piedmontese Protestants. Its phonetics were also chosen to conjure up associations of violence and grief: the repetition of the long *o* and *n* sounds in "stones," "moans," "groans," and "Babylonian woe" re-create in some small sense the plaintive cries of victims falling before the sword.

Themes and Meanings

From the first word, the reader is able to condense a powerful minimalist sentence that sets the tone for the entire sonnet: "Avenge." Milton may be addressing God, but not the loving, forgiving shepherd of the New Testament. With this particular prayer,

Milton is looking forward and backward to invoke the God of blood and vengeance: backward to the Old Testament deity who pronounced "I will make mine arrows drunk with blood and my sword shall devour your flesh . . . he will avenge the blood of his servants" (Deuteronomy 32:42-42) and forward to the apocalyptic prophecies found in John's visions, "O Lord . . . avenge our blood on them that dwell on the earth" (Revelation 6:10).

Lines 3 and 4 credit the massacred Waldensians with following true Christian principles while England was still finding its way, worshiping "Stocks and Stones." These mysterious and ambiguous stocks and stones evoke several images: material wealth in the form of livestock and precious stones; pagan idolatry with the livestock signifying an animistic deism and the stones signifying graven images (the golden calf being a primary example); or even the harshness of seventeenth century justice, which utilized cruel public stocks to ridicule offenders and stones to press out their confessions. If one puts credence in the latter explanation, then the sonnet's call for revenge has been undercut. Is a society that employs such barbaric means to preserve its civil order closer to the Waldensians or to the army that cut them down?

Lines 10-13 employ another of Milton's signature devices of conflating classical and biblical allusions into a single poetic image. In the poem, the blood and ashes of martyrs are sown over fields, held by the "triple Tyrant," to reproduce one hundred-fold. The reader is expected to associate the myth of Cadmus, who sowed dragon's teeth to create an army of warriors (as Cromwell is calling on the combined forces of Protestant Europe to battle the Papacy), with the parable of the sower found in Matthew 13 (the seed that fell on good ground brought forth as much as one hundredfold) and theologian Tertullian's famous phrase, "The blood of the martyrs is the seed of the Church." The triple Tyrant is generally assumed to refer to the pope's mitre with three crowns.

Again, Milton seems to deliberately undercut his own arguments, as though he were divided about what he ought to feel, what stance he ought to take. In the Cadmus tale, the brother warriors fell among themselves in a bloody civil war. In Matthew, the parable of the sower is followed immediately by the parable of the thorns that sprang up among the good seed and had to be cast into the fire. In addition, Tertullian, like all Montanists, held that Christians should welcome persecution, not flee from it. His dogmatic tendencies ultimately led him into heresy. One may see that each of Milton's allusions attach destructive consequences to Cromwell's call for retribution and to the disunity among the Protestant factions. Although Milton was dismayed and angry about the massacre of the saints at Piedmont, and his initial reaction was to lash out with violent and furious language, the reader may also believe that Milton included in his poem hints that Cromwell's call for a holy war against Rome was not the Christian way to reform.

Tony A. Markham

SONNET XIX

Author: John Milton (1608-1674)
Type of poem: Sonnet
First published: 1673, in *Poems upon Several Occasions*

The Poem

John Milton's Sonnet XIX, sometimes known as "When I Consider How My Light Is Spent," opens with the narrator reflecting on the fact that he has become blind before half his life has been lived. He is profoundly distressed at the prospect of no longer being able to use his greatest talent, writing, and fears that God might be displeased and punish him for not using it—just as, in a biblical parable, God punished the servant who had not used the money entrusted to him but had hidden it instead. He asks himself whether God could possibly expect the same service from him, being impaired, that God expects from those without an overwhelming handicap.

As he is posing this question in his mind, Patience, personified, answers by reminding him that God does not have to depend on humanity's work or its gifts; rather, those who serve God best are those who "Bear his mild yoke." The narrator acknowledges God's exalted position and the fact that multitudes of people all over the world stay busy night and day doing things that God bids them do; nevertheless, he concludes that those who "only stand and wait" can also serve God in a way that is worthy.

Forms and Devices

In Sonnet XIX, Milton opts to replace the verbal luxuriance of the Elizabethan sonnet with classical precision and the Petrarchan, or Italian, form in crafting this tight poem. With fourteen rhymed lines of iambic pentameter, the sonnet is divided into two parts by rhyme scheme: The octave is rhymed *abba abba*, and the sestet is rhymed *cde cde*. The structure of Sonnet XIX is masterful. A basic structural principle is paragraph rather than sentence, and this sonnet is, in effect, a verse paragraph. Also in typical Italian form, the sonnet's rhetorical structure follows its rhyme scheme. The octave presents a problem—how a man deprived of his sight can please God and obey God's admonition to use his talents to the fullest—and the sestet offers a solution or a resolution: He can serve in other ways and still please God. Milton employs personification to provide for a response to the narrator's anguished question. Patience interrupts to put an end to his foolish question at the *volta*, or the turn at the sestet.

Various critics have commented on Milton's use of puns and have identified a number of them in this short poem. In the opening line, Milton uses the word "spent," which evolved from the Indo-European form meaning "to spin," through the Latin meaning of "weigh," into Middle English "pensive," and through Old French to the modern English "expend," "ponder," or "spend." In the context of the rest of the poem, all these meanings are relevant. In the second line, Milton refers to his plight in "this dark world and wide." Darkness in this sonnet immediately suggests his blindness;

however, Milton was also a man with deep religious conviction, and he would have been aware that darkness was a cliché in much religious writing for sinfulness and ignorance.

One of the most obvious plays on words is the use of "talent." When the poet makes a reference to "that one talent which is death to hide," simultaneously one associates the word both with Milton's great skill as a writer of prose and poetry and with the biblical passage commonly known as the parable of the talents in Matthew 25 to which the poem clearly refers. The "talent" was a type of coin used in biblical times.

In line 4, the word "useless," familiarly used to indicate that something is not serving a valuable purpose, also is related to "usury" and is associated with money not earning any interest. In the same line, the word "bent" carries the idea of being determined to do something but also has the etymological background of being bonded or bound, in this case to Milton's feeling of divine-given vocation to writing. The words "light denied" in line 7, in addition to the obvious suggestion of blindness, can also refer to spiritual light or to inspiration for the poet. The phrase in lines 11 and 12, "his state/ Is kingly," can be associated with greatness, power, and stateliness as well as with territory.

Following the example of Edmund Spenser, one of the greatest nondramatic poets of the Elizabethan era, Milton developed the characteristic of using archaic words, particularly in his earlier work. One such example in Sonnet XIX is "fondly," which in medieval English meant "foolish" or "naïvely credulous." Even by Milton's time, the word was taking on its later meaning of "affectionately."

Unlike various poets before and after him, Milton did not feel compelled to end an octave precisely at the end of a line, as with line 8 of this sonnet. Here, he practices enjambment, in which he carries over a sentence into line 9 and then introduces the contrast with the word "but" in the middle of the line.

Although he could write simple subject-verb-object clauses when such was required, Milton often preferred involved syntax. In Sonnet XIX, he uses subordination, inversion, and a delayed subject and verb. The complexity of the opening adverbial clause ("When I consider . . . lest he returning chide") contributes to a building of intensity to a climax at which the speaker, feeling either angry, despondent, or impatient, speaks the direct object in the form of the question ("Doth God exact . . .?") before qualifying it with the main clause ("I fondly ask").

Themes and Meanings

Sonnet XIX is deeply concerned with the plight of one who wishes, and is even determined, to do God's will but, because of circumstances beyond his own control, finds that he may not be able to continue doing it. He wonders if he will be punished by God for not being able to use to the fullest the talent with which God has endowed him.

The metaphor around which the sonnet is developed is the parable of the talents in Matthew 25:14-30. In this parable, the Kingdom of Heaven is compared to a master, who, before departing to a faraway place, distributes among three servants various sums of money (talents). They are to invest or otherwise use the money to earn more so that they can report a worthy gain when the master returns. Two of the servants do so: The one with five talents produces ten, and the servant with two doubles his. The third servant, however, is fearful and hides his one talent for fear that, if he fails to use it profitably, he might lose even the little that he has. When the master returns and hears his excuse for not having increased what he was given, he is angry and commands that the unprofitable servant be cast "into outer darkness."

Milton believed fervently that his genius for writing was a God-given talent, and when he became blind, it was a reasonable reaction to wonder what consequence there might be for not using his gifts in God's service. The poem proceeds, then, from grief through questioning—"Doth God exact day-labor, light denied?"—to resignation and acceptance.

Patience reminds the distraught poet that God does not require human work or even gifts to maintain God's kingly position; rather, those who serve God best are those who "bear his mild yoke." This reference to a yoke is to a passage in Matthew 11, in which Jesus invites all those with burdens to take on his yoke because it is easy and his burden is light; in so doing the "heavy laden" will find spiritual rest and comfort. The yoke was used, literally, over the necks of oxen to keep them astride as they performed their work in the fields. Figuratively, God's yoke is to keep humankind joined to God so that God shares much of the burden and humans do not have to carry it alone.

The reply that Patience makes is stated in the terms of the hierarchy of angels that Milton cites in *Paradise Lost* (1667, 1674)—that some are angels of contemplation rather than of action. Thus, "waiting on" God can be a means of service just as in the account in Luke 10:38-42, in which Mary and Martha invited Jesus into their home. Martha bustled about preparing refreshments but Mary just "sat at Jesus' feet, and heard his word." When Martha objected to Mary's inactivity, Jesus told Martha that Mary's wishing to simply commune with God was "the good part." Sonnet XIX not only is among Milton's masterly poems in its structure and its rich use of word play but also delivers a powerful message and speaks with an authoritative voice.

Victoria Price

SONNET XXIII

Author: John Milton (1608-1674)
Type of poem: Sonnet
First published: 1673, in *Poems upon Several Occasions*

The Poem

John Milton's Sonnet XXIII, which begins "Methought I saw my late espoused saint," is an Italian or Petrarchan sonnet—with a rhyme scheme of *abbaabba cdcdcd*—that offers an autobiographical dream vision of the poet's imagined reunion with his second wife, Katherine Woodcock, whom he married on November 12, 1656. Woodcock died on February 3, 1658, not quite four months after giving birth to a daughter, Katherine, who survived her mother by only one month. Most scholars posit Katherine Woodcock as the subject of Milton's dream in this poem, but some believe that the sonnet memorializes Milton's first wife, Mary Powell, who died on May 5, 1652—three days after giving birth to a daughter, Deborah—while others argue that the poem commemorates both wives.

Critics have also held the opinion that Sonnet XXIII is not an autobiographical poem, but an idealistic work that traces a movement from pagan legend to Christian doctrine, thereby enacting a drama of the poet's personal salvation. Although the sonnet's ambiguity permits all these possible readings, the strongest evidence in the poem supports interpretations of Katherine as the subject of Milton's dream about a wished-for reunion with his "late espoused saint" as one who was "washed from spot of childbed taint." While both Mary and Katherine died after giving birth, only Katherine lived until the end of the period of purification according to "the old Law" of Leviticus 12:2-8.

Sonnet XXIII confronts not only these losses of interpersonal relationship but also the poet's own loss of the faculty of sight. Milton was totally blind at the time of his marriage to Katherine. His dream of her, which is the sonnet's main subject, momentarily allows the poet what had been denied but so strongly desired in life: full sight of his beloved's face. The work's first twelve lines present five different apparitions of Katherine and three corresponding conditions for her possible return from death, all underscored by Milton's conviction "yet once more . . . to have/ Full sight of her in heaven without restraint." However, the sonnet's concluding two lines, which shape a sixth vision of and fourth possibility for recovering the beloved, qualify the poem's scenarios for reunion through the bittersweet image of Katherine who, upon reaching to embrace the dreaming poet, wakes Milton from his vision of "Love, sweetness, goodness in her person," thereby hastening her own disappearance: "But O as to embrace me she inclined/ I waked, she fled, and day brought back my night."

In keeping with the conventions of most English poetic elegies written in the sixteenth and seventeenth centuries, Milton's elegiac sonnet crafts relationships between three fundamental components of the mourning process: lamentation, praise, and consolation. Each of the poem's imagined reunions with the beloved intertwines expressions of sorrow, love, and solace—though not necessarily in that strict order—thus achieving at each step a synthesis of those three emotional and rhetorical dimensions of grief. For example, in the fourth of these visions (lines 9-11) the poet fancies seeing his beloved once more in heaven, where she will appear "vested all in white, pure as her mind." This articulation of praise and love for Katherine's virtue quickly incorporates a qualification for their potential meeting in heaven—"Her face was veiled"—which implies lamentation and Milton's sorrow for his physical blindness during their life together. Although emotionally ambivalent and rhetorically ambiguous, this semblance of the beloved as both luminous and shrouded hinges upon the consolation that the faculty of imagination may permit the poet to see beyond the veil: "yet to my fancied sight,/ Love, sweetness, goodness in her person shined." Milton's solace at this particular moment in the sonnet thus joins together praise and lamentation through the image of Katherine's mind.

Forms and Devices

In Sonnet XXIII Milton shapes the Petrarchan form through the use of two key poetic devices: simile and conceit. Milton's dream-as-poem offers six distinct visions of Katherine, each signaled by a simile, which together shape four possible scenarios for her imagined return: the first theme informed by a classical legend; the second, by Hebraic law; the third, by Christian faith; and the fourth, by secular humanism. In the first simile Katherine is compared to Alcestis, who, after giving her life to save her husband, Admetus, was rescued from the underworld by Hercules ("Jove's great son"): "Methought I saw my late espoused saint/ Brought to me like Alcestis from the grave."

Katherine is next likened to a mother who, in accordance with Leviticus 12:2-8, has neither touched any sacred objects nor entered any places of worship for a period of eighty days after giving birth to a daughter: "Mine as whom washed from spot of childbed taint,/ Purification in the old Law did save." By way of the next two similes, the sonnet then links this Old Testament condition for Katherine's purification with New Testament principles of redemption and Christian virtue: "And such, as yet once more I trust to have/ Full sight of her in heaven without restraint,/ Came vested all in white, pure as her mind." These classical, Hebraic, and Christian themes culminate in the following image of Katherine as one who embodies Renaissance humanist ideals of "Love, sweetness, goodness" that shine within her person "So clear, as in no face with more delight." The poem's final simile grounds those ideals in a tangible desire for relationship—Katherine's imagined gesture of reaching toward the dreaming poet—that ironically disperses his vision and awakens Milton to the reality of both her absence and his own sightlessness: "But O as to embrace me she inclined/ I waked, she fled, and day brought back my night."

In each case, Milton's similes both initiate and join together these six apparitions of Katherine that collectively determine the poem's thematic progression from pagan lore to Old and New Testament doctrine to secular humanist principles. This rhetorical movement in turn underscores the sonnet's central conceit that Katherine's spirit embodies the best elements from all four cultural traditions that conclude in the poem's image of her mind's singular virtue: "So clear, as in no face with more delight." The sonnet thus invests Katherine's spirit with Protestant tenets of the soul's indwelling grace and covenant of redemption in a characteristic gesture that distinguishes most, if not all, of Milton's poetic works from "On Shakespeare" (1632) to *Paradise Lost* (1667, 1674), in which the poet places essential moral teachings from classical, Hebraic, and other cultural, literary, and religious traditions in the service of Protestant reform and secular humanist ideology. Since that conceit is such a driving force in this sonnet, Milton elides the poem's syntactical division between octave (*abbaabba*) and sestet (*cdcdcd*), thereby working within Petrarchan formal conventions to achieve a fluid synthesis of Katherine's changing semblances against the sonnet's more predictable rhyme scheme.

Themes and Meanings

Milton's careful attention to this balance between poetic form and poetic devices in Sonnet XXIII illustrates his chief concern with merging the Greek notion of poetry as *poiein* ("to make or craft") with the Roman idea of the poet as *vates* (a priest or diviner). Just as this elegiac poem works within the metrical conventions of the Petrarchan sonnet in order to make (*poiein*) a perfect pattern, the poem's similes and central conceit underscore the poet's experience as a visionary (*vates*)—an artist, that is, who can not only craft a good poem, but who can use poetic form as a vehicle for revealing sacred truths. In nearly all of Milton's writings (prose and verse alike) this tension between poetic making and divining reveals a larger cultural and philosophical conflict about the poet's social responsibility that was much debated in sixteenth and seventeenth century England. Was the poet a rhetorician (in the tradition of Cicero) or a religious visionary (in the tradition of St. Augustine)?

As a record of Milton's dream, or fancied sight, Sonnet XXIII places the poet in both of those roles through the work's subtle fusion of classical legends, Hebrew and Christian doctrines, and humanist ideals that culminates in a private vision of his beloved's spiritual perfection. However, of all the themes working within this sonnet that explore the poet's competing roles as orator and diviner, the most poignant is that of the relationship between physical (or external) blindness and spiritual (or inward) vision. The poem announces this particular thematic tension from the very first line— "Methought I saw my late espoused saint"—and articulates the substance of that conflict until the very last line, when the dream vision is broken: "I waked, she fled, and day brought back my night."

Whereas the poem's first three scenarios for Katherine's imagined recovery offer positive consolation for the poet's confrontation with loss, the sonnet's final glimpse here of the disappearing beloved presents a more complex solution that paradoxically achieves a diminished solace through resistance to consolation. Although Katherine flees as Milton wakes from dreaming, his reversion to physical, external blindness— "day brought back my night"—suggests both a qualification of consolation as well as an open, diurnal movement toward his ongoing remediation of loss by which new apprehensions of the beloved may appear "yet once more" when the poet returns—through dreams—to spiritual, internal sight. Though fleeting and veiled, dreams embody redemptive power for Milton and serve as bridges between the secular and sacred realms. The sonnet's final and transitory image of Katherine foretells of Milton's "Full sight of her in heaven without restraint," thus infusing personal vision with religious significance.

W. Scott Howard

SONNET XXVII

Author: Pablo Neruda (Neftalí Ricardo Reyes Basoalto, 1904-1973)
Type of poem: Sonnet
First published: 1959, as "Sonnet XXVII" in *Cien sonetos de amor*; English translation collected in *One Hundred Love Sonnets*, 1986

The Poem

Although Pablo Neruda calls the fourteen-line poems in the volume *One Hundred Love Sonnets* sonnets, he uses the traditional sonnet form in widely different ways—from a virtual free-verse order within the framework of a sonnet (as in "Sonnet XXVII") to the more conventionally strict forms; a sonnet is traditionally a lyric poem of fourteen lines, highly arbitrary in form, and adhering to one or another of several set rhyme conventions.

In the first stanza of "Sonnet XXVII," the speaker of the poem addresses his beloved. Opening the stanza with the word "naked," the speaker compares the simple lines of his beloved's naked body to the simplicity of one of her hands. He goes on to describe her body with the following adjectives: "smooth, earthy, small, transparent, round." Continuing the description, the speaker, in the final line of the stanza, in an apparent contradiction to the roundness emphasized earlier, compares his beloved's body to a slender grain of wheat, conjuring up images of another image of earthiness.

The second stanza begins also with the word "naked." The speaker continues to use metaphorical language to express his emotional response to his beloved's body. The first metaphor of the stanza declares that the woman's body is "blue as a night in Cuba." Metaphors of earthiness introduced in stanza 1 are continued in the next line: "you have vines and stars in your hair." The beloved's naked body is also compared to the sacredness of a beautiful summer day; it is "spacious and yellow/ as summer in a golden church."

The third stanza, like the previous two, opens with the word "naked." The lover likens his beloved's naked body to one of her fingernails. Her body is "tiny," "curved, subtle, rosy." It is only tiny, however, at night; at daybreak, her body retreats to a different place, to an "underground world."

The final stanza describes this underground world as "a long tunnel of clothing and chores." In the daylight hours, the beloved's body loses its brilliant light: It dons clothing, loses its earthiness; that is, it "drops its leaves." The delicate, almost magical shape and form of the woman's body at night becomes transformed, by daylight, into something more mundane. Her body is now merely a "naked hand again."

Forms and Devices

Although the volume *One Hundred Love Sonnets* was dedicated to Neruda's third wife (the greatest love of his life, Matilde Urrutia) as an affirmation of his love for her, it is not only to her that Neruda sings in these sonnets but also to the things that make up his life with her. Neruda's love for Matilde fuses in these sonnets with his love of nature.

The subject of "Sonnet XXVII" is woman in nature, cosmic woman, woman surrounded by the force and attributes of nature. Neruda as a nature poet is essentially an observer of his surroundings as well as his own emotional attachment to those surroundings. The inner world of his own psyche is often described in terms of the external world of nature and matter; it is formed and expressed through images and metaphors taken, in a process of synthesis, from the poet's external environment. In this way, Neruda is both a modern poet of nature and a poet of the human condition.

The basic images of "Sonnet XXVII" equate the beloved's body with some aspect of the natural world. In the process of linking woman to nature, Neruda's metaphors "explode" the human body, subject it to a peculiar tension, and extend it. For example, the unexpected imagery in the first stanza describes the beloved's naked body as having "moon-lines, apple-pathways." The poet describes the roundness of the woman's body by comparing its shape with that of objects in nature; it is also as slender as "a naked grain of wheat."

The poet builds a bridge between the human body and the universe; the woman's body is felt to be an important part of the cosmos. The beloved is a being endowed with supernatural powers; she has "vines and stars in . . . [her] hair." The beloved is, in this line, literally part of the earth, part of the universe from which she has come. Her sexuality transcends her individual nature, and the relationship between the speaker and his beloved transcends two individual people. The relationship becomes laden with philosophical consequences.

Woman's sexuality is described not only through nature imagery but also in quasireligious metaphors. In the second stanza of the poem, the beloved's body is described as "spacious and yellow/ as summer in a golden church." In these lines, sexuality, nature, and religion fuse. The color of the woman's body and its spaciousness trigger a memory in the mind of the speaker: being inside a vast church on a golden summer day. The woman's body is described not only lovingly but also with reverence and awe by the speaker.

Themes and Meanings

In Neruda's earlier love poetry, *Viente poemas de amor y una cancion desesperada* (1924; *Twenty Love Poems and a Song of Despair*, 1969), love is described as both a joyous and a perilous experience. There is often a shadow lurking in the background, an indefinable threat, a romantic foreboding. In the mature Neruda of *One Hundred Love Sonnets*, however, there is only one tone; it is pure joy, sensuality, union, ecstasy, and triumph that inspire these poems. Love, Neruda seems now to say, can be explored in all of its enchantment without the fear of suddenly losing it.

The major themes of "Sonnet XXVII" are love, passion, and eroticism—but, as previously mentioned, always linked with nature. Neruda's relationship with nature is essentially sexual. Sex, for Neruda, is a way of entering the world, of conquering and being conquered by the world. It is a path to knowledge.

The poem is dominated by a purely erotic tone. Although it is the beloved's body that is glorified in this poem, the speaker's love transcends the body. He is unwavering in his devotion, and a sense of contentment and peace permeates the poem.

The speaker sees his beloved as part of two worlds: the world of night and the world of day. The woman is both day and night, as she is both round and slender (in the first stanza). The two colors used to describe the beloved's body in the second stanza are blue ("blue as a night in Cuba") and yellow ("yellow/ as a summer in a golden church"); thus, she is both darkness and light. The woman's body is described as a world in itself, as well as being part of the world of nature.

The final stanza describes the "underworld" to which the beloved descends after the night is over. There is a sense of regret in the speaker's tone when he must let her go and cross over into that world. This underworld is not, however, a place of darkness and death. In Neruda's poem, the underworld to which the woman returns is a place crowded with daylight and practicality. The woman emerges from the glorious and erotic night, her "clear light dims," and this extraordinary mortal resumes the tasks of an ordinary woman once again.

Genevieve Slomski

SONNET 18

Author: William Shakespeare (1564-1616)
Type of poem: Sonnet
First published: 1609, in *Sonnets*

The Poem

This fourteen-line poem begins with a straightforward question in the first person, addressed to the object of the poet's attention: "Shall I compare thee to a summer's day?" After a direct answer, "Thou art more lovely and more temperate," the next seven lines of the poem develop the comparison with a series of objections to a summer day.

William Shakespeare develops the "temperate" elements of his comparison first, leaving the "lovely" qualities for later consideration. His first criticism of summer is that in May rough winds shake the "darling" buds. This objection might seem trivial until one remembers that the poet is invoking a sense of the harmony implicit in classical concepts of order and form which writers of the Renaissance emulated. His use of the term "darling" extends the harmonious concept to include the vision of an orderly universe embracing its creations and processes with affection.

Such terms apply only to the ideal universe, however. In nature's corrupt state, after Adam's fall, all sublunary (earthly) forms and events fail to adhere to their primal harmony. Hence, rough winds shake the May buds and, as the next line indicates, summer is too short. Sometimes the sun is too hot; at other times the day becomes cloudy.

In lines 7 and 8, the poet summarizes his objections to the summer day by asserting that everything that is fair will be "untrimmed," either by chance or by a natural process. The most obvious meaning here is that everything that summer produces will become less beautiful over time. The word "fair," however, seems to mean more than merely beautiful to the eye and, like the words "lovely" and "darling," comprehends all desirable qualities. Here, too, the poet invokes the concept of sublunary corruption. Although he is apparently still discussing the disadvantages of a summer's day when compared to the person he is addressing, he is at the same time creating a transition to the next section of the poem by introducing the second element of his comparison, that comprehended in the word "lovely."

The last six lines of the sonnet detail the advantages of the person addressed, indicating no diminution in the durability or fairness of that individual. The reason lies in the "eternal lines to time" that Shakespeare creates in his sonnet, knowing that the poem in which the person is memorialized will last through all time.

Although in the concluding couplet Shakespeare gives a direct statement of the theme, he uses the pronoun "this" to carry the weight of meaning and gives no verbal referent to the pronoun. Yet in making the poem itself the referent, the poet creates the object that will transmit the immortality of its subject to eternity.

Form and Devices

This poem is a sonnet, a poem consisting of fourteen lines in iambic pentameter, a form created by Petrarch, an Italian poet of the fourteenth century. A Petrarchan sonnet usually contains eight lines sketching a situation (the octave) and six lines applying it (the sestet). The form was modified by Sir Thomas Wyatt and Henry Howard, earl of Surrey, appearing in poetic anthologies during the mid-sixteenth century. They and other poets created the English sonnet, consisting of three quatrains followed by a couplet, rhyming *abab, cdcd, efef, gg*. In this form, the eight-six division is occasionally maintained, as in Sonnet 18, but the concluding couplet summarizes the theme.

The sonnets of Shakespeare, taken as a whole, may be said to form a sonnet sequence: a series of sonnets, usually addressed to a woman for whom the poet has conceived a passion. From Petrarch's time on, the conventions of the lover's complaint pervade the imagery of these sequences, but their originality of imagery and conceit generally transcends the limitations of the troubadour traditions from which they derive. The women of these sequences have themselves become widely known: Petrarch's Laura, Sir Philip Sidney's Stella (Penelope Devereux), and Edmund Spenser's Elizabeth Boyle have achieved the kind of immortality that Shakespeare's Sonnet 18 contemplates.

It is thus ironic that the object of Shakespeare's own sequence should be unknown. The poems themselves range over many topics, including the beauty and desirability of marriage for a young man, a love triangle, a "dark lady," and several philosophical and moral problems. They form a unique source of speculation on Shakespeare's life in addition to being poems of great power.

In Sonnet 18, Shakespeare sets up his comparison by rhetorically introducing the basis for a simile that will underlie the structure of the whole poem: the comparison between the person who is the object of the poet's attention and a summer's day. The first image, of rough winds shaking May's buds, is stated directly. In the next line, however, the poet uses the metaphor of summer's lease being too short, aptly indicating the transitory nature of a season and, by extension, a year and a life.

The use of metonymy in "eye of heaven" (the sun) illustrates the power of that device: The eye is usually thought of as the agency for perception and character; here the central focus of the sky seems central to the concept of nature itself. Personification of this eye enhances the subject of the poem as a whole, for dimming his gold complexion implies hiding the beauty of the individual whom the poet addresses—something the poet intends to prevent.

The personification of death in line 11 curiously treats the word "shade," often used to describe those who have died. Here it seems to signify, instead, the atmosphere of death—the shadow that hovers over those who come within its influence, which the poet's lines are about to dispel.

Themes and Meanings

As in his plays, Shakespeare's sonnet introduces several themes reflecting Renaissance thought. The most important of those here is the belief that everything under the moon was corrupted by Adam's fall from grace. Thus, although the sun (the "eye of heaven") moved in an uncorrupted sphere above the moon, the earthly influence upon its shining could make it either too hot (line 5) or too hazy (line 6). A corollary of this fall was the consequent mutability of the sublunary creation. For Shakespeare the change was not lateral; rather, it involved a progressive degeneration of beauty, created by chance or by the influence of time on nature (lines 7, 8).

In Shakespeare's Sonnet 18, one may thus discern Renaissance beliefs about nature. One can also see remnants of medieval thinking. This combination appears most obviously in the poet's treatment of the Ovidian tradition. The Middle Ages had interpreted Ovid (43 B.C.E.-17 C.E.) as a moral poet whose Metamorphoses (c. 8 C.E.) contained a cosmology based on Greek and Roman myths. The Renaissance, on the other hand, saw him as an erotic poet whose *Amores* (c. 20 B.C.E.; *Loves*) and *Ars Amatoria* (c. 2 B.C.E.; *Art of Love*) provided the model for Petrarch and later sonneteers.

In Sonnet 18 one finds both the moral and erotic suggested in the words "lovely," "darling," and "fair." Emphasis on the physical beauty of the person addressed is tempered by hints that this beauty outshines that of the natural universe itself; through the poet's lines, it becomes one with Plato's eternal forms. Missing from this sonnet, however, is that part of the Petrarchan tradition that sees the lover complaining of his mistress's rejection and displaying his own despair or resolution resulting from it. In its place one finds the central theme of mutability, the imperfection and impermanence of the sublunary world, infusing the first eight lines and providing the foil for the rest of the poem.

In contrast to the mutability theme, the concluding sestet proclaims Shakespeare's art as the antidote to time and change. The poet's consciousness of his own genius, although placed here within a tradition maintained by several of his predecessors, transcends the limitations of the fallen world. *Ars longa, vita breve* (art is long, life is brief) becomes the underlying theme, arrayed in Shakespeare's unique and comprehensive poetic language.

Russell Lord

SONNET 19

Author: William Shakespeare (1564-1616)
Type of poem: Sonnet
First published: 1609, in *Sonnets*

The Poem

William Shakespeare's Sonnet 19 is a traditional English sonnet (traditional because Shakespeare made it so), consisting of a single stanza of fourteen lines, rhymed according to a standard format. Like the other 153 sonnets by Shakespeare, Sonnet 19 has no title.

In the first quatrain, the poet addresses time as a devourer, handing out a series of defiant invitations to time to perform its most destructive acts. First, time is instructed to "blunt" the "lion's paws," which gives the reader an image of enormous strength reduced to impotence. In line 2, the poet moves from the particular to the general, invoking time as a bully who forces the earth, seen as the universal mother, to consume all her beloved offspring. Line 3 echoes line 1. It gives another image of the strongest of nature's creatures, this time the tiger, reduced to weakness. Time, seen as a fierce aggressor, will pluck out its teeth. No gentle decline into age here. In line 4, the poet moves to the mythological realm. He tells time to wreak its havoc by burning the "long-lived phoenix." The phoenix was a mythical bird that supposedly lived for five hundred years (or a thousand years, according to some versions) before being consumed in fire. The phoenix was also said to rise from its own ashes, but that is not a meaning that the poet chooses to develop here. The final phrase in the line, "in her blood," is a hunting term that refers to an animal in the full vigor of life.

The second quatrain begins with a fifth invitation to time, couched in general rather than specific terms: "Make glad and sorry seasons as thou fleet'st." This takes the invocation of time's destructive power to a more refined level, because it alludes to the human emotional response to the hurried passage of time: Seasons of gladness and seasons of sorrow form part of an ever-recurring cycle. Lines 6 and 7 seem to continue the poet's willingness to allow time full sway to do whatever it wants wherever it chooses.

In line 8, however, the argument begins to turn. Having built up a considerable sense of momentum, the poet checks it by announcing that there is one limit he wishes to place on time. It transpires that all the concessions the poet has made to time in lines 1 through 7 are one side of a bargain the poet wishes to strike. The terms are now forcefully announced, as the poet attempts to establish his authority over time. He forbids time, with its "antique pen," to make furrows on the brow of his beloved. The friend must be allowed to go through life untouched ("untainted") by the passage of time. Anything less would be a crime, because the lover is an exceptional being who must represent to future ages the pattern of true beauty—an eternal beauty that stands outside the domain of time.

In the final couplet, however, the poet seems to acknowledge the futility of his demand, yet he remains defiant. In spite of the wrongs that time inflicts, the poet's friend will forever remain young because he will live in the poet's verse.

Forms and Devices

The sonnet is a highly concentrated work of art in which the poet must develop and resolve his theme within the strict confines of the sonnet form. Sonnet 19, like all Shakespeare's sonnets, follows a standard pattern. It consists of three quatrains and a concluding couplet, and it follows the rhyme scheme *abab, cdcd, efef, gg.*

The meaning of the sonnet is reinforced by the variations Shakespeare makes in the meter. This takes the form of a subtle counterpoint between the regular metrical base, which is iambic pentameter, and the spoken rhythm—what one actually hears when the sonnet is read. For example, in the first quatrain, the theme of the destructiveness of time is brought out more forcefully by a series of metrical inversions.

In the third foot in the first line ("blunt thou"), a trochee is substituted for an iamb, resulting in a strong stress falling on the first syllable. This gives "blunt" a much stronger impact than it would otherwise have, especially as the rest of the line follows a regular iambic rhythm. In line two, the last foot is a spondee rather than an iamb, resulting in two heavy stresses on "sweet brood." The emphasis on the "sweetness of what time destroys" makes the work of time seem even more harsh. Line 3 is a very irregular line, echoing the turbulence of the sense. There is a metrical inversion in the first foot (it is trochaic, not iambic) that serves to highlight the word "Pluck." This recalls, through assonance, the "blunt" of line 1. Both of these are forceful words that express the way in which time assaults the natural world. The second foot of line 3 is a spondee, and the assonance contained in "keen teeth" adds to its prominent impact in the line. The fourth foot of this line is also a spondee, making the "fierce tiger" very fierce indeed. Line 3 in particular, with its high number of stressed syllables, brings out the idea of time as an aggressive, fearsome warrior going to battle against all living things.

The meter of the second quatrain is more regular than the first. The speedy passage of the end of line 5 ("as thou fleet'st") echoes the sense, and this is emphasized again by the heavy stress on "swift" in line 6. In the third quatrain, the turbulent rhythm and harsh consonants of the earlier part of the sonnet vanish as the poet turns his attention to the friend. The smooth and regular iambic rhythm of line 12, for example, "For beauty's pattern to succeeding men," suggests the perfection of the friend.

Time makes a forceful reappearance in the first line of the couplet, with the spondee, "old Time," prominently positioned immediately before the caesura. This makes the triumph of the last line, in which the poet obtains his victory through the power of his pen (a contrast to the seemingly all-powerful "antique pen" of time), all the more striking and effective.

Themes and Meanings

In this sonnet, the poet faces up to one of the most fundamental facts of human existence: the transience of all things, even those of greatest power and beauty, and including those most loved. In seizing on this theme, Shakespeare echoed a passage from Ovid's *Metamorphoses* (c. 8 C.E.), a source he turned to often: "Time, the devourer, and the jealous years that pass, destroy all things and, nibbling them away, consume them gradually in a lingering death."

The conflict between beauty and time, and the anguish of the lover who fears the touch of time on his beloved, is a major theme of the whole sonnet sequence. In sonnet 16, for example, the friend is reproved for not making sufficient effort to "Make war upon this bloody tyrant Time." In sonnets 1 through 17, the poet proposes a solution. He enjoins his friend to marry and produce progeny, so that he will live again through his offspring. Sonnet 12 states that nothing can stand against time "save breed." In Sonnet 19, however, this solution is implicitly abandoned because all of earth's "sweet brood" will be devoured by time. Here "brood" recalls the "breed" of sonnet 12, but the significance of the term has altered completely.

The battle against time is made more intense in this sonnet by the absolute value that the poet attaches to the friend. He is the very archetype of beauty, "beauty's pattern to succeeding men." Such an ideal view of the lover is repeated at other points in the sonnet sequence. Sonnet 106 states that all the beauty of past ages was only a prefiguring of what the friend now embodies. In Sonnet 14, the poet claims that the most fundamental values in existence are bound up in the life of his friend, and cannot endure after his demise. Sonnet 104 reveals that future ages will not be able to produce anything to match the beauty the friend embodies. It might perhaps be said that the poet sees in the friend what William Blake would later describe as the "Divine Vision." This presence of an absolute, transcendental element in the relative world of time and change fuels the dramatic tension that gives Sonnet 19, and others, a stark and poignant power.

Bryan Aubrey

SONNET 30

Author: William Shakespeare (1564-1616)
Type of poem: Sonnet
First published: 1609, in *Sonnets*

The Poem

The opening lines of William Shakespeare's thirtieth sonnet ("When to the sessions of sweet silent thought") evoke the picture of a man sweetly and silently reminiscing, living once again the pleasant (or "sweet") experiences of his past. The situation, however, soon shifts from silence to a sigh and from pleasantries to a lament for projects never completed, desires never fulfilled. The angst of this cannot be confined to the past but bursts into the poet's present consciousness. He suffers intense nostalgic pain for the wasted time that can no longer be reclaimed. Old woes are reborn, exacerbating a fresh hurt.

The second quatrain of the sonnet expands this idea, but the pain is heightened as the author thinks of the people who will never again come into his life. This brings tears into the eyes, as once again the pain of loss is relived. The vanished sights lamented are the faces of friends who have disappeared into death and the emptiness of love that is no more, but also suggested are places, possessions, and events that can never be re-experienced.

The third quatrain adds little new content, but increases the weight and significance of the poem's central idea: The act of remembrance recalls old griefs into the present where they become as painful in their rebirth as they were the first time they were experienced. It is as if the persona of the poem were caught in a psychological trap from which there is no escape and in which his mind, as if dragging chains, moves "heavily from woe to woe," unable to escape from the images that repeat "the sad account of fore-bemoaned moan." Though the account has been paid up in the past, the debt of pain is reopened and he must pay the entire amount again.

After twelve lines of bewailing the symptoms of the persona's condition, the final couplet of the sonnet moves abruptly to the solution. The cure is carefully coordinated with the disease, for just as the patient's woes were initiated by remembering the past, so are they dissipated by the thought of his current "dear friend," which restores all the lamented losses and ends all the reborn sorrows.

Forms and Devices

This sonnet is an "English," or "Shakespearean" sonnet—that is, it is composed of three quatrains and a couplet of iambic pentameter, rhymed *abab, cdcd, efef, gg*. What is different about the structure of this sonnet is that there is far less development from quatrain to quatrain than is usual for the overall collection. Shakespeare most often develops his sonnets by moving his argument in three quite distinct steps to its concluding couplet, or by developing three quite different images to be tied neatly together in the closing lines. This sonnet, however, has far more repetition than differentiation from quatrain to quatrain. The differences are subtle: The quatrains quietly move from wailing to weeping to grieving, a progression that is hardly noticed.

What makes this one of Shakespeare's most loved sonnets is not its structure but its music, achieved in part through the rhymes, but even more distinctively through the repetition of consonant sounds. In the first quatrain of the sonnet there are no less than twelve sibilant sounds, which, rather than hissing, evoke the music of the wind. The sound is repeated in the last line of the sonnet, surely an intended recapitulation to increase the feeling of completion. The fourth line of the poem introduces a series of alliterated *w* sounds: "And with old woes new wail my dear Time's waste." These sounds introduce the rhythm of wailing, which is repeated in line 7, "And weep afresh love's . . . woe," and again in line 10, "from woe to woe." Repeated liquid sounds in line 7 add a languid sound to the line—"love's long since canceled woe"—and repeated *m*'s add both softness and length to lines 8 and 11: "And moan th' expense of many," and "fore-bemoaned moan." A lengthening of sound comes in the repetition of *fr*'s in "friends" and "afresh" in lines 6 and 7. The poem's alliteration enhances the meaning of the text and emphasizes both the standard iambic pulse and the variations from this standard in lines 1, 6, and 7.

Another device evident in this poem is what seems to be a calculated use of ambiguity. In the first line, the word "sessions" denotes a meeting of a legal court, but in context it also suggests a mere period of time. Thus "thought" could represent the judge presiding over the session or merely describe the activity of a designated period of time. Again the persona, the "I" of the poem, could be the judge, summoning his remembrances to stand trial. In the fourth line, the word "new" could be an adjective modifying "woes," which were once old and have now become new, or it could act as an adverb modifying "wail." It is not beyond possibility that "my dear" could be a noun of address, since the final couplet makes it clear that the sonnet was addressed to a "dear friend," though it seems more probable that "dear" is an adjective modifying either "time" or "waste."

"Time's waste" could be read as either the person having wasted his time or (more likely) as time, the destroyer, having laid waste to items and qualities of ultimate value to him. "Expense" in line 8 could be read in its most usual modern sense as cost, the money spent, or simply as loss: something that is spent is gone. "Fore-gone" in the ninth line probably means simply past, as having gone before, but could also carry the connotation of "given up," or "taken for granted." In the tenth line, "tell" could mean to relate, but more likely has the older meaning of "count" or "tally." "Account" could mean a mere story, a financial account, or the final accounting at the last judgment. This accumulation of ambiguity engages the reader's mind, focusing it on the form and keeping it from wandering; it also enriches the poem by suggesting alternative readings.

The dominant metaphor of the poem is the comparison of a period of reminiscing to the session of a court of law, but even so it is not meticulously carried out in the nature of an Elizabethan conceit. Words such as "canceled," "expense," "grievances," "account," and "losses . . . restored" may suggest court language, but the idea is not worked into the syntax. Other uses of figurative language enriching the poem are an eye "drowned" in tears, friends "hidden" in night, a woe "canceled" as if it were a debt, and an "account" of moans that needs to be settled.

Themes and Meanings

Shakespeare's Sonnet 30 is a beloved, often-remembered, often-quoted poem simply because it is an exquisite description of the pain of nostalgia, an experience which is common to most of humankind. The human psyche does not want to let go of the experiences of its past, even when that experience was exceedingly painful, or perhaps especially because it was painful, since somehow the hurt has increased the meaning of the moment. It certainly has increased its intensity. The release which dissipates such remembered pain is also a welcome experience, and the reader of Shakespeare's sonnet experiences that release as the tension built up in the first twelve lines of the poem disappears in the recollection of a current, fulfilling friendship.

The poem is meaningful also because of its inclusion in the most famous collection of sonnets in the English language, if not in any language. Though almost no scholars believe that Shakespeare himself was responsible for the order in which the sonnets were printed, this poem does belong to the early group which were addressed to a young man. It also has a close relationship with the sonnet immediately preceding it and the one that follows, pointing to the probability that these were written together. Sonnet 29 has the same thought progression as 30, as the poet laments the fact that Fortune has not been kind to him and wishes that he might change places with anyone a bit higher on her wheel. When the thought of his friend intrudes on this meditation, however, all is made right: The lark announces day, the earth sings, and he would change places with no one. Sonnet 31 is largely an explanation of the thirtieth. "Losses are restored" because those whom the author "supposed dead," whom he "thought buried," are alive in his friend, who contains all of their virtues. The friend is the grave containing all of their lives, "Hung with the trophies of my lovers gone,/ Who all their parts of me to thee did give." In this realization, the poet discovers a new, integrated personality, for what he used to find by dividing his love among many, he now finds in only one person who contains in himself all of those who have gone before. Though Shakespeare's Sonnet 30 stands alone, perfect in its own merits, that unity is more fully appreciated in the context of its neighbors.

Howard C. Adams

SONNET 35

Author: William Shakespeare (1564-1616)
Type of poem: Sonnet
First published: 1609, in *Sonnets*

The Poem

Sonnet 35, "No more be griev'd at that which thou hast done," is written to a young man, the poet's friend and nominal addressee or auditor of sonnets 1 through 126, by far the largest section of Shakespeare's sonnet sequence. The friend presumably is the "Mr. W. H." of the inscribed dedication of Thomas Thorpe's 1609 printing of the sonnets. This mysterious figure's identity has never been incontrovertibly established, although the scholarly consensus has focused on two candidates: Henry Wriothesley, third earl of Southampton (1573-1624), and William Herbert, third earl of Pembroke (1580-1630), both of whom were patrons of the poet-dramatist.

The true identity of the young man is of relative unimportance critically; in fact, some scholars have suggested that the youth might even be an idealized literary figure rather a real person. However, Sonnet 35 argues, as do some related sonnets, that the friendship is at times strained and certainly less than idyllic, giving it the semblance of an actual relationship. Although the young man's looks bear the stamp of perfection, he is not without character flaws. This poem arises from some unidentified hurt inflicted on the poet by the friend, the source of a momentary estrangement that is dealt with in Sonnets 33 through 42.

In Sonnet 35, the friend is grief-stricken by his trespass, and the poet attempts to assuage his friend's guilt through clever sophistry, reasoning that he himself must bear some of the responsibility for his friend's offense. Because the friend's transgression seems to involve sexual betrayal, a "sensual fault," scholars have traditionally speculated that the friend may have seduced the poet's mistress or been seduced by her, although a few commentators have concluded that the sexual suggestion is homoerotic.

If the wrong done the poet is moot, its effect is not. The friend is "grieved" by it. The poet argues, through parallel examples, that the faults of men have analogues in nature, even in the most beautiful of things: roses and buds, silver fountains, sun and moon. These images of nature's perfection are no less subject to flaws than humans are. The rose stem bears wounding thorns, clouds and eclipses dim the beauty of moon and sun, canker worms devour sweet buds, and the water of the silver fountains may, at times, grow muddy. The poet then argues that he is also blameworthy, since he excuses his friend's fault with his flawed comparisons and his faulty logic, which speciously justify his friend's betrayal. He is thus corrupted by his need to excuse his friend's faults.

Line 8, one of the most difficult of lines in Shakespeare's sonnets, has frequently been emended to read "Excusing thy sins more than thy sins are," with its implication that the friend's transgression was not significant enough to require the poet's reasoned defense, one that turns the wounded party into the wrongdoer's chief advocate. The poet, drawn by the conflicting demands of "love and hate," is put in the untenable position of defending the "sweet theefe" who has stolen his mistress's affections, and he chastises himself as an "accessary" to the friend's crime.

Forms and Devices

Sonnet 35 is in the English or Shakespearean sonnet form, as are all but three of the poems in Shakespeare's sonnet sequence. This form consists of fourteen iambic pentameter lines arranged as three quatrains and a couplet, rhyming *abab cdcd efef gg*. Sonnet 35 is a very regular example. Its phrasing is rigorously maintained by end-of-line punctuation marking full caesuras; Shakespeare employs no enjambment or run-on lines. Each line is a whole syntactical unit, usually a dependent clause. The rhymes, too, are regular, although modern pronunciation turns "compare" and "sins are" of lines 6 and 8 and "Advocate" and "hate" of lines 10 and 12 into apparent sight rhymes rather than true rhyme. There is also some metrical inversion, beginning in line 2, with "Roses," a trochee. Similar variations in meter occur in lines 3, 6, 8, 10, 13, and 14. Metrical inversion is common throughout Shakespeare's sonnet sequence. It is often used to counterpoint the basic iambic scheme, which might otherwise become too monotonous.

The sonnet's regularity complements its basic idea. The poem takes the form of logical discourse, of a legal argument, ostensibly rational rather than emotional. Although the poet admits to using what elsewhere he calls "false compare" (Sonnet 130), he starts out to justify his friend's betrayal by arguing that nothing is perfect. In the manner of much Elizabethan verse, the lyric uses multiple examples from nature, although as either analogies or analogues they are clearly strained if not completely inappropriate. The fault of the young man lies in his own character, whereas the analogies in nature involve such phenomena as an eclipse of the sun or moon and the destruction of a flower bud by a canker worm. Such "flaws," except for the rose's thorns, are not intrinsic in the object but are introduced by some external or invasive presence. However, at a metaphorical level, that presence—the shadow on the sun or the mud in the water of the silver fountain—might be interpreted as the "Dark Lady," the poet's mistress and the corrupting influence on the young man. Elsewhere in the sequence, including Sonnet 34, Shakespeare uses the sun as metaphor for his friend—thus, when read in sequence, Sonnet 35 takes advantage of resonant associations established in the lyrics preceding it.

In the reasoning that follows the examples of lines 2 through 4, the poet turns the argument against himself, claiming that he is flawed for "authorizing" his friend's wrongdoing through an involuted reasoning that uses "sence" or logic to justify his friend's "sensuall fault." He thereby becomes both plaintiff and the offender's advocate, a paradoxical situation arising from the "civil war" that pits his feelings of "love and hate" against each other. These ambivalent feelings are very succinctly expressed in the vivid "sweet theefe" oxymoron of the last line. There is perhaps a hint of self-contempt in the alliterative use of sibilants in lines 7 through 9, the hissing sound of words in phrases like "salving thy amissse" and "excusing their sins," tingeing the poem with some self-disgust. Ironically, although the poet is clearly the wounded party, he seems more willing to forgive his friend than he is himself for doing so. Such convoluted sophistry was part of the rhetorical tradition so much admired by Shakespeare's contemporaries. It provided evidence of a poet's invention and wit, though to a modern ear it may seem somewhat contrived and insincere.

Themes and Meanings

Sonnet 35 investigates the conflicting demands of erotic love (*eros*) and spiritual love (*agape*), a familiar Elizabethan theme. Friendship, because it is based on reason, was perceived as a higher order of love than that based on physical attraction, and although it might exist between members of the opposite sex, it was generally restricted to relationships within the same sex, since, for heterosexual men and women, that exclusiveness would preclude carnal attraction and preserve the love's purity. One test of such a friendship, exploited by Shakespeare in both lyrics and plays, is the threat posed by sexual jealousy. Since a man's will can be corrupted by desire, he could betray a friendship by engaging in a sexual liaison with his friend's mistress, as seems to be the situation behind Sonnet 35 and related sonnets dealing with the temporary estrangement of the poet and the young man. That the friendship can survive the conflicting demands of *eros* and *agape* is evidence of its enduring strength.

The poem also reflects an idea prevalent in much of Shakespeare's work, one that suggests a great generosity of spirit and ensures the poet's lasting place among the world's most humane and forgiving writers. Humankind is susceptible to sin, having, as Friar Laurence in *Romeo and Juliet* discloses, both "grace and rude will," two opposing factions that correspond to reason and appetite. Susceptible to sin, humans will err and therefore must be forgiven. Capable of sin themselves, those victimized by it must be merciful, since, as Portia explains to Shylock in *The Merchant of Venice*, mercy is an attribute of God himself and is a quality that transcends retributive justice. Humankind is thus enjoined to forgive the sinner while condemning the sin. As Hamlet tells Polonius in *Hamlet*, if people were given only their just desserts, none would "scape whipping." It is this belief that is the ethical lodestone of the New Testament.

Sonnet 35 seems to reflect a testing of the poet's belief in the necessary charity of the human spirit at a very personal level. The act of forgiving exacts its toll, primarily because the poet's pride resists the humiliation attendant upon manufacturing such a tenuous excuse for his friend's behavior. Shakespeare's sonnet vividly captures a sense of the struggle between the poet's wounded ego and his need, from love, to forgive his friend.

John W. Fiero

SONNET 55

Author: William Shakespeare (1564-1616)
Type of poem: Sonnet
First published: 1609, in *Sonnets*

The Poem

Sonnet 55 is one of a collection of 154 sonnets written by William Shakespeare and expresses one of the major themes of these sonnets: Poetry is eternal and will immortalize the subject of the poem. The tone of the first quatrain, or first four lines, reflects the extreme confidence of the poet: His "powerful rhyme" is compared to durable marble and solid, gilded memorials that mark the graves of princes. The monuments for the Elizabethan royals and aristocracy often consisted of a full-length portrait of the deceased carved in high relief on the stone cover of a coffin. The sonnet is compared not only to the lastingness of stone but also to an enduring image of the deceased. The poet asserts that his portrait of the young man, written in verse on fragile paper, will outlive even the marble memorials of princes, which will inevitably become neglected, "unswept stone" with the inexorable passage of time. In this sonnet, Shakespeare gives time a character. In this case, time is "sluttish," suggesting that it is dirty and careless. "Sluttish" can also mean whorish. Time, then, cares for no individual; it is immoral and will, in its slovenly and whorish manner, pass. The grand memorials will become eroded, and the people memorialized will eventually be forgotten. However, the subject of the poem will "shine more bright" than the time-smeared monuments and live not in effigy but in essence in Shakespeare's verse.

The second quatrain intensifies the poet's declaration. The imagery of long-forgotten, cold stone monuments gives way to active, deliberate devastation. The young man will be remembered despite the wrack and ruin of "wasteful war." When marble statues topple and stone buildings and other "works of masonry" are destroyed, the poetry will live on. Not even the flaming sword of mighty Mars, the god of war himself, is able to "burn/ The living record" of the young man's memory. The final quatrain contains the powerful image of the young man striding like a Titan through time "'Gainst death and all oblivious enmity." He will "pace forth" and be not only remembered but also praised in the eyes of "all posterity" even to posterity's end. His memory will outwear the world and survive "the ending doom," the Apocalypse itself.

The couplet—the final two lines of the poem—draws a conclusion and sums up the ideas that have accumulated with each successive quatrain. The young man will live in "this," the poet's verse, until Judgment Day. On that day, the bodies of all humanity are to be resurrected and reunited with the soul, and judgment will be passed as to which souls will suffer in hell and which will rise to heaven. He, too, will face his individual judgment and will "arise" to heaven rather than be damned to hell.

Forms and Devices

Sonnet 55 is one of a series of 154 sonnets written in the first person—the first 126 are addressed to a young man, and the remaining sonnets (127-154) are addressed to or refer to a dark lady. A rival poet is a third character in the drama of the sonnets. Some scholars believe that the sonnets tell a story that is a reflection of Shakespeare's private life, while others claim that the sonnets are a literary exercise. In either event, the accumulated sonnets tell a story of love, lust, separation from the beloved, betrayal, repentance, and self-loathing.

Sonnet 55 is typical of the form that has become known as the Shakespearean sonnet. Its fourteen lines generally consist of three quatrains (three sets of four lines each), the first of which puts forth a poetic idea that the two following quatrains explore and develop. The quatrains are followed by two final lines (a couplet) that punctuate, draw a conclusion to, or make an ironic comment on the ideas the poet has been exploring in the quatrains. The lines are written in iambic pentameter, and the rhyme scheme of the Shakespearean sonnet is *abab cdcd efef gg*.

Although each sonnet, as a rule, can stand on its own as an individual poem, it is a good idea to look at the sonnets that surround it. Sonnet 54 sets up Sonnet 55 by bringing up the idea that the essence of a person may be distilled by poetry in the same manner that the essence of a rose may be distilled. After death, the substance of the rose or of the person may perish, but it lives on by virtue of its remaining essence. The first quatrain of Sonnet 55 elaborates the idea that the young man will live perpetually in the poet's verse. The imagery of fragile flowers gives way to grand marble and elaborate, gilded stone monuments. The final line of the quatrain is thick with alliteration and vivid imagery that tells of "unswept stone, besmeared with sluttish time." The contrast implies the passage of a very long time—centuries, perhaps—and reinforces the power of the verse that will eternalize the essence of the young man's brightly shining self.

The second quatrain elaborates the idea of the durability of poetry through the use of images of war and destruction. Overturned statues and "broils" (battles) that "root out the work of masonry" summon up the image of a city left in ruins. The introduction of Mars, the ancient god of war, suggests once again the passage of ages. Shakespeare's use of the word "record" evokes the image of record books and reminds the reader that a poem is written on paper that is easily destroyed by the fires of war. Yet the essence of a poem lies not in the paper upon which it is written but in the ideas and emotions expressed by the poet, who contends that his rhyme is so powerful that it will outlive even this dire threat of destruction.

The third quatrain puts the idea of eternity in the foreground. The lines speak of death, oblivion, and the "ending doom." Most people's memories fade into the oblivious mists of time. However, the young man of the sonnets will keep pace with the time. As time progresses, this praise, this poetry, this essence of the young man will keep pace with its passage. Even to the end of days, when posterity's posterity has outworn the world, men will remember and praise the young subject of the verse—he will live in their eyes, the window to their souls. The "So" of the final couplet announces the summing up of the ideas and the themes of the sonnet. The phrases "ending doom" and "the judgment" are references to the Christian belief in the Last Judgment. On this day, after the Second Coming of Christ, the world and time will come to a violent end. This suggests that the essence or the life force of the young man, distilled in the poet's words, will outlive life itself.

Themes and Meanings

The idea that verse would ensure the poet's immortality is a common Renaissance theme that came to the Elizabethans via Latin poets such as Ovid in his *Metamorphoses* (c. 8 C.E.; English translation, 1567) and Horace in his odes. Shakespeare puts a twist on this idea by claiming that his poetry will guarantee the undying fame of the subject of the poems rather than the author himself. The motif of immortality in the sonnets is expressed differently in the first seventeen poems, in which the poet urges the young man to marry and procreate so that he will continue to live through his children after his death. Beginning with Sonnet 18, and in several sonnets thereafter, the notion that the ineluctable power of poetry will ensure perpetual remembrance is expressed. The relentless passage of time is a major theme of the collected sonnets, and time plays an active role. Time will age the beautiful young man to whom the sonnets are addressed. With the passage of time, summer roses will wilt and die. However, just as the perfume, or "essence," of the rose can be distilled and kept long after the rose is gone, so too can the essence of the young man, his physical and spiritual beauty, be distilled in poetry and remain long after his death. Poetry is time's most effective enemy.

Scholars have gone to great lengths to discover the identity of the young man who was to be immortalized in the sonnets. The dedication of the 1609 printing of the collected sonnets to a "Mr. W. H." as "the onlie begetter of these insuing sonnets" has been cited as evidence that the young man was, in fact, a living person and perhaps a patron of Shakespeare. Henry Wriothesley, earl of Southampton, and William Herbert, earl of Pembroke, are persons most often considered as the potential "Mr. W. H." There has also been great speculation as to the identity of the "dark lady" and the "rival poet" of the sonnets. The great irony is that it is Shakespeare himself who is immortalized in the sonnets and none of the collection's major players. The "beautiful young man" who was to live until doomsday in the verse of the poet has long been forgotten, while Shakespeare lives on.

Diane M. Almeida

SONNET 60

Author: William Shakespeare (1564-1616)
Type of poem: Sonnet
First published: 1609, in *Sonnets*

The Poem

Sonnet 60, like all sonnets, is a fourteen-line poem of one stanza, rhymed according to a traditional scheme. The sonnet is one of 154 untitled sonnets by William Shakespeare, each of which adheres to the form of what is referred to as the English, or Shakespearean, sonnet.

The first quatrain consists of an extended simile, comparing the passage of human life to the onward movement of waves rushing to the seashore. Each wave pushes the one in front of it, and is in turn pushed by the one that follows it. Each following the other in close succession, the waves struggle forward.

The second quatrain introduces a new thought, more directly relating the passage of time to human life. The newborn baby, once it has seen the vast light of day, quickly begins to crawl. This is the first stage in its growth to manhood. Once the human being is "crowned," however—that is, attains in adulthood its full stature as a royal king, the summit of the natural order—he is not allowed to rest and enjoy his status. The heavenly bodies, which have ruled his destiny since the day he was born, conspire against him to extinguish his glory. The same process that resulted in the gift of birth and growth is now responsible for change and decay.

The third quatrain develops the idea of time as destroyer, highlighting three lethal actions that time performs. First, time tears. It "doth transfix the flourish set on youth," which means that it pierces through the attractive outward appearance, the flower, of youth. Second, time imprints itself; it creates furrows ("delves the parallels") in the brow of the beautiful. Third, time is all-devouring. It consumes the most valuable and most prized things that nature produces. Nothing at all can stand against time, whose scythe will mow down everything.

It seems inevitable that time will be victorious, but in the final couplet the poet attempts to salvage what he can. He believes that at least one thing can survive the onslaught of time. In future times, his verse will "stand," if all else has fallen. At the same time, the poet reveals what has prompted his meditation on the destructive nature of time: his love for the youthful beauty of his friend. The poet's verse will always ring out in praise of this beauty, in spite of the devastation wrought by the "cruel hand" of time.

Forms and Devices

The frequent occurrence of *s* sounds in the first two lines (on no fewer than seven occasions) suggests the sound of the incoming waves as they break on the shore. The final two *s* sounds, in "minutes hasten," are placed closer together than the others, and this suggests the increasing speed and urgency of the passage of time.

The second quatrain is remarkable because it fuses three distinct sets of images: child, sun, and king. "Nativity" is at once the birth of a child and the rising of the morning sun. The child that "Crawls to maturity" is also the ascending sun, and "crowned" suggests at once a king and the sun at its zenith in the sky. This thought would have come easily to an Elizabethan mind, at home with the idea of an intricate set of correspondences between the microcosmic world of man and the macrocosmic heavens. The same image occurs in Sonnet 33 and Shakespeare's play *Richard II* (c. 1595-1596).

At this point of maximum strength and power, the man-king-sun faces an assault on his position, as "Crooked eclipses 'gainst his glory fight." "Crooked" suggests the plotting of rivals to usurp his crown; "eclipses" is an astrological reference, suggesting an unfavorable aspect in the heavens that will bring about the inevitable downfall of the man-king, as well as ensuring the downward passage of the sun as it loses its glory over the western horizon. "Crawls" (line 6) and "Crooked" (line 7) are given added emphasis by the trochee at the beginning of each line and by alliteration, which also links them both to "crowned" at the end of line 6. The rising and falling rhythm of the final line of this quatrain, "And time that gave, doth now his gift confound," sums up the idea conveyed in the first three lines.

The third quatrain is introduced by a trochee, "Time doth," which gives notice that time is to be the direct subject of this part of the sonnet. Another trochee in the first foot of line 11 emphasizes the consuming aspect of time, and Shakespeare again makes use of a trochaic foot, "Praising," in the first foot of the second line of the couplet. This paves the way for the defiant flourish with which the sonnet ends. The fact that the phrase "Praising thy worth" is followed by a caesura slows the line down and leaves this phrase echoing in the reader's mind, a magnificent counterpoint to the "cruel hand" of time that the sonnet has labored to convey. Labored is the appropriate word here, since the struggle of all sublunary things depicted in this sonnet is hard and unrelenting. Images of struggle begin in the first quatrain, as the waves "toil" and "contend" with each other. The slow struggle of the man upward is suggested by the caesura placed after "Crawls to maturity," and this struggle lasts far longer than his brief moment of glory, which dissolves after another fight.

Themes and Meanings

This sonnet is closely related to sonnets 63 through 65, and many others in the sonnet sequence, which also bemoan the inexorable advance of time and pose the question: How can beauty survive, given that all created things are transient and travel their allotted course to death? The theme of these sonnets was in part inspired by a passage from Ovid's *Metamorphoses* (c. 8 C.E.): "The baby, first born into the light of day, lies weak and helpless: after that he crawls on all fours, moving his limbs as animals do, and gradually, on legs as yet trembling and unsteady, stands upright, supporting himself by some convenient prop. Then he becomes strong and swift of foot, passing through the stage of youth till, having lived through the years of middle age also, he slips down the incline of old age, towards life's setting. Age undermines and destroys the strength of former years." This passage gave Shakespeare the image of "Nativity, once in the main of light,/ Crawls to maturity," and the passage that follows in Ovid, "Helen weeps . . . when she sees herself in the glass, wrinkled with age," may have suggested to Shakespeare the image of "delves the parallels in beauty's brow."

Shakespeare is not content to leave the world, or his friend, to mutability. The attempt in this sonnet to immortalize the friend through the poet's verse is also a theme of many other Shakespearean sonnets, including numbers 19, 55, 63, 65, 100, 101, and 107. Some readers may find the resolution of the problem, which is accomplished in the final two lines of the poem, unsatisfactory. How can the hope expressed in the couplet somehow outweigh the remorseless pressure that has been built up in the first twelve lines? It might be argued that a poem about a beautiful person now dead is a poor substitute for the presence of the living person. The same argument might be applied to the solution proposed in sonnets 1 through 17, that the friend should marry and produce offspring, and thereby achieve a kind of immortality, but it should be pointed out that these are secular poems. The poet refuses to take refuge in any belief system that will soften or remove the effect of mutability. In this sonnet, as in others, there is no Christian heaven in which the lovers can look forward to another meeting, and the thought is not Neoplatonic; the friend is not described as a shadow or reflection of an eternal form, existing in an ideal world not subject to change. On the contrary, in this sonnet the human and the natural worlds are inextricably intertwined; the images of the devastating effects of time can be applied equally to both human and nonhuman realms. The poet thus works towards his triumph, limited though it may be, entirely in the terms that the natural order offers.

Bryan Aubrey

SONNET 65

Author: William Shakespeare (1564-1616)
Type of poem: Sonnet
First published: 1609, in *Sonnets*

The Poem

The opening quatrain of William Shakespeare's Sonnet 65 asks how beauty can resist that power in nature which destroys brass, stone, earth, and the sea, since beauty is less durable and powerful than any of those. The earth and sea together cannot withstand death, the dismal ("sad") state that overpowers everything in nature. In the third line, mortality becomes "this rage"—a violent anger, even a kind of madness, that opposes a most fragile supplicant, beauty. If the earth itself is no match for this force, beauty seems to have no hope of lasting, since its strength is no more than a flower's.

The second quatrain repeats the opening question, beauty now characterized by another of nature's insubstantial and temporary forms, "summer's honey breath," which the poet sees as the victim of an assault by a "wreckful siege" in the form of "battering days." The "earth" alluded to in the opening line is represented here as "rocks impregnable," and brass has been replaced by "gates of steel." Neither of these substantial forms can withstand time's battering and corrosive force. Though asking a question, the speaker implies that any resistance to time is doomed and, further, that natural things are in constant battle with a force that nothing survives, least of all something as evanescent as summer's breath.

The third quatrain begins with an expostulation that expresses the poet's feelings as he confronts the prospect of time's onslaught: "O fearful meditation!" Even flight is futile, for beauty, now represented as a jewel, cannot escape being encased finally and forever in "Time's chest." Time is then characterized as the swift runner whose foot cannot be held back. No outside force—no "hand"—can or will reach out and rescue beauty from time's onward thrust. At the close of the third quatrain, beauty is not only a doomed supplicant but also a helpless victim of time's plundering. At this point, the poet appears to have accepted the inevitable annihilation of beauty by time's relentless onslaught.

The final couplet offers hope, however—the written word. Mere ink, imbued with the poet's love, offers the only defense against Time's annihilating power, for the poet's words have the miraculous ability to reflect beauty's splendor in a timeless state.

Forms and Devices

The sonnet's fourteen lines form three quatrains and a concluding couplet, rhyming *abab, cdcd, efef, gg.* Known as the Shakespearean (or English) sonnet, this arrangement differs from the Italian (or Petrarchan) sonnet in adopting a different rhyme scheme and dividing the sestet (the final six lines) into a quatrain and a couplet. The third quatrain addresses the poem's subject somewhat differently from the first two quatrains (which correspond to the octave of the Italian sonnet), and the couplet offers a final comment on, or a summary of, the foregoing argument. A typical line consists of five stresses, or ten syllables, called iambic pentameter: "Since bráss, nor stóne, nor eárth, nor boúndless séa." An extra syllable is occasionally added to the line, as in lines 2, 4, and 10. Within this highly patterned world, Sonnet 65 achieves myriad effects.

Wordplay creates much of the poem's irony by combining multiple meanings into one word. The "sad" in line 2 characterizes the personified "mortality," sad because it is his duty to destroy things; at the same time, "sad" expresses the poet's own feelings regarding this destructive force. In the third line, "this rage" ironically plays on the idea that mortality, usually thought of as a dormant state, is a violent passion, even a madness. Shakespeare twists the traditional conventions by assigning such a passion, not to the lover, but to the force that destroys beauty. Irony is implicit, too, in the reference to "boundless sea," which is nevertheless "bound" by "mortality." Though the tone of the sonnet may not be entirely serious—Shakespeare seems close to mocking the tradition of the forlorn lover in the line "O fearful meditation! where, alack"—any playful spirit the poem may have is sobered by the ominous nature of the subject.

The poem's principal imagery focuses on the various forms given the chief antagonists, "Time" and beauty, though beauty is depicted in images that suggest insubstantial form (a mere "plea" and "summer's honey breath"), a passive hardness ("jewel"), and a helpless victim (Time's "spoil"). Time is personified variously, too, as a force that "decays," keeps jewelry in a chest, has a swift foot, and plunders his victims. When the poem wants to suggest the delicate, impermanent nature of beauty, imagery is deft—"flower . . . summer's honey breath." When it wants images of strength, it is prolific—"wreckful siege . . . battering days . . . rocks impregnable . . . gates of steel."

Numerous sound effects underscore the poem's doleful tone. Repetition of words (such as "nor" and "O" and structures—the five questions, for example—suggests the relentless assault of "this rage" as well as the urgency of the speaker's mingled hope and fear. Apt alliteration—"steel so strong" and "none, unless"—and vowel sounds reinforce the meaning. The sound of "brass" and "stone" suggests more durable qualities than those of a flower and honey breath, and the phrases "rocks impregnable" and "gates of steel" sound "harder" than the more mellifluous sounds of "miracle have might" and "my love."

Themes and Meanings

Shakespeare's central theme is the opposition between the transitory, delicate nature of beauty and the devastating effect on beauty of mortality and its principal instrument, time. The opening questions seem rhetorical, indirectly arguing the poet's conviction that beauty is no match for aging and death. The final two lines dispel the gloomy predictions implicit in the questions, however, by pointing to the power of the written word to sustain its subject—in this case, beauty. As the poem advances through the first two quatrains, the changes in the images of time suggest an increase in the implacable strength of time, which only "o'er-sways" in the second line but turns to a "rage" and then a "wreckful siege of battering days" attacking such impressive things as "rocks impregnable" and "gates of steel."

The final two lines, by opposing "black ink" with the light which the poet's love emits, leave the reader with the central conflict of the poet's vision: light (beauty) is opposed by darkness (black ink), and therefore utter annihilation. The balancing imagery of the final line suggests a resolution to this conflict and so ends the poem on a bright note, literally on the word "bright" itself: The poet's love, expressed in this written sonnet, is the one force that can successfully oppose time and death. The word "still" in the last line introduces a paradox. If "my love" is "still," meaning lifeless, it cannot "shine," yet it does, or might; if it is indeed motionless, it cannot "still" be shining, yet it may, in "black ink," and in that form, it can forever oppose the destructive motion implicit in the phrase "this rage." The poet's skill is the only force that can reverse the effects of aging and stop time's forward motion, which carries all things to their death. The poet's hand becomes the "strong hand" (line 12) that can indeed hold time's "swift foot back." The surprise is that the strength is not physical but poetic.

A more subtle surprise is that, while appearing to address what male lovers are expected to address, a beautiful woman, Shakespeare here focuses on beauty, perhaps in keeping with the poem's general air of indirection—rhetorical questions develop the poet's subject all the way to the final couplet in place of direct argument. The poem seems to suggest that to be any more direct, by addressing his beloved directly, he would "expose" her to time's onslaught. By remaining as "hidden" and insubstantial as "Time's best jewel," the object of his love may be saved. If the "black ink" of his poem draws a curtain of darkness before the face of his beloved, her beauty may nevertheless shine through the love that the poem expresses.

In keeping with the delicate indirection of the poem, the poet makes only slight references to the sexual aspect of his love, principally in the third quatrain, where "impregnable" subtly suggests where the poet's mind is going—time is a ravager of beautiful women, one way or another. Hints of ravishment continue as the poet references "gates of steel" and concludes in his using "spoil" (plundering) that beauty cannot "forbid."

The structure of the final line reflects brilliantly the poem's resolution, the inky blackness of annihilating time at one end of the line and, at the other, the redemptive light of the poet's love. Between these two states is the poet's "love," the fulcrum that forever separates and balances them.

Bernard E. Morris

SONNET 73

Author: William Shakespeare (1564-1616)
Type of poem: Sonnet
First published: 1609, in *Sonnets*

The Poem
This fourteen-line poem, which is divided into three distinct quatrains (four-line stanzas) followed by a couplet (two lines), is addressed to the poet's lover and comments on the approach of old age in the speaker. As in all the Shakespearian sonnets, the voice is that of the poet. The lover has sometimes been interpreted as the unknown "Mr. W. H." to whom the first quarto edition was dedicated, but Samuel Taylor Coleridge surmised that the lover must be a woman.

The poet opens by stating that his lover must behold him at the time of life corresponding to late autumn, when almost no leaves remain on the trees and the birds have flown south. The poet's calling attention to his old age might seem incongruous, since many lovers might try to hide the fact from their companions. Yet, in this relationship, William Shakespeare not only is being forthright but also seems to be seeking the sympathy of his dear friend.

In the second quatrain, the image shifts from the time of year to the time of day. He chooses twilight, the period between sunset and darkness, to reflect his state. "Twi" originally meant "half," so "half-light" signifies a period of diminished abilities and activities, again calling for the sympathy and understanding of the poet's friend. The second half of the quatrain brings forth more forcibly the associations of darkness with death and emphasizes the immanence of that mortal state in the poet's life.

The third quatrain moves from the world of seasons and time to the more restricted compass of natural phenomena—the way a fire burns itself to ashes and then is smothered by those ashes. As the magnitude of the image decreases, the force of its message concentrates, concluding with the very picture of a deathbed.

The concluding couplet sums up the purpose of Shakespeare's revelation of his decreasing powers: to request that his friend love more strongly because of the short time left to the poet. Critics have been concerned with the word "leave" in the last line, since it might be thought to indicate that the lover is the one to depart. Some have even commented that "lose" might better convey the idea. Certainly the death of the poet would cause a separation to occur, however, and the lover would have to "leave" him.

Forms and Devices
This poem, a sonnet, consists of fourteen lines of iambic pentameter. The form, which was created by Petrarch, an Italian poet of the fourteenth century, usually consisted of eight lines sketching a situation (octave) and six lines applying it (sestet). The form was modified by Sir Thomas Wyatt and Henry Howard, earl of Surrey. They

and other poets created the English sonnet, which consists of three quatrains followed by a couplet, rhyming *abab, cdcd, efef, gg*. In this form, adopted by Shakespeare and frequently called by his name, the couplet summarizes the theme.

Shakespeare's sonnets range over many topics, including the beauty of a young man, the desirability of his marriage, a love triangle, a dark lady, and several philosophical and moral concerns. In addition to their poetic power, they remain a unique source of biographical speculation.

Sonnet 73 contains three distinct metaphors for the poet's progressive aging. The first of these is the implied comparison between his state and the time of year when a few yellow leaves, or none at all, remain on boughs shaking in the cold winds, deserted by the birds that usually inhabit them. One might be tempted to compare this directly with graying and loss of hair, but it is more probably to be taken generally as a reference to the aging process. William Empson has pointed out manifold connotations of the "bare ruined choirs" in his *Seven Types of Ambiguity* (1930), evoking images of ruined monastery choir stalls made of wood and infused with the atmosphere of stained glass and choirboy charm, showing how that richness is unified by the way that the poet's subject relates to his narcissistic affection.

The second quatrain moves from the time of year to the time of day. Again there is a metaphor: The poet's likeness is that of a day fading in the west after sunset. Instead of the yellow of the first quatrain, there is the black of night's approach, a more sinister prospect. There follows a personification within the metaphor, naming night as death's second self, in essence creating a new metaphor within the first as it envisions night, which "seals up all in rest." The word "seals" suggests the permanent closing of a coffin lid, providing a finality that is only slightly relieved by the knowledge that the reader is actually seeing not death, but night. Some critics have suggested that the word "seals" suggests the "seeling" of the eyes of a falcon or hawk, a process of sewing the eyes of the bird so that it would obey the falconer's instructions more exactly. This suggests an even more forcible entry of death into the metaphor.

Structurally, this concept would close the octave of a Petrarchan sonnet, and although the English sonnet has ostensibly eliminated the eight-six division, the vestiges of a division remain, since the poet moves from his year-day metaphors to another kind of figure in his next quatrain. Here, the metaphor involves a complex process rather than a simple period of time. The afterglow of a fire gradually being choked by the ashes of its earlier burning becomes the description of Shakespeare's aging. The ashes of the fire's earlier combustion are the poet's own youthful dissipation, hinting an extravagance of which we know nothing biographically except the metaphorical statement made here. Although there is no specific color named, one senses the red of a glowing fire, enhancing the yellow and black of the previous descriptions. The concluding couplet moves from metaphor to direct statement, summarizing the purpose of the poet in revealing so frankly his approaching old age. After the richness of the preceding lines, it might appear almost anticlimactic, yet it is important to the structure of the form, lending finality to the whole.

Themes and Meanings

As do his plays, Shakespeare's sonnets introduce themes reflecting Renaissance thought. In order to understand them, one must realize what the term "Renaissance" implies. The word was introduced into art criticism by John Ruskin in *The Stones of Venice* (1851-1853), when he referred to a return to "pagan systems" in Italian painting and architecture during the fourteenth century. Essayist Walter Pater extended the meaning of the term to include all phases of intellectual life. Scholars have associated with the Renaissance such phenomena as Neoplatonism, humanism, and classicism. Recently, they have also deduced that medieval traditions were not utterly displaced; there was no sharp dividing line.

Perhaps the most obvious theme in Sonnet 73 is that of mutability, deriving from Greek and Roman philosophers, but strained through the theological thinkers of the Middle Ages and modified during the Renaissance. Basically, it describes all "sublunary" phenomena (those beneath the moon, thus corrupted) as subject to change. Thus they lack the permanence both of biblical perfection and of Platonic ideals.

In this sonnet, Shakespeare's consciousness of himself and of his beloved friend remains rooted in mortality and mutability. Unlike the idealized relationship portrayed in earlier sonnets, here there is a strong consciousness of the changes that old age brings to the poet and to his relationships with others. Here is resignation in the face of the inevitability of death and his permanent separation from his beloved. Time becomes omnipotent. It controls all natural processes, and no expedient of art can resist it. The most one can do is to express a heightened affection for one who is soon to pass away.

If one examines the consistency with which Shakespeare has joined his three sets of images, one may glimpse something of the coherence created by the poet's genius. The words "bare ruined choirs" of the first quatrain are strengthened in the second into the words "Death's second self." In the third, what was previously merely a metaphor for sleep has become metaphorically a deathbed. The concluding couplet may be considered a further step still, since it translates metaphorical references to death into personal ones referring to the poet's own approaching end.

It has been shown that the poet uses a variety of colors within the quatrains of this sonnet: yellow, black, and red (glowing). These colors have suggested to other poets images of death and pestilence. Shakespeare uses them to describe metaphorically his approaching old age. Thus he maintains the theme of inevitable change and sublunary corruption throughout.

Russell Lord

SONNET 76

Author: William Shakespeare (1564-1616)
Type of poem: Sonnet
First published: 1609, in *Sonnets*

The Poem

The first quatrain of the sonnet consists of two questions that address a supposed problem with William Shakespeare's own verse—its utter conventionality, barrenness of thought, and monotony (it is "far from variation"). A more ambitious or imaginative lover, he says, would express himself with variety and surprise ("quick change"). The second question implies that, in keeping with the fashion ("the time"), the poet should employ better "methods" and new "compounds." Besides being destitute of invention, it seems that he lacks a pleasing spirit of adventure. The second quatrain questions the poet's motives or common sense in writing verses that are "ever the same" and have a familiar appearance ("noted weed"), since it can easily be known who wrote them and where they were sent ("did proceed"). In matters of love, the implication is, discretion is the soul of wit.

Having presented one side of love's coin in the first eight lines of the sonnet, the poet turns the coin over in the third quatrain, answering the implied charge of triteness and lack of imagination. Actually, he argues, by writing always of one subject, "you and love," he is being clever; instead of wasting his effort by trying always to invent new words, he devotes his "best" to simply dressing up the old and thereby finding continued use in what has already been used. Expressing his love in verse is in fact like spending money, and words are like coins. His subject, "you and love," enables him to give familiar words new meaning, to reuse those that have been used before. The benefits of this kind of recycling are too obvious to argue: less effort, less waste, greater efficiency.

Lest his beloved not be convinced by this curious way of looking at his verse, Shakespeare in his final couplet points out that his method is the very principle upon which the sun operates, returning again and again, ever the same yet always new. What better model can a poet have than the sun itself? His verse repeats what has already been written, or spoken, but like the sun, it brings with it a new look, the difference being the poet's "love."

Forms and Devices

Unlike the Italian (or Petrarchan) sonnet, the Shakespearean (or English) sonnet is divided into three quatrains and a couplet, rhyming *abab, cdcd, efef, gg.* The first two quatrains introduce and develop the subject of the poem to the end of the eighth line, where a pause occurs. The third quatrain addresses the subject from a some-what different perspective, concluding the poet's argument in line 12. The couplet sums up the foregoing argument or, as in Sonnet 76, delivers a final statement that clenches the matter.

Each line of the sonnet regularly consists of five stresses, or ten syllables, called iambic pentameter. In Sonnet 76, lines 1, 3, 5, 8, and 12 are irregular. All these lines except line 1 combine iamb feet (in which the stress falls on the second syllable) with trochees, two-syllable feet whose stresses fall on the first syllable of each foot: "Whý with the tíme do í not glánce asíde," for example. The last four syllables in the first line vary the conventional line even further, placing the stresses and unstressed syllables in pairs (illustrated here within brackets): so bár[ren of néw príde]." These variations subtly contradict the poet's conceding that his verse is conventional.

Structurally, the poem develops as an argument. The first eight lines challenge the poet with three questions, which he answers in the third quatrain and final couplet with a witty rejoinder that demonstrates his skills as a noteworthy opponent. Within this debatelike format, Shakespeare's logic weaves a paradox, which ironically displays those very qualities and skills that the questions imply he lacks. His verse is deficient in "new-found methods" and "compounds strange," yet his poem is a compound of wit, logic, and sophisticated argument: By writing always of his "love" and "dressing old words new," the poet transforms old coin into new and in that way gives his "love" permanent currency ("still telling"). While seeming to admit his artistic failings through the first twelve lines, the poet's conceit—that writing and loving are like reusing the same words and spending money—cleverly demonstrates those skills he appears to admit not having.

The poem's rich wordplay is evident in simple puns, such as the use of "time" (line 3) to mean poetic meter and the time in which the poet lives; the double meaning of "O, know" (line 9); and the more subtle play on seed in "proceed" (line 8). Its more important role is developing at least three arguments simultaneously by playing on the various meanings of spending, telling, inventing, and arguing.

This wordplay is evident in how the poet suggests various roles for himself. As an actor, he might perform a "quick change" (line 2), develop a new style of acting ("new-found methods"), or stay with the familiar mode and dress ("noted weed"), performing his "best" by "dressing" old words in new ways. In this conceit, he ironically hints that his words are nothing more than memorized speech and that he is "acting" the part of the lover, ending with the ambiguous compliment of repeating ("telling") again and again "what is told (line 14)."

As a dealer in coin, on the other hand, he might make "quick change" or deal in new "compounds" (metals or coinages); his words, being coins (punning further on the notion that words are coined), reflect the value of his name, and he spends the word-coins that have been spent before (line 12). Finally, as the poet-logician, he debates the question of his method with a skillfully reasoned argument: His "love" and the words in which he expresses it are the same "coin" that he counts out and spends, making new currency out of the old or, like the sun, returning always the same but always new.

Themes and Meanings

The principal metaphor of the sonnet equates words with coins that the poet counts out, or spends, as he writes verse. Line 2 suggests that the poet's verse is unacceptable as currency, "far from . . . quick change." In line seven, "tell" plays on the idea of counting out the poet's name as if it were coin. The metaphor of spending continues in line 12 and concludes in the last line, where the twin actions of counting out ("telling") and being spent ("told") are brought together. Because "telling" also means revealing, the poet conducts a simultaneous argument, that to write verse is to reveal his love to the world, and he ends with a pun on "told," which conflates these two meanings and conclusively demonstrates the poet's skill in both writing and "spending," for he brings his argument to a close at the very point where it and his love are "told"— summed up, counted out, and revealed.

The idea that lovers should not let others know their secret runs through the puns already mentioned, especially the use of "tell," which suggests revealing a secret and hints at verbal indiscretion. The last line plays on this notion by asserting that the poet's "love," represented by this poem, continues to reveal publicly—so long as it is read—the fact of his love and its valued substance, which is already reckoned and revealed ("told"). If his verse is as repetitious as the sun, it is also as visible as the sun.

A third argument is evident from the first line, where "pride" suggests an animal in heat. This idea is continued in the reference to "birth" (line 8) and to spending and being spent (line 12), giving "new and old" (line 13) the additional meaning of generation. From old words come new life, as the old generation procreates the new.

The theme of the old producing the new unifies the various arguments of the poem. As an actor, Shakespeare is challenged to invent new "methods" instead of keeping "invention in a noted weed" that is "ever the same." His "best," however, is to dress "old words new." As a dealer in "coin," he is perhaps expected to make "quick change," seek "new-found methods" and "compounds strange" so as to avoid having "every word . . . tell" his name—that is, reveal its commonplace value. The third quatrain asserts the poet's superior value, the ability to spend "again what is already spent." Writing verse confers upon him a power, like the sun's, of continuously returning, by being read again and again, each time his verse shedding upon the world the brilliant light of his "love." The old generates new life by simply returning (being read or "told" again). The act of writing verse goes beyond even the procreative act, however, for the old is not replaced by the new; rather, the old and the new unite forever in the poem, which is "still" reckoning and revealing what has already been revealed and reckoned.

Bernard E. Morris

SONNET 87

Author: William Shakespeare (1564-1616)
Type of poem: Sonnet
First published: 1609, in *Sonnets*

The Poem

In his cycle of 154 sonnets, Shakespeare directs the first 127 to a handsome young man usually identified as his patron, Henry Wriothesley, the earl of Southampton (1573-1624). Sonnet 87 concludes a series of ten known as the Rival Poet group. It is unknown who the rival poet was, and in fact it is possible that he never really existed. Among Shakespeare's contemporaries who have been suggested are Edmund Spenser, Christopher Marlowe, Samuel Daniel, and others, although because certain lines in Sonnet 86 seem to allude to George Chapman, he is the most favored candidate. On the other hand, some of the sonnets in the series, for example, Sonnet 85, suggest that more than one poet may rival Shakespeare for the young man's attentions.

Throughout the Rival Poet group, the writer reveals an increasing amount of self-deprecation as he realizes that he is losing out to his rival. Sonnet 87 thus brings the competition to an end by renouncing the speaker's claims to the young man. It is a moving farewell but not an unambiguous one: Shakespeare's sonnet operates at several levels simultaneously. Although the speaker recognizes that the young man has grown quite beyond his ability to hold, and that he no longer deserves his favor, his sense of regret and loss is sharp. If the relationship was once based upon an acknowledgment of reciprocal worth, or deserving, that no longer appears to be true. The young man apparently overvalued the writer's qualities and, since he now can more clearly see their true worth, has withdrawn his love.

The final two lines of the sonnet express the speaker's regret most poignantly. For him, the relationship with the young man has been like a dream, in which he ruled like a kind of sovereign or prince. Now that the young man has withdrawn his love, the speaker has awakened to reality. It is a brutal awakening, at once destroying the "flattery" with which his "dream" deluded him.

Forms and Devices

Shakespeare's sonnets differ from the Italian (or Petrarchan) form of the sonnet. Unlike Italian sonnets, his have three quatrains followed by a single couplet—instead of an octave (eight lines, rhyming *abba abba*) followed by a sestet (six lines, usually rhyming *cdcdee*). In some of Shakespeare's sonnets the octave-sestet form may still be discerned, but Sonnet 87 is not among them. Sonnet 87, moreover, is unusual not so much in having all its lines end-stopped, but in the number of weak, or feminine, endings—twelve of a possible fourteen. These weak endings are generally held to be more appropriate to a comic poem (such as George Gordon, Lord Byron's poem *Don Juan*) than to the solemn occasion that this sonnet ostensibly describes.

The poem begins with a firm "Farewell" and proceeds through the next twelve lines to explain, if not to justify, the parting of the two friends. The weak line endings signal and tend to underscore the ironies and ambiguities that pervade the sonnet. These devices bespeak the speaker's underlying reluctance to let go as well as his sense of undeserved dismissal. The words "too dear" in the first line state that the young man is too precious or of too high a rank for the speaker, but they may also imply that his friendship costs too much. The last word in the line, "possessing," introduces further ambiguities involved in the legal and commercial language of the next eleven lines. The second line is fraught with ambiguity; it may be interpreted to signify (among other possible meanings) "Very likely you know how highly I regard you," "You probably know your own worth very well," and "You know how much you deserve to be loved." The "charter" in line 3 is a legal metaphor for privilege that his noble rank or intrinsic value bestows on the young man, a privilege that allows him to sever with impunity their relationship. Hence, the speaker's "bonds" (ties plus legal covenant) are all "determinate"—that is, ended and outdated, as applied to legal bonds, but also circumscribed.

In the second quatrain, the speaker explains how all this has come to pass. His "possession" of the young man was in the first place made possible only by the latter's voluntary granting, which the speaker's merits perhaps did not justify. Since those "riches," or the "fair gift" of the young man's favor, were insufficiently deserved, they revert, as in any legal or commercial arrangement, to the owner. "Fair" conveys a multiple ambiguity: "handsome," "legally equitable," "desirable," and perhaps "flattering." The "patent" in line 8 refers to a license or exclusive privilege that the young man had granted the speaker, which now returns intact to the grantor.

By the third quatrain the underlying resentment bordering on hostility becomes more acute. The young man had freely given himself, possibly without knowing how much either he or the receiver of his love was "worth." The misjudgment thus has led to a withdrawal of his "great gift," his love, once he has evaluated the relationship more precisely. By framing the situation in terms that carry suggestions of commercial trading, the speaker reveals his bitterness that their relationship—or any such relationship—should be measured in this way. The resentment deepens further, since "misprision" in line 11 signifies "contempt" as well as "error": What once was mutual affection has now turned into near despising, mutual or otherwise.

The final couplet summarizes the speaker's attitude in succinct terms, using a quite different but nonetheless appropriate metaphor. It has all been like a dream, and on awakening, the poet sees the reality of the situation. If in dreaming he felt like a king, possessing the "fair gift" of the young man (with a possible pun on the sexual significance of "had"), upon awakening he sees himself and the situation for what they are: He is not at all like royalty, and their friendship was merely illusory. Since "king" may also refer to the young man, the further implication is that the young man is something less than the speaker believed while he was dreaming. The emphasis on "matter," with which the poem ends, conveys disgust both in its ambiguity and in its enunciation, for "no such matter" means "nothing of the sort" but also "real substance" (as opposed to illusion), with a further allusion to the sexual sense of "matter" (as in Hamlet's reference to "country matters" in *Hamlet* 3.3.111).

Themes and Meanings

As the valediction to an affair or to a deeper personal relationship, Sonnet 87 conveys the mixed feelings, thoughts, and emotions that often accompany such moments. Although it is grouped among sonnets that have as their object, or auditor, a young man, the sonnet itself does not specify a particular person or sex. Removed from its immediate context, then, it has a more universal application and resonance. By the kinds of diction and metaphors it uses, it reveals a subtlety and sophistication worthy of any profoundly affected friend or lover faced with the ending of something once— and perhaps still—highly esteemed and cherished.

The ambiguities noted in the previous section reflect the kind of ambivalence typically found at the breakup of an affair. Examining the sonnet closely, one sees that the renunciation may be occurring on either side. In *Shakespeare's Wordplay* (1957), M. M. Mahood remarks: "Either Shakespeare is saying: 'You are so good and great that you may well end our friendship on the ground that there is no corresponding worth in me,' or he means: 'Because of your social advantage over me, you exact too high a price for our friendship, so I have decided to break free.' In addition, there is a strong hint of the meaning: I have lavished affection on a creature who is just not worth it." On the other hand, as Mahood recognizes, Shakespeare may be saying all three things at once. Contradictory feelings at such times are perfectly natural, and Shakespeare accordingly may be expressing them in this sonnet.

As in many of his poems and plays, Shakespeare shows himself to be aware of the ironies in human experience. That one can love a person who is undeserving of that love is one such irony; that one can praise a person while at the time being aware that the praise may not be fully—or at all—deserved is another. Both are found in Sonnet 87. The young man, handsome and attractive in many ways, may be too full of himself, too aware of his own "worth," to merit the kind of devotion the speaker in the sonnet is foolishly willing to give him. The situation, however, cannot continue. In the context of the Rival Poet sonnets, Shakespeare as the speaker of the sonnets cannot compete with the other poet to whom the young man has turned. Nevertheless, the speaker knows his own worth, or rather the value of his love, which unlike the young man's is neither shallow nor fickle. On this count alone he may deserve more, though the young man fails to recognize it, and their relationship therefore seems doomed.

Jay L. Halio

SONNET 91

Author: William Shakespeare (1564-1616)
Type of poem: Sonnet
First published: 1609, in *Sonnets*

The Poem

Sonnet 91 by William Shakespeare is a relaxed work when compared to its predecessor, Sonnet 90 ("Then hate me when thou wilt, if ever, now"). The initial quatrain
of Sonnet 91 is clear; it remarks that there are those who glory in birth, skill, wealth,
strength, and worldly possessions.

The poet is establishing in the first quatrain a platform from which he will depart.
The seemingly sardonic nature of this introduction becomes clear with the reference
in line 3 to the "new-fangled ill"—a description of clothes that are fashionable but
ugly. The unattractiveness of material possessions serves as a metaphor that is related
to the implicit ugliness of the other attributes mentioned. The second quatrain begins
by excusing the vanities of those who prize the attributes listed in the first quatrain.
The narrator simply says that each person's "humor"—personality or temperament—
finds some joy that it particularly prizes. The quatrain ends, however, with the speaker
turning to his own preferences. He interjects that none of those individual tastes suit
him. Further, he states, he is able to do them all one better in "one general best."

That "general best" is named in the first line of the third quatrain, where the narrator identifies it as the love of the woman he loves. He then explicitly states that his love
means more to him than high birth, skill, and material wealth or possessions. This idea
separates him from those mentioned in the first quatrain, for he has put his love above
all else. The narrator, however, omits a comparison with the strength that is prized by
some in the first quatrain.

In the final couplet, Sonnet 91 abruptly assumes a paradoxical tone. The apparent
adulation of the previous quatrain gives way to the narrator's recognition of the power
that his lover holds over him and of the vulnerable, if not tenuous, position in which he
has placed himself. The narrator admits that this love makes him "wretched" in one
respect: He recognizes that his lover can take from him what he desires most—she
herself. The end result of such an action would leave him even more wretched.

The departure in the last couplet from the initial quatrains illustrates the irony of love:
One is wretched while in love and one is wretched when love has ended. The other attributes first mentioned and then disregarded by the narrator are all elements in which
the possessors have some kind of control; they are all theirs to lose and cannot be taken
from them. All those attributes either must be relinquished by neglect or bad decisions
or must be willingly released. This is not the case with love. The final couplet of Sonnet
91 illustrates the vulnerability of one who succumbs to love. Once this has occurred, the
lover is at the mercy of his beloved; it is the one whom he adores who holds his happiness. The narrator fears that he may one day lose the one thing he holds dearest.

Forms and Devices

The poem's form is that of a conventional Elizabethan sonnet. Each of its fourteen lines contains ten syllables. The poem consists of three distinct quatrains; the first two are complete sentences, and the third is directly linked to the concluding couplet. It begins with a series of images highlighted by the cadence which is produced by Shakespeare's steady use of anaphora in the first quatrain.

The extensive repetition of "some" (seven times in four lines) stresses the idea which will be refuted by the following two quatrains and couplet. This technique strongly links the lines of the initial quatrain. When this link is broken in the second and third quatrains, the isolation of the narrator is raised to a peak that climaxes in the final couplet.

The anaphora also seems to debase those who are primarily interested in things other than love. This attitude produces a certain irony in the poem's shift to the singular in the second and third quatrains, where an image of superiority is produced. The narrator, who seems to be deriding those who care so much for items and ideas which cannot reciprocate their affection, actually appears pompous by placing himself above the others.

This technique also produces an oxymoron which is as startling as it is ironic. Love should not be a wretched affair, yet the psychological realism of this emotion is often just that. Love does cause pain and concern as well as a feeling of contentedness. The usual practice of the sonneteer was to glorify love; the heights of this devotion could reach nearly absurd proportions. Shakespeare chooses to vary from this technique, and the result is a shocking revelation which clearly illustrates the point.

Shakespeare's use of surprise or negation in the closing couplet further elaborates the nakedness a lover feels when he expounds his feelings for his beloved. The effect elicited by this negative couplet is a stark contrast to the usual pouring out of love and devotion found in the sonnets of Petrarch and others. It is the very twist of this conclusion that ties the sonnet into an organic whole and makes the poem so effective. All the attributes mentioned in the initial quatrain parallel the emotions of the final quatrains and couplet.

As different as this conclusion may be, Sonnet 91 retains many of the elements which are traditionally included in the genre. The anaphora of the initial quatrain gives way to the expected love analogy. Certainly the narrator adores and idolizes his beloved. The explication of such emotions is the normal function of the sonnet form. It is the irony of the poem's shift in the closing couplet that differentiates it from more traditional sonnets.

Themes and Meanings

Shakespeare's Sonnet 91 exemplifies how vulnerable lovers become when they put their love above all else. He has slightly altered the traditional Elizabethan sonnet from a form which glorifies love to one which exposes it as a deeply disturbing emotional experience. While countless Elizabethan poets employed the traditional techniques of composing sonnets, Shakespeare uses his control of language and images to twist the form and create an unusual and moving piece.

The pining and lamentation for lost or unrequited love, a theme prevalent in many traditional sonnets, is replaced by a psychological examination of the process of love. Further, Shakespeare has developed the first quatrain in such a way that it heightens the poem's surprise conclusion. This technique depends on several items, which the poem fails to explore, to present this viewpoint. Shakespeare never clearly states that any of the scenarios noted in the first quatrain are excessive or covetous. Indeed, many of the traits are honorable: One's name is one's identity, for example, and it is paramount that artists be skilled. In retrospect, the elements listed in the initial quatrain are normal characteristics of life.

People become admired for certain values and scorned for others. Yet, in any society, high values are placed upon birth, wit, wealth, beauty, and material possessions. Those items do not seem to fit in a love poem, however, except to serve as grounds above which love can be elevated. Thus, it is expected that once those attributes are mentioned, they will be acknowledged as foolish, and the author will demonstrate that love is much better.

Shakespeare does follow this to a point, but then he breaks from tradition. The narrator claims that he is better off than others because he has obtained love. Yet love is not a measurable attribute; one may determine another's "worth" in terms of name, artistic ability, and sporting prowess, the elements mentioned in the opening quatrain and downplayed in the third. Moreover, love can be more decimating than those others when it is lost.

This raises the question of the value of love, which is answered by Shakespeare's omission of strength from the characteristics downplayed in the third quatrain. It is the strength of the feelings between the two lovers that creates both the thrill and the torment of love. The energy that exists between lovers clearly surpasses the power which comes from one's social standing, vocation, and sporting ability. It is love that bridges the gap between these characteristics, for it does not care about their value. Sonnet 91 demonstrates Shakespeare's superb ability to stray from the normal path and manipulate the language to express deep emotion in a way which ironically heightens the psychological trauma of love.

R. T. Lambdin

SONNET 94

Author: William Shakespeare (1564-1616)
Type of poem: Sonnet
First published: 1609, in *Sonnets*

The Poem

Sonnet 94 is a typical English or Shakespearean sonnet: fourteen lines of iambic pentameter rhymed *abab, cdcd, efef, gg*. This rhyme scheme effectively divides the poem into three quatrains and a closing couplet, unlike the Italian or Petrarchan sonnet, which tends to be structured as an octave and sestet. In Sonnet 94, William Shakespeare's first-person voice of the lover extols the virtue of stoic restraint and suggests that acting on emotions corrupts the natural nobility of a person's character and, thus, compromises identity itself.

The first line opens the poem with a subject and a restrictive clause that describes the stoic character: Such persons have the power to act, to hurt others, but refuse to do so. The next three lines of the quatrain elaborate on this quality through a series of restrictive clauses: Though such persons may seem to threaten to act, they do not; they move others to act but are themselves unmoved, show little emotion, and restrain themselves from temptation.

Having defined the subject with these restrictive clauses, this rather long opening sentence finally arrives at the verb in line 5: "do inherit." Persons who can exercise such restraint are the proper recipients of grace (divine assistance or protection) and, in turn, protect the earthly manifestations of grace ("nature's riches") from waste. Those who can restrain their emotions and actions, moreover, are in control of their own identities—that is, they are not fickle or quick to change but constant. Such persons truly may be said to follow the advice voiced by Polonius in *Hamlet* (c. 1600-1601): "To thine own self be true." Others, the poem continues, rightly must be subservient to the virtues kept alive by such stoic characters.

In line 9, the formal "turn" in the sonnet, the poem shifts to a new conceit, that of the "summer's flower" as a metaphor for human identity. Though as an individual one recognizes one's value to oneself as self-evident in the fact of one's existence, one's life also has a value to the age and community in which one flourishes: The flowers of summer are "sweet" to the summer itself and contribute to making the summer the pleasant season it is. The speaker adds, however, that if that flower allows itself to be corrupted, then the value of that flower's identity—not simply to itself, but to its community as well—becomes lost, and, in that event, even weeds seem more dignified.

The couplet reiterates this point: Virtue may be corrupted by actions—"Sweetest things turn sourest by their deeds"—and such corrupted virtue is far more damaging to a community than the baseness and vices of individuals—"weeds"—who had no potential for beauty and virtue in the first place.

Forms and Devices

The most striking device in the opening five lines of Sonnet 94 is the repeated use of the word "do" in the sense of "perform" ("do none," line 1); as an intensifier ("do show," line 2); in both senses ("do not do," line 2); and finally, again, as an intensifier to emphasize the verb ("do inherit," line 5). Although the poem is about persons who restrain their actions, this repetition of the most basic word for performing an action, "do," suggests that actions are being performed. In fact, though, if one looks at the grammar of this first sentence, one sees that all but one of these instances of the word are contained within restrictive clauses, and the main verb of the subject "they" is restrained, as it were, until the second quatrain: "do inherit" in line 5. The sentence thus echoes the sense that the "thing they most do show," like the appearance of grammatical action in "do," is restrained. When one does get to that main verb, moreover, it is a verb not of doing but of receiving, of inheriting.

The poem introduces its most significant metaphor in the second quatrain. The speaker compares this stoicism to legal inheritance and ownership of land, land that is then cultivated and made productive. Ownership of land was, in the sixteenth century, a traditional privilege of the nobility, although this rapidly was changing as members of the mercantile middle class accumulated more and more wealth. In lines 7 and 8, this metaphor depicts the relationship between the stoic personality and others in terms of social rank: The former is a lord for whom others are but servants. (It should be noted, however, that both types are, in effect, "stewards," with some serving the stoic's "excellence" and the stoic himself serving to protect "nature's riches.")

The third quatrain makes a surprising leap from these images of land and social rank to the image of the summer flower. The suddenness of this shift from one image to another seemingly unrelated one is characteristic of Shakespeare's methods in the sonnets. It is also perhaps one reason that his contemporary, Ben Jonson, said of Shakespeare, *sufflaminandus erat* (that he needed to put on the brakes, to restrain his free ways with the language). One need not share, however, in Jonson's criticism of his illustrious friend. Instead, one should see this leap as a device that, like metaphor itself, leads one to new and surprising perspectives on its subject.

The natural beauty of the flower is also responsible to its environs, as the stoic is to nature's riches and as others are to the stoic himself. Additionally, its natural beauty, like the nobility of the stoic, can be so corrupted by "deeds" that it becomes inferior to those of less beauty or those of lower social rank—"weeds." The final rhyme of these two words, "deeds" and "weeds," makes emphatic the connection between unrestrained action and the corruption of personal identity and social responsibility.

Themes and Meanings

Shakespeare viewed nature in terms of its benefits to human society. On its own, nature produces wild, unweeded, overgrown fields and woods that neither please the aesthetic sense nor feed a community as effectively as the gardens and crops produced by horticulture, by "art." Nature, therefore, must be nurtured by human industry in order to be beneficial to society. In his poetry, too, Shakespeare's images of nature do not focus on the natural environment in its own right, but have ulterior poetic motives that refer the reader to human experience.

In one of his last plays, *The Tempest* (1611), Shakespeare uses gardening and careful husbandry as metaphors for political and romantic relationships: Friendship and marriage are means of nurturing natural sexual desires into a morally productive relationship; charity, forgiveness, and restraint are means of nurturing desires for political power and possession into an ethical and productive political state. In this play, too, the reader sees noble characters who, because they are unwilling to restrain their greed for power, seem less noble than their social inferiors who "seek for grace." These are the themes of Sonnet 94.

Nobility, as a political status, was passed through inheritance; its attendant personal virtues of honor, strength, and moral rectitude were, it was thought, genetic, passed through the blood. What Shakespeare suggests here is that true nobility is neither inherited nor inherent, but achieved. Political power that is beneficial to others is achieved by first having power over oneself, having the power to hurt, but having the restraint not to exercise such power.

Humans must first and foremost be "lords and owners of our faces." Conversely, if society is to be mutually beneficial, that responsibility for having control over one's own identity is not solely a responsibility to oneself, but also a responsibility to those with whom one lives. The flower produced by summer gives summer its character and has the potential, if corrupted, to make summer seem rank with decay rather than, as it should be, redolent of birth, growth, and life.

James Hale

SONNET 106

Author: William Shakespeare (1564-1616)
Type of poem: Sonnet
First published: 1609, in *Sonnets*

The Poem

In William Shakespeare's Sonnet 106, the speaker calls upon the glories of the past to illustrate the present. He perceives that the beauty of his lover has been prophesied by the pens of authors who are now long dead. The initial quatrain establishes the tone as one of courtly elegance. The references to "chronicles," "ladies," and "knights" all recall the glorified stereotypical image of a time long past, when a knight was obligated by the chivalric code to behave bravely in the battlefield and solicitously in the community.

This highly elevated rhetoric establishes the mood of Sonnet 106, yet the elegance seemingly gives way to irony in the juxtaposition of adjectives in line 4: "Ladies dead and lovely knights." The "beauty" of line 2 has been usurped by the truth of mutability: The ladies are literally dead; they live only as images created by the words of the old rhymes. Further, it seems that the adjectives describing the ladies and the knights have been willingly transposed. The common conception of the lady or mistress in the old poetry was of a fair and lovely creature of inspiration; it was the valiant knights who died for her.

The introductory octave continues with a shift in the second quatrain, where the narrator personifies beauty in the form of a coat of arms which accentuates the erotic images of his love's finest attributes: foot, lip, eye, and brow. These common physical, and even sexual, images initiate a change from the spiritual to the physical. The second quatrain concludes with a vivid image: The narrator visualizes that the earlier poets would have expressed just such a beauty as his love. Thus the initial octave establishes the background from which the sestet will depart.

The sestet begins, in the third quatrain, by connecting the past with the present: The praises of the poets from an earlier age become actual prophecies. The narrator perceives that futuristic visions of his beloved provided the impetus for the old poets' works; however, this idea is quickly amended. Even though those authors were guided by divine inspiration, they were still unable to praise or describe the beauty of the narrator's lover adequately.

The concluding couplet emphasizes the futility of such an effort in the composition of love poems. It is clear that the authors of the past, now long dead, have transmitted their words along to the authors of the present. Yet their adoration remains an enigma; it is impossible for an author to describe his love truly by using mere words.

Forms and Devices

Sonnet 106 conforms to the Elizabethan fourteen-line stanzaic form. Each of the lines contains ten syllables, and the poem consists of two sentences. The first encompasses the initial octave, and the second, the final sestet. This form is similar to Shakespeare's Sonnets 32 and 47. The initial octave may be broken into two distinct quatrains. The first initiates the work with a "when" clause that, while syntactically logical, cannot stand alone.

The second quatrain counters the first with a "then" clause. Through this syntactical convention, logic is used first to divide and then to unite the initial octave. The final sestet similarly depends upon its syntactical sequence first to answer, then to expand upon, the logic conceived in the initial octave. Despite its unification, the sestet is composed of both a distinct quatrain and a concluding couplet.

The quatrain of the sestet begins a new sentence that remarks on the evidence put forward in the preceding sentence. It states that despite the worthy stature of the poets who composed the earlier works, their attempts at prophecy fall short: They were incapable of capturing the beauty of the narrator's beloved in words. The main point of the work, however, is the narrator's own seeming inability to put his love's beauty into words.

The sonnet uses alliteration, particularly of the *s* sound, throughout the poem. Shakespeare also creates effects by expanding or contracting the number of syllables that appear between certain repeated sounds. In the couplet, for example, a pulsating alliteration emphasizes the poem's conclusion; the "praise" of line 14 represents a compression of the *pr* and *ay* sounds previously heard in the "present days" of line 11. There is also an expanding alliterative pattern in the placement of *b* and *pr* sounds. In line 9, the pattern begins with "but prophecies." The sound is stretched in line 13—"behold the present"—and stretched even further in the final line: "but lack tongues to praise."

Sonnet 106 exhibits Shakespeare's uncanny ability to manipulate language into poetic form; the poem is not as simple and straightforward as it may appear. In line 3, the narrator refers to the "beautiful old rhyme" of bygone days, yet he is speaking a poem that both echoes and modifies those old rhymes, a poem that will one day take its place in the canon to which they belong.

Themes and Meanings

Sonnet 106 is in many ways a typical love poem filled with conventional techniques. While it does not offer significant insight into the many mysteries of the sonnets, it does provide a glimpse of an idea far too often overlooked in much criticism—that Shakespeare and other Elizabethan writers depended upon the authors of the past. It is often perceived that the literary works of Renaissance England rely solely upon the classical traditions or spring from an author's sudden burst of inspiration. Sonnet 106 proves that is not true, for it clearly displays Shakespeare's debt to medieval authors and their works.

Shakespeare was influenced by the work of Geoffrey Chaucer, whose "The Knight's Tale" from *The Canterbury Tales* (1387-1400) is a major source for the plot of *A Midsummer Night's Dream* (c. 1595-1596). While Shakespeare somewhat alters the myth surrounding the marriage of Hippolyta and Theseus, the Chaucerian influence is abundant. This type of borrowing is continued in Sonnet 106. In this poem, Shakespeare clearly reminds readers of his debt to the older works. He also shows an understanding of the themes of many of the ancient texts: ladies, knights, courtly love, and chivalry.

It is clear that perceiving beauty is one thing, while putting those visualizations into words is quite another. Thus, ironically, the narrator fails miserably in his quest—yet he is also successful to some degree. Despite his omission of any physical description, he has captured at least a part of his love's essence, and he is honoring her with a poem. Like the women who were glorified in literature long before her, she, too, has been given eternal life.

Sonnet 106 also has a consciousness of the theme implicit in the phrase "this our time" (line 10). The sonnet constantly reinforces the idea that what lovers can do is mandated by their particular era; what has previously occurred affects them, so they cannot ignore the past. Yet, after their death, they are doomed to become faint images for other authors to wonder about. At best, they can attempt an understanding of the ideals and the images of their present. This theme, introduced in Sonnet 106, is furthered in the more famous Sonnet 107 ("Not mine own fears, nor the prophetic soul"). The message of Sonnet 106 is clear, and its technique is conventional. It is of particular value because it shows an aspect of Shakespeare's work that is too often overlooked: its debt to medieval authors.

R. T. Lambdin

SONNET 116

Author: William Shakespeare (1564-1616)
Type of poem: Sonnet
First published: 1609, in *Sonnets*

The Poem

Sonnet 116 is generally considered one of the finest love poems ever written. In this sonnet, William Shakespeare raised the theme of romantic love to the status of high philosophy. At a time when love between man and woman was not often recognized as essentially other than a form of family obligation, Shakespeare spiritualized it as the motivator of the highest level of human action. Love of that kind has since become the most sought-after human experience.

The poem is a regular English sonnet of fourteen lines arranged in three quatrains and a concluding couplet. It begins by using the language of the Book of Common Prayer marriage service to make an explicit equation of love and marriage. It not only suggests that marriage is the proper end of love, but it also goes beyond to make love a necessary prerequisite. The quatrain continues by describing the essential constituents of the kind of love that qualifies. Such love does not change under changing circumstances; in fact, constancy is its first element. It continues even when unreciprocated or betrayed. Further, true love does not depend on the presence of the beloved, but actually increases during absence.

The second quatrain uses a series of metaphors to flesh out the character of proper love. Its constancy is such that it not only endures threats but actually strengthens in adversity. Its attractive power secures the beloved from wandering, and it sets a standard for all other lovers. Although conspicuous and easily identifiable, its value is inestimable. Aspects of it can be measured, and many of its properties are tangible, but it resides in another dimension, unassessable by normal instruments in space and time.

The third quatrain considers the constancy of true love under the threats of time and aging. It declares that love is unaffected by time. To begin with, love far transcends such mundane physical characteristics as size, appearance, condition, and shape. For that reason, it ignores physical changes caused by age or health. It defies time and everything in its power, including death. True love operates in the realm of eternity. Not even death can part true lovers; their union endures forever. Because love has the capacity to raise human action to this exalted state, it alone enables humans to transcend temporal limitations. Humankind becomes godlike through love.

The sonnet ends with a simple couplet which transfers the focus from the ethereal region of eternal, transcendent love to the routine present of the poet-speaker. He merely observes that if he is ever proved wrong, then no man has ever loved. It seems a trivial conclusion, until one recognizes that this is exactly the feeling that allows men and women to continue to fall in love and to endow that feeling with meaning.

Forms and Devices

In spite of being one of the world's most celebrated short poems, Sonnet 116 uses a rather simple array of poetic devices. They include special diction, allusion, metaphor, and paradox. All work together to reinforce the central theme.

Shakespeare establishes the context early with his famous phrase "the marriage of true minds," a phrase which does more than is commonly recognized. The figure of speech suggests that true marriage is a union of minds rather than merely a license for the coupling of bodies. Shakespeare implies that true love proceeds from and unites minds on the highest level of human activity, that it is inherently mental and spiritual. From the beginning, real love transcends the sensual-physical. Moreover, the very highest level is reserved to "true" minds. By this he means lovers who have "plighted troth," in the phrasing of the marriage service—that is, exchanged vows to be true to each other. This reinforces the spirituality of loving, giving it religious overtones. The words "marriage" and "impediments" also allude to the language of the service, accentuating the sacred nature of love.

Shakespeare then deliberately repeats phrases to show that this kind of love is more than mere reciprocation. Love cannot be simply returning what is given, like an exchange of gifts. It has to be a simple, disinterested, one-sided offering, unrelated to any possible compensation. He follows this with a series of positive and negative metaphors to illustrate the full dimensions of love. It is first "an ever-fixéd mark/ That looks on tempests and is never shaken." This famous figure has not been completely explained, although the general idea is clear. Love is equated with some kind of navigating device so securely mounted that it remains functional in hurricanes. It then becomes not a device but a reference point, a "star," of universal recognition but speculative in its composition; significantly, it is beyond human ken.

In "Love's not Time's fool," Shakespeare moves on to yet another metaphorical level. To begin with, love cannot be made into a fool by the transformations of time; it operates beyond and outside it, hence cannot be subject to it. This is so although time controls those qualities which are popularly thought to evoke love—physical attractions. Shakespeare conjures up the image of the Grim Reaper with his "bending sickle," only to assert that love is not within his "compass"—which denotes both grip and reckoning and sweep of blade. Love cannot be fathomed by time or its extreme instrument, death. Love "bears it out"—perseveres in adversity—to the "edge of doom"—that is, beyond the grave and the worst phase of time's decay.

The final device is a conundrum in logic. It establishes an alternative—"If this be error"—then disproves it. What remains, and remains valid, is the other. It also bears a double edge. If this demonstration is wrong, Shakespeare says, "I never writ," which is an obvious contradiction. The only possible conclusion is that it is not wrong. He proceeds then to a corollary, "nor no man ever loved," which is as false as the previous statement.

Themes and Meanings

In this sonnet, the theme is the poem. Shakespeare presents an argument, forcing the double conclusion that love transcends normal human measures and that it represents the highest level of human activity. Yet, as a famous love poem, it is highly unusual: It is not a declaration of love but a definition and demonstration. It still accomplishes the object of a love poem, however, because the inspirer of this statement could not possibly be flattered more effectively.

Sonnet 116 develops the theme of the eternity of true love through an elaborate and intricate cascade of images. Shakespeare first states that love is essentially a mental relationship; the central property of love is truth—that is, fidelity—and fidelity proceeds from and is anchored in the mind. The objective tone and impersonal language of the opening reinforce this theme. This kind of love is as far removed from the level of mere sensation as any human activity could be. Like all ideal forms, it operates on the level of abstract intellect, or of soul. Hence it is immune to the physical, emotional, or behavioral "impediments" that threaten lesser loves. It is a love that fuses spirits intuitively related to each other.

The poem proceeds to catalog a number of specific impediments. The first involves reciprocation. Does true love persist in the face of rejection or loss of affection? Absolutely, even though those might be sufficient grounds for calling off a wedding. True love endures even the absence of the beloved: not that the heart grows fonder in such a case, as in the cliché, but that it operates independently of physical reminders. Such love stabilizes itself, as if possessing an instinctive self-righting mechanism. Shakespeare himself uses this kind of gyroscopic and autopilot imagery; like the navigational devices to which he alludes, true love serves as a standard for others, maintains its course under stress, and guarantees security against storm and turmoil.

This imagery duplicates the sequence of promises exchanged by true lovers in the marriage service that Shakespeare quotes in the opening of the poem. True love vows constancy regardless of better, worse, richer, poorer, sickness, health—all the vagaries of life and change. The simple series, however, seems to minimize the intensity of love necessary to do this. On the contrary, love is absolutely secure against external assault. In particular, it holds firm against the ravages of time. Since the poem begins by dissociating love from the limits of time, this should not be surprising, especially since the marriage service insists on the possibility of love surviving time and its consequence, change. So strong is the popular belief that love is rooted in physical attractiveness, however, that the poem is forced to repudiate this explicitly. It does it in the starkest way imaginable, by personifying time as the Grim Reaper and by bringing that specter directly before the eyes of the lover. This happens; the threat is real, but the true lover can face down even death.

The marriage service does that also, by asking the thinking lover to promise fidelity "until death do us part." Shakespeare's poem uses imagery to give form to this belief that true love has to be stronger than death, set as a seal upon the lover's heart.

James Livingston

SONNET 129

Author: William Shakespeare (1564-1616)
Type of poem: Sonnet
First published: 1609, in *Sonnets*

The Poem

Sonnet 129 is a typical Shakespearean sonnet in form, written in iambic pentameter with twelve lines rhymed *abab, cdcd, efef,* and a closing couplet rhymed *gg.* Unlike the majority of William Shakespeare's sonnets, however, it is not addressed to a particular individual but is directed to an audience, as a sermon is.

The first line is the only one that presents any difficulty in interpretation. Shakespeare sometimes compressed a large meaning into few words, creating an impressionistic effect. Although this opening line appears a bit garbled, it is easy enough to understand and well suited to the mood of the poem. It creates the impression of a mind overwhelmed by a whirlwind of bitter reflections.

He is obviously talking about sexual lust. The first line states that lust is shameful and spiritually debilitating. The rest of the poem simply expands upon this idea. The torrent of adjectives and short descriptive phrases that follows suggests the different ways in which sexual lust can lead to tragic outcomes. The reader may evoke specific illustrations from personal experience or from the world's literature which, from the Bible and Greek mythology to modern novels such as Vladimir Nabokov's *Lolita* (1955), is full of warnings against lust.

Each word or phrase in the opening lines suggests different scenarios. For example, the word "perjur'd" suggests the lies men tell women, the most common being "I love you" and "I want to marry you." Lust drives people to say many things they do not mean. The word "perjur'd" also suggests the humiliating experience of having to lie to the fiancé or spouse of one's lover, who might even be a personal friend.

The word "bloody" suggests even more serious outcomes of sexual lust. The outraged husband who discovers his wife in bed with another man may murder her, or him, or both. Lust also may lead to bloody abortions and suicides. "Full of blame" suggests the painful aftermath of many affairs based not on love but on lust. The woman blames the man for deceiving her; he blames her for leading him on, for allowing herself to become pregnant, or for confessing her adultery to her husband. "Full of blame" in Shakespeare's time probably suggested the great danger of contracting syphilis or gonorrhea, and in recent times it suggests the modern plague of acquired immune deficiency syndrome (AIDS).

The closing couplet of the sonnet alights gracefully, with the juxtaposition of "well knows" and "knows well." The tone is like the calm after a storm. It is not a happy conclusion but a truthful one. Humanity repeats the same mistakes generation after generation. Sexual passion is hard to control and leads to much of the tragedy that human beings experience.

Forms and Devices

There are two important things to notice about the structure of this sonnet. One is that, except for the closing couplet, it consists of a single run-on sentence. The other is that it is built around a single simile, which takes up the seventh and eighth lines. The effect of crowding most of the poem into a single outburst is to leave the reader with a feeling of agitation mirroring the conflicting emotions that accompany sexual lust. Run-on sentences are often the targets of English teachers' red pencils, but at times such sentences can be extremely effective.

Shakespeare often filled his sonnets with metaphors and similes, as he did in his famous Sonnet 73, in which he compares his time of life to winter, to sunset, and to a dying fire. In other sonnets, however, he deliberately avoids metaphors and similes in order to obtain the maximum effect from a single striking image. This is the case in another of Shakespeare's most famous sonnets, Sonnet 29, which begins, "When in disgrace with fortune and men's eyes." After complaining at length about his miserable condition, the speaker changes his tone entirely and says that, should he happen to remember the friendship of the person he is addressing, his state, "Like to the lark at break of day arising/ From sullen earth, sings hymns at heaven's gate." These are two of the most beautiful lines in English poetry, and they are more effective because they are not competing with any other imagery in the sonnet.

In Sonnet 129, the dominant image is contained in the lines

> Past reason hated, as a swallowed bait
> On purpose laid to make the taker mad.

After this—but without starting a new sentence—the poet launches into another tirade, echoing the word "Mad" at the beginning of the next line and rhyming it with "Had" at the beginning of the line after that. These devices arouse apprehension because it seems as if the speaker may actually be starting to rave.

People do not set out poisoned bait to kill human beings. The kind of bait Shakespeare is referring to is commonly used to kill rats: They are driven mad with thirst or pain and run out of the house to die. One of the reasons the image is so striking is that it implicitly compares people motivated by uncontrolled lust to the lowest, most detested animals. Sonnet 129 is unlike most of Shakespeare's other sonnets and in fact unlike most other Elizabethan sonnets, which are typically full of references to love, the moon, the stars, and other pleasant things. This strange sonnet on lust has a modern, experimental quality to it which foreshadows the cacophony and deliberately shocking ugliness of much twentieth century art.

Themes and Meanings

Shakespeare was not a deeply religious man. The moralistic tone of this poem seems so out of character that one distinguished Shakespearean scholar, A. L. Rowse, suggested that Shakespeare did not intend it to be taken seriously but wrote the sonnet as a sort of private joke for his circle of friends; yet its emotional effect is so powerful that it is hard to believe that Shakespeare was not writing with true feeling. It has also been suggested that Shakespeare wrote the sonnet after discovering that he had contracted syphilis from a liaison with a prostitute—or possibly from the mysterious "Dark Lady" mentioned in some of his other sonnets.

The theme is simple and clear. The poet is preaching a brief sermon on the dangers of sexual lust. These dangers have been a subject of literature since the stories of Samson and Delilah and of David and Bathsheba, recorded in the Old Testament. The Trojan War, which led to the destruction of a whole civilization and was described in both Homer's *Iliad* (c. 800 B.C.E.) and Vergil's *Aeneid* (c. 29-19 B.C.E.), was reputedly caused by Paris's lust for Helen, the wife of Menelaus. In Shakespeare's own long poem *The Rape of Lucrece* (1594), the story is told of how the Etruscan rulers came to be driven out of Rome because of Sextus Tarquinius's rape of Lucrece and her subsequent suicide.

In Leo Tolstoy's novel *Anna Karenina* (1875-1877; English translation, 1886), the heroine throws herself under the wheels of a locomotive after she has left her husband and children and ultimately finds herself deserted by her faithless lover. In Henrik Ibsen's play *Gengangere* (1881; *Ghosts*, 1885), a promising young man dies because he inherited syphilis from his profligate father. In Anton Chekhov's best short story, "Dama s sobachkoi" (1899; "The Lady with the Dog," 1917), an adulterous relationship leads to endless mental torture for both parties involved. In Theodore Dreiser's novel *An American Tragedy* (1925), lust leads to murder and death in the electric chair.

As Shakespeare wrote, the world well knows that sexual intercourse without love is often a grave disappointment and can lead to torment in a wide variety of forms. Unfortunately, many people have to learn this truth by bitter experience.

Finally, a political statement might be read into this sonnet. The fact that it departs from the norm and is not pretty and soothing might be taken to indicate a view that art should serve a higher purpose than merely helping the genteel elite to pass their leisure hours. Its denunciation of sexual lust might be read as an indictment of the aristocracy, whose favorite pastime, as shown by so many of the songs, poems, and paintings of the period, was playing at the game of love. Thus, it might be seen as foreshadowing views that led to the English Civil War which began only twenty-six years after Shakespeare's death and changed the course of history.

Bill Delaney

SONNET 130

Author: William Shakespeare (1564-1616)
Type of poem: Sonnet
First published: 1609, in *Sonnets*

The Poem

Sonnet 130 is a blazon, a lyric poem cataloging the physical characteristics and virtues of the beloved, in typical English or Shakespearean sonnet form—three quatrains and a couplet in iambic pentameter rhymed *abab, cdcd, efef, gg.* The first-person voice of the poem should be understood as that of a dramatic persona; even if William Shakespeare means it to represent himself, he nevertheless has to create a distinct personality in the language, and from this distance, the reader has no way of knowing how accurately this might describe the man. The speaker describes his beloved in comparison with, or rather in contrast to, natural phenomena. In the love poem tradition, as it emerged in English poetry in imitation of the sonnets of fourteenth century Italian poet Petrarch, poets often compare their beloveds to the elements of nature. In this sonnet, Shakespeare takes the opposite tack by describing his beloved as "nothing like" the beautiful productions of nature or art.

Her eyes, the poet begins, do not shine like the sun; nor are her lips as red as coral. When compared to the whiteness of snow, his beloved's breasts seem "dun," a dull gray. The "wires" of line 4 refer to gold spun into golden thread, and his beloved's hair, if the metaphoric description of hairs as golden wires is valid, can only be seen as black, or tarnished beyond all recognition.

The damasked roses of the fifth line are variegated roses of red and white, and such, the poet continues, cannot be seen in his woman's face. Perfume, too, is an inaccurate simile for his lover's breath, since most perfumes are more pleasing. The word "reeks" in line 8 simply means "breathes forth" in Elizabethan English, although our modern sense of the word as denoting an offensive smell certainly emphasizes Shakespeare's point of contrast.

At the ninth-line "turn"—the formal point at which sonnets typically introduce an antithesis or redirect their focus—the speaker continues in the same vein, noting how music has a more pleasing sound than his lover's voice, though he also introduces an important point: None of these contrasts is to suggest that he finds his beloved any less pleasing. He loves her voice, as he does her other characteristics, but honestly he must acknowledge that music is, objectively speaking, more pleasing to the senses.

Lines 11 and 12 dismiss conventional descriptions of women as goddesslike. Who among mortal men has ever witnessed a goddess in order to make such similes in the first place? All this lover knows is what he sees, and his mistress is, like him, quite earthly and earthbound, walking on the ground.

The sonnet's couplet then explicates the point of the above contrasts. The lover's objective comparisons of his beloved with nature and human artifacts of perfume and music, however unfavorable to the woman, do not change his subjective perception of her: She is as rare as any of those women whom poets describe with comparisons that exaggerate, and thus belie, human beauty.

Forms and Devices

The effect of the formal division of the Shakespearean sonnet, the four quatrains and closing couplet, is to pile up examples of a single idea—that the beloved's beauty is really not comparable to the productions of nature and human art—so that by line 12, the reader wonders if there is anything at all about the woman that can be seen objectively as beautiful. The last two lines then provide a memorable explication of that idea: Objectivity and actual beauty are really no concern of the lover. While lines 11 and 12 dismiss comparisons to heavenly beauty as meaningless—mortals have no experience of the metaphysical world on which to base such similes—Shakespeare uses the mild expletive "by heaven" in line 13 to suggest in contrast that the impassioned subjectivity of the lover is itself metaphysical in origin, a kind of grace.

The speaker's attitude in this poem is strikingly antimetaphoric, and lines 3 and 4 subject two conventional metaphors to examination by deductive logic. Line 3 begins with a premise, "If snow be white," and concludes that the woman's breasts are "dun." In technical terms, the rhetorical device employed here is an "enthymeme," a syllogism in which one of the terms is left out and must be inferred by the reader. One may reconstruct the full syllogism thus: Snow is white; my lover's breasts are dull gray; therefore, my lover's breasts are not like snow. Since snow is in fact white, one can concur with the conclusion's logic and deny the validity of the simile "women's breasts are white like snow." Line 4 offers another enthymeme beginning with the premise "If hairs be wires" and concluding that the woman's hair is black, or tarnished, wire. The full syllogism here would read: Hairs are golden wires; my lover's hairs are black; therefore, my lover's hairs must be tarnished.

The conclusion follows logically, but the metaphoric premise is untrue: Hairs are not wires, and if the woman is judged on the basis of this premise, one can only conclude by denigrating the woman's physical characteristics as sullied examples of an ideal: tarnished gold. This is what Shakespeare means by "false compare"—unjust comparisons that not only ignore the possibility that the woman may be beautiful in her own right, but also miss the value of the beloved in the eyes of her lover: To him, she is, if not golden, at least as "rare." That the poet has his persona subject love and beauty to deductive logic at all tells the reader something important about the lover's attitude and about the overall meaning of the poem.

Themes and Meanings

The ostensible subject of this sonnet is the so-called dark lady of the later sonnets, a woman with whom the speaker of the poems is having a passionate sexual affair. The first 126 sonnets are addressed to a man, in whom the speaker denies having sexual interest. (See Sonnet 20, where the speaker notes that the male beloved has "one thing to my purpose nothing.") These sonnets to and about the man attempt to consider the dimensions of platonic love, "the marriage of true minds" (Sonnet 116), without the compromising motive of sexual desire. In contrast, the sonnets addressed to the dark lady suggest that once sex enters into the relationship, the possibility of achieving a higher, platonic love is virtually lost. Indeed, the speaker and the dark lady engage in quite a sordid affair.

Although the poem focuses on this woman, its main subject is perception itself and the methods by which poets represent love. Poets often concern themselves with the nature of their art and, in creating new ways of seeing human experience, question the validity of the poetic conventions of their predecessors. This poem prompts some very fundamental questions about poetic devices. What does metaphor actually tell about the objects on which it focuses? If poetry attempts to bring one closer to what is true in the human experience, why is it that most poetic conventions are falsehoods? Love is not a rose, beloveds are not heavenly goddesses, lovers do not die from being rejected by their beloveds. As the character Rosalind, in Shakespeare's play *As You Like It* (c. 1599-1600), remarks in response to the "poetic" language of her lover: "men have died from time to time, and worms have eaten them, but not for love."

In Sonnet 18, when the poet asks of the male beloved, "Shall I compare thee to a summer's day?" the answer—no—calls attention to the inadequacy of conventional metaphors and similes to describe accurately not the beloved, but the subjective nature of love. In the case of Sonnet 18, however, such comparisons are insufficient, the lover suggests, because they are not superlative enough. Here, he suggests the opposite: They are too superlative to give a realistic picture of his beloved. Such metaphors and similes are, after all, mere lies—poetic lies, perhaps, but lies nevertheless. Although clearly in love with the woman, this lover seems poignantly aware of the way she really looks, beyond his love-inspired subjectivity.

Sonnet 130 provides logic instead of metaphor, objectivity instead of hyperbole. In one very important sense, this focus on actual physical appearance seems appropriate to the affair between the speaker and the dark lady: Throughout the sonnets that represent this affair, Shakespeare continually stresses the point that their relationship is based primarily, almost exclusively, on physical appearance and physical attraction—on what Sonnet 129 calls "lust in action."

James Hale

SONNET—TO SCIENCE

Author: Edgar Allan Poe (1809-1849)
Type of poem: Sonnet
First published: 1829, in *Al Aaraaf, Tamerlane, and Minor Poems*; collected in *The Complete Works of Edgar Allan Poe*, 1902

The Poem

In Edgar Allan Poe's later collections, "Sonnet—To Science" appears with a footnote describing it as one of "the crude compositions of my earliest boyhood." The same footnote excuses its republication with reference to "private reasons—some of which have reference to the sin of plagiarism, and others to the date of Tennyson's first poems." Alfred, Lord Tennyson, had been born in the same year as Poe and had published his first volume of poetry, *Poems by Two Brothers* (in association with his brother Charles), in 1827, the same year in which Poe's earliest publications appeared.

The sonnet's rhyme scheme follows the English, or Shakespearean, form rather than the Italian, or Petrarchan, sonnet form. Its substance, by contrast, has more in common with the Italian tradition, which characteristically involves the posing of a question, than with the English tradition, which tends to be more meditative. Where the Petrarchan sonnet would usually supplement an interrogatory octave with a responsive sestet, however, "Sonnet—To Science" maintains its inquiring tone throughout the three quatrains and the concluding couplet.

"Sonnet—To Science" addresses its object from a point of view solidly anchored within the Romantic movement, likening science's keen-eyed inquiry to a vulture whose wings cast a shadow of "dull reality" upon the landscape of the imagination. It asks how the poet, having discovered such a predator "upon [his] heart," can possibly love the scientific revelation or concede its wisdom. It is only natural, the sonnet suggests, that poets should flee the shadow of dull reality in search of better and brighter pastures, lit by "jewelled skies."

The last six lines of the sonnet add detail to the charges presented in more general terms in the first eight. Like a prosecutor engaged in cross-examination, the sonnet demands an accounting of specific sins. Has science not dragged Diana (a Roman goddess associated with nature and birth) from her "car"? (Diana was associated in Rome itself with moonlight, so the car in question is the moon.) Has not the Hamadryad (a type of nymph associated with oak trees) been "driven . . . from the wood" and the Naiad (a species of water nymph) from her "blood"—the blood in question being the stream or spring embodying her spirit? Has science not banished the Elfin— the Anglo-Saxon fairy race—from their pastoral haunts? And has it not, in consequence, robbed the poet of the "summer dream" which might otherwise have visited him in the shade of the tamarind tree?

The accusative tone of these questions implies that they are rhetorical—that they do not actually require an answer because it is obvious that each charge is correct. The fact remains, however, that no answer is given and that the questions are questions rather than statements. The poem preserves a margin of uncertainty, which the poet's voice invites the reader to share. "Sonnet—to Science" is a poem that seeks to address a problem and thus to define the problem's nature. As might be expected of a poem composed at the outset of an adventurous career, it is essentially open-ended. It is setting out an agenda rather than delivering a verdict.

Forms and Devices

Although Poe was well aware in his later years that he had been born in the same year as Tennyson, he probably was not conscious of the fact that he had also been born in the same year as Charles Darwin, whose theory of evolution was not published until ten years after Poe's death. It was Darwin's science which finally picked the bones of mythology clean, extrapolating in the process Tennyson's key image of "nature red in tooth and claw" ("In Memoriam," 1850).

Whether or not he was aware of Charles Darwin, however, Poe would certainly have been aware of Charles's grandfather, Erasmus Darwin (1731-1802), who was renowned in his own day as a poet as well as a naturalist. Erasmus Darwin frequently reported his scientific discoveries in poetic form, and his earlier publications—including *The Loves of the Plants* (1789)—are not ashamed to formulate his discoveries as news conveyed by nymphs and elemental spirits. The imagery of "Sonnet—to Science" implies a stark contrast between myth and science—a frank enmity expressed in the violence with which it treats Diana and the dispossessed nymphs—but the implication is more tentative than it may seem.

By choosing the metaphor of a shadow-casting wing to represent science Poe admits—and then re-emphasizes in the vital eighth line—that science has its own soaring imagination and its own admirable courage. The first line, too, concedes that science is a "true daughter of Old Time," the time in question being that which brings self-knowledge and reveals previously hidden truths—and perhaps also the time that heals wounds.

The concessions of the first and eighth lines would be more generous were it not for the fact that the shadow-casting wing of science is attached to a vulture: a bird of ill-omen more disreputable even than a raven. The third line makes it explicit, however, that Poe conceives science as a predator, not as a scavenger, and this is re-emphasized in the second part of the poem. Science drags, drives, and tears; it does not sit around waiting for myth to die of natural causes. It is, in fact, more like an eagle than a vulture. There is a hesitation here, if not an outright ambiguity.

Themes and Meanings

Even in this early work, Poe seems to have been considering—albeit a bit reluctantly—the possibility that he might align himself with those Romantics who celebrated the awesome revelations of the scientific imagination (among whom Percy Bysshe Shelley was the most outstanding) rather than those who viewed the intellectual and industrial revolutions with mournful regret. He never did resolve that dilemma, and that was greatly to the advantage of his work. No other nineteenth century American writer fled as far as he "to seek for treasure in the jewelled skies," and the flight in question began in the poem which follows "Sonnet—to Science" in his collected works: the brilliantly bizarre "Al Aaraaf."

The first footnote to "Al Aaraaf" links it to Tycho Brahe's "new star," which revealed once and for all that the heavens are not fixed and finished, but the imagery of the long poem is as rich and exotic as anything Poe was later to produce. Other footnotes set Classical references and scientific references side by side, but not as Erasmus Darwin might have done. Poe never lost the sense of a vital and violent struggle between the hallowed glories of mythology and the new revelations of science; he never could combine the two without a keen awareness that he was doing something paradoxical. But Poe was a very paradoxical man, and he took pride in that fact. He conceived of his own self as something deeply divided, echoed that division in many of the characters with whom he populated his phantasmagoric tales, and saw it reflected in the war between science and romance for possession of the modern imagination.

"Sonnet—To Science" is a very modest poem by comparison with the works for which Poe is best remembered. It lacks all trace of the greatness of his best work, yet it is an interesting poem, both in the context of its time and in the context of the career that grew from it. Even as an adolescent Poe was aware of the overarching importance of the march of science and was concerned with calculating its costs and rewards. "Sonnet—To Science" emphasizes the costs, but it does not do so blindly or blandly; it has intelligence enough to acknowledge that the imaginative predations of science are not without a certain grandeur as well as an ominous inevitability.

Toward the end of his life, Poe was to expand greatly on his perception of the problem posed in "Sonnet—To Science" in the long poetic essay *Eureka* (1848). *Eureka* protests against the reductionist method of science while celebrating the magnificence of its revelations. Like "Sonnet—To Science," *Eureka*'s first concern is the astronomers who dethroned Diana and the other deities embodied in the heavens. In a sense, "Sonnet—To Science" is the more prophetic work in that it proceeds to pay more attention to the disenchanting effects of biological science.

In answer to his own not-quite-rhetorical questions, Poe decided that if science was neither lovable nor entirely wise, then the duty of the poet was to take arms against it and fight for the conservation of the Elfin and their classical analogues. The heroic quality of that mission was never properly appreciated in his native land, where nonbelievers in science and technology preferred to sequester themselves within the walls of religious fundamentalism. In the lands where the fugitive Elfin and the Dianic mysteries were still remembered, however, and their force still felt, Poe's progress from sonnet, "Sonnet—to Science," to epic, *Eureka*, via the most scenic route imaginable, has been celebrated with all appropriate reverence.

Brian Stableford

SORDELLO

Author: Robert Browning (1812-1889)
Type of poem: Narrative
First published: 1840; revised and collected in *The Poetical Works of Robert Browning*, 1863, 1868, 1888

The Poem

Sordello is commonly described as the least comprehensible poem written in the English language. Its publication caused the author unending troubles with the critics of his day. Robert Browning wrote it between the years 1833 and 1840; he apparently wrote four different versions, each with a somewhat different purpose in mind. The version most often read today is a poem of 5,982 lines in iambic pentameter, rhyming in couplets, and including running titles that summarize the action.

Browning's historical sources for the story appear to have been Dante's *Purgatorio* and the *Biographie Universelle* (a popular nineteenth century biographical dictionary) that was in his father's library. Sordello was a Mantuan poet and warrior of the early thirteenth century, and thirty-four of his poems in the Provençal language are extant. His age at the time of his death remains uncertain (some historical accounts describe him as middle-aged, others as old), but Browning chose to have his character die at the age of thirty.

Other characters who figure in the drama include the Lady Palma; the minstrel Eglamor, whose place at court Sordello tries to usurp; the Ghibelline leaders Taurello Salinguerra and Ecelin; Ecelin's wife, Adelaide; the literary critic Naddo; and Palma's fiancé, the Guelf Count Richard of St. Boniface.

Before the actual story gets under way, in book 1 Browning introduces a speaker who promises to tell the story but who first paints an elaborate picture of a street scene in Verona in the twelfth century. He explains the history of the political battles between the Guelfs (supporters of popular liberation headed by Pope Henricus III and affiliated with the Este family) and the Ghibelline aristocracy (Frederick II and the barons of the Austro-German empire). He also apologizes for not using his usual dramatic monologue narrative technique and discusses Dante, who was Browning's principal source for the story. Around line 400 he finally introduces Sordello.

The rest of book 1 shows the young Sordello in the town of Goito in the domain of the tyrant Ecelin, aspiring to become a great poet. As though he is naïvely fitting himself to some classical pattern, he finds himself ready, at the end of the canto, to fall in love.

In book 2, in order to win the love of the Lady Palma, Sordello pits himself against Eglamor in a poetry contest. When Sordello wins, Eglamor dies of grief. This convinces the younger man that he is himself quite talented, and he briefly experiences a sense of victory. Eglamor's death over such a defeat, however, convinces Sordello that this more experienced minstrel, like many others, had been writing poetry strictly for popularity, and that Sordello's victory is, therefore, hollow. He decides to attempt the writing of a poetry that will be more subjective yet clearly directed to the ennoblement of humanity. The critic Naddo ridicules the young poet and suggests that the world does not need more half-baked philosophers, especially among writers of poetry. Disheartened but not defeated, Sordello leaves the court of Taurello Salinguerra.

In book 3, Sordello first spends a year alone, recouping his energy and idealism. Then Naddo recalls him to court and asks him to write a public poem celebrating the impending marriage of Palma to Count Richard of St. Boniface, which would secure peace between the Ghibellines and the Guelfs. Sordello, however, professes his own love for Palma. She discovers the secret of Sordello's birth but does not reveal the truth to him. She professes her love for him. Following her suggestion, the two move to Ferrara and become politically active in support of the Kaiser. Salinguerra helps them. Sordello's musings prompt the narrator to digress from the story and discuss the role of the poet in society, with some reference to his or her affiliation not only with the socially prominent but also with the suffering poor.

Book 4 seems principally a further exposition of the twelfth century history of the conflict between the Guelfs and Ghibellines, but it focuses particularly on the psychology and history of Salinguerra. His service of Ecelin is discussed. The reader learns that Adelaide, Ecelin's wife, revealed to her husband that Salinguerra was, in fact, Sordello's father. Discovering this, Ecelin had retired from the world and entered a monastery at Oliero, announcing, at the same time, the proposed marriage between Count Richard and Palma (mentioned above). Salinguerra had been in Naples, preparing to depart on a crusade with Emperor Frederick II, and he hurried back to Ferrara when he heard what Ecelin had done. Count Richard attacks him, but is imprisoned. This leads Sordello to condemn both parties in his heart. He asks whether solidarity between individuals of all classes might be more important than loyalty to any party.

Though he does not align himself specifically with the Guelfs, in book 5 Sordello embraces the democratic cause of the people and intercedes with Salinguerra, encouraging the leader to use his great power to help the poor of northern Italy. Salinguerra scorns the advice and tires of the long speech, but he offers to abdicate in favor of the idealistic poet. At that point Palma reveals that Salinguerra is Sordello's father. The poet is now left with a crucial ethical dilemma: Can he enforce his ideals by assuming the power of a tyrant?

Somewhat shorter than the others, book 6 reveals that Sordello died at the end of the former book, unable to resolve the conflict with which he is there presented: He is a Ghibelline ruler by birth, but a Guelf democrat by instinct. Before his death, he crushes Salinguerra's badge beneath his feet. Beyond this brief exposition, book 6 is a discussion of the question of Sordello's successes and failures as both a poet and a leader. Much of the answer, the narrator suggests, must await the next life. There is, therefore, little sense of closure at the end of the poem.

Forms and Devices

Structurally, *Sordello* is organized into two halves, the first dealing more or less with the young man's development as a poet, the second half with his development as a politician. Temporally, however, the poetic development lasts for more than thirty years, and the political for only three days. The first three books, therefore, are something of a digression from the action promised in the opening. This combination of anticipation and discontinuity becomes a persistent—and initially annoying—device that thematically stitches the poem together while appearing structurally to tear it apart.

Unlike Browning's other distinctive poems, which are, in most cases, dramatic monologues, this early effort is narrative. That description can be misleading, however, since the poem does not set out, in simple expository form, the story of a particular Mantuan poet. Alfred, Lord Tennyson, wryly noted that the poem begins with the line "Who will, may hear Sordello's story told," and ends with the line "Who would has heard Sordello's story told," but both statements, in his opinion, were lies. Anyone approaching the poem without some idea of the story will be quickly frustrated by the extensive digressions from the plot and the juxtaposed sequence of incident.

This latter device, in fact, is not far from the *progression d'effet* later used by the modern novelist Ford Madox Ford in his novel *The Good Soldier* (1915). It may at first appear that Browning's narrator is suddenly remembering an important detail that had slipped his mind. This can disconcert the reader, who expects a more obvious competence in straightforward storytelling, but it is Browning's attempt to force reassessments of events and to make any one view of history seem relative. As noted in the next section, this formal device mirrors one of the poem's themes. Digression, while potentially frustrating, should therefore be viewed as an essential device in Browning's decision to step back from the onrush of heroes and villains. He wants a psychological portrayal of the artistic temperament and its development and must, therefore, show reflective activity as it happens.

The use of ellipsis, the breaking off in the middle of sentences, further slows the action; this, coupled with the complexity and length of some other sentences, the extensive use of enjambment and strong caesuras, have led critics to suggest that some of the poem's difficulties and stylistic variety are the result of transforming an early version of the poem in blank verse into one in rhymed couplets. This reference to the earlier versions of the poem (there were three before the final one) helps explain the frequent confusion over whose consciousness is being depicted—Sordello's, the narrator's, or Browning's. The dreamlike atmosphere of the narration that results, joined to the rather esoteric historical knowledge demanded of the reader over such a lengthy poem, discourages many potential readers.

Despite these challenges, though, as the Victorian Edmund Gosse noted, the poem has "passages of melody and insight, fresh enough, surprising enough to form the whole stock-in-trade of a respectable poet." An effect Browning seems to desire in his use of colloquial diction and parenthetical expressions, one that he perfected later, is the sound of ordinary language despite the metrical straitjacket. The delineation of character that Browning would later perfect is certainly here in much of *Sordello*, as is the energetic description of locale. This "word-painting," Browning's great success at visualizing his events, would have been particularly appealing to his contemporaries—those, that is, who could get through the dense and allusive narration (another Victorian, Jane Carlyle, said she had read the poem cover to cover and could not decide whether Sordello was a person, a book, or a town; yet another, Douglas Jerrold, feared as he read it that he had lost his mind).

This reference to mind is actually of the greatest significance, since the greatest formal success of the poem is its early, pre-twentieth century experimentation with the representation of consciousness. The poetic devices that caused such confusion in the Victorian period and that continue to distress the casual reader are not far short of the fixation on the portrayal of mental states found in the works of James Joyce or Joseph Conrad.

Themes and Meanings

Sordello invites a political interpretation, since it is so heavily involved in the politics of the twelfth century. Viewed allegorically, it can be described as Browning's critique of the bourgeois class in England that considered itself liberal in its republican sentiments, while maintaining a political alliance with the aristocracy. In a note to a friend, however, Browning protested that the historical setting of Sordello was somewhat arbitrary and was simply a backdrop to a more immediate drama that was not notably political: "The historical decoration was purposely of no more importance than a background requires; and my stress lay on the incidents in the development of a soul." Though the setting is medieval, the ideas being discussed are very much of the nineteenth century, and they are more psychological than political.

To his interest in portraying a young poet's consciousness, Browning added the Victorian preoccupation with duty. On one hand, therefore, he follows the Romantic tradition of examining degrees of poetic inspiration in the types of poetry one may be called upon to write. On the other hand, considering the Romantic tradition of the isolation of the artist from society, Browning's spokesman becomes increasingly and emotionally preoccupied with the question of the role of a poet or of any artist in the political world.

Sordello, like the earlier *Paracelsus* (1835), offers Browning an opportunity to mull over the sort of poetry that he wants to craft and to confront the possibility that the higher the poetic aspiration, the greater the chance not only of perceived failure among his contemporaries, but also of genuine failure in the eyes of history. In book 1, he discusses two approaches to poetry. The first is a validation of the world and its manners, and the artistry that results from such an attitude is an imitation of that world. The second approach, the less popular path, seeks instead to better the world and to do so in an original and possibly misunderstood manner. Such an approach leads to a poetry that challenges the reader far more than may be welcomed.

Especially in book 5, Sordello discusses three types of poets, each important in his or her own way. First there appear epic poets who use individuals as allegorical representations of good and evil, and thereby teach a moral lesson. Then there are dramatic poets, who drop allegory for greater realistic representation; the moral judgment of the actions of their characters is left up to the reader. The third sort, the synthesist, deals with interior action and uses the physical only so far as necessary. Such a poet is a "Maker-see," and, as in the case of Sordello's homiletic intervention with Salinguerra, seeks to awaken others to their responsibilities to the rest of the world.

Briefly put, the question that Sordello comes gradually to ask is this: Beyond the personal satisfaction of successfully wooing a beautiful maiden or the acclaim attendant upon the success of a popular public poet, what sort of impact can and should a poet have in the rough world of wars, economics, and vengeance?

In this early poem the question of love, here the love of the Lady Palma, does not receive the complex psychological treatment that it does in later Browning poems. Already contained in *Sordello*, however, and blossoming into full flower in such later poems as "Andrea del Sarto," is the ancillary question of the inevitability, and possible benefit, of human fallibility in any committed activity in the world. For Browning, to have loved and lost seems, in some sense, even better than to have loved and *not* lost, and in *Sordello* there is already a clear preference for imperfection over perfection.

Sordello's sudden death in the midst of his crisis of conscience, and on the verge of what might have been a great political success, leads to a question that was already assuming great importance in Browning's mind. Beyond one's possible role as a poet, what would constitute a "successful" life? For someone such as Sordello, Browning's narrator suggests, success cannot take the form of political power. It must derive from the ethical force that leads others to act in responsible and generous ways. The true leader, as Sordello in some sense is, therefore serves as a prophet.

Especially if he is a poet, his real task is to embody a new consciousness, a new idea, that will someday take root in those more politically powerful; they, in turn, will change governments and all social structures that enslave. For the Browning of *Sordello*, therefore, the successful poet is not necessarily the one whose poetry is immediately accessible, beautiful, or even didactic. Sordello helped others see the conflict not only between Guelfs and Ghibellines but within each individual as well. That job accomplished, his brief life was a success.

John C. Hawley

SORTING, WRAPPING, PACKING, STUFFING

Author: James Schuyler (1923-1991)
Type of poem: Lyric
First published: 1969, in *Freely Espousing*

The Poem

"Sorting, wrapping, packing, stuffing" is a poem in free verse, its sixty-five lines divided into seven stanzas of varying lengths. The title strongly suggests the poem's method and tone by signifying busy activity, the four consecutive participles accumulating into a sense of hurry and culminating in a sense of fullness. The poem is written in the first person, yet the role of this person is not so much to reveal his character or emotions as to be the instigator and then the witness of the poem's events. He appears to the reader more as a performer than as a speaker.

"Sorting, wrapping, packing, stuffing" begins with a disorderly catalog of tacky domestic trivia, such as "dirty socks in dirty sneakers." The atmosphere is one of carelessness and transience; then this atmosphere is startlingly transformed by the ringing of a "great bronze bell." The sound elevates the tone of the poem to one of importance, of some unnamed crisis in which the soiled ephemera of the opening lines must be reassessed and sorted out. This emergency surprises the speaker in the midst of his own domestic trivia, just as he is making some instant coffee and a sandwich. Suddenly he is compelled to judge and to rank his belongings, to choose from among them those he will rescue from the still unnamed crisis. The madcap pressure of his situation is epitomized by what is apparently his most prized possession, "a blue fire escape": How can such an object be packed and, itself a means of rescue, be rescued? This pressure prompts the speaker to make avowals that are simultaneously tongue-in-cheek and profound, avowals that express the impregnability of the human heart even as they attest its ordinary materiality: "All there is/ is blood and thump."

Offering no transition, the speaker announces that it is now the next day and that the fire escape has somehow been successfully packed. There is no diminution of the crisis, however, because every next day is still a today, and every future eventually becomes a critical present, an ordinary but strident domestic situation of weeds and weather. The speaker considers the conventional escape of a trip to Florida, but chooses to remain in his city, there to dwell among the unexotic but irrepressible details of the life he apparently knows so well. This decision seems to elevate the status of everything in sight to a stellar level, and the speaker's life comes "unpacked," illuminated, as though his rubbish were the Milky Way or the northern lights.

This transformation is celebrated by a hurried sequence of nonsense exclamations punctuated by promises of further revelations. Abashed by the chaos, the speaker quickly calls a halt to the sequence, declaring that the "time is getting out of hand," a phrase that, in this case, is literally true. The poem concludes as it began, with a catalog, this time of imaginary books whose comic titles suggest the reconciliation of seriousness and absurdity, of imaginary and ordinary life, a reconciliation that, it is now obvious, has been the poem's purpose all along and that is affirmed by the closing words' declaration that "the world will fit."

Forms and Devices

A founder of the New York school of poetry (along with John Ashbery, Kenneth Koch, and Barbara Guest), James Schuyler expertly employs the most characteristic technique of that group: a verbal equivalent of the methods of such painters as Jackson Pollock and Franz Kline. As these painters treat their canvases as fields across which the paints move nonrepresentationally in unpremeditated patterns, so does Schuyler treat his page as a white expanse over which his words are free to group and regroup without being restricted to any conventional narrative or expressive plan. Schuyler trusts that words, having definitions, can never become meaningless, and so he literally finds his meaning in the actions of language—the sorting, wrapping, packing, stuffing of his title, for example. Schuyler desires for his words the freedom of stars, which can be imagined in countless changeable variations called constellations. This is perhaps the reason that his blue fire escape becomes a Milky Way when it is unpacked.

Schuyler's action technique does not signal a complete divorce from conventional poetic devices; it is instead a reanimation of those devices. Chief among these in "Sorting, wrapping, packing, stuffing" is the key metaphor of the "blue fire escape." Like Schuyler's words, it seems at first to be an object of use reduced to nonsense. What possible point is there in painting a fire escape blue? How could it get into someone's eye, much less be removed therefrom by a druggist? Most tellingly, how could it be packed and carried off in an emergency, only to be unpacked somewhere else? The answers to these questions provide much of the poem's meaning and prove that Schuyler's nonsense is really the elevation of the mundane to the level of true metaphor, since here a usually unregarded means of exit is transformed, by the poet's affectionate attention, into an entrance into new worlds of perception and understanding.

Schuyler's other principal poetic devices all participate in this process of transformation. The catalog was originally a convention of epic poetry, as in the catalog of ships found near the beginning of Homer's *Iliad* (c. 800 B.C.E.). Schuyler employs catalogs, such as the one that opens "Sorting, packing, wrapping, stuffing," in order to constellate ordinary or absurd articles into sudden clusters of meaning invested with the kind of dignity that accompanies meaning. His catalogs are more than lists; they are challenges to one's perception of one's own individual methods of sorting and categorizing in the creation of meaning, just as, upon viewing a Jackson Pollock painting, one is challenged to perceive a pattern in seemingly accidental drips and swirls of paint. In a similar device, Schuyler embeds these catalogs within the larger context of a continuously shifting poetic tone and vocabulary. His unexplained transitions from narrative to declamatory to nonsense language and then back again charge his poem's atmosphere with a busy energy that compels readers to keep their eyes constantly moving forward, their interpretive faculties constantly revising and so enlarging their understanding of the poem.

Themes and Meanings

As do all of Schuyler's best poems, "Sorting, wrapping, packing, stuffing" radiates an unselfconscious love for the world and all its minutiae. Its uniquely energized way of paying attention to its subject matter advocates the dignity of mere being. Schuyler's voice is one that rejoices in the transitory nature of things, the inevitable, unpredictable differences between one day and the next that so many other poets lament. Appearing frivolous at first, Schuyler's poems turn out to be meticulously, movingly faithful life studies of our extraordinary ordinary lives, studies in which it is a joy simply to say the names of things out loud.

For Schuyler, the acts of seeing and imagining are simultaneous, virtually identical in their purpose of recognizing the dignity of things and nature, recognizing, in keeping with this poem's title, that each object—stone or weed or article of soiled clothing—is a thing unto itself, larger in its reality than any abstract category in which we might wish to wrap and pack it. The stuff of life is just that—stuff. This stuff cannot be estranged from the human heart (itself a mundane reality of "blood and thump"), which so fervently and so mysteriously cherishes it. All dwell together in a time that is eternally the present. Schuyler rejects both nostalgia and anticipation as attitudes that subordinate the world to fixed interpretations, rejects them in favor of celebration, finding in those things that others commonly ignore—the fire escape that may be a galaxy, the "brown bat" droppings that may be a source of light and warmth—the literal material of the marvelous. In this eternal present, it is abject folly to seek to flee time and change as one might flee a New York winter by vacationing in Florida. Time and change accompany everyone everywhere, and so it is far better freely to accept and to choose change, as Schuyler chooses to "slip into this Ice Age remnant granite boulder," one of the many left behind by the glaciers in what is now New York's Central Park.

From the perspective that Schuyler's poem recommends, there can be no contradictions, no mutually exclusive options, for such things arise only from abstract principles of logic. Just as any two words may be typed beside each other, so any two objects may combine to form new landscapes of new meanings. This is the theme of Schuyler's closing booklist. *"The Great Divorce Has Been Annulled"* celebrates the end of paralyzing distinctions and definitions that shrink the world, a world that Schuyler's poem believes to be a perfect fit.

Donald Revell

SOURDOUGH MOUNTAIN LOOKOUT

Author: Philip Whalen (1923-   )
Type of poem: Meditation
First published: 1960, in *Like I Say*

The Poem
  "Sourdough Mountain Lookout" reflects on Philip Whalen's experience as a fire lookout in the Cascade Mountains in the western United States. The poem does not develop ideas or narrative in a linear fashion; instead, it wanders and loops in a manner that suggests the natural course of the thoughts of someone ruminating on experience. In his notes on poetics in *The New American Poetry 1945-1960* (1960), Whalen describes his poetry as "a picture or a graph of a mind moving, which is a world body being here and now which is history . . . and you." The title names the mountain where Whalen was a lookout in the summer of 1955. The poem is dedicated to Kenneth Rexroth, a poet of the generation before Whalen's. Rexroth influenced and encouraged the poets of the San Francisco Renaissance, including Whalen. Rexroth also helped make Chinese and Japanese poetry known in the West through his translations and essays. Since "Sourdough Mountain Lookout" makes a number of references to Buddhist and Asian topics and since Rexroth shared an interest in mountaineering, the dedication is quite appropriate.
  "Sourdough Mountain Lookout" has a loose, associational form. It is a series of more or less developed notations reflecting on Whalen's experience as a lookout. It divides into roughly forty verse paragraphs, including several that are only one line long. On a larger scale, the poem may be seen as divided into four sections of unequal length. These divisions are marked by quotations that set a tone for that section. The quotations are introduced by the source's name in capital letters. There are section quotations from the Greek philosophers Heraclitus and Empedocles and from the Buddha. Whalen quotes other figures as well, including his grandmother, eighteenth century English writer Samuel Johnson, and another Forest Service employee.
  The poem differs slightly in its published versions. In *On Bear's Head*, it has an epigraph from the ancient Chinese writer Tsung Ping that anticipates the tone of Whalen's poem as a meditative reflection on mountains. The epigraph does not appear in *Like I Say*. In *The New American Poetry 1945-1960*, the poem includes a transliteration of a Sanskrit mantra as well as Whalen's colloquial translation. The epigraph from Tsung Ping not only establishes a tone for the whole poem but also governs the first section. Whalen begins by stating that he always says he will not return to the mountains. This opening makes it clear that he is reflecting on his experiences as a lookout but that his perspective includes more than just that experience. In seven paragraphs, this first section establishes the feeling of being on the mountaintop. The details of fog, lakes, and animals establish the setting, with Whalen placed firmly within it: His "bootprints mingle with deer-foot" in "the dusty path to the

privy." Whalen assumes a very human and ordinary persona throughout the poem so that despite its concern with elevated topics, it never becomes ponderous or self-serious. Consistent with Whalen's general attitude in his poetry, "Sourdough Mountain Lookout" is playful and relaxed.

Forms and Devices

The language of "Sourdough Mountain Lookout" is colloquial and casual without being slack or unclear. Whalen uses colloquial American language much as a music composer such as Aaron Copland may use folk tunes for formal compositions; the spoken language becomes the medium for thought and perception that rise beyond the rather cloudy level of ordinary awareness. The first three lines set the tone and attitude for the remainder of the poem: "I always say I won't go back to the mountains/ I am too old and fat there are bugs mean mules/ And pancakes every morning of the world."

Whalen varies line length and paragraph length expressively. The longer lines include more poetic language:

> Morning fog in the southern gorge
> Gleaming foam restoring the old sea-level
> The lakes in two lights green soap and indigo
> The high cirque-lake black half-open eye

These lines describe the fog in the gorge with respect for what it is while still keeping in mind the process of change that is a major theme of the poem. The language is careful and exact without fancy effects. The only unusual term, "cirque," is chosen not for poetic effect but for geological accuracy. The poem's shorter lines are terse and tightly focused. A later passage of seven lines falls into a syllabic pattern. The first two and the last three lines have four syllables each, and the third and fourth lines have eight syllables, accommodating polysyllabic words: "There was a bird/ Lived in an egg/ And by ingenious chemistry/ Wrought molecules of albumen/ To beak and eye." This paragraph draws the reader's attention to the specifics of avian reproduction to express the theme of change. These two passages illustrate Whalen's skill in combining different types of diction in the same poem as well as his skill in writing in different modes. The quotations he includes extend the dictional range of the poem from the colloquialism of his father and grandmother to the aphorisms of the philosophers.

Whalen makes little use of metaphor or simile in the poem. The figurative language that he does use does not call attention to itself. An example is his description of the fossil of a palm frond as a "centipede shadow" and a "limestone lithograph." Generally, Whalen uses literal language but loads it with meaning. Toward the end of the poem, however, he uses an emphatic metaphor that extends into symbolism. The mountains surrounding him are a "circle of 108 beads." The description of the circle of beads is developed in detail. Whalen is referring to a string of *mala* beads used by both Hindus and Buddhists in meditation. As a string of prayer beads, the mountains acquire a specific meaning for Whalen as they become the means by which he meditates.

The next-to-last paragraph of the poem gives a colloquial American translation of the mantra of the Heart Sutra. A very brief Buddhist scripture, the Heart Sutra is an important text in Zen as well as in other Mahayana Buddhist schools. A translation more literal than Whalen's would read "gone, gone, gone beyond, gone all the way beyond, awareness, bliss." Its position at the very end of the poem suggests the mantra's importance to the poem's meaning.

Themes and Meanings

The style and structure of "Sourdough Mountain Lookout" not only reflect and express Whalen's Buddhist views but also express his way of thinking. Whalen speaks for himself in the poem as a witness to his experience. He clearly does not take himself seriously, a stance appropriate to any spiritually oriented poem and especially to a Buddhist poem. In the Buddhist view, the "self" is unreal, an aggregation of various elements. The quotation from the Buddha expresses this view: "All the constituents of being are/ Transitory." That being the case, the constituents of this poem are also transitory, as Whalen's loose, notational style suggests. He does not try to create a poem as an eternal monument to his experience; instead, his poem is a loose, tentative testimony to what is passing and ephemeral. About halfway through, Whalen suggests that like Buddha and Jesus, he is preaching on a mountain: "Flies & other insects come from miles around/ To listen" to Whalen tell them and the reader that all things are transitory. Whalen's awareness ranges from the very rocks of the mountains to the sun, from the flies that come to listen to him to the brontosaurus that has left fossils in the rocks. The sun flames in the background of the poem as the unavoidable fire that burns and transforms all things. In referring to Heraclitus, Whalen introduces a Western philosopher of change to match the Buddha's sense that all things are in flux. The second quotation from Heraclitus presents the world as a system of transformations that flow without ceasing.

In the first lines, Whalen says he is too "old and fat" to go up the mountain again. In the last two lines, he says that he has never left: " 'Four times up,/ Three times down.' I'm still on the mountain." He is still on the mountain because his experience of transcending the world of flux remains with him. The mantra that just precedes these lines expresses and engenders that experience. The Heart Sutra teaches that "form is emptiness, emptiness is form." Whalen implies that he has somehow incorporated that teaching and that it stays with him. Written about fifteen years before Whalen formally became a Zen Buddhist monk, "Sourdough Mountain Lookout" clearly expresses the Zen teaching that samsara, this world of change, is nirvana, the world of freedom.

Gene Doty

SOUTHERN CRESCENT

Author: Dave Smith (1942-   )
Type of poem: Lyric
First published: 1989; collected in *Cuba Night*, 1990

The Poem

Dave Smith's "Southern Crescent" is composed of five sections varying in length from twenty-nine to forty lines each; additionally, a six-line epigraph introduces the poem and appears before the numbered sections start. The poem is an amalgamation of elegiac, narrative, and lyrical poetry. The epigraph is in fact a quotation from a rail-road brochure dated 1891 and is an advertisement for the Crescent, a train whose route takes it from Washington, D.C., across the Potomac River and into the mountains of Virginia and other places to the south.

The poet-persona and his wife are traveling on this train in the wake of what appears to be the recent death of his father-in-law. The poem records descriptions of what the couple see from the train window and of their dialogue and thoughts. In so doing, it manifests a progress of their acceptance of the man's death, which has evidently occurred because of his uncontrolled alcoholism. It is the Christmas season, a matter which further enhances the setting.

In the first section the poet sets forth that he and his wife are on a passenger train leaving Washington and headed south. He gives more than one dozen images to paint the countryside (that is, the universe of the poem) as a dismal, empty, hopeless and endless place, one populated by people who reflect their environs. He speaks, for example, of "slimy mattresses, asylums of fires,/ disemboweled dolls, beercans" and claims that those who are here are those whom mainstream society has left behind.

The second part reveals that the poet's wife and father had been from Pennsylvania, where there is now an abandoned house, presumably because of the father-in-law's death. The speaker makes here one of the prime assertions of the poem: "How unreal/ death makes anything/ we know." This is antithetical to what is usually said of death, that it makes everything real or that it brings people back to reality. This point is further accented and made concrete when he notices that his wife's foot is on a cardboard box which "she put him in, the urn/ as unremarkable as garbage." Presumably, the cremated corpse does not provide reality of death for either the wife, the reader, or the speaker.

The middle section provides flashbacks to an episode in which the couple had made love while decorating the Christmas tree and while the wife's father was dying. It also refers to the funeral, at which the priest had indicated that the father-in-law, an alcoholic, had loved himself. The priest is suggesting that the dead has acted selfishly; then, the daughter and her husband reenact this same selfishness in their lovemaking.

A classical allusion to the River Styx occurs in the fourth section when the train crosses a river on its further descent into hell. Here the speaker sees things such as "a shack/ cluttered with life's junk" and an old man—something of a ghost of the father-in-law—gives him "his horny middle finger." Clearly, the point is that the father-in-law will haunt and control and work evil from death.

The concluding section continues with references to this old man "giving me the finger" as the speaker later tells of the event to his wife in a discussion about love. He is unable to make her understand the significance of the event, probably because he does not reveal that, in his mind, there is an explicit connection between the old man and her father.

Forms and Devices

The poem displays an amalgamation of several poetic forms. Ostensibly and primarily, it is lyrical in the sense that it works to create a singular impression and emotion; specifically, the subject is death. It also is something of an elegy in the sense that it is a tribute written to commemorate and meditate about the dead. Moreover, it contains characteristics of a formal ode since the various sections could be viewed as stanzas performing the functions of the chorus, strophe, antistrophe, and epode. Finally, it almost succeeds as a narrative poem because it is organized around the events of the poet and his wife as they travel.

The central metaphor of the poem derives from its title. The Southern Crescent is a train that becomes a vehicle carrying the poet and his wife into their descent into "hell" as they bury his wife's father. The terrain the train travels through is the ash heap of modern society, replete with "fields once/ green now the vomit/ of rust, wormy dog-bodies,/ spraycanned annunciations/ of glory in garbage that won't quit." As they cross the river, presumably the Potomac, they are greeted by a creature from hell who is somehow a cross between the devil and the dead father-in-law. His gesture signifies their continued damnation.

As in much modern poetry, the poet relies primarily on images to create and sustain his mood as well as to document his intended meaning. All the stanzas within the five major sections are rich in imagery. These images are interspliced with flashbacks, thoughts, conversation, the present action of the narrative, and authorial intrusions. Without exception, all the images are bleak, dismal, and hellish. They come mainly from that which is visible to the poet as he looks out the window of the train to study the landscape that is hell. In the opening lines of the poem—"The Crescent, silver as tinsel in vacant lots,/ pistons through dawn-glow/ and corrugated roofs ripped/ from rowhouses by the bums"—the poet makes use of everything visible to him from the train window, including not only physical objects such as houses but also the people themselves.

Themes and Meanings

While the central meaning of this poem is to be found in the poet's experiences with death, other matters are taken up as well. Specifically, the poet is concerned with the effects of his father-in-law's life upon his wife and upon their relationship. What are the residual effects of his alcoholism? The suggestion is that if his wife had not been able to achieve a successful relationship with her father, she cannot, now, accomplish one with her husband. They talk of love: "Like us/ He loved what/ he knew how to love." The point is that they do not know how to love each other, either. Hell, among other things, means an inability to love. The priest points out that he had lived "so long alone," but the poet and his wife are also alone, even though they are together.

How does one experience and deal with death in a world in which the ash heap of all social order is the only reality? The poet here, through his images, creates a world in which alienation and despair are the governors of human experience. These people consciously recall characters in T. S. Eliot's poems of wastelands. In a universe where life is meaningless, can death itself assume or provoke meaning? How does one descend into a kind of further, existential hell if one is in hell already? The husband and wife, like her father, realize that they cannot: "When I lean to kiss you/ I am full of words/ the dead have spoken." The poet entertains the idea that death in this land of "vacant lots," "slimy mattresses," and "disemboweled dolls" offers no more than the prospects of life in such attitudinal environs.

The reader may wonder why the devil is interchangeable with the ghost of the dead father-in-law, and why this devil-like character simply gives forth the "horny middle finger" instead of performing some sort of expected action of a figure from a classical hell. The suggestion is that the father-in-law is not dead—or, at least, it is for the poet to consider that this man's life will continue to interfere with a successful relationship between him and his wife. Finally, they are unable to communicate because of the shadows of the dead, alcoholic father-in-law. In the last section they attempt conversation; the poet tries to explain to his wife what he had seen and what it means (the man with the "horny middle finger"). Yet while he can utter the words, she cannot grasp their meaning. They are left alone not merely in a world where they do not experience love and meaning, but in a world where these things are impossible.

Carl Singleton

SPANISH IMAGE OF DEATH

Author: César Vallejo (1892-1938)
Type of poem: Lyric
First published: 1939, as "Imagen Española de la Muerte," in *España, aparta de mí este cáliz*; English translation collected in *Spain, Take This Cup from Me*, 1974

The Poem

In his "Spanish Image of Death," César Vallejo issues an unusual command: the command to call Death, the alien figure whose personification functions as the central metaphor of the poem. While it may be understood in one reading as a poem lamenting the horrors of war, more broadly the poem confronts a question that preoccupied Vallejo throughout his poetry: the question of the role of the poet. The battle against Death in the poem, then, becomes the battle of human passion—spearheaded by the poet—against extinction.

Death is foremost, as the title makes clear, an image, which even before the first line highlights the question of the poet's, the image-maker's, powers against her. The poem opens with the speaker, the poet, sighting Death as "she"—the first detail readers learn about Death is her femaleness—steps through Irun, a Basque town near the French-Spanish border which was ferociously attacked by Fascist troops in 1936. She presents a bizarre sight, certainly, with her long skinny legs making "accordion steps" and curses flowing constantly from her mouth, yet the speaker recognizes her instantly, and has apparently spoken of her before. He describes her with precision: "her meter of cloth that I've mentioned,/ her gram of that weight that I've not mentioned." This focus on what the poet has and has not mentioned again raises the question of his powers, which are the powers of witness and the immortalization, through poetry, of the witness's observations.

The tension between these two adversaries is heightened in the second stanza when readers learn that not only is the poet seeking Death, but also is Death seeking him, establishing this mutual seeking early on as the main spine of the poem. "Call her! Hurry! She is searching for me," he cries, insisting that one's only chance of defeating her is to beckon her willingly, gaining strength in the courage this action requires. It is not possible to deceive her, at least not permanently; she "well knows where [he] defeat[s] her,/ what [his] great trick is."

As the poem proceeds, this reciprocal searching continuing almost like a game, the poet takes comfort in asserting that Death is "not a Being," not the omnipotent entity she is traditionally conceived of as, but a simple, brief occurrence not superior to any other and not provoking "orbits or joyous canticles." Furthermore, she is worthy of assistance and may be chastised (her cursing suggests a moral transgression). By engaging her in these ways, the poet finds himself identifying with her: "by calling her . . ./ you help her . . ./ as, at times, I touch myself and don't feel myself." The final stanza reasserts, with renewed urgency, the poet's obligation to call to Death because his "tears for her must not be lost." He must seek her out before she can exhaust his passion; he must go willingly into his tomb before she can reveal the true impotence of his "great trick," namely, poetry.

Forms and Devices

"Spanish Image of Death" revolves around the personification of Death; as she becomes human she also becomes vulnerable. Her weaknesses lie, like the human's, in her contradictions. Her "audacious time" has little effect, resulting merely in an "imprecise penny," and she creates "despotic applause," to which she is, however, deaf. On one hand she is utterly ineffectual; on the other in her humanity she becomes doubly formidable, as the poet is forced to identify with her and she becomes capable of understanding him. The interaction with Death is portrayed in images of war; the poet locates himself "among the rifles" and "on the parapets" and asserts that Death must be followed "to the foot of the enemy tanks." Death easily enters these places, however; she cannot be stopped by the weapons of war. She does seem somehow thwarted by irrationalism, as she "walks exactly like a man"—strong, assured, rational—and "stops at the elastic gates of dream." Vallejo may be suggesting that irrationalism, or passion—for what is more rational than to abandon passion against the fact of one's mortality?—is the poet's greatest strength. The poet's task, then, becomes Vallejo's plea, to call to Death.

It is a horrible task, and Vallejo is painfully aware of its horror; hence the forceful tone of "Spanish Image of Death," with its every stanza punctuated by exclamation marks. Such an ardent tone is required to invoke such an irrational act, and one must not merely call Death, but call her "with fury." While Death seems to seek the individual speaker, who is referred to in the first person, the speaker rallies his listeners like a general rallying his troops. The spirit of camaraderie becomes one of the human's strengths against Death. "We," Vallejo insists, must follow her in unity, and he entreats both "comrade" and "lieutenant" to join him in the descent to the tomb.

The erratic structure and choppy rhythm of the poem further intensify the anxiety Vallejo wishes the reader to share in. The poem consists of seven stanzas containing from two to eleven lines of greatly varied lengths, from three to twelve words each. Vallejo also uses repetition in the poem, most often the repetition of his plea to "Call her!"—indicating the speaker's uncertainty that his listeners will obey. That there is a call issued to her, however, is clear when in the third stanza Death responds ("from hearing how we say: It's Death!"), and the importance of this response is stressed by repetition: "She shouted! She shouted! She shouted her born sensorial shout!" It is significant that Death is not indifferent to the speaker, because this endows the speaker with some power. She even plays the games that a temptress might play, when she "pretend[s] to pretend to ignore" the speaker. Here she resembles the poet's elusive muse, but Death is an ironic muse, whose aim is not to inspire but to smother.

Themes and Meanings

"Spanish Image of Death," collected with fourteen other poems in *España, aparta de mí este cáliz*, presented by Vallejo as poems about the Spanish Civil War, seems also to be principally about the war. The title and the reference to Irun, the town devastated by the war, nationalize the death which is the focus of the poem, and war images form a majority of the poem's imagery. However, earlier versions of the poem lacked any references to war, and some critics have come to believe that it was written earlier than the outbreak of the Civil War and that Vallejo added the war references in order to work it into the fabric of the *España* collection.

Regardless, with Vallejo the Spanish Civil War, and any war, is much more than a political event; it is suffering and death and dismemberment ("global enigmatic fractions [that] hurt, pierce") of the unity he so values. With this in mind, the poem becomes an expression of Vallejo's compassion for humankind far wider than the specific political issues at hand. The poet-speaker, then, embodies both the individual human and the soldier—Vallejo would count both as members of humankind—who either defended or attacked Irun.

The battle described in "Spanish Image of Death" may be the battle of the Spanish Republicans against the Fascists, but it is also the battle of life against death, of creativity against stagnation, of courage against fear as well as the attempt on the part of the poet not to uphold one over the other, but to fuse them. When the poet admits that "at times, I touch myself and don't feel myself," he is acknowledging his inability to become whole, the stubborn separateness of his body and spirit.

The solution, Vallejo maintains, is unification through passion. By calling with tears and fury to Death (Vallejo also makes allusion to the Spanish secular tradition of engaging in dialogue with Death) and not attempting to hide from her, the poet embraces the fullness of the life-death cycle. Not only this, but the poet must approach Death with an intense awareness of his body: "From her smell up, oh god my dust . . ./ From her pus up, oh god my ferule." In so doing, he embraces the body for precisely what it is—dust and iron—and through this courage may gain the power to fuse it with his soul, or at least to find out if such fusion is possible.

Finally, in experiencing "Spanish Image of Death," one of Vallejo's greatest and most stirring poems, it should be remembered through whose eyes Death is observed: the poet's, the martyr-witness, who resists Death with his power to immortalize through words. Whether this power is a worthy rival, Vallejo does not conclude; instead his challenge to the poet is to find the answer, for if resurrection is ever to occur, death is necessary.

Tasha C. Haas

THE SPANISH TRILOGY

Author: Rainer Maria Rilke (1875-1926)
Type of poem: Lyric
First published: 1927, as "Die Spanische Trilogie," in *Gesammelte Werke*; English
translation collected in *Poems, 1906 to 1926*, 1957

The Poem

Rainer Maria Rilke wrote "The Spanish Trilogy" in Ronda, Spain, between January 6 and 14, 1913. He had seen El Greco's dramatic painting of Toledo in 1911 and made the trip to Spain to see the landscape. The opening lines of the poem capture his great enthusiasm for the rugged countryside, which is full of movement and charged with portent on a windy night. Rilke's engrossment in the landscape is reflected structurally in the complex, long first sentence of the poem, which spans all twenty-four lines of part 1. Its repeated prepositional phrases beginning with "from" convey a sense of involvement in an active, synthetic process, the purpose of which is revealed in an infinitive clause without subject: "to make one Thing." Something is happening to the poet. In a moment of heightened awareness, he becomes one with his surroundings. His impassioned language, "Lord Lord Lord," reveals his rush of ecstacy. His clever closing simile, comparing the "Thing" with a meteor, emphasizes the speed and significance of the occurrence.

Part 1 is written in a rhythmic iambic pentameter without rhyme. In the original German, all lines have a masculine ending except for the last line, whose extra, unaccented syllable gives a sense of graceful completion to the last word: "arrival." Part 2 is, by comparison, more introspective, more involved in the human condition. Its twenty-two lines are divided into three stanzas. The poet has been in the presence of the extraordinary, which he must accept with imperfect understanding. Rilke managed to write all of part 1 without naming a subject. Now, in part 2, he humorously likens himself to a servant who does not dare to ask, "Master, why this banquet?" He makes the same point more seriously in the second and third stanzas, choosing the likeness of a shepherd. The man is necessarily so alert and so observant that he is bombarded with "world": He has "world each time he lifts his head;/ each time he looks down—world." Again the repetition of a word, in this case "world," lends an emotional element to the description.

Part 3 returns to the first-person point of view and relaxes the metric scheme. Its twenty-one lines of free verse sound more like conversational commentary. The poet is resolving to use his memory of the shepherd to his advantage when he returns to the city of Paris, France. At the end of the poem, Rilke resorts to a more pastoral, idealized picture of the shepherd, even describing him as majestic and godlike. The four-line coda at the end of the poem explains that the image Rilke retains of the shepherd is, for him, a means of accessing inner peace, of returning to a most meaningful experience, a moment of oneness with the universe that was so intense he would happily have died afterward.

Forms and Devices

Since the three parts of "The Spanish Trilogy" are different in tone and content, Rilke relies on structural similarities to unify the poem. Each of the three parts begins with anaphora. In part 1, lines 1, 3, and 5 proceed from the same preposition: "From this cloud," "from these dark clustered hills," and "from this stream in the valley." Lines 2, 4, and 6 complement that with epistrophe, all ending with "(and from me)." Rilke has introduced the two main components, the landscape and the poet, from the left and the right and uses the rest of the stanza to combine them. In part 2, the first two stanzas begin with the identical rhetorical question "Why must a man." In part 3, Rilke uses the repetition of "Let me" at the beginning of lines 1 and 4 to lead in the poet's resolution. The anaphora at the beginning of each part of the trilogy helps to underline the sequence of the parts. First the poet has an extraordinary experience, then he has a period of questioning, and finally he decides his further course of action.

Rilke provides the reader with a wealth of images in the course of the poem. The image of the shepherd is given extended treatment in parts 2 and 3 and can also be inferred in part 1 from the mention of the flock. Yet Rilke cautions, in the coda, against seeking hidden meaning in the figure of the shepherd: "Let him be whomever you wish." He is interchangeable, simply a means to an end. The poet is not so much interested in the shepherd as in the elements and forces in the midst of which he appears: night and day, the earth and sky, old age and youth, this world and the next; in short, the universe in its totality. The "Thing" of part 1 is both "earthly and cosmic." In part 2, the shepherd takes "all the galaxies/ into his face." In part 3, he is "like the day itself" with space thinking for him. These are grandiose, mind-expanding images.

In "The Spanish Trilogy," Rilke is dealing with something very real but at the same time elusive. It can only be indicated as an abstract "Thing" or approximated through analogous descriptions. Rilke ends each stanza with a striking simile. The position of the similes provides structural unity, and each of them makes the meaning more precise. For example, the simile at the end of part 1 that compares the "Thing" to a meteor shows the substantial becoming insubstantial. It emphasizes the transitory nature of the experience and its subsequent inaccessibility while leaving no doubt in the reader's mind about the actual event. The image used in the final simile of the poem is scaled down considerably from that of the first. For the poet, evoking the memory of his Spanish experience has the same stabilizing effect as placing a stormlamp around a fluttering candle. This is the fire of the meteor in more manageable form. Implicit in the simile are elements of volition and control, of quiet domesticity, duration, and fulfilment. The poet has come a long way in the course of the poem.

Themes and Meanings

Rilke was in his late thirties when he wrote "The Spanish Trilogy." In 1910, he completed his novel *Die Aufzeichnungen des Malte Laurids Brigge* (*The Notebooks of*

Malte Laurids Brigge, 1930), felt exhausted, and wondered whether he could continue writing. Another major project, *Duineser Elegien* (1923; *The Duino Elegies*, 1930), was also proving more difficult than expected, and, at the time of his trip to Spain, Rilke was entertaining alternative career plans. For this reason, some critics have interpreted "The Spanish Trilogy" as dealing specifically with the "processes of poetry, as Rilke experienced them," as a three-stage description of the creative process: First, poets have an intense experience; second, they struggle with the materials of that experience; and third, they feel the satisfaction of successfully converting the essence of the experience into a permanent form, a poem that effectively communicates their sensations and perceptions to others. While this approach is too narrow to do justice to the entire poem, it does have merit. Rilke had written a short prose piece a year earlier titled "über den Dichter" (about the poet), in which he describes a situation that presented itself as an allegory for the role of the poet. Sailors rowing a becalmed boat upstream are energized when a man standing at the bow bursts into song. His voice connects them with the distant goal that only he can see. The poet, for Rilke, is the person who can make that connection and convey that vision to others. If this insight is applied to "The Spanish Trilogy," the poet is the person who, in the turmoil of the big city, can recall the calm of a pastoral scene. People who are not poets also calm themselves through recourse to special memories, and this is what Rilke is recommending. He does not expect that his experience of the shepherd will have a similar effect on others, but he does suppose that others have their own significant sources of peace and harmony: "Let him be whomever you wish."

The last lines of the poem, which must be included in any comprehensive interpretation, go far beyond any comment on writing. They place Rilke's Spanish experience in the order of the ultimate considerations of life and death: "May death/ more easily find its way." In Ronda, Rilke felt extraordinarily at one with the world. A few weeks after writing "The Spanish Trilogy," he wrote "Erlebnis" (experience) 1 and 2, prose pieces that also describe states of unusually heightened awareness. He remembers how, in a garden by the sea, he felt the subtle vibrations of the life force itself in a tree trunk and how the blue of a periwinkle was of inexhaustible significance. A bird call was simultaneously outside and within him. Once privy to this transcendent state, he had a new perspective on everyday life since he had, in a sense, overcome its restrictions. "The Spanish Trilogy" is written with the knowledge of universal harmony. Having glimpsed the massive forces that contain life and death, the poet quietly accepts their sovereignty.

Jean M. Snook

SPARROW HILLS

Author: Boris Pasternak (1890-1960)
Type of poem: Lyric
First published: 1922, as "Vorob'evy gory," in *Sestra moia zhizn': Leto 1917 goda*; English translation collected in *Selected Poems*, 1983

The Poem

"Sparrow Hills" is a lyric poem consisting of five stanzas of conventional quatrains, with the regular rhyming scheme *abab*. The title refers to a hilly section of Moscow situated on a bend of the Moscow River. At the time of the writing of this poem (1917), Sparrow Hills was an area on the edge of Moscow, but now it is completely inside the city limits, near Moscow University. The poem is written in the first person, with Boris Pasternak addressing directly either the reader or himself, now describing the scenery, now expressing his thoughts and feelings or giving a friendly suggestion, even a warning. The poem is set in the summer, which is especially luxuriant in both the open and the wooded countryside. The persona begins by exhorting the unknown listener or reader to submit himself to the charms of nature, to let his breast be kissed as if "under a tap," for the summer will not always be so gallant and one will not be able to dance to accordion music night after night.

In stanza 2, the poet suddenly switches to musing about old age, saying that he has heard all kinds of terrible prophecies about it—"no face in the grass,/ No heart in the ponds, no God in the trees." There will be nothing in old age to inspire one toward the stars. After he has conditioned the reader with this mild warning, in the third stanza the poet exhorts him all the more to liven up and partake of this beauty. "Where are your eyes?" he asks good-naturedly. The poet's goal seems to be to convince his reader to look around and to realize that the world is at the high noon of its development and that clouds, heat, woodpeckers, pine needles, and pinecones can all inspire elevated thoughts and gentle feelings.

In the fourth stanza, the poet reinforces the pastoral charm of the scenery. The rails of the streetcars end here simply because they can go no farther, for beyond that line is a holiday atmosphere; the glade rolls on, grass hugging the branches.

In the final stanza, the poet allows nature itself to tell the reader that the world is always this accessible—one need merely ask the thicket, the fields, and the clouds pouring down transfigured light on the people in their summer clothes. The poem ends on a very positive, invigorating note, just as it has begun. Its message has been delivered, and the reader's prospects of heeding it are hoped to be improved.

Forms and Devices

In a poem centered almost entirely on nature, it is not surprising that "Sparrow Hills" abounds in nature images, representing the main device used here by Pasternak. The images are reinforced by metaphors carefully selected to fit the atmosphere of the poem.

It is also not surprising that, since the poem takes place in the summer heat, most of the images should be connected with water as the source of the most satisfying relief. In the very first line, Pasternak uses the metaphor of a breast being soothed by the kisses of invisible rain, as if under a tap. Further images centering on the refreshing effect of water follow. When the poet exhorts the soul to come to life, he wants it to bubble up in foam, and when clouds, woodpeckers, pine needles, and pinecones are called on to display their "Sunday best," they cluster in fleecy sprays, inspiring creative thoughts. In the final verse, the poet also hails the soothing power of water in the form of light that descends from the clouds like vapor.

Auditory images are also abundant, as if to underscore the teeming, seething nature of a hot summer. The summer "bubbles up," everything is astir, and the thoughts evoked by the summer scenery are effervescent. The sound images complement the sight images and vice versa.

Other images deal with spatial delineation between the two worlds—that of the city and that of nature. As revealed in the first three stanzas, the poet emphasizes through water images the beneficial aspects of nature providing relief in the summer heat. Next, he turns to the city by way of the metaphor of the rails stopping at the foot of Sparrow Hills. There is no place for them beyond that point. From there on, it is the pines, the clearings, the holiday spirit as expressed metaphorically by the word "Sunday."

By constantly shifting his focus between nature and humankind and by combining complementary images and metaphors, Pasternak achieves a certain unity of purpose and creates a compact, well-defined poem.

Themes and Meanings

"Sparrow Hills" is a lyric apotheosis of the beauties of nature. Pasternak wrote numerous poems extolling nature, including the other poems in the same collection *Sestra moia zhizn (My Sister, Life,* 1959), but this poem is among his best, if not the best, in that respect. Some of his most powerful images are to be found in "Sparrow Hills."

For Pasternak, nature represents the best things that life has to offer. It has a soothing and healing power that is there for the taking. Even the frightening specter of approaching old age cannot diminish the beneficial power of nature, as illustrated by the poet's dismissal of the "terrible prophecies" concerning old age. All one has to do is to be attentive to the signals coming from nature, and the vital forces in man will be released.

Yet Pasternak is not merely praising the beauties of nature. He is also warning humankind not to be so blind, as, for example, when he asks rhetorically, "Where are your eyes?" The veiled warning of the potential for incalculable loss is contained in the final stanza, where he bestows on nature the power to light up the whole world (metaphorized by "noon"), all holidays ("Whitsunday"), and all motion ("walks"), all of which can be lost if humankind is indifferent or abusive. Life has always been like that, and nothing will ever change it. The woods know it, the clearings know it, the clouds know it—only human beings seem to be blind to it. They can ignore nature, however, only at their own risk: the risk of the loss of vital energy and of the very reason for their existence.

In reality, the poet is addressing himself, hinting at his own negligence of the vital link with nature. As a creative artist, he can gain much more than others from an intense commitment to all reality, when, in the words of Rimvydas Silbajoris, the heat of the poet's passion melts down the barriers between different categories of phenomena. Therefore, nature, as the depository of these phenomena, represents the best source of creative power, and thus the summer heat and the heat of creation are used by Pasternak as similes.

"Sparrow Hills" was written in the summer of 1917, a few months before the October revolution. Although Pasternak probably was not predicting it, the disintegration of the country and of the fabric of Russian life was already in progress, having started with World War I and continued with the revolution of February, 1917. People were in danger of losing their spiritual compass and of forgetting the basic values that had nourished them so far. Until then, the Russians had been known to be in uncommonly close contact with nature, especially because the vast majority of them lived in rural areas. Seen from that perspective, "Sparrow Hills" seems to express the poet's plea to his countrymen—and to himself—to revert to communing with nature, as they had done for centuries.

Seen within the entire opus of Pasternak, especially when complemented by the poems of *Doctor Zhivago*, in which nature also plays a decisive role, "Sparrow Hills" fits into the large mosaic of Pasternak's poetry as a shining and important tessera.

Vasa D. Mihailovich

SPEAK

Author: James Wright (1927-1980)
Type of poem: Lyric
First published: 1968, in *Shall We Gather at the River*

The Poem

James Wright's poem "Speak" is a lyric lament in five rhyming stanzas. Wright combines a common, colloquial language with an Old Testament rhetoric to describe, through contemporary, personal examples, the state of a lost world. The poem also stands as an imperative plea to the God who is the "you" of the poem to reveal himself. The speaker says, "I have gone every place/ Asking for you."

Part of the pleasure and the success of the poem depends on the reader not knowing at the beginning that the poem is an address to God. The first stanza begins with the speaker in search of someone, to whom his words are addressed, and he is worried about the consequences of his search. "Wondering where to turn/ And how the search would end." The stanza's last image is one of foreboding: "And the last streetlight spin/ Above me blind." In those moments at the end of his quest, will he have fallen, blind and defeated, or will blindness bring vision?

Stanza 2 answers that question. What the speaker has sought has not been found, and there has been no revelation. The speaker has returned from his search with an earned wisdom, but it is of a world where the reality is one of heroes cast down and battles lost. He refers first to a May, 1965, heavyweight title fight lost by the reigning champion, Sonny Liston. "Liston dives in the tank/ Lord, in Lewiston, Maine." His other example is of Ernie Doty "drunk/ In hell again." Although the poem does not say so, the poet has explained (in reference to this poem and others in which Doty appears) that Doty was a distant family friend; he was convicted and then executed for rape and murder.

Stanza 3, in emotional language, moves readers forward to yet a third example of someone whose life is an emblem of failure: "And Jenny, oh my Jenny/ Whom I love." Because one is told that the speaker has developed this intimacy, her failure proves to be the most shocking. The promise of redeeming love has failed her, or she has rejected it, living as a prostitute and even abandoning her own child "In a bus-station can." She seems to suffer no remorse, as she "sprightly dance[s] away/ Through Jacksontown."

As stanza 4 begins, the speaker places himself inside this blighted urban landscape. He too has been one of the failed, one of the transgressors, who "got picked up/ A few shrunk years ago/ By a good cop." He speaks now with an ironic detachment: "Believe it, Lord, or not." By including himself among the damned, and being able to joke about it, he offers at least a momentary way of confronting the pain. The speaker modifies and expands the scope of his ability and perhaps his responsibility: "I speak of flat defeat/ In a flat voice." The last stanza provides a summary and a slight shift of focus. The speaker and the poem have moved beyond explanation and examples. The voice becomes pure lamentation, almost accusation.

Forms and Devices

The sense of the speaker measuring his experience and his argument adds an important quality to the poem's success. The form of the poem contributes to this effect. It is written in accentual-syllabic meter, with an iambic base meter. The eight-line stanzas are rhymed *ababcdcd*, with the fourth and eighth lines as two-beat lines and the others as three-beat lines. Since the fourth line of each stanza is also end-stopped, each stanza seems to be made up of two quatrains. The voice, then, seems carefully paced, holding to a middle ground that could be called "flat."

The slant rhyme also plays its part in the overall design. John Frederick Nims, in his widely used *Western Wind: An Introduction to Poetry* (1974), describes the effect as like that of a flatted "blue note" in music, one that expresses a modified and controlled sadness. Against this norm, the poem's moments of runaway emotion stand out. An important example comes in stanza 3, when the speaker is describing Jenny, a lost soul whom he loves: "And Jenny, oh my Jenny/ Whom I love, rhyme be damned." The poet not only allows the second line of the stanza to expand to four beats but also follows through on his promise by dropping the expected *b* rhyme in line 4, matching "damned" with "old."

Along with the metrical and rhyming skill with which Wright crafts the poem, one can locate its success in the blended rhetorical voices. Wright combines an elegant Old Testament language with a tough, contemporary jargon. He borrows directly from the texts of Ecclesiastes ("And saw under the sun/ The race not to the swift/ Nor the battle won") and Psalms ("Lord, I have loved Thy Cursed,/ The beauty of Thy house"), changing them only slightly to fit his needs. He moves from the slang voice of "Liston dives in the tank" to the odd nursery-song rhythms of Jenny's tragic story: "She left her new baby/ In a bus-station can,/ And sprightly danced away/ Through Jacksontown." The voice of stanza 4, in its humor and plain diction, approaches the sound of pop music or perhaps slapstick:

> Which is a place I know,
> One where I got picked up
> A few shrunk years ago
> By a good cop.
> Believe it, Lord, or not.

In a poem titled "Speak," this variety and richness of voices reflects the speaker's shifting emotions and needs. Instead of preparing "a face to meet the faces that you meet," as did T. S. Eliot's Prufrock, Wright's character in this poem matches the voice to describe his psychic and spiritual challenges.

One of the poem's strategies—suspense—is more conventionally found in fiction, but Wright uses it with success here. Often Wright's poems offer the reader a clear understanding at the outset of the setting and what the story will be about. "Sitting in a

Small Screenhouse on a Summer Morning" is a good example. In "Speak," the reader overhears the speaker's complaint, directed toward a "you," but is not told who that "you" is. One then reads on, hoping to discover both the identity of the "you" and the nature of the quarrel. When the playful use of "Lord" as a mild and appropriate expletive in the early stanzas gives way, at the end, to the direct invocation of God, the reader more clearly understands the speaker's Job-like cry for a voice, for God to "speak." Only through such a manifestation could the speaker grow beyond the "flat defeat" to which he has become a witness.

Themes and Meanings

"Speak" might be fairly considered Wright's *ars poetica*, a creative expression of his philosophy of poetic form and theory. It contains the central themes and approaches regularly found in his work: the outcast and tragic characters who are so often his subject; the search for meaning and redemption inside a blighted landscape; and the poet's role within this world, as he or she tries to find a commensurate language and emotion to at least face if not overcome its challenges. Wright, like many of the poets influenced by the new critical style of the 1940's and 1950's, knew how to use the accentual-syllabic tradition to write lyric poetry of love and inevitable loss.

He also knew that the world he had grown up in—filled with factories, poverty, pollution, and the people of industrial river towns—deserved its place within the body of English poetry. He would be the people's champion, speaking in a "flat voice" of what would often be their wasted lives, their "flat defeat." In talking about them, he raised them up as tragic heroes.

Like the romantics before him, Wright affirms what is ultimately good within each person. One critic described Wright's work as a clash between a "romantic's world vision and a classicist's aesthetics." What makes this poem and the body of Wright's poetry worthy of careful attention has its roots in this clash. In elegant, lovely, and compassionate language the poet asks the reader to identify with, and thus understand more completely, the failures of a modern world. By doing so people might come to a deeper understanding of themselves.

Michael Burns

SPEAK, PARROT

Author: John Skelton (c.1460-1529)
Type of poem: Satire
First published: 1545, as "Speke, Parrot," in *Here after foloweth certayne bokes cöpyled*; collected in *John Skelton: The Complete English Poems*, 1983

The Poem

"Speak, Parrot" has been regarded as John Skelton's masterpiece, a brilliant tour de force which links his strong sense of moralism, keen observations of contemporary court and political events, and his extraordinary poetic talents. It is a long poem, over 520 full or partial lines in its definitive modern edition. While it is written largely in blocks of seven-line stanzas with a consistent *ababbee* rhyme pattern, it is also interspersed with various other line lengths and rhyme patterns, and it includes snatches of dialogue, much of it in languages other than English.

"Speak, Parrot" is typical of much of Skelton's work. It is a commentary on public events that would have primarily interested the court of Henry VIII but also would have had wider political implications. As court poet (essentially the same as the modern poet laureate) Skelton would have been expected to produce such works. In addition, the poem carries a strongly moralizing element, which again is characteristic of Skelton's verses. The combination of the two threads produced a rich, densely compact poem presented in a brilliant but sometimes enigmatic style.

The poem is one of Skelton's most difficult to understand, not only because of its vocabulary and organization but also because it is an extended allegory, many of whose meanings and references are presented in veiled imagery that would have been familiar to a limited number of persons at the time the poem was written and that has become fainter over the years. Still, the work retains a vigorous sense of form and meaning that makes it accessible to the modern reader.

In large part a political satire on life and affairs in the court of the English king Henry VIII, the poem takes as its central target Cardinal Thomas Wolsey, Henry VIII's most important minister. However, a number of other topics, including new ways of teaching Latin in English universities and the moral decay of the times, are included. Because of this range of subjects, and because "Speak, Parrot" has a structural pattern that, like its language, is rather freely and loosely assembled, the work has been termed a "gallimaufry," or confused medley. With "Speak, Parrot," this is literally true, since the poem presents several different rhyming and rhythmic patterns as well as shifting from English to Latin with sometimes bewildering frequency.

However, this seeming confusion is deliberately manipulated by Skelton to suit his satirical purpose. Because of the open nature of the poem, it can address any subject freely and move from one to another without bothering with strictly logical consistency. Because of its hidden and allegorical nature, it can suggest and imply more than it openly states.

The "Parrot" of the title is the narrator of the poem and may be identified with Skelton. Within the poem, as a "byrde of Paradyse," Parrot is a special pet of the ladies at the court, who beg him to speak to them: " Speke, Parott, I pray yow,' full curteslye they sey,/ Parott ys a goodlye byrde and a pratye popagay'" [prattling popinjay]. As a prattling popinjay, or chatterbox, Parrot is given leave to speak freely, much in the tradition of court jesters or royal fools, and he takes full advantage of this, especially in his attacks on Cardinal Wolsey.

The poem moves from the general to the particular. Its early stanzas set the context, placing Parrot in the court of Henry VIII and Catherine of Aragon, then still Henry's wife. Parrot is established not only as witty but also as learned: He knows a number of languages, including Latin, Hebrew, and Chaldean (the languages of the "New Learning," or Renaissance) as well as Dutch, French, and Spanish (the languages of contemporary diplomacy). In addition, in the poem Skelton has Parrot imitate Scots and Irish accents. As Parrot modestly remarks, his mistress Dame Philology gave him the gift "to lerne all langage and hyt to speke aptlye."

Having confirmed his linguistic abilities, Parrot uses them to paint a picture of contemporary abuses—the most important of the traditional roles of satire. He attacks the new method of teaching in English schools, especially Oxford and Cambridge Universities, where Greek is displacing the traditional Latin, and Latin itself is taught in a fashion that makes it less useful than before. On one hand, Skelton is defending the old order, while on the other he is covertly attacking Cardinal Wolsey, who openly supported the New Learning, especially the teaching of Greek. Having finished with this pedagogic matter, Skeleton has Parrot signify a change in subject by presenting his version of "My proper Besse," a popular song of the period which had both an amorous and a moralistic meaning: It could be interpreted either as a lover's carnal desire for his beloved or the soul's longing for God.

Skelton then shifts the poem again, giving Parrot a series of envois in which he comments again on contemporary events, especially Wolsey's diplomatic mission to France and Belgium during 1521. These attacks finished, the poem concludes with Parrot, in highly rhetorical and mannered language, railing against the abuses and excesses of the times, including those in the royal court, the church, and contemporary English life.

Forms and Devices

Like so many Tudor and early Elizabethan poets, John Skelton made highly conscious and conspicuous use of rhetorical techniques and devices. These are central points of "Speak, Parrot," as are the frequent Latin phrases and quotations which would have been easily read and quite familiar to his courtly readers.

The basic structure for most of the poem is a seven-line stanza, with a steady but varying meter that is not quite iambic pentameter but which provides a sense of order and regularity. It is against this sense of order that Skelton places what he, as a moralist and satirist, sees as the disorder of the world: the decline of learning in the universities, abuses of the clergy in the church, and, above all, the inordinate power and malign influence of Cardinal Wolsey over the court and the entire kingdom.

The three most noticeable rhetorical devices throughout "Speak, Parrot" are alliteration, anaphora, and antithesis. They bring artistic variety to the poem and help underscore its themes and meanings. The first, alliteration, appears early, in line 3 of the poem, when Parrot describes himself as "Deyntely dyetyd with dyvers delycate spyce." It is found throughout the work, as in line 60, where Parrot notes that "Melchisedeck mercyfull made Moloc mercyles," as well as near the end of the poem, in line 357, when one reads, "Go, propyr Parotte, my popagay."

Anaphora is similar to alliteration. The latter is the repetition of a sound within a line, while the former is the repetition of a word or words at the beginning of successive lines or phrases. This device is used throughout the poem but is generally limited, as in lines 205 through 207, which follow the same format: "Parrot is no pendugum," "Parrot is no woodecocke," "Parrot is no stamerying stare." However, as the poem approaches its climax and Skelton wishes to underscore the work's satiric content, he uses a highly anaphoric pattern to present and emphasize his message:

> So many morall maters, and so lytell usyed;
> So myche newe makying, and so madd tyme spente;
> So myche translacion into Englyshe confused;
> So myche nobyll prechying, and so lytell amendment.

This is the pattern—constantly recycling the same limited set of words to introduce lines and phrases—for the final ten full stanzas of "Speak, Parrot." It presents the culmination of Skelton's argument to the reader in a fashion that is both powerful and memorable.

The impact is increased because the anaphora is frequently found with another rhetorical device, that of antithesis, in which two contrasting ideas are linked by being presented in similar grammatical and syntactic form. Thus, in the example above, "So many morall maters" is both joined to and contrasted with "so lytell usyed," as "So myche newe makying" parallels "so madd tyme spente." Antithesis allows Skelton to set the positive and negative aspects of contemporary life side by side, emphasizing how people should behave as opposed to how they actually act. The rhetorical pattern reinforces the moral meaning and the use of anaphora, with its insistent repetition, further strengthens the lesson that Skelton, through Parrot, is teaching his reader.

Finally, Skelton makes skillful use of languages other than English, but none more so than Latin. The second—sometimes first—language of any educated person during this period, Latin was regarded as the tongue for knowledge and artistry—although, as "Speak, Parrot" itself notes (and to some extent laments), Greek was quickly becoming a respectable rival.

Because of this universal knowledge of Latin among his readers, Skelton could lace his poem with Latin throughout, beginning with the opening epigraph, which can be translated, "The present book will grow greatly while I am alive; thence will the golden reputation of Skelton be proclaimed." In other words, Skelton is staking out a bold claim for himself and his work: It will last, and the poet will long be remembered. This is a familiar conceit in European poetry, its most memorable statement was by the Roman poet Horace, echoed in William Shakespeare's Sonnet 55: "Not marble, nor the gilded monuments/ Of princes, shall outlive this powerful rhyme."

Skelton closes his poem with another Latin epigraph, which is a slight variant of his opening lines. Now it is Parrot himself, rather than the book, which will live and preserve Skelton's memory and message. Parrot, the created character who points out abuses and condemns them, will ensure the fame of "Skelton Lawryat/ Orator Regius" (Skelton the poet laureate, orator of the king).

Themes and Meanings

Although "Speak, Parrot" is one of Skelton's greatest poems (perhaps his masterpiece, according to a number of scholars) it is a difficult poem to read and understand. Its themes are masked by its allegorical method, which hints at but does not always openly disclose its references. In addition, Skelton's languages (since he includes a goodly portion of Latin, French, and other tongues) can be difficult, even obscure.

There are valid reasons for this difficulty, chief among them the fact that "Speak, Parrot" is a poetic satire—an attack on what Skelton felt to be the follies and abuses of the times. Specifically, he is concerned with the state of education in English universities, the conduct of the court of Henry VIII, and the position and activities of Thomas Wolsey, cardinal of the Catholic Church and Lord Chancellor of England, about whom he is particularly vehement.

Skelton was closely connected with the higher education of his day. A graduate of Oxford, he had served as both court poet and as tutor to Prince Henry, who later became king, and in 1512 he was appointed *orator regius* (orator of the king). He was recognized with a number of honorary academic degrees, or "laureated," by colleges and universities in England and in Europe. In all these areas he was greatly concerned with the education of the rising generation, especially in Latin, which was still the universal language of any educated person. In "Speak, Parrot" Skelton attacks the new fashion of favoring Greek over Latin:

> In Achademia Parrot dare no probleme kepe,
> For *Greci fari* [Greek] so occupyeth the chayre,
> That *Latinum fari* [Latin] may fall to rest and slepe.

Parrot goes on to state his fear that in addition to supplanting Latin, Greek studies will replace the "Tryvyals and quatryvyals" (the Trivium and Quadrivium, the traditional "seven liberal arts"), which had been the basis of European learning since the early Middle Ages. Skelton, through Parrot, takes an essential conservative position, accepting the place of Greek in the New Learning but insisting that the older ways are better than the new.

The poem's second major theme concerns abuses in contemporary England, especially in the court of Henry VIII. Skelton, who was an ordained priest, had a strongly moralistic streak and deplored the excesses of his day. He attacks these same abuses in other of his works, such as his earlier poem "The Maner of the World Now a Dayes" and the later "Colin Clout." In "Speak, Parrot" he reaches a sustained pitch of feeling, especially in the long set of closing stanzas that speak of "So manye bolde barons, there heartes as dull as lede" and "So hote hatered agaynste the Chyrche, and cheryte [charity] so colde." Clearly, in many ways the times are out of joint in Henrican England.

One great reason this is so is Thomas Wolsey, cardinal and Lord Chancellor. To Skelton, Wolsey seemed to embody all the abuses and excesses of the times. Wolsey's accumulation of wealth, titles, and power must have made him seem the very personification of the seven deadly sins, especially those of avarice, gluttony, and, above all, pride. Having risen from humble beginnings (his father was a butcher), Wolsey had, through his brilliance and ability, made himself indispensable to the young king. In 1521, when "Speak, Parrot" was most likely composed, Wolsey was in Europe on a delicate diplomatic mission to France and the low countries, seemingly to mediate a peace between France and the Holy Roman Empire, but more likely to support Emperor Charles V, who had promised Wolsey help in his quest for the papacy. Skelton was greatly offended by such blatant political maneuverings, which subordinated England's welfare to Wolsey's personal ambition. His distaste for Wolsey is clear throughout the poem, especially when he declares that Wolsey "caryeth a kyng in hys sleve." The reference to Henry VIII, whose dependence on his chief counselor was well known, is clear. When Skelton describes Wolsey himself, his invective is scathing:

> So rygorous revelyng, in a prelate specially;
> So bold and so braggyng, and was so baselye borne;
> So lordlye of hys lokes, and so dysdayneslye [disdainfully];
> So fatte a magott, bred of a flesshe-flye.

The image is clear and highly unflattering. Skelton, himself a clergyman and a social conservative, is highly offended by Wolsey's inappropriate, even scandalous behavior. Perhaps the worst aspect of that behavior, and the major offense against which Parrot speaks, was his meteoric rise from his humble beginnings.

Michael Witkoski

THE SPIRIT OF THE AGE

Author: Friedrich Hölderlin (1770-1843)
Type of poem: Ode
First published: 1800, as "Der Zeitgeist"; in *Sämtliche Werke*, 1846; English transla-
tion collected in *Some Poems and Fragments*, 1966

The Poem

"The Spirit of the Age" is a short ode of twenty lines. An ode is a poetic form derived from a Greek model (ode means "song" in Greek); it was often used by the Romantic poets for lyric poetry of high seriousness. Friedrich Hölderlin called this poem
a "tragic ode," meaning that it combined the lyricism (or personal tone) of the ode
with the heroic or fateful tone of the tragedy.

The title of this poem might be better translated as "The God of Time," for "Zeitgeist"—literally, "time-god" or "time-spirit"—means here both the élan (mood or
spirit) of a time period, such as William Hazlitt was later to describe in a work by that
title (1824), and a sort of divinity that Hölderlin invokes.

The poem contains five stanzas of four lines each, with no rhyme scheme. The meter is irregular (a mixture of iambs and dactyls) but somewhat consistent: In each
stanza but one (the fourth), the first two lines have five feet and end with a stressed,
"masculine" syllable, and the last two lines have four feet and end with an unstressed,
"feminine" syllable.

The first stanza is an invocation of the god of time, who is, the poet says, "above my
head." This god seems rather frightening and threatening, like the "dark clouds" in
which he dwells. The same mood is continued in the second stanza, where the poet describes being tempted to ignore this god by pretending to be still a boy, innocent and
unknowing, and by looking at the ground and into a cave, involved in earthly things,
away from the god above. He calls the god "the all-shattering," he who shakes and
convulses everything.

By the third stanza, there is a sudden reconciliation of opposites and a resignation
to the rule of this god. Twice the god of time is called not "the shatterer" but, simply
and naïvely, "Father." No longer wishing to avoid seeing him, the narrator now asks
for his own eyes to be opened. By accepting the god, the narrator becomes truly innocent, not through ignorance, but through open-eyed, knowledgeable faith.

In the fourth stanza, where the rhythm varies slightly from that of the rest of the
poem, there is a shift to natural imagery; the maturation of the narrator is compared to
the ripening of grapes to make wine, and the movement of the god is compared to a
"mild spring air" in which "[mortal] men" are "wandering/ In orchards calmly." This
stanza flows directly into the fifth stanza without a sentence break, but there is nevertheless another sudden shift here: The mood returns to that of the beginning of the
poem, but with an important difference. Now the "Shaker" is seen as a teacher of the

young, as one who teaches the old to be wise, representing a threat only to those who
are "evil" or "bad."

Forms and Devices

Although the poem is written in the first person, there is an aesthetic distance between the poet Hölderlin and the narrator of the poem. This means that the poem has an
impersonal, universal quality to it rather than the ambience of a highly personal experience. Even in the first line, there is an air of generality or of repeated, lasting experience,
not of a one-time occurrence: "Too long above my head you have governed there."

In fact, the narrator does not appear in the last two stanzas, where the god who is
addressed is described in terms of his effect on "us," "youths," and "older men"—
generalized terms—not on the "I" of the beginning. Throughout the poem, there is
more emphasis on the "you" to whom the poem or invocation is addressed than on the
"I" who relates or prays. This structure is appropriate to both the form of the poem as
a "tragic ode" and the meanings of the poem. A tragic mood must have universal—
not merely individual—validity, and the meanings of this poem, as will be demonstrated, have to do with the significance of the self in terms of the whole society.

The original Greek ode (the Pindaric ode), upon which this poem is loosely based,
consisted of three sections: a strophe, an antistrophe, and an epode. Since music, poetry, and dance were united in Greek art, these poems were chanted and danced by a
chorus, which moved up one side of the stage for the strophe, down the other side for
the antistrophe, and remained standing for the epode. This structure still exists (if only
abstractly) in "The Spirit of the Age": The first two stanzas manifest strife and conflict; the third and fourth stanzas show a growth and change in attitude, and then a vision of one's being within the universal context of the natural world; and the final
stanza returns to the original conception of the god, but with a vision that looks toward
the future and an understanding of the significance of the threatening god.

Several sets of opposites work within the poem to show the original lack of unity of
the poetic voice. The god in the clouds "above my head" is contrasted with the "ground"
and the "deep cave" on which the narrator at first wishes to concentrate. Such a contrast
of the spiritual and religious with the physical and earthly is common in Western poetry.
Another contrast is that of original blindness with open-eyed recognition.

This leads to a slightly more confusing contrast in the poem: that between youth
and age. At first, boyhood seems to represent ignorance, for the narrator wishes,
wrongly, one may assume, to return to boyish naïveté. Shortly thereafter, he refers to
himself as "stupid" ("Poor craven") in this context. Yet the reader then sees that youth
can also be viewed as a time of potentiality, of grapes not yet ripe, of wisdom not yet
attained. Since the poet now addresses the god as "father," one can see that it is not
childlikeness that is criticized here, but willful ignorance. Like William Wordsworth
in his famous poem "Ode: Intimations of Immortality" (1807), Hölderlin calls for a
return to youthful innocence insofar as this means a turning away from worldly concerns and from what Wordsworth termed "the light of common day"—human reason
and reasonableness, the petty mundane things that make one forget one's immortality

and divine nature. Neither Romantic poet desires an abdication of responsibility or a return to childish dependence, but rather a movement toward a new, more highly developed state in which child*like* (not child*ish*) awareness is mingled with adult consciousness to create a better world.

Themes and Meanings

Hölderlin's background in the Pietistic religion of the eighteenth century, which stressed a personal, mystical, self-observing religious experience, is very evident in his poetry. Yet he was later to adopt the pantheistic beliefs of the followers of the philosopher Baruch Spinoza, and his poetry cannot be understood fully without reference to this theory.

Hölderlin felt that God manifested himself in all natural phenomena, a system of belief that did not necessarily contradict orthodox Christianity but did alter some of its doctrines. In "The Spirit of the Age," the god that is invoked is not really the Christian God, but something more like the Greek divinities that inhabited all of nature. Thus the poem under discussion mingles a pantheistic conception with traditional Christian imagery.

The god in the clouds of stanza 1 clearly evokes the brooding spirit who moves over the waters in Genesis. This god, like the Christian God, is a "father" who teaches (stanza 4) and who puts the spirit of life into mortal man (stanza 3). The image of ripening grapes recalls the wine of the Christian Last Supper; for Hölderlin, however, wine meant more than this. In his poem "Bread and Wine" (1807), a clear reference to the Last Supper, Hölderlin mixes in imagery of the Dionysian "drunkenness" (Dionysus was the Greco-Roman god of the grape harvest and wine) that he associated with the "drunkenness" or loss of purely rational capabilities of poetic inspiration. This poem, too, is an appeal to the gods of poetic, not religious, inspiration.

All this is not to say that Hölderlin was completely abstract and cut off from the historical occurrences of his times. The poem's final stanza reworks the Christian parable of the separation of the sheep from the goats, making it clear that the gods punish only those who are "evil" and therefore deserving of punishment. For Hölderlin, this had a very real significance. In a time when his country was under the rule of people he thought were tyrants (the nobility) and was threatened by attack from abroad (by Napoleon), political right-mindedness was of extreme importance. Hölderlin wanted a democratic government, which he thought could be effected through poetry. By achieving a unity with nature, such as can be seen in this poem, a new level of consciousness could be reached. By contemplating the divinity with open eyes instead of concentrating on worldly affairs, humans could return to a natural state, a "Oneness" with the universe, from which they have "fallen" (again, the concept is Christian) as a result of limited knowledge and vision. Although this attitude must certainly seem very naïve and even ignorant in the twentieth century, for the Romantics it represented a radically new way of perceiving man's place in the universe. It is in part because of their vision that humanity now has the luxury of considering it outmoded and wrong.

Laura Martin

THE SPLENDOR FALLS

Author: Alfred, Lord Tennyson (1809-1892)
Type of poem: Lyric
First published: 1850, in the third edition of *The Princess*

The Poem

"The Splendor Falls" was written in 1848 shortly after Alfred, Lord Tennyson visited Killarney in Ireland. The poem describes a sunset in mountainous country. The scene is glorious: The setting sun illuminates an old castle and the snow-capped peaks beyond. The surface of a nearby lake reflects the light, as does a waterfall seen tumbling from a cliff. In the scene, too, is a "scar," or cleft in the rock face, from which the echoes of sounds emerge, first strongly, then with decreasing intensity.

Celebrating the joy of the scene, the speaker calls for bugles to blow, so that the echoes may set off a clarion call heralding the wonders of the day's end. There is a magical quality about the scene, suggested by the castle and the mountains "old in story," and further emphasized by a reference to the "horns of Elfland," a fairy kingdom. Highly romanticized, the sunset scene evokes moods of elation, wonder, and even excitement. In the final stanza, the speaker says to an unidentified listener—clearly his own beloved—that, unlike the echoes from the fissure along the cliff wall, the echoes of their love will not diminish.

The poem succeeds on its own merits as a lyric by creating a mood and evoking powerful emotions in readers. However, its initial publication as one of the songs interspersed into a longer blank-verse narrative warrants some attention. In 1847, Tennyson published *The Princess*, a story focused on women's rights, women's education, and the proper relation between the sexes. The tale of Princess Ida, who many centuries earlier had abandoned the world of men to establish a college for women, is not told in a straightforward manner. Instead, Tennyson begins in the present time by creating a party of young men and women who are asked to invent a story in which each of the seven members of the group would tell one part, building on what others have said before them.

The resulting medley of Ida's love affair with the Prince, framed by an introduction and conclusion in which the poet narrates the stories of the modern young men and women who invent her character, met with mixed success. Readers of the 1847 edition complained that the disparate stories did not coalesce well into a single tale, so Tennyson decided to include songs between each part to link the sections thematically. "The Splendor Falls" appears between the third and fourth sections of the poem, shortly after the Prince has invaded the walls of Princess Ida's college and won her love. The third part of *The Princess* ends with a scene in which the Prince, Princess Ida, and their friends have just completed an amateur geological trek through mountainous terrain, having quit to observe sunset in the region. Hence, within the longer poem, the lyric is used to echo both a sense of the scenery and the mood of the young lovers.

Forms and Devices

"The Splendor Falls" is a deceptively simple lyric. At first glance the poem appears highly structured. It consists of three stanzas, each containing a quatrain rhyming *abab*, followed by a rhyming couplet. Each line of the quatrain appears to have four beats and generally follows the pattern of an iambic tetrameter. The couplet contains one five-beat line followed by a six-beat line.

Upon examination, however, it becomes clear that hardly any line in the poem consists exclusively of regular iambic feet. Where regular lines occur, Tennyson almost always follows them with a variation. For example, the opening line is a regular iambic tetrameter: "The splendor falls on castle walls." The second, however, contains an extra syllable, because of the feminine rhyme: "And snowy summits old in story." The next two lines are both irregular: "The long light shakes across the lakes,/ And the wild cataract leaps in glory." In the first of these lines, the words "long light shakes" all require a stress; in the second, two unstressed syllables precede two that require a stress. Readers will find this pattern repeated throughout the poem. The effect is that the individual lines strive to destroy the exceptionally tight structure created by the rhyme scheme and the stanzaic pattern of the lyric.

Tennyson uses the highly structured stanza pattern and rhyme scheme as but one means of creating a sense of regularity against which the metric variations seem to be in conflict. The couplets at the end of each stanza are essentially the same. Only one variation occurs: Line 5 in the second stanza is altered from "Blow, bugle, blow, set the wild echoes flying" of the first and third stanzas to "Blow, let us hear the purple glens replying." The final lines of each stanza are identical, suggesting the action of the echoes described by the poet throughout the lyric.

The auditory and visual imagery of the poem creates a vivid experience of the close of the day. Readers can visualize the castle atop a cliff, beside which there runs a cleft in the mountain where echoes reverberate. The image of water sparkling in the sunset is captured in active verbs: The light reflecting on the lakes "shakes," and the waterfall pouring from the side of the mountain "leaps in glory." The repetition of key words and phrases, made most obvious in the final lines of each stanza, suggests a sense of continuance about the pattern of this natural event. The subtle irregularities, however, create the sensation that something extraordinary is taking place.

Sophisticated readers may find parallels to William Wordsworth's "Ode: Intimations of Immortality," in which the poet tells of "cataracts blow[ing] their trumpets from the steep," and babes come into the world "trailing clouds of glory." Like the soul in Wordsworth's poem who achieves immortality through communing with nature, the lovers described briefly in "The Splendor Falls" can become immortal through their love.

Themes and Meanings

Because this poem is often published apart from the longer narrative in which it originally appeared, it is possible to develop both a general and a specific interpretation for it. Like many lyrics, "The Splendor Falls" is not constructed principally to tell a story, but rather to evoke particular feelings in readers. Many poets equate the passing of the day with the passing of a life, or of some bond between individuals, such as love. In fact, Tennyson himself used both daybreak and sunset to suggest certain human emotions. In stanza 7 of his most renowned work, *In Memoriam* (1850), he expresses his speaker's pain at the loss of a good friend by describing sunrise in stark terms: "ghastly through the drizzling rain/ On the bald street breaks the blank day." In "Crossing the Bar," an often-reprinted lyric written late in his life, Tennyson gives readers clear indication that the "sunset and evening star" referred to in the poem represents the end of his life.

In "The Splendor Falls" the suggestive visual and auditory imagery, repetition and variation of key words and phrases, and linking rhyme scheme all work to create a vivid picture of the setting sun's effect on the landscape. Colors change on the walls of the castle, sounds echo from the cataract, all heralding the passing of the day. Tennyson does not suggest, however, that the end of the day is a time of sorrow or loss, as is the case in many poems. Rather, this is a glorious time when nature is both active and triumphant: The "wild cataract leaps in glory," bugles set "the wild echoes flying." The poet contrasts the glorious dying of the day with the enduring love of the speaker and his beloved. While the echoes from the bugles eventually fade away and the day slips into evening, the "echoes" of the lovers who witness the splendor of the sunset "roll from soul to soul,/ And grow for ever and for ever." The implication is that human love can outlast even the death of lovers, who may live forever in the "echoes"— that is, the stories—told about them.

Such a theme was common among Victorian poets and has been borrowed almost directly from the late Middle Ages and the Renaissance. Suggestions that love lives beyond death are present in the works of Dante, whose *La divina commedia* (c. 1320; *The Divine Comedy*, 1802) contains a beautiful passage about the lovers Paolo and Francesca, who, even in hell, exhibit the passion that drove them to their illicit affair. In more than one of the sonnets in his famous sequence, Shakespeare celebrates the immortality his friend will achieve by being commemorated in his verse. It is not surprising, then, that Tennyson chose to use the image of the echo as a means of suggesting not only the general premise that love may outlast death, but also the specific notion that the newfound love of the Prince and Princess Ida will be celebrated for all time.

Laurence W. Mazzeno

SPRING AND ALL

Author: William Carlos Williams (1883-1963)
Type of poem: Lyric
First published: 1923, in *Spring and All*

The Poem

"Spring and All" is a short descriptive poem in free verse. The scene described is not what the title would lead one to expect: It is a muddy field populated by a few trees and bushes beside "the contagious hospital," Williams's phrase for a sanitorium that isolates people with contagious diseases. This unlikely setting becomes the occasion for one of poetry's oldest tasks—the description of springtime.

The poem begins with a series of prepositional phrases, followed by some noun phrases. The uninviting landscape is wet and cold; the leaves are "dead" and the vines "leafless." At line 14, however, something changes. Spring is personified as a drowsy slumberer awakening. The next verse paragraph introduces an ambiguous "they," which "enter[s] the new world naked." Though that phrasing understandably may remind one of newborn babies, the context suggests that the speaker is referring to emerging spring growth, the puny stems of grass and weeds that arise from the mud into the "cold, familiar wind." The reader realizes that this unlikely landscape represents the very beginning of spring. The ground is wet from rains or melting snows, and the first harbingers of the more conventionally celebrated spring are making their appearance.

The speaker then enumerates some of the new growth and anticipates the appearance of "the stiff curl of wildcarrot leaf." The coming of new growth is described as a kind of definition whereby individual plants take on clarity and individuality from the undifferentiated muck from which they sprout. The final lines celebrate this process as possessing "stark dignity" and representing a "profound change," presumably from nonexistence to life. The new growth is described as downward as well as upward: the roots "grip down," and the plants "begin to awaken." Though the scene has not changed much from the initial, uninviting landscape, the final word "awaken," echoing the life-giving associations of the earlier "quickens," seems appropriate for a poem of spring.

Forms and Devices

"Spring and All" is primarily descriptive. As such, it abounds in imagery. Though the imagery is rich and detailed, it is not lush in the traditional manner of poems to spring. No blossoms, buzzing bees, or sweet perfumes animate the poem. Instead, the imagery focuses on precision, on a realistic rather than romantic evocation of natural detail. The clouds are "mottled" and driven by a wind that the poet notes comes from the northeast. Brown is the most common color; the word appears twice and is relieved only by "reddish" and "purplish." The items delineated early in the poem seem to be distributed randomly: "patches of standing water," "the scattering of tall trees," "twiggy/ stuff of bushes." After the appearance of spring in line 15, objects take on definition and are enumerated "one by one," as individual living things. Though the clarity of outline characteristic of the latter part of the poem contrasts with the "broad" indiscriminate waste of the first half, the description is still unreservedly spartan. No romantic effusion is permitted.

The stark visual imagery is complemented by the tactile imagery of coldness. The wind is twice described as "cold," and the word "cold" modifies "they"—presumably new spring plants—of line 16. This repetition is significant: The warmth of spring is only anticipated in the poem. The birth of spring is a harsher process, but it is also a familiar one, repeated every year and undergone by all living things. This quality is expressed by the unusual word choice of "familiar" to describe the cold wind of line 19. The pain of passing into existence is shared by all of the animate, natural world; it is a familiar coldness. The bleak landscape into which the blades of grass emerge is the world's stage on which all creatures have their day. The presence of a hospital nearby connects the images of birth with those of death: The cold wind that welcomes the new plants casts a chill over the suffering souls in the hospital, who may not live to see another spring. The setting unites birth and death.

The adjective "naked" suggests human birth, and, indeed, one can read this poem (written by a pediatrician who assisted at hundreds of deliveries) as a poem about the birthing process. Perhaps the ambiguous words "and all" of the title connect the traditional images of spring to the conditions that precede it and connect the burgeoning of the natural world with the human life cycle. The title "Spring and All" thus unites the typical Williams understatement—a sort of a shrug—with a celebration of universality.

In a poem dominated by natural imagery, abstract terms such as "dignity" and "profound" in the concluding lines stand out. These more abstract words, with their connotations of importance, contrast with the realist assembling of drab natural details that characterizes the poem. "No ideas but in things" is Williams's famous dictum, and here it implies that the assertions of the final lines must be earned by the painstaking description earlier in the poem. The poet is a clear-eyed observer, who, by paying attention to the early signs of spring growth in a muddy field, is allowed a glimpse of "the profound change" represented by coming alive. The concreteness of the bulk of the poem supports the abstraction of its conclusion.

Consistent with the refusal of the poem to engage in poetic effusiveness about spring is the virtual absence of figurative language. There is no metaphor in the poem, unless one takes "naked" figuratively. Spring is personified, but even that figure of speech undermines traditional associations by stressing the "sluggish/ dazed" quality of the season. More subtly, the new growths are personified by being granted uncertainty and the ability to feel the cold.

Williams plays with the sounds of words throughout the poem. The consonance of *r, s, t,* and *f* works effectively in the following lines to suggest the roughness of the scrubby landscape: "All along the road the reddish/ purplish, forked, upstanding, twiggy/ stuff of bushes and small trees." The most meaningful wordplay is the sound echo that transforms "leafless" to "lifeless" between the third and fourth stanzas. These similar sounding words have similar meanings, but the latter is qualified by the phrase "in appearance," which marks the turning point of the poem and the introduction of spring. The leafless landscape appears lifeless but, on closer examination, reveals itself to be full of the early growth.

Line endings significantly add slight (and unexpected) pauses. The line and stanza break after "fallen" (lines 6-7) illustrates a typical characteristic of Williams's verse. The break makes the phrase "standing and fallen" ambiguous: Does it modify the "dried weeds" or the "patches of standing water"? Williams uses unusual line breaks to create an expectant pause after "tomorrow" (line 20) and to break the phrase "dignity of/ entrance" over two lines (24-25). These may seem minor points, but they are important in free verse. Since meter does not determine where lines end, the poet must have a different and distinct rationale—or he or she might as well be writing prose. Williams often breaks lines in mid-phrase (or, as he does famously in "The Red Wheelbarrow," in mid-word). The effect is to slow the reading, to force the reader's attention to detail, and to call attention to the poem as a made object.

Themes and Meanings

The most important theme of "Spring and All" has already become apparent: The poem demonstrates that the awe-inspiring process of coming to life is a springtime miracle visible in the details of the thawing landscape. They come alive through close observation by the poet, who commits them realistically to language. The poem should be read in the context of a whole history of poetry heralding springtime. Writing in the early twentieth century, Williams looks for a way to treat a virtually hackneyed topic with freshness. For Williams that freshness comes from unadorned simple language and closely observed detail.

The time of the poem's publication suggests another useful context for interpreting it. The poem appeared in 1923, the year after T. S. Eliot's famous poem, *The Waste Land* (1922). Williams felt that Eliot's *The Waste Land* took poetry in the wrong directions: away from American traditions and language and toward the European, and away from direct language and imagery and toward highly allusive quotations from literature and mythology. Williams's evocation of a wasteland landscape in the opening lines (including the word "waste," opening line 5) hints that this poem may be a response to Eliot's work. In particular, the poem echoes the imagery of a depleted natural landscape with roots struggling to survive—images from the beginning of Eliot's poem. Where Eliot's use of roots becomes a metaphor for cultural traditions, however, Williams's use of roots is organic, suggesting rootedness in the natural world. In this light, it makes sense to read the penultimate paragraph as Williams's statement of a poetic credo. Then the concepts of "definition," "clarity," and "outline" make sense: The natural world offers to Williams a model for poetic expression. Poetry will quicken or come to life—freeing itself from the morbid excesses of late nineteenth century ornamentation and avoiding the arid excesses of Eliot's appeal to scholarship—by faithfully outlining and defining the stuff of the world.

Christopher Ames

SPRING RAIN

Author: Boris Pasternak (1890-1960)
Type of poem: Lyric
First published: 1922, as "Vesennii dozhd," in *Sestra moia zhizn': Leto 1917 goda*;
English translation collected in *My Sister, Life and Other Poems*, 1976

The Poem

"Spring Rain" is a short poem of twenty-four lines that are broken into six stanzas of four lines each. Set in the spring following the February beginning of the 1917 bloodless Russian Revolution, the poem is written as if the speaker were not a participant but simply a witness to the urban scene recorded. While there is no reference to an "I," the last line of stanza 6 contains the word "our," which by implication broadens the voice. In the quotation from Nikolaus Lenau's poem "Das Bild," the epigraph to *Sestra moia zhizn': Leto 1917 goda*, the volume in which "Spring Rain" first appeared, "my beloved girl" is named as someone whom the poet wishes to draw into the experience of the poems. The "our" could be interpreted to mean the poet and the beloved girl of the epigraph.

From the beginning line, rain takes on properties beyond that of mere water falling from the sky. The speaker anthropomorphizes the downpour such that it first grins at a wildflower, then sobs, and then soaks things as diverse as the hard shine of vehicles and breeze-blown flora. In the last two lines of the stanza, the speaker sets the scene: The action is outside at night, near a theater where a crowd of people is being managed by a policeman.

The effects of the rain and the moonlight, the positive transforming powers, are described in the next two stanzas. Drops, called both "tears" and "damp diamonds," touch everything, including the people gathered, arousing joyfulness. Moonlight bathes the scene in white, capturing the drama of the historical moment in a plaster-like silhouette. A question begins the fourth stanza, and in its unfurling, the heightened emotion of the crowd finds expression. "The minister's" refers to Aleksandr Kerensky, who was the minister of justice in the government that was set up after the abdication of Czar Nicholas II. His charismatic address has melded the assemblage together in unity of spirit.

The series of denials that begin both stanza 5 and stanza 6 erases the scene's carefully constructed details in order to focus on two observations by the poem's speaker. What remains to look on is the momentousness of what has taken place to bring about the uproar. The speaker places the triumph of revolution in context by drawing an illustration from ancient Rome, suggesting the disparity between hopeless entrapment in the dark catacombs of the past and freedom of movement in the city's heart of public commerce in daylight. This is one measure of the feeling of liberation that is unleashed by the ongoing revolution.

Yet the speaker does not restrict his elucidation to the boundaries of his country, for in stanza 6 he links the rain and the moon to the rest of Europe, intimating that what has begun in Russia will, like unstoppable tides, come to Europe's troubled shores as well. The fullest meaning of the rain as a symbol of the spiritual impetus and energy that the speaker finds in the revolutionary air is finally expressed with approval as the speaker makes the street outside the theater the "forum." He returns to his original anthropomorphism, describing the rain as "proud" of its Russian geography.

Forms and Devices

Boris Pasternak's poems contain many metaphors and metonymies. As a young man, Pasternak considered a career as a professional musician. He devoted more than six years to the study of composition but abandoned the pursuit when he became convinced that he lacked the required technical skill. The musical training greatly influenced his poems, however, and the artistry of sound design, as well as rhyme and meter, guided his word choice and resulted in intricate metaphoric and metonymic usage. "Spring Rain" falls among the group of poems in which the poet found parallels in nature to convey his theme and discovered an abundance of metaphors and metonymies to both strengthen the poem's form and add crisp originality to its imagery.

In stanza 2, first a simile—the raindrops as tears filling a throat—and then a metaphor—"damp diamonds" burning—is followed by the metonymy of "eyelids" to imply the congregation in the street.

The pallor cast by the moon is metaphorized, along with the moonlight-silhouetted urban scene, as a plaster sculpture in which the congregation in the street again is represented by metonymies. This time, there is a series: "queues, tossing dresses, . . . enraptured lips." The "fingertips" and "aortas and lips" of the next stanza are also pieces representing wholes. The government minister has raised his hands in his moving oration and has unified the emotional and verbal response of the people.

The last two stanzas employ the device of negative parallelism, wherein the first two lines of both stanzas begin with a list of what is not to be considered from the scene previously presented. These stanzas also contain elaborate metaphors. In stanza 5, the description of finding a way out of catacombs is used as a metaphor for the atmosphere of the revolution, implying a turning from a past mired in persecution and secrecy toward a future filled with openness and public deeds.

The metaphoric pattern of stanza 6, the most interwoven, again suggests that the street in front of the theater is the "forum" of ancient Rome, thus bringing to the reader's mind that great empire and its epic magnitude. The rain, previously allowed human characteristics of mood and whim, is now metaphorized as "the surf of Europe's wavering night" that feels "proud of itself." A complex web of metaphors, as "wavering night" is a metaphor as well, stands for what Pasternak perceived as a healthy unrest calling the revolution to traditional European civilization as it did to Russia. The final words, "on our asphalt," display metonymy as well. "Our asphalt" broadens to mean all of Russia as the incubator of a dynamic revolutionary spirit.

With regard to structure, "Spring Rain" can be divided into two parts. The first three stanzas focus on the details of the scene, such as the rain, the flowers and trees, and the crowd. The following three stanzas turn from concrete detail to focus on the atmosphere of history in the making. The language of liquids, mostly water, permeates both halves, however, and acts as an artful unifier.

Rain sobs, soaks, and congregates in "puddles." It is like tears, and it is "damp diamonds." Clouds, themselves collections of moisture, feel a wet form of happiness. Hiding in "enraptured" is the sense of being carried away, or filled, both suggestive of liquid action. Further on, blood rushes "in a flood" just before a "blinding emergence," which can be seen as something akin to a flood. Lastly, the crowds "roar" precedes "surf," two words often connected by a sound link, and rain feels proud "on our asphalt," a metonymy which allows a characteristic of water to be part of the image, in the idea of the wetness that has covered the street.

Themes and Meanings

"Spring Rain" is a poem about dynamism and the energy that is formed by unifying individuals. Pasternak uses the atmosphere of liberation in the spring immediately following the first 1917 revolution in Russia as a vehicle to illustrate the exhilarating effect that such a cataclysmic, monumental event has on the collective human spirit. Electrified air, exuberant crowds, nature dazzled with wetness—all point toward a positive release of pent-up grievances which is created from hope for the future and the unifying glory of national pride.

The lightning-rod revolution, in combination with a summer love affair (with a woman never specifically identified), inspired Pasternak to capture the everyday events in a poetic history which became the cycle of poems called *Sestra moia zhizn'*. Olga Andreyev Carlisle, in her prologue to the translation of this work, entitled *My Sister, Life and Other Poems* (1976), quotes Pasternak's remarks about the period forty years later:

> During the remarkable summer of 1917, in the interlude between the two revolutions, it appeared as if not only the people participated in the discourse, but together with them also the roads, the trees and the stars, the air, free and unlimited, carried this ardent enthusiasm through thousands of versts and seemed to be a person with a name, possessing clear sight and a soul.

"Spring Rain" is but one of fifty poems in a narrative cycle which celebrates the romance of life. In its entirety, the cycle is a discourse between the poet as character and the poet as author. "Policeman's Whistles," the companion to "Spring Rain" in the cycle, directly opposes the enthusiastic applause for revolution of "Spring Rain" and tells instead of the suffering and vulnerability of the individual striving for identity in the revolution's whirlwind of change.

Virginia Starrett

A STAFFORDSHIRE MURDERER

Author: James Fenton (1949-   )
Type of poem: Narrative
First published: 1983, in *The Memory of War and Children in Exile: Poems, 1968-1983*

The Poem

"A Staffordshire Murderer," James Fenton's dense, often enigmatic narrative poem, explores the aberrant mind of a nameless serial killer as he prepares to kill yet again. Despite expectations that a man who at poem's end brutally knifes a helpless victim would be quite emotional, Fenton's killer—and the poem itself—is intricately cerebral, even calm. Even as he strolls about the gardens near Lichfield's magnificent three-spired cathedral to select his victim (his "accomplice"), the killer pauses to observe ducks and flowers. Erudite, he ponders historical references that reveal his familiarity with the blood-soaked history of the Staffordshire countryside—he acknowledges the shadow-company of these other "Staffordshire murderers" who wait metaphorically alongside him.

The poem deliberately frustrates any clear narrative line. Fenton only indirectly indicates the action: the wait for the victim; the abduction and removal of the victim by van to the killer's house; and then the killing itself, accomplished in the ninety-ninth line of a one-hundred-line poem. In deploying a series of intricately related digressions that cohere only loosely, like a cubist collage, Fenton reveals an interest in the mind of the murderer rather than in the bloody act itself—that is, after all, redundant to the point of cliché as attested not only by the killer's allusions to the bloody history of the Staffordshire region but also by his acknowledgment of his own previous killings.

Thus, the real horror of the poem is not the murder but rather the mind that creates the context that makes such an act inevitable, acceptable, even logical. Fenton never intrudes to suggest any wider moral frame that might temper the ghastly event by suggesting that such evil will be punished—the poem closes only with the killer's flush of triumph and the disquieting expression of his creepy logic: that he is liberating the victim into a "new life."

Forms and Devices

The poem rejects the traditional notion that poetry is confessional, thus tightly bound to its poet. This poem, rather, is a voyeuristic projection and speculation: Fenton himself is no murderer. Influenced by the psychoanalytical poetry of W. H. Auden, Fenton's poem effectively effaces the poet. As such, the poem is best approached as an experiment in what language can do, specifically whether it can contain the dark logic of murder itself.

Thus, without authorial intrusion, the killer reveals his character indirectly through the vehicle of his labyrinthine speculations. It is not always possible to determine exactly the reference or to follow the killer's obscure train of thought. Passages with clear narrative intent shift without transition into fragmentary speculations that in turn shift into historical and literary glosses. To so deliberately frustrate the reader's traditional act of "understanding" a poem is a strategic necessity to convey the inaccessible logic of the mind of a serial killer. Fenton cannot allow clarity; his subject will not permit it. The poem consistently maintains this distance from the reader. Fenton is not interested in creating psychological depth that might encourage sympathy for either the killer or the victim.

"A Staffordshire Murderer" is a sort of interior monologue without the interior, a monologue without the "I." The killer never even directly contemplates what he is preparing to do; it is all surfaces. The killer observes one thing, and the reader must draw from that apparently random observation the interior workings of the killer's mind. For instance, in the park, the killer observes a mallard swimming not only diagonal but also backward, an unnatural motion that suggests transgression against the mainstream, not unlike the heinous act the murderer is about to commit.

The reader is further distanced by Fenton's unstable pronouns, which are difficult to clearly identify. As the killer moves from his reflections near the cathedral to the actual killing, he apparently changes from the sympathetic "you" to the distant "he"; the victim, however, moves from "he" to "you," thus presumably pulling the reader into sympathy with his predicament. Yet the victim remains so stubbornly nonparticularized that such emotional investment cannot be made easily. Reader identification is thus intentionally thwarted as Fenton experiments more with poetic effect: How can a poem talk about something without directly talking about it? Not surprisingly, he repeatedly deploys figurative language and euphemism as insulating devices. For instance, the killer recasts the abduction into palatable euphemism: He appreciates the victim "bequeath[ing]" his body to his "experiment." Even the murder itself is repackaged into sunny personification—"The blade flashes a smile."

Formally, the poem is organized into twenty-five apparently neat quatrains. Yet such a tidy appearance is deceiving, much like the figure of the killer himself calmly watching ducks. Like the killer, the poem is barely restrained anarchy. Its free verse does not sustain rhythm or rhyme. It avoids the subtle language devices that create the harmonics of free verse—alliteration, consonance, assonance, internal rhyme, slant rhyme. It is necessarily unmelodious, jarring, cacophonous. Each elastic line moves to its own length as if patternless, much like the killer's restless mind.

Themes and Meanings

Fenton once commented that the postwar poets' most workable posture is not as the reliable voice next door giving depth to the familiar. Rather, the poet acts as a visitor, an alien-outsider who interacts with the familiar landscape like an anthropologist or, in the most extreme expression, like an invader. Fenton termed such poetry "Martianism," and, in this poem, he functions in such a mode, observing with detachment the murderer's mind-set without tidily rendering a theme or two. The reader is left to observe the act of the poem itself, how the poem conducts its lexical experiment:

What would a killer think, a logical act, as he prepares to kill, a most illogical act?

In the first twenty-eight lines, the killer, his van nearby, meditates without irony on the ghastly intimacy that exists between killer and victim. Although he acknowledges his fears, he also finds such fears stimulating and the act unstoppable—he compares his fear to the last whirring seconds before a clock strikes the hour. He is coolly philosophical, impeccably epigrammatic, extending well-turned bromides to his to-be-selected victim, such as "every journey begins with a death" and that while a "suicide travels alone . . . the murderer needs company." Suddenly, the killer abandons narrative to speculate on the rapid changes in the geographical makeup of the Staffordshire countryside, how so many trees now stand nearly underwater with fish in their branches and how elsewhere, virtually unnoticed, an entire pond suddenly drained dry, killing its fowl with nature's cool precision. Thus, the killer meditates on the inexplicability of change and the inevitability of sudden extinction.

That pattern of violent, sudden change is extended within the killer's logic to history itself as he then ranges about more than a thousand years of bloody acts that each center about the Staffordshire district: William Palmer, the infamous poisoner of Rugeley, a physician hanged in 1856 for killing his family over a gambling debt; James Rush, who in 1848 shot his family in Stanfield Hall; the devastating havoc wreaked on the centuries-old Lichfield Cathedral by the Puritan Oliver Cromwell during the bloody English civil wars; and the deaths under the order of the Roman emperor Diocletian (c. 245-316) of more than a thousand Christians in the fields around Lichfield. It is reminder that against such a vast and violent backdrop, the killer's anticipated act shrinks in its barbarity and even in its significance. Moreover, these others acted out of self-serving agendas. By contrast, Fenton's murderer kills without motive, without provocation, aesthetically a purer act. At any rate, the killer rationalizes, death quiets everyone, the infamous and the good, poisoners and preachers (he mentions specifically hymn writers Ira Sankey and Dwight L. Moody and the religious leaders John Wesley and George Fox). Thus, by his logic, it is easy to dismiss death. He even offers a digression in which a knifing victim, whose attacker speaks Elizabethan diction, moves, bloodied and dying, through the Lichfield marketplace. Violence, the reader begins to see, has long rested at the dark heart of the Midlands.

The poem returns abruptly to the present. "It is hot." Even as the reader surmises that the killer is in the process of actually abducting the victim, the killer trains his attention on the healthy growth of cowparsley, the fetid bubbling water in the canal, and the clumsy movements of a slow-flying coot as it hurries across the towpath. The heavy chiming of the cathedral and a final bit of encouragement—"Keep calm"— closes off the abduction, which itself happens without actually being recorded. The poem then quickly cuts to the killer's house, where he dispassionately shows the victim the niche in his basement where he will dispose of the body before bricking it up. Now in complete command ("God and the weather are glorious"), the killer sardonically brags to the victim about the long, perhaps exaggerated, record of his other murders before the killing is done.

Spending one hundred lines locked within this killer's logic is a disquieting experience. When the killer observes that "History murders mallards, while we hear nothing// Or what we hear we do not understand," he surely indicates the effect of the poem itself. A mind such as this demands scrutiny—in a violent age such realities cannot be ignored. It is, Fenton suggests, the sobering responsibility of such an age to grapple with just such a monstrous mind.

Joseph Dewey

STAMP COLLECTING

Author: Cathy Song (1955-   )
Type of poem: Lyric
First published: 1988, in *Frameless Windows, Squares of Light*

The Poem

Cathy Song's "Stamp Collecting" is a lyric of three unequal stanzas. Its easy flowing and conversationally cadenced verse lines muse in a whimsical and wittily urbane tone of voice on postage stamps and what stamps can reveal about the countries that issue them. Ostensibly about the hobby of stamp collecting, the poem is also about geopolitics.

The opening stanza of the poem begins with the commonplace observation that many of the least wealthy nations issue the most eye-catching of postage stamps. These countries tend to produce commodities of trifling value for the world market, such as bananas, T-shirts, coconuts—and pretty postage stamps. The speaker of the poem takes as an example the island nation of Tonga, tucked in the South Pacific between New Zealand and Fiji. Tourists to Tonga may well expect to view dramatic natural beauty such as waterfalls or exotic birds, but the particular mystery they are guided to is merely oversize bats hanging upside down from fruit trees. The stamps of Tonga depict fruits—bananas pictured to look as exotic as seashells, pineapples dramatized to resemble erupting volcanoes, papayas colored to look like goat skulls.

The second stanza continues in a similar vein. Developing nations, which often have only lesser products to sell to the world, produce postage stamps that strain to be impressive. The stamps illustrate their nations' faith in postcard-like snapshots of their efforts at progress and modernization: images of new dams, pictures of young native doctors sporting stethoscopes, scenes of recently built medical schools that unfortunately succeed only in looking like American motels.

In the third and final stanza, the speaker of the poem turns to consider the postage stamps of wealthier countries. Their stamps are more mundane and predictable. Within this group, nevertheless, there are differences. The more fortunate of these countries can boast of native assets such as tigers or queens. The Japanese, for instance, can issue stamps boasting of their cherry blossoms. The less fortunate of these developed countries, however, who can boast of neither royalty nor exotic fauna nor enticing flora, can only print bleak, stark stamps that discourage beauty and fancy. In their stamps the landscape of such countries seems to be frigid and icebound, and their stamps tend to celebrate factories, trams, and airplanes. At the same time, their stamps seem to scorn the rest of the world and to promote themselves as irresistible forces of history.

Forms and Devices

The poem is written in unrhymed cadenced verse and in the language of intelligent conversation. Its lines flow with a smoothly pensive rhythm that indicates a speaker musing wittily and with gentle irony on his or her subject.

The poem also proceeds by comparison and contrast. "The poorest countries" (stanzas 1 and 2) are contrasted with the richer countries (stanza 3)—presumably, the former category includes the developing nations of the Third World while the latter includes the developed Western democracies and the Soviet bloc. Paralleling this contrast, the "prettiest" stamps of the poorer countries are contrasted with the "predictable" stamps of the wealthier. Again, the lightweight "impracticality" of the products of the poorest nations (bananas, coconuts, T-shirts) is juxtaposed against the heavyweight value of the developed nations (factories, trams, airplanes). Furthermore, within this overarching series of oppositions are subsidiary contrasts. For instance, within the description of the developing nations, there is, on one hand, the South Pacific nation of Tonga whose stamps are efforts to make their fruits look exotic and dramatic, and on the other hand, a Latin American country whose stamps are also attempts to make their doctors and hospitals appear progressive and modern.

Within the category of the developed nations also, contrasts appear. The "lucky" or capitalist countries are those that have aristocracy ("a queen") or resources of nature (cherry blossoms or tigers); on the other hand, there are the more "pity"-inspiring or socialist countries that have only statues of athletes and resources of industry (factories and planes) on their stamps. With such comparisons and contrasts, Song conveys a sense of balance, creates opportunities for elaboration, and uses the opposing terms to comment on each other tacitly, if not explicitly.

Vivid imagery is an important device for this poem, as it is for Song's other works. The banana stamp of Tonga is exquisitely described through a simile comparing it to an extravagant "butter-varnished seashell." Similarly, Tonga's fruit bats, or flying foxes, as they are also called, are most aptly described in another simile comparing them to "black umbrellas swing[ing] upside down." The quality of poverty prevalent in some developing nations is brilliantly captured in the image "mule-scratched hills," evoking a picture of an arid, barely arable land from which generations of peasants have eked out a marginal subsistence.

Song's word choice, along with her imagery, also evinces a playful wittiness. The image of a Tongan pineapple stamp resembling a "volcano [with] a spout of green on top" will bring a chuckle to the reader amused by the witty hyperbole and the exaggerated grandiosity of the comparison. Similarly, the aptly phrased image of the socialist countries' "athletes marbled into statues" conjures up associations with the artificial, steroid-fed human specimens who represented Eastern European nations at games during the Cold War era. These socialist countries are also personified as "turn[ing] their noses upon the world"—a wittily suggestive pun on "upon" that suggests snobbishness (as in turning up one's nose at a contemptible object) as well as aggressiveness (as in siccing hounds upon a quarry), while also hinting slyly at the unforgiving nature of these nations which do not turn their cheeks but turn up their noses at others. The word "climate" is another example of double entendre used in characterizing the socialist countries, for it not only denotes the harsh winters of Russia and Eastern Europe but also connotes metaphorically the intellectually and politically repressive regimes that dominated these communist states.

Song also employs some teasingly allusive words in her poem. For instance, the developing nations have "mystery" and their people "believe"—terms connoting a religious-like faith. The developed nations, however, appear to have lost this sense of religious awe and faith; they are only "predictable" and "stark."

Themes and Meanings

The themes most frequently associated with Song's poetry have been those related to women's concerns (mother-daughter relationships, pregnancy and childbirth, family dynamics), or to art and aesthetics (Georgia O'Keeffe's paintings, Utamaro Kitigawa's woodblock prints), or to ethnicity (the travails of immigration, the stereotypes of Chinatown ghettos). "Stamp Collecting" is a departure; in this poem, Song makes a foray into the arena of world politics and expresses a view on the geopolitical forces prevalent during the 1970's and 1980's.

The comparisons and contrasts upon which "Stamp Collecting" is constructed derive from a certain view of the comparative economic status of the world's nations. Song's poem employs a north-south view of the world in which the developed nations of the First World and the Soviet bloc are of the north while the poorer, developing nations of the Third World are of the south. Song's poem points out the inequities of such a dichotomy. Song forthrightly names Japan as an example of a nation of the north, while she is more circumspect in identifying others, merely mentioning the presence on their stamps of queens (such as Great Britain's or Holland's) or factories (such as the Soviet Union's or Poland's). Similarly, Tonga is overtly named in the poem as a nation of the south, while the Spanish phrase "Facultad de Medicina" serves to conjure up images of any Latin American banana republic of the south.

The speaker of the poem observes that the nations of the south produce commodities of low valuation in the world marketplace, exemplified by cash crops such as pineapples and coconuts or sweatshop products such as T-shirts. The nations of the north, however, produce goods of high valuation in the world marketplace, such as trams and airplanes. This juxtaposition of products leads the reader to speculate on the justness of the valuation of these commodities. After all, are not food and clothing (coconuts and T-shirts) more basic and essential to sustaining life than speed and flight (trams and planes)? If so, there seems to be a distortion (possibly a perversion) of values when the world marketplace puts a lower value on that which is more basic to life than on that which is less so.

The attitudes of the nations are also being implicitly compared through their stamps. The nations of the south are attempting to please, striving to gain recognition through their melodramatic representations of the little they have (pineapples exaggerated into volcanoes) or the pathetic pictures of the little they have achieved (tawdry medical colleges). The capitalist nations of the north, however, project symbols of power and imperiousness (tigers and queens) or of escape into the heady cherry-blossom gardens of economic success ("the Japanese . . . : like pollen, they drift, airborne"). The north's socialist states also arrogantly flaunt their marmoreal champions and boast of their factories with chilly invidiousness.

Song's poem, then, starts with so seemingly trivial and flimsy a subject as postage stamps but quickly extrapolates from that several compelling and saddening truths about the geopolitics of the power, arrogance, and wealth of nations. It moves the reader to sympathize with the vain efforts of poorer nations and to question the vanity of richer ones. It invites the reader to examine the world's inequities.

C. L. Chua

STANZAS FOR MUSIC

Author: George Gordon, Lord Byron (1788-1824)
Type of poem: Lyric
First published: 1816, in *Poems*

The Poem

"Stanzas for Music" is a brief lyric poem of sixteen lines, one of five that Byron wrote with the same title. As its title suggests, it was written to be set to music, and its musical qualities have bearing upon its theme and structure.

The poem is written as an address by the poet to a person with whom he is infatuated. It is couched in feminine references and is most conveniently discussed as a love lyric to a woman, but it is important to note that the gender of the addressee is never specified. For that matter, the word love is never mentioned. The tone of the poem is one of adoration, and the poet carefully chooses words and images to evoke emotions that transcend feelings of simple affection. In the first two lines, for example, he creates a persona for his addressee by comparing her favorably to "Beauty's daughters." By alluding that she is more enchanting than the children of a personified ideal, he endows her with a godlike presence. He reinforces this apotheosis through the application of synecdoche, the use of a part or element to suggest a whole. The only aspect of the addressee that the poet describes is her voice, and just as readers are able to infer the totality of the Old Testament God from his manifestation as a disembodied voice, so can they envision a being of divine nature from the phenomena for which the woman's voice alone is responsible.

The poet conveys the majesty of his subject by comparing her effect upon him to the effect of a supernatural influence upon the ocean. He attributes "magic" to her and imagines that she has the power to leave the ocean "charmed" to stillness. Throughout the poem, the poet treats these powerful subjective impressions as objective reality: The woman has "magic" because her effect upon him can be understood in terms of natural phenomena that are beyond ordinary human control.

The poem is rich with sensory images. The poet begins by comparing the woman's "sweet voice" to "music on the waters" whose sound causes the waves to pause. In the absence of their sound and movement, a striking visual tableau presents itself: an ocean whose waves "lie still and gleaming" as "the midnight moon is weaving/ Her bright chain o'er the deep." The sensuality of these images notwithstanding, their impact on the poet transcends the physical and achieves a spiritual quality. As he tells the woman, "the spirit bows before thee,/ To listen and adore thee." Ultimately, the poem is a paean to a person who inspires near-religious veneration in the poet.

Forms and Devices

In "Stanzas for Music," there is a fundamental tension between form and content that contributes to the poem's effect. The poem was written to be set to music; this fact is evident from its songlike structure. Its sixteen lines are broken into two stanzas of eight lines apiece. Each stanza is thus composed of a quatrain followed by two rhyming couplets, not unlike a song in which each verse is followed by a chorus. The poem is composed with musical precision and balance: It begins with a subjective observation, supports this observation with objective description, and concludes with an image that synthesizes its subjective and objective elements. The theme of the poem, however, refuses to be contained within such a tidy structure.

The poet hopes to elaborate the overwhelming emotion his subject excites in him through a series of similes that evoke the awe and splendor of the natural world: "like music on the waters/ Is thy sweet voice to me:/ When, as if its sound were causing/ The charmed ocean's pausing." Similes, though, are at best only approximations. They suggest equivalence through powerful comparisons, but they do not fully capture the uniqueness of what is being compared. There is an ineffable quality to the woman that resists definition, and it is this quality which earns the poet's adoration.

The tension between the poem's form and content is mirrored in Byron's use of nature imagery. Like other poets of the Romantic era, Byron often described his characters and their endeavors in terms of the natural world in order to elevate and exalt them. The Romantics saw the natural world as a secular manifestation of the divine that superseded theological interpretations of godliness. A good example can be found in the third canto of *Childe Harold's Pilgrimage*, in which Byron uses the inexorable and immutable ocean to symbolize the tide of time upon which human destiny is borne. When Byron uses natural phenomena to describe the influence of the woman addressed in "Stanzas for Music," he transfers their divinity to her. Indeed, he suggests that she transcends their divinity because she can arrest them in their course. By implying that her voice can quell the winds and still the waves, he attributes awesome power to her. Nevertheless, her command over nature is depicted as gentle, rather than violent. In response to her voice, "the lull'd winds seem dreaming" and the swelling ocean's "breast is gently heaving,/ As an infant's asleep." Her effect upon nature at its most volatile is that of a mother to a sleeping newborn child. Hence the poet's adoration of her, through "a full but soft emotion" that differs from simple worship or respect for nature's majesty. Although powerful forces underlie the poem's imagery, its mood is one of tranquility and serenity.

Themes and Meanings

"Stanzas for Music" is a poem concerned with idealized love. In his definitive *Byron: A Biography* (1957), Leslie Marchand proposes that Byron's inspiration for the poem was John Edleston, a choirboy to whom Byron formed a romantic attachment while at Cambridge and whose death in 1811 inspired the five elegiac "Thyrza" poems. Byron created the female persona Thyrza to express, as he said in his diary, "the violent, though *pure*, love and passion" he felt for Edleston. His description of Thyrza in " If Sometimes in the Haunts of Men'" as "too like a dream of Heaven,/ For earthly Love to merit thee" corresponds to the platonic ideal of a love that transcends sexuality at the core of "Stanzas for Music." There is no physical dimension to the love articulated in the poem. Despite Byron's use of vigorous natural imagery, the intense feelings the poem conveys occur on a purely emotional level and almost entirely within the poet's imagination.

Love is the theme of many lyrical poems, but it has a special significance for Byron and the Romantic poets. "In the broad Romantic application of the term love,'" Meyer H. Abrams writes in *Natural Supernaturalism: Tradition and Revolution in Romantic Literature* (1971), "all modes of human attraction are conceived as one in kind, different only in object and degree, in a range which includes the relations of lover to beloved, children to parents, brother to sister, friend to friend, and individual to humanity. The orbit of love was often enlarged to include the relationship of man to nature as well." In "Stanzas for Music," Byron describes the ideal love of the poet for his beloved in terms of several of these relationships. In a different context, the amorous feelings of lovers, the affection of mother for child, and humankind's awe at the mystery of nature might seem very different emotions that bear little relationship to one another. In the poem, however, Byron presents them as flowing from a single pure source. In keeping with the poem's musical format, one could say that the various manifestations of love Byron addresses in the poem are harmonic expressions of the same theme.

"Stanzas for Music" is an example of what Abrams refers to as "natural supernaturalism," the Romantic poets' tendency "to naturalize the supernatural and to humanize the divine." The poem ennobles the person to whom it is addressed by endowing him or her with uncommon powers that are all the more extraordinary for their unconscious expression. It frames supernatural experience in terms of natural phenomena that are universally recognized and understood. In essence, the poem suggests that a love relationship as strong as that known to the poet offers the same emotional fulfillment as an encounter with the divine. It is worth noting that Byron wrote this poem shortly after another love lyric entitled "Stanzas for Music" was published in *Hebrew Melodies*, a collection of verse written to be set to traditional synagogue music. Byron clearly perceived an association between love and religious experience. Although the poem is steeped in the ideology of Byron and his time, the reverent tone and emotional intensity of "Stanzas for Music" make it seem as timeless as a devotional prayer.

Stefan R. Dziemianowicz

STANZAS FROM THE GRANDE CHARTREUSE

Author: Matthew Arnold (1822-1888)
Type of poem: Meditation
First published: 1855; collected in *New Poems*, 1867

The Poem

"Stanzas from the Grande Chartreuse" is a philosophical poem of thirty-five stanzas, each of which contains six lines of iambic tetrameter verse, rhyming *ababcc*. The poem is deeply personal, describing Matthew Arnold's own struggles to find a faith that would give his life meaning.

The poem begins as a narrative. The setting is a mule trail in the Alps, and the time is right before dark on a windy, rainy autumn day. Arnold, a guide, and an unnamed companion or companions are riding slowly up the trail toward the monastery of the Carthusians, who provide shelter and food to passing travelers such as those in Arnold's party.

In the next segment of the poem, Arnold describes the ascetic way of life inside the monastery. The monks devote themselves to prayer, to penitence, and to the study of religious texts. Their only "human" work is growing the plants from which they make their famous liqueur, chartreuse.

At the monastery, Arnold thinks about two faiths that he has rejected: the Christianity represented by the Carthusians and the rationalism that the teachers of his youth presented as a substitute. Believing in neither, Arnold can only suffer. Arnold then thinks of Romanticism, which seemed to offer a new faith. Three Romantic writers— the English poets George Gordon, Lord Byron, and Percy Bysshe Shelley, and the French author of the romance *Obermann* (1804), Étienne Pivert de Sénancour—are all mentioned as examples of Arnold's predecessors, who were willing to suffer to lead human beings to a better life but who left nothing but literary works describing their agonies.

In the final seven stanzas, Arnold defines his state of isolation and of intellectual uncertainty in dramatic terms. He and those who share his sense of alienation are compared to children who live in an abbey. Although they catch sight of passing soldiers, although they hear the sounds of revelry, they have been conditioned to live another kind of life. They cannot obey the calls to "action and pleasure"; they must remain in the cloister, to which they are accustomed.

Forms and Devices

Arnold had a gift for clarifying and dramatizing his often-complex ideas through the use of imagery and metaphor. The beginning of "Stanzas from the Grande Chartreuse" is an example of his technique. On one level, the description of the trail to the monastery captures the reader's attention. On another level, however, the images combine to suggest the poet-speaker's state of mind. The time of day and the season both conventionally symbolize the approach of death. Furthermore, the stream below sounds "strangled"; the mists that arise from it are "spectral," or ghostly. The frightening supernatural is further invoked by the description of the rapids below as a "cauldron." The "scars" on the rocks and the "ragged" trees add to the total picture of fearful desolation, a desolation that is less objective than subjective. This is nature as perceived by a troubled and apprehensive human being.

In the description of the monastery that follows, Arnold again selects images that will emphasize his own reactions. At first, the monastery looks like a "palace," and Arnold rejoices that "what we seek is here!" Literally, he means food and shelter, but more profoundly, his words suggest the faith for which he is searching. Even though the monastery is full of activity, however, the fact that its motivating force is dead, at least to the poet, is emphasized by references to silence, to cold, to the "ghostlike" monks, and to death. After the Mass, the monks bury their faces in their cowls; at night, they lie in the beds that will become their coffins. To the poet, as to his rational teachers, the monastery is in fact merely a *"living tomb."*

Sometimes, instead of using clusters of images to dramatize his perceptions, Arnold explains his philosophical stance by the use of an extended metaphor. For example, he compares himself to a Greek, far north of his own land, looking at a marker in an ancient Germanic language, a marker that evidently is the remains of some long-vanished religion, such as that of the monks. The Greek remembers his own gods, as Arnold recalls the devotion of his rational teachers. To this Greek wanderer, however, those gods are in reality as nonexistent as the Germanic gods represented by the stone before him.

Similarly, in the final section of the poem, Arnold depends on a comparison to make his point. This extended simile is signaled by the opening words, "We are like children. . . ." The significance of the two groups who ride by is indicated in line 194: One represents "action," the other "pleasure." Both groups are on their way somewhere; both are purposeful, in pursuit of something. In contrast, the thoughtful "children" such as Arnold somehow lack the power to leave their refuge. Their alienation is suggested by the fact that they are "forgotten," that they remain "secret" and enclosed, among the graves of the dead, in a "desert" dominated by the dead. Only the candles on the altar give them a glimmer of hope.

Themes and Meanings

Explicitly and implicitly, in "Stanzas from the Grande Chartreuse" the poet has explained the predicament of a person with spiritual aspirations in the modern world. Even though he respects the faith of the Carthusians and, by extension, of other Christians, Arnold cannot embrace it. As his images of the monks and the monastery suggest, the poet believes that faith is dead.

On the other hand, while Arnold still respects the teachers of his youth, their rationalism has not given him a basis for living. Similarly, he cannot see any lasting benefit from the passion of the Romantics, whose descriptions of their own pain did not in any way lessen the pain of future generations.

Evidently, the poet believes that his world is given over to the pursuit of pleasure and of material progress. In ironic phrases, he praises the men of action, who dominate nature, who "triumph over time and space." Certainly, they are energetic, but as he politely rejects them, the poet is suggesting that all their pride and all their energy are purposeless and superficial.

Having rejected Christianity, rationalism, Romanticism, and materialism, Arnold seems to have very little left. He is in a kind of limbo, "Wandering between two worlds, one dead,/ The other powerless to be born." Yet, the poem is not totally pessimistic. One must recall the poet's identification with children in the imagined abbey, who "watch those yellow tapers shine,/ Emblems of hope over the grave."

One source of optimism is the future. Perhaps an age will come when humanity can be wise but not hard-hearted, happy but not dedicated to trivial pleasures. Evidently, most of the great intellectual leaders of Arnold's time placed their hope in such a future time. As the Greek hero Achilles retreated to his tent when he could not prevail against Agamemnon, these leaders have given up the fight; they "wait to see the future come."

There is another source of hope in Arnold's poem: the fact that there are still idealists in the world, people who yearn to believe. Above all, this is the significance of the final metaphor. Although the abbey is deserted, as long as the children of faith listen for "accents of another sphere," they may hope to be rewarded. As long as there is a saving remnant of would-be believers who continue to keep their vigil, there will be a chance for humanity and for a new faith to make life meaningful.

Rosemary M. Canfield Reisman

STATION ISLAND

Author: Seamus Heaney (1939-   )
Type of poem: Meditation
First published: 1984, in *Station Island*

The Poem

"Station Island" is a long meditation on Seamus Heaney's own poetry. The poem sets forth a series of encounters with "ghosts" or remembered figures, many of them from Heaney's own life, some from his reading. The poem takes its title and major setting from Station Island in County Donegal, a devotional shrine; the "stations" there are fixed locations of prayer. The poem is, briefly, a parallel to Dante's *Purgatorio* (c. 1320).

The "I" of the poem is Heaney himself. A few of the ghosts are identified by the text or by Heaney's notes. What is more important is what they say to the poet—the advice and counsel they give him about how to write and how not to "break covenants and fail obligations" to himself, to his art, and to his culture.

Part 1 seems to take place largely in memory. The boy Heaney, on his way to church, encounters an old man, breaking the Sabbath by collecting wood. It is Simon Sweeney, head of a family of tinkers who camped near Heaney's boyhood home. Heaney, hearing bell-notes which are both part of the remembered Sunday and part of the procession on Station Island, sees "a crowd of shawled women," who may very well be his fellow pilgrims. Like the poem itself, the crowd grows into a larger crowd of "half-remembered faces." Heaney sets out "to face into my station." Sweeney, however, is not done with him yet: "Stay clear of all processions" is his shouted advice—processions of religion, politics, and literary and cultural conformity.

Part 2 seems to occur on shore, before Heaney has taken the ferry ride to the island. Seated in his car, he is approached by an angry ghost, who proves to be the nineteenth century Irish novelist and folklorist William Carleton. Carleton was Catholic by birth but converted to the (Protestant) Church of Ireland. Much of his writing records the life of rural peasantry and the sectarian hostilities evident in it even more than a century ago. He is connected to Station Island by way of his first published work, "The Loch Derg Pilgrim," which describes his own visit to the shrine.

Heaney admits that he has read the "Pilgrim." Carleton, perhaps somehow having read Heaney's own accounts of the current sectarian violence in Ulster, is struck by the long persistence of such violence.

Heaney tries to reject the model of Carleton and goes on to suggest how closely his own Derry upbringing imitates the peasant life observed and described by Carleton. It is another example of persistence, yet seemingly a less threatening one than the persistence of the Ribbonmen (Catholic nationalists) and "Orange bigots" (Protestants claiming a loyalty to England) whom Carleton notices. Carleton begins to show some of the self-doubt that will shortly overcome Heaney as well, condemning his conversion as the act of a "turncoat." He has been a man who followed Sweeney's advice and refused to follow the expected processions. A part of what Carleton goes on to advise—"Remember everything and keep your head"—is advice that Heaney seems long before to have followed. Maybe he acknowledges this in his enigmatic last message, a strange and not very pleasant metaphor for an art rooted, like Heaney's, in the details of a particular rural way of life.

Part 3 finds Heaney hearing in the devotions of the present a direct continuation of the religious devotions of his childhood. The ghost here is Heaney himself, as a child saying his prayers with the family and rather mischievously hiding in a large oak sideboard. There he finds the family's relics of a dead aunt.

Part 4 is built around renunciation, first as part of the present pilgrimage, second in the life of a young priest who became a missionary. Heaney's memory of the priest is ironic; he can recall how the priest became a kind of "holy mascot." The priest, in turn, accuses Heaney of a kind of a nostalgic return to the Catholic life within which he was reared. The priest wonders if Heaney is endeavoring to take "a last look" at the sources of his own life and mind or is only returning to the devotional habits of his childhood.

Part 5 may in part be a response, since it begins with "a last look" at his schooling in Anahorish school, and especially at Barney Murphy, a master there who taught Latin to Heaney. Murphy and another unnamed schoolmaster soon give way to two of Heaney's literary "masters," first the Ulster novelist and short story writer Michael McLaverty, and finally the loud voice of the poet Patrick Kavanagh. Kavanagh speaks rather dismissively of Heaney's accomplishment as a poet. Perhaps he represents that nagging voice which prompted Heaney to move from his basically lyric poems into longer ventures such as "Station Island" and *Sweeney Astray* (1983).

Part 6 seems to take its cue from Kavanagh's final rude and sarcastic remark about chasing women. Again Heaney looks back, into the world of adolescent lust and at an unnamed girl whom he pursued in those days. The present world of the pilgrimage interrupts this reflection and suggests other, more "literary" lines of thought—the pastoral verse of Horace, then the love poetry of Dante.

Part 7 forcefully interrupts the mood of reverie; the ghost here is not some beautiful girl or the poet himself as a rather foolishly lovesick boy, but the victim of a sectarian killing. The poem offers a straightforward account of the murder of the ghost. In one sense, the poem is important for what it does not say. The victim, a small-town shopkeeper, was in fact the Catholic victim of a reprisal killing. The killers were off-duty Protestant policemen. The poem itself invokes no sectarian labels whatsoever; Heaney refuses to follow in that "procession" which is the self-generating cycle of sectarian victimization in his native Ulster. The encounter and the poem that records it cannot wholly escape politics or political commitments; confronted with the existence of such victims as this, Heaney feels guilt over his own, less direct part in the politics of civil rights in Northern Ireland. He asks forgiveness, but none is offered.

Part 8 finds the poet-pilgrim still on his rounds. There he encounters two ghosts from his own past, and the note of guilt deepens. The first ghost is that of one of

Heaney's friends, an archaeologist who worked near Belfast. Heaney regrets now his inability to talk satisfactorily with the man during his final stay in the hospital. Again he can find no forgiveness. A second ghost appears, that of Heaney's cousin Colum McCartney, another victim of sectarian violence and the subject of the poem "The Strand at Lough Beg" in *Field Work* (1979).

McCartney, like many of the other ghosts, is angry; he does not find Heaney's having remade his death into poetry at all a consolation, and indeed rebukes him for his commitment to poetry rather than to the sectarian struggle which cost McCartney his life. Worse still, he says, "You confused evasion with artistic tact"—once again, he did not find the correct words, as he had not with his dying archaeologist friend. The result was a "whitewash" job, prettifying the "ugliness" of the actual killing and hiding it behind "the lovely blinds of the *Purgatorio*." Part 9 hears another sectarian voice, that of an Irish Republican Army (IRA) hunger striker. The ghost drives Heaney all the way to "self-disgust"—the emotional low point of the poem—and prompts another apology for lack of full commitment. Heaney goes further: "I hate where I was born."

Yet as part 10 shows, he is not finished with his own past; more gently and lovingly, he recalls a mug used in his bathroom, once used as a prop by some traveling players near his childhood home. Part 11 again looks back, to an unnamed priest who urges Heaney to translate the Spanish mystic and poet Saint John of the Cross—perhaps as partial answer to the entrapment in the personal and cultural which Heaney seems to feel. The greater part of this section is in fact, just such a translation—of a poem explicitly about the "fountain" of faith and eternal life in God, but implicitly about the fountain of poetic inspiration.

In part 12, Heaney returns to the shore, but he is not done with ghosts quite yet. A final figure appears; it is James Joyce, who rebuffs the poet's effort to discuss his *A Portrait of the Artist as a Young Man* (1916). Joyce offers advice which echoes Sweeney's. Against Carleton's insistence that Heaney attend to and remember the details of Irish life, Joyce argues for a freer path. The poem as a whole thus ends with the notes of radical self-doubt and "Irishness" as an obligation rejected unequivocally.

Forms and Devices

The poem moves through a variety of forms. There is occasional rhyme and near rhyme in the five-line stanzas of part 1 and the quatrains of part 3 and part 10; there is a careful approximation of Dante's terza rima in the tercets of parts 2 and 12, and less elaborately in part 7. The translation from Saint John of the Cross in part 11 is in short rhymed stanzas with a refrain. Ironically, Colum McCartney rejects poetic elegance generally (part 8) in elaborately rhymed verse. Parts 5 and 6 are written in ten- or eleven-syllable free-verse lines.

The most evident and consistent device is the appearance of what Heaney calls "Presences," which are in fact recollections and imaginations—"ghosts," but more accurately enactments of Heaney's own self-accusing voice.

Themes and Meanings

Several questions repeatedly arise in the poem, all of which bear directly upon the body of Heaney's own work. What relation should a poet and his work bear to the poet's own past? Can a poetry, like that of Heaney's mentor and friend Robert Lowell, which arises from intensely and often mysteriously personal experience, be satisfactory? The poem examines what relation a poet's work must bear to the (in Heaney's case, harsh) political realities of his culture. It asks how, if at all, a poet may respond to the chilling fact of death. The poem is a prolonged meditation on Heaney's commitments, especially to himself and to Ireland. He hears firmly given advice about going his own way and speaking in his own voice; but how, in practical terms, is such advice to be followed?

These questions often are cast in the language of obligation, which makes them particularly pressing in the tortured world of Ulster, where almost any speech is political. The poem's final advice seems to be in favor of an independence of voice and mood, but that is perhaps offset by a prevailing concern about failure.

John Hildebidle

THE STEEPLE-JACK

Author: Marianne Moore (1887-1972)
Type of poem: Lyric
First published: 1932; collected in *Selected Poems*, 1935; revised in *Collected Poems*, 1951; revised in *A Marianne Moore Reader*, 1961

The Poem

The six-line stanzas (thirteen in all) of "The Steeple-Jack" look oddly ragged at first glance, until one sees that each stanza's pattern is rigorously maintained throughout. Because the poem reads in straightforward sentences, the subject of the whole is easy to identify. A speaker with much information at his or her disposal is providing the reader with a description, full of out-of-the-way details, of a charming New England seaside town. Throughout the poem, the town is described as a peaceful, safe haven; the ocean's waves are "formal," and fishnets are "arranged" to dry. All sorts of people could find refuge here, from waifs to prisoners to presidents. Even a storm is no more dangerous than "whirlwind fife-and-drum" music.

In the course of praising the town as a place of unassuming beauty and inviting elegance, this speaker names three people who are, or would be, "at home" here, "each in his way": first, the German painter Albrecht Dürer, whose close-viewing artistic sensibilities were also Marianne Moore's; second, an out-of-town college student named Ambrose, who also likes to look at the town from a hillside perch; and third, the town's own steeplejack, C. J. Poole, who repairs the steeple on a local church—no doubt one of those picture-postcard churches North American readers associate with New England. Moore published a revised version of the poem in 1961, shortened to eight stanzas, in which the student appears only briefly and is not mentioned by name. The steeplejack has set out two signs in front of the church where he is working; one gives his name, and the other warns, "Danger." The steeplejack's precarious position high in the air provides the only note of tension in the poem, and it hints that—no matter how secure things may appear—there is no haven that is completely safe.

Forms and Devices

In "The Steeple-Jack," Moore uses an idiosyncratic meter that is typical of her verse—a meter that is neither counted in metrical feet nor grasped as "free verse," but rather consists of an exacting syllable count in each line. What the eye cannot see nor the ear hear is that there are exactly eleven syllables in the first line of every stanza. There are ten syllables in all the second lines, thirteen syllables in all third lines, and eight syllables in all lines 4 and 5. Most of her poetry uses this odd method, in which there is an apparently arbitrary syllable count from line to line of an opening stanza which is then rigidly adhered to in subsequent stanzas. This remarkable versification is a Marianne Moore invention; no one writing in English verse had used it before. Most readers do not ever discover it, and no reader, short of counting out the syllables and keeping a record, can grasp by ear the peculiar method. Her famous poem "Poetry" uses a line count of exactly, and preposterously, nineteen, nineteen, eleven, five, nine, and seventeen syllables, repeated five times. The poet must often go to great lengths to keep score. Many lines throughout Moore's opus end in mid-word or on a dangling "the." In "The Steeple-Jack," this delightful event occurs at the end of stanza 3.

Moore loved hiding form inside this mind-boggling tactic. One senses from the liveliness of her poems that Moore devised her method for the sheer fun of it, but in addition to such sport, Moore's use of hidden formal properties is related to several of her themes.

Themes and Meanings

One of Moore's themes in "The Steeple-Jack" is boldly stated early in the poem: "it is a privilege to see so/ much confusion" (lines 23-24). In listing the special features of the town, Moore has placed the banalities of lighthouse and town clock right alongside very painterly specifics, such as the exact names of the changing color of the sea. These two vantage points—the banal and the artistic—cannot be brought together easily without her medium: language. A faith in the aesthetics of odd and ironic juxtapositions places Moore squarely in the high modernist tradition of T. S. Eliot, Ezra Pound, and Wallace Stevens. The speaker, looking down on this tiny whaling town, loves employing, as richly as she can, her strange language palette. Poetry has a reality of sound all its own. On a stroll through this town, anyone might enjoy the flowers, but it is Moore's special privilege to bombard the ear and the language eye: "snapdragon and salpiglossis." It is especially within her province to rhyme however she wishes, and she wishes to rhyme some very unlikely words, rhyming "diffident" with "serpent," and "fishing-twine" with "trumpet-vine." These kinds of rhymes are not for convenience; they make frames of reference collide. Such collisions are only possible through the poet's special language tools. Trust Moore to have learned how many whales have been said to have washed up in this town from time to time; she then gives the reader the pleasure of all eight whales at once—in a kind of surreal timeless image. This poem is as much about its own bravura as it is about the real town it describes. In fact, one purpose of the poem may be to help one question what is meant by a "real" place. Fundamentally, place is something larger than what can be noted as buildings and population.

Understanding this underlying theme and meaning—how poetry bountifully gathers reality in its own way—will help readers understand what happens when Moore finally arrives at the ostensible topic of the poem: There has been a steeplejack on top of the church the whole time. Part of the poem's meaning is to disclose the steeplejack's odd connection to the "ring lizard" and "little newt/ with white pin-dots on black horizontal spaced/ out bands."

For one thing, ring lizards and newts and Mr. Poole provide an odd grouping which, in part, releases readers from stereotypes of comfortable New England towns with sugar-bowl-shaped summer houses and sugar-coated sentimentality. Usually one does not think of waifs and stray animals as being tolerated easily in such a place. Moore would have readers see the postcard notions of New England as one frame of reference among many others that bring fresher vision. There is the vision of the painter, of the student, and of Mr. Poole—each removed and elevated. Mr. Poole is so high up he needs a sign to alert the ordinary passerby.

Once readers hear this urbane and amused tone in Moore, they are faced with exactly what makes her challenging and complicated. Her last odd gathering under the church portico, for example, of waifs, children, animals, and prisoners is made altogether lopsided by her fifth category in the list: presidents. Presumably, like everyone else, presidents may also find release from their normal frame of reference (other politicians who have moral agendas). Poetry is a "place" where one can travel, at least in the mind and soul, far beyond the ambitions and one-dimensional concerns of politics and business. There is a poetic sphere—a sphere of sight, sound, and accuracy—which has little to do with piety or judgment. The accuracy of the newt's markings and Mr. Poole's hand-painted signs provide a reader at times, if by no means always, with a larger truth from which one needs to be at some distance in order to see and enjoy. One must not presume that Moore, for her own convenience, has deliberately ignored small-town stuffiness or prejudices. Few have any illusions that the citizens of such towns actually permit waifs to stand on church doorsteps for long. Nothing is pat in Moore's thinking, either. Something above small-town mentality is more important and vital to the speaker—and to Ambrose, Dürer, and the steeplejack: elegance. Elegance is a key word and underlying theme of the poem.

One rarely knows how to account for elegance ("of which the source is not bravado," line 50). Moore suggests that true elegance eludes human strivings and pride. Elegance is achieved by a poetic ordering of the sort she has managed here, in which the world is not judged nor the hypocrisy in people proved. Moore's is the studious, meditative elegance achieved by disinterested love. Like Mr. Poole, she puts out her danger sign and then goes ahead and climbs that faulty steeple—always in need of repairs, yet always a symbol for humankind's highest spiritual transportation from one small frame of reference to another, larger one. From the top one will have, at the very least, a spectacular view and, at the very most, a new way of seeing and believing.

Beverly Coyle

STELLA'S BIRTHDAY, 1727

Author: Jonathan Swift (1667-1745)
Type of poem: Epistle/letter in verse
First published: 1728, as "Stella's Birth-day. March 13. 1726/7," in *Miscellanies*; collected in *The Poems of Jonathan Swift*, 1958

The Poem

"Stella's Birthday, 1727" is a verse epistle, or letter written in verse. It is the last in a series of birthday poems written by Irish satirist Jonathan Swift for his beloved friend Esther Johnson. Swift met Johnson ("Stella") when she was a child of eight. The daughter of a retainer to Swift's friend and patron Sir William Temple, Johnson served not only as one of Swift's most important correspondents but also as his literary muse. Swift's charming custom of presenting Johnson with the gift of a verse epistle commemorating her March 13 birthday began in 1719 and resulted in a series of "Stella's Birthday" poems culminating in the final poem of 1727.

Johnson died on January 28, 1728, at the age of forty-seven, after years of intermittent poor health. Swift's touching birthday poem of 1727 is both a moving testament to a woman who exemplified for him the feminine ideal of decency, modesty, and prudence, and a tender valedictory to a dear friend. On learning from a servant on January 28 that Johnson had died "about six in the evening of this day," a heartbroken Swift recorded in his journal that he had lost "the truest, most virtuous, and valuable friend, that I, or perhaps any other person ever was blessed with." The following day, still grief stricken, he notes sadly in his journal, "My head aches, and I can write no more" (*On the Death of Mrs. Johnson*, 1765).

Swift begins the poem by assuring Stella that despite her failing health and his own advancing age and increasing infirmities, he intends, as always, to celebrate her birthday with optimism and joy: "This day, whate'er the Fates decree/ Shall still be kept with joy by me:/ This day then, let us not be told,/ That you are sick, and I grown old." Although Swift seeks throughout the poem to cheer his ailing friend by recalling her past acts of generosity and compassion, he also attempts to assuage his own pain at the possibility that she is dying. Unlike the earlier "Stella's Birthday" poems of 1719 and 1721, which are informed by a mood of playful optimism and satirical whimsy, the final 1727 poem contains an air of unrelieved morbidity expressed in a series of pointed questions implying that the person most in need of cheering is not Stella but Swift. In reminding Stella of the lasting value of her past acts, he asks,

> Does not the body thrive and grow
> By food of twenty years ago?
> And, had it not been still supplied,
> It must a thousand times have died.
> Then, who with reason can maintain
> That no effects of food remain?

Swift suggests that true virtue has permanence, nourishing both the virtuous individual and the lives of those who have been touched. These lines reflect the poet's pained awareness not only that he is losing his dearest friend but also that the world is losing an exemplary human being, and it is this sobering realization that haunts the moving central sections of the poem.

Beginning with line 15, the poet beseeches Stella not to dwell on present miseries but rather to take comfort from having lived an unblemished life. In line 18, he urges Stella to "look with joy on what is past." Later, still intent on raising her spirits, he gently challenges her not to dwell on the bleakness of the future but rather to derive satisfaction from a lifetime of virtuous achievement: "Say, Stella, feel you no content,/ Reflecting on a life well spent?" "Virtue," as Swift is at pains to remind Stella, himself, and the reader, can, if properly recalled, "assuage/ Grief, sickness, poverty, and age."

As proof of Stella's exemplary conduct and as a means of paying tribute to her integrity and decency, Swift provides a brief but eloquent catalog of her virtues. He extols her selflessness in ministering to the needy and sick, reminding her that had it not been for her compassion, others less fortunate would surely have died of disease or want: "Your skilful hand employ'd to save/ Despairing wretches from the grave;/ And then supporting with your store/ Those whom you dragg'd from death before." He praises her "gen'rous boldness" in staunchly defending the reputation of "an innocent and absent friend" against the idle gossip and malicious slurs of others. He commends her "detestation" of "vice in all its glitt'ring dress" and, finally, notes with awe her remarkable "patience under torturing pain/ Where stubborn stoics would complain." In thus enumerating Stella's many virtues, the poet establishes for both his subject and the reader that here is an individual of extraordinary merit worthy of everyone's esteem.

Although Swift seeks throughout the poem to repel darker thoughts of Stella's death, he confronts, at the conclusion, the likelihood that she is dying. In the final section, Swift implores Stella to pity those who, like himself, will suffer most from losing her: "O then, whatever Heav'n intends,/ Take pity on your pitying friends!/ Nor let your ills affect your mind,/ To fancy they can be unkind." The poem ends with a deeply moving tribute in which the poet expresses both his desire to change places with the dying Stella and his gratitude that he is at least able to tell her so:

> Me, surely me, you ought to spare,
> Who gladly would your suff'rings share;
> Or give my scrap of life to you,
> And think it far beneath your due:
> You, to whose care so oft I owe
> That I'm alive to tell you so.

Forms and Devices

A standard eighteenth century verse epistle, "Stella's Birthday, 1727" is written entirely in couplets: forty-four pairs of rhymed eight-syllable lines. This poetic form helps convey the intimate, almost conversational tone of the poem while providing a tightly controlled frame for the poet to express his innermost thoughts. Despite the regularity of the meter and the rigidity of the rhyme scheme, the form is not as confining as it may appear. Swift takes advantage of the epistle form to speak directly and concisely to Stella. The poem's lines are short, to the point, and virtually devoid of imagistic language or extended metaphor. Rather than masking his message in rhetorical flourishes or elevated language, Swift employs the more direct and humble address of the letter writer and friend. For example, late in the poem he urges Stella not to abandon herself to despair but rather to gain strength from the visible effects of her past virtuous actions:

> Believe me, Stella, when you show
> That true contempt for things below,
> Nor prize your life for other ends,
> Than merely to oblige your friends;
> Your former actions claim their part;
> And join to fortify your heart.

This is not to suggest, however, that Swift wholly abandons the use of poetic device or diction. At various points in the poem he uses metaphor and personification to convey the active importance of "Virtue" in Stella's life. In line 62, for example, he likens virtue to a "nutriment that feeds the mind," and later, in lines 73 and 74, he equates the personified Virtue to Janus, the mythological god possessing two faces, one looking forward and one backward.

Themes and Meanings

On one important level, "Stella's Birthday, 1727" is Swift's heartfelt tribute to a much-loved and dying friend. Yet, like virtually all of Swift's works, "Stella's Birthday, 1727" contains satiric elements that allow the central message of the poem to operate on a more universal level. The speaker's voice is both intensely personal and broadly didactic. One of the central issues raised in the poem is the importance of virtue, "by all sages understood/ To be the chief of human good." The poet thus paradoxically uses the twin occasions of Stella's forty-seventh birthday and her impending death to reflect broadly on the importance of a virtuous life well lived.

The Stella of Swift's poem is a model of rectitude, courage, and moral decency, and, as such, she stands as a shining example to all human beings. Stella's willingness to place the needs of others before her own, her devotion to truth and honor, her many charitable deeds, and, above all, her keen understanding of what it means to be a friend all mark her as an individual of the highest moral character and thus worthy of emulation. Swift's personal anguish at the thought of losing so beloved a friend ultimately contains a larger message: that true virtue is an irreplaceable commodity and that those who possess it, such as Stella, need always to be reminded of their value to others. In the concluding lines of the poem, Swift pays lasting tribute to a woman he regarded as the embodiment of virtue, decency, and moral rectitude, a woman he once described, in *On the Death of Mrs. Johnson*, as having "all the softness of temper that became a lady, [and] the personal courage of a hero."

Jacqueline Lawson

STEPCHILD

Author: Garrett Kaoru Hongo (1951-   )
Type of poem: Dramatic monologue
First published: 1982, in *Yellow Light*

The Poem

"Stepchild" is a dramatic monologue in free verse divided into seven sections. Section 1 was first published in *The Nation* under the title "Evacuation." The complete poem under the current title was published in Garrett Kaoru Hongo's poetry collection *Yellow Light*. The title thematically suggests how Japanese Americans feel they are treated in the United States. It also calls the reader's attention to the narrator's relationship with his parents, which, according to the narrator, is built on "lies" and "fairy tales."

In part 1 of the poem, the narrator urges the reader to revisit the experiences of 120,000 Japanese Americans during World War II. Under President Franklin Delano Roosevelt's Executive Order 9066, they were evacuated from the West Coast and put in relocation camps. The narrator then places the Japanese American internment in a larger picture. He lists the discriminatory laws against Asian Americans in the history of the United States: the Chinese Exclusion Act of 1882, a bill passed by the United States Congress that made it illegal for Chinese laborers to come to or stay in the United States; California's Alien Land Law of 1913, which prevented the Issei (first-generation Japanese immigrants) from purchasing land and obtaining leases for more than three years on the basis that they were aliens ineligible for citizenship; and the 1922 United States Supreme Court ruling that stipulated that Japanese immigrants were not eligible for citizenship in the United States (referred to as "the Exclusion Act of 1921" in the poem). Unmentioned by Hongo is the Immigration Act of 1924, also known as the Asian Exclusion Act, which was directed against Japanese and Asian Indian immigration.

Parts 3, 4, and 5 describe the narrator's eagerness to find out what happened to thousands of Japanese immigrants after they arrived in the United States. In part 3, the narrator talks to his parents. He is very upset that he has been fed "fairy tales" about the Nisei (second-generation Japanese Americans) "emerging full-grown/ Americans at birth." Since the narrator cannot find truth from his parents, he decides, in part 4, to do some investigation on his own. He examines stories, brief chronologies, photocopies of documents, records, newspapers, and documented newsprint with "genealogies,/ obituaries, births, driver's licenses,/ land sales, moving sales, leases,/ and Evacuation! Must Sell!' sales." The narrator is shocked by the fact that he is able to find only "ten or twelve books/ a handful" that accurately portray the Asian American experience.

As a result of his research, the narrator becomes very angry. "The Dragon" wants him to scream; the "Shark" wants him to kill, "to tear at the throats of white children."

He then remembers, however, that his wife is also white, "a descendant of Menno-nites/ and Quakers/ who nursed the sick" at the Manzanar and Gila River Japanese American internment camps and who "rowed the long boats/ of their outrage, their protest,/ into the shoals of storms/ gathering on the peaks/ of Heart Mountain." In the last section of the poem, the narrator reconciles with the past, with his feelings, and with the environment. He is at peace with himself and the world.

Forms and Devices

Dramatic monologue consists of words spoken by a fictional character to a silent audience at a critical moment of his or her life. Sometimes these speakers reveal as-pects of their own personalities of which they are unaware. "Stepchild" uses the form of dramatic monologue effectively. In the poem, Hongo creates a persona who feels frustrated about being cut off from history. Sometimes the narrator appears to be talk-ing to the reader; other times he is talking to his parents or himself. The form con-cretely objectifies a person's loneliness and frustration in his search for truth. The nar-rator's attempt to learn about his family history has been obliterated by "lies" and "fairy tales." He feels alienated from a society that has denied him the opportunity to connect to history and to his ethnicity. He is trapped in a situation in which a false sense of security has secluded him from knowing who he really is.

In "Stepchild," the metrical device of free verse is used to celebrate the human aspi-ration for freedom and dignity. The narrator's determination to reclaim his sense of history and identity leads him to writings by people who have the courage to speak the truth. In parts 4 and 5, the narrator quotes directly from Japanese American writer Tokio Akagi, Japanese American artist Paul Chikamasa Horiuchi, and Filipino Amer-ican writer and activist Carlos Bulosan, turning prose into poetry and form into mes-sage. Bulosan's autobiography, *America Is in the Heart* (1973), has been hailed by many as a book that has stripped the recording of Asian American history of its eu-phemism and verbiage. The quotations serve as a bridge between the narrator and the part of history he has never been told, filling a gap left in his heart by the lies people have been telling about themselves, about their families, and about the past. They also situate the narrator firmly among other writers with whose experience he can empa-thize.

"Stepchild" abounds with images of violence. The mother who takes part in the evacuation has a mouth "like crushed rose petals/ fresh with the shock of lipstick." Af-ter "all the veins had collapsed/ from the needles of a thousand mine shafts,/ after all the rail was laid/ and the last spike driven through," the Chinese laborers were "chased back home to Frisco/ or shipped to Kwantung"; if "they refused to be herded,/ they were buried where they stood." The narrator has learned that Japanese American "his-tory is bitter;/ a farmer's thick arm/ slashed on the spiked teeth/ of barbed-wire fences." However, something "stopped the telling./ Someone pulled out the tongues/ of every Nisei/ raped by the felons/ of Relocation." The narrator's anger makes him want to kill, "to tear at the throats/ of white children,/ exterminate them/ like the An-gels of Auschwitz." The poem ends, however, with the narrator's realization that

"There is always a need/ to hate, a need to find/ victims for that hatred." In part 7, he makes peace with himself, with the past, and with the environment. He thinks about nothing for a change except "what it is that flowers from itself and shakes the yellow dust of thought/ onto the red cloisters" of his heart and his passions.

Themes and Meanings

Asian Americans have stereotypically been labeled the "model minority." Many Japanese Americans who were interned during World War II feel too ashamed and embarrassed to talk about that part of history. Except for books such John Okada's *No-No Boy* (1957) and Jeanne Wakatsuki Houston and James D. Houston's *Farewell to Manzanar* (1973), there are not many history or literary books providing honest portrayals of Japanese Americans' experiences in the relocation camps. Hongo is a Yonsei (fourth-generation Japanese American), and "Stepchild" is apparently based on his personal experience. It portrays a person's anger at finding out about the discrimination and mistreatment his parents and grandparents have experienced.

The title of the poem has a strong bearing on Hongo's thematic preoccupations. Following along the same line as Okada's *No-No Boy*, it reveals the confusion many Japanese Americans experienced during and after the relocation camps. According to Chinese American scholar and writer Frank Chin, the experience of the narrator in *No-No Boy*, Ichiro, is based on that of Hajiime Akutsu, a Nisei who participated in the resistance movement in the relocation camps and who demanded constitutional and legal rights for Japanese American internees during World War II. In Japanese, both Ichiro and Hajiime mean "firstborn." The name is appropriate for a whole generation of people who struggle with the confusion about their relationship with both the mainstream culture and their ethnic culture.

What is also interesting about the title "Stepchild" is that it reveals the narrator's ambivalent relationship with his parents. The narrator grows up in a house where people believe that Japanese American internment is "to laugh at,/ its lesson best told/ in a fairy tale/ about the Nisei/ emerging full-grown/ Americans at birth." Eventually, however, the narrator learns of the bitterness of Japanese American history, and no one knows that part of history better than the grandfather "who spent the years/ of his internment/ sealed in the adobes/ at Leuppe in Arizona,/ sleeping on packed earth floors/ under sheepskin blankets,/ and twisting the iron bars/ of his cell."

"Stepchild" represents an effort to search for a connection with history and to reclaim a person's sense of identity. The narrator's discovery in his search for truth can very easily lead him into outrage and hatred. Revenge, however, "blisters" the narrator's tongue and "works in these words, says,/ Teach a Blessingway.'" By reclaiming the past, the narrator has reached peace with himself and with the world. He revels in a scenery where "the sun blonds nothing/ but the sands outside [his] window/ and melons ripening on the sill,/ the yellow ones [they] call bitter."

Qun Wang

STILL, CITIZEN SPARROW

Author: Richard Wilbur (1921-   )
Type of poem: Lyric
First published: 1950, in *Ceremony and Other Poems*

The Poem

Like many other poems in English, some of them quite famous, Richard Wilbur's "Still, Citizen Sparrow" takes as its subject, at least partially, a bird—in this case, a vulture. It does so, however, by addressing itself to another bird, a sparrow.

The use of the opening word, "Still," suggests that the reader is entering the poem at a point where the speaker has already been talking to the sparrow, in a way presumably sympathetic to that bird's belief that the vulture is an "unnatural" creature. This negative characterization is undoubtedly based, for the most part, on the vulture's habit of feeding on dead flesh, "carrion." The use of "Still," however, indicates that the speaker now wishes to qualify whatever he has conceded before the start of the poem proper. In fact, the poem will make a case for the vulture and his mode of existence. This view needs to be argued, not simply because the sparrow thinks otherwise, but also because many human beings share the sparrow's view, responding to this scavenger bird with revulsion, both because of its appearance (its bald head is registered here by the term "naked-headed") and the nature of its diet.

The vulture is presented as rising into the air, bearing the dead flesh he has seized. The initial part of his flight is seen as clumsy (he "lumbers"), but very quickly Wilbur creates an effect of contrast. Once the vulture has ascended to a very high point ("the tall/ Tip of the sky"), he appears to move with effortless ease (he "lie[s] cruising"). In fact, the poem makes an extremely positive judgment of the vulture, saying that there is no more beautiful bird in the sky. Part of the bird's appeal at this point in the poem (the second stanza) lies in its alertness, presumably with respect to detecting creatures who have died.

The vulture is seen as in some way supporting nature, and the sparrow is asked to forgive this scavenging bird, because it rids the earth of dead things. It thereby jeers at changeability ("mutability") by removing evidence of one of its chief manifestations, the change from life to death.

Having devoted half of "Still, Citizen Sparrow" to the vulture, Wilbur then uses the second half of the poem to give his version of a story found in the Bible. Because the inhabitants of earth were wicked, according to the Old Testament, God decided to destroy the world by causing a great flood. Humanity, however, was not to be entirely wiped out; it would survive in the form of Noah and his family. In order to withstand the Flood, Noah was directed by God to create a boat, an ark. According to legend, when the floodwaters subsided, Noah's ark came to rest on Mount Ararat.

The sparrow (along with the reader) is asked to "forget" Noah's activity in building the ark as well as his ability to look down on the drowned world. Rather than make a negative judgment of Noah, the sparrow is asked to empathize with the difficult position of the man, who had to live with the experience of seeing almost everything he knew brought to an end and who had to preside over the surviving small world of the ark and its inhabitants. The sparrow is told that, put in the same position, it would rather have died along with its world. Noah, however, chose to live and is to be seen as the father of humanity.

Forms and Devices

An "apostrophe" is a device often found in poetry. It is an address, usually of an elevated nature, to someone or something not literally present or, if present, not literally capable of hearing or understanding. Yet its use presumes, for the purposes of the poet, that the being or object addressed will hear and comprehend. The apostrophe constitutes a kind of theoretical communication with the reader of the poem; the ultimate audience of the apostrophe, the reader, overhears, so to speak, the words being uttered. "Still, Citizen Sparrow" falls into the category of apostrophe. What makes the employment of this device unusual here is that the apostrophe is not addressed to its initial central subject, the vulture, but is directed instead to another sort of bird, one of the most commonly seen, the sparrow. As such, Wilbur's poem contrasts with two famous works where the bird-subject is directly addressed: John Keats's "Ode to a Nightingale" and Percy Bysshe Shelley's "To a Skylark." In neither of these cases is the poet confronted with having to defend a bird commonly regarded with revulsion, as Wilbur is.

The sparrow is startlingly addressed as "citizen." This is one of several instances in the poem of a notable or unusual diction. Another example is the term "watch-fuller," which is an invention, or coinage, on Wilbur's part, one that would seem to violate convention. He uses it instead of the "correct" form—"more watchful"—to dramatize the vulture's admirable alertness. Other examples of unusual diction are found in the phrases "frightfully free" (used to describe the vulture) and "bedlam hours" (used to describe the poem's second central subject, Noah, as he goes about building his ark). In the first case, a negative term is conjoined to a positive one, the freedom in question perhaps that of the vulture's being able to soar on the basis of feeding off the dead; in the second instance, a word most often used as a noun, "bedlam" (meaning a madhouse), is used as an adjective. Other phrases of note include "rotten office" and "carrion ballast." The first of these uses "office" in its sense of "duty" or "function," attaching to it the adjective "rotten," which can be seen as doing double service. It could constitute a pejorative comment on the vulture's function, as seen by the sparrow; it could also refer to the rotting meat the vulture is willing to consume. The term "ballast," which usually refers to heavy material placed in the bottom of a ship to give it stability, is here made to refer to the carrion the vulture eats and carries with him into the sky. It gives his flight a stable foundation.

Another device Wilbur uses is that of allusion—reference to well-known material drawn from history, literature, mythology, and the Bible. In this poem, the allusion is to the biblical story of Noah. Incorporating that story as he does, Wilbur is making use of yet another device: apparent discontinuity of subject matter. Without warning, the sparrow (and therefore the reader) is asked to shift focus from a scavenger bird to a biblical character. The reader may wonder what one thing has to do with the other, but the poet seems to be leaving it to the reader to close this apparent gap.

There is a notable use of sound patterning, particularly alliteration, in the poem. Alliteration is employed to intensify the effect of certain phrases, such as "the tall/ Tip," "frightfully free," "Devours death," and "mocks mutability."

Themes and Meanings

The unusual nature of the apostrophe in "Still, Citizen Sparrow," the poem's use of striking words and phrases, and its sudden switch of focus are all congruous with the unusual perspectives it is attempting to convey. Wilbur's poem is trying to shake up the sparrow's preconceptions and, ultimately, those of the reader as well.

The sparrow may be said to be a representative of the norm, an ordinary "citizen," having conventional responses both to the vulture and to the idea of cataclysmic destruction. This common bird is presumed to feel repugnance in both cases, being put off both by the vulture's feeding on what has died and by the prospect of surviving in a world where everything one has known has come to an end. The sparrow, according to the poem, would have been only too willing to die along with its world if it had been in Noah's place.

In the view of the poem, which modulates from making a positive aesthetic judgment of the vulture to a positive moral judgment of that bird as well as of Noah, both the scavenger and the biblical character are capable of confronting death and enabling life to continue—the link between the poem's seemingly unrelated subjects. The vulture participates in a physical cleansing of the earth, while Noah participated in a moral cleansing of the same. Neither of them is a "nice" figure. The bird eats rotting meat, while Noah agrees in effect to see his fellow humans killed without having to share their fate. Niceness is not a premium for the poem, however, although it may be for the sparrow, which is viewed as living at a relatively low level. Both the vulture and Noah are placed at a height, the elevated position being ultimately that of the hero, the unusual being, who can confront and absorb the awful, which is part of the necessary rigors of life. It is a difficult endeavor but one that is required if life is to continue. The hero may in some way be a repugnant figure, one who has to be forgiven, but he does what must be done, and in that sense humankind is indebted to him—"all men are Noah's sons."

Alan Holder

STILL FALLS THE RAIN

Author: Edith Sitwell (1887-1964)
Type of poem: Meditation
First published: 1941; collected in *Street Songs*, 1942

The Poem

"Still Falls the Rain" is a meditation on suffering in the world. This poem begins with a reference to the bombing of England by the Germans during World War II, then spins a tapestry of references to suffering throughout the history of the world. The thirty-four lines of the poem are divided into seven stanzas, perhaps to symbolize the seven days of the week and thereby emphasize the comprehensiveness of the suffering Christ still endures. The title of the poem is repeated six times throughout the poem, the number six traditionally being associated with humankind, which was, according to Genesis 1, created on the sixth day of creation.

The poem begins with a somewhat ambiguous and somber allusion to the rain that could refer to a typical rain of water or to a rain of bombs during the air raids. Whichever rain is intended, the allusion is related to the sacrifice of the "Starved Man" or Christ upon the cross so that the rain is finally seen as a flow of blood from Christ's side. The years since the birth of Christ (1,940 at the time the poem takes place) are represented by nails in the cross, thus indicating that Christ suffered for all the sins of the world committed after his death as well as before it.

The poem makes several allusions to biblical accounts related to Christ's betrayal, Crucifixion, and ministry on earth. "The Potter's Field" or "Field of Blood" is the plot of land purchased with the thirty pieces of silver that Judas Iscariot received for betraying Christ and later returned to the Jewish leaders before he hanged himself in despair, as detailed in Matthew 27:3-10. The "worm with the brow of Cain" alludes to the mark placed on Cain after he murdered his brother Abel, as described in Genesis 4. The plea for mercy on "Dives and on Lazarus" refers to the parable of Jesus, given in Luke 16:19-31, about a rich man (traditionally called Dives) and a beggar named Lazarus. In this parable, the rich man lives for himself and ends in Hades where he is tormented with flames, while the poor man ends in the bosom of Abraham, or in heaven. The poet's plea is for both the innocent and the guilty, since the two are often hard to distinguish this side of eternity.

By stanza 5, the rain and the blood of Christ on the cross are presented in parallel lines, emphasizing how he suffers for all creation. The number five is traditionally associated with the five wounds of Christ (two in his hands, two in his feet, and one in his side), making the fifth stanza an appropriate one for this reference to how Christ "bears in His Heart all wounds." The second line of the sixth stanza refers to some of the final words of the self-condemned Faustus in Christopher Marlowe's play *Doctor Faustus* (1588), in which Faustus made a pact with the devil in exchange for twenty-four years of power and fame much as some leaders during World War II bargained with their lives for the sake of worldly gain. In contrast to all these human failings, in stanza 7, the final words of Christ in this poem are those of benediction or blessing as he offers forgiveness at the price of his own life.

Forms and Devices

Edith Sitwell uses a free-verse form for this poem, but she still includes a wide variety of rhymes, including scattered end rhymes. For example, the four lines in stanza 1 end with the words "Rain," "loss," "nails," and "Cross," the first and second forming a half-rhyme and the third and fourth forming a perfect rhyme. In stanza 4, in contrast, the five lines end with the words "Rain," "Cross," "us," "Lazarus," and "one," the middle three words rhyming while the outside two are again a half-rhyme, this time in a form sometimes called consonance. Because the pattern of rhyming is varied throughout the poem, the music of the poem underscores the unpredictable nature of life in the twentieth century.

As noted in the previous section, this poem makes careful use of biblical allusions. No fewer than fifteen of the thirty-four lines contain direct allusions to biblical accounts or concepts, and many of the other lines contain statements consistent with the Christian perspective. These allusions, combined with carefully modulated rhymes and the repeated refrain "Still falls the Rain," give this poem a liturgical quality as it moves from contrition to confession to benediction. In the preface to her book *The Canticle of the Rose* (1949), Sitwell notes that she thought of her poems as "hymns of praise to the glory of life." "Still Falls the Rain" is part of this hymn tradition. The title and refrain also contain a pun on the word "still," which can mean "yet" or "without motion," as if to say the observations in this poem are about a timeless moment that is at once perpetual and complete. This pun emphasizes the eternal nature of Christ's sacrifice even though it took place about two thousand years ago.

One can also see in this poem evidence of the influence of the Symbolist movement from France. T. S. Eliot helped Sitwell discover the genius of this movement in poetry. The Symbolist movement, as interpreted by Eliot, sought to create "objective correlatives" that would use images, either verbal or visual, to indirectly evoke a certain emotional state or response. Because of the subtlety of this approach, the emotional impact is all the greater for its subterranean arrival. In this poem, the collection of images such as "hammer beat," "Tomb," "worm," "Starved Man," and "Baited bear" evoke a feeling of suffering and near despair. In contrast, the music of the poem propels it forward to the concluding benediction so that the final note is one of hope above despair. These two contrary emotions are conveyed or evoked indirectly.

Themes and Meanings

"Still Falls the Rain" represents one of the first serious poems Sitwell wrote after she completed *Gold Coast Customs* (1929). Her decade of relative silence was broken by the encouragement of her brother Sacheverell Sitwell and by the arrival of World War II. Rather than rail at Germany and the other wartime enemies of Great Britain, Sitwell focuses on the larger issues of suffering and absolution as related to all humanity. She prays for Dives and Lazarus, the undeserving as well as the deserving. She acknowledges that Christ suffered for all people and that each year of life (rather than just the war years) is in some sense a cause for his death on the cross. The scene she paints of wartime England becomes a portrait of all history in which humanity is in continual need of redemption. The portrait of Christ at the end of the poem is one of unceasing love and sacrifice. The crimes and griefs of the world seem innumerable, yet the love of God exceeds them all. Thus, in spite of the war era being treated in this work, this poem is very positive in its confidence in God's ability and willingness to act in a chaotic world.

Beginning with this poem and others of the World War II era, the reading public in England began to recognize that Sitwell was a poet of considerable depth and spiritual insight. This poem is dense with historical allusions and profound in its theological statements. Her readings also gained notoriety, especially one given in the fall of 1944. She and her two brothers, Osbert and Sacheverell, were giving a poetry reading at the Allied Forces' Churchill Club in London that was heavily attended by numerous notable literary figures. Just as Sitwell began to read "Still Falls the Rain," a warning sounded that a "doodle bug" or "buzz bomb" was heading toward London. Edith refused to halt her reading, even when many thought of heading for shelter. Her voice and demeanor kept them spellbound as she spoke against the impending doom. She finished her reading as the bomb exploded in the distance, and the audience burst into deafening applause.

Sitwell's poetry reflects her heroic posture of facing the terrors of life with an unflinching conviction that faith and poetry will triumph in the end. In recognition of her valiant spirit and fine poetry, Sitwell was named Dame Commander of the British Empire in 1954. The endurance of "Still Falls the Rain" is proof that such honor was well deserved. Between 1940 and 1949, she wrote an impressive array of poems of striking intensity and beauty, including "Invocation," "An Old Woman," "Eurydice," and "The Song of the Cold." Among these poems, "Still Falls the Rain" stands as one of her finest works.

Daven M. Kari

STILL TO BE NEAT

Author: Ben Jonson (1573-1637)
Type of poem: Lyric
First published: 1616, in *Epicœne: Or, The Silent Woman*

The Poem

"Still to Be Neat" is a song sung by the character Clerimont in one of Ben Jonson's most successful and highly praised comedies, *Epicœne: Or, The Silent Woman*. Clerimont is a rowdy co-conspirator of Sir Dauphine Eugenie, a young man who is to inherit a fortune from his self-centered uncle, Morose. Morose, wishing to disinherit his nephew, marries Epicœne, a young woman whose future children, he plans, will receive his estate instead of Dauphine. At the end of the play, it transpires that Epicœne is actually a young man hired and trained by Dauphine for the role of wife to Morose.

The song is in two stanzas of six lines each. Like the plot of the play, it concerns appearances which can belie reality. The first stanza could be paraphrased as, "Lady, although because of cosmetics you are lovely on the surface, you may not be beautiful at all underneath." The second stanza says, "I prefer a woman whose surface is simple and unaffected, unadorned, but who is lovely within." One key to understanding the poem is to know that the word "still" here really means "always" and carries a concessive sense: "Still to be neat" could therefore be paraphrased. "Although you always appear neat." "Neat," "dressed," "powdered," and "perfumed" describe the cosmetic artifices employed by a woman in high society to make herself beautiful to the eyes of admiring, eligible men.

The "hid causes" of art could be either a natural, inner beauty or merely cunning strategies of self-adornment. Since the lady is always seen covered with powder, perfumed, and clothed in fancy, carefully arranged dress, it is to be presumed that she hesitates to show herself without the protecting artifice of cosmetics. Therefore, even though one has not discovered art's "hid" cause, one may conclude that it is not natural beauty, but cunning and conceit. She is not entirely as sweet as she appears; her beauty is hollow and not "sound."

"Give me a look, give me a face/ That makes simplicity a grace" is a sort of rationalist motto. It means that the singer prefers a woman whose face and figure ("look" may refer to how she looks overall) are pleasing in themselves. Simplicity is exactly the opposite of artifice and implies a lack of adornment. Grace is used in a double sense; it means "graceful," but it is also a word for "virtue," as in the cardinal virtues recommended by religion. So, just as simplicity—a sense of straightforwardness and lack of design, lack of a hidden agenda—is a moral virtue, so a simple face without makeup is graceful and lovely.

"Loosely flowing robes" are contrasted with clothes that are always ("still") "neat." The hair, rather than being powdered and piled up in a fashionable coiffure, should hang loose in "sweet neglect." "Adulteries," like most of the key terms in this song, also has two meanings: sexual dishonesty and adulteration. Literally, art or artifice in a woman's makeup is something unnecessarily added to her natural beauty—an adulteration of her physical virtues. If "art" here refers to the fine arts in general, then to use artistic devices to hide the fundamental situation is to make an adulteress of art. Although these "adulteries" of high fashion, makeup, and dress may attract a man's attention ("they strike mine eyes"), they do not win his heart.

Forms and Devices

Poems that express a sentiment, impression, or moment of contemplation are called lyrical, which opposes them to narrative poetry, which tells a story. This poem, however, is literally a lyric—that is, it is the words to a song. This must be remembered in considering the form of the poem. First, one should note that the lyric is performed by a fictional character and therefore is not directly the voice of the author. Clerimont sings this piece in the midst of a play about deceptive appearances when he has special knowledge that the object of the play's attention, Epicœne, is not really a young girl at all, but a boy in disguise.

Lines which are broken in the middle by repetition alternate with lines which contain no caesura; the rhythm matches the structure of the melody. The second stanza repeats exactly the pattern of the first, with strong syntactic caesuras in lines 7, 9, and 12. In the first stanza, therefore, there is a special accent which picks up the words "neat," "dressed," "powdered," and "perfumed" and matches them with "not sweet" and "not sound." The same pattern occurs again in the second stanza: "look," "face," "flowing," and "free" match with "mine eyes" and "my heart." In the same way, "art's hid causes" and "adulteries of art" are parallel in the song pattern. Such resonances, repetitions, and echoes are characteristic of the genre of poetry called ballad or song. They occur naturally when words are well-matched with music. Merely to think both stanzaically and melodically will produce structures this strict.

What is peculiar to Jonson in this poem is the plainness and straightforwardness of the language—the seeming lack of metaphor or simile. "Still to Be Neat," like its theme of honesty and directness, seems to avoid the usual ornamental figures of speech and tropes that are the natural tools of poetry. Every word can be taken literally, as if this song were merely prose that happened to have a meter and rhyme. The simplicity, however, is itself a poetic effect, an artifice. Most of the key words invite a double reading—are, indeed, almost puns. For example, if the word "art" is taken to mean not "artifice" but the fine arts such as poetry, then "Still to Be Neat" could be read in a second way as a poem about the writing of poetry itself. Then the sartorial imagery becomes symbolism, not literal reference, and the word "adulteries" becomes a powerful statement about morality in aesthetics. "Eyes" become symbolic of superficial perceptions in which value and beauty are separated, whereas "heart" refers to a more authentic response, implying a more authentic poetry.

Themes and Meanings

If one accepts this "symbolic" interpretation of "Still to Be Neat," this elegant little song becomes a typical statement of Ben Jonson's position on the nature of art and language. Jonson lived in a time when the natural philosophy of thinkers such as Francis Bacon and Thomas Hobbes, who were attempting to develop what would today be called a scientific view of reality, engaged in a critique of figural language. When poets employ symbolism and figures of speech to ornament the expression of their meaning, they are moving away from direct reference—from the clean and uncluttered literal designation which would be the ideal of the scientific revolution in the seventeenth century.

This distrust of linguistic embellishment, of poetic fancy and ornament, was based on a philosophy that placed nature before art. Western civilization's new-found confidence in its ability to know the natural world through direct observation and experimentation was replacing a medieval approach to nature as a sort of text written by God. Jonson seems to accept the change in values and tries to reflect it in the rhetoric of his poetry. As Arthur F. Marotti says in his article "All About Jonson's Poetry," "Jonson reveals an hostility to sensuous imagery as well as metaphoric inventiveness, which are to him impediments to communication, a disguising of subject matter he would like to represent in a more direct way."

Jonson's great comedies express the concept in the vaster field of general human morality. In his most famous comedies, *Volpone* (pr. 1606, pb. 1607), *Epicœne*, and *The Alchemist* (pr. 1610, pb. 1612), he represents gullible characters who are easily fooled by appearances and are at the mercy of scoundrels who take advantage of their uncritical acceptance of convincing language and their unpenetrating observational powers. His highly polished epigrams and eulogies often warn of art's ability to deceive. It is ironic that this poem, whose theme is a praise of directness and lack of artifice, makes full use of artistic indirection and double entendre to praise the same thing in poetry.

Robin Kornman

THE STONE HARP

Author: John Meade Haines (1924-   )
Type of poem: Lyric
First published: 1971, in *The Stone Harp*

The Poem

"The Stone Harp" is a free-verse poem of twenty-five lines divided into six stanzas. The title, evocative of a mysterious sound, illustrates John Haines's tendency toward surrealism, a quality noted in many of his poems from the 1971 collection *The Stone Harp*. Haines homesteaded in Alaska (1947, 1954-1969) and established himself as a nature writer. He published this volume, an assortment of mystical and loosely political poems, to mixed reviews. Although he was caught up in the political atmosphere of the late 1960's, he has noted that he was probably too far removed from the events to communicate effectively about them. Perhaps this situation accounts for the somewhat ethereal quality of his work at the time.

"The Stone Harp," Haines says, "was inspired . . . by the sound made by a sudden drop in winter temperatures at my old homestead outside Fairbanks: a very loud humming in the telephone wires, pronounced enough to vibrate in the pole itself." To him, this suggested the earth as a harp with telephone wires as strings. The first stanza describes it thus:

> A road deepening in the north,
> strung with steel,
> resonant in the winter evening,
> as though the earth were a harp
> soon to be struck.

From this simple image, Haines weaves a metaphor that works on several levels, but its essence reflects nature's basic indifference to the struggles of humankind. Stanzas 2 and 3 use a dreamlike sequence to intensify the original image and further evoke the cryptic sound.

In the fourth stanza, the poem shifts to a more specific subject, although indirectly enough to have received varying interpretations from different scholars. "Now there is all this blood/ flowing into the west" seemed to some to refer to the construction of the Alaskan oil pipeline. (In this interpretation, the stanza's final line, "that ship is sinking," could be read as an eerie prediction of the *Exxon Valdez* disaster.) However, Haines himself has asserted that the stanza's flowing blood and sinking ship refer to the Vietnam War.

The final two stanzas shift from universal to more personal reflection. Haines likens himself to the wind, "a drifter/ who walked in from the coast/ with empty pockets." Use of the words "empty pockets" imparts both hope and hopelessness. The five lines of the last verse circle back to the title image of the harp. Left standing on a road at twilight, the poet creates a sound similar to the wind strumming "a stone harp" with "a handful of leaves."

Forms and Devices

The best nature writers, of which this poet is arguably one, possess a sense of "negative capability." The phrase, originating with John Keats, does not imply fatalism (although most nature writers, including Haines, find their work inevitably linked with death), but rather an emptiness, a waiting-to-be-filled quality. One sees this quality developing in Haines's memoir of his Alaskan homesteading years, *The Stars, The Snow, The Fire* (1989). The book is filled with the observations of a careful man surviving alone in the last great American wilderness, and there is much of the watcher, the thinker, and the patient hunter portrayed there. Wendell Berry writes that Haines's poems seem "to have been made with a patience like that with which rivers freeze or lichens cover stones" (*The Wilderness of Vision: On the Poetry of John Haines*, ed. Kevin Bezner and Kevin Walzer, 1996). Indeed, "The Stone Harp," a relatively short poem, took more than two years to assume its final shape.

The beginning stanza uses the metaphor of the earth as a harp about to be struck. Haines then engages the reader's senses with simile. After setting a scene of waiting silence, he introduces sound, emphasizing it with a two-line second stanza that reads, "As if a spade/ rang in a rock chamber:" The colon establishes a bridge to the next stanza, and the resulting momentum carries the reader more easily through the most obscure imagery of the poem. Stanza 3 ends with another reference to sound, as a figure "tries to sing." The allusion to singing subtly underscores the poem's readable, almost songlike quality, produced through an unobtrusive use of alliteration and consonance.

The fourth stanza portrays the anguish of the Vietnam War: "It was not in my nature to speak directly of such things, but to find a way to suggest them . . . a ship going down, and blood draining across the sea" (Haines, in *Living Off the Country*). The third line, "ragged holes in the waterline of the sun," describes Haines's observation of dark clouds appearing like holes in the sky and provides an exceptionally threatening image.

Much effective free verse ends with a striking metaphor that provides a flash of deeper knowledge, and this poem is no exception. Haines reinforces the figurative image in stanzas 5 and 6 with simile in the last verse. The final few lines describe a poet's words as no more than the scratching of wind-blown leaves against stone, easily ignored by the natural world and humankind alike.

Themes and Meanings

Kevin Bezner (*The Wilderness of Vision*) asserts that "Haines has continued to write a variation of the same poem, making it finer and finer." Though this is perhaps an oversimplification, it echoes the belief of many that Haines's poetry reflects a deeply personal attempt to define and refine a fresh archetype of humankind's place in the world. Many nature writers bemoan the effect of civilization upon the natural world, and their writing consistently and pessimistically argues that the earth would be better off without its human "parasite." Haines, having lived in the wilds, writes from a different perspective. His critical writings refer repeatedly to the need for authenticity and sincerity, and indeed he seems tenacious in his honesty. He refers to art as "a version of the truth." As a poet, Haines served an internship in the pre-language world of the wilds, and his voice is the voice of experience—of a man who has run trap lines throughout a brutal Alaskan winter. His work exhibits a solid sense of time passing, the slow wheeling of the seasons, and the inevitability of both winter and spring, of death and life.

Noteworthy too are the repeated references to stone, root, and leaf in much of Haines's work, including this poem. To a poet coming of age in an unforgiving wilderness, the images evoked by these three parts of the natural world are plain yet unending in their possibilities. Stone is hard, cold, unyielding, but it can be broken by a living root. Roots are necessary before leaves can exist. Leaves enable a plant to thrive, yet when leaves die and blow away, the root still lives, guarding its life-blood unseen below the cold frozen earth. Haines continually plumbs this endless cycle in graceful and revealing ways.

Close inspection of the ending of "The Stone Harp" reveals a double meaning that nicely illuminates the mind of the writer. The wind is both poet and wind. As wind, it ignores the efforts of civilization, continuing to blow the leaves across the landscape as it has always done. As poet, it almost abdicates the work of the writer, for the poet's words make only a sound as faint as a rustle. Such implicit simplicity and self-deprecation stand at the heart of Haines's poetry and to a large extent constitute its power.

Sue Storm

THE STONE OF HEAVEN

Author: Jane Hirshfield (1953-   )
Type of poem: Ode
First published: 1988; collected in *The October Palace*, 1994

The Poem

"The Stone of Heaven" is a free-verse ode of thirty-two lines arranged in five stanzas. The stanzas range from two to sixteen lines of irregular length. The last stanza, a sixteen-line hymn to the earth, includes human beings in its praising and naming and is marked by many repetitions of initial words in succeeding lines (anaphora). The voice of the poet serves as a guide in the first two stanzas of the poem, signifying a place ("here") where the earth is the many greens of jade (known as the stone of heaven in China). She further specifies the place in the next stanza, identifying it as the home of the "Flemish Masters," painters of the fifteenth century known for the brilliance and depth of their colors; the poet's voice takes on the tones of an enamored tourist as she describes the town, the houses, and the wine.

In the closing line of the second stanza, she compares the detail in the paintings to brightly colored, leaping fish. A reader familiar with Jane Hirshfield's Buddhist imagery will recognize the appearance of fish in the poem as a kind of shorthand for the abundance of life. This is reinforced in the following image of the woodthrush who sings not in order to fill the world with his song but because he is overflowing with the world's abundance. From here the poem moves to instruct the reader in the many forms of this abundance, striking another of Hirshfield's Buddhist keynotes: Human beings are not the center of the universe ("But the world does not fill with us"). On the contrary, the world generates its own continuous spectacle of sights and sounds. It is "a carnival tent, a fluttering of banners."

The last long stanza is a celebration of the whole world in its abundance and variety, beginning with human beings as multitalented creators. The poet refers to humans as bakers, sword dancers, seamstresses, and glassblowers. Then she apostrophizes the forces in the universe ("whirler of winds"), the mighty sea ("boat-swallower"), and the earth's powers of renewal ("germinant seed"). Returning to the colors of jade with which she began, Hirshfield extends the palette to include the plain colors of earth seen in other minerals, animals, plants, and rippling water. She names the brilliant and the nearly colorless: "roof flashing copper, frost-scent at morning, smoke-singe of pearl." Her catalog embraces the visible signs of creation and those invisible to the naked eye ("flickering helix," "barest conception"). From "the almost not thought of, to heaviest matter," from north to south ("glacier-lit blue to the gold of iguana"), her naming encompasses all of creation. In naming and in seeing the things of this world, she concludes that humans "begin to assemble the plain stones of earth."

Forms and Devices

Its form and structure and the treatment of its subject mark "The Stone of Heaven" as a free-verse ode in the Pindaric mode of encomium, or a poem in praise of something. The classical Pindaric ode includes a paean (a hymn of praise) as Hirshfield does in the final stanza of "The Stone of Heaven." Like the classical ode, it is characterized by apostrophe and anaphora. The poet has set herself the task of praising the whole world (animal—especially human—vegetable, and mineral), including the four elements: earth, fire, air, and water. Throughout the poem, she juxtaposes nonhuman with human creativity in imagery that is predominantly visual and emphasizes color; its palette ranges from brilliant, intense colors to the near colorlessness of smoke and water.

Hirshfield begins by juxtaposing certain colors of jade with human creations (paintings). She refers to jade as the Chinese do: It is a religious symbol, "the very stone of Heaven." The effect of the implicit metaphor that follows ("And here, in the glittering/ hues of the Flemish Masters") is to place the viewers of the scene and the reader in both the paintings and the town: "we sample their wine;/ rest in their windows' sun-warmth,/ cross with pleasure their scrubbed tile floors." Thus the following simile of the leaping and darting fish depicts the colors of both the paintings and the town: "Everywhere the details leap like fish—bright shards/ of water out of water, facet-cut, swift-moving/ on the myriad bones." Fish also symbolize plenty in Buddhist iconography, and thus they, together with the stone of Heaven, perform a dual function: poetic device and religious symbol.

The singing woodthrush is the poet's counterpart in the animal world and the embodiment of the world's abundance. His importance is emphasized in the two-line stanza devoted to him: "Any woodthrush shows it—he sings,/ not to fill the world, but because he is filled." This and the following stanza are transitional, leading into the hymn, a version of a classical paean, with which the poem ends. In encompassing the whole universe in a carnival metaphor, Hirshfield personifies it, emphasizing its spectacle and its amazing feats: "It spills and spills, whirs with owl-wings,/ rises, sets, stuns us with planet-rings, stars." In the long final stanza of the poem, she praises human beings as well as the forces in the universe:

> O baker of yeast-scented loaves,
> sword dancer,
> seamstress, weaver of shattering glass,
> O whirler of winds, boat-swallower,
> germinant seed,
> O seasons that sing in our ears in the shape of O—

Together with the woodthrush's song, this depiction of the wind and the "arpeggio" of ripples it creates in a pond ("we name them arpeggio, pond") provide the few but vivid sound images of the poem; the wind's "O" and the pond's arpeggio are synthetic images, fusing sight and sound. The repetitions characteristic of the classical paean form the very scaffolding of this final stanza as the poet shifts to naming, beginning each of the next five lines with "we name." The poet then shifts the initial repetitions to "from" for three lines, then to "naming," and finally to "seeing." This is the only place in the poem where she actually uses the word "see," though the poem attempts to dazzle the reader with its visual imagery from the outset.

Themes and Meanings

The linked themes of "The Stone of Heaven" are the overflowing abundance and creativity of the universe and the unity of all life. Hirshfield sees the former in every object from the most microscopic to the grandest. In keeping with her Buddhist ideas, the poet celebrates all forms of life from the minute salt crystal and the microscopic helix within the cell to the mighty forces of the earth and the heavens. She uses jade, a stone of widely varying colors, to symbolize the unity of all creation. The colors named in the poem range from yellow to shadings of green to azure blue. Though many traditions other than the Chinese have attached religious significance to jade, the Chinese call it the stone of heaven, and it has been used extensively to symbolize both heaven and earth in religious rites. As the embodiment of the power of heaven, jade plays a large part in funeral practices as well. Taoist belief is even more specific, ascribing cosmic power to jade. The history of jade's religious importance in Buddhist thought can be seen in the theme of Hirshfield's poem in several ways. Her very first naming of the stone in the poem's opening lines connects it to both heaven and earth. She calls it "the stone of heaven," but the jade she names is the common type dredged up on the riverbank and named after the colors of familiar earthly products—muttonfat, kingfisher, and appleskin.

The moral of this celebration is implied in the two-line stanza devoted to the woodthrush who sings because he is overflowing with the world's abundance. Similarly, the job of human beings is not to fill up an otherwise empty universe but to express its plenty. This lesson in perspective and—one could say—in ecology culminates in the naming and praising of the poem's last stanza. Humans may not be the center of the universe, but they are privileged. They are the painters and the poets (the namers), and they make crude matter into objects of beauty and utility. Humans have also been given the power of scientific discovery and the secrets of the cell. As namers and makers, it is "our" (this explains Hirshfield's use of the inclusive pronoun "we" throughout the poem) job to fully apprehend the multifaceted world in all its beauty. To "begin to assemble the plain stones of earth" may be read as instructions for building a heaven on earth now that humans have named it and begun to truly "see" it. Finally, the power Hirshfield accords language and the artist (the namer or the poet) should be mentioned, for it is great and is announced in the reference to the Flemish painters early in the poem.

Sandra Cookson

STOPPING BY WOODS ON A SNOWY EVENING

Author: Robert Frost (1874-1963)
Type of poem: Lyric
First published: 1923, in *New Hampshire: A Poem with Notes and Grace Notes*

The Poem

"Stopping by Woods on a Snowy Evening" is easily one of the most famous, as well as one of the most anthologized, of Robert Frost's poems. It consists of four quatrains that have the following rhyme scheme: *aaba, bbcb, ccdc, dddd.* The poem's central narrative is simple, and the scene is understated, even stark, bare of elaboration or detail. A traveler pauses late one snowy evening to admire the woods by which he passes. He reflects that the owner of the woods, who lives in the village, will not see him stopping to "watch his woods fill up with snow."

The speaker interrupts his reflections by imagining that his "little horse must think it queer" to stop without a farmhouse nearby on the "darkest evening of the year." In the third stanza, the speaker expands this conceit, suggesting that anxiety over the untoward action causes the horse to shake his harness bells "To ask if there is some mistake." Then, by way of contrast, the speaker notes that "the only other sound's the sweep/ Of easy wind and downy flake."

Something about the woods compels the speaker's interest, and by the poem's end, as most critics note, one has the sense that there is more to these woods than meets the eye. In the last verse, the speaker acknowledges that the "woods are lovely, dark and deep." He seems reluctant, however, to pursue this insight more deeply, since he immediately observes that he has "promises to keep,/ And miles to go before [he] sleep[s]." Nevertheless, the central focus of the poem is not the woods. Of more importance is the inward drama of the speaker as he reflects about and understands—or fails to understand—why he stops and why he finds the woods so captivating.

The poem ends, then, ambiguously. The reader learns very little about the speaker—either where he is coming from, where he is going, or why he stops. The speaker, however, does not permit himself to reflect too deeply about the occasion, either. One can only speculate, and this is perhaps the full intent of the poem's title: "Stopping by woods" is a gratuitous action, a grace note, an imaginative possibility. The reader, like the speaker, is always "stopping" by woods, and the reader, like the speaker, can choose to make the most of them or to go on.

Forms and Devices

Robert Frost wrote to Louis Untermeyer in 1923 that "Stopping by Woods on a Snowy Evening" would be his "best bid for remembrance." Frost's instincts were correct, but like Walt Whitman's famous "Captain, My Captain," Frost's poem is often remembered for all the wrong reasons. Part of its appeal, surely, is its simple and accessible narrative, which contains only sixteen words that are more than one syllable.

In addition, Frost's end-stopped lines, accentuated by the insistent rhyme, make the poem easy to remember.

Frost, born in California, worked hard at developing the persona for which he is now mostly known—the farmer-poet from New England, the writer of Currier & Ives miniatures. "Stopping by Woods on a Snowy Evening" is Frost's most memorable "genre study" in his "New England" manner, though examination of the poem reveals nothing distinctively regional about it at all. Despite Frost's reputation as a regionalist, his lyrics are generally so underdescribed that they tend toward allegory or parable. "Stopping by Woods on a Snowy Evening" is an example of Frost's art in this respect: It gains its power by suggestion and implication, in its stark understatement, powerfully conveying a depth and fullness of human experience. It is, as Frost remarked, "loaded with ulteriority."

Criticism of the poem has generally treated it allegorically or biographically, and it is easy to see why. Like "The Road Not Taken," another frequently misread lyric, "Stopping by Woods on a Snowy Evening" is almost earnest in its simplicity, though close attention to the text shows it to be more crafty than at first it appears. For example, as is often the case in Frost's first-person lyrics, the speaker of the poem is not to be mistaken for the poet himself, nor is the "I" in a Frost lyric always credible or aware of the complexity of his reflections.

Thus, in this poem, the speaker indicates that his horse thinks it "queer" for them to stop, though it is evident that whatever the horse may think or feel, it is the speaker who projects his own anxiety onto the horse. The poem is constructed as the speaker's reflections of the event, and the first line indicates the speaker's sense that the woods are owned. Thus, some nameless feeling of impropriety or perhaps social violation keeps him from his ease. Consequently, his abrupt dismissal of the wood's allure and his lofty response that he has "promises to keep," though idealistic and possibly true, sounds like a dodge. Mistaking the speaker for Frost himself, one could miss the author's implied criticism of the speaker's sentimentality—who avoids the issue of why he stops by taking refuge in rhetoric and cliché.

To read "Stopping by Woods on a Snowy Evening" as simply a story about a weary traveler longing for the comforts of home, or even to allegorize it as the journey of Everyman, is to miss the subtle qualities that identify it as a Frost lyric. For one thing, Frost balances the onward rhythmic pull of the verse against the obvious stasis of the poetic scene itself: The speaker never arrives, nor really leaves; he is simply always stopping. Frost also arranges the natural scene so as to heighten the drama of the encounter and to reveal its symbolic density. Finally, Frost's sense of dramatic and contextual irony undercut the simplicity of the narrative. After all, despite the speaker's confident assurance about where he is going and the miles he has yet to go, his restiveness (projected onto the horse) and the vagueness of the future "promises" he must keep reveal his assurance to be, in a word, a fiction. This is an important point for Frost. Frost celebrated the necessity of imaginative extravagance in human affairs, but he knew well enough that the imagination traps as well as frees.

Themes and Meanings

Whatever "Stopping by Woods on a Snowy Evening" means, it is evident that the poem makes meaning; it has suffered many designs upon it, and even Frost thought that critics had pressed it too much for meaning. Nevertheless, the poem contains tensions and oppositions that are characteristic of Frost's symbolic terrain in general and of his poetics as well.

Woods are a pervasive image in Frost's poetry, evident in his earliest poems as well as in his last. Dark and unowned, woods are a metaphor of life's wildness, and Frost contrasts them, generally, with places owned by human beings and made artful by their craft. Domesticated spaces such as pastures, clearings, even homes, show the presence of human beings; in these places they make themselves at home, spiritually and physically. In "The Constant Symbol," Frost observes that "strongly spent is synonymous with kept." The human spirit must risk and spend itself, paradoxically, in order to fulfill its nature.

Poets risk themselves and their skill as they create a poem out of the wildness of language. Consequently, readers of Frost's verse, like the speaker stopping to watch the woods fill with snow, find themselves in a typically Frostian place: The poem is a partly wild, partly domesticated place, demanding risk and commitment, involvement and acceptance. Poems, like woods, are lovely, dark, and deep, but only if one will risk entering them more deeply and will let them work upon the imagination.

"Stopping by Woods on a Snowy Evening," then, directs one's attention to that moment when one stops, or at least pauses, between two equally delicious possibilities, and this insistence upon human choice is characteristic of Frost. The "woods" that are "lovely, dark and deep" echo and suggest other sorts of "woods"—the "woulds," the limits, conventions, and oughts by which poets and readers alike live and write. Fenced around with social convention and imaginative need, facing wild woods and dark choices, one must balance and choose.

Frost commented that "Stopping by Woods on a Snowy Evening" is a "commitment to convention." It is also a commitment to risk and to extravagance, especially imaginative extravagance, in order to possess something aesthetically—the woods, for example—that one cannot possess or "own" in any other way. The poem is about patterns and predictability, about rhythms and the complex ways human beings respond to patterns. It contrasts the horse's habituated responses to the human, if less predictable, response of the speaker. The human being must be able to break conventions and rhythms as well as create them. The poem is, finally, about more abstract conventions and rhythms, those of knowledge and understanding, or those of history and the movement of time; it is about how one discovers beauty within these rhythms. It also is about smaller patterns—social manners and expectations, habits enforced by hunger and sleep. The poem is about the boundaries and limits within which human beings live and—Frost's denials to the contrary—the limits within which one must die.

Ed Ingebretsen

THE STORY OF OUR LIVES

Author: Mark Strand (1934-   )
Type of poem: Narrative
First published: 1972; collected in *The Story of Our Lives,* 1973

The Poem

"The Story of Our Lives" is a 201-line narration divided into seven numbered sections. Although the title suggests a history, the poem plays with the discrepancy between what one would expect in a story and the speaker's reluctance or inability to share substantial narrative details. To be sure, traditional narrative elements exist: The speaker reveals that the poem takes place in a room that looks out onto a street, and there are characters. The plural pronouns "we" and "our" in the poem hint at a married couple whose life is not so much told as lived, a life upon which the speaker meditates. Another important "character" exists and speaks in the poem: the book that contains the story of their lives from which the poet quotes; fifty-six lines (28 percent of the total) are italicized as coming from this book. In other words, another important tension in the poem lies between the story in the book that the speaker quotes and the story that arises from his own meditations.

The poem's seven sections suggest an ironic, archetypal period of creation. Although stories usually record past events, this poem, written mostly in the present tense, presents an unfolding of events. Sections 1 and 2 both begin with the line "We are reading the story of our lives." In the first section, the couple is sitting on the couch reading, "hoping for something/ something like mercy or change." The first notes of barrenness are sounded: "it would seem/ the book of our lives is empty." In the second and longest section (forty-six lines), the speaker and the woman continue to read and write (live) the story of their lives as the theme of separation is introduced: "when I lean back I imagine/ my life without you, imagine moving/ into another life, another book."

A dreamlike mood pervades the third and fourth sections, while a tone of yearning pervades the fifth section in which the speaker says, "If only there were a perfect moment in the book." Simultaneous with this yearning, however, is a desire to retreat: "Each moment is like a hopeless cause./ If only we could stop reading." In the sixth and shortest section (sixteen lines), the book chronicles the contradiction between intent and inaction: "*They would patch up their lives in secret:// They did nothing.*" The final section ends by pointing toward hope as the speaker says "yes to everything" and the book records that "*They were determined to accept the truth./ Whatever it was they would accept it./ The book would have to be written/ and would have to be read.*"

Forms and Devices

Mark Strand's "The Story of Our Lives" plays at pushing language to its limits. One device with which the poet attempts to accomplish this is the use of patterns of assertion and contradiction. Many lines blatantly run against each other: "so much seemed to vanish,/ so much seemed to come to life again." In another instance, the characters vow to patch up their lives and then do nothing. When the speaker says, "I say yes to everything./ You cannot hear me," one wonders what good a universal affirmation is if the person to whom he is speaking does not hear it. Toward the end of the poem, the couple is "horrified by their innocence," and, two lines later, they are "determined to accept the truth"; the juxtaposition of active and passive reactions pushes language against itself.

A variation of this strategy is the use of sentences that contradict each other only if read in a certain way: "If only we could stop reading./ *He never wanted to read another book*." If the second clause is interpreted as meaning "he wanted to read *only* this book," it contradicts the meaning "he was tired of reading all books." Another instance of contradictory language based on interpretation is the assertion that "The book will not survive./ We are living proof of that." Since the poem postulates that "they *are* the book," how can they be living proof of the book not surviving? Yet another variation of this device of pressing language to its limits is seen in the tendency toward solipsism, the idea that the self is the only thing that can be known and verified: "We say it is ideal./ It is ideal." What "we say" is truth. Another instance is the line "We study what we remember." Memory and analysis seem to be contrasting rational functions.

These examples of language confronting itself in "The Story of Our Lives" show the surreal leanings of the poem. Strand suggests the play between the real and the imaginary: "The rugs, the furniture,/ seem almost imaginary now."; the room looks onto a street but "There is no one there,/ no sound of anything"; and "The furniture in the room is never shifted." The woman in the poem falls in love with the man across the street because she knows "that he would never visit." The use of the absolute negatives "no" and "never" applied in these circumstances throws readers into a fantasy world where the language of their experiences is being applied to physical and social phenomena that do not follow. Everywhere in the poem, images of waking are set up against images of sleep and dreaming.

Strand's minimalist style strips events and language to essentials. However, there is a troubling quality to these essentials. Taken alone, the assertions seem simple and reasonable enough, but Strand combines them in such a way as to create a distressing, alienated world. The cadence of simple sentences builds a surface rhythm of reasonableness. The author, however, couples images and assertions in such a way that readers feel the world undermining itself, shifting beneath them as if a constant, though subtle, earthquake was making their most basic assumptions unstable.

Themes and Meanings

Strand's chief theme is the exploration of the mind working through language to define the nature of the self. The attempt to reconcile two opposing selves is perhaps best seen in the relationship between the book and the speaker's supplement to and commentary on the book. The closing two lines of the poem read "*They are the book and they are/ nothing else.*" Yet the previous two hundred lines have attempted to explore the reality that their life must be, or at least wants to be, more than the book. For example, at one point the speaker awakens and believes that there is no more to their lives than the book, but the woman disagrees and then goes back to sleep, attempting to elude the control of the linguistically constructed self.

The key tool in this exploration is language. Because language is such a problematic tool, however, writing provides hopeless hope. Language can construct the self, but anything constructed by language is suspect. At a key moment, the speaker says of the book, "It describes your dependence on desire,/ how the momentary disclosures/ of purpose make you afraid." The pronouns "you" and "your" have three possible antecedents. In the structure of the poem, they most literally refer to the woman. They could also be used as a universalizing substitute for "I" and "my." Finally, they could refer to the reader being directly addressed. At any rate, language exists, the passage tells readers, essentially to express desire ("momentary disclosures of purpose"). Those descriptions and disclosures make readers afraid for two reasons: First, language expresses the self's wishes, making them public and permanent; second, another self or part of the self realizes the discrepancy between what is meant or felt and what is said. The speaker says that they keep "hoping for something,/ something like mercy or change,/ a black line that would bind us/ or keep us apart." Language is the black line that both unifies and severs.

For Strand, language is the source not only of hope but also of hopelessness—hopelessness because it will not stay pure and straight; it is, by its nature, contaminated, inadequate. When the speaker says, "I write that I wish to move beyond the book,/ beyond my life into another life," he embodies this paradox. Both the world of the book and the world of "the life" are the world of language, of writing. There is a strong undercurrent in the poem flowing toward the idea that hope comes in love or feeling: "what I feel is often the crude/ and unsuccessful form of a story/ that may never be told." It may never be told because, for Strand, there are only crude language and unsuccessful forms of telling stories. Yet the desire to get beyond language and story always exists. The poet is finally a problematized king: "*A bleak crown rested uneasily on his head./ He was the brief ruler of inner and outer discord,/ anxious in his own kingdom.*"

Scott Samuelson

THE STORYTELLER'S ESCAPE

Author: Leslie Marmon Silko (1948-   )
Type of poem: Narrative
First published: 1981, in *Storyteller*

The Poem

Leslie Marmon Silko's "The Storyteller's Escape" is one of the story-poems included in *Storyteller*, Silko's somewhat autobiographical compilation of stories, photographs, and poems. The work is set in the southwestern United States, specifically in the Laguna area near Albuquerque, New Mexico. In "The Storyteller's Escape," the storyteller is a Native American woman who explains why stories are important. Her statements are alternated with third-person comments and bare descriptions of episodes in the storyteller's life. The free-form stanzas move, more or less, visually in a righthand direction across the page.

The poem begins with the storyteller's assertion that "With these stories of ours/ we can escape almost anything/ with these stories we will survive." This woman—acknowledged by her people to be their storyteller—knows all her people's stories of escape and keeps them both to help the living and to remember the dead.

The people consider her best story to be the one of her own escape from an unnamed enemy. As usual during an enemy attack, the people leave their homes to hide. This time, the enemy is so close that there are no possibilities for rest stops. The old woman muses that in earlier escapes, she had been healthy and fast, leaving the slower villagers behind. However, this time, she is the one who slows under the heat of the sun and who must sit down in the shade to rest. Her main concern is not the enemy, but herself and her story: She fears that no one will know what happened to her or be able to tell her story; thus, no one will remember and grieve for her.

Making the best of her situation, she tries to think of a story to distract herself. She creates a story in which a child looks back, remembers her, and creates a story for her. The child's story explains that the old woman plans to outfox the enemy—by dying before she can be caught. When finally the sun moves away from the old woman, she imagines it beating down on the enemy. She waits through the night until dawn and, knowing she might encounter the enemy yet, returns to the village. She believes this is truly her best escape story. Yet it is the child who must ultimately tell this story, since the old woman died that day.

Forms and Devices

The form of this poem rejects traditional Western ideas of page formatting and of poetic formats that use rhyme scheme, standardized line length, and regular stanzas of lines neatly tucked underneath one another on the page. Instead, the lines of the stanzas of this poem stretch from left to right across the page in nonsymmetrical stanzas. A stanza might—or might not—start at the left margin, indent the next line, then have the next line start on the left margin again. Some stanzas do not ever touch the left margin.

This antitextual representation represents the oral nature of the storytelling that this poem mimics. Laguna storytellers do not speak in iambic pentameter or rhyme; instead, they speak in phrases and sentences of varying length, the length chosen to represent the characters in the narrative and to create the appropriate emotion—tension, laughter, surprise—in the listeners. The offset stanzas allow space for the reader to imagine the storyteller changing voices between the third-person sections and the first-person dialogue.

The poem is unified by the simplicity of its diction (mostly one-syllable, everyday words) and repetition of words, phrases, and situations. For example, the repetition of "always before," as the old woman remembers earlier flights from the enemy, serves to increase the nostalgia and heartbreak of the situation. She describes the ones who had faltered and been left—the sick, the pregnant, the crippled, the old—but "this time," she is among that unfortunate group. Even her decision to stop and rest, an act of defeat, becomes a ritual, for she gives up on the afternoon of the fourth day; four, with its connection to the cardinal directions and winds, is a number often repeated in ceremonial acts.

Neither the setting nor the enemy is delineated in the poem, although both are integral to the narrative. The storyteller's Laguna audience does not need the surroundings depicted; instead, the narrator can mention the lava rocks, hills, and Dough Mountain to evoke the Laguna region for her people. The sun becomes the narrator's focus for description. Although the overwhelming heat of the sun is the immediate reason for the storyteller's pause in the shade, the sun is never described in hostile terms. Instead, the sun is a "hat," a "shawl," and finally, as it leaves, a "butterfly." Even when the speaker wishes the enemy to be disabled by the heat, she refers to the sun as a "blanket." The enemy, too, need not be described, since the actual enemy—be it a hostile tribe, a colonizing culture, or government regulations—is not important: Any enemy can be eluded if people cling to their stories.

Themes and Meanings

The old woman's occupation as storyteller, as well as her conscious efforts to remember stories, create stories, and be remembered in her own story, reveals a recurrent theme in Silko's works: that a common heritage of stories helps people survive. The stories build, continue, and eventually transform the tradition of the community. People survive in cohesive groups because they know and value the same stories. They remember their loved ones and their heroes and know themselves through stories. The old woman, who had guarded and transmitted the Laguna heritage all her life, "could die peacefully" if she knew that someone would tell the story of her final days.

The creative, transformative power of stories is most boldly illustrated when the old woman reflects, "I just might as well think of a story/ while I'm waiting to die" and begins a new story. At this point, the storyteller acts like "Thought Woman" (also known as "Grandmother Spider"), a Laguna creator figure who creates by thinking; as the storyteller narrates, she simultaneously tells of and creates the child A'moo'ooh (this Laguna term of endearment means granddaughter).

In the new story, A'moo'ooh looks back with pity on the storyteller slumped in the shade, knowing how the old woman hates the enemy and contemplating what the storyteller is thinking. At this point, the narration of the story is assumed by the child. Reconsidering the poem in the light of the narration of A'moo'ooh, readers might now suspect that A'moo'ooh (perhaps grown older) has actually been the narrator throughout. This realization broadens the implications of the practice of storytelling, as readers wonder whose story this actually is and how long this story has been told. As A'moo'ooh completes the old woman's story, she completes a cycle of storytellers— while starting another. She achieves the storyteller's escape by telling the story. The storyteller momentarily believes that her escape and achievement will be to die before the enemy can find her, but readers know that the real escape is that the story lives on. The enemy could not kill the story.

When the storyteller exults that she has fooled the enemy, she emerges as what is often called a trickster character, a complex figure known for mischievous pranks and comic or coarse behavior. However, the often-contradictory trickster is also a culture hero who can create and teach. Coyote, the Laguna trickster figure, is known for his protean ability to adapt and to persevere. Significantly, "The Storyteller's Escape" is situated in *Storyteller* within a group of stories about Coyote. When the storyteller creates the A'moo'ooh story, she mimics Coyote's divergent thinking and willingness to change in order to survive; as she plans to "die just to spite" the enemy, her thoughts even sound like Coyote: "I'll fix them good!/ I'll fool them!/ I'll already be dead/ when the enemies come." When she declares that "this one's the best one yet," she shows a Coyote-like pride in both the story she will tell and the fact that the story relates her own exploits. It is only after she makes the resolve to die that the she finds real relief from the sun.

This narrative poem merges well with the other segments of *Storyteller*, since the details of the child and the sun as butterfly imagery echo the details in "Aunt Susie Had Certain Phrases," a story near the beginning of the volume. The other poems and narratives in the volume offer examples of outsiders trying to steal or stamp out the Laguna heritage, suggest ways in which stories convey heritage and heighten the meaning of everyday life, and illustrate traditional tales of the Laguna people; the cumulative effect is to underline the importance of "The Storyteller's Escape." The poem is not about the survival of just one individual through stories, but about the continuity of a people through stories.

Kathryn A. Walterscheid

STRANGE FITS OF PASSION HAVE I KNOWN

Author: William Wordsworth (1770-1850)
Type of poem: Lyric
First published: 1800, in *Lyrical Ballads, with Other Poems*

The Poem

"Strange Fits of Passion Have I Known" is one of six short lyrics generally classified as the "Lucy poems." William Wordsworth wrote all six between 1799 and 1801, and each speaks about a young woman or young girl who has died. (In "Lucy Gray," it is a young girl who has died; in others, including "Strange Fits of Passion Have I Known," Lucy is older and seems to be spoken of as a lover.) Whether Lucy represents a specific person in Wordsworth's life is not known; the poet's close friend Samuel Taylor Coleridge speculated that the poet may have been inspired to write these works when "in some gloomier moment he [Wordsworth] fancied the moment his sister might die" (David Perkins, *English Romantic Writers*, 1967). Since Wordsworth was very close to his sister Dorothy, this explanation is plausible, but it is not necessary to offer a biographical interpretation for any of the Lucy poems; they can all be read as explorations of the impact of loss on the speaker, an emotion both universal and particularly poignant.

In "Strange Fits of Passion Have I Known," the speaker describes a moonlight ride through the English countryside as he travels toward the home of his beloved Lucy. The "strange" fit of passion he wishes to explain to the reader is the rather ironic premonition of death he feels as he rides through the moonlight toward Lucy's cottage. In the opening stanza, the speaker takes the reader into his confidence ("I will dare to tell" of this experience, he notes in line 2); this story is not for everyone, he suggests, but "in the Lover's ear alone" (line 3) can he express his feelings.

The speaker's story is a simple one. At a time when the object of his love looked "Fresh as a rose in June" (line 6), he traverses the countryside toward her cottage. Over "paths so dear to me" (line 12) the speaker's horse carries him toward the object of his travels. All the while, the speaker himself keeps his eyes fixed on the moon, which lights his way as it descends from its point high in the sky, where it sits as the journey begins.

In every stanza except the first and last, the moon is mentioned specifically; in the fourth, fifth, and sixth stanzas, it is described as descending in the night sky, finally dropping behind the roof of Lucy's cottage as the speaker approaches. The passage of the moon in the night sky prompts the speaker to engage in a fantasy, one which he cannot explain logically but which grips him nevertheless. As he watches the moon pass out of sight behind Lucy's cottage, he experiences what he describes as a "fond and wayward" thought (line 25): "O mercy!. . ./ If Lucy should be dead!" (lines 27-28). On that strange, ironic note, seemingly out of context with the idyllic scene depicted throughout the first six stanzas, the poem ends. Unquestionably, this "strange fit"—the choice of words becomes clear to the sensitive reader in this final stanza—is prompted by the speaker's passion for his lover and has no basis in logic; it captures the feelings that often overwhelm one who is passionately devoted to another.

Forms and Devices

As he does with many of his early compositions, Wordsworth uses the ballad stanza form in "Strange Fits of Passion Have I Known" to achieve a note of rustic simplicity. His technique is deliberate and has a historical explanation: In the eighteenth century, most poets relied on elevated language and formal devices that reflected the influence of classical literature. Wordsworth and Coleridge made a conscious effort to transform poetry into something more simple and direct, in which human emotions could be expressed directly in language that all people would understand. Wordsworth states these principles in his famous Preface to the second edition of *Lyrical Ballads, with Other Poems* (1800); there, he describes poetry as "the spontaneous overflow of powerful feelings . . . recollected in tranquillity." A poet is not some seer invested with special divine powers; rather, Wordsworth says, he is "a man speaking to men."

"Strange Fits of Passion Have I Known," and all the Lucy poems, exemplify Wordsworth's premises about the nature of poetry. The language is direct and virtually free of literary tropes. The only simile the poet uses is the rather clichéd "Fresh as a rose in June" (line 6), which he says describes the way Lucy looks to him every day. Even his use of adjectives and adverbs is limited. Only in characterizing the path of the moon in the night sky does Wordsworth attempt to suggest change and motion through choice of descriptors: that sphere is variously "sinking" (line 15), "descending" (line 20), and finally "bright" (line 24) as it drops out of sight behind Lucy's cottage. The result of such sparseness of verbal decoration, coupled with the sparseness of the ballad stanza itself (quatrains of alternating lines of four and three beats), focuses the reader's attention on the action in the poem. Much of that action is simple mental reverie, but the growing state of anxiety which the speaker feels as he approaches Lucy's cottage is made apparent to the reader through the simple language and rustic form of this ballad.

Themes and Meanings

"Strange Fits of Passion Have I Known" is one of several poems in which Wordsworth explores the experiences of solitude and loss. Personifying the idea of solitary beauty in the figure of his chief character, Lucy, the poet uses his reactions to the girl's growth in the country and her death to examine his own attitudes about the value of life and the importance of nature in shaping life.

The very simplicity of Lucy's lifestyle has strong appeal for Wordsworth. Looking back over almost two centuries of poetry shaped by Romantic ideas about the importance of nature and its prominent place as a counter to the evils of civilization, it may be hard to imagine the significance of Wordsworth's achievements in this and the other Lucy poems. Wordsworth's contemporary Francis Jeffrey, editor of the influential *Edinburgh Review,* thought that in "Strange Fits of Passion Have I Known" the poet was trying to handle the "copious subject" of "Love, and the fantasies of lovers" in "one single thought." It is "improbable," Jeffrey thought, that any reader would comprehend Wordsworth's meaning from such a simplistic endeavor (*Edinburgh Review*, 1808).

Such an opinion would hardly be considered tenable in the twentieth century. The tenets of Romantic poetry, which include a recognition of the power of unadorned speech, have gained considerable ascendancy in literary criticism, and twentieth century readers are much more likely than Jeffrey was to sympathize with Wordsworth's intent in this poem. The direct statements concerning the speaker's idle reverie have an immediacy of impact that makes the poet's central ideas easily understandable. This poem is about the simple joys of love and the intensity of feeling that one person can have for another; it emphasizes the tremendous sense of attachment such a feeling provokes. At the same time, the poem serves to remind readers of the tremendous sense of loss that follows the death of a beloved. Wordsworth has carefully woven into his lover's reverie the possibility of such impending doom through his consistent references to the descending moon; its path through the night sky serves as a symbol for the fading lover whose death is foreseen at the end of the poem.

It would be unwise to make too much of this single lyric, however; taken in the context of the series of Lucy poems, it serves to give readers a glimpse into the kind of simple but sincere passions that characterize the life of rustics, a group of people Wordsworth greatly admired. By extension, these passions are ones that Wordsworth attributes to all people of genuine sensibility. These passions are, in his opinion, what define individuals as truly human and what make life worth living.

Laurence W. Mazzeno

STRANGE MEETING

Author: Wilfred Owen (1893-1918)
Type of poem: Elegy
First published: 1919; collected in *Poems by Wilfred Owen*, 1920

The Poem

"Strange Meeting" is a short elegy lamenting a soldier-poet's participation in World War I, the most cataclysmic event that had occurred up until that period in recorded history. The poem is written in the first person; it can be safely assumed that Wilfred Owen and the narrator are the same person and that this is Owen's private journey into hell.

Drawing from many trips into the underworld by characters in earlier literature, Owen seems to escape the horrors of the battlefield; he enters a "profound dull tunnel" where the sounds and scenes of the war are not evident. Noticing that he is not alone, Owen probes one of the "sleepers," awakening one who seems to recognize him and bless him: "By his dead smile I knew we stood in Hell."

Entering into a discussion with the awakened sleeper, Owen informs him that there is no reason to mourn, since the guns and deaths from the battles above are divorced from their presence. The sleeper replies that even though this is true, he grieves over "the undone years,/ The hopelessness." The sleeper, too, had been a soldier-poet—in fact, he is Owen's alter ego, and he realizes the effect he might have had on society if he had not been killed but had been allowed to live and continue writing poetry.

The alter ego holds that World War I, considered at that time as the war to end all wars, is only the beginning of conflicts that will plague men for eternity. The calamity is that "Now men will go content with what we spoiled"; worse yet, if they do not accept conditions, they will simply go to war again, with nationalism dominating human progress. The only slight hope that the alter ego has is that the legacy left behind by the dead might be able to exert influence on the populace "with truths that lie too deep for taint." Leaders would therefore not be able to falsify the reality of war and would not be able to force war upon society.

The alter ego knows that the true duty of the soldier-poet is to inform the public, and he would have gladly given his all to accomplish this goal. Unfortunately for him (and society), he was killed before he was able to do this. Even if he had not been killed, he is afraid that his sensibilities would have been permanently warped by the horrors of war, because the "Foreheads of men have bled where no wounds were."

Owen's alter ego finally identifies himself, in the last five lines, as the man whom Owen had bayoneted to death the day before. Owen then realizes that he too is dead and is bonded with his alter ego, who closes with "Let us sleep now. . . . " Eternity then begins for Owen.

Forms and Devices

By looking formulaically at the structure of "Strange Meeting," one can look at the introduction, the body, and the epilogue separately and can trace the devices Owen uses to produce his desired effect.

In the three-line introduction, Owen draws extensively from the traditional dream-vision poetry of the Romantic period, but he also bases this descent on several incidents from his actual experiences. It has been recorded that Owen once spent more than fifty hours trapped in a caved-in dugout with his only companion a mutilated fellow officer. He also had an almost surrealistic experience when he was a young child with his family in a misty Irish wood; he was haunted in his dreams by both experiences. His preoccupation with the terror of being trapped underground or in a "profound tunnel" manifests itself in the entry into the netherworld of the poem.

In the body of the poem, antithesis is evident throughout. The newly initiated dead man (Owen, even though he does not yet realize that he is dead) is rejoicing at being away from the horrors of the battlefield and questioning his alter ego about why he should mourn now that they are safe and "no blood reached there from the upper ground." The alter ego, conversely, is mourning the lost opportunities to influence society positively through poetic works and language that will educate the public about the futility and folly of war. No sacrifice would have been too great for the alter ego except that of dying and not fulfilling his duty as a poet. He says, "I would have poured my spirit without stint/ But not through wounds; not on the cess of war." Ironically, the price he had to pay was the only one he was unwilling to pay—death—and he mourns.

The alter ego is also mourning the Pandora's box that he believes World War I has opened. Using the "tigress" as a metaphor for the world as a jungle and man as the relentless carnivore, the alter ego is imagining a world in which only the strong will survive, by subjugating the weak. He sees no hope for humankind, because the world and progress are retreating from aggression.

Antithesis is also highlighted in the closing lines as the alter ego addresses Owen by saying, "I am the enemy you killed, my friend." This juxtaposition of opposites, enemy and friend, transcends the animosity of nations and advocates the universal brotherhood of man. It is ironic that this brotherhood is only recognizable and reconcilable after death; on the battlefield Owen was so committed to killing his "enemy" that he had to frown in concentration to accomplish his task.

Themes and Meanings

The central theme in "Strange Meeting" is the futility and horror of modern war. There is no chivalry or honor, which the traditional poets found in war; instead, there is only suffering and death. Owen is attempting to inform the public of the horrors of trench war as seen by the common man in an effort to motivate this self-serving public into a front to force an end to World War I and to be aware enough not to allow another war to happen.

"Strange Meeting" was the end result of a metamorphosis undergone by Owen and other World War I soldier-poets. They went through many changes as their exposure to the war and trench life increased. Initially they wrote patriotic verse, designed to help build a united front opposing the aggressions of Germany. This quickly changed as they began to realize the grim realities and arbitrariness of war. As their frustrations grew, they lashed out at those they saw as either profiting from the war or misguidedly supporting it. Their final stage reflects the sadness and waste of any war at any time no matter what side the combatants and populace are on. Owen was no exception; "Strange Meeting" is perhaps his most poignant poem and strongest antiwar work, crowning his short list of achievements.

Owen is not only lamenting the terrors his generation must face; he is also sadly prophesying future conflicts between nations. He is attempting to show the public the waste such conflicts create, but he realizes the futility—no matter what the truth is nor how it is presented, there will always be those who will strive to go "Into vain citadels that are not walled." It will be the common man who will pay the ultimate price for the conquest of nations.

"Strange Meeting" is a moving elegy for the unknown dead of all nationalities who shared suffering and deprivations for their nations and gave their lives in a conflict very few understood. War is nothing more than murder between strangers, and modern technology raises it to new levels of proficiency. Owen and his alter ego—both soldier-poets, both dead—have concluded their journeys; they are now sleeping together as comrades, even though they were proclaimed enemies by the uniforms they wore. Those differences have been overcome by the universal brotherhood of man. As fellow poets, they know they have been cheated by death of the influence they may have provided. Owen can only hope that by showing their human bond amidst the horrors of war, he can exert some slight influence to urge the world to a warless future.

Stephen H. Crane

STUMBLE BETWEEN TWO STARS

Author: César Vallejo (1892-1938)
Type of poem: Meditation
First published: 1939, as "Traspié entre dos estrellas," in *Poemas humanos*; English
translation collected in *The Complete Posthumous Poetry*, 1978

The Poem
    "Stumble Between Two Stars" is a short poem of forty-five lines divided into nine
irregular paragraphs that range from eleven lines to one line in length. The title affects
a reading of the poem since the word "stumble" is the only indication of movement in
the poem. It is possible, but by no means certain, that César Vallejo intends to suggest
that the meditation which follows is based upon observations made during a walk
along city streets.
    The poet's "stumble" consists primarily of observations and the emotional re-
sponse that those observations provoke. Thus, in the first two stanzas, the poet turns
his attention to "people so wretched" that they have lost their bodies, and by implication, perhaps their souls as well. The poet's description of them certainly echoes that
of Dante's lost souls.
    The second stanza continues the observation of these wretched people. The poet em-
phasizes their doomed condition. They were born to death; every hour of life is death. In
their wretchedness, not even language is available to them, for their alphabet is frozen.
    This wretchedness moves the poet to a cry of pity in the third stanza and begins the
incantatory litany that constitutes the bulk of the poem. In the next five stanzas, the
poet delivers this litany in an almost hypnotic chant, as he calls up those who are "beloved" and details their characteristics. There is a decided echo of the biblical prophets in this chant, as the poet mixes the prophetic voice of vision with that of lamentation. That the biblical prophets were considered spokesmen for God is no doubt part
of Vallejo's intention here: The poet is in essence the voice of God expressing both
pity and tenderness toward the wretched. It is, nevertheless, an ironic God who speaks
through the poet, and the tenderness affected offers rather cold comfort to the blighted
souls accounted for in the litany.
    It is certainly an odd collection of souls that the poet calls forth. Most seem to suffer
an obvious physical poverty or torment or misery, such as hunger and thirst; others
suffer more subtle spiritual or psychological ailments; and some suffer from what appear to be relatively minor complaints. Regardless of the source of their woes, they all
are demeaned in some way, reduced to an almost subhuman condition. The poet feels
pity at the sight of them.

Forms and Devices
    The logic of "Stumble Between Two Stars" is that of Surrealism. Therefore, in or-
der to make sense of the poem, it is essential to understand some of the basic aspects

of surreal metaphors. The Surrealist poet seeks to discover new realities by linking unusual or incompatible objects. Through swift association and arbitrary metaphors—the more arbitrary the better—a deeper reality can perhaps be glimpsed. Contradictions may be apparent in such linkages, but the Surrealist meaning resides precisely in those contradictions. Vallejo, for example, uses adjectives that are not usually associated with the nouns that they modify in his poems. It may not be normal to speak of people with "hair quantitative," but by connecting mathematics or statistics with the human body, Vallejo can make an unusual and subtle point: The wretched people, in this instance, are demeaned, treated in cold statistical terms. Perhaps, too, this concept of quantitative hair is meant to be connected to the biblical statement of Jesus that the hairs of one's head are numbered. Thus, the apparently arbitrary connection of adjective and noun—initially bizarre and esoteric—reveals many possible layers of meaning.

In 1926, Vallejo wrote two articles that urged poets to abandon the false, stylized poetry predominant at the time. In "Poesia Nueva" ("New Poetry") and "Contra el secreto profesional" ("Against the Professional Secret"), he called for poets to avoid simple mimicry of style and instead to embrace nontraditional techniques. In his own work, Vallejo met this call by inventing a unique poetic language that confronted the chaos in the world by approximating and reflecting it. One way in which this language reflected the chaos was by adopting the aesthetics of cubism. In art, Cubism was a movement led by Pablo Picasso and Georges Braque that broke an object into simple geometric shapes and re-presented various views of the object simultaneously. Similarly, Vallejo's poetry attempts the re-presentation and recomposition of not only particular images, but also of the language used to communicate that imagery.

In "Stumble Between Two Stars," for example, Vallejo creates new images by fragmenting familiar ones into parts. The result is a surrealist version of synecdoche and metonymy. These two rhetorical devices, by which parts become representative of the whole, are transformed by Vallejo's irrational vision. In presenting imagery, Vallejo consistently focuses on unusual aspects of the image—in this case of the many "beloved" people who are called forth. The aspects that Vallejo chooses are decidedly unusual. Vallejo concentrates on eccentric imagery in an attempt to parallel the ambiguity inherent in contemporary experience. The aesthetic of this poem thus mirrors the irrational world that the poet experiences. Through surrealist metaphor and the off-center use of synecdoche, he conveys in language the chaotic, bizarre, and often incomprehensible nature of life in his age.

Themes and Meanings

"Stumble Between Two Stars" expresses the sense of alienation and despair that distinguishes much of the great literature that came out of the Paris literary scene of the 1920's and 1930's. Vallejo spent the last fifteen years of his life (1923-1938) in Paris. Vallejo, however, lived a poverty-stricken, bohemian life, moving from hotel to hotel. His experience with poverty and his association with Marxist groups influenced his poetry. Thus, Vallejo, perhaps more than any other artist in Paris, was sensitive to the degradation of human life and the trauma of living a meaningless and gratuitous life on the fringe of society. Vallejo is truly the poet of the *Lumpenproletariat*.

His wretched people—and Vallejo includes himself among this group—are doomed from birth. These people are born in sarcophagi; they constantly suffer; they do not even have the recourse of language, for their alphabet is frozen. Although Vallejo seems to suggest initially that this wretched multitude is condemned to its own Dantesque circle of the Inferno, his incantation of pity for them does offer the hope of something better—purgatory at least, if not paradise. By calling them "beloved," Vallejo offers his own blessing and holds out some measure of hope, however small, for his fallen, weeping fellow wretches. The poet's litany calls to mind the Sermon on the Mount and the Beatitudes that Jesus recites in Matthew. It also brings to mind the chantlike tone of American poet Walt Whitman. The similarities between Vallejo and Whitman may at first seem tenuous, the former being the great bard of democracy, progress, and possibility, and the latter being the poet of personal anguish who wrote of those who suffered under the very forces that Whitman celebrated. On another level, each poet attempts to name the nameless, to identify the hidden, and to give voice to the voiceless.

It is difficult to supply a precise meaning for Vallejo's imagery, since the words in the text are not limited to the meanings that they have in everyday usage. Often, Vallejo simply plays with words and their sounds, and he ends up with phrases such as "the sanchez ears" in line 15. Such wordplay is lost in translation. It is not necessary to find a single correct meaning behind each metaphor or image in the poem, for a basic theme of Vallejo's work concerns one's inability to grasp fully whatever meaning does reside in the world around him or her. His poetry confronts the chaos of the world with a chaos of its own—a chaos of fragmented images and broken syntax. By detailing the drudgery, the poverty, and the physical misery that define human life, Vallejo voices the frustration that is inherent in the human condition. It is a world where hunger can only be satiated by thirst, that is, one deprivation replaced by another—and even that dubious solace often proves unavailable. The poet bemoans the fate of those who have no spiritual control, who have lost part of what defined them as individuals. They no longer remember childhood. They are deep in debt. They fall to the ground, neither dead nor alive, and are not even allowed the comfort of tears. "Stumble Between Two Stars" is a poem full of the anguish, compassion, and hope that Vallejo had for his fellow humans.

Stephen Benz

THE STURGEON

Author: Raymond Carver (1938-1988)
Type of poem: Lyric
First published: 1989, in *A New Path to the Waterfall*

The Poem

"The Sturgeon," written in free verse, consists of fifty-six lines, which are divided into five stanzas or verse paragraphs. The title bluntly states the apparent subject of the poem; as with other poem titles in this posthumous collection—"Wine," "Suspenders," "Lemonade," "Letter," and "Summer Fog," for example—Raymond Carver does not force the title to mean anything. It simply names the object on which Carver decides to focus the poem.

The poem is written in the first person, and the speaker is the poet himself reminiscing about his father and the stories his father told him. The poem begins, however, with an objective description of a sturgeon. Unlike some of the more embellished nature poems by Marianne Moore or Elizabeth Bishop, Carver baldly describes the fish's habitat, body, and habits: "the sturgeon is a bottom-feeder/ and can't see well." He continues, "The sturgeon/ lives alone . . . and takes/ 100 years getting around to its first mating." This is not a baroque style to say the least; Carver's words are as close to prose as poetry is likely to get.

The second stanza moves this description out of a timeless world into a specific moment in time with the description of a specific sturgeon. It seems the opening journalistic description was imitating or recalling "a sketch . . . of its biography" of a nine-hundred-pound sturgeon the author and his father saw "winched up in a corner/ of the Agricultural Exhibit Building." At this point, where the poem will lead can only be guessed.

The third stanza, like the first, has the first-person persona removed from the description. Again, only the facts about the sturgeon are here: "The largest are netted/ in the Don River/ somewhere in Russia." The knowledge displayed about sturgeons is encyclopedic, and the style of the poem is reminiscent of the language of a common reference book. Carver has let the air out of the grand style of poetry writing.

The flat language is used to tell a tall story in the fourth stanza, in which the narrator and his father reappear. The reader discovers that apparently Carver is writing—"I am quoting"—from memory or from an imaginary recollection of the "particular specimen . . . killed in the exploratory dynamiting/ that went on in the summer of 1951," when Carver was twelve or thirteen. The poem picks up pace with the father's description of a hooked sturgeon that fights to a standstill a team of horses fastened to the line.

Carver, however, does not like pyrotechnics—he cuts the story short: "I don't remember much else—maybe it got away." All he can remember is his father beside him "staring up at that great dead fish,/ and that marvelous story of his, all/ surfacing, now and then." The concluding stanza does not resolve any of the principal questions a reader might have about the poem, but it does raise new ones about the importance of the story to Carver as a boy and as a man recollecting it and about what the poem says about the presence of memory in poetry. It is also interesting to consider whether William Wordsworth's definition of poetry fits here, for example, whether this poem is an instant of "emotion recollected in tranquillity" or whether Carver is trying something different.

Forms and Devices

Carver is known primarily as a brilliant short-story writer, although his poems are also well regarded by many. His poems owe much to the short-story genre, as is clearly evinced in "The Sturgeon." The poet uses a plain style, with descriptive details that shy away from metaphor or simile, and a narrative to hold the work together. Carver also takes Wordsworth's words about poetry quite literally: Wordsworth argued, in his 1800 preface to *Lyrical Ballads*, that poets should write in a "language really used by men" and that there should be no "essential difference between the language of prose and metrical composition." Carver seems intent on blurring whatever norms or conventions separate the two genres. This poem reads in places as if it were a reference work; his use of figurative language in the poem—"Mosslike feelers hang down over/ the slumbrous lips"—occurs in the section in which he is apparently quoting from an unnamed source rather than being "poetic."

One of the primary distinctions between a short story and this poem—besides the line breaks—is the fact that the narrator is Carver himself; this poem is not, he insists, fiction, although the fact that Carver cannot quite recall the events central to the poem slurs this distinction. The other central poetic technique used here is the juxtaposition of the simple, descriptive sections (parts 1 and 3) and the parts that are devoted to the capturing of memory (parts 2, 4, and 5). It is this juxtaposition that forces the reader to wonder about the point of joining together the story about the hanging fish, including "its biography—which my father read/ and then read aloud" and Carver's silence about his feelings for his father. The reader is left wondering whether this poem is about grief, and, if so, where the true emotion lies.

Themes and Meanings

In some ways, this poem resists interpretation. It seems to want to remain on the surface, on the level of description only. As with much minimalist fiction, however, there is a hint of another world beneath the poem's prosaic language. Perhaps in the same way that the sturgeon is brought up out of the depths and hung up to dry, this memory that Carver is dragging out of the subconscious is on display for all to see.

What makes this story/poem interesting is the narrator's inability to piece together the story entirely. Yes, he remembers chapter and verse descriptions of the huge fish, but he admits to only partial knowledge of the significance of the memory: "I don't remember much else—maybe it got away/ even then." The memories surface "now and then," and he cannot capture the past in its entirety; it is this honesty that is so winning in the poem. The reader believes a poet who admits fallibility. Also, the poem accrues some tension by this paralleling of encyclopedic fact and incomplete memories, if in fact anything happened—anything "significant"—when he actually stood with his father "staring up at that great dead fish."

Although the poem rejects the traditional devices of poetry—metrics, metaphors, images, or lush sounds—in some ways the poem can be seen as an old-fashioned allegory. The poet is similar to the team of horses in his father's story that is trying to drag the fish—or in the poet's case the memory—up to the surface, but the poet is not even sure who wins in this battle.

The poem does manage to capture a glimpse of a father-son relationship, one that Carver wrote about often in his essays and poems. The relationship is not a warm one or one in which great truths are passed from father to son; there exists one story about horses versus a fish that flashes in the poet's mind, but beyond that the reader is given a picture only of two males staring at a dead fish. The reader is left to decide whether the fish is emblematic of memory or the father in some way or whether the depths at which the fish lives are symbolic of the quiet, almost chilling depth of feeling—the unexpressed feeling—that exists between Carver and his father. It is not a poem that expresses itself; it is as reticent as some men are, as muted and oblique as some relationships between father and son.

Perhaps in Carver's inability to bring the memory of the fish into sharper focus for the reader, he is allowing a glimpse into the world of a man who, like the fish, "lives alone." The accumulation of factual information about the fish is one way to form a bridge of communication, but essentially the poem suggests that there is a central loneliness even in the most intimate relationships. The "marvelous story" of the father that surfaces in Carver's memory "now and then" is a gift that the poet cherishes, but the relationship itself seems as mysterious and strange as the sturgeon, "something left over from another world," now that the poet's father is dead. The poem does not wear its heart on its sleeve, but there is silent mourning in the recollection of what has been lost and perhaps of what was never quite there.

Kevin Boyle

A SUMMER NIGHT

Author: W. H. Auden (1907-1973)
Type of poem: Lyric
First published: 1934, untitled; collected as "A Summer Night 1933," in *Look, Stranger!*, 1936

The Poem

"A Summer Night" is a lyric of ninety-six lines, divided equally into sixteen stanzas (a later version has only twelve). On a June evening, the poet-speaker lies on the lawn, looking at the constellation Vega and aware of the moon beginning to rise. He feels fortunate to be here: a place and time of erotic happiness and fertile friendships. He is an equal lying here each evening with his friends; enchanted, each is called forth, as flowers are drawn by light into fullness of blossom.

These are experiences that will later be recalled when the friends are separated. These evenings, when beastly emotions are tame and there is no consciousness of death, will be important to remember when emotions may be violent and times are chaotic. There is one friend among these others whom the speaker regards as his beloved; their eyes exchange affection, and each is present for the other through the passing of each day.

The second phase of the poem (stanzas 6 through 12) begins when the poet becomes aware of outside pressures threatening to destroy his happiness. He considers the larger world, that part which lies under the light of the rising moon. There, many others in all their variety are also lying at rest. The moon, however, looks down impersonally upon all objects, not discriminating between "churches and power stations," not capable of enjoying the art that its light illuminates in the great galleries of Europe. Indeed, the moon is unable to respond to anything except gravity.

Somewhat like the moon itself, the poet and his friends look out from their island of happy contentment as if from a garden secure against the pains and sufferings that exist in the world. In their tranquillity of love, the friends do not know, and do not want to know, about the threats to Poland or anywhere else in the world. They do not want to think what might be in store for England; they indulge themselves as if on "picnics in the sun."

Inside the wall of their garden, the friends are protected from the sight of "gathering multitudes" whose physical distress is separated from the happy friends' metaphysical debates and limited charity. Even as he distinguishes his garden retreat from the world outside, the speaker is aware that he and his friends are nevertheless being driven down a path that they have not chosen. Their energies have been sapped, their contentment has drained them of the power to direct their own lives. They would give all they have enjoyed from their youthful past, if they could keep alive that happy contentment forever.

In the last phase of the poem, however, their tranquillity is broken by the force of events outside their happy garden. Each of them has been made small by the overpowering flood of violence, as if each had been a river dreaming of itself as the whole reality, when suddenly the great ocean overwhelmed all and revealed how inconsiderable each really is. Each is confronted by the great and horrifying fact of death as it crashes through the "dykes of our content." Still, even ocean floods eventually retreat. While mud yet covers the devastated landscape, some "shy green stalks" will peep through, as "stranded monsters gasping lie" scattered about the landscape. Sounds of rebuilding will disturb the monsters, but those sounds will join the sight of green wheat to promise renewal amid destruction.

The speaker imagines such a future ahead for him and his friends who lie outside this June evening. He resigns himself to loss of private happiness, accepting a future strength in the rebuilding that will come after violence. That future strength that will rise through the mud of political chaos will be the product of his own, and his friends', present happiness in love; it will be like the happy cry of a child through whom the "drowned voices of his parents rise/ In unlamenting song." That strength of a new civilization, like the art nourished by tradition, will be a calm after a storm, a strength born of patience and loving forgiveness.

Forms and Devices

The short lines, repeated rhyme scheme, and brief stanzas of "A Summer Night" are appropriate for the meditative mood of carelessness that governs this poem. Despite the brief interruption of imagining apocalyptic events, the poem is a sustained reflection upon the virtues of friendship, simplicity, and provincial tranquillity. The lyric is therefore like the ode practiced by the Roman poet Horace (65-68 B.C.E.), who sang his songs of happiness in rural retreats to his farm, where he could put great historical events into controlled perspective. Such a lyric may therefore be called a Horatian ode, with its repeated brief stanzas moving through a landscape of tranquil emotion and considered thought.

The devices employed to move the poem in this way are shifts in meter to mark changes in feeling and perspective, variations in the rhymes, and links of sound by alliteration and assonance. The first stanza, to illustrate the shifts of meter, contains two strong pauses and one weak pause before stopping with the period at the end. The first strong pause, a semicolon, occurs at the end of a line, while the second occurs in the middle of a line. The second stanza offers one strong pause and four weak pauses to balance the rhythm of the first stanza. Within the simple and uniform stanzas, thus, are shifts of feeling conveyed by shifts of rhythm.

There are subtleties of rhyming to complicate the appearance of uniformity and simplicity of the *aabccb* scheme. Masculine rhymes (space/place) are varied with feminine ones (summer/newcomer) and mixed ones (bed/overhead). In addition, there are slant-or partial-rhymes (hiding/pleading, wretchedness/distress), which cause a wrenching of the feelings beneath the prevailing tranquillity. Finally, harmonies of sound within stanzas are made by echoing consonants and vowels: In the third stanza, the consonants of "equal" link "colleagues" and "calm," while the vowel of "with" links "in" and "sit"; the play of these links continues in "light" and "hiding," "light," "leaves," and "logic," and "leaves" and "pleading."

In addition, image as symbol is a major device in the poem's development. The image of the moon, which is barely noticed (by the poet's "feet") in the first stanza, becomes prominent in stanza 6, where a new phase of awareness begins and where the speaker's imagination is identified with the moon's light. Sunlight provides a balancing image, hinted at early as the power forcing flowers into blossom and late as the energy summoning wheat from the mud of devastation. Similar balancing of images, to create a rounded or symmetrical form to the poem as a whole, appears in the mention of "lion griefs" early and "tigress . . . motions" late, "forest of green" early and "shy green stalks" late.

Themes and Meanings

Such balancing of sounds and images expresses the meaning of the poem as a balancing of feeling against numbness, of love against hate, and peace against violence. The enchanting light of the moon reveals beauties it cannot appreciate, but it serves well as a vehicle for the poet's humanizing imagination: Everything is made equal by the moonlight, as in a political sense, all should be equal in the human community; but the humanizing of that light allows for political equality to support aesthetic quality and civilized values. The sun provides energy for life, but the imagination provides ethical direction for that life: "The murderer" can see himself "in his glass" by aid of the sun's light, but only an ethical imagination can "forgive the murderer in his glass."

Themes of love and friendship, retirement, nature, and nurture work together to create a harmony of balanced reconciliation between various forces of opposition. Love among friends provides a resource of strength to be drawn upon when hate threatens: Thus, civilization can survive violence on account of its base as communion (community). Retirement behind walls of security appears to be a retreat from reality, because it seems to exist at the expense of a world of suffering; however, it proves to be the source of emotional strength needed for rebuilding after the walls have been broken down. Nature is a calm source of life, even in the worst of times, although it cannot be the end (as either goal or threat) of life. For that, human imagination is required. Instincts (of hunger or sex) may be natural, but their satisfaction will need something more than nature.

Auden, in 1933, anticipated the terrors of World War II. He imagined the need to create sources of strength from which to draw in future need. His poem refuses to surrender loving human commitments in the face of threat and want.

Richard D. McGhee

SUMMER NIGHT

Author: Joy Harjo (1951-   )
Type of poem: Lyric
First published: 1986; collected in *In Mad Love and War,* 1990

The Poem

"Summer Night" is a thirty-five-line poem visually arrayed so that alternating lines dominate either the right-or lefthand side of the page. The poem, written in free verse, describes the persona's impressions of a balmy summer night spent waiting for a lover to come home. In an autobiographical piece, Joy Harjo wrote that she had wanted the poem to capture the feel of a humid Oklahoma night and the impressions of her family's home.

The narrative opens with a description of the nearly full moon and flowers. In the night, children can be heard playing; their parents' laughter and music can also be heard inside the house. The narrator observes this world, listening to its sounds and feeling its rhythms while she waits, once again, for someone to return home—something that apparently is a common occurrence.

Although the poem is not divided into stanzas, the beginning of line 17 marks a shift in perspective from the neighborhood and other people to focus on the emotions of the speaker. The narrator talks of loneliness and of what it feels like to be waiting in the dark on a humid, heavy summer night. Everyone else is sleeping, and it seems that they are all sleeping with someone: Even the night itself is cradled in the arms of day. The narrator sees herself as the only thing without a partner.

The poem's final section is marked by the unseen intrusion of the person she has been waiting for, a return heralded by the scent of a honeysuckle brushed by the person, whom Harjo describes as blooming out of night's darkness. The poem concludes, giving no indication of whether the reunion is pleasant or what problems cause this unnamed individual to be away so often—or even, precisely, who he or she is.

Forms and Devices

The arrangement of the alternating lines that dominate either the right-or left-hand side of the page is an important device for several reasons. To capture the languid rhythms of a humid night, Harjo spreads the words across the page so that they almost lazily descend down the page with blank spaces joining succeeding lines. This wispy visual form also makes the poem seem drowsy and heightens the feeling of warm oppressiveness that can occur on a hot, sticky midsummer's night. Harjo begins the poem by describing the "humid air sweet like melon," a heaviness that dominates most of the first fifteen lines of the poem. The open, alternating visual array also adds a drifting, floating aspect to the poem and helps to portray the wandering, semi-focused attention of someone sitting in the dark listening to the night sounds and waiting. Finally by alternatively pushing the lines right and left, Harjo builds tension, because this placement is unnatural or unfamiliar. The tension helps underscore the narrator's own subtly expressed tension gained from waiting for someone's return.

Not only does the poem's visual sprawl embody the tensions and laziness of the summer night, but it also makes a powerful nonverbal statement about the speaker's isolation. All lines in the poem—with the exception of one—follow the alternating pattern: After the narrator tells the reader that everyone has a partner with whom to sleep, the reader's attention is turned to the narrator's own isolation in line 28 ("Everyone except me"). This is the only line of the poem that is centered on the page. To further heighten the feeling of loneliness, Harjo has made the previous two lines very short, creating a visual blankness above line 28 so that it truly stands all alone.

Harjo is a blues fan and saxophone player; "Summer Night" re-creates some of the cadences of that music. The slow, languid musical rhythms of the lines drift from one topic to another in much the same way that blues spills from harmony to harmony. Harjo gives a bluesy rhythm to her poetry by making use of numerous sentence fragments, a technique that mirrors musical phrasing. Each fragment is the equivalent of a tone, and the combination of these fragments establishes much of the poem's feeling of languor, isolation, and loneliness—in other words, the blues. Harjo underscores this aspect of the poem by mentioning the "wornout records" of the children's parents in line 8 and by equating her own loneliness with "an ache that begins/ in the sound of an old blues song." Just as blues songs sing about people who have been abandoned and who are heartbroken, "Summer Night" works as a blues lament for an unfaithful lover.

"Summer Night" is a poem that circles back on itself: The poem opens with a description of the almost full moon hanging melonlike in the night sky above sleeping flowers. This leaves the reader with the unstated impression of a perfumed night. The poem then moves inward to more and more specific, personal references: first to the darkened neighborhood where only voices in the night can be distinguished, then to a family's home and the intimate sounds of music and laughter, and finally to the narrator's self, which Harjo equates to a darkened home with one light burning patiently through the night. From this point, the poem remains on the level of the abandoned individual and is concluded and moved full circle when the returning lover is described as a "flower of light," echoing the flower image of the poem's second and third lines.

Themes and Meanings

In "Summer Night," Harjo talks of loneliness and anticipation in such a way that the reader is lulled into this sadness by the sleepy rhythms and sprawled lines that propel attention into the middle of the poem and, metaphorically, into the speaker's darkest, most secret private places. It is in the middle of the poem that the speaker confesses her loneliness. Because she says that this waiting "happens all the time, waiting for you/ to come home," she reveals that the loneliness is deep and of long duration. This mood of waiting and watchfulness is intensified by the placement of line 16 ("to come home") on a separate line far to the right of the page.

Harjo calls the narrator's loneliness an "ache" that starts in a blues song. By mentioning this particular type of music, Harjo enables the reader to draw on all the associations that contribute to the power of the blues. Traditional blues is itself a cry for a lost love, a plea for a lover's return, a lament for ill treatment; "Summer Night" is Harjo's blues. In her essay from *I Tell You Now: Autobiographical Essays by Native American Writers* (1987), Harjo says that she wanted "to sustain a blues mood, pay homage to the blues . . ." and that she hears "the sound of a sensuous tenor saxophone beneath the whole poem." Thus, the theme of loneliness is reinforced and its poignancy heightened by the one-time mention of blues in line 18. The poem is a lament, the blues; it is a plea for reunion.

Metaphors also serve to intensify the emotion of "Summer Night." The narrator equates her feelings of loneliness with "a house where all the lights have gone out/ but one." By placing the words "but one" alone on a line at the far right-hand side of the page, Harjo reinforces this isolation. The loneliness—the light mentioned in line 20— burns through the night into the "blue smoke of dawn." The metaphor of smoke calls to mind a spent candle or a lantern guttering out, perhaps in the same fashion as the persona's hope for the absent lover's return.

The low ebb of the poem is the narrator imagining herself as the only person or thing alone—even the night's "sound of a thousand silences" has itself for company. The fact that the night sounds are now quiet implies that they are at rest, peaceful, satisfied. Only the narrator remains awake, watchful, and alone.

Despite the narrator's isolation, at this point the poem's mood grows more affirming: The perfume of a bruised honeysuckle literally sweetens the air; the lover has returned. The poem concludes with the lover radiating light, a light that blooms to fill the darkness. Although Harjo never alludes to why the two people have been separated, and there is no resolution of whatever conflicts caused one person to be absent for an entire night, the poem ends on a positive note; the night is now described as "miraculous."

Melissa E. Barth

SUMMER ORACLE

Author: Audre Lorde (1934-1992)
Type of poem: Dramatic monologue
First published: 1976, in *Coal*

The Poem

An oracle is a prophecy or prediction of the future transmitted through a priest. Audre Lorde's "Summer Oracle" is a prophecy transmitted through the voice of an African American lesbian poet. The poem is a prophetic meditation on the consequences of hopelessness. In the first stanza of this thirty-seven-line poem, the reader is given the world without hope: "Without expectation/ there is no end/ to the shocks of morning/ or even a small summer." At first it is difficult to grasp how the two basic and utterly unremarkable moments of beginning can be experienced as "shocks." Yet in the world of the hopeless, where the morning leads to the inevitable night and the summer to the inevitable winter, there can be no "expectations" of the sort that make morning and summer emblems of hope and transformation.

The oracular voice of the poet begins in the second stanza to characterize and prophesy the world without "expectations." What is described are expectations, but they are ones of fire and insurgency: "Now the image is fire/ blackening the vague lines/ into defiance across the city." The oracle has presented an image, a way to understand what had in the first stanza been merely undefined "shocks." "Defiance" defines the city, and the definition operates both in the sense that it gives meaning to the city and in the sense that it makes it visible. The sun, which had in the first stanza been a shocking reminder of a morning or a summer without expectations, has now become the "sun warming us in a cold country/ barren of symbols for love." Once the definition of violence and defiance has been given to the cold and barren city, it begins to be possible to imagine something else: It becomes possible to imagine love, or at least the symbols for love.

In the next and longest stanza of the poem, Lorde shifts from addressing a social audience to addressing a specific "you" (a member of the barren city now defined with the image of fire). The defining force of defiance is personified, or made into a humanlike actor in the oracle's vision. The earlier stanza had ended with a hope for "symbols of love," but this stanza proclaims that Lorde has "forsaken order" and instead imagines "you into fire/ untouchable in a magician's cloak."

With the introduction of the "magician's cloak," Lorde begins to link the world of the occult and the supernatural with the world of political transformation. The magician (who is also the force of defiance) is "covered with signs of destruction and birth." These are the ancient alchemical signs of the transmutation of base metal into gold, but they are also the revolutionary symbols of apocalyptic transformation: The destruction of the old is joined with the renewing force of birth. The cloak is "sewn with griffins and arrows and hammers and gold sixes." The griffin is a linking of the lion and the eagle; the "arrows and hammers" balance warfare and carpentry. Each emblem operates in two realms: the political and the supernatural.

The new force in history that Lorde has summoned can find no companionship among other ancient magicians and warlocks. Since a warlock is a male witch, the force of history is marked with the signification of the male gender. The new force is not adorned as was the old one: "no gourds ring your sack/ no spells bring forth peace."

The poet who speaks with divine inspiration has brought the "image of fire" into being and has given it the trappings of prophecy, numerology, and alchemy. She has also created the image for destruction and rebirth. The abstract symbols on the cloak do not take into account the real, practical, and human concerns of summer: "I am still fruitless and hungry." The individual human needs are not met. She is "fruitless." Even the fruit is fruitless: "peaches are flinty and juiceless/ and cry sour worms."

The final two stanzas bracketing the long central section return the reader to the poetic fact that "The image is fire." Now one is able to understand more fully specifically what (apart from being a force of defiance and an alchemical magician) the image is and what it means. The second to the last stanza links the image to "the blaze the planters start" in the sugar fields after the harvest; the planters "burn off the bagasse from the canefields/ after a harvest."

In the final stanza, again Lorde says that "The image is fire." It is, she writes (mixing street language with the supernatural and occult), "the high sign that rules our summer." The fire, the sun, and the comradely sign of friendship among urban young men are linked together. The linking of these elements turns the supernatural warlock of the long central stanza back into the potentially violent city. The image is fire, Lorde continues: "I smell it in the charred breezes blowing over/ your body." The body is the city landscape she had described in the first stanza: "blackening the vague lines/ into defiance across the city." The work of the poem has been to turn those vague lines of defiance into accessible language. The body she smells in the fire is "close/ hard/ essential/ under its cloak of lies." The lies are the fictive devices of an ancient way; the truth is the actual historical experience of purifying destruction.

Forms and Devices

As a dramatic monologue, Audre Lorde's "Summer Oracle" is in the tradition of modern poetry that emphasizes the seemingly natural cadences of spoken language while it participates in the resonant and historically significant language of classical prophecy. As an oracle or prophecy, it is in the tradition of an African American rhetoric of spirituality and political empowerment.

One striking example of the use of "natural" language to suggest a spiritual realm is that of the "high sign" in the last stanza. At one level, the high sign is a slang expression for the glance or gesture meant to be a warning of impending danger—it is therefore a kind of oracle in itself. In addition, Lorde evokes the elaborate greeting young men give one another in the street or the high sign with which they celebrate an important shared achievement; it suggests friendship and community. Finally, Lorde's use of the phrase points directly to the sun, the transforming life source which is the most immediate and compelling—the highest sign of all. It is, she writes, "the high sign that rules our summer."

The dramatic monologue, as is customary, is addressed to another person, a persona for the community for whom the poem is a prophecy. While she imagines him in the third stanza as wearing on his cloak the magical symbols of the occult, in the last stanza the inherited symbolic world is revealed to be a "cloak of lies."

While Audre Lorde uses few of the elaborate devices associated with traditional poetry, her "Summer Oracle" draws on the power of poetic statement to inspire and awaken. This power is realized by means of the juxtaposition Lorde makes between the extremes of destruction and survival. Linking such emotional extremes is characteristic of the sublime or the power to envision and communicate a sense of greatness to a reader.

Themes and Meanings

"Summer Oracle" is about envisioning the future; it conveys a sense of impending disturbance and political unrest in the ghettoes of the United States, but it also, by the end, suggests the possibility of purification and personal authenticity. The necessary rebirth can come only after the old historical forces have in some way been destroyed. This is made clear in the image of the canefields burning after the harvest—the burning of the crushed sugarcane refuse is a stark analogy to the destruction that the poem forecasts for the city. When the poem begins, the future is seen as shocking, unmapped by hopes and expectations. As the poem progresses, the indistinct sense of the city is replaced by precision, defiance, and the warming of a "cold country" that had been without the "symbols of love."

Lorde is able to look at her city and the people of her city and say to them that she is able to "imagine you into fire." The theme of fire in its many forms (as the sun, as the magical fire that the warlock's fingers draw, as the burning canefields, and finally as the burnt body from whom "charred breezes" blow back to the poet) gives Lorde the multiple visions of fire as destroyer and purifier. Finally the "Summer Oracle" foretells itself and holds within itself the warning and promise of urgent political change.

Sharon Bassett

THE SUN RISING

Author: John Donne (1572-1631)
Type of poem: Lyric
First published: 1633, in *Poems, by J. D.: With Elegies on the Authors Death*

The Poem

"The Sun Rising" is a lyric poem divided into three stanzas of ten lines each. Each stanza is further divided into two quatrains, respectively rhyming *abba* and *cddc*, and a couplet rhyming *ee*. The title, "The Sun Rising," suggests an aubade, a song sung by lovers upon parting at morning; John Donne, however, renders a parody of the tender love songs written for such occasions. Parting from his beloved is the last thing the speaker of the poem desires to do. Moreover, the title allows for a physical image of the sun actually getting out of bed, an action that the lovers refuse to follow.

In this poem, Donne uses both personification—figurative use of language in which human qualities or feelings are attributed to nonhuman things—and apostrophe—a figure of speech in which a personification is addressed—when the poem's speaker addresses the sun in all three stanzas. The persona or speaker in this poem is the lover who argues with the sun about the power of love to exist outside time and space.

In the first stanza, the speaker irreverently rebukes the sun, whom he calls a "busy old fool" and a "saucy pedantic wretch" for daring to disturb the lovers as if they were mere "schoolboys" or "sour prentices." Donne's allusion to King James I's passion for early hunting outings (line 7) is often used for dating this poem after 1603, the date of James's ascension to the throne of England. The stanza ends with the lover claiming, in the couplet, that perfect love is not bound to the progression of time.

The second stanza begins with an apparent reversal of tone. The lover seems to flatter the sun when he exclaims, "Thy beams, so reverend, and strong." This statement is undercut and reversed in the next lines, however, by the lover's claims that he can obliterate the sun by merely closing his eyes and that his mistress' eyes can blind even the sun's brilliance. He tells the sun to make its appointed daily journey around the earth and discover that all the wealth and power the world has to offer are contained in the bed where the two lovers are resting. (Writing in the seventeenth century, Donne knew quite well that the sun does not make a daily revolution around the earth but uses the image for the sake of the argument.)

The last stanza continues the outrageous qualities that the lover claims for the love between him and his mistress. The two become all states and all rulers, while "Nothing else is." The speaker then changes his apparent dismissal of the sun in the first stanza and invites the sun to join the lovers in the bedroom, arguing that the duties of the sun to warm the world are fulfilled by warming them. The invitation gathers the force of a mild command in the couplet, making the reversal from the opening stanza complete: "Shine here to us, and thou art everywhere;/ This bed thy center is, these walls, thy sphere."

Forms and Devices

The power of Donne's poetic voice is characterized by his dramatic monologue and intensified by his use of the present tense. His approach in "The Sun Rising" illustrates the immediacy that such a voice creates. His speaker (the lover) and his addressee (the sun) are strongly characterized; the present tense allows the reader to experience a progressive development of the speaker's claims and arguments. The inclusion of such mundane things as curtains and beds and the juxtaposition of schoolboys and kings create a strong scene.

The claims that Donne makes for the exclusiveness of love in "The Sun Rising" are created by his expert manipulation of hyperbole, the trope of exaggeration. In the first stanza, the lover elevates mutual love to dimensions beyond the confines of time, while simultaneously dismissing hours, days, even seasons, as mere "rags of time." In the second stanza, the hyperbolic assertions gather force as the lover piles his exaggerations in quick succession; the mistress' eyes are more brilliant than the sun's beams; both Indias—one is not enough—are contained in her; and the bed sleeps all the world's kings and their wealth.

Having reached the near pinnacle of hyperbolic manipulation in the second stanza, Donne makes his most exuberant but logical leap in hyperbolic argument in the third stanza: "Nothing else is." This affirmation of love independent of the world obliterates anything and anybody but the lovers in their bed and bedroom, which now has attained cosmic dimension as well as cosmic significance.

In conjunction with his manipulation of hyperbole, Donne uses meter and intricate syntactical arrangements to convey the superiority of the love portrayed in "The Sun Rising." He employs an uneven syllable count in his lines by varying his line length from short, pithy lines with four syllables to longer iambic pentameter lines. His manipulations of the syllable count allow Donne to operate with different levels of stress and syntactical arrangement. The terse four-syllable lines create a forceful tension in each stanza.

In the first and second stanzas, these short lines are questions addressed to the sun. In the first stanza, "Why dost thou thus" follows its subject—the sun—but Donne delays its completion by syntactical inversion so that the sun literally has to push through windows and curtains, the intervening adverbial phrases, to find its verb. The lovers are not only protected by the physical presence of windows and the like but also isolated by syntax.

In the second stanza, Donne reverses the syntactical arrangement, starting with the direct object instead of the subject, although the reader does not know that until the short second line is read. Whereas in the first stanza the short line questions the sun's authority, in the second stanza this line denies the sun its authority.

The force of the short line is especially immediate in the third stanza as it embodies the ultimate hyperbolic claim of the separateness of love: "Nothing else is." The power of carefully chosen syntactical structure in line 1 of the third stanza illustrates the relevance of such syntax to the understanding of the poem and affirms that attention to such matters can assist the reader to a heightened appreciation of the poem. By syntactical placement of "She" at the beginning of the line and "I" at the end, Donne traps the whole world and its power structure between the lovers: "She is all states, and all princes, I."

Themes and Meanings

The theme of love in all its rich variety fascinated Donne, and he expressed this fascination in the range of attitudes and responses to love in his *Songs and Sonnets*. Heir to the Petrarchan code of the abject lover prostrate before his proud and unrelenting mistress, Donne parodies this tradition in poems such as "The Blossom" and "The Funeral." He advocates promiscuity in lighthearted poems such as "The Indifferent" and writes a witty seduction poem in "The Flea." He questions the constancy of men and women in such cynical poems as "Loves Usury" and "Womans Constancy," and he portrays love that is both physical and spiritual in poems such as "The Good-Morrow," "A Valediction: Forbidding Mourning," and "The Ecstasy."

"The Sun Rising," although it does not explicitly blend body and soul, is nevertheless an argument for the grandeur of love that can combine spiritual and sexual love in perfect equality. Donne insists that the sun has no power over perfect love, reasoning that, since the lovers are the world, the sun will fulfill its duties by remaining in the bedroom; he outrageously asserts that "Nothing else is," testifying to the superiority of a love that is "all alike."

The power of hyperbole, the trope chosen by Donne to embody the separateness of love, lies in its forcible straining of the truth and its ability to go beyond truth to express an ideal. Hyperbole, however, can also overshoot its mark and become an empty affectation, undercutting the ideal it is intended to defend. Eminently aware of the dangers inherent in the hyperbole, Donne manages to push each hyperbole in this poem to its limit so that the mistress, the reader, and the sun are convinced of the unsurpassing beauty of the beloved and the sacredness of mutual love.

Another theme found in Donne's love poetry is the juxtaposition of the sacred and the profane, mirroring secular love in divine concepts and expressing spiritual truths by linking them to secular experiences. In "The Sun Rising," the speaker calls the sunbeams "reverend," an adjective that alludes to a level higher than the physical; by analogy, the mistress also takes on more than physical characteristics. The lovers mirror in their mutual love the Incarnation, since in them the world and its material and spiritual values are contained: "All here in one bed lay."

Ultimately, the poem asserts neither that earthly love mirrors heavenly love nor that mutual love that is both physical and spiritual is the only valid perspective on love. The serious portrayal of love in this poem is but part of the rich variety of human experiences that Donne offers readers of his poetry.

Koos Daley

SUN STONE

Author: Octavio Paz (1914-1998)
Type of poem: Lyric
First published: 1957, as *Piedra de sol*; English translation collected in *Sun Stone*, 1963

The Poem

The title *Sun Stone* refers to the massive calendar stone of the ancient Aztecs. The well-known Aztec calendar measured the synodical period of the planet Venus (the period from one conjunction of the planet Venus with the sun to another). For the ancient Mexicans, Venus was one of the manifestations of the god Quetzalcoatl, the plumed serpent. The calendar begins, as the poem does, at day 4, *Olín* (movement), and ends 584 days (and exactly 584 lines) later at day 4, *Ehécatl* (wind), the conjunction of Venus and the sun: the end of one cycle and the beginning of another. Each of the poem's 584 lines is composed of eleven syllables (hendecasyllables).

Since the Aztec calendar cycle of fifty-two years always begins with *acatl*, the year of the east, it indicates not only the beginning of the world but also the birth of the sun and the dominance of Quetzalcoatl, who, after he is sacrificed, appears in the east as the morning star. The symbol of the east, then, is one of rebirth and resurrection. The opening (and closing) six lines set the poem's tone by describing the world of nature and its rhythms (life and death, day and night). Into this harmonious world, man, the poem's speaker, and history intrude in the fourth stanza.

Stanzas 4 through 9 are a hymn of praise to the speaker's beloved, in which the woman's physical attributes are described in abstract terms. She is ultimately likened to a rain goddess ("all night you rain, all day/ you open my chest with your fingers of water"). In the concluding stanza of this first hymn, the speaker wanders through the corporeal geography to which he has ascended from his abstractions and returns to the first landscape. Youth, growth, beginnings, dawn, vegetation, and water are all clearly attributes of the east echoed in the poem's opening.

With the stanza beginning at line 67, there is a transition that continues to praise the beloved's body and a parallel continuation of nature imagery. Now, for the first time, nature becomes ominous ("a mountain path/ that ends in an abrupt abyss"). The speaker's shadow, his identity, is shattered, and he tries in vain to recover the fragments.

The next two stanzas focus upon the total disintegration of the speaker's personality. Everything that he sees and touches, everything that he is, evaporates, as does time. In his despair, he declares: "I tread my shadow in search of a moment."

In lines 98 and 99, the speaker continues his search, but with less loneliness and fear. A group of girls is shown leaving school, coming out of "its pink womb," an image suggesting birth. One temporarily unnamed girl is at the center of a litany in the lengthy stanza that follows (lines 109-141). More than representing an individual, however, she becomes a composite of all women.

As the east was the dominant spirit of the introductory section of the poem, the western point of Aztec cosmology is invoked here. The west, known as Cuiatlampa, was the place of women and residence of the goddesses and demigoddesses, including the goddess of childbirth. Octavio Paz uses birth imagery and the nameless girl who represents all women (including Melusine and Persephone) to extend the direction of his Aztec calendar to the west. This section ends, like the section on the east, with a return to the nameless, faceless, and timeless moment (lines 146-152).

Instead of moving to north and south, as might be expected, Paz shifts the main weight of the poem's meaning to the remaining pre-Columbian cardinal (and symbolic) point, the center. This symbolic center in the first half of the poem is evoked through the reduction of the speaker's consciousness to his center, to the awareness of his own effort to understand. This shift to the center is preceded, however, by a disintegration of the perception of the "real" world, involving the speaker's figurative dismemberment: "I pick up my fragments one by one/ and go on, bodiless, searching and groping." The speaker is first led and then destroyed by a feminine figure.

In the stanza headed by line 142, at the quarter point of the poem, an invocation of time occurs that fuses its positive aspects, the goal of the search, with the negative, the impossibility of its attainment. All of time becomes encapsulated into a single moment that the speaker attempts to find, capture, and express.

Time's circularity resumes, after the stanza break between lines 194 and 195, with a further development of its destructive features. The unidentified woman who is addressed seems to portray the opposite characteristics of the sensual vision of line 41. Instead of being a rescuer from time's forces, she is now the instrument of time's punishment. Addressing her, the speaker says: "and your sharpened words dig out/ my chest and desolate and empty me." The only definable reality is the speaker's awareness of his own awareness: "awareness pierced by an eye/ which sees itself looking at itself until it is annihilated in clarity." The conclusion of the first half of the poem suggests that the speaker has not progressed in his quest, since he continues to be imprisoned by his own awareness—the only successful weapon against time.

In the second half of the poem, the direction of the speaker's experience moves outward rather than inward. Society, rather than the individual psyche, is its main subject. This change is further intensified by the images of violence in the bombing of Madrid. In the midst of this bombardment, a couple seeks security and peace by making love. In this act, they display a process of integration that is in direct contrast with the speaker's earlier disintegration; the couple is united and untouched by time, invulnerable in "a single body and soul."

The experience of love is dominant in the poem's second half; love becomes life's goal. It is the symbolic center that unites the poem's structure. The tone, in contrast to the first half of the poem, is optimistic. Both halves, however, share the speaker's desire to transcend time and reality.

After a catalog of caricatures of professions and types, followed by a long discourse on history that leads to questions about its meaning, it becomes clear that the speaker has reached a philosophical dead end in his search. He abandons a direct treatment of time in the concluding section of the poem and transfers his anguish instead to the meaning of life and the understanding of the individual's place in it. The prayer of the conclusion (beginning with line 533) is anticipated in the summoning of Eloise, Persephone, and Mary (history, mythology, and Christianity) to reveal their true identities so that the speaker may find his.

Ostensibly addressed to a pre-Columbian deity, the prayer is, in its urgency, the most emotionally charged section of the poem. The anguish of the litany stems from the speaker's hope that he (and humankind) may be released from the narrow confines of time. The prayer is granted (lines 574-583), and the speaker enters a paradise, constructed of the intricate water imagery of the poem's final six lines. With the description of the river that is both source and terminus, the poem concludes with an adverb and a colon that promise infinity: "a course of a river that turns, moves on,/ doubles back, and comes full circle,/ forever arriving:"

The colon contributes to the circular structure of the poem by creating the expectation of continuation. If the reader is not aware at first reading that lines 585-590 are repetitions of the first six lines, then the colon dramatically returns him to the beginning.

Forms and Devices

A major feature of *Sun Stone* is its circular structure. The poet achieves this circular structure through his use of language and by drawing upon Mexican tradition, specifically, Aztec mythology. Transcending Mexican history and setting the poem in a universal dimension, time (the poem's theme), like the poem's structure, becomes cyclic. Endings become beginnings, for man and for nature.

The closing of the poem's cycle with line 584, the synodic course of Venus, recalls the connection with the Aztec calendar system. Particularly noteworthy are the five days at the end of the solar year that do not fit into a regular unit and yet somehow must be counted before a new year can begin. In a system otherwise so symmetrical, the Aztecs dreaded these odd days, called *nemontemi*, the "nameless" or "unfortunate" days. Thus, the final five lines of Paz's poem, since they occur outside the final line count as a refrain, draw a comparison with the *nemontemi*.

In Aztec mythology, the world had been destroyed and re-created four times. The entire Aztec cosmology, therefore, was not only elaborately cyclical but also fragile, for the circular movement could be halted at any juncture. Any moment of ending and beginning, of which the concluding lines are a symbol, was regarded with awe and, finally, with a reverence that culminated in the worship of the forces of renewal. This is the same effect achieved by Paz at the end of his poem.

Although the entire Aztec calendar is composed of interlocking cycles, the deity who is most specifically charged with the process of renewal after destruction is Quetzalcoatl. His calendar sign is 4, *Ehécatl* (wind); in his hand, the deity carries the wind jewel, a round section of conch shell with five segments.

The use of Aztec myth at the poem's conclusion to symbolize the forces of destruction and renewal is linked with the intention of the epigraph (a quotation from the opening lines of the poem "Artémis," by Gérard de Nerval; these lines emphasize the uniqueness of each moment of love and its ever-repeating rhythm, which returns always renewed—like the planet Venus evoked by Paz), and suggests that destruction and renewal, like the two halves of the poem that each dominates, are both separate and identical. The first half of the poem analyzes time and reality through a process of disintegration; the second half attempts to achieve the same objective through the opposite process of integration and synthesis. The two halves of the poem are, therefore, opposite sides of the same reality. The poem's conclusion, which applies to both halves, is that any discernible meaning, whether negative or positive, must be derived from the process of circularity.

Themes and Meanings

Sun Stone is essentially a quest or a pilgrimage in which the unnamed speaker attempts to define his identity. Ostensibly the subject is love, or, more specifically, the beloved. Transcending the experience of love, however, is the real theme of the poem: time and its relationship to reality. In describing his own feelings of love and those of lovers in general, the poem's speaker attempts to describe love in terms of its transience and permanence, illusion and reality. In the poem, the speaker attacks the moment and surrounds it in his quest for its permanence—a permanence that he feels is capable of revealing his true identity to himself.

Throughout the poem, there are many reminders of time's circularity, which is both a dilemma and a symbol of disorientation. Whether the present is meaningless because it is prolonged interminably, or whether events, both personal and historical, lack significance because they are endlessly repeated, the poet's reaction to time's circularity is summed up in line 498: "each minute is nothing forever." The first lines of the final stanza express his reaction to the dilemma: "I want to continue, to go farther, and I cannot:/ the moment plunged into another and another."

Considered against the backdrop of linear time, which extends itself in measured units both forward and backward, is the poet's (and the Aztecs') conception of time as circular. Yet the awareness of the moment that is simultaneously first, last, and unique brings no resolution, no peace of discovery. On the contrary, it implies to the poet that there is an ultimate reality, a timeless realm, which he searches for beyond all other realities, and which is evoked by several experiences of love dramatized in the second half of the poem. The brief attention that the poet gives to the concept of the timeless paradise is in inverse relation to its importance as the poem's emotional goal, which is defined in the penultimate stanza (lines 562-570). Above all other descriptions of time in the poem, this one holds the most abiding hope of a final fulfillment.

Genevieve Slomski

SUNDAY AFTERNOONS

Author: Yusef Komunyakaa (1947-   )
Type of poem: Lyric
First published: 1991; collected in *Magic City*, 1992

The Poem

Written in free verse, "Sunday Afternoons" is a relatively short poem of thirty-five lines divided into seven stanzas. The title refers to the day and time of the week when the poet's parents excluded their children from the family house and locked the doors to ensure their privacy while they had sex. This poem is just one of a number of verse compositions, most of them collected in the volume *Magic City*, wherein Yusef Komunyakaa explores his and, by extension, the readers' shared childhood. In this regard, most children have memories of coping with the mystery of forbidden access, of engaging in the frustrated attempt to decode the parental sounds heard on the other side of closed doors.

Using the first-person plural pronoun "we," the poem is told from the perspective of the poet and his siblings when they are excluded from the monitoring parental presence and left to their own devices. Even in the confines of the family yard, however, the children discover their own innate animal nature by identifying, in the second and third stanzas, with the sometimes wild creatures that cross their field of experience. They become "drunk" on mayhaw juice and terrorize nesting birds. After this exercise of animal spirits and animal cruelty, the children, in the fourth stanza, refocus their attention on the house and their shared realization that there is something going on inside, something to be interpreted solely by auditory evidence. What they hear are the parental cries of passion and anger. With the words "We were born between Oh Yeah/ and Goddammit," the poet summarizes the trajectory of his parents' marriage.

It is at this point that the first-person perspective shifts from the plural to the singular, "we" becoming "I." For the last three stanzas, the collective experience is replaced by the personal vision of the dreamer-child who will one day become the poet-adult. While his brothers heed the parental stricture to stay away from the house, Komunyakaa remains at the screen door, persisting in his attempts to discover the truths of the bedroom and of the adult world. Yet despite his stubborn and ultimately transfiguring refusal to abandon his need to find answers, his quest is marked by a quiet sadness. This is in keeping with the general climate of all the poems contained in *Magic City*. Magic is a two-sided coin, and the poet reinforces that contention by presenting the reader with enchanted childhood memories that combine the elements of delight and horror.

Forms and Devices

In both the poems about his childhood in rural Louisiana and his celebrated compositions on his Vietnam War experience (*Dien Cai Dau*, 1988), Komunyakaa displays the Romantic trait of finding correspondences between humanity and the natural world. Set free in the yard, for example, the children mimic, in their engagement with the landscape, the pattern of many adult relationships. First, they are intoxicated by the juice of the mayhaw and the crabapple. The ripe fruit embodies that period of sexual fertility that adolescence will bring. Then, the children feel "brave/ As birds diving through saw vines." Similarly, future hormonal urges may lead to the potentially painful risk-taking that is also a component of adolescent experimentation. Finally, they observe dogs in heat, and this image of feverish intensity is followed by the children holding speckled eggs in their hands as a hawk circles overhead. Thus, natural images of puberty and fecundity foretell the end of the state of sexual latency the children now experience. Most of the poems in *Magic City* explore this engagement with the natural world. In a 1994 *New York Times* interview, Komunyakaa recalled his hometown of Bogalusa, Louisiana, as a "place where there was vegetation all over. There was a chemistry going on in the landscape and I identified with it, so I kind of look for that wherever I go."

In the second half of the poem, when the poet refocuses on what may be taking place inside the house, there is an acknowledgment of the consequences of sexual union, the recrimination that sometimes follows procreation and the enforced union of the partners. Gospel music can be heard playing on the radio, as "Loud as shattered glass/ in a Saturday-night argument/ About trust and money." In this instance, the music is intended to camouflage the sounds of passion, but, to the children, the music recalls parental arguments about infidelity and finances that have sometimes turned violent. Komunyakaa has written elsewhere about his parents' troubled marriage and his father's anger and propensity for abuse. The poem "My Father's Love Letter," also collected in *Magic City*, recounts the poet's memory of writing a letter for his father to his estranged wife, promising that he would never beat her again. The boys, in their yard gambols, prefigure their father's inability to understand the full ramifications of his nature as a sexual being, the fact that the consequence of just one episode of sexual congress may be the often-unanticipated responsibilities of being a husband and a father.

To enhance the realism of his message, Komunyakaa uses the vernacular. This poem, for example, uses the Southern names for various flora: The poet writes "mayhaw" instead of "hawthorne" and "saw vines" instead of "green briars." The use of these regionalisms enforces the sense of a localized landscape rendered through the filter of the poet's memory. Also characteristic of Komunyakaa's work is the layering of simile upon simile. Some critics have accused the poet of overusing this device while others have praised him for his inventiveness in this regard. In the last poetic sentence of "Sunday Afternoons," for example, there are two similes. The first one is rather hackneyed: "Like a gambler's visor"; the second is nothing short of inspired: "like a moon/ Held prisoner in the house." Komunyakaa is also fond of enjambment, or the use of run-on lines. Sometimes, in fact, the lines in this particular poem run on not only within stanzas but also between stanzas. The poet is quoted as saying that for him enjambment, represents "extended possibilities." For this reason, the device is most appropriate when used in poems without narrative closure, such as "Sunday Afternoons," wherein the identity of the child protagonist is not fixed but is in the open-ended process of becoming.

Themes and Meanings

The theme of the outsider pervades the poem. As an African American raised in the segregated South, Komunyakaa would naturally be drawn to this concept of exclusion, and the reader finds evidence of this theme in the poet's other works. "Between Angels and Monsters," another poem collected in *Magic City*, tells how Komunyakaa and his boyhood friends helped set up the big tent for a traveling circus; they stood "like obsidian panthers in a corner of the white world." Even as a soldier in Vietnam, as evidenced by the poem "Tu Do Street" from the volume *Dien Cai Dau*, the poet confronts exclusion in the informally segregated bars and brothels of Saigon. When he enters a bar patronized by white soldiers, Komunyakaa writes, "I'm a small boy again in Bogalusa. 'White Only' signs and Hank Snow."

Banished from the house and prohibited from viewing the bedroom behavior of their parents, the poet's brothers retreat from the screen door. The child-poet, however, stands his ground to gaze into the light from his dark vantage point. The speaker yearns for the knowledge he will need to interpret the adult mysteries, so he bends toward the light like a phototropic plant. In this case, however, it is not the sun that he glimpses but the dresser mirror cut in half "like a moon/ Held prisoner in the house." The moon is not a source of light but a reflective surface, and it may be that the poet wants the reader to comprehend that the knowledge sought by the child is already within.

Regardless of the parental efforts to "latch the screendoors/ and pull Venetian blinds," the children unconsciously carry within themselves, as reflected in their behavior in the yard, the seeds of adult sexuality and the latent awareness of its sometimes troubled consequences. One can also argue that, like the poem "Out of the Cradle Endlessly Rocking" by nineteenth century American poet Walt Whitman, this work chronicles that single moment when the child-poet recognizes his difference from others, even from his own family. His brothers shy away from the house, but the poet who was then a child struggles stubbornly for a view of what has been denied. Unlike the others, the poet seeks vision. From this childhood experience, one can trace Komunyakaa's career as a seer and an interpreter.

S. Thomas Mack

SUNDAY AT THE APPLE MARKET

Author: Peter Meinke (1932-   )
Type of poem: Lyric
First published: 1977, in *The Night Train and the Golden Bird*

The Poem

In "Sunday at the Apple Market" Peter Meinke uses free verse to portray the gaiety and freedom associated with a Sunday afternoon visit to an orchard to stock up on apples. The seventeen-line poem depends on images to suggest all the sensory pleasures of such a visit.

Meinke uses punctuation and capitalization sparsely, yet the reader can readily see separate introductory, middle, and concluding sections. The first two lines that introduce the subject indicate the open form of the poem. The opening "Apple-smell everywhere!" contrasts with the slower pace of the second line: "Haralson McIntosh Fireside Rome." This opening gives the reader entrance to the general atmosphere of the orchard market, one focused on the olfactory sense. The middle of the poem—lines 3-15—presents seven snapshots describing the orchard market scene: a shed with cider presses, ladders leaning against the now fruitless apple trees, apples of several colors stacked high in a barn, people gathered around a "testing table," "dogs barking at children," doting couples, and people loading their cars with the apples. The last two and a half lines provide the conclusion. They begin with a reiteration of the prevalent apple smell but then leave all sensory diction to provide commentary: "making us for one Sunday afternoon free/ and happy as people must have been meant to be."

Forms and Devices

"Sunday at the Apple Market" begins with an overview and ends with a comment, but the main body of the poem is dependent on images. The middle section follows the goal and the technique of the American Imagist poets prominent early in the twentieth century. The emotional impact of the poem comes directly from the images. Meinke involves all five senses in describing his scene. Beginning with the "Apple-smell" of the first line, Meinke soon turns to visual images of the orchard market; in the middle of the poem, as the people are introduced, the images suggest sound, taste, and touch as well as sight and smell.

In addition to having images central to the poem, the Imagist poets often concentrate their focus using common, though precise, diction and free verse. All these characteristics help to define Meinke's poem. One method of compression is Meinke's creation of new compound words out of ordinary words: "Apple-smell," "cider-presses," "applechunks," and "appletrees." The word apple or apples or the name of one of the fruit's varieties occurs ten times in this seventeen-line poem, keeping the subject in tight focus. The scant use of capitalization and punctuation also suggest compression. Capitalization appears only in the introductory or concluding sections, and three commas are all that punctuate the body of the poem.

In this way, the images flow into one another, allowing the reader to visualize the scene as if it were spread on a canvas. The first three images suggest to the reader a still life; once the people are introduced "laughing" and tasting the apples, the still life transforms into a more vibrant scene. The snapshot images that constitute the body of the poem vary in length, but frequent repetition of participles and compounds or items in a series binds the views, making the already compressed picture seem even more tightly constructed. The "old ciderpresses weathering in the shed" parallel the "old ladders tilting at empty branches"; likewise, the "boxes and bins" of an early image lead later to the "bushels/ and baskets and bags and boxes" that appear in the last image of the body of the poem.

The last two lines of the poem depart from the method of the Imagists. The obvious rhyme contrasts with the body of the poem, which has only one exact end rhyme, working more with alliteration. Instead of speaking through an image, the conclusion provides direct commentary. The point of view in the poem becomes apparent when the speaker says the scent of the fruit makes them "free/ and happy." The poem can then be seen as the speaker's sense impressions of the visit and his philosophic comment that the visit is actually a brief respite from the normal pattern of life.

Themes and Meanings

"Sunday at the Apple Market," with its predominantly joyous mood and just the end suggestion of caution, fits the tone of Meinke's collection *The Night Train and the Golden Bird*. As the title may suggest, the collection mixes poetry of darkness with poetry of light. The first twenty-five poems—many of which deal with sadness, loss, disease, and death—follow the heading "The Night Train." The remaining twenty-five poems—including "Sunday at the Apple Market"—follow the heading "The Golden Bird." Yet the two sections of the collection aren't complete contrasts. Several of the poems in "The Night Train" section contain subject matter that lightens some of the dark views. Additionally, the dark tone of the early poems occasionally makes its way, sometimes unexpectedly, into those in "The Golden Bird" section, as with the concluding comment in "Sunday at the Apple Market."

Although the poem focuses on a joyous slice of life, the concluding comment says, through implication, that such joy is not the norm. The body of the poem is light and carefree, with the sensory details clearly making the mood positive. The reader is left, though, to ponder the implication of the conclusion: Why is such an atmosphere rare? These people are joyous on "one Sunday afternoon." They clearly have the desire and ability to enjoy the simple pleasures of life. Yet the conclusion implies that time spent in this way is minimal. Mixing the light with the serious or the positive with the negative is not unusual for Meinke.

The poetic vision that inspires the simple and common diction of "Sunday at the Apple Market" is directly expressed in "The Heart's Location," the poem that opens "The Golden Bird" section of the collection. Suicide is the subject of "The Heart's Location" as it is the subject of both the first and last poem in "The Night Train" section. Yet here suicide is treated lightly, as a foolish thought. The speaker in "The Heart's Location" finds life worth living in order to "search/ for . . . a poem full of ordinary words/ about simple things/ in the inconsolable rhythms of the heart." The mixture of positive and negative is here, as it is in "Sunday at the Apple Market"; the speaker in both poems recognizes the dark but is still enchanted with the light. The possibilities of joy remain despite the knowledge that joy is sometimes difficult to maintain.

Two other American poems that "Sunday at the Apple Market" may bring to mind are Hart Crane's "Sunday Morning Apples," from *White Buildings* (1926), and Robert Frost's "After Apple Picking," from *North of Boston* (1914). All three titles with their reference to apples suggest the simple delights of a rural experience. Crane's free-verse poem, with its dedication to the painter William Sommer, shows the influence of the Imagists. The poem ends with a description of a still life that the apples inspire. Frost's poem, on the other hand, is clearly more philosophic, more of a contrast in form and tone to "Sunday at the Apple Market." Frost uses end rhyme, and the mood of his poem is throughout more somber; instead of the conviviality of Meinke's scene, Frost's speaker ruminates in isolation, and instead of Meinke's gaiety and activity, the Frost poem speaks of tiredness and sleep and suggests death.

"Sunday at the Apple Market," although clear and easily accessible, contains some of the mix of forms and ideas that Meinke frequently uses. Basically written in open form, the poem ends with an obvious exact rhyme; predominantly upbeat in tone, the concluding commentary adds a touch of dismay at the unspoken weekday life of the Sunday apple enthusiasts. From everyday life, Meinke suggests deeper philosophic concerns. Yet the power of the sensory details in the body of the poem leaves the reader with a positive response to the life Meinke portrays in the poem; the possibility of such freedom and gaiety is affirmed.

Marion Petrillo

SUNDAY MORNING

Author: Wallace Stevens (1879-1955)
Type of poem: Meditation
First published: 1915; revised in *Harmonium,* 1923

The Poem

In its final form, "Sunday Morning" consists of eight self-contained, fifteen-line strophes, written in Wallace Stevens's customary version of blank verse. The speaker's meditation on life, death, and change is presented through a description of a woman who prefers the world of the senses to "The holy hush of ancient sacrifice" associated with religious practice, but who is not really sure that she can be satisfied with temporary delights.

The stage is set with a description of the woman's Sunday morning, when the effects of vibrant colors and relaxation are dissipated by the call of religious services. The poet, however, questions why the woman should be distracted from her enjoyment of life by a religion that is available "Only in silent shadows and in dreams." Rejecting the pallid consolations of spiritual belief, the speaker says that she must find divinity "within herself."

In the third strophe, Stevens evokes Jove as a representative of the inhuman gods of ancient religious belief. Jesus, because he was partly human, was a step forward but not the final stage in the evolution of divinity. Humans should recognize that their own divinity should be enough, since it is the only thing upon which they can finally rely. If they accept that there is nothing beyond this world, they will be able to enjoy the world for what it is: "The sky will be much friendlier then than now// Not this dividing and indifferent blue."

The woman speaks in the fourth and fifth strophes, saying that although she finds contentment in earthly beauty, she still needs "some imperishable bliss." The poet responds that permanence is not only impossible, it is also unnatural and undesirable. The fifth and sixth strophes use vivid imagery to present the major theme that "Death is the mother of beauty" and that impermanence is essential to the human ability to perceive beauty.

The final sections of "Sunday Morning" present images conveying what the poet regards as proper celebrations of the bonds between humans and the natural world. In the last strophe, the woman hears a voice that denies the divinity of Jesus, and the poem ends with the poet's final evocation of the transitory beauties of the world.

Forms and Devices

"Sunday Morning" is composed of self-contained strophes, all of the same length; the order of the final version is different from that of the poem's original form. The basic line in all Stevens's longer poems is a solemn and somewhat heavy blank verse, employing iambic pentameter and making use of echoing sounds rather than end rhyme. In the second strophe, for example, successive lines begin with the words "Passions," "Grievings," "Elations," and "Emotions." At several points in the poem, the verse has a majestic quality and an intensity that are used to emphasize the strength of the poem's message. This is especially the case in the final seven lines of the poem, where deer, the whistling cry of quail, and the sweetness of ripening berries represent the attractions of the natural world.

"Sunday Morning" makes much use of assertions and rhetorical questions that are designed to cast doubt on the validity of traditional religious belief. The poem, however, presents its message primarily through imagery, much of it evoking bright colors, movement, and vivid tastes and smells to provide a contrast to the dimness and insubstantiality of spiritual appeals. Death, as it brings "sure obliteration," is an active and positive force, imaged through verbs such as "strews," "shiver," and "stray impassioned." Passion and other strong emotions are possible only because one knows that life is only temporary. The description of a human ritual in the seventh section makes use of energetic images: "Supple and turbulent," "boisterous," "savage."

On the other hand, in an imagined paradise, there is "no change of death," but only rivers that never reach the sea, ripe fruit that never falls from trees; the images associated with religion and dreams of an afterlife are sinister and lifeless: "haunt of prophecy" and "old chimera of the grave."

Stevens's fondness for obscure words and unusual phrasings is less marked in "Sunday Morning" than in many of his other poems, but it is evident in such words as "chimera" or "mythy," in the opening phrase ("Complacencies of the peignoir"), and in the following lines from the final strophe: "Or old dependency of day and night,/ Or island solitude, unsponsored, free,/ Of that wide water, inescapable." There are few similes in the poem, and most of the metaphors are subtle, such as the use of "measures" in the second section to suggest both musical divisions and ways of measuring.

Stevens, however, makes considerable use of personification, not only by ironically imaging death as an active force, but also by giving being to emotions such as sorrow and passion. In some places, he deliberately uses archaic words and phrases to suggest that religious belief is out of date: "such requital to desire," for example, or the lines "Neither the golden underground, nor isle/ Melodious, where spirits gat them home."

Themes and Meanings

Stevens's lifelong conviction that poetry and poets must take the place of religion and priests to provide form and meaning for human life is implicit in "Sunday Morning," not explicit, as it would become in his later poetry. "Sunday Morning," however, does clear the way for those poems, and it establishes basic themes that Stevens would employ in all of his subsequent work.

The most important of these themes is the idea that human perception of beauty requires the recognition that everything earthly is temporary. Everyone will die, everything will change; permanence must be recognized as an illusion. Christianity, Judaism, or any religion promising permanence is false because it envisions a paradise that is something like our earth but without the inherent changes in earth's life and circumstance.

This does not mean that religious emotion must be stifled, only that it must find a more appropriate outlet. This new form is presented in the seventh strophe, and it amounts to the worship of nature and the integral connection between humans and the rest of the natural world. The men in this image, dancing in an orgy, celebrate the sun as the natural source of life, present with them, and the tune they chant is composed of the objects in the world around them.

At the time he wrote "Sunday Morning," Stevens had not yet developed fully the idea that all systems of order are necessarily fictions, fulfilling a need all humans have for fictions that will make life seem comprehensible. Since religion, in his view, had failed to provide a meaningful order, poetry would have to do so. This idea would receive extended treatment in works such as *Notes Toward a Supreme Fiction* (1942). While celebrating "chaos," "Sunday Morning" also anticipates the later theme by suggesting that aspects of religion, such as worship and ritual, are important to human existence.

"Sunday Morning" has remained one of Stevens's best-known poems. Written at the beginning of his career as a poet, this poem introduces the themes that would dominate his verse, and it establishes a unique poetic manner. It is most memorable, finally, for its vivid use of color and action imagery and for its romantic evocation of the natural world.

John M. Muste

A SUPERMARKET IN CALIFORNIA

Author: Allen Ginsberg (1926-1997)
Type of poem: Narrative
First published: 1956, in *Howl and Other Poems*

The Poem

"A Supermarket in California" is a short poem in free verse, its twelve lines divided into three stanzas. The title suggests a bland setting—not the expected source of a poem. The title and setting prove ironic, however, as Allen Ginsberg demonstrates that for most people in America, exploration goes no further than the local grocery store.

The poem is written in the first person, which is typical of Ginsberg's work; he writes very personally of his visions and experiences in America. Ginsberg is speaking in the first person not only to share his immediate sensuous experiences but also to invoke, by using this perspective, the American poet in whose footsteps he is attempting to walk: Walt Whitman.

In fact, Ginsberg speaks directly to Whitman in the poem's first line as he wearily trudges down the streets of suburban California, "self-conscious looking at the full moon . . . shopping for images." He enters a bright "neon fruit supermarket" (line 2) as if here he might find the same image of America—the diversity and freedom, the limitless, democratic possibilities—that Whitman saw. What he sees in the market, however, is only the multitude of fruit and the families shopping together as if this were the richest experience they could share.

At the end of stanza 1, Ginsberg also spies the twentieth century Spanish poet Federico García Lorca standing by the watermelons. The sighting of García Lorca—a homosexual like Ginsberg and, many suspect, Whitman—creates a smooth transition to stanza 2, where Ginsberg chides Whitman for "eyeing the grocery boys" (line 4). In his mind he hears Whitman asking mundane questions about food prices, about "who killed the pork chops," and if anyone will be his "Angel"—that is, will follow him (line 5). There is no response, but Ginsberg continues following the elder poet past aisles of canned goods, perhaps trailed by the store detective, who has noted Ginsberg's suspicious appearance.

Stanza 2 ends with the poets tasting delicacies along the way but buying nothing. At the beginning of the final stanza, they find themselves with no place to go, since in an hour, when the store closes, they will be given their freedom again. Ginsberg looks to Whitman for advice and direction, and even "touches" Whitman's book (presumably *Leaves of Grass*, 1855) for inspiration.

He gets no response and thus finds himself out on the "solitary streets," with the "lights out in the houses," where he and Whitman will "both be lonely" (line 10). He asks if it is possible that their walk will be a pleasant memory of "the lost America of love" (line 11), meaning the freer, untamed America of Whitman's day, since, as he notes, they will also have to walk past the same blue cars in the same driveways, house after house. The poem ends on a note of despair as Ginsberg asserts that when Whitman's journey ended, he found himself by the mythical waters of Lethe, one of the rivers in Hades. "What America did you have then," he asks Whitman, and since the poem began in the first-person singular and shifted to the plural in stanzas 2 and 3, as if the two are journeying together, he seems to be including himself in this haunting question.

Forms and Devices

What is most noticeable about the form of "A Supermarket in California" is its free verse, which again alludes to Whitman, the founder of the free verse style. Ginsberg even more closely associates himself with Whitman by exploiting the complexity of the structure and rhythm of this form. Whitman's famous self-referential poem "Song of Myself" (1855) is the particular model for Ginsberg, as both poems employ convoluted sentence structures and lines that cannot be contained within one line on the typical printed page.

Each line of "A Supermarket in California" "contains multitudes," as Whitman said of himself in "Song of Myself" (line 1326). For example, the first line invokes Whitman himself, sets the poem down on a suburban street in America, describes the speaker as having a "headache," being "self-conscious," and looking at "the full moon," which, though traditionally a sign of lunacy, functions even better here to contrast with the artificial "neon" light of the supermarket in the next line. Outdoor America is easily traversed, in contrast to Whitman's idea and to the reality of America in the nineteenth century.

The third line also supports this premise as it speaks of various fruits, families spending time shopping, and finally the homosexual poet García Lorca. By using García Lorca, Ginsberg points to two clear distinctions between the average American and the poets mentioned: the poets' confusion and despair over the loss of the art and beauty of unspoiled America and their sense of alienation at deviating from the sexual norm of America.

Rhythmically, "A Supermarket in California" also matches "Song of Myself" through the use of opening repetition. Each of the first three lines of stanza 2 begins with the first-person-singular pronoun followed by an active verb: "I saw you, Walt Whitman . . .;/ I heard you asking questions . . .;/ I wandered in and out." The last line of that stanza, while switching to first-person plural, only varies the same pattern: "we strode down the open corridors." This rhythmic pattern works as well in the last stanza through Ginsberg's questioning of Whitman, similar to Whitman's questioning of his readers in "Song of Myself": "Where are we going . . .;/ Will we walk all night . . .;/ Will we stroll dreaming." The repetition of certain patterns serves as an incantation in which Ginsberg tries to break the spell that suburban, homogeneous America has on its citizenry.

Finally, the supermarket is an obvious metaphor for Ginsberg's view of the final product of what Whitman had seen as the great promise of America's vast, unexplored frontier. The age of exploration in nineteenth century America pushed the frontier to the Pacific Ocean. Whitman advocated following America's paths and thereby exploring and finding oneself—one's imaginative and spiritual potential. All Ginsberg has found at the end of the frontier is a neon-lit supermarket full of people who seem to have nowhere else to go or who have lost the drive to explore. Thus, the potential of America has been transformed, or has "progressed" to that of easy shopping.

Themes and Meanings

Ginsberg uses Whitman and his "Song of Myself" as an ironic counterpoint to "A Supermarket in California," though the irony is shaded by Ginsberg's remorse for himself, Whitman, and America. For Ginsberg, America in the twentieth century has reneged on its promise of opportunity, freedom, and liberty. Where Whitman in the nineteenth century found and celebrated diversity in the American people, as he sings in "Song of Myself," Ginsberg finds only homogeneity. Where Whitman saw an endless horizon of land to explore—the pageant of the American landscape—Ginsberg sees only "solitary streets," houses with their lights out, "blue automobiles in driveways," and "the neon fruit supermarket."

Thus the images of America that Ginsberg sees are not the ones he is "shopping for." This town and supermarket exist everywhere in the United States, each market and each town, in their design and emphasis on materialism, trying to keep up with all the others. America's melting pot has become an all too grim reality.

Try as America might to obscure its differences—its variety of people and their desires, ambitions—it cannot hide all of its parts. The very fact that poets such as Whitman, García Lorca, and Ginsberg, who have deviated from the norm sexually as well as artistically, exist testifies to this truth. That Ginsberg still wants to write about America, even in lamentation, indicates the emotional attachment and investment he has made in the country, as well as the force with which he has believed in Whitman's dream. No matter how hard the mainstream tries to homogenize and tame the wild, "barbaric yawp" (as Whitman put it) within us, Ginsberg and others continue to sound it out loud and strong.

In the final stanza, though, he is faced with the troubling question of where to go to find his joy and inspire his innermost being. His remorse for himself, Whitman, and America surfaces in the parenthesis of this stanza when he "touches" Whitman's "book" (*Leaves of Grass*). Instead of being comforted and inspired, as Whitman intends in "Song of Myself" when he tells his readers not to fear taking the journey through America, for he (Whitman) will go with them, Ginsberg can think only of his "absurd" walk through the supermarket, perhaps followed by the store detective who is a symbol of the watchful eye of the nation's conformity. As he leaves Whitman in Hades at the poem's end, asking the "lonely old courage-teacher, what America/ did you have" then, one suspects that ultimately Ginsberg believes that he is the one who is left alone on the shore of "the black waters of Lethe."

Terry Barr

SUPERNATURAL LOVE

Author: Gjertrud Schnackenberg (1953-   )
Type of poem: Lyric
First published: 1982; collected in *The Lamplit Answer,* 1985

The Poem

Like many lyric poems, Gjertrud Schnackenberg's "Supernatural Love" contains a narrative element, a sort of dramatic situation that provides the framework for this meditation on the nature of supernatural love. At the end of this brief story of a young child and her father, the reader is invited to see the similarities between divine love and human love, similarities which the poem's ambiguous title suggests from the beginning.

The poem opens as the narrator visualizes herself as a four-year-old child as she and her father work in his study. She is cross-stitching a sampler text while her father looks up word origins in the dictionary. The intertwining of the needlework, the etymologies, and the text of the sampler create the thematic web of the poem. The poem hints that carnations are present in the room. In any event, the narrator has apparently said that she calls carnations "Christ's flowers," although she can give no reason why. Curiosity has led her father to look up "carnation" in the dictionary. As he does so, the child notes how his eyes look through the magnifying glass he holds. In return, she peers at him through the eye of the needle and then returns to work on the word "beloved." Later it becomes clear that her sampler has a religious motto and that "beloved" is one part of it.

From the dictionary, the father learns that the root of "carnation" is the Latin word *carn,* meaning "flesh," perhaps because the flowers are commonly pink or red. Since the child cannot explain the source of her version of the name, the father goes on, noting the dictionary's information that carnations are a variety of clove. When he looks up "clove," he learns that the word has its roots in the French word *clou,* meaning "nail." At about that moment, the child accidently stabs herself with her needle, running it into her finger clear to the bone. When she cries out in pain, her father gently touches the wound, just as earlier he had gently touched the words on the page.

In addition to these actions, Schnackenberg records the words of the sampler's motto, "Thy blood so dearly bought," and two other sentences, the origins of which are not entirely clear. One is *"Child, it's me,"* which the child hears in the squeak of her scissors; the other is punctuated as an isolated sentence in quotation marks in the poem: "'The obligation due to every thing/ That's smaller than the universe.'" In the context of the rest of the poem's references, the first of these sentences may come as Christ addresses the little girl. The second is treated as if it is part of the dictionary's entry and must be read as a commentary on the word "carnation."

Forms and Devices

"Supernatural Love" is written in nineteen three-line stanzas of iambic pentameter. The three rhyming words of each stanza share a single rhyme sound. The three-line stanza (called terza rima when it rhymes *aba, bcb,* and so on) was most notably used by the medieval poet Dante Alighieri (1265-1321) in his long narrative poem *The Divine Comedy,* in which he used it to honor the doctrine of the Trinity—the Christian doctrine of the essential unity of God as Father, Son, and Holy Spirit. Schnackenberg, as a poet who frequently uses formal structures, would be well aware of the traditions of this verse form. In this poem, the triplets harmonize with the poem's theme of supernatural love, love which in Christian doctrine was expressed by God's appearing in human flesh on earth in the person of Jesus.

In the poem, this theme emerges from a network of images concerning the carnations, their roots (both real roots and etymologies), flesh, blood, and nails. The "iron-fresh" scent of the flowers floats up to the child narrator, a scent she calls "drifted, bitter, secret ecstasy." In a context which has already united the flowers with the idea of Christ, this reference to iron and bitterness inevitably suggests the crucifixion, a reference which is reinforced when the father's dictionary identifies cloves with a word for "nail." Significantly, the father reads the definition twice, "as if he hasn't understood," just as the child, who cannot yet read, does not understand the text she is cross-stitching. Moreover, the dictionary's reference to cloves as a spice also suggests the spices with which Jesus's body was prepared for burial. The very *X*'s of the child's cross-stitching use the Greek letter *chi,* the first letter of the Greek word for *Christ* and a traditional abbreviation of Christ's name. This union of images is what makes the narrator say, "The incarnation blossoms, flesh and nail." The pun on "blossom" is one of several puns in the poem, including the "cross" stitching of the child's needle work and the "roots" of both words and flowers.

As the child twists the threads of her work "like stems," she accidently jabs herself. She has been working the phrase *"Thy blood so dearly bought,"* an explanation of Christian understanding of the meaning of the crucifixion—Christ's blood was the high price paid for human salvation. Now the blood being shed is the child's; it reminds her of the threads she has been working with, and she calls for her father using the intimate "Daddy daddy," which is undoubtedly intended to recall for the reader Jesus's use of a similar word (*Abba*) in addressing his heavenly father. In response, her father gently touches her injury, just as before he gently touched the dictionary's page. Now the italicized *"Child, it's me,"* which earlier seemed to emerge from the flowers and the child's scissors, sounds like a reassurance both from her father and from Christ himself; it is the sort of thing a loving parent might say to an injured child.

Themes and Meanings

This poem is the last in a series of three poems on religious themes that conclude Schnackenberg's volume *The Lamplit Answer.* Their theme makes them rather uncommon in the corpus of twentieth century American poetry. Religious poets such as John Donne and George Herbert flourished in seventeenth century England, but twentieth century America has been a basically secular place for poems. Perhaps that is why Schnackenberg has chosen to explicate a very basic concept of Christian theology in this poem—the concept of supernatural love. The poem's title suggests the mystery of divine love, God's love for human beings. It also suggests other remarkable loves, such as the love parents feel for their children. In the New Testament, Jesus used parent-child love to illustrate the nature of divine love, thus establishing a tradition of imagery.

Implicit in this image is the idea that the loved creature cannot understand such love. Children cannot grasp the depth of their parents' love for them any more than human beings can grasp the depth of God's love. Thus the child in the poem cannot read the text she is cross-stitching, and even the father seems not to understand what he reads in the dictionary.

At this point it seems useful to look again at the images of the poem's opening. The father gazes at the room through the magnifying glass almost like God looking at the world as he touches a word which seems to ring like a "distant, plucked, infinitesimal string." The message of that string seems to refer to "The obligation due to every thing/ That's smaller than the universe." Although that sentence can scarcely be part of the definition for "carnation," it is relevant to the concept of "incarnation," which Christians have understood to be the result of God's love for creation—the decision to take on human flesh and eventually to undergo the agonies of crucifixion. At the same time the father looks through the magnifying glass, the child peers at her father through her needle's eye and receives a sort of miniaturized vision—the sort a butterfly might have, she muses—thus reinforcing the suggestion of her smallness in comparison to her father.

When the child wounds herself while stitching the "perfect text" and calls for her father, he touches her wound with the same hand which earlier had touched the "obligation due" text, and the themes of the poem are drawn together. The father is moved by love for his child and concern for her pain. Such concern is the nature of supernatural love. The child has perceived this dimly, perhaps, in her naming carnations "Christ's flowers," and the idea is reinforced by the etymologies that the father has uncovered. Supernatural love is the mystery at the root of everything; it is the "lamplit answer" that this poem names.

Ann D. Garbett

SURPRISED BY JOY

Author: William Wordsworth (1770-1850)
Type of poem: Sonnet
First published: 1815, in *Poems*

The Poem

"Surprised by Joy" is a short lyric written in the form of a sonnet about a person who continues to grieve over the death of a loved one. Late in life, William Wordsworth told a friend that the "Thee" to whom he refers in line 3 was his daughter Catherine, who died in June of 1812. He also may have been thinking of his son Thomas, who died later that year. Wordsworth meditates on this dramatic and highly emotional experience in such a way that his meditation also becomes a dramatic and significant experience in itself. (Most readers find it necessary to read this poem several times before its time scheme and its implications become clear.) The poem opens with the poet describing a vivid, past experience: He had a joyful thought. "Joy" is an important word to Wordsworth and can suggest not only a happy feeling but also a life-giving, mind-altering, deeply emotional, and profound sense of harmony and well-being. A moment of such joy "surprised" the poet, implying that it came suddenly and without warning. It surprised him (as the reader understands from the rest of the poem) because, previously, he had not been joyful.

After being surprised by joy, the poet turned with impatience to share his new and highly emotional state of mind (his "transport"). As illustrated elsewhere in his work, when Wordsworth feels a joy, he often wishes to communicate with someone else. The phrase "impatient as the Wind" implies that he turned quickly, forcefully, and thoughtlessly to someone he assumed was standing beside him, a person who had often stood beside him in the past as his daughter must have done. However, when he turned joyfully to his daughter, he realized she was not there to share his emotion because she was dead. The poem breaks into an exclamation ("Oh!") to communicate the excruciating pang of sorrow Wordsworth felt at that time in the past and also the emotion he feels when he thinks about it later as he writes this poem. He had turned to share his joy with "Thee" in vain because, as he knew and still knows, she is buried in a tomb that is both "silent" (she cannot hear her father) and beyond "vicissitude" (she has been removed from the change or mutability of mortal life).

Lines 5-9 can be read either as a report of the poet's original experience or as his later thoughts about that experience. Either way, Wordsworth tells the reader that his "faithful love" (not just a momentary feeling) is what made him think of his daughter. Why the poet should insist on his faithfulness becomes clear in the next three lines: He feels guilty. He asks how he could have been so unfaithful as to have forgotten the "most grievous loss" of his dear daughter even for a moment, for "the least division of an hour," for a unit of time long enough for him to have had a joyful thought. Although his daughter is now beyond vicissitude, the poet laments his own changeable nature.

He does not answer his question, but he seems to hope that his unfaithfulness will somehow be excused. Remembering his daughter proves his "faithful love." Beginning with the middle of line 9, the later, more meditative Wordsworth reflects on his earlier experience. "That thought's return" (that is, suddenly recalling that his daughter was dead) once caused a pang second only to the one he felt when he first learned she had died. In all cases, he is affected not only because a loved one is dead but also because he has lost the thing he loved more than anything else ("my heart's best treasure").

Forms and Devices

"Surprised by Joy" is a fourteen-line Italian sonnet, though Wordsworth somewhat modifies its traditional form. The usual break in sense between lines 8 and 9 actually occurs in the middle of line 9. Wordsworth's rhyme scheme is not as rigid as usual: In a strict Italian sonnet, lines 3 and 4 would rhyme with lines 6 and 7, and in this poem they do not. In line 11, "return" may have been pronounced by Wordsworth to rhyme perfectly with "forlorn." Wordsworth's modifications are appropriate to the dramatic progress of the poem, for it is both a dramatic utterance full of the fits and starts that proceed from a disturbed yet thoughtful mind and a controlled reflection on what that utterance means to the poet.

The dramatic complexities are communicated by the poem's jumbled syntax. Line 1 begins calmly enough with a participial phrase, but, halfway through, the poet provides a dash to show that his mind interjects a clause to describe what he did after joy came over him. This account is, in turn, interrupted partway through line 2 with a dramatic interjection ("Oh!"), followed by a string of phrases and appositions that modify "turned." What technically may be a sentence in lines 1-4 may strike readers as less than grammatically stable because of its two dashes. Such patterns persist. The statement in line 5 contains an interruption ("faithful love"), and a dash at the end of the same line implies that the question in line 6 is an interruption, a shift in the poet's thinking. The poet's thought and mood shifts again in the middle of line 9. His statement about his "worst pang" is no sooner uttered than qualified by a string of dependent elements that extend to the end of the poem. In short, the poem's somewhat chaotic grammar helps express the poet's mental anguish and communicates the freshness of his experiences when he was surprised by joy, when he reflects on that experience, and when he first knew of his daughter's death. Despite its informality of structure, the poem is moderately formal in diction ("transport," "vicissitude," "beguiled," "grievous"). It uses tropes only to reflect simple emotional experiences. A simile ("impatient as the Wind") describes the poet's reaction to joy, and a metaphor ("heart's best treasure") suggests his first reaction to his daughter's death.

The intensity of Wordsworth's complex experience is communicated by the emphatic nature of the verse. Readers can hear the poet's voice stress such words a "Wind," "Oh!" "tomb," "love," "power," "hour," and "blind." Some of these stresses are caused by words themselves; they often have long vowels, deep or strident, that are seldom clipped off. The rhythm of the lines themselves works up to stresses, as in the haste with which line 7 ("Even for the least division of an hour") speeds to its conclusion. Readers sense a relaxation of tension toward the end of the poem. Its more pensive tone is caused by its verse, which is less emphatic and more regularly paced.

The tone of this poem is complex, a mixture of emotion and restraint. The poem communicates the anguish Wordsworth felt in the past and feels in the present. At the same time, the poet shows the psychic control of a mature adult. Perhaps one way he expresses this mixture of emotion and control is by filling a strict form such as the sonnet with irregularities of syntax and heavy emphasis. The poem's juxtaposition of anguish and control suggests how much the poet's maturity has cost him.

Themes and Meanings

This poem is not simply one that remembers the death of a loved one. It is both about death and about remembering that death. Even though Wordsworth the poet often wrote about transcendental influences and Wordsworth the mature man entertained thoughts of Christian immortality, such matters are not part of this poem. The poet thinks of his daughter in two ways: in her grave and in his memory. Her body is buried in a tomb, a physical spot where all is silent. The Wordsworths once lived across the road from the church where Catherine was buried, but Mary Wordsworth was so affected by seeing her daughter's grave so close to her home that the family had to move. In this poem, however, memories are more potent reminders than graves. The impact of "Surprised by Joy" comes first from its vivid rendering of a moment of joy, immediately followed by the realization that the loved one with whom the poet needed to share that joy to make it complete was not present. Most readers will remember similar moments. The full meaning of the poem embraces not only that moment but also subsequent reflections on that moment as well as other memories it calls forth. The poem is about the way a human being's emotional life is an interactive mixture of immediate and remembered (but no less vivid) emotional experiences.

George Soule

SWEENEY AMONG THE NIGHTINGALES

Author: T. S. Eliot (1888-1965)
Type of poem: Lyric
First published: 1918; collected in *Poems*, 1919

The Poem

"Sweeney Among the Nightingales" is a modernist lyric poem of forty lines, divided into ten quatrains and focusing on Sweeney, a brutish modern man in the company of disreputable women ("nightingales") in a café (also perhaps a brothel) at night. The poem ranks with the finest of T. S. Eliot's early poetry, as the author himself wrote to his brother, Henry, when it was later included in *Poems* (1919): "Some of the new poems, the Sweeney ones, especially 'Among the Nightingales' and 'Burbank' are intensely serious, and I think these two are among the best that I have ever done. But even here I am considered by the ordinary Newspaper critic as a Wit or satirist, and in America I suppose I shall be thought merely disgusting."

"Sweeney Among the Nightingales" is very much a serious commentary on the paltriness and insensitivity of modern humanity by comparison with the tragic grandeur and mighty passion of ancient heroes such as Agamemnon, who headed the Greek conquest of Troy and who returned home to die violently by his own wife's hand. Elements of satire and comedy are present to teach, through muted ridicule, a genuine disgust for the coarseness and coldness of the modern sensibility as personified by Sweeney and the equally detached call girls and owner of the café.

In the title, the nightingales connote prostitutes around Sweeney but also refer to a Greek tale about the transformation of lust into mythic beauty: Philomela, who was ravished and had her tongue cut out by her sister's husband, King Tereus, wove the story of the rape into a tapestry that she sent to her sister, Procne. In revenge, Queen Procne served her own son as a stew for the unsuspecting king to eat. Just as the enraged Tereus was about to kill the fleeing sisters, the pitying gods transmuted Philomela into a lovely swallow, Procne into a beautiful nightingale, and Tereus into an ugly hawk.

The poem's Greek epigraph, from Aeschylus's *Agamemnon* (458 B.C.E.), "ah, I am struck a deadly blow and deep within," is the first of two cries by King Agamemnon as his wife, Clytemnestra, stabs him to death in his bath while throwing robes over his dying body.

The animality of Sweeney and his tipsy female companions, frolicking distrustfully in a café, is unredeemed by any mythic transformation or tragic elevation. In myth or legend, lust-ridden violence was resolved in mythic beauty (as in the tale of Philomela and Procne) or by divine justice (at the end of Aeschylus's *Oresteia*, 458 B.C.E.); here, it has degenerated to crude and trifling gestures of estrangement and indifference between the modern sexes. Apelike Sweeney's facial features have a sinfully bestained ("maculate") and bizarre animality that are even uglier than Tereus's transformation into a hideous bird. Unlike the pitiful ebbing of Agamemnon's strength and life from his wife's dagger blows, Sweeney's sprawling posture betrays only a careless eroticism (lines 1-4). Sweeney's sexually inviting sprawl becomes a trap for a woman who falls from his lap to the floor; she falls with absolute indifference (line 11-16).

Sweeney, the modern man, is as benighted as the beclouded, moonlit sky that obscures his vision of great myths surrounding death, the constellations Orion (the hunter) and "the Dog" (the hunter's dog), and the gates of horn in Hades, through which accurate dreams and prophecies ascended to mortals. He stands outside the gates of underworld prophecy, living in a becalmed sterility of "hushed" and "shrunken seas."

There is an absence of connectedness among the café's customers. Sprawling Sweeney, an effete low-life vertebrate, stiffens sexually but musters only enough energy to decline the call girl's "gambit," or sexual overture, because he is distrustful of a conspiracy between two women, one of whom is a degenerate version of the biblical Rachel who apes Clytemnestra's murderous gesture by tearing café fruit (lines 16-28). Instead, Sweeney walks outside and stands apart, loosking in with a stupid grin, as the host and another customer converse in indifference and detachment. All these people are estranged, aimless, and oblivious to the great myths of pagan transmutation (the singing nightingales), Christian resurrection (reverenced at the nearby "Convent of the Sacred Heart"), ritual regeneration (ancient sacrificial killings of old priests by their successors in the "bloody wood" of Nemi), and divine justice. All these myths revolve around a pattern of sacrifice and ultimate exaltation sorely missing in a feckless, mundane modernity.

Forms and Devices

The stylistic devices of "Sweeney Among the Nightingales" are typical of Eliot's best early poetry, culminating in *The Waste Land* (1922), and relate to modernist literary conventions that he popularized and developed from Metaphysical and Symbolist traditions of poetry in, respectively, the early seventeenth and late nineteenth centuries.

No simple label describes Eliot's early poetry. He consciously rebelled against what he termed the "dissociation of sensibility"—the supposed breakdown of a fusion of intellect, emotion, and imagination in poetic creation—since John Milton's time and especially under the flabby subjectivity of early Romantic authors. Eliot reacted with a demand for a Metaphysical wit (a sharp conceit or alert poetic consciousness apprehending the many-sidedness of anything), for dense allusiveness (embracing all cultural history as a backdrop for modernity), and for telling irony (contrasting past grandeur and present squalor, ancient myth and modern mediocrity).

Eliot saw in the Metaphysical poets of seventeenth century England a fusion of intellect and feeling and sought to capture this fusion in a conceit such as the image of a disgustingly lax modern Sweeney aping the tragic posture of dying Agamemnon as strength and life ebb from the king's body ("Apeneck Sweeney spreads his knees/ Letting his arms hang down to laugh").

Eliot was drawn also to the ideas of Théophile Gautier (1811-1872), who aspired to a poetry of highly wrought artifice and impersonality, devoted to artistic beauty for its own sake (*l'art pour l'art*) and devoid of bourgeois utilitarian didacticism. Most of these traits can be found in "Sweeney Among the Nightingales," except that Eliot seeks less an aesthetic escapism for beauty's sake and more a classical perspective on the mundane ugliness of modernity.

Coming later, the French Symbolists cultivated an aristocratic impersonality, intense craftsmanship, and a care for precise imagery and suggestiveness in a poem's words as they combine to create new sensations and meanings not communicated by the individual words themselves. The combination of precision, symbolic suggestion, and ironic mockery found in a witty, urbane speaker in the poetry of Jules Laforgue (1860-1887), for example, directly anticipated Eliot's early style.

"Sweeney Among the Nightingales" is a highly crafted work written in chiselled iambic tetrameter quatrains (end rhyming in the second and fourth lines), containing alliteration and assonance and some very compressed metaphors (such as an implicit comparison of Sweeney to a giraffe, an odd animal stained or "maculate" with sin). There are precise imagery and a compressed suggestiveness of meaning springing from repeated juxtapositions of words and phrases; the juxtapositions lend a descriptive vividness and a mythically rich range of allusion that embrace a broad cross-section of Western cultural experience as a backdrop for Sweeney, the modern swain (and swine), who is a dime-store degradation of the legendary King Agamemnon.

As Eliot wrote in "Tradition and the Individual Talent" (1919), the modern poet must surround his subject matter with a revealing historical sense of past tradition: "[T]he historical sense compels a man to write not merely with his own generation in his bones, but with a feeling that the whole of the literature of Europe from Homer and within it the whole of the literature of his own country has a simultaneous existence and composes a simultaneous order" for the modern chaos of the poet's subject matter. With its Homeric-Aeschylean frame of reference, "Sweeney Among the Nightingales" could have been written with this passage in Eliot's mind.

Themes and Meanings

"Sweeney Among the Nightingales" is about the depraved coldness, callousness, and cowardice of modern life as embodied in Sweeney's uneventful encounter with two call girls in a sleazy café setting. Sweeney's evasion of an assignation is ironically compared to mighty Agamemnon's tragic confrontation with a wife of legendary infamy.

The poem demonstrates Eliot's characteristic method of presenting his meaning through multiple parallels and contrasts. There are complex ironies and analogies generated between the comically inconclusive seduction of Sweeney in a nonheroic present and the tragic but regenerative violence against Agamemnon, mythological Philomela and Procne, and Christ, the crucified redeemer of humankind. In heroic times, lust, betrayal, and violence sprang from passions of love or hate and became embodied in meaningful myths of sacrifice and redemptive transformation. The shabby animality of Sweeney, however, eluding the conspiratorial advances of tipsy call girls in a café-brothel, is unrelieved by any such epic significance, sacrifice, or regeneration.

Despite the multiplicity of mythic allusions in the poem, Eliot's ironic conception of Sweeney (a Celtic surname in keeping with Eliot's condescending view of a slovenly, sensual Irishman) depends principally upon two conflated classical descriptions of Agamemnon in Homer's *Odyssey* (c. 800 B.C.E.) and Aeschylus's *Agamemnon*. According to the *Odyssey*, Ulysses in his descent to Hades meets Agamemnon, who recounts his slaying at a banquet table: "You have seen many die in single combat or in battle, but never one who died as we did, by the wine bowl and the loaded tables in a hall where the floor flowed with blood. Cassandra's death-shriek rang in my ears as she fell. Clytemnestra slew her over my body. I tried to lift up my hands for her, but they fell back. I was dying then." Eliot modernizes this Homeric account in an ironically mundane fashion by having Sweeney sit at a fruit-filled café table with a futile sprawling gesture of relaxed arms, letting a latter-day Cassandra fall to the floor.

Imposed on the Homeric account is the Aeschylean portrayal of the climactic death scene in *Agamemnon*, in which Cassandra, the captive Trojan prophetess and mistress of Agamemnon, prophesies the king's murder and her own slaying, but to no avail: "Oh for the nightingale's pure song and a fate like hers. With fashion of beating wings the gods clothed her about and a sweet life gave her and without lamentation. But mine is the sheer edge of the tearing dagger" (lines 1146-1149). Cassandra's cry for a different destiny is the inspiration for Eliot's own poem, which is the ironic inversion of the "nightingale's pure song" and is similarly dependent on the Philomela legend for a contrasting mythic perspective on the action at hand.

Aeschylus's Agamemnon is compared to a lion, dies with rich robes thrown over him by his wife, and falls with legs buckling under him, as vengeful Clytemnestra calls him a philandering "plaything of all the golden girls of Ilium" worthy of lying beside his slain mistress Cassandra in bloody death. Eliot's Sweeney is compared to odder animals; he, too, relaxes his body muscles—if not in death, then in an uneasy assignation with the woman who falls off his lap. Another woman harmlessly reenacts Clytemnestra's violent tearing motion, as the "liquid siftings" of Agamemnon's torrential bloodletting "stain the stiff dishonored shroud" (lines 38-40) spread over him in the bath by Clytemnestra.

Thus, classical prototypes provide a rich and pervasive mythic texture for "Sweeney Among the Nightingales," down to the most minute details of Eliot's description of characters, gestures, situations, and setting. Indeed, Sweeney's innocuous café food of "oranges,/ Bananas figs and hothouse grapes" possibly reverberates with ironic overtones of the horrid cannibalistic fare served in the two principal myths underlying the poem. In the Philomela myth, Procne turned her son into a stew for tyrannical Tereus to consume. As part of the Agamemnon legend, the father Atreus had a brother dine on his own two sons in imitation of the crime of Tantalus, their ultimate ancestor. For Tantalus committed the sin of trying to trick the gods into eating his son and thereby cursed the entire family line down through Agamemnon.

Sweeney's café fruit is a pale counterpart of the sumptuous repast denied Tantalus in Hades in retaliation for the horrible human meal offered the gods. Tantalus is doomed to eternal hunger in Hades by being deprived of "pears, and pomegranates, and apple trees with their bright fruit, and sweet figs, and luxuriant olives above his head" (*Odyssey*, XI: 582-592). Sweeney is one of Eliot's modern antiheroes who parody classical prototypes for an ironic portrayal of mediocrity and meaninglessness in the present.

Thomas M. Curley

SWIMMING BY NIGHT

Author: James Merrill (1926-1995)
Type of poem: Lyric
First published: 1961; collected in *Water Street*, 1962

The Poem

"Swimming by Night" begins, not surprisingly, in the middle of things: "A light going out in the forehead/ Of the house by the ocean" signals to the reader that the poet is already in deep water. James Merrill is presumably swimming in the ocean off the coast of an island in Greece, where he spent nearly two decades living half of each year. He wrote a prose version of this poem in *The (Diblos) Notebook* (1965), in which Sandy, the protagonist in a novel—which Sandy is writing himself, in one of those nice double gestures that Merrill adores—explains that "What one *can* use is the poetry of the night, the lights running across black water toward us from the mainland." Because the swimmer is "Without clothes, without caution," the poem and the poet are deeply committed to some kind of self-discovery.

There is a double darkness of ocean and of night, a "warm black" in which the poet and the reader are plunged. With "Wait!" in the second line of the second stanza, the poem and the poet draw attention to the contrast of surface and depth, both in ocean and in understanding. The poet seems to say he is going to take this slowly, by degrees—"Where before/ Had been floating nothing, is a gradual body"—and that body is the poet's own, as well as his craft.

It is important to know that Merrill enjoyed considerable freedom from certain real pressures of life. His father was an immensely wealthy stockbroker, who gave his son a large fortune before the boy was six. Infinite options surface in this poem as a kind of exotic and liberating chance to be out of one's own element. Thus this lyric meditation, which is only three sentences long on the page, might represent the entire lexicon of Merrill's imagination. In the middle of the poem, where the poet's awareness of his body metamorphoses into the figurative "body" of his work, irony and characteristic playfulness produce lines that condense swimmer and poet as "Yours, risen from its tomb/ In your own mind." The poet is self-conscious at his nakedness in the poem (and in every poem in *Water Street*, since he has doffed the cloak of elaborate conceits), where a "Haunting nimbleness" constantly threatens to expose how confidently he can and does move through the vastness of possibilities—creative, intellectual, athletic, and experiential.

It is obvious that "Swimming by Night" will not end in a toweling off on the sand. The last half of the poem, a single sentence floating up and down on the "evening's alcohol," turns into myth as Merrill evokes the sorcerer's apprentice in his "master's robe." The poem does not so much conclude as burst into "the star running down his cheek."

Forms and Devices

"Swimming by Night" is essentially lyric in design and character, a poem expressing subjective feeling and the personal emotions of the poet. In addition, this poem exemplifies the melodic quality of lyric poetry with quite broad repetition of initial
sounds, or alliteration ("forehead," "feints," "fade," "floating") and slant-rhymed endings ("ocean" with "caution," "feed" with "bed"). Merrill employs the useful technique of periphrasis, talking around a subject through diction, where stars are "feints
of diamond" and one's own reflection in water is "astral with phosphor."

Like so many of the poems in *Water Street* "Swimming by Night" can be read as an
extended metaphor. Although the emphasis on linguistic devices to supply the music
as well as the meaning of poetry is quite traditional, Merrill's work is unusual because
he no longer preserves the conventional boundaries between art and life. Here Merrill,
the powerful swimmer and poet, extracts a subtle implication from the ordinary situation of a swim. In "Swimming by Night" the boundary between the surface of the
water and dissolution into it are completely erased as the poet becomes part of the
ocean of life. The poet-observer and the poetic image become one and reflect each
other as Merrill is reflected in the ocean's water. In fact, the water in this swim helps to
dissolve the usual limits between the real and the imaginary for Merrill, as though
water were indeed the poet's element as well as language.

There is a natural colloquial trace in the poem's "Wait!" that, along with feminine
line endings of one stressed and one unstressed syllable throughout the poem, lends a
modern rhythm to Merrill's obvious command of established patterns of versification.
In some ways "Swimming by Night" is about figurative language, where "By this
weak lamp/ The evening's alcohol will feed" the role that language must play in any
poem, especially in this one.

There is a rare opportunity with "Swimming by Night" to observe the way a prose
fragment can be transformed by the techniques already familiar to the practiced
poet—ellipsis and compression—into a poetic meditation. Juxtaposition of a prose
passage from *The (Diblos) Notebook* reveals the exact images conjured in precisely
the same words:

> To swim then: one's limbs, stippled with phosphorescence, bringing to mind—to my
> mind—ectoplasm, the genie conjured up out of oneself, floating & sporting, performing
> all that's asked of it before it merges at last into the dark chilled bulk of its master's body
> stumbling over stones to sleep.

In the poem the swimmer becomes "astral with phosphor," and "the genie chilling
bids you limp/ Heavily over stones to bed" as the poet dissolves the usual limits between poetry and prose.

Themes and Meanings

Merrill's *Water Street*, in which "Swimming by Night" is collected, has long been
regarded as a distinct break with the remote, symbolist, decorative patterns that domi-

nate his earlier verse, in *First Poems* (1951) and *The Country of a Thousand Years of Peace and Other Poems* (1959). Poems in *Water Street* are concerned with domestic, personal, even intimate experiences: Merrill's own sickness and health, his inspiration, his imagination, his passions for ideas and for people. The formal and metrical preciseness he embraced in earlier volumes is not discarded entirely here, however, but blended seamlessly into a new concentration on themes "of love and loss." The opening poem in *Water Street*, "An Urban Convalescence," is often quoted for its explicit description of this new direction that Merrill intends to take in his work: "the dull need to make some kind of house/ Out of the life lived, out of the love spent."

"Swimming by Night" compresses several poetic themes common to Merrill. He liked to regard a poem as an opportunity to see double. He both finds his psychological depth in this swim, a form of self-knowledge, and loses himself as he merges with water, or submerges his body, in dreams of escape. Other poems carry the same message, as when, in "The Drowning Poet," Merrill explains that "To drown was the perfection of technique/ The word containing its own sense, like Time." The ritual of immersion in language as in water permits the poet to grasp his own senses. In "the far break/ Of waves," with their implied waves of emotion as well, the poet is carried onward and inward at the same time. Water for Merrill is both adventure and risk: "Plunging past gravity" he can enjoy both the actual and the imaginative dimensions. With any other poet one might ask whether the ocean is threatening to engulf him. However, the reader is reassured by the "master's robe" of language worn here as protection against the harsh elements, as one might depend upon God's presence in the midst of a troubled life.

If in "Swimming by Night" one wanted to detect further evidence of Merrill's evident amusement in playing with language (and with his reader's understanding of it), then the preference he has for keeping things in suspense, which this poem does both literally and figuratively, crowns all the other tropes. The unconscious is both on the surface of the poem and underneath. Each line resonates with meanings from myth and history, with tones and overtones of other poems—Merrill's own and those of poets of other times. Finally, the "spinning globe" is Prospero's, who, in William Shakespeare's *The Tempest* (1674) is a sorcerer of the most dramatic kind, to use as much as "word" is part of "world."

Kathleen Bonann Marshall

THE TABLES TURNED

Author: William Wordsworth (1770-1850)
Type of poem: Lyric
First published: 1798, in *Lyrical Ballads*

The Poem

"The Tables Turned" is subtitled "An Evening Scene on the Same Subject," indicating that it forms a pair with the poem published immediately ahead of it in *Lyrical Ballads*, "Expostulation and Reply." A reader should understand one to understand the other.

In "Expostulation and Reply," William Wordsworth's friend Matthew, finding the poet sitting on a stone, urges him to quit dreaming and to read those books through which the wisdom of the past sheds essential light on the problems of the present. William replies that while he sits quietly, he feels the force of "Powers" which give his mind a "wise passiveness." By implication, this passiveness is more precious than the knowledge that can be gained by reading.

"The Tables Turned" is a short lyric poem of thirty-two lines arranged in eight stanzas. It takes the form of an address by a speaker (who most readers will agree is Wordsworth himself) to a friend, the Matthew of "Expostulation and Reply." The scene is presumably that of the other poem ("by Esthwaite lake") in England's Lake District; by its subtitle, "An Evening Scene on the Same Subject," one may assume that the events of the poem take place later in the same day.

Wordsworth metaphorically turns the tables on his friend, for this time it is Wordsworth who makes the confrontation. The poet's general argument has not changed: The mind is much better off when it responds to the influences of nature than when it takes on intellectual tasks. The central concern of the poem is to develop this contrast and this argument.

In stanza 1, Wordsworth forcefully yet playfully urges Matthew to stand "Up! up!" lest he "grow double" in the "toil and trouble" of reading. In stanza 2, the poet paints a picture of the glories to be seen in nature as the sun appears above a mountain and gives the "long green fields" their "sweet evening yellow." From stanza 3 on, nature is embodied specifically in the sounds of birdcalls in the woods—the music of the linnet and the "blithe" song of the throstle (or thrush).

Wordsworth is interested in more than simply giving the reader specific images of nature, however; most of the poem is given over to an argument. The "dull and endless strife" of reading books, the preachers' wisdom they contain, and even the "ready wealth" they may bring are not so sweet and wise as a bird's song. The argument becomes more intense in stanzas 7 and 8, where the poet's objections to books widen to include most kinds of knowledge found in books, especially that "barren" knowledge which comes from rational (perhaps scientific) analysis, by which "Our meddling intellect/ Misshapes the beauteous forms of things—/ We murder to dissect."

In contrast, Wordsworth urges Matthew, "Let Nature be your teacher" by responding to bird songs, by deriving "Spontaneous wisdom" from them in a state, not of dull toil, but of "health" and "cheerfulness." The poet states his program for wisdom in stanza 6: "One impulse from a vernal wood/ May teach you more of man,/ Of moral evil and of good,/ Than all the sages can." Because this is so, Wordsworth ends his poem in stanza 8 by calling on his friend to "come forth" from his books with an alert heart ready to receive nature's lessons.

Forms and Devices

"The Tables Turned" contains eight quatrains of a specific kind; they are "ballad stanzas." Such a stanza generally has four lines of alternately eight and six syllables, which rhyme *abab*. Many of the poems published in *Lyrical Ballads* are written in this kind of verse. This was the stanza in which many folk ballads were composed, so to choose to write in it signaled that a poet was departing from the usual poetic form of the eighteenth century, the heroic couplet.

The poem begins playfully. The poet remonstrates with Matthew, calling forth a fanciful image of his friend's growing double over his books with a witty implication that he is behaving like, and perhaps coming to resemble, the witches in William Shakespeare's *Macbeth* (1606), with his "toil and trouble." The next three or four stanzas are also light in mood. The poet continues to use the imperative voice to call upon his friend to come away from books, and he uses most of the poem's vivid visual images in so doing. Most of the poem's few metaphors (bird as preacher, nature as teacher) occur in stanza 4. In each, the amount of semi-serious and abstract assertion increases: from none in stanza 2 to almost all of stanza 5.

In the climax of the poem, stanzas 6 and 7, the reader finds almost no images, no metaphors. The poet is serious, not urgent or playful. Stanza 6 states the positive side of Wordsworth's argument. Its language has a grand and prophetic simplicity; its rhythm is appropriately regular and calmly emphatic. Stanza 7 states the negative: It is more cacophonous, irregular in rhythm, and polysyllabic than stanza 6. Its final line ("We murder to dissect") is the poem's most forceful in meaning and most dramatic in presentation. The poem ends on a somewhat less intense but hopeful note, as it returns to the imperative to call Matthew forth and to define how he will attain the insights the poet has described.

Themes and Meanings

When Wordsworth chose to employ the ballad stanza, he not only broke with the poetic practice of serious English poetry of the past, he also implied that he held new values. If those values were not (at least in this poem) the values of common folk, they were at least quite different from those common to educated persons in the eighteenth century.

Matthew, the representative of older values, has been identified in part with William Taylor, Wordsworth's boyhood schoolmaster. Wordsworth once said that this and the poem that preceded it "arose out of conversation with a friend" (possibly William Hazlitt) "who was somewhat unreasonably attached to modern books of Moral Philosophy."

It is precisely the kind of ideas about moral philosophy found in books that Words-worth attacks in this poem. In the all-important sixth stanza, Wordsworth asserts that when a person is affected by a perception of beauty in the natural world in springtime ("an impulse from a vernal wood"—a bird song), that person is made immediately and intuitively sensitive to what is good and what is evil. This kind of moral intuition is more to be trusted than judgments made on the bases of philosophical systems.

The seventh stanza describes what such systems do. They reject what can be learned from the pleasing ("sweet") impulses of nature ("the lore which Nature brings"). Instead, these systems encourage the mind ("Our meddling intellect") to an-alyze ("dissect") the "beauteous forms of things." This last phrase is somewhat vague; presumably the mind attempts to analyze not only the beautiful impulses from nature but human actions as well. In either case, before the mind can analyze, it must kill: "We murder to dissect." The action of the logical mind destroys what it touches and defeats its own purpose of discovering moral principles.

Wordsworth criticizes how the logical mind operates upon moral questions. Some readers also take the powerful statements in stanza 7 to apply to the analytical mind in all of its operations. Although elsewhere he expresses different opinions, here Words-worth seems to have much in common with other Romantic poets, who generally val-ued imaginative understanding much higher than logical and rational thought.

George Soule

A TALE OF TWO GARDENS

Author: Octavio Paz (1914-1998)
Type of poem: Lyric
First published: 1969, as "Cuento de dos jardines," in *Ladera este*; English translation
  collected in *The Collected Poems of Octavio Paz: 1957-1987*, 1987

The Poem

"A Tale of Two Gardens" is a long poem in free verse that evokes the concept of rebirth and renewal found in the return to a timeless beginning symbolized by images of
gardens. The poem uses garden imagery to represent key and dynamic moments in
Octavio Paz's life in Mexico and India. As the title of the poem indicates, there are
two gardens in the work. The first is associated with Paz's childhood in Mixcoac,
which is now a part of Mexico City. The second garden is located in India, where the
poet served as an ambassador from Mexico for a number of years. This garden also
provides the setting for the author's second marriage. The poem is written in the first
person and genuinely reflects an intense personal experience with universal implications. The beginning of the piece immediately establishes the garden not so much as a
place but as a moment outside of normal time and space. It is depicted as a void, an archetypal center through which the rivers of cosmic life flow.

The first experience in the garden occurs during the poet's childhood. It is a time of
idyllic vision that only the innocence of youth can create. As the protagonist leaves
his youth, he also symbolically abandons the garden and its transpersonal nature. The
garden of childhood becomes a ruin for ants to harvest. The protagonist's return to the
garden during adulthood represents a return to that magical center abandoned after
childhood. This time it is in a garden in India under a neem tree that awareness is again
expanded and a universal experience is achieved through passionate and erotic love
with the woman he married; the poet depicts her as Almendrita, the "Little Blond Al-
mond" of fairy tale in the children's book by the same name. This passion turns everything into rivers that cover the world, destroying the old and creating the new. Contradictions that come from opposites are symbolically resolved. Even the contradictions
of life and death find common ground in the realm of the Great Mother as expressed
by a variety of feminine deities in Indian lore. The two gardens of the poem are active
places of wonder that carry the protagonist away from his human condition to partake
of the universal source. When the protagonist leaves India at the end of the poem, he
does not leave the garden behind because "there are no more gardens than those we
carry within."

Forms and Devices

The poem develops around the garden as a central image. The garden is part of the
life and everyday history of the protagonist. The memory of the garden in Mixcoac includes the grandfather with whom he spent much time as a boy and the fig tree that

was the center of life there. The garden in India includes the memory of his marriage to his new wife and a neem tree that plays the same role in India as the fig tree did in Mixcoac. However, this image is also presented as both symbol and metaphor. As a symbol, the garden manifests the archetypal center of authentic being. As a metaphor, the garden provides the method by which the protagonist is able to achieve a transformative experience and renew his spiritual condition.

It is the image of the garden as a symbol that provides the mythical setting for the magical moments in the protagonist's life. In it, the fig tree is depicted as the mother goddess whose opened trunk reveals "the other face of being,/ the feminine void," and the neem tree resolves all contradictions: "The other is contained in the one,/ the one is the other." The garden as the setting for the other side of being teaches the protagonist "to wave . . . goodbye" to himself. To return to the garden is to return "to the beginning of the beginning." The garden represents both Prajnaparamita, "Our Lady of the Other Bank," the Indian goddess of perfect wisdom, and Yakshi, the goddess of trees and plants.

The garden as a metaphor begins with the notion that "A house, a garden,/ are not places:/ they spin, they come and go./ Their apparitions open/ another space/ in space,/ another time in time." In another passage, the speaker states that "a garden is not a place:/ it is a passage,/ a passion." The garden is a "Mumbling river" that "flows through the night." The image of the garden acts as a bridge that brings together the concrete and the universal, a manifestation of the dynamic process that leads to magical transformation. The story of the protagonist's union with Almendrita is a story of universal fulfillment. It takes the form of a water-filled journey that destroys the old reality and creates a new world. The journey symbolically resolves all human contradictions. "We don't know where we're going," says the speaker, "to pass through is enough,/ to pass through is to remain." That is, the paradox associated with passing through and remaining is resolved. The garden as a transformative metaphor is confirmed when the speaker states that "there are no more gardens than those we carry within." The garden as passion and as passage is the way by which one reaches self-realization. This self-realization is described in the poem as "the other bank." Once the garden completes its work and allows the protagonist to reach a new level of existence, it disappears only to appear again when the next renewal experience is sought. "The garden sinks," states the speaker in conclusion, "The signs are erased:/ I watch clarity." The garden has transported the protagonist to his ultimate destination. Clarity and wisdom are achieved at the conclusion of the journey.

Themes and Meanings

"A Tale of Two Gardens" is about an archetypal journey to achieve spiritual renewal and a vision that transcends the contradictions caused by the rules of human existence. Adam and Eve's biblical Garden of Eden is an example of that undifferentiated original state of innocence sought by the poetic experience. The journey motif provides both the theme and structure for the work. The concept of the archetypal journey is very much a variation of anthropologist Joseph Campbell's "adventure of the hero" as well as the process of individuation outlined by psychoanalyst Carl Jung. In it, the hero travels to the center of a magical reality to obtain the secrets that symbolically resolve human contradictions. The garden represents such a place.

The garden in Mixcoac manifests the realm of the protagonist's original state of innocence. In that environment, the boy is nurtured. "The garden for me," says the speaker, "was like a grandfather./ I clambered up its leafy knees." The fig tree is then depicted as the mother and the feminine void that dominates the center of that magical world. The protagonist then grows up. Natural innocence is left behind and the garden of his youth no longer exists. The garden as a universal center becomes available again when, as an adult, the protagonist comes in search of its magical gift. What the protagonist achieves in the garden this time is expressed both intellectually and through erotic passion. Intellectually, the protagonist comes to understand the garden as a transformative experience that resolves the paradox of the "one" and the "other" to make both the same. The paradox of life and death is resolved in the notion that views "death is expansion." Finally, the denial of self and the expansion of self are brought together by the concept that sees that "self-negation is growth."

Erotically, the adventure with Almendrita, the symbol of feminine principle and the protagonist's opposite, results in the poetic inundation and destruction of the old reality and the creation of a new world by their love and their archetypal union as representatives of the masculine and the feminine principles. The poem is populated by Indian deities of love, passion, and wisdom. They serve to communicate to the reader that the work is not only a love poem but also a powerful instrument of change and renewal with archetypal implications. In "A Tale of Two Gardens," intellect and passion combine to construct a superior work of art. Symbol, structure, metaphor, and theme come together to provide a way of transcending the human condition.

David Conde

TAR

Author: C. K. Williams (1936-   )
Type of poem: Narrative
First published: 1983, in *Tar*

The Poem

"Tar" is a poem divided into three stanzas, set around the poet's own experience of the Three Mile Island nuclear-reactor accident. In March, 1979, this accident threw many people around the nation (and especially people in Pennsylvania, where the poet lived and where the reactor is located) into a state of alarm over the danger of a full-scale nuclear meltdown that would have unleashed a cloud of deadly radioactive gases over a wide area.

As the poem begins, the juxtaposition of the nuclear accident, mentioned in the first line, with the workmen who are mentioned in the second line seems incongruous, and, in fact, it seems to be this incongruity that has attracted C. K. Williams's attention. He talks about wandering out to watch the men at work to distract himself from the news that he spent most of the night watching.

As the poem progresses in the second stanza, as the official denials of danger from the nuclear-reactor accident seem to him more confused and less trustworthy, and as he sees that the work the men do on his roof is "harrowingly dangerous," watching the roofers and their work becomes not so much a way of avoiding thinking about the nuclear accident as a way of confronting it. That is, the dangerous work of reshingling his roof becomes a metaphor for the precariousness of living in the nuclear age.

By the third stanza, the events of this day have convinced him of the inevitability of a disastrous nuclear mishap. "We'd understood," he says, "we were going to perish of all this . . . if not soon, then someday." As the narrator—who is clearly Williams himself—reflects on the whole incident, he tries to understand why these roofers stay so clear in his mind, while the rest of the events have become such a haze to him. Not only did the glitter of the metal they were working with stay in his mind, but the carats of tar that formed in the gutter, "so black they seemed to suck the light out of the air," became for him an appropriately threatening image of the fear he felt that day, and the graffiti—"obscenities and hearts"—that the children in the neighborhood write with these pieces of tar stays in his mind as an expression of the chaos of this experience.

As becomes clear in the first stanza, when Williams discusses watching the news for long hours, the terror of an accident like this happening nearby is amorphous and hard to grip mentally. By the end of the poem, however, he realizes that his memory has found a form for this terror by selecting images of the whole experience, especially the images of the workmen.

Forms and Devices

C. K. Williams is known for a narrative style of poetry that has an organic and almost casual sound to it. A poem such as "Tar" (and most of the poems in the collection of the same name) does not force language into self-consciously "poetic" forms. Instead, it tries to shape a poem out of the rhythms of natural-sounding speech.

The careful reader, however, will not let the casual sound of the language lull him or her into overlooking the careful shaping of the poem. Although true to Williams's style of poetry, the central metaphor, in which he thinks of the Three Mile Island accident in terms of the work that was done on his roof that day, is not presented self-consciously as a metaphor, but rather as a coincidence; this metaphor constitutes the heart of the poem. When the narrator says he never realized how "matter-of-factly and harrowingly dangerous" it is, he is referring literally to the work of tarring and shingling a roof, but there is also a clear figurative level being worked out on which he is referring not only to how dangerous nuclear plants are, specifically, but also to how dangerous life in the nuclear age is.

The things that make the work on the roof particularly dangerous are the decaying materials, the rusty nails that have to be pulled out, the under-roofing that crumbles under the weight of a workman, and the old furnace that is kept burning to heat the tar. The extent to which he sees the crumbling of these fairly simple tools and materials as stand-ins for the nuclear power plant becomes clear when a "dense, malignant smoke shoots up" from the furnace, reminding him of the danger of radioactive gases being released from the nuclear core of the Three Mile Island plant. The furnace is adjusted rather crudely by a workman hitting it with a hammer.

When the poet looks inside the heated tar pot, he sees a "Dantean broth" and compares the tar to the images of hell presented in *Inferno* (c. 1320). The bubbling tar looks bland, almost like licorice, in the crucible in which it is cooked, but when spilled, it "sears, and everything is permeated." Again, the comparison to the "crucible" within the power plant is clear; the water that is used both to cool the nuclear core and to convey the tremendous amount of heat it takes to operate the turbines in the plant is innocuous so long as it is kept contained. If this water were to be spilled as radioactive steam, however, it, like spilled tar, would permeate and contaminate everything around it.

The middle stanza ends when the men go to lunch, leaving the air above the roof "alive with shimmers and mirages." Literally, Williams is referring to the shimmer of heat rising from the hot tar on the roof, but this image also completes the comparison the stanza has been developing by implicitly referring to the cooling tower of the Three Mile Island plant, which, in news reports of the accident, was prominently displayed giving off heat and radioactivity.

Themes and Meanings

Although the themes of the poem are developed throughout, it is in the third stanza especially that they are brought into the forefront. When the poet says that by the afternoon "we'd understood:/ we were going to perish of all this, if not now . . . then someday," it is clear that the image of the battered furnace boiling a "Dantean broth" and spewing "malignant smoke" into the atmosphere has become more than a metaphor for the potentially lethal technology of the Three Mile Island plant. This furnace and the nuclear accident happening not far away are both images for him of the precariousness of life in late twentieth century America.

For a moment, he has a clear and bleak vision of a future generation cursing "our earthly comforts . . . our surfeits and submissions." That is, the demand for earthly comforts will eventually lead to the destruction of the planet when the increasingly complicated technology that has been developed to sustain an American lifestyle rich with such comforts backfires.

The mention of "the president in his absurd protective booties, looking absolutely unafraid, the fool," is a reference to a tour of the plant that President Jimmy Carter took when the crisis was winding down but was by no means over. Some frequently reprinted photographs of this tour showed Carter wearing no special protective clothing other than some protective footwear, but smiling and looking confident. Within this poem, Williams seems to see the president's confidence as a part of the larger social machinery that is malfunctioning. Rather than facing the danger with an examination of the larger social forces that have led to such a breakdown, the president responded with a display of confidence that Williams clearly thinks was misplaced.

The most vivid image the poet retains from this incident is of the workmen "silvered with glitter from the shingles, clinging like starlings beneath the eaves." Calling a comparison of the workmen to birds "clinging . . . beneath the eaves" the most vivid image of this incident suggests that the relative helplessness of birds who try to find a home in a building they have no real power or control over is, to Williams, a situation akin to the dilemma of residents of twentieth century America who live in a society that is reliant upon technologies that most people can neither understand nor control.

The image with which the poem actually ends, "obscenities and hearts" scribbled with hardened lumps of tar on sidewalks by the children in the neighborhood, has a number of meanings. On a very basic level, this is a reassuring image, in that the light-heartedness of children scrawling graffiti is something of a relief from the heavier images and issues with which the poem has been dealing; even after a crisis such as this, one might read the poem as saying, children will be children. Coming as it does at the end of a poem called "Tar," however, this image of "obscenities and hearts" being scribbled with lumps of tar "so black they seemed to suck the light out of the air" takes on additional meaning. Williams seems to be suggesting that one danger of such a baffling crisis is that such things as scrawled obscenities can seem to be the only possible response, and the very magnitude of the crisis can make any other response seem reduced to the level of unoriginal, quickly scribbled graffiti on the sidewalk. Against the backdrop of these scribblings, the poem itself emerges as an attempt to try to find lasting truths from these images he recalls from a brush with what had threatened to be a national (if not a worldwide) calamity.

Thomas J. Cassidy

THE TASK

Author: Denise Levertov (1923-1997)
Type of poem: Lyric
First published: 1982; collected in *Oblique Prayers: New Poems with Fourteen Translations from Jean Joubert*, 1984

The Poem

"The Task" is a twenty-five-line poem composed of two stanzas written in free verse, which Denise Levertov herself would describe as "organic poetry." The poem discusses the character and—as the title implies—the work of God. The opening six-line stanza presents a false image of God as an uncouth and somewhat threatening old man "always upstairs, sitting about/ in sleeveless undershirt," his arms folded over his rumbling stomach. He is asleep and probably snoring since she concludes the stanza with the lines "his breath from open mouth/ strident, presaging death" (an image suggestive of the "death rattle"). The stanza ends with an ellipsis, as if the description was unfinished, and the second stanza interrupts and proceeds to correct this image of God.

In the corrected image, God is depicted as a weaver working at his loom "in the wilderness," described as a "huge tundra room" with no walls and a "sky roof." However, he is not far away; he is just next door. His work is absorbing and loud, and he seems to be in some hurry to finish it. The sounds of human screams and prayers come through the clamor of his task, but the poem is somewhat ambiguous about the kind of attention God pays to them. He "hears far-off" humanity's screams and "perhaps listens for prayers in that wild solitude." Ultimately, humans "can't stop their/ terrible beseeching," but "God/ imagines it sifting through, at last, to music." The poem concludes with the task complete, the loom quiet, and "the weaver at rest."

Forms and Devices

Concerning the forms of her poems, Levertov, in *The Poet in the World* (1973), distinguishes between free verse, which rejects precast or reusable forms in favor of freedom from all bonds, and her "organic poetry," which, having freed itself from imposed forms, voluntarily submits to the forms that content reveals and imposes on it. The form of "The Task" is an outgrowth and expression of its contents. The poem's two-stanza structure permits the contrast of the false image of God with the corrected image. The first stanza begins conversationally with the words "As if," implying the conditional character of the description and establishing a skeptical tone. The reader understands immediately that this is not the true image of God. The second stanza begins with a resounding "No," specifying—in no uncertain terms—a contradiction to the first stanza.

The controlling metaphor of the second stanza is God as a weaver whose work is weaving a great garment. The structure of the stanza is loomlike: Elements of both sense and sound are threaded into the poem, not in prose sentence order but in alternating and somewhat irregular arrangements that only present a finished pattern in the fully woven poem. For example, visual images of the wilderness in the first two lines of the stanza are followed by a line combining the introduction of the loom with a picture of berry bushes, which in turn is followed by a line in which "rain" and "shine" are juxtaposed to the aural image of the "clacking and whirring" loom. Human screams, introduced in lines 14 and 15, are commented on in lines 21 and 22; likewise, God's listening, introduced in lines 15 and 16, is related to human voices in line 19. The "hum of bees, not the din" that he hears in line 13 is echoed by his imagining human "beseeching" as "music" in line 23. Similarly, line length at the center of the second stanza is patterned, with pairs of longer lines alternating with shorter lines. Line breaks seem to be determined by emphasis, with key words such as "solitude," "woven," "task," "God," and "music" occurring at the ends of lines.

These devices illustrate Levertov's ideal of the elements of a poem working together to create "a kind of extended onomatopoeia" that imitates "not the sounds of an experience . . . but the feeling of an experience" (*The Poet in the World*). However, the poet also uses onomatopoeia in the traditional sense of using words that sound like their referents: a stomach rumbling, the loom clacking and whirring, and the bees humming. In her description of the false image of God, repeated sibilants (as in "sleeveless undershirt, asleep") sound like breath passing through dentures, and the assonant sounds of the dull, open vowels intensify the image of the open-mouthed sleeper.

Themes and Meanings

Levertov begins her poetry collection *Oblique Prayers* with a note explaining that the book and the sections within it represent a thematic rather than a chronological order. The order of the fourth and final section, "Of God and Of the Gods," seems to represent the Judeo-Christian Creation story: not just the initial Creation of the biblical account but also an active and continuous creation that finds completion in the individual believer's life. "The Task" stands exactly at the center of the fifteen poems that comprise this final section and can be fully understood only in its relationship to the others. The first seven poems account for the creation of the natural world: of rivers, of "earth-gods," of trees and flowers. In most of these poems, God is designated as unknowable, at least to "the gods." In "The Avowal," God is named "Creator Spirit" and man is placed in the natural context. In the next poem, "The God of Flowers" (which precedes "The Task"), though the god of flowers cannot know God, her work pleases him and he "watches and smiles."

Levertov has referred to God and the gods in poems written before this collection, notably in *Candles in Babylon* (1982), and has written much overtly Christian poetry since; however, "The Task" was her most explicit and most nearly orthodox poem about God at the time of its publication. The poem implies much about the character and work of God. That God is "in the wilderness next door/ —that huge tundra room, no walls and a sky roof—" implies that while God may be unbounded, neither he nor his whereabouts are unknowable. He seems near and exists not apart from but within the created world.

Since the poem follows a catalog of Creation in the first seven poems, the task of the title seems to be the work of Creation itself. Elsewhere in *Oblique Prayers*, Levertov uses images of knitting to represent re-creative acts, as when she describes an old gray sweater being conjured into a poem: "it and your need for it," she writes, "are/ the knit and purl of the poem's rows/ re-raveled" ("Grey Sweaters"). The reader is prepared then to regard the task in which God, without raw materials, "hurries on with the weaving:/ till it's done, the great garment woven" as Creation. However, God is involved in this poem with more than the creation of the natural world. The poem affirms that while God is "absorbed in his work," he "hears far-off" human screams and "listens for prayers." Though he "hurries on with the weaving," the human voices are "clear under the familiar/ blocked-out clamor of the task." The human cries are not annoying or irrelevant. Though they leave the lips or hearts as "terrible beseeching," they become, like the spacious hum of bees, the music that accompanies God's work.

At the end of "The Task," the loom is idle, suggesting the completion of God's task, but the implication of the last seven poems is that God's creative work is not finished. These final poems outline a kind of apostolic succession from Saint Peter to the poet and a sequence of belief from spiritual dryness to transcendent joy. In the final poem, "Passage," God's spirit, walking "upon the face of the water" and moving the meadow grass, provides new life not only to believers but also to their world.

Gaymon L. Bennett

TEARS, IDLE TEARS

Author: Alfred, Lord Tennyson (1809-1892)
Type of poem: Lyric
First published: 1847, in *The Princess*

The Poem

Though often printed as a separate poem, "Tears, Idle Tears" is actually part of *The Princess* (1847), a long poem in which Alfred, Lord Tennyson explores questions of feminism and the proper roles of the sexes. In fact, the lyric is not titled at all in the original publication; rather, the first words of the opening line have come to serve as an identifying tag for the poem.

While one need not be familiar with *The Princess* to appreciate "Tears, Idle Tears," some understanding of the dramatic situation in which the lyric is presented may help explain its theme and account for its particular imagery. This lyric is sung by one of the maidens residing at the castle of Princess Ida, an independent young woman who has retreated from society with some of her female colleagues to found a school from which men are excluded. She is pursued there by the Prince, who is in love with her; he infiltrates her castle disguised as a woman. At the moment in *The Princess* when this song is sung, Ida, her friends, and the Prince are relaxing at sunset. Hence, the mood of this lyric, that of sober melancholy, seems appropriate for the setting in which it appears.

Even if one is not familiar with *The Princess*, however, "Tears, Idle Tears" can be read as a powerful statement about the impact of the past. In the poem, the speaker laments the passing of time that has robbed him of the chance to relive cherished experiences. This meditation is brought on by a sudden unexplained welling-up of tears in the speaker's eyes. The cause for the speaker's feeling of sadness cannot be determined, and he never hints directly at what might be the source of his own tears; instead, he tries to explain how he feels by comparing his feelings to a series of events that produce similar emotions in others.

In the middle two stanzas, the speaker focuses his attention on these "days that are no more"—a phrase that serves as a kind of refrain in the final line of each stanza of the poem. He first compares his feelings about bygone times to the experience one has when anticipating the arrival of friends from afar, and then seeing them sail away beyond the horizon as they return to faraway lands. In the third stanza, the speaker likens his emotions to those of a dying man who sees a summer dawn and hears birds piping outside his window. In the final stanza, the speaker compares his feeling for the past to that of "remember'd kisses after death" (line 16)—though it is not clear who has died and who lives on—and to the recollections of one's first love with all its passion and all its regret.

Forms and Devices

One might expect that if a poem's first line speaks of tears, the poem would be about uncontrolled emotion. Perhaps Tennyson is relying on such an initial response to create a certain tension in "Tears, Idle Tears," for there is little sense of wild abandon in these lines. On the contrary, all the formal devices and literary tropes suggest a great sense of emotional restraint.

As he does in most of his compositions, Tennyson relies on several formal devices to convey a note of restraint. The blank-verse lines and the extensive use of enjambment create a meditative, conversational atmosphere. Each of the stanzas is linked to the others, however, by a closing phrase: "the days that are no more." This refrain develops in readers a sense of anticipation and fulfillment and establishes a common thread to each of the images described in the stanzas: All are intended to remind the reader of the passing of time and the losses that come with such passing; by implication, the reader is reminded also of the inevitability of death.

Even more than these formal devices, the imagery of "Tears, Idle Tears" focuses the reader's attention on the melancholy calm and the sense of irony that comes with the mature contemplation of life's passing. Each stanza concentrates on a single example that illustrates a sense of loss. In the first stanza, the poet presents an individual looking out at "happy Autumn-fields" (line 4)—certainly a time for bittersweet memories, as autumn traditionally suggests an impending ending—and reflecting, as the seasons change, on times past. This reflection brings these "idle tears" to the eyes.

In the second stanza, the sense of loss is compared to the feelings one has when good friends come to visit and then leave. This is the most complex image in the poem. There is a sense of joy at seeing the "glittering on a sail" (line 6) as the ship bringing the friends tops the horizon; that feeling is balanced with the sadness that sweeps over one when those same friends depart. Of particular interest are the words Tennyson chooses to describe the arrival and departure of the ship: the friends appear to be coming "up from the underworld" (line 7), and when they depart, the ship carrying them seems to sink "below the verge" (line 9). This voyage carries symbolic overtones; it is as if the voyage represents the passage of life itself.

That same image is carried forward and made explicit in the third stanza, where the speaker suggests that his idle tears are like those of the dying man who sees a summer dawn. This individual knows that he will not see many (if any) more, and the melancholy produced by that realization is the source of his tears. Similarly, in the final stanza, the tears are likened to those that well up in people who recall with joy and regret a love affair that has ended with no hope of renewal. The individual who experiences such feelings is living a "Death in Life" (line 20): He is alive, but he knows that a part of him—the part that shared those happy times in the past—is gone forever. The realization of his loss is the cause for what appears to be unexplained melancholy and the source for his "idle tears."

Themes and Meanings

Within the context of *The Princess*, this lyric provides Tennyson with an opportunity to show the immaturity of his heroine, who rebukes the maiden singing the lyric. Recognizing that the song's purpose is to remind the listeners of the sadness that comes from reflecting on the past, the Princess rejects that attitude explicitly and vehemently, saying that "all things serve their time . . . let the past be past." She even calls such reminiscences "fatal to men" and recommends that the company "cram our ears with wool" to avoid hearing such maudlin thoughts. As the long narrative poem progresses, however, the Princess comes to realize that a mature contemplation of the past is an important attribute of sensitive adults.

Viewing the lyric outside the context of the long poem in which it first appeared, readers should see that Tennyson's major theme is the sadness and irony that accompanies such reflection on bygone times. There seems little hope or optimism in these lines; every image suggests the futility and even the incomprehensibility (on an emotional level, if not on an intellectual one) of coping with lost time. It is important to note, however, that no image in the poem suggests that these feelings of sadness result from missed opportunity. Rather, the images convey a sense that they come from the realization that pleasurable experiences of the past may never be enjoyed again. Tennyson told his friend Frederick Locker-Lampson that the poem was motivated by "the yearning that young people occasionally experience for that which seems to have passed away from them forever" (Hallam Tennyson, *Memoir*, 1897). Such a remark is consistent with Tennyson's persistent infatuation with the past, and with his constant recognition that man is not able to relive past times and experiences. Though "Tears, Idle Tears" is not a part of Tennyson's most famous long poem, *In Memoriam* (1850), it shares the same mood as many of the lyrics that make up the poet's elegy to his dear friend Arthur Henry Hallam, who died suddenly in 1833. Tennyson spent almost two decades composing poetry inspired by feelings of loss at the death of Hallam; composed in the mid-1840's after a visit to the region where Hallam is buried, "Tears, Idle Tears" shows the same characteristics of restraint in its presentation of emotion and the same penetrating insight into the nature of loss that the poet expresses so poignantly in his major elegiac work.

Laurence W. Mazzeno

THE TEETH MOTHER NAKED AT LAST

Author: Robert Bly (1926-   )
Type of poem: Meditation
First published: 1970; revised in *Sleepers Joining Hands*, 1973; further revised in *Selected Poems*, 1986

The Poem

"The Teeth Mother Naked at Last" is a long, frequently subjective, meditation on the American involvement in the Vietnam War. It describes the "harm" the war has done to America and to Americans "inwardly." The poem is divided into seven numbered and self-contained sections ranging in length (in the final *Selected Poems* version) from eight to fifty-three lines. Each section is divided into stanzas of uneven lengths. Several sections are further divided into subsections, separated by asterisks, and section 3 contains two paragraphs of prose. One part of section 2 was originally published independently, in quite different form, in *The Nation* (March 25, 1968), and another part of this section originally appeared in Robert Bly's play, *The Satisfaction of Vietnam* (1968).

The title refers to one of the "mothers" that make up the mystical cult of the Great Mother, which first appeared in ancient times. The Teeth or Stone Mother attempts to destroy consciousness and spiritual growth and has come to stand for the destruction of the psyche in Jungian psychology.

The poem begins with airplanes and helicopters ("death-bees") lifting off from the decks of ships and flying over Vietnamese villages to bomb the people huddled in the "vegetable-walled" huts. This massive destruction, without mercy even for innocent children, is seen as the end result of what has happened in the American political system. The voices of soldiers are heard ordering the killing of "anything moving," and the reed huts of the Vietnamese villagers are set afire. The war, with its wanton death and destruction, is defended and even rationalized by political and religious leaders and political and religious institutions back home in America. These rationalizations are "lies," however, and these lies "mean that the country wants to die." Things have already gone so far that even objective truths (such as the name of the capital of Wyoming, the number of acres of land in the Everglades, and the time the sun sets on any given day) now can be lied about by the president and the attorney general. This kind of corruption of the facts, in addition to the travesties and literal horrors of the war, are detailed primarily in the first three sections of the poem. "This," readers are told, "is what it's like for a rich country to make war."

The transitional fourth and fifth sections suggest a literal, structural, and thematic turn in the poem. The fifth and shortest section begins with the most pertinent question of the whole poem: "Why are they dying?" Since, as has been seen and shown, there is no rational reason given, nor any answer available, the remaining sections of the poem move beyond the rational, into the mystical or metaphysical realms, in an attempt to deal with the atrocities inherent in war psychologically. In this sense, although the clear focus of the poem remains fixed on the Vietnam War, the poem expands this focus to a treatment of the psychological accoutrements of war in general.

The sixth section of the poem, which describes the burning of innocent children, is the most graphic and the most condemnatory. The speaker finds himself suddenly forced backward through the evolutionary chain, to the consciousness of his "animal brain," which allows for a more emotional and less intellectual way of dealing with existence. Such a place in the psyche is also the place where poetry has its source and, thus, this movement down into the depths of the psyche prepares the reader for the poetic paean of the last two sections of the poem.

At the beginning of the seventh section the speaker says that he wants to sleep without being awakened. In his apocalyptic dream vision, from "waters" deep beneath the surface of self and consciousness, "the Teeth Mother, naked at last," rises up and points to the possibility of both a political and a psychic renewal, one which may vitiate the problems posed both by the war in Vietnam and by war in general.

Forms and Devices

If "The Teeth Mother Naked at Last" is thought of as political satire, it may also be seen to combine elements of several of the traditional kinds of satire. It is a formal satire in that it makes a direct frontal attack on its adversary, naming names. At the same time, Bly combines elements of the two traditional varieties of satire: the Horatian (through his use of informal diction and the long Whitmanesque line) and the Juvenalian (through the gravity and seriousness of the threat posed and the hoped for serious and positive reaction solicited). Further, using another traditional satiric device, Bly approaches his theme indirectly via the third-person point of view—although, significantly (after slipping in and out of the first and third persons) the point of view shifts dramatically to the first person in the short, climactic fifth section, and it keeps to that point of view throughout the rest of the poem. This shift in the point of view, from the third person to the first, forces the theme and meaning of the poem to the immediate moment and puts it in terms that make it definitively personal.

One of the most conspicuous poetic devices in the poem is Bly's vivid, often surprising and startling (if sometimes arbitrary or gratuitous) use of imagery and metaphor. Bly is known for his interest in, and his often obsessional use of, "deep images"—that is, images that combine or fuse disparate or unlikely elements and often attempt to connect the physical world with the psychic or spiritual world. Such images are clearly in evidence throughout this poem and they come to climax at the very end of it in such lines as "Let us drive cars/ up/ the light beams/ of the stars."

Another conspicuous device (which Bly here appropriates for the first time in his work) is the long line, which he discovered in the poetry of Walt Whitman. This long line, and the form his poem takes are, according to Bly himself, most appropriate for "public" and "political" poetry because, as he says in his essay "Whitman's Line as a

Public Form," "The subject of political poetry is power, and . . . I felt drawn to a line that handles power . . . directly."

Finally, in a poem of this length, what is perhaps most important is rhythm. As "The Teeth Mother Naked at Last" moves smoothly through its themes and through the nightmares of the landscape of war, there are logical and imaginative "leaps" in the lines, as well as seemingly irrational associations. These "leaps" are intended to suggest and parallel similar leaps and irrational shiftings in the political and social fabric of a society attempting to justify its involvement in war. Such imaginative "bullets" are Bly's own "bombing raid" on warmongers.

Themes and Meanings

The main theme of "The Teeth Mother Naked at Last" is the age-old theme of the terror and the horror wrought by war. This poem reminds one of other powerful antiwar poems, both about the Vietnam War and other, earlier, wars. Now that war involves the prospect of and, indeed, the inevitability of, mass destruction—including the innocent as well as the "guilty"—the issues have become more demanding, just as the terrors have become more terrifying. There is, then, a greater pressure to protest. Bly's poem leads the way.

"The Teeth Mother Naked at Last" is a poem that demands a response and a reaction. In form and theme, in its large and small design, it forces the reader toward making a response, toward a reaction, and toward taking action.

Like many of Bly's shorter antiwar poems in *The Light Around the Body* (1967), "The Teeth Mother Naked at Last" is didactic, propagandistic, and controversial, both in terms of its theme and its "meaning" or significance. It is a political, social, even psychological analysis of the malaise of modern society, which came to a climax in the Vietnam War—a war here seen and described as the latest, the most immediate, and the most terrifying example of man's inhumanity to man. In forcing these issues on the reader, Bly is attempting to awaken readers from the sleeplike state in which they have existed and continue to exist, to awaken them to what they are doing to themselves as well as to others by allowing such things as the Vietnam War to occur, and to motivate them toward taking positive action (life-giving instead of life-taking) to see that such wars never happen again.

In order for this to happen, however, men and women must be able to understand themselves to the depths of their beings; they must be able to acknowledge the Teeth Mother, "naked at last," and they must be able to deal with her in appropriate political and psychological ways. This is what the final lines of Bly's poem imply. Humans must, yes, move outward into space and explore the outer reaches of the universe, but even more important, they must simultaneously travel through the depths of their own inner psychic "spaces" and make, if necessary, even a martyr's sacrifice for what they find there, for what they must most believe in.

Here, then, is the shock of recognition and realization, the full and final realization of the significance and the power of the "Teeth Mother" who has hidden away in Western culture and in everyone's own individual psychic selves for so long, buried so deeply that only something like the Vietnam War could force her, "naked at last," back into view, demanding to be seen and heard. "The Teeth Mother Naked at Last" is Robert Bly's most important poetic response to the demands forced out into the world by the Teeth Mother.

William V. Davis

TELLING THE BEES

Author: John Greenleaf Whittier (1807-1892)
Type of poem: Ballad
First published: 1858; collected in *Home Ballads and Poems*, 1860

The Poem

Originally published as "The Bees of Fernside," "Telling the Bees" is a poem of fourteen quatrains, or stanzas of four lines each. Each stanza displays *abab* rhyming, which means that the first line rhymes with the third and the second line with the fourth, a typical pattern for a ballad. A note written by John Greenleaf Whittier precedes the poem, informing readers that on farms in Essex County, Massachusetts (Whittier's home), a custom dating from colonial times was long observed: When a death occurred in the family, someone would "tell the bees" kept on the farm about the death and drape the hive with black crepe to allow the insects to mourn for the deceased. At one time people believed that not doing so would cause the bees to leave, frightened by a death they did not understand.

This poem uses a first-person narrator, a young man who is distinct from Whittier. He is reminiscing a year after the events he describes, walking down the same path he took the previous June. Twelve months earlier, he was going to see his sweetheart, Mary, after being away a month, which, he adds, seemed to be a year without her. The young man's remark ironically suggests the year of grief which began on the day he recalls. As he walks, he describes the earlier trip. He steps through an opening in a tumbled wall and crosses a brook. He comes within sight of Fernside, Mary's farm, and notices the red gate, tall poplar trees, brown barn, and white horns of the family's cattle showing above a stone wall. He sees the beehives kept near the barn, the spring flowers by the brook, and describes the "sweet clover-smell in the breeze" from the meadows nearby. It is a beautiful spring day, much like the one he recalls from the previous year.

The speaker reminisces that a year before, he took a drink from the stream, admired the blossoms, and brushed off his coat, preparing to see Mary. However, as he drew near, he saw a servant girl draping the beehives in black and singing to the bees. Despite the sun's warmth, he felt chilled, knowing that the crepe meant a death had occurred. He assumed that Mary's frail grandfather had died, and he felt pity for the sadness she must feel. However, as the young man came closer to the house, he heard Mary's dog whining from the house and saw her grandfather sitting on the porch, resting his chin on the end of his cane. At the same moment he finally made out the words the servant sang, and he realized that it was Mary who had died. The poem ends with this realization.

Forms and Devices

Ballads, in general, are narrative poems modeled on English and Scottish folk songs. Such poems are generally more effective at depicting action than thought or feeling; emotions are typically shown through the depiction of situations and deeds rather than through a discussion of mental states. Accordingly, despite the first-person narration, Whittier relies on sensory details and setting to develop the emotion of "Telling the Bees." The young man, going to see his beloved, mused happily on the scenery along the path. Everything was familiar, friendly, and warm; these details allow the reader to sense the speaker's past joy, equating the bright day and fragrant vegetation with young love.

Similarly, the subsequent shock and grief are neither described nor portrayed. Instead, the reader is presented with the contrast of the living, pleasant colors (the hues of the flowers along the brook as well as the red, green, brown, and white of the farm) with the somber black being draped about the beehives. The birds' songs contrast with the sad voice of the hired girl. At that point, the narrator says, he felt cold, as if he were walking on a snowy day in winter (itself a contrast with the sunny June weather). Even here the narration dwells not upon the emotion but its physical manifestation, the chill and shiver that people feel as they anticipate bad news. The narrator regarded the loss of life as sad but not unexpected, for Mary's grandfather was obviously unwell. Observed detail, rather than description, then communicates the final destruction of the speaker's comfort, as if the reader can see through his eyes and hear through his ears the events leading to the realization. First, Mary's dog cried for its owner, and then the grandfather appeared on the porch, staring into space as if heartbroken. Finally, the words of the dirge sung by the "chore-girl," "Mistress Mary is dead and gone," became audible. The young man's emotions at the loss of his sweetheart, whom he expected to see after a month's absence, strike the reader even though the feelings are never described.

Also effective in engaging the imagination is the use of detail. As with the colors, a few traits of the day are suggested, but most are omitted, allowing the mind's eye to create the scenes more easily from individual experience. The pasture smells of clover, as do most meadows in the late spring; in this, and similar details, Whittier allows the reader to fill in the larger picture from memory. Such personalized scenes help the reader to experience vicariously the sadness of the young man. Everything else the speaker notices is unchanged—even the tumbled wall through which he walked many times before is still in the same state of disrepair, and the flowers near the brook are still overgrown with weeds; only Mary is missing. The sun is the same, the fields and cattle are the same, but the person who gave everything meaning for him is gone.

Themes and Meanings

Scholars have pointed out that Whittier combines the custom of telling the bees about a death in the family with a description of his own family farm. He wrote the poem as a memorial tribute to his mother, Abigail Hussey Whittier, who died in December, 1857, three months before its publication. She had lived on the family farm most of her adult life. Whittier, who sometimes has been viewed by critics as artificially sentimental, here weaves details from his own life into a masterful evocation of grief and loss. His almost conversational tone, which contains very little "poetic" diction, helps the reader imagine the scene through which the narrator walks. He does not depict emotion, but rather draws the reader into the situation so skillfully that one feels something of the young man's loss.

Whittier's self-discipline, which allowed him to express his profound sorrow in a brief poem, also helped him make that poem powerful. Instead of pouring out the lamentation that might seem natural to a grieving person, Whittier kept direct expressions of emotion out of the poem, focusing instead on details of the physical world to suggest the emptiness which the bereaved feel. Further, by having the speaker reminisce a year later, Whittier was able to show someone who still mourned Mary but who could ponder his situation without the despair and confusion which would be associated with a more recent death.

Even though the poem was a tribute to his mother, Whittier chose not to make the lost loved one a mother, but rather a sweetheart (named for his elder sister, Mary Whittier Caldwell). By fictionalizing the loss in this way, the poet both kept his personal sadness private and made his perceptions more accessible for a wide range of readers. As innumerable songs, legends, and literary works attest, the fear of losing a lover is common. It is easy to imagine such a loss, which makes the shock accessible for a wide range of readers, young and old. In the ensuing years, as he continued to contemplate the death of his mother and later of his sister Mary, Whittier wrote many religious or inspirational verses. In "Telling the Bees," however, he took a different approach, expressing sadness for lost joy in this world rather than hope for the next. Although it is not overtly about Abigail Whittier, "Telling the Bees" expresses the feelings her son experienced at the time of her death.

Critics generally consider "Telling the Bees" one of Whittier's best works. Much of his poetry was occasional, written for specific situations, and it has not always been admired by later readers. Much of what is still well known, such as Whittier's numerous religious poems, was similarly written for specific audiences. However, "Telling the Bees" relies upon such basic experiences as a beautiful spring day and the expectation of a happy reunion to emphasize the suddenness and absoluteness of death. By employing such universal events, the poem draws its force from the basic shock of the contrast of life and its end.

Paul James Buczkowski

TELYRIC

Author: Andrei Codrescu (1946-   )
Type of poem: Lyric
First published: 1987, in *Cottonwood Commemorative: River City Portfolio 1987*;
collected in *Alien Candor: Selected Poems, 1970-1996*, 1996

The Poem

In thirty-four lines the narrator of "Telyric" describes being prepared for an outdoor television presentation. A television performer, the narrator is clearly poet Andrei Codrescu himself. Elsewhere, Codrescu has explained that he wrote the poem while working on a documentary about baseball for a Minneapolis television station.

In the poem a "professional TV person" tells the narrator where to stand and shields him from the sun with a "silver shield"—presumably a metallic umbrella, such as is used for reflecting sunlight in outdoor shooting. The "nuclear-trained soundman" wires the narrator to himself and brags about the "top-secret clearance" he once had while "shut four years inside a sewer pipe," when he indulged a drug habit. An old man stops to ask whether the narrator is famous. He spits in a monumental fountain built by the Immigration and Naturalization Service. The fountain is reputed to have been controversial in an earlier time, when its ornamentation shielded terrorists. The British cameraman shooting the narrator proudly wears a T-shirt immortalizing the life of a Scandinavian plastic surgeon, Tord Skoog, that is worn "from Patagonia to Maroc."

The narrator feels the self-consciousness of the performer, his media personality on display in the sunshine as if he were a large puppet. He mentions a sports hero also on display, Dennis Martinez, the "new national hero of Nicaragua" (a Baltimore Orioles pitcher whom Codrescu interviewed for the documentary). Public notice and adulation conceal rather than reveal, distorting the narrator's sense of self. The electronic connections to the media equipment allow the narrator to communicate with the outside world, but they provide no psychological or intellectual understanding, no "sense." A television person waves to the narrator, signaling him to begin his performance. The narrator walks toward her, overcoming his lack of familiarity in his youth with the conventions of television performance. He puts on his television personality and delivers his first line into the bright light of the sun. His "tinfoil trembles like Skoog's fjord."

Forms and Devices

The language of "Telyric" synthesizes and blends complex experiences into units of poetic discourse. An example of this technique is the title, which by this process of blending forms a new word as "television lyric" becomes "telyric." Such formations are known as portmanteau words—words formed by telescoping pairs of existing words, such as "electricity" and "execute" to make "electrocute" or "breakfast" and "lunch" to make "brunch." However, Codrescu's title is also humorously oxymoronic in that "television" and "lyric" usually suggest contradictory contexts. "Lyric" connotes music and deep emotions—a far cry from the utilitarian banality of television.

Apart from the poem's title, the blends in "Telyric" connect the awkward social and psychological feelings involved with being in the camera's eye with the events of the production itself. The narrator's observations and memories are linked to the physical setting of the production, as when the fountain in which the geezer spits triggers memories of a long-past (and absurd) contretemps [the fountain] "said years ago/ to have been an object of controversy/ capable of shielding terrorists."

Codrescu is a master of a comic *reductio ad absurdum*, carrying the seemingly straightforward if silly—"capable of shielding terrorists"—into the completely ridiculous: "in the goldfish rolls of its Dubuffet clusters." (Jean Dubuffet was a French artist who designed large sculptures noted for their apparent disorder and spontaneous vigor.) The T-shirt worn by the British cameraman not only promotes a Scandinavian plastic surgeon—an unlikely subject in itself—but follows his life from "humble beginnings/ to an obituary in the *Scandinavian/ Journal of Plastic Surgery*"—a publication most people may be excused for never suspecting existed. The comedy is capped by the Scandinavian doctor's notoriety via T-shirt "from Patagonia to Maroc" (which are separated by the Atlantic Ocean).

The synthesizing language merges the narrator's "telyric self" and "large puppethood," the metaphor suggesting how awkward, graceless, and controlled the television self feels while under the control of the wires (literally audio cables) of the production crew. The solitary narrator "bends" like a puppet in the glare of the sun, as if on stage in a spotlight. However, the setting is outdoors, perhaps prompting the baseball comparison ("A window of light is in the dugout roof . . ."). The baseball allusion continues when the narrator "throw[s] the first pitch into the sun," punning on the idea of a television pitchman and on his role of pitching his own television performance, which is itself a documentary about baseball. The narrator's "tinfoil," recalling the "silver shield" which the producer used to shield him from the sun in the first lines, "trembles," suggesting his nervousness. This, in turn, recalls another association, the sunlight shining on the water in the fjords of Scandinavia, a reference to the Scandinavian plastic surgeon, Skoog.

The mind of the poet links experiences and associations, even if they have little in common except surface features. The narrator, here surely identified with Codrescu, who grew up television-deprived in communist Romania, walks toward the producers in the convention of the casually strolling television commentator, across the "narrows/ of the TV-less childhood." "Narrows" suggests the strait or constricted passage between two different pieces of land or countries, here possibly two different ways of life, the media-less land of Codrescu's youth and the modern American broadcast culture.

Exaggeration is also used as a comic technique. The sound man is "nuclear-trained," with "top-secret clearance." He claims to have spent "four years inside a sewer pipe," apparently doing military surveillance. His self-promotion is an ironically skewed boastfulness technically proficient persons might be tempted to indulge. In response, the narrator challenges the engineer with an ironic question, "Top-hat clearance?" Playing on "top clearance," "top-hat" suggests the absurd image of a vaudeville performer, rather than a daring spy. The laconic answer, "our army's stoned and theirs is drunk," is a classic cynical exaggeration about the Cold War standoff between Americans and Soviets.

Command forms of verbs accentuate how little control the narrator has over his public self, as he is told to "stand here," "go on," and "put on the shield." The poem also builds on the idea of things seeming to be open while remaining closed. The narrator is "shielded" from the sun; the sound man has spent four years in a sewer pipe; Dennis Martinez is "concealed" in a dugout; the narrator is "bent" and constricted by the "narrows." Again these references reinforce the two selves in the poem: the apparently open tele-self and the closed reality of each individual. Unexpected echoes and resonances link the disparate imagery. The umbrella-like shield of the opening comes up again in the verb "shields," referring to protecting terrorists. The narrator "bends" in the sunlight while Skoog "rises." The British cameraman "shoots" the narrator while the terrorists presumably might try to shoot from the protection of the fountain.

Themes and Meanings

Codrescu's "telyric self" is at odds with the narrator's inner being. Like a puppet, he is manipulated and maneuvered into the best physical position for his performance. The narrator's relationship with his production crew is thus purely utilitarian and mechanical, as no one asks about the content of his presentation. The old man's question, "He somebody famous?" sums up the situation: The telyric self is famous; however, the inner self is unconnected to sense but rather connected to a situation rich in a feeling of fraudulence and replete with chaotic images, from Skoog's history as a plastic surgeon to baseball player Martinez to the passing "geezer" to the production crew.

The multiple nationalities represented in the short poem suggest both the confusion of many unconnected cultures and their being brought together by television. The Romanian Codrescu, Nicaraguan Martinez, the British cameraman, the Scandinavian Skoog, Patagonia (Argentina), and Maroc (Morocco). The connection between the fountain and the Immigration and Naturalization Service seems appropriate given this multicultural cast.

Whether "Telyric" reveals Codrescu's heartfelt feelings or is merely another witty performance—a poetic performance commenting on a television performance by a media-wise commentator—is immaterial. From the reader's perspective, the poem's value lies in its evocation of the awkward, uncomfortable feeling of being in the spotlight. The real self becomes a bogus one when an unnatural role is required; random thoughts and observations, "real" though they may be, are unacceptable when acting as conventional commentators must in their television personas. Codrescu himself refers to the "weirdness" of television and his beginner's wonder at it. The poem thus raises the theme of honesty in the roles people play and emphasizes the disjunction between immediate sensations and the consistency that is expected in social situations.

Andrew Macdonald

TEMPLE NEAR QUANG TRI, NOT ON THE MAP

Author: Bruce Weigl (1949-   )
Type of poem: Narrative
First published: 1979; collected in *The Monkey Wars*, 1985

The Poem

Bruce Weigl's poem "Temple near Quang Tri, Not on the Map" is a narrative poem set in Vietnam during the Vietnam War. Through the description of a temple and of a "small man" inside it, Weigl creates a tense, tightly woven poetic illustration of an essential misreading of Vietnamese culture and custom. The misreading costs men their lives and costs a nation a war.

The poem consists of thirty-eight lines divided into four stanzas. The title serves to locate the scene as a place "not on the map"; such a statement suggests that the temple is somehow outside the realm of Western understanding. In addition, the title reveals that the setting of the event is a traditional sacred space.

In the first stanza, the narrator, who is a member of a patrol of American soldiers, approaches a Buddhist temple. The time of day is dusk, and there are birds in the ivy climbing the temple wall. The word "ivy" is repeated three times in the first stanza, suggesting that the temple is somehow hidden behind the green vegetation.

The speaker and his group move into the temple in the next stanza, following the lead of the "point man," the member of the patrol charged with going first in dangerous situations. Once inside, the men handle a variety of sacred objects, including a "white washbowl," "stone lanterns," and "carved stone heads." It is not clear whether or not the men handle the objects with respect. The narrator says that everything they investigate "is clean." Because these are soldiers looking for the enemy, it would seem that Weigl's use of the term "clean" here has nothing to do with cleanliness and everything to do with the absence of the enemy.

The last line of the second stanza introduces a "small man." In the next stanza, the narrator describes the man in what can be interpreted only as an act of prayer: "He is bent over, his head/ rests on the floor and he is speaking something." The gaze of the narrator shifts from the man to the commanding officer ("CO"), who fires at the wall of the temple to see if there is rice hidden there by Viet Cong.

The last stanza begins with the word "But," often an indication that the poem has reached some sort of turning point. In this case, although the CO has ordered the men to leave the temple, some of the men approach the small man and force him to sit upright. When they do, however, they discover that the man has booby trapped himself: "his eyes/ roll down to the charge/ wired between his teeth and the floor." In the last sentence, the birds "burst off the walls," indicating that there is an explosion and implying that the small man has killed himself in order to kill several members of the patrol.

Forms and Devices

Weigl very carefully chooses a series of images to describe the temple in the jungle. The cumulative effect of the images is to render the temple inscrutable and hidden. For example, in the first stanza, the ivy covers the outside of the temple thickly. Hidden within the ivy are sparrows. In a very potent image, the birds' wings become "calligraphy." Calligraphy, artistic or creative handwriting, both reveals and hides the meaning of the words it renders. The image, then, is an early clue that the temple is not necessarily as it appears. The ivy is also "thick in the grottoes." A grotto is a structure that appears to be a cave but is really of human construction. As the jungle hides the Viet Cong and their tunnels, so too does the ivy hide the sparrows and the temple.

Further sacred images appear in the second stanza, when the Americans make their way to the interior of the temple. The objects the Americans handle have little meaning for them. They search the objects for evidence of the enemy, but the stone faces reveal nothing. The Americans search the entire temple, declaring it clean. Weigl plays on the word "clean" here. On the one hand, the Americans view the area as secure, clean of enemy contamination. To the Vietnamese, the temple is clean in the sense that it is a place of prayer and holiness; soon it will be clean of the American presence as well.

Two important auditory images contribute to the contrasting depictions of the small Vietnamese man and the Americans. In the first, the small man speaks as he rests his head on the floor. The sound of his voice quietly fills the temple with words that the Americans cannot understand. Because this is a temple, the reader might assume that he is whispering prayers. The second auditory image is that of the commanding officer's gun; "he locks and loads and fires a clip into the walls." The CO does this to check for rice hidden in the walls, a sign that the temple is a Viet Cong supply station or hideout. The noise of the gunfire, however, seems somehow at odds with the silent temple, save for the sound of the small man's prayers.

In the last stanza, Weigl uses irony and surprise to complete his portrait. When the men, who have declared the temple "clean," get close to the small man, they discover that he has a charge in his mouth, ready to blow them all up. Nothing in the poem has prepared the reader for the shock of this moment, as the small man's "eyes roll down to the charge." Like the Americans, readers fail to understand the importance of the small man's prayers. Ironically, the detail the Americans fail to take seriously leads to their deaths.

Themes and Meanings

Weigl, a veteran of the Vietnam War, has a long history of interest in the Vietnamese language and culture. In 1994, along with Thanh T. Nguyen, he helped to select and translate a group of poems from the diaries and letters of North Vietnamese and Viet Cong soldiers. This project reveals his long-standing desire to render the Vietnamese culture intelligible to Americans.

In his poem, Weigl leaves clues that "Temple near Quang Tri, Not on the Map" is about the ways Americans repeatedly made mistaken assumptions about Vietnamese history, culture, and people during the Vietnam War. Misunderstandings such as those alluded to in the poem led to the loss of lives, time and time again, as Americans stumbled into situations of which they had insufficient knowledge.

The title is the first clue. That the temple is "not on the map" suggests a viewpoint other than that of a local resident. The map referred to is one constructed by American cartographers, based on incomplete knowledge. Further, because the temple is "not on the map," it is located somehow outside the realm of Western rules and law. The American patrol is on foreign soil, not graphed nor charted by American mapmakers.

In the second stanza, Weigl describes the birds' wings as "calligraphy." This word has important meaning in the poem. As noted earlier, the image hints at the hidden or esoteric nature of the temple. At a deeper level, calligraphy also refers to the way most Asian languages are put on paper. The beautiful symbols are painted onto paper with a special brush and with the calligrapher's special skill. French missionaries, however, many years ago rendered the Vietnamese language into Western-style text, using their own Roman lettering rather than the Asian pictographs, which fell out of use. Consequently, the birds' calligraphy suggests that the spirit that inhabits the temple is precolonial, before the European invaders turned Vietnam into a colony. The man who waits inside is the spirit of Vietnam, hidden, waiting to destroy all invaders.

The men also fail to read the sacred symbols in the second paragraph. Although they open the stone heads, all they see are carved stone faces, faces that reveal nothing to them. Likewise, Americans have been reported as saying again and again that they never knew who the enemy was during the war. They were unable to read the faces of the Vietnamese people.

Not only do the Americans fail in their reading of the calligraphy and the stone faces, but they also fail to understand the sacred nature of the temple. They choose to fire into the walls, looking for Viet Cong stash, thereby violating the rule of sanctuary associated with sacred space. They further fail to understand the prayers uttered by the small man. Again, the Vietnamese language confounds them. Perhaps they believe that the small man is a monk praying for his own safety, frightened by the American guns. Indeed, during the war, the small stature of Vietnamese people often led Americans to discount them or stereotype them as helpless children.

Finally, the Americans in this poem are guilty of the biggest mistake made by Americans during the war: their failure to recognize that the Vietnamese would rather face death than endure the French and American presence on their soil. The small man in the poem is indeed saying his prayers, but he is saying prayers in anticipation of his own suicide. He represents the Vietnamese people, seemingly harmless or "clean," but ready to take their own lives if it means taking a few Americans with them.

"Temple near Quang Tri, Not on the Map," then, is a poem about one culture's inability to read another. The Americans could not read the symbols, the language, or the people of Vietnam. This failure leads the American patrol in the poem to their deaths and, ultimately, the American forces in Vietnam to their defeat.

Diane Andrews Henningfeld

10 JANUARY 1934

Author: Osip Mandelstam (1891-1938)
Type of poem: Lyric
First published: 1964, as "10 yanvarya 1934," in *Sobranie sochinenii*; English translation collected in *Selected Poems*, 1974

The Poem

The poem "10 January 1934" is about the distinguished Russian poet, novelist, and thinker Andrey Bely, one of the leading Symbolists in the first two decades of the twentieth century. Although Osip Mandelstam subscribed to a different poetic creed, he respected Bely's poetry highly, and the two became close friends for a brief time in 1933. When Bely died soon thereafter, Mandelstam wrote a cycle of seven poems in honor of his friend and fellow poet; "10 January 1934" is the central poem of the cycle. Like so many of Mandelstam's poems, it was published posthumously.

The poem consists of nine stanzas. The title itself precisely locates the poem in time—the day of Bely's death. Mandelstam's subjective persona reveals immediately how he felt about the loss of his friend, being "haunted by a few chance phrases" of the departed poet. He speaks of "the rich oil of my sadness," borrowing the metonymy from the old Russian epic *Slovo o polku ígoreve* (c. 1187; *The Lay of Igor's Campaign*, 1919), thus retracing the roots of Bely's heritage back several hundred years. A striking metaphor follows: "the dragonflies of death." They are black, and, even though their eyes are blue, the blueness is black at the same time. Through a series of rhetorical questions, Mandelstam comments on the essence of Bely's poetry. Mandelstam asks where a leading poet ("the first-born") belongs now that he is gone, wondering at the evaluation criteria and hinting at Bely's place among the foremost of Russian writers. Where, now, is the "tiny hawk" of soaring flights of Bely's spirit? Mandelstam then emphasizes Bely's erudition and his deep study of Russian verse, the firmness of his beliefs, and the straightforwardness of his words "honestly weaving back and forth"—an undisguised barb at the rigidity of thinking of the Soviet officials who caused Bely much suffering in the last two decades of his life. His path was paved by centuries-old wisdom of his predecessors ("solutions of three-layered salts"), by idealistic German philosophers who had a significant influence on his thinking, by Russian "mystical" thinkers, and, finally, by the Russian thinker-poet Vladimir Solovyov, who honed his thought and chiseled his verse.

In the fifth stanza, Mandelstam suddenly shifts his attention, as if rudely awakening from his reverie. The funeral music "leapt from ambush" like a "tiger . . . hiding in the instruments"; its impact was not so much to be heard and to soften things but to jar everyone and direct attention to the deceased. (In the Russian burial custom, the casket is left open until it is lowered into the grave.) As if removing the mask from the dead, the music brings back to life the muscles, "the drumming/ forehead," the "fingers holding no pen," "the puffed lips," "the hardened caress," and "the crystallized calm and goodness." While the other funeral participants seem to react normally under the circumstances (there is even an engraver in the crowd to make a death mask), Mandelstam is grieving, "hanging on my own eyelashes." He turns, increasingly, to his own feelings, "swelling, ripening, reading all the parts of the play/ till I'm picked." With the final words of the poem, Mandelstam identifies fully with his departed fellow poet, expecting to follow him along the same sorrowful path because "The plot is the one thing we know."

Forms and Devices

The poem "10 January 1934" consists of nine quatrains rhymed *abab* in Mandelstam's customary interchange of eleven-syllable (*a*) and ten-syllable (*b*) lines. The poem teems with images and metaphors, as do most of Mandelstam's poems. The most expressive metaphor is the aforementioned dragonfly, a colorful, translucent insect that is a frequent symbol in Bely's poetry. In "10 January 1934," it is a dragonfly of death, befitting the occasion. Here, it represents the effervescence of Bely's talent; the irony of it is that it is very much alive even as the poet lies dead (his poetry survives him). Another metaphor is a "tiny hawk that melts deep in the eyes," a reference to Bely's powerful gaze. Nadezhda Mandelstam, Osip's widow, also speaks, in *Hope Against Hope* (1970), of the luminescence and electric charge of his eyes, of the electrifying effect he had on those he came in contact with, and of his ability to inspire new and exciting ideas in them. The swiftness of Bely's mind is depicted by the metaphor of a skater leaping into a blue flame, indicating his fearless forays into dangerous territory. His thoughts and words were sharp like "blades in the frosty air" and sonorous like "the clink of glasses in a glacier," crackling with lucidity and precision and "weaving back and forth" with astonishing dexterity and speed. The mourners gather at Bely's funeral, shoulder pressing shoulder, the fur on their coats breathing. Their health ("red ore boiling"), blood, and sweat are used as a contrast to the immobility and finality of death.

Finally, the predicaments of both Bely and Mandelstam are presented as a play with an all-too-familiar plot. Mandelstam sees the fate of Bely, as well as his own, reflected in an imaginary play, a tragedy, no doubt, as reflected in his comment about himself hanging "on my eyelashes"—a symbol, borrowed from Italian poet Dante Alighieri, of unspeakable suffering.

Themes and Meanings

The main theme in "10 January 1934" is the role and fate of a poet. By writing this requiem to Bely, Mandelstam writes not only an apotheosis of him but also a sad commentary on his difficult and even tragic fate in the society. By enumerating Bely's great achievements, he makes the forlorn appearance of his funeral stand out all the more. In this eulogy of a man who was among the leading poets of the beginning of the twentieth century, only to be neglected and hounded out of existence after the Bolshevik Revolution, Mandelstam sums up the callousness of a system that frivolously throws away its best people. Thus, the fate of a talented, independently minded poet is decided by the indifference and callous practicality of the modern age. Indeed, the poem is, in effect, "the effigy of the dying age," as Omry Ronen observes in *An Approach to Mandelstam* (1983). There are a number of poems in which Mandelstam addresses this theme: "The Age," "Wolf," and "Ariosto" come readily to mind. In all fairness, he was interested in this theme before he became the target of persecution, as attested in his book of prose, *Shum vremeni* (1925; *The Noise of Time*, 1965). He was also concerned with the impact of the modern age on the development of Judeo-Christian civilization, primarily on the spiritual plane and independent of political factors. In "10 January 1934," however, his preoccupation with the age syndrome culminated after he became aware of the destructive impact that "the age of the wolf-hound" had on Russian culture in general and on poets in particular. For Mandelstam, this interaction became, literally, a matter of life and death.

Coupled with the castigation of the modern age is the theme of Mandelstam's own fate. He spent the last years of his life warning about the pernicious effects of tyranny and eventually became consumed by it, both figuratively and literally. It is not coincidental that he subtitled one poem from the Bely cycle "My Requiem," which, as it turned out, was a clear premonition of his own death. Jennifer Baines writes in *Mandelstam: The Later Poetry* (1976) that Bely's death made Mandelstam visualize "the possibility that he would be thrown unceremoniously into a hole in the ground, with none of the last respects or funeral rites accorded to Bely." Unfortunately, this is exactly what happened to Mandelstam four years later in a concentration camp in Siberia; his grave has never been identified.

The entire poem is a minute record of Mandelstam's impressions of and reactions to Bely's funeral, as if he were looking at his own burial. This is clearly indicated in his matter-of-fact statement of resignation at the end of the poem, "till I'm picked." Thus, by binding his fate to that of Bely, Mandelstam universalizes the sacrifice they made at the altar of struggle against tyranny and elevates the heroic role of the poet in his ruthless society to the level of a modern Greek tragedy.

Vasa D. Mihailovich

TENEBRAE

Author: Paul Celan (Paul Antschel, 1920-1970)
Type of poem: Lyric
First published: 1959, as "Tenebrae," in *Sprachgitter*; English translation collected in *Poems of Paul Celan*, 1988

The Poem

"Tenebrae," a poem in free verse, consists of twenty-two lines. The Latin title refers to the period of darkness prior to the death of Christ. The term also points to the idea of an eclipse, the cause of such darkness, as well as night and death. In this context, although with no specific reference, the association to Nazi death camps, an experience elemental to Paul Celan's life and work, cannot be avoided.

The poem begins with a declaration of apparent proximity to God. The use of "we" as the subject pronoun provides a tone of universality. The second line clarifies this relationship as one not only of proximity but also of attentiveness. This idea is further developed in the second stanza. Line 3 implies that this connection is the result of a process, a means to an end, perhaps toward some higher purpose. In line 4, however, the reader finds that the process is one of defilement. Bodies are clawed while those same bodies claw in anguish. Furthermore, the poem compares this experience to God's experience, an apparent reference to Christ on the cross.

In line 7, God is called upon to pray. In the following line, the plea turns slightly surreal, roles are reversed, and God is instructed to direct his prayers "to us." As line 9 refers back to the first stanza, it becomes clear that such proximity and the horrific condition described are in some measure related. In the fourth stanza, the bodies are twisted. Still, the exclamation "we went" implies that they have arrived at this condition of their own volition. They are bent down as if having submitted themselves at this crater. The fifth stanza, a single line, reveals that the purpose of gathering there is to be watered like lambs or cattle.

In lines 14 and 15, the reader finds that it is blood that fills this watering hole, blood shed by God himself. In line 16, another single-line stanza, the pool of blood radiates with light. Now God's image is reflected in the blood and cast into the eyes of those huddled there. In line 18, eyes and mouths are "open and empty," drained of life. Finally, lines 19 and 20 tell of drinking from the trough and consuming both the blood and the image cast in it. "Tenebrae" moves toward its conclusion by repeating the directive "Pray, Lord." In the final line the repeated declaration of proximity takes on new meaning. Clearly, the "nearness" alluded to in the poem refers not to a closeness to God but to something horrible eclipsing this sense of immediacy.

Forms and Devices

"Tenebrae" uses several devices common to Celan's poetry. A sparsity of words as well as the poetic tone suggest absence more than presence. Five of the nine stanzas contain one or two lines, contributing to the barrenness of its appearance on the page. Multiple meanings balance the thin word usage and add to the poem's complexity. Common also are the new meanings that a single word or its root take on as the poetic voice proceeds. For example, in a few brief lines readers go from being at hand to having been handled to hands clawing. Thus what begins as a reference to attentiveness is quickly transformed into violation by a single allusion.

Celan also describes events in terms of their opposites. In the darkness of the poem, images, scenes, and roles are inverted and confused. This takes on seemingly strange proportions when describing the relationship with God. He appears without omniscience. Although the idea that "we" are near provides a sense of movement toward God, he is directed to "pray to us." While the poem is clear that "we went," implying that arrival at such a state is of "our" own free will, the reader may ask if events are running contrary to God's will. What challenges the reader's sensibility is the dilemma of attributing the situation to God's absence or his apparent indifference to humanity.

The most striking inversion is that of the Christian imagery presented in the poem. The association of Tenebrae to the Passion of Christ is represented in the Catholic liturgy of the same name performed during Holy Week. Both the victims' suffering compared to the suffering of God and the common essence that the image of God and the blood itself take on evoke Christian symbolism. Because such images are easily associated with Christianity, some critics have concluded that the scene in the poem relates directly to the Crucifixion. However, this one-dimensional understanding draws the reader to surface conclusions that correlate neither to the poem's angry tone nor to the circumstances it describes.

Celan's poem constructs the horrific with the vocabulary of Christianity, the vocabulary accessible to him yet distinct from a Christian construction. The use of this imagery serves to express a marginal syntax with a central language. Yet because the vocabulary is recognizable, the reader is easily drawn to accept the obvious that eclipses a deeper explanation. In "Tenebrae," the ornaments that decorate the world may be Christian, but it is the juxtaposition of Christianity with Jewish symbolism, as well as surreal forms and existentialist doubts, that heightens the poem's meaning.

Themes and Meanings

"Tenebrae" is a poem of shadows, of multiple meanings eclipsing one another. This juxtaposition of meaning using single images provides it with layers of context. Beyond the Christian facade are Jewish underpinnings. Likewise, behind the symbolism of normative Judaism one finds reference to the Kabbala, the Jewish mystical and esoteric tradition. Finally, both Surrealism and existentialism play important roles.

The poem reads like a strange, surreal prayer. Anger and loss predominate in describing the relationship with God. The use of the pronoun "we" flows naturally in Jewish thought and practice, in which regulations strictly mandate communal prayer. *Ashamnu*, literally "we have sinned," is the prayer that runs alphabetically through the list of transgressions asking for forgiveness on Yom Kippur, the Day of Atonement.

The use of "we" establishes the importance and culpability of all people in the face of God.

It is not clear that the condition described is the result of any specific sin. In fact, the angry tone of the poem implies that an injustice has been done against humanity. As the poem proceeds, it seems that "we" have acted out of obedience to God. "We" are near, and "we" went to the trough like cattle, bent over, submitted to be watered, and drank as directed. Yet this violation continued. The Lord, the shepherd, shed the blood of his own flock. "We" even drank it in obedience to God. The drinking of blood is an important allusion because it carries radically different significances for Judaism and Christianity. In Christian doctrine the blood of Christ gives life, while in Judaism the consuming of blood is strictly forbidden. Thus in a Jewish context, to drink blood at the crater is to violate one of God's commandments.

Thus not only is God's covenant with Jews eclipsed by the revelation of Christ, but also the Christian notion is eclipsed by the overriding existentialist tone realizing the absence of God. For the existentialist, this absence is a point of departure not toward nihilism but toward constructing new meaning. The poem reads: "your image into our eyes, Lord." The image of God and the faces of those staring into the pool become one. Likewise, when the eyes and mouth appear empty, God too is drained of life— another eclipse. Finally, the people depicted in the poem drink not only the blood but also the image in the blood, their own image, which in the poem inverts creation back to humanity as it sees itself and the God it created.

The multiple eclipses of "Tenebrae" are found not only in the juxtaposition of imagery but also in the language of the poem used to construct it. While in Christianity Christ is the incarnation of the Word in the flesh, within Judaism (accentuated in the Kabbala), words, the letters that form them, and even the spaces between them are thought literally to make up creation and the mystery behind it. The construction of the poem, Celan's use of a minimal number of words, and, more important, the use of a single vocabulary to describe seemingly contrary explanations all reflect a deep sense of distance from the dominant notion of God. If the central eclipse evokes the Passion of Christ, in Celan's poem it is the mythic Passion that is eclipsed—not only by a seemingly Godless reality but also by the realization of humanity's role in constructing it.

Steven Clotzman

THE TENNIS COURT OATH

Author: John Ashbery (1927-   )
Type of poem: Lyric
First published: 1962, in *The Tennis Court Oath*

The Poem

"The Tennis Court Oath" is a poem in free verse, its forty-nine lines divided into six stanzas of varying length. The title has a double suggestiveness, only one aspect of which turns out to be relevant to the actual poem. The Tennis Court Oath was a key event of the French Revolution, an event in which the commoners (or Third Estate), having been locked out of a meeting of the Estates General, gathered in a nearby tennis court and vowed there to stand together until the Constitution could be reformed. John Ashbery's poem in no way retells or even refers to this incident. The title is also that of a famous painting by the French painter Jacques-Louis David, one in which the oath-taking is seen in an extremely heroic light. David never completed the painting, and this irony of heroism combined with incompleteness is very relevant to the methods of this poem, a poem whose first-person speaker remains permanently "incomplete."

The key to enjoying this difficult poem is found in its very first line. The phrase "What had you been thinking about" offers perspectives from which to view the many unfinished sentences and narratives that arise and disappear willy-nilly throughout the piece. The phrase asks a question that can never be completely answered, because one person's thoughts can never be completely transferred to the mind of another; thoughts are unique and finite events. Because it is "thinking" itself that this poem wishes to penetrate, it rightfully proceeds as a stream of consciousness, a flow of partial and only partially comprehensible incidents, images, and assertions.

The first stanza initiates the stream of consciousness with phrases of sinister import, such as "the face studiously bloodied" and "a terrible breath in the way," whose tones are of paradox and obscurity. Someone is not elected, though he or she "won the race." There is a fragmentary journey concealed not only by incompleteness but also by literal "fog and drizzle," and the journey is threatened with failure by a horse's fatigue. No wonder, then, that the stanza ends, "I worry." The promptings of hidden danger and violence and of unreached destinations cannot help but conjure a mood of anxiety—the sort of anxiety which, in other circumstances, might well prompt one to ask a friend or lover (the theme of hopeless love surfaces briefly in line 4), "What had you been thinking?"

Through the ensuing stanzas, the poem gathers dizzying momentum, leading the motifs of danger and journey through many variations. In the second stanza, an insect's head becomes a grotesque mirror that reflects breathing and dancing, while the journey is transformed into both a postal correspondence and a camping trip. Stanzas 3 and 4 bring one to a house in which one is approached (but never reached) by a nameless woman. Then, in the final two stanzas, one is outdoors once again, responding along with "the doctor and Philip" to some indistinct but bloody emergency, perhaps inside the house that had been so briefly entered. In the end, "there [is] no turning back but the end [is] in sight." The stream of consciousness becomes a dream, part of a fevered illness that is past now. True to its nature, the poem does not conclude but rather disappears through a dark hole, inscrutably "glad" to have made its inscrutable journey.

Forms and Devices

Virtually all the elusive but memorable effects of "The Tennis Court Oath" are products of its central technique: its stream-of-consciousness approach. In the modern period, such innovative novelists as James Joyce, William Faulkner, and Virginia Woolf employed this technique as a means of probing beneath the social and dramatic façades of their characters in order to illuminate psychological motives and complexities which might otherwise have passed, as do most thoughts, out of existence unremarked. In novels, stream of consciousness usually has a context within the wider frame of setting and plot. In poetry, however, it appears unframed and so challenges the reader with the suddenness of surprise. Thus, Ashbery's technique has much more in common with the aleatory or "automatic writing" methods of André Breton and other French Surrealist poets of the early twentieth century. Since the poem's title refers, however ironically, to an incident of French history and was indeed composed during Ashbery's ten-year residence in Paris, its use of a characteristically French poetic technique seems entirely appropriate.

The principal effect of aleatory poetry is one of disruption. By rejecting conventional expository techniques, by rejecting even the conventions of syntax and grammar, it forces readers to abandon their usual habits of reading and thinking and so to improvise new ways of understanding that will, of necessity, be unique to each individual poem. Every aleatory poem is a category unto itself, and this absolute originality is a primary aim of the technique. Nothing but "The Tennis Court Oath" teaches one to read "The Tennis Court Oath." It accumulates rather than unfolds, as its fragmentary lines—by not completing their thoughts—trigger new fragments via undisclosed motives of free association and private emotion. Amid these fragments, readers become co-authors of the poem, sorting and combining the fragments according to their own experiences and states of mind. In this way, the poem becomes an event of potentially infinite variety, as opposed to an object to be dutifully comprehended, and this is clearly another aim of the aleatory poet: to win an active instead of a passive readership and so gain a permanent timeliness for the poem.

One may think of "The Tennis Court Oath" as one thinks of a collage. The lines, like newspaper clippings, once removed from an ordinary narrative context, placed alongside other lines similarly removed, and then arranged in an explicitly suprarational sequence, challenge a reader to make the connections which the artist refuses to make on the reader's behalf. The effect is atmospheric rather than thematic, similar to that of a dream whose emotional atmosphere lingers in the mind long after the incidental details of the dream have faded away. Everything in "The Tennis Court Oath" is a potential metaphor, and each image stands willing to allow any reader to use it as a key to his or her interpretation of the dream that is the reading of the poem.

Themes and Meanings

On one level, "The Tennis Court Oath" is a poem about the possibilities of poetry itself. For John Ashbery, the purpose of poetry is not communication in the sense of a message delivered or of an idea expressed. It is, instead, communication as the continuous encounter between ideas and things in language on the page and in language in the mind. In the fragmentary rhetoric of this poem, one can never be certain whether a given word is the object of one verb or the subject of the next. One does not know what to subordinate to what, just as one cannot determine plot from subplot or reality from dream in the inconstant landscape of the poem's progress. For Ashbery, this indeterminacy represents the liberation of poetry from poetic precedent, a chance for the poem to be read only by its own and its readers' own lights. The poem becomes an exemplary act of literary sabotage, a bomb tossed into the anthologies that readers carry in their minds from one work of literature to another.

Yet the theme of "The Tennis Court Oath" resonates beyond the limits of poetry alone. Its stylistic indeterminacy, when applied to its enigmatic journeys, emphasizes the uncertainty of all travel, the intriguing if unsettling reality that not all destinations are reached or even known. As the poem is enriched by incompleteness, so too may the actual journeys of life be enriched by liberation from fixed objectives. Since the only absolutely certain point of arrival is death (a point anticipated by the poem's allusions to violence and melodramatic murder), perhaps it is best to postpone arrival, just as Ashbery's sentence fragments strive to postpone the inevitable, final punctuation mark.

This poem works to revise accepted notions of interpretation as well as those of anticipation. As the ends of things are entrusted to uncertainty, so too are the precise identities of objects and events encountered en route to the ends. This is why the poem moves restlessly back and forth between tones of menace and of slapstick, images of blood and of surreal vistas of candy and pink stripes. Every stanza can be several, utterly contradictory stanzas, depending upon which words a given reader chooses to emphasize. It is the final randomness of such emphasis that calls into doubt the possible accuracy of any interpretation of any circumstance. For Ashbery, experience is too quick and too complex to be contained by interpretation. Language can only pursue reality, never apprehend it. In "The Tennis Court Oath," this pursuit becomes a wild, improvisational dance to the limits of coherent writing.

Donald Revell

TERENCE, THIS IS STUPID STUFF

Author: A. E. Housman (1859-1936)
Type of poem: Meditation
First published: 1896, in *A Shropshire Lad*

The Poem

"Terence, This Is Stupid Stuff" takes its title from the first line of poem sixty-two of A. E. Housman's first and most important collection of poems, *A Shropshire Lad.* The poem is divided into four verses of varying length and purpose that, taken together, provide an apology or defense of what is generally regarded as Housman's pessimistic poetry.

The speaker of the first stanza addresses the poet's persona, Terence, who is the ostensible author of the preceding poems. Clearly, the speaker is unhappy with the sort of poetry Terence composes. In fact, he reminds the poet that he seems to be in reasonably good health considering his general consumption of food and drink. Terence's companion in life has no patience with poetry that speaks of broken hearts and broken lives. Further, he accuses Terence of having such a dismal view of life "melancholy mad" that his poetry is endangering the sanity and well-being of his friends, even to the point of being life-threatening. His counsel is that Terence take up a happier mode of existence: "Come pipe a tune to dance to, lad."

In the next two stanzas the poet ("Terence") takes up a lively defense of his work. First, he reminds his friend that if he's looking simply for pleasure, he's come to the wrong place: Breweries are a better place to find solace from life's troubles. Moreover, the poet suggests that the making and consuming of beer is a national endeavor, one in which the upper classes profit from the manufacture of beer consumed in great quantities by the common man. The poet questions why else the great breweries of Burton were built on the river Trent and why the English grow hops if not for the manufacture of ale. He reminds the first speaker that ale does a better job of blunting reality than poetry, for not even the great poet John Milton, whose masterpiece *Paradise Lost* (1667, 1674) sought to explain the human condition in terms of God's intentions, provides much in the way of alleviating human suffering.

He flippantly replies that "ale's the stuff to drink/ For fellows whom it hurts to think." Terence does not, however, address his friend condescendingly; in fact, he tells of his own encounter with drunken euphoria and its subsequent rude awakening. He reflects that the temporary state of well-being induced by too much drink is pleasant enough but does not last. Self-deception only to be followed by weary resignation leads nowhere but back to the starting point to "begin the game anew."

Then, if there is no respite from the often-unpleasant realities of life ("Luck's a chance, but trouble's sure"), one must prepare to "face it as a wise man would,/ And train for ill and not for good." This advice, however, is not given lightly, for it comes from the wisdom of experience, of having suffered and plunged into escape only to find pain inescapable. Thus, Terence offers his friend a recipe for survival in a not-so-pleasant world. Yet, it is an opportunity not only to endure but also to prevail.

In the last stanza, the poet recounts the myth of Mithridates, a North African potentate who, when offered a choice of death by his Roman captors, chose poison. The Roman offer was considered an act of mercy, for the Romans frequently employed more imaginative and painful means of death on their enemies. In this case, it proved to be more merciful than intended, for Mithridates was unaffected by his captors' efforts to dispatch him. By ingesting small portions of differing poisons from infancy and continuing the process throughout life, he had developed an immunity that left him untouched and the Romans frightened and frustrated, for "Them it was their poison hurt." The parable of Mithridates draws a parallel between the elegiac reflections of the poet and the poisons ingested by Mithridates. Neither are pleasant, but both provide a bulwark against the sad mischances of life. More to the point, the verse Terence makes acts as an antidote to the pervasive sadness of life that rescues one from despair.

Forms and Devices

Much of the appeal of Housman's poetry derives from its apparent simplicity. The adoption of the persona of Terence Hearsay, a country lad from Shropshire whose conversational candor makes Housman's poetry immediately accessible to the reader, accounts for much of the continuing popularity of *A Shropshire Lad*. It is difficult to imagine having an acquaintance with poetry without having encountered "When I Was One-and-Twenty" or "To an Athlete Dying Young." These poems express the loss of love, youth, and life in a manner so simple and direct that they have become staples of English textbooks and classrooms. Yet one must be careful not to mistake simplicity of style for lack of sophistication. The animus of the classical scholar Alfred Edward Housman informs the poetic voice of Housman's Terence. The simple yeoman's reflections on the demands of life draw on a breadth of knowledge and experience beyond that which one associates with rural life. Nowhere is this more apparent than in "Terence, This Is Stupid Stuff."

In this poem, the contrast between form and content provides a bridge between reader and scholar/poet. The opening stanza questions the very nature of Terence's poetic efforts as his unnamed friend challenges the entire body of work. Moreover, the challenge is put in such a way that the reader can easily recognize it from one's own adolescent struggles with sad words about dead people who never seemed to get it right—"It gives a chap the belly-ache." The conversational tone engages the reader and plays into the all-too-human avoidance of the unpleasant.

Terence, however, is up to the challenge. In the manner of a country lawyer, he grants the questioner's premise that poetry is not the place to turn to for some fun or a respite from daily drudgery. He plays on class consciousness—"Oh many a peer of England brews/ Livelier liquor than the Muse"—and gives thanks for the existence of the upper class, which brews beer for the lower class, for "malt does more than Milton can/ To justify God's ways to man." In this stanza is the poet's first direct allusion to

Milton, and it serves several purposes. It continues the folksy intimacy established between Terence and his reader, and it permits the reader to believe that Terence really
shares the common prejudice against poetry and gloomy reflection. Finally, it serves
to remind the reader of the fall from grace, that Eden and man have become separated,
that humankind lives with suffering, and that not even Milton's poetic explanation can
dull the edge of sorrow ("Ale, man, ale's the stuff to drink/ For fellows whom it hurts
to think").

Yet, for fear that the reader will be put off by so harsh an assessment, Terence con-
fides that he, too, has searched for relief in drunkenness—and found it to be a lie. The
tone of confidentiality and the assumption of shared misery make the reader predis-
posed to accept the poet's conclusion. Life is hard, and one had better "train for ill and
not for good."

Oddly enough, this Shropshire lad has a knowledge of classical literature that he
disclaims by saying, "—I tell the tale that I heard told." After all, his surname is Hearsay; he is only repeating the tale of Mithridates, whose story merely happens to be an
illustration of the narrator's point.

Housman successfully hides the scholar/poet behind the mask of his adopted persona, Terence, whose tone of convivial fellowship invites the reader into an exploration of critical theory (such as the purpose and uses of poetry and why it should be
read) as old as Aristotle.

Themes and Meanings

The essential truth revealed in *A Shropshire Lad* is the discovery that the human
condition is subject to mutability and death. Nothing escapes the ravages of time,
which claim youth, love, and, finally, life. That is precisely why Terence's unnamed
companion objects to the poet's gloomy verse. He wonders why a poet would want to
subject the reader to a treatise so morbid as to suggest mental instability ("moping
melancholy mad") and a world that apparently does not allow for redemption. Similarly, he wonders about the point of such "tunes as killed the cow."

Housman's poetic persona addresses the question from several perspectives; for example, he grants that poetry in general is not the place to turn for frivolity. If escape is
sought, he suggests ale. The problem with hiding in alcohol is that it is temporary and
deceptive—"Heigho, the tale was all a lie."

Unlike Milton, Terence's verse makes no attempt to "justify God's ways to man."
Yet Housman was as acutely aware as Milton of the painful consequences of humanity's fall from grace. For Milton's age, untouched by the intellectual consequences of
the scientific revolution of the eighteenth and nineteenth centuries, there was comfort
in the hope of eternal salvation. This "vale of tears" would surely be exchanged for
eternal bliss. By the end of the nineteenth century, the foundations of faith had been
eroded by scientific discovery. The fruit of the tree of knowledge had been too completely consumed to sustain the simple religious faith of the preceding age. In the
Shropshire where Terence lives, corpses decay and flowers fade. For Housman's generation, "Paradise" had been irredeemably lost. The question arises as to the sort of

reconciliation that can be made between so bleak a prospect and the worth of human existence. Housman's response is clear. Self-deception is temporary at best. The truth of life will show itself regardless of whether one chooses to acknowledge it. If humanity must live with pain and loss, they must be faced, for in the last analysis avoidance is not possible. In acknowledging the hard circumstances of life, one is better prepared to face the "embittered hour" and "the dark and cloudy" days that are a part of the human condition.

The tale of Mithridates with which Housman closes the poem serves as a parable. The poisons consumed by Mithridates fortify him against catastrophe. He survives where others would perish, exactly as the reader will survive the awaiting catastrophes of life having taken an antidote in the form of Terence's painful verse, which may produce "belly-ache" but will "do good to heart and head/ When your soul is in my soul's stead."

That, then, is not only the purpose of Housman's verse but also the essence of literature itself: to prepare one for the inevitable sorrows of human existence, to face tragedy with dignity, to prevail against the "slings and arrows of outrageous fortune" as long as one is sustained by the breath of life.

David Sundstrand

THE TESTING-TREE

Author: Stanley Kunitz (1905-   )
Type of poem: Poetic sequence
First published: 1971, in *The Testing-Tree*

The Poem

"The Testing-Tree" is a poetic sequence divided into four sections, each written in supple free verse with no stanza breaks. The lines themselves are prepositional phrases or noun clauses and are generally enjambed, giving the reader a sense of flowing, forward movement. The title, the same as that for the entire volume of poetry in which it was originally published, is mythic, suggesting the biblical Tree of Knowledge where Adam ar.•: Eve are tested and Ygdrassil, the tree of wisdom from Norse mythology. The title is also specific, being emblematic of the tree where the narrator played games and in which he carved his name. Each sequence within the poem operates on both levels—the mythic and the local.

In section 1, the narrative "I" recalls the imaginary games and challenges of childhood in which reality, "the Academy ballpark/ where I could never hope to play," is juxtaposed against the imaginative life in which "magic Keds" bring "the prize of the mastery" and the speaker is the "world's fastest human." The speaker recalls these imaginative visions with concrete nouns ("flying skin," "crouching start") and makes these experiences vivid for the reader, while the quotidian events of daily life are only hinted at in the first three lines of the section before being abandoned in favor of the imaginary, which offers more potential and fulfillment. It is the "magic" that is able to project the speaker beyond a rather banal present into a realm of imagination; the speaker is master over the "given course."

Section 2 opens with a renewed search for this magic that takes the narrator away from home. Instead of leading toward the ballpark and imaginary fame, the magic in this section leads the narrator down a secret path leading to the woods. The path leads away from the "drainage ditch" of society and civilization of the first section to nature and solitary sojourn reminiscent of American Indians and legend. The trail is a "right of passage" and the narrator practices his "Indian walk." The magic conjures up in the narrator a sense of communion with nature, and the "umbrageous trail" leads away from the pressures of school and home.

In section 3, the trail leads the narrator, who walks with "deliberate" steps, through an abandoned quarry into a clearing where the "testing-tree" of the title stands. The narrator has inscribed his name in the tree as if to claim ownership. Yet despite this "ownership," the boy is "in the shadow" and prays for a blessing. The boy imaginatively plays a symbolic game of life in which he seeks to hit the tree "for love, for poetry,/ and for eternal life." Taking stones from his pocket, the narrator hurls them at the tree, his "tyrant and target," hoping to hit it and secure for himself the illusory joys unavailable to him in sections 1 or 4.

A mythic reading of the poem gains more resonance as, in section 4, a "recurring dream" haunts the narrator in which the family life of childhood metamorphoses into natural images: The mother appears "wearing an owl's face." The sacred space amid the vegetation of section 3 is invaded again by a presence from society. These figures of his family make him feel guilty, and he asks, "why should I be blamed?" when he notices the dirt sifting slowly down into a well "where an albino walrus huffs." The mother figure points with a "minatory" finger, and the narrator seems to attempt to avoid this finger of blame by escaping back into his sacred world of the "umbrageous trail" and his "testing-tree"; the dream, however, keeps recurring and will not let him return. The figures of family and society relentlessly pull the boy away from his solitude in nature.

Forms and Devices

References to mythic symbols abound in Stanley Kunitz's poem. The primary recurring image is that of various types of paths: a "stretch of road" in section 1 and an "umbrageous trail" in section 2; though there is no direct naming of a path in section 3, its presence is implied as the narrator winds by the stone quarry into a clearing. This clearing is the end of the trail, and "the inexhaustible oak" stands as the final test for the narrator. For the moment, the metaphor of paths is suspended as the narrator enters the shadow of the great tree and throws his stones of destiny in an attempt to wrest a blessing from it. The relapse is momentary, however: In section 4, the poet returns to the metaphor of paths. This time it is in the form of a highway unfurled, and the narrator instead wishes for the trail. The highway is associated with a mechanistic element of society that has so far been absent in the poem: A Model A car and a military tank with turrets dominate this path. Combat and industrialism intrude into the haven of consciousness offered by nature in section 3. The repetition of the road imagery indicates its centrality to the meaning of the poem, and it becomes a metaphor for the journey, the heroic quest, on which the narrator embarks.

The poem's imagery, however, is not limited to that of a journey. In section 3, the "target," or the end of the trail, is reached. This section abounds in rich symbols: an oak, stones, acorns, and a watchtower. Some of the symbols are made explicit (the stones "changing to oracles," for example), but many are left implicit, to be decoded by the reader. Traditionally in Celtic mythology, acorns were seen as seeds of prophecy: If a seer ate them, he could be given the voice of prophecy. Such a reading, with both biblical and Celtic overtones, is underscored by the presence of the name Jehovah, the highest name that can be invoked for prophecy and wisdom within the Hebraic tradition of prophets. "Bless my good right arm" the narrator asks of an absent figure who represents both a physical father and God the Father, Jehovah. The poem functions on a literal level with a boy, stones, and a tree, and on a symbolic level with a narrator, oracles, and the tree of wisdom.

Themes and Meanings

"The Testing-Tree" is a poem about humanity as a paradox, dwelling in the mortal reality of time and space yet cognizant of the infinite and "eternal life." A child's innocent games and flights of imagination and a mature man's quest and his fight to hold on to memories portray the narrator's effort to combat the ephemeral nature of humankind. He is both flesh and spirit, and the journey of this poem seeks to transcend the limitations imposed on the spirit by the flesh through receiving prophetic power at the base of the proverbial oak of wisdom. This search bears a resemblance to William Wordsworth's search in his epic poem *The Prelude: Or, The Growth of a Poet's Mind* (1850) for a way in which the mutable consciousness of humanity can imprint itself into the immutable realms of nature. The "inexhaustible oak" contains the blessings and secret wisdom that are the object of the quest in all the various paths, trails, and highways within the poem.

Another central tension in the poem is that between society and the individual. In the opening section, the narrator feels the pull of society as he imagines himself a baseball hero or a world-class runner, yet all this disappears as the boy crosses the "nettled field" and enters the "long teeth of the woods." The mossy, dark woods offer solitude broken only by signs of "rabbit life." The narrator must undergo a test of solitude and face the forces of legend contained within the oak. Again, the road is a significant image in this drama between self and other. It is straight and confined, and it implies the presence of a purpose or a final destination. Once the narrator has reached his "tyrant and target" in the clearing, he must return to family and society as evidenced by the figure of his mother in the opening of section 4. He realizes that "It is necessary to go/ through dark and deeper dark/ and not to turn." His escape from time, exemplified by his crossing of the field of wild nettles on no given path, is brief. The narrator rises up out of time and out of societal space when entering the clearing, but he can do nothing else except fall back into them in section 4. As a human being, he is limited by the circumstances of family and history. The tragedy of this reality is expressed in the words "dark" and "deeper dark" and the chilling term "necessary." In desperation, the narrator asks, "where is my testing-tree?" Finally, in the closing lines, the self of the poet reiterates a hopeless demand to return his stones. The self longs to return to the tree and hurl its oracles against the tree of wisdom in an anguished attempt to transcend mere matter and to play a game of keeps with eternity.

Tiffany Werth

THAT MOMENT, WHICH YOU COULD LOVE, WHAT OF IT

Author: Dave Smith (1942-   )
Type of poem: Lyric
First published: 1976; collected in *Goshawk, Antelope*, 1979

The Poem

"That Moment, Which You Could Love, What of It" is a short free-verse poem, its forty-one lines divided into six roughly equal stanzas. The unusual title indicates both an acknowledgment of the fleeting nature of experience and an irreverent tone. The absence of a question mark following the title heightens the impression of irreverence, but the poem's serious intent eventually supersedes any initial hints of flippancy or cynicism.

The poem is written in the second person. Although in general usage the second person is employed for direct address, in modern poetry it is often used, paradoxically, as a form of the first person. Dave Smith has chosen to refer to himself as "you" as a way of transcending himself and of including the reader intimately in his vision and experience, an intimacy that would be far less intense had he chosen "I."

The poem begins with the poet reporting primarily on the time of day—dusk—and the weather—unchanged, below freezing. There is more, however, in the first stanza; when dusk appears with "a newspaper under its arm, gray/ overcoat flapping," readers rightly begin to feel that they are in for an extraordinary experience.

In the second stanza, the poet takes us from a memory of snow and ice "hunched in the aborted grass" through a swift-moving chain of associations to an immediate perception, in the stanza's last line, of the objective reality of ice on his window. Just as a window separates weather and other exterior elements from indoor space, the iced-window image separates the poet's descriptions and impressions of the outdoors from those of his room—"your room."

In the third stanza, the voice of a singer, "the diva," enters the room via the radio and commingles with hanging plants and aquarium water. In the fourth stanza, after the diva is overcome by static, and as Smith describes some objects in the room, the reader is drawn closer to the emotional heart of the poem. On a table near empty salt and pepper shakers, there are "tracks/ in what you poured out/ circling on themselves." Again, as with dusk and unchanging weather, the poet shows his poignant awareness of the passage of time. He had poured the condiments "playfully/ at first, then desperate for what/ was the beginning."

In the fifth stanza, a climax is reached, both literally and in literary terms. Using highly charged diction—and with dusk's "overcoat/ left in a corner" adding resonant allusion to earlier images—Smith recalls a sexual encounter. The memory of "her/ cry riding the one long note/ of your breath" recalls the diva's song. When the poem alludes to itself in this way, it in effect transforms itself from a seemingly haphazard series of images into a logical progression. Continuing the memory, in a reference to the salt, the pepper and the radio, the poet states, "something trackless, nor of wires/ received, envelops you." The poem ends with a sweeping question: "Who/ would not risk everything for this . . . ?" The open-ended "this" can refer both to the recollection on which the poem focuses and to the poet's, and therefore the reader's own, human capacity to recall valued moments, as if the process itself were as valuable as any single experience.

Forms and Devices

Dave Smith's poetry is one of solemn extremes. There is nothing jocular—no offhand urbanity or self-mockery—and "That Moment, Which You Could Love, What of It" does nothing to break the pattern. The poem's diction, its ventures into metaphor and its imagery progressively intensify the poem's meaning.

The poem opens explosively with a striking first line—"Today, bitch of a day, trembling"—introducing readers to a stark diction that continues throughout the poem. The opening is followed almost immediately by an equally striking personification of dusk, which "rounds corners,/ a newspaper under its arm, gray/ overcoat flapping." This figure, exemplifying an extreme form of metaphor, shows Smith's deftness at taking creative risks. In the second stanza, a simile—"snow . . ./ hunched in the aborted grass/ like terror"—is followed by an almost blinding series of metaphorical leaps: snow on a branch is seen as "one snaking/ tongue [which] flares in a small bush/ lost in winter." Within two short lines of verse, snow becomes a snake, a tongue, and a flame. The effect is startling.

These metaphorical pyrotechnics go far toward establishing the poem's imagery. In the third stanza, the visual images broaden to include the aural. Thus, the diva's song transforms, in a peculiar metaphorical connection, into "coilings" and "tendrils" of potted plants hanging in the room. Conversely, the prevailing image of the fourth stanza, loose pepper and salt that "you poured out," is devoid of metaphorical connection, in keeping with the stanza's resigned mood. The associations return, however, with "the fierce blaze of light" that opens the fifth stanza, reminding one of the image of snow as a tongue of flame in a bush.

With this blaze of light, the poet's memory of an ecstatic sexual experience bursts explosively into the poem, and Smith's abrupt diction—"blaze," "cry," "breath," "surge"—is equal to the task. His reliance on one-syllable words heightens the tension: "you/ know a surge in the earth," the poem intones, and the reader knows a climax has been reached. The "she" of the memory is intentionally vague, the moment is brief, and the only remaining image afterward is the aural one of "the beautiful diva/ straining notes like moments/ so rare nothing dies."

After such intensity, it is fitting that the poem end with a rhetorical question—a syntactical device otherwise absent in the poem. This sudden, final shift is tantamount to an admission that the language employed to convey the experience—like the experience itself, and its participants—is both exhausting and exhausted, a sign of Smith's thoroughness in lyrically capturing his deeply felt emotion.

Themes and Meanings

"That Moment, Which You Could Love, What of It" is a poem about people's awareness of the passage of time. Bruce Weigl, in *The Giver of Morning: On the Poetry of Dave Smith* (1982), emphasizes Smith's "recognition of the inevitability of time [moving] forward." Such an awareness may well be the mental function which most distinguishes us from all other species. The isolation of the enigmatic "you" in a room recalling meaningful and highly personal events is thus emblematic of all humanity, or people's isolating capacity to anticipate, with objective detachment, their own deaths.

Smith addresses this theme throughout the poem, beginning with the dissolution of day into a peculiarly human incarnation of dusk. Memory, by separating now from then, is a reminder of time's passage. With a highly charged memory at its heart, "That Moment" makes the same separation, but in Smith's hands, memory is a salve as well as a source of distress. By asking "Who/ would not risk everything/ for this. . . .?" Smith is celebrating both the reader's capacity to recall and his own ability to render his remembered experience into artistically satisfying lyric poetry. In short, Smith's life work of writing is for him a sacramental transformation.

Other poets have made the same point, but what distinguishes this poem from many contemporary poems on the same theme is the poem's allusion to a story in what is traditionally regarded as a sacred text. The metaphorical image of snow as a tongue of flame in a bush evokes the burning bush that appears to Moses in the Book of Exodus. In this way, Smith offers his readers an enriching expansion into levels of meaning that greatly enhance our experience of the poem.

For one thing, the allusion infuses the poem with important metaphysical underpinnings that are entirely in keeping with its theme. Any meaningful meditation on the passage of time puts one in touch with the prospect of death. Even more important, when Smith brings the matter up again with "the fierce blaze of light" that introduces his memory of a sexually ecstatic encounter, he is mixing the sacred with earthly sensation in a crucial way. His message is that human contact, however fleeting, is of paramount redemptive value.

Ultimately, the poem's response to the seemingly irreverent "What of It" of the title is its solemn insistence that a "moment which you could love" is more valuable than virtually everything. Herein lies the logic of the poem's concluding lines: "Who/ would not risk everything/ for this, even as darkness rushes/ over the fish, the salt, the snow?" The question is so broad, so globally encompassing, as to suggest a breathlessness, as though Smith, like Moses, were struck dumb by the power of his vision.

Jonathan Daunt

THAT NATURE IS A HERACLITEAN FIRE AND OF THE COMFORT OF THE RESURRECTION

Author: Gerard Manley Hopkins (1844-1889)
Type of poem: Sonnet
First published: 1918, in *Poems of Gerard Manley Hopkins, Now First Published, with Notes by Robert Bridges*

The Poem

"That Nature is a Heraclitean Fire and of the comfort of the Resurrection" is a sonnet in accentual hexameter with three codas of two and a half lines plus one final half-line. The cumbersome title names the first and last of the three topics the sonnet treats; the grammatical structure of the title—a noun clause plus a prepositional phrase—suggests the lack of parallelism of the two topics named. The clause "That Nature is a Heraclitean Fire" refers to a vision of nature through the eyes of the fifth century B.C.E. Greek cosmological philosopher Heraclitus, for whom process was the fundamental fact of the cosmos and fire was the fundamental symbol or element; this topic occupies the first nine lines. The phrase "of the comfort of the Resurrection" refers to an article of Christian faith, the reunion after death of Christ's physical body and human soul comprehended as a model for the eventual resurrection of each believer; this topic occupies the final lines, from lines 16 to 24. The unnamed topic is the individual human's death.

The first section bulges beyond the Petrarchan or Italian octave (the *abba, abba* rhyme scheme of the first eight lines) into the ninth line. It presents a picture of the summer cycle of rainstorms and drying out of the landscape (the poem was written in Ireland on a late July day in 1888). The first four lines might present the thunderstorm itself—the different shapes of clouds moving together ("throng"), the lightning ("glitter"), the warlike array ("marches"), the rain ("roughcast . . . dazzling whitewash . . . Shivelights and shadowtackle"). If the lines describe the sun drying the landscape the next day, however, the glittering is that of sun on the clouds, and the "Shivelights and shadowtackle" are a pattern of sun-daggers and ship's rigging on dark ("roughcast") and bright ("whitewash") walls alike—or is that another picture of the dark and bright sides of clouds? Lines 5-9 describe the warm wind drying the sodden earth, the puddles and wheel-tracks turning from ooze to dough, from crust to dust. Humanity makes a late impact in this section, for some unseen workmen have left their footprints in the mud during and after the rain. As the fire-driven cosmos destroys and re-creates itself over and over, all the species are transfinite in time. When any particular component of the total pattern is lost through struggle and metamorphosis, it is replaced in due course with a suitable equivalent.

The second section, lines 10-16, contrasts logically with the cyclic opening. A person is utterly unique, he or she has no equivalent, and therefore no other person can serve as a replacement. Each sacred human spark of the Heraclitean fire is "selvéd"—self-possessed—as no individual entity in any other species can be; so when a spark goes out, the loss is irreparable.

The third and final section of the poem does not follow rationally from the natural experience of the first fifteen and a half lines. As the sonnet's form surprises the reader with line 15 on, so its content in this last section leaps into being nonlogically, by faith. Speaking for himself and for every believer, Gerard Manley Hopkins asserts the eschatological transformation into immortality of the mortal side of Christ and humans (1 Corinthians 15).

Forms and Devices

The poem exemplifies Hopkins's experimentation with sonnet form; John Milton's "On the New Forcers of Conscience" provided a model for the codas. Heraclitus said that the basic world element, fire, moved out from the sun and condensed successively into air and water; then half the water thickened into earth and half rarefied into smoke, fiery stormclouds, waterspouts, and souls. The half that had become earth thinned into sea and air, and everything ultimately returned to the sun. The world was thus a steady-state cosmos in which "the way up and the way down are one and the same."

The key images in lines 1-9 are therefore those that combine two of the four elements—"bright wind" (fire and air), clouds (air and water), and "ooze . . . dough, crust, dust" (water, in lessening quantities, mixed with earth). Man finally appears only to realize that the Heraclitean bonfire is his "bone" fire, his funeral pyre. The sonnet's octave-plus-one-line, which describes a world of species, employs a large number of plural and collective nouns.

The word "But" (line 10) is the *volta* (Italian for "turn") that moves the poem from the world of species to the world of individual humans, where "he"—man in the sense of a man, not the species man—becomes central. Heraclitus tags along for a few more lines, for he was among the first people to become even slightly aware of the individual as such, separated from the communal matrix. The human spark of the bonfire is the only being in the cosmos capable of grasping the world's order, intelligibility, and beauty, noted Heraclitus: "Most men do not comprehend the things they happen upon, nor do they understand what they have experienced, though they seem to themselves [to do so]." All too soon, time beats man level (as the wind beats the "masks and manmarks" of line 14 into dust), and "his firedint [flint striking steel], his mark on mind" are soon gone.

The second transition is more a *salto*—less a turn than a leap to a totally new and unexpected level: "Enough!" The shipwreck image of "foundering deck" picks up from earlier words such as "shadowtackle" (line 4), "ropes" (line 5), and "drowned" (line 13), and it may contain a faint but lovely echo of Shakespeare's Sonnet 116, lines 5-8. The reader should note the auditory ("clarion . . . trumpet-crash") and visual ("beacon . . . beam") images that announce the presence of the risen Christ in the poem. One may also wish to read the "eternal beam" (line 19) as the horizontal beam of Jesus' cross, the only effective negative to the transfinite (and ultimately idiotic) up-is-the-same-as-down churning of the Heraclitean funeral pyre, where the individuals burn so their species may live. Flesh and mortality are then remanded to the "residuary worm"; many medieval wills bequeathed "my soul to God and my body to the worms."

Themes and Meanings

Because it deals with the eternal philosophical problem of the one and the many— the one species embodied in many individuals—the poem is characterized by plurals and collectives in lines 1-9 and by "man" and "he" in lines 10-16; these are the two sides of the coin of nature. The poem's version of Heraclitean nature, however, is not philosophical so much as phenomenological or experiential. It fits very well with the experience of the nineteenth century, which had cast off the earlier mechanistic models of the universe and favored instead organic, vital models. These often took a developmental form; but like most religions, Catholicism at that time was very wary of Darwinism, so Hopkins turned to this Greek philosopher, whose process was cyclic, not evolutionary.

If all individual material beings exist only temporarily, then nothing in the material world possesses permanent validity or authenticity; thus, only if human bodies become eternal can meaning be intrinsic to the material world. Mere belief in the survival of a spiritual soul leaves the material world absurd. By affirming Christ's resurrection as a pattern for his own, Hopkins creates a theology of history and can acquiesce in death as the necessary precondition for a rebirth to a diamondlike permanence.

Thomas J. Steele

THERE IS A GARDEN IN HER FACE

Author: Thomas Campion (1567-1620)
Type of poem: Lyric
First published: 1617, in *The Third and Fourth Booke of Ayres*

The Poem

Thomas Campion's song "There Is a Garden in Her Face" consists of three stanzas in the same metrical pattern. The poet compliments a lady on her beauty in the most extravagant terms. However, he feels it necessary to warn her suitors, himself included, that the lady will not permit anyone to approach her more closely until she indicates that she is ready for him to do so. At first reading, the poem appears to be no more than another elaborate tribute of the sort that Elizabethan and Jacobean courtiers and courtly poets were expected to produce. However, the lines in which suitors are warned away suggest that the reason the lady is so unapproachable is not that she is innocent or overly virtuous; it is simply that she is holding out for the highest price. Thus, while ostensibly praising the lady, the poet is actually exposing her and, by extension, the society that has produced her.

In the first stanza of the poem, the lady's face is called a "garden" filled with flowers, specifically, white "Lillies" and red "Roses," a conventional description of the white skin and pink cheeks found so frequently among English girls. The poet also mentions "pleasant fruits" and specifically "Cherries." When in the second stanza he goes on to say that the cherries "enclose" two rows of pearls, obviously he is describing the lady's red lips and her white teeth. The first stanza ended with a caution: "none may buy" those cherries unless the lady signals her permission. At the end of the second stanza, the warning is even more specific: even men of the highest rank must respect the lady's wishes.

In the third stanza, the lady's features are again described in flattering terms: her "Eyes" resemble "Angels," and her well-shaped eyebrows are like "bended bowes." However, the emphasis here is not on the beauty of those features but on their roles in keeping trespassers away from her lips. The eyes, then, are not just angelically beautiful; they also function as guardian angels. The brows are not just lovely; they are well-armed and poised to attack. If someone attempts to touch those lips, the eyebrows can "kill" an intruder with "piercing frownes." The final line of the song is the same as that with which the two previous stanzas ended. Again readers are reminded that no one may "buy" the lady's cherry-red lips "Till Cherry ripe themselves doe cry."

Forms and Devices

It is important to remember that Campion thought of "There Is a Garden in Her Face" as a composite work, which like his other songs aimed at a fusion of poetry and music. Campion's words had been circulating for at least a decade before the fourth volume of "Ayres" appeared in 1617; they had even been set to music and published by others. However, because Campion thought of each of his songs as an integrated whole, he waited to publish "There Is a Garden in Her Face" until he had composed his own musical setting for it. Any analysis of the song, therefore, must take into account both Campion's words and his music.

The poem has a simple, regular structure. It is made up of three six-line tetrameter stanzas, each of which begins with four lines that rhyme alternatively and concludes with a couplet. The first lines of these couplets differ from each other in fairly significant ways, but the second line, with which each stanza ends, is in every case the same.

In the music that he composed for his poem, Campion pointed out the importance of the couplet by inserting a double bar before it, indicating that it is a refrain. However, the first line of the refrain, which varies from stanza to stanza, proceeds at a very slow pace. By contrast, the metrical pattern breaks up in the second line, proceeding in irregular snatches. Moreover, the line "Till Cherry ripe themselves doe cry" is expanded considerably, now becoming, "Till Cherry ripe, till Cherry ripe, till Cherry ripe, Cherry ripe, ripe, ripe, Cherry ripe, Cherry ripe themselves doe cry." It has been pointed out that whenever "Cherry ripe" appears in the song, the musical notes reproduce the cries of London street vendors.

However, there is nothing particularly original about Campion's metaphors themselves. They are simply Petrarchan conceits, extravagant comparisons in the tradition established by the Italian poet Petrarch and still flourishing in the Elizabethan period. Many of Campion's contemporaries described their ladies' complexions in terms of lilies and roses, and it was not unusual to think of their lips as cherries; indeed, that metaphor was especially apt, since ripe fruit almost asks to be brought to one's mouth. It has even been suggested that Campion borrowed this metaphor from a song by Thomas Morley, number 16 in the *First Booke of Balletts to Five Voyces* (1594), in which the lover observes that cherries are subject to decay and therefore should be tasted at once.

Petrarchan tradition also dictates the gender clichés in "There Is A Garden in Her Face." The lady is perfection itself. She is superlatively beautiful, worthy of being worshiped by all the men around her. She is also as powerful as a goddess, capable of dealing a death blow with a mere frown of displeasure, and, like a goddess, completely in command of her passions, fully in control of her future. By contrast, the Petrarchan lover presents himself as totally submissive to his lady, totally dependent upon her for his own happiness. He can only admire her, praise her, and await her pleasure. However, though Campion's persona assumes the manner and the mannerisms of a conventional Petrarchan lover, expressing himself in conventional Petrarchan conceits, the words and music of the refrain suggest a very different meaning.

Themes and Meanings

"There Is a Garden in Her Face" is built upon the contrast between artifice and reality. All the Petrarchan elements in the song come from a world that is a construct of the human imagination, a world in which women are meant to be worshiped and, indeed, deserve no less. Campion reinforces this idea with references to his lady's goddess-like power and even with religious images, referring to his lady's face as a "heav'nly paradice," to her eyes as "like Angels," and to her lips as "sacred." Men are so in awe of these goddesses or saints that they are willing to adore them without making any demands upon them. The ladies who live in this imaginary world appear to be emotionless; it is only their lovers who burn, freeze, and sometimes die, perhaps of a broken heart, perhaps, as Campion suggests here, destroyed by the lady's frown.

With the repeated word "buy" and the cry of the cherry-seller, however, the poet catapults the reader into the real world. If someone will eventually "buy" those cherry-red lips, then the lady's distancing herself is not a matter of saintlike behavior but a commercial calculation. Although the reference to a real cherry-seller is so minimal that one who looks only at Campion's words might miss its significance, in the musical setting the repetition of "Cherry ripe" and of the single word "ripe," echoing even the intonation of a street vendor, makes it clear that the vendor's cry is more than just a useful comparison drawn from the real world, as are the lilies and roses the poet mentions. Like the street vendor, the lady is peddling her wares. Like the cherries, she will be most valuable when she is at her prime, in other words, fully ripe. At that point, she will be sold to the highest bidder. That is the way marriages are made in the real world, and everyone who reads Campion's words or hears his song is well aware of that fact.

Certainly the poet does not mean to suggest that the lady he praises so highly it not beautiful. However, the reader would recognize that the tribute is somewhat perfunctory and that the metaphors are both conventional and exaggerated. Although Campion is willing to indulge the lady for a time, even to assume the role of a Petrarchan lover, he makes it clear that after an excursion into the world of make-believe, one must return to reality. The reality is that the lady's behavior is just as artificial as the language in which she is described. Thus "There Is a Garden in Her Face" is essentially an ironic work, in which words and music collaborate to expose a society that pretends to idealism but in actuality is coldly materialistic.

Rosemary M. Canfield Reisman

THERE'S A CERTAIN SLANT OF LIGHT

Author: Emily Dickinson (1830-1886)
Type of poem: Lyric
First published: 1890, in *Poems*

The Poem

Emily Dickinson's poetic strategy is governed by her belief that truth must be approached indirectly in order to be understood most fully. In "The thought beneath so slight a film" (poem 210), for example, she insists that the "film," or embodiment in a work of art, allows the idea to be "more distinctly seen," and she uses two similes (lace revealing breasts and mists revealing the Alps) as examples. In "Tell all the Truth but tell it slant" (poem 1129), she explains more fully why "success in circuit lies": "the Truth must dazzle gradually/ Or every man be blind." Again she uses a simile, this time the way adults explain the phenomenon of lightning to children (in a metaphorical and "kind" manner), to express a truth figuratively which cannot be expressed literally.

"There's a certain Slant of light" is the fullest and most complicated rendering of this idea; in it, she uses dramatic metaphors and similes not only to suggest her own literary methodology but also to express the dynamic interrelation she sees between people and nature. One of the interesting aspects of her first line (as in all her poems, used by editors as the title) is that it is the word "Slant" which is capitalized, and no other, not even "light," though there are fourteen internal capitalizations in the poem. The focus is not on the light itself, but on the angle it takes at a particular time of day (late afternoon) during a particular season (winter) in a particular place (rural Massachusetts). Stanza 1 shows that this angle of light "oppresses" rather than uplifts the poetic voice, and perhaps the reader as well, just as does organ music in a great cathedral.

Though this oppression is the chief characteristic of the angle of light, it suppresses and depresses as well. It gives "Heavenly Hurt," which leaves no external scar, but makes a person internally different, for it changes what the world means to the person. These changes, wrought by nature, are to Emily Dickinson often more profound than those changes caused by other people, or by oneself.

In stanza 3, Dickinson indicates that this hurt, and the changes that come with it, cannot be taught, or learned from any human teacher, because it comes from the "Air" as an "affliction," which brings with it the "Seal Despair." In stanza 4, she extends the metaphor to indicate its effect on nature. When the slant of light comes, even the landscape listens, and shadows hold their breath; when it leaves, it leaves behind, for both human observer and nature, an experience of distance which is like "the look of Death," or a sense of vacancy, absence, and isolation.

Forms and Devices

Dickinson is well known for her idiosyncratic use of capitalized words and dashes at the end of most lines, and both are used in abundance in this poem. The primary use of capitalized words within a line is for emphasis; it is Dickinson's own way of indicating to the reader that one should pay especially close attention to a particular noun (nouns are capitalized much more often than any other part of speech). The dashes not only accentuate the rhythm of the poem, they also give the reader a sense of openness, extension, and ambiguity that is often less comfortable than the more traditional period. While not evident here, in other poems Dickinson commonly used exclamation points at the end of some lines for emphasis.

A more important and certainly much more influential device is that of slant rhyme (also called off rhyme, partial rhyme, or near rhyme). Slant rhyme (in which the final consonant sounds are the same but the vowel sounds are different) is frequently used when a poet wishes to negate, deny, or counter something, often a traditional value or idea. Here, for example, Dickinson uses slant rhyme in the first and third lines of each stanza (light/heft, us/difference, and listens/distance), and conventional exact rhyme to end the second and fourth lines (afternoons/tunes, scar/are, despair/air, and breath/death). Thus, what might have been a rather traditional poem of sixteen lines, divided into four quatrains rhyming *abab*, becomes a signature statement in free verse.

Dickinson uses a number of other poetic devices, including alliteration, assonance, and sibilant sounds, and her use of metaphor and simile is especially striking. In stanza 1, the visual perception of the light on a winter afternoon is compared with the sound of organ music in a cathedral; each has an oppressive weight and power in this particular situation that it would not have in any other. In stanza 2, she creates the metaphor "Heavenly Hurt," an oxymoron perhaps, and certainly a paradox: It might mean that the hurt is sent from heaven, that it is a kind of delicious pain, or both. In the context of her other poems, one can guess that she means the reader to see both suggestions. There is a similar paradoxical ambiguity in stanza 3: Does the fact that despair is sent "of the Air" (not "from" the air) mean that it is sent from God or from nature? Perhaps for Dickinson, God and nature are finally so inextricably interwoven as to be inseparable. Personification is another common device in Dickinson's poetry; here the landscape listens and the shadows hold their breath. All nature, it seems, not only the human part, is attentive to this awesome quality of light.

Themes and Meanings

Dickinson as poet is committed to an aesthetic point of view shared in large part by other American Romantics such as Henry David Thoreau, Nathaniel Hawthorne, and Herman Melville. She speaks for the indirect vision in art and literature, one that resists the reduction of truth to any logical definition or comprehensive statement. As with Hawthorne's idea of the "neutral territory" where the actual and the imaginary meet, Thoreau's search for "the hound, the bay horse, and the turtle dove," and Melville's (and Ralph Waldo Emerson's and Walt Whitman's, for that matter) sense of objects as "pasteboard masks," Dickinson's assertion is that only the use of metaphorical rather than direct language will allow the writer, and thus the reader, to "pierce the veil" of the material world and gain some sense of the spiritual reality which is behind it.

Another major theme in her poetry as a whole is reflected in this poem: the idea that people are deeply wedded to the physical world. For Dickinson, the landscape has the power to affect a person deeply and permanently; for example, external weather may cause changes in one's "internal weather." What is more (and here she differs sharply from Emerson, Thoreau, and Whitman), these changes may not always be pleasant or positive ones. In this poem, for example, the speaker has been hurt and oppressed enough by this slant of light so as to feel despair. She experiences the fading of the light much as she experiences that sense of isolation, estrangement, and separation that comes with seeing death.

These two ideas come together as a paradox: How can one resolve the tension between appreciating and transcending the physical world? Dickinson seems to be suggesting in many of her poems that first one must come to a full appreciation of the physical world; then one may be able to push through and beyond it to where the meaning lies.

In this, one of the very finest of her poems, Emily Dickinson has created a metaphor in which feeling and abstraction are fused. It is a metaphor that vividly expresses what for her was the spiritual fact that seasonal changes in the external world often parallel spiritual changes in the internal world. These changes may be negative as well as positive; they may bring despair as well as hope.

Clark Mayo

THEY ARE ALL GONE INTO THE WORLD OF LIGHT!

Author: Henry Vaughan (1622-1695)
Type of poem: Elegy
First published: 1650, in *Silex Scintillans*

The Poem

"They Are All Gone into the World of Light!" (the poem is known by its first line), consisting of ten rhymed (*abab*) stanzas, is at once a lyrical expression of faith and an elegy for friends who have passed away. A meditation on death, it juxtaposes the world of light that follows death with the world of darkness that is the fate of the living. It culminates with a two-stanza prayer in which the speaker requests that God renew the fallen world and either give him spiritual insight here or take him to heaven, where there are no impediments to vision.

In the first four stanzas, the speaker establishes and develops a contrast between the fortunate dead who live in a world of light and his own unfortunate life in a world of darkness, a contrast at odds with the reader's usual associations of life with light and darkness with death. The speaker, however, looks beyond death, merely a transitory stage in this poem, to life after death. Despite the imagery of darkness, bondage, and blindness, the poem reflects the speaker's faith—there is no real tension, no uncertainty, no doubt. Even though he has "sad thoughts," the speaker's thoughts do "clear"; the memory of the departed "glows and glitters in my cloudy brest," lending some light or "beams" to his obscured vision. The dead walk "in an air of glory," but his "days" (his life, the times, the temporal) are "dull," "Meer glimering and decays," reflecting the nature of the fallen world.

In the second four stanzas the speaker addresses "Dear, beauteous death" as a "jewel" that shines, extending beyond the "dust" traditionally associated with death. The "dust" becomes the "mark," the border beyond which lie mysteries that could be apprehended if man had more than "first sight," or physical vision concerning natural phenomena. The speaker contrasts the bird-watcher's knowledge "if the bird be flown" with his ignorance about the current whereabouts of the "flown" bird. Although the fallen of humanity may not apprehend glory directly, there are "strange thoughts" that do "transcend" physical sight and provide limited access ("peep") to spiritual truth. This section concludes with such a "strange thought," the image of a confined star being released from a "Tomb" to "shine through all the sphære."

This liberating image leads directly to the concluding two-stanza prayer to the "Father of eternal life," a description that applies directly to the life after death "they" all enjoy. The speaker asks God likewise to restore this "world of thrall," a world of sin, to the "true liberty" of the world before the lapse. This request is reiterated in the last stanza, in which God is urged to disperse the "mists" from his perspective, or "remove me hence unto that hill,/ Where I shall need no glass," a spiritual elevation after which the speaker will need no mechanical aids for his imperfect sight. This "removal" clearly is the culmination of an event alluded to in the first stanza, in which the speaker sits "lingring here" behind his friends.

Forms and Devices

Although Henry Vaughan wrote some secular verse, he is known primarily as a religious poet indebted to Metaphysical writers, notably George Herbert, whose *The Temple* (1633), a collection of religious verse, served as a model for Vaughan's *Silex Scintillans* (Parts I and II, 1650, 1655). Vaughan was influenced by the hermetic philosophy of his twin brother Thomas, by the Welsh countryside in which he spent most of his life, and by Christian theology as revealed in the Bible and in the writings of the church fathers. All are reflected in "They Are All Gone into the World of Light!"

The metaphors and imagery of the poem derive from Christian doctrine, primarily from the resurrection story. The eighth stanza, which precedes and leads to the concluding prayer, provides an analogy to Christ's death and resurrection: A "star" is confined, appropriately, to a tomb but is released by "the hand that lockt her up," surely the hand of the "Father of eternal life." After release, the star will "shine through all the sphære." The "star," moreover, is to be seen in juxtaposition to the earthly "Sun" which leaves its "faint beams" on "this hill," itself juxtaposed with "that hill" at the end of the poem. Since the reference to the "Sun" would have suggested the "Son," Christ, to his seventeenth century readers, Vaughan thereby prepares his readers for the Son's coming, which follows the "Sun's remove" in the second stanza.

Vaughan's use of juxtaposition extends to the stanza involving the bird-watcher, who may detect if the "fledg'd bird" has left the nest. This knowledge, which depends on the physical senses, cannot detect where that bird sings. Implicit is the idea not only that there is another, transcendent vision unavailable to man, but that the spiritual vision is associated with God, who notices even the flight of the sparrow. Another related association involves the bird/nest analogy with the flight of the soul from the body at death. This analogy encapsulates the theme and subject of the poem. Seen from the perspective of resurrection, even the paradoxical reference to "high humility" contains a double meaning. The oxymoron suggests that the dead, having been humbled by death, are now raised in the world of light; it also calls to mind Christ, the servant/King who resolves all paradoxes.

What light "glows and glitters"—Vaughan often uses alliteration to slow the pace and call attention to words—is associated with the star, the spiritual Son who is also light. The fallen world is transfigured by Christ, who can partially dispel the "mists" and clouds of the temporal world, making some light and insight available through His sacrifice. That sacrifice destroys death's power—as John Donne wrote, "Death, where is thy sting?" From Vaughan's point of view, death legitimately can be termed the "Jewel of the Just," because the faithful, "just" Christian looks to death as a reward, bringing eternal life and light.

Themes and Meanings

Vaughan's use of juxtaposition, within lines or stanzas, is particularly appropriate since he is concerned with the gulf between "they" and "I," a separation established in the first two lines of the poem: "They are all gone" parallels "And I alone sit lingring here." "Lingring" itself suggests that his proper place is not "here" on "this hill," but "there" on "that hill." By the end of the poem the speaker, through a series of associated opposites, overcomes any trepidation he may have felt and looks forward to his "removal" from this earth.

The speaker's contrast between two kinds of vision, a common Renaissance notion, clearly establishes the superiority of the spiritual realm over its physical counterpart. Even with the light derived from Christ's sacrifice, the speaker cannot see clearly those sights that are most meaningful to him. Like the bird-watcher, the speaker has visual access to the natural world and can apprehend and draw conclusions from physical data; he can see not only "the hill," but also his "dull days." Those days are not literally "dull," nor is his "brest" literally "cloudy"—these are insights expressed metaphorically about his condition. The "mists" and "clouds" are common metaphors for sadness and grief, but the speaker's feelings about his dead friends transcend graveside gloom. The "clouds" and "mists" are impediments to spiritual vision—he is "blind" to the "mysteries" which the dead can "see."

In this "world of thrall," the speaker's vision is limited to an awareness of his condition and of the state of the fallen world; even "here" some "strange thoughts" or perceptions allow a "peep" into glory. The speaker can transcend ordinary themes or concerns, but will be able to "see" glory directly only after death. When he requests, "Resume thy spirit from this world of thrall/ Into true liberty," the speaker refers to his own spirit being "resumed" or renewed much as the speaker in John Donne's "Holy Sonnet XIV" requests that he be made "new" and states, "Except You enthrall me, never shall be free." One of Donne's "meditations" on death contains a biblical quotation that informs Vaughan's treatment of vision in this poem: "For now we see through a glass, darkly; but then to face: now I know in part; but then shall I know even as also I am known" (Corinthians 13:12).

Since the first alternative of the last stanza, the dispersal of "mists," seems as unlikely as the face-to-face vision, the speaker's only recourse is the reiteration of "Resume thy spirit": "remove me hence unto that hill." God's intervention is required since the speaker cannot, even with mechanical aids like a "glass," himself attain the vision he seeks. The "removal hence" is to the "world of light."

Thomas L. Erskine

THEY FLEE FROM ME

Author: Sir Thomas Wyatt (1503-1542)
Type of poem: Lyric
First published: 1557, as "The lover sheweth how he is forsaken of such as he some-
time enjoyed," in *Songes and Sonnettes* (known as *Tottel's Miscellany)*; collected in
Collected Poems, 1969

The Poem
"They Flee from Me" is a short lyric poem of twenty-one lines divided into three
rhyme royal stanzas—seven lines rhymed *ababbcc.* As in many of Sir Thomas
Wyatt's lyrics, the first-person voice of the poem, not Wyatt himself but a dramatic
persona whose impressions the reader needs to examine critically, complains of a beloved who has left him for another lover.

The opening stanza depicts the beloved as a deer—a conceit or extended metaphoric image, which Wyatt and later English poets borrowed from the sonnets of the
fourteenth century Italian poet Petrarch. Wyatt compares the woman to a wild deer
who once risked danger to feed from the hand of the poet and so grew tame under his
gentle charity. Yet now, apparently forgetful of that time and the poet's gentleness, the
deer ranges wildly, seeking "food" elsewhere. That the woman continually seeks new
sources of this food suggests that she has become promiscuous.

In the second stanza, as the poet remembers times past when his beloved acted differently toward him, the poem takes on a wistful tone: The poet remembers with pleasure ("Thanked be Fortune") that there were twenty such times when she desired him,
and he recalls one time especially, when she actively sought and seduced him, rather
than he her. The poet recalls the scene in vivid, sensual detail, describing his lover's
appearance and actions, and he ends the stanza with a direct quotation of her gentle
and playful words to him.

The third and final stanza opens by commenting on the dreamlike sequence of
events described in the previous stanza. The poet's wishes and desires were gratified
so fully that the experience seemed like a dream—but it was not: He was wide awake;
it really happened. The poet's tone, however, becomes increasingly bitter as he compares that time with the woman's present behavior. Ignoring him now, the woman
seeks other lovers, indulges in "newfangleness" and a "strange fashion of forsaking";
that is, she has become inconstant and promiscuous. One hears the speaker's bitterness most strongly in his suggestion that she has rejected him *because* of his gentleness. In the sarcasm of the final lines, he asks rhetorically how she may deserve to be
treated since she has treated him "so kindly."

Forms and Devices
The poem creates its overall effect primarily through a series of striking metrical effects, vivid images, and changes in tone. The irregularity of Wyatt's meter has led

some critics to believe that many of his lyrics, including "They Flee from Me," were written for music, and that the verses conform to a musical melody now lost rather than to an internally generated rhythm. In reading the poem as it stands, alert to the changes in line length and positions of metrical stress, one can sense the drama that Wyatt's rhythm creates:

> When her loose gown from her shoulders did fall,
> And she me caught in her arms long and small,
> Therewithal sweetly did me kiss,
> And softly said, "Dear heart, how like you this?"

> It was no dream: I lay broad waking.

The poem also suggests the inappropriateness or irony of the metaphors which the speaker uses to describe the woman. The conceit that Wyatt borrows directly from Petrarch, the image of the woman as a deer, although sustained through the first stanza, begins to give way already in the second line's reference to "naked foot." This creature is no deer but a real woman, and this lapse in the conceit suggests that the image may not be entirely appropriate. Moreover, the word "stalking" in the same line makes it unclear who is the hunter and who is the prey. In contrast to the speaker's depiction of the woman as "meek" in the first stanza, she seems distinctly less so in the second.

Already in the first stanza, then, Wyatt gives readers the sense of a complex sexual relationship quite unlike that between a wild deer and the feeder whose gentle behavior domesticates the animal. Also, unlike the idealized woman/deer in Petrarch's poetry—a woman whose ideal virtue and chastity make her an unattainable object of sexual desire—this woman seems very sexual indeed, more coy than meek. Although the speaker claims to have lured her, the reader sees in the second stanza that the speaker himself is the one being "lured," the one who puts himself in danger of being abandoned.

The second stanza not only drops the conceit of the woman as a deer but also focuses on the details of the actual affair, giving readers a vivid picture of how the woman appeared, how she disrobed, how she approached the lover, and even how she spoke to him. These detailed images allow the reader to experience the affair vicariously and see firsthand her behavior toward the poet. After hearing in the first stanza how gentle the speaker was with her, one sees more forcefully how gently, and how effectively, she has lured him.

Nevertheless, the lover's "gentle" behavior has not guaranteed his being treated in kind, and the tone of the final stanza changes strikingly from the dreamlike wonder of the second stanza to a bitter sarcasm hinted at in the first stanza's complaint—he has not been "kindly served." The last line's question of what his lover might deserve for having treated him so sounds plainly vengeful. The reader is left wondering who has changed most; the woman, who has gone from "gentle, tame, and meek" to dismissive and aloof, or the lover himself, who moves from gentleness and wonder to bitterness and vengeful reproof.

Themes and Meanings

Love poetry, rather than the soggy expression of sentimentality the popular imagination may conceive it as, often deals incisively with sexual politics—that is, with the confrontation of two egos in a social relationship. "They Flee from Me" examines a sexual relationship that has ended from the male lover's point of view. It also reveals the wounded ego that ungraciously finds the woman's freedom a cause for complaint. Rather than ask the reader to sympathize with the lover's hurt, however, the poem allows one to distance oneself from the speaker's concerns in order to see that his ways of thinking about the woman and about women in general—the "they" of the first line—is itself as much to blame for the relationship's demise as anything the woman has done.

Having opened the poem by considering the woman as a wild deer, the lover ends by deriding the woman for having remained wild and at liberty. He has failed to domesticate her, as one might very likely fail to domesticate real wild animals. One might reasonably question the lover who thinks of his beloved in such terms. The lover fails to realize that he is castigating the woman for acting naturally. If indeed she has come to him freely, and if he has enjoyed her free expression of sexual desires, how can he then deride her for enjoying the freedom to continue to seek the objects of her desire? If there is any truth to the metaphor of the deer with which he began, then the lover fails to see that any attempt to domesticate such a creature will ultimately be foiled by its natural desire to remain wild. Yet the complexity of this deeply human relationship finally belies the metaphor.

Wyatt himself seems to have been involved romantically at one point with England's future queen, Anne Boleyn, and his poems often seem to reflect life in Henry VIII's promiscuous court. Whether that is true, this poem certainly moves away from the idealized beloved of Petrarchan convention. Influenced by and commenting on the poems of Petrarch, the love-poem tradition in sixteenth century English poetry often presents a conflict between Neoplatonic ideas of beauty—the idea that outward beauty is a reflection of inner goodness and virtue that moves others to be virtuous—and the fact that physical attractiveness stimulates carnal desires that move men and women to cast off the virtues of chastity and sexual restraint. Yet Wyatt, although he often borrows freely from Petrarch, translating and imitating his poems more or less loosely, seems unconcerned with presenting the drama of these contradictory drives. Rather, he uses the language of Petrarch to represent a society in which promiscuous sexual pursuits are a given and virtue is largely a matter of social manners, affectations, and pretensions.

James Hale

THINKING OF THE LOST WORLD

Author: Randall Jarrell (1914-1965)
Type of poem: Meditation
First published: 1965, in *The Lost World*

The Poem

"Thinking of the Lost World" is a long (ninety lines) free-verse meditation that imitates the associative structure of reverie. The last poem in Randall Jarrell's last book of poetry, it almost demands to be read with the three-part poem "The Lost World" in the same volume. "Thinking of the Lost World" begins with a deliberate echo of Marcel Proust and the madeleine pastry in *À la recherche du temps perdu* (1913-1927; *Remembrance of Things Past*, 1922-1931), partly because Proust was one of Jarrell's favorite authors, but primarily because Jarrell himself is interested in a similar project: recovering the past through imagination. In this sense, the title becomes doubly evocative, referring at once to the 1925 film based on an Arthur Conan Doyle short story ("The Lost World") and to the poet's lost world of childhood, part of which he spent in Hollywood in the care of his grandparents and great-grandmother, "Mama and Pop and Dandeen."

At this point in his career, partly influenced by his friend Robert Lowell's autobiographical experiments in *Life Studies* (1959), Jarrell confronts his own past head-on in the poems, infusing them with an intensely personal tone, risking the charge of sentimentality. In a voice alternately diffident and emphatic, he invites the reader to undertake this trip through time to his childhood, assuming that even though the experience is singular, its universality will be enhanced by the very act of memory. The poem, therefore, like the life it describes, "meander[s]," starting with a moment in the poet's present and drifting by associations back through one memory after another, "world after world."

As he sits with his wife and cat, in a scene of domestic bliss, Jarrell's taste of chocolate tapioca sparks a recollection of childhood, which in turn sparks the desire to remember even more. He recalls how they had returned to Los Angeles at one time to find it changed utterly; that scene dissolves, over the span of an ellipsis, into an even more remote time. Change and death are confronted and defeated through a series of vignettes in which the poet remembers and, in some cases, addresses such figures from his past as the mad girl whom he drove with her mother to the hospital in Daytona: "If I took my eyes from the road/ And looked back into her eyes, the car would—I'd be—."

An element of irony attaches to the "Lost World" in the title. Jarrell recovers his Lost World through an asserted imagination, almost an act of faith: ". . . All of them are gone/ Except for me; and for me nothing is gone." Finally, he is able to see the changes wrought by time as "miraculous" rather than as the "pain" the speaker feels in the much earlier "90 North" (from *Blood for a Stranger*, 1942).

Forms and Devices

Jarrell aspires to a verse that is colloquial, emotional, and rooted in particulars. Especially in the poems of his last book, *The Lost World* (1965), the reader finds the dramatic monologue, the speech, as the dominant form. Rarely do the poems revolve around specific metaphors or strive for the imagistic concision so often attributed to the style of the high modernists. John Crowe Ransom, one of Jarrell's early mentors, cannot recall Jarrell's ever using the term "metaphor."

Jarrell is, however, the poet of allusion and reference, not only as a way of calling to mind another context for his own poem but also of reminding readers that the context no longer exists. Whether it be a passage from the Gospel, a veiled reference to William Shakespeare (Hamlet's "undiscovered country"), or a simple borrowing from a silent film, the allusion is a reminder of something absent; in a poem about recovering the "lost," this strategy is indeed appropriate. The echo of Proust at the beginning of the poem is as much a quotation as the lines from Mark 9:24 ("I believe. Help thou/ Mine unbelief."); both are "memories" that tinge the poem with a subdued ruefulness the poet works to overcome. At the same time, Jarrell's speaking voice gives form to a playful, wide-ranging intelligence to which quotation comes naturally.

Some images, such as the "chicken's body" going around in circles, are drawn from Jarrell's other poems, in this case "The Lost World," and cannot be explained without them. In the earlier poem, the young boy's grandmother wrings a chicken's neck, and, in his first encounter with the reality of death, he looks on horrified as the creature flops about. In the present poem, that moment produces one of Jarrell's rare metaphors as the chicken's body becomes "a satellite" bearing the mad scientist of science fiction lore (also present in the earlier poem). The horror of his youthful reaction has been transformed by the older poet's imagination into an image that both recalls a fantasy that once thrilled the boy and suggests a far grimmer reality of which the older poet, in the midst of the Cold War, must be aware.

The fleeting narrative recollections give the poem its movement, the act of "thinking" its action. For example, when the now gray-bearded poet hears a boy call him Santa Claus, he waves back, pleased, because "It *is* miraculous/ To have the children call you Santa Claus." When his hand drops back to the steering wheel, however, he is perplexed: "Where's my own hand? My smooth/ White bitten-fingernailed one?" That simple gesture seems to span the years between youth and age, and the poet recognizes that the passing of time is partly responsible for miracles.

Themes and Meanings

"Thinking of the Lost World" can register somewhat deceptively upon a first reading, for its impulse seems nostalgic, and nostalgia—that attitude of longing for the past—is always tinged with a certain gloom. The conclusion might tempt readers to deem the whole enterprise an indulgence in despair—unless, that is, they challenge any facile explanation of the "emptiness" and the "nothing" that suddenly prevail in a poem abounding with people, places, and things.

When the speaker recognizes in his own hand the hand of his grandmother, he realizes also that time has wrought a transformation, that the past is resilient and potent as long as he is, but only through the agency of the imagination. Those "gray illegible advertisements" somehow have to be "legible" for the soul to memorize them. For "soul," one might substitute imagination, and it functions by imposing on the "nothingness" a meaning. The mature poet trades one "emptiness" for another, his present for his past, but he recognizes that all is fraught with meaning and simply awaits the touch of the creative power. That power is his act of faith, his "belief" or his "crystal set" that will allow him a communion with the Lost World. In truth, then, he has lost "nothing," as one can see in his playful manipulation of that word in the final lines. It is the kind of imaginative and witty wordplay that suggests not only a reconciliation with the past but also a reinvigorated imagination as the means to it.

Jarrell, unknowingly near the end of his career (he died when struck by a car in October, 1965), finds that William Wordsworth's Romantic axiom is never more true: The child *is* father to the man. In *The Lost World*, and particularly in "Thinking of the Lost World," he returns to the source of his poetic power—the imagination. For the child that power enlivens the dull and ordinary, changing reality into something with an almost magical appeal. For the fifty-year-old poet, it once again makes possible the child's impulse, that urge to transform the world and, in the process, one's own life. The protagonist effects a compromise with the cold facts of aging and impending death by convincing himself that nothing is ever lost, that his "thinking" can bestow a substance and reality on the past by making it the occasion of poetry—"the nothing for which there's no reward."

Nelson Hathcock

THIRTEEN WAYS OF LOOKING AT A BLACKBIRD

Author: Wallace Stevens (1879-1955)
Type of poem: Poetic sequence
First published: 1917; collected in *Harmonium,* 1923

The Poem

"Thirteen Ways of Looking at a Blackbird" is a sequence of thirteen Imagist poems written in variable syllabic verse. Line length varies from two to ten syllables, but the norm is four to eight syllables per line, thus approximating in English the line lengths of Japanese forms such as the haiku, the senryu, and the tanka, all of which utilize five- and seven-syllable lines. In effect, Wallace Stevens's series is a sequence of Japanese-style Zen poems. The unifying factor in the series is the image of the blackbird, which appears in each of the numbered sections of the set; each poem otherwise stands on its own and offers an insight either into "the nature of the universe," as does the haiku, or into "the nature of mankind," as does the senryu.

Each short poem in the series has its own subject, focus, and thesis, though all are related. The subject of the first, for example, has to do with existence and perception; the second, with perspective. The fourth poem makes the Zen Buddhist point that "all things are one thing." Number 5 discusses the differences between statement and implication. In the ninth poem, the theme is that the universe is a series of concentric circles extending outward to infinity. Number 12 is close to what the Japanese call a "katauta"—a short, emotive question and its intuitive answer. It would be a katauta if the first line were phrased in the form of a question—"Is the river moving?"—the answer to which is, "The blackbird must be flying."

These poems are quite unusual for Stevens, for they are Imagist in the style of his friend and correspondent William Carlos Williams, rather than in Stevens's normal style, which was Symbolist. That is to say, these poems exemplify Williams's dictum that there should be "no ideas but in things" and do not deal in what Carl Jung called "archetypes," or manifestations in language of the basic drives of human nature, such as love (Eros), wisdom (Athena), or power (Zeus).

Forms and Devices

Each of these short poems is basically a metaphor, though most of them also contain other sensory devices, such as descriptions and similes. A metaphor is essentially a language equation: A = B. The first part of the equation is the subject (called the "tenor"); the second part is the object (called the "vehicle"). It was William Carlos Williams's belief (as well as the belief of others of the school of twentieth century poets called Imagists) that, if one chose the proper object or vehicle, one would not need to mention the subject or tenor at all, for one would have chosen what T. S. Eliot called the "objective correlative"—that object which is relative to the idea being expressed. Thus, the idea would be clearly stated in the image itself.

For example, in poem number 5, which is really an embodiment of the theory stated in the paragraph above, there is a double tenor: "inflections"—that is to say, statements (denotations)—and "innuendoes," or implications (connotations). The speaker does not know which he prefers. He gives an example of each. The metaphorical vehicle of inflections is "The blackbird whistling"; the vehicle of innuendoes is the silence "just after" the blackbird has stopped whistling. The reader is left to decide which he or she prefers—the sound of the blackbird's whistle or the silence in which the overtone of the whistle hangs suspended like an echo.

Poem number 2 is a simile, not a metaphor. A simile does not make a strong equation between a tenor and a vehicle, but a comparison between dissimilar things with a point in common. The speaker says that he "was of three minds"—he was vacillating among three alternatives, much like a tree in which one can see three blackbirds doing three different things. Thus, the tree becomes an embodiment of the state of the speaker's mind.

Poems number 4 and 9 are neither similes nor metaphors; they are statements, but the assertions are also endless lists by implication. If one were standing in a prairie, for example, where one could see a long way, one might, as in number 9, be able to follow a bird flying so far that eventually the eye lost track of it and could no longer see it. That would be the edge of a circle, the circle of sight; yet the bird is still flying, assumedly, and when it finally lands, that would be the edge of another circle. The horizon beyond that is yet a third circle. The earth's orbit around the sun is a fourth, the solar system is a fifth, and the edge of the universe is a sixth; the edge of infinity would be the last. Stevens never says anything beyond pointing out the edge of the first "of many circles," however; all else is implied.

Similarly, poem number 4 begins a list: One man plus one woman "Are one." Upon consideration of this statement, the reader may well agree, for one is useless without the other and cannot exist separately for any length of time. Then Stevens adds a third item to the list: a blackbird. The reader may agree that, if two different things, such as a man and a woman, are in reality one thing, then it is possible that a third different thing, such as an animal, is also part of the same thing, the same "oneness." If the reader accepts this third item in the list, then all other items Stevens (or the reader) might have added, by implication, are one thing. This is a Zen Buddhist concept, that all things are one. It points out the Japanese character of this poetic sequence.

Themes and Meanings

The first poem in the series sets the overall theme of the sequence. Like poems 4 and 9, it represents a list, but it is also an objective correlative, the vehicle of an unstated metaphorical equation. The list consists of "twenty snowy mountains," a blackbird, and the blackbird's eye, but it also contains one other item not mentioned. Every poem has a narrator (the narrator of numbers 2, 5, and 8, for example, is "I," the author). Although there is no "I" in the first poem, someone is looking at this vista, so a fourth item in the list is the narrator. There are other things one might add by implication; if the narrator can see "twenty snowy mountains" in the distance, that means that his field of vision is deep and vast. The color white is specified in "snowy," as is the color black in "blackbird." Closeness is also implied, for the blackbird is close enough to the speaker to be seen clearly; in fact, it is so close that the narrator can see not only the blackbird's eye but also the eye moving—it is, in fact, "The only moving thing," so stasis is implied as well as motion. These are the contrasts of the poem: vastness (mountains) and smallness (blackbird, blackbird's eye); distance and closeness; whiteness and blackness; motion and stillness. One may ask why the poet is speaking only of contrasts and why an eye is mentioned. Is it what the blackbird sees that is important? What does the blackbird see? No doubt it sees the narrator, but by the same token the narrator is using his own eyes to see the blackbird in its environment and to see the blackbird's eye in the act of seeing him.

Thus, the subject of the first poem in the sequence is "seeing." The theme of the poem might perhaps be put into these words: "Seeing is an act of perception on the part of a living creature." The poem, like all the other poems in the sequence, has to do with the nature of existence. They are celebrations of life, but life seen with a cold eye—the clear eye of the existential poet, for Stevens believed that people ought to look directly and unswervingly at life, accepting it unflinchingly and without religious or sentimental props of any kind.

Poem 7 says this almost in so many words. The "thin men of Haddam" are the citizens of Haddam, Connecticut (Stevens lived in Hartford). The speaker of the poem asks the people why they "imagine golden birds." He asks what is wrong with the real life that is objectified in the blackbird that "Walks around the feet/ Of the women" of Haddam.

The thirteenth and last poem of the sequence is a coda, a summing up and an ambiguous climax; it is itself the last item in the list of short poems that Stevens has compiled. What is happening has happened and will continue to happen. The blackbird sat waiting for the extraordinary things of everyday life to occur. The implication is that there are many more than these thirteen ways to look at the blackbird and for the blackbird to participate in the actions of life. The season is winter, as it is in the first poem and in others of the series. One thinks, perhaps, of another early Stevens poem, "The Snow Man," in which Stevens said that "One must have a mind of winter" with which to regard the realities of existence.

Lewis Turco

THIS AFTERNOON, MY LOVE

Author: Sor Juana Inés de la Cruz (Juana Inés de Asbaje y Ramírez de Santillana, 1648-1695)
Type of poem: Sonnet
First published: 1690, as "En que satisface un recelo con la retórica del llanto," in *Poemas*; English translation collected in *Sor Juana Inés de la Cruz: Poems*, 1985

The Poem
"This afternoon, my love," from the group of poems "De Amor y de Discreción" ("Of Love and Discretion"), is a classical sonnet. It is composed of an envelope-rhymed octave followed by an *ababab* sestet—embodying, according to the rules of the sonnet, "the statement and the resolution of a single theme," here given in the caption "She Answers Suspicions in the Rhetoric of Tears." This description establishes that a woman in love is pleading with a jealous lover.

Although all her love poems were commissioned, and it is therefore impossible to tell whose poetic "voice" is speaking to the reader, Sor Juana Inés de la Cruz prefers to speak in the first-person singular (the "she" of the caption refers to herself in an ironic distancing effect) but to emphasize the second person, the one to whom the speech is addressed. By utilizing this strategy, the poem pretends to deal with a particular case but in fact deals with the universal significance of that case.

Sor Juana was the most learned person in New Spain, but she was highly conscious of the limits of intellect and reasoning. She may here, following her elder contemporary, the French philosopher Blaise Pascal, be asserting the superiority of the "reason of the heart" over the "reason of the mind," but one cannot be quite sure. As she does frequently, she starts out in this poem resigned to the powerlessness of arguments to overcome irrational feelings such as jealousy. Consequently, she wants her lover "to see her heart" directly. This gesture of baring herself, of allowing the other to see her intimate being passing from rigidity to melting ("liquid," "undone," "molten"), may or may not have erotic connotations. Sor Juana is a master of the indeterminate.

Balancing such oppositions as words and reasoning versus heart is her favorite, and typically Baroque, stylistic device; in her case, testimony to the lifelong struggle between feeling and intellect, fantasy and reason, carnal love and love of God. The heart is traditionally considered the seat of love, and from it all power derives. When arguments failed, "Love came to the help of my intentions" (a literal translation) and achieved "what seemed impossible" by means of a magic potion: tears "which my melting heart distilled in copious drop" (translation by Frank J. Warnke, *Three Women Poets*, 1987).

In the sestet, she urges her lover to drop all foolish doubts and arguments, using—tongue in cheek—the rational "argument" that emotion, or irrationality, is the ultimate "proof": "Since thou hast seen and touched a liquid rare—My molten heart caught up between thy hands."

Sister Juana is extremely modern—one might even say deconstructionist—in her ironic inversion of word content: "Rhetoric" is the Aristotelian "art of persuasion," which means well-wrought arguments, articulate words. The "rhetoric of tears" is the revenge of the inarticulate, the triumph of anima over animus. This triumph is staged, however, by a supremely lucid anima.

Forms and Devices

Quintessentially Baroque, this poem contains in a nutshell the spirit of the period: its penchant for theatricality, trompe-l'oeil techniques, and playful forms masking metaphysical anxiety. Using linguistic devices, Sor Juana produces a seemingly light-hearted disclaimer of her own—supposing that the poetic voice is her own—sentimental involvement.

Having spent her later adolescence at the court of the viceroy of New Spain before entering first a Carmelite then a Hieronymite convent, Sor Juana was superbly versed in European literature and philosophy, including ancient Greek, and she was a master of Baroque literary forms. Her Spanish thus suffers little in translation; she is a catalyst of "intertextuality." This poem brings to mind the archetypal Baroque poet, John Donne, with whose work Sor Juana may have been familiar.

Forms—particularly the illusion-creating devices and mirror effects of Baroque poetry—are hardly dissociable from their content, especially in Sor Juana's work, since formal and stylistic prestidigitation was so well suited to Sor Juana's temperament, which was both profoundly serious and coquettishly playful.

Her love poems are modern in the sense that they are, as it were, "written under erasure"; that is, she is pulling the rug from under her own statements, leaving the erasure and the not-quite-erased statement side by side to form an *indécidable* (something that is indeterminate or undecidable). Jacques Derrida might count her among his spiritual ancestors: Sor Juana was besieged by ontological doubts that she saw reflected in language, which she viewed as an unreliable expression of truth. She was certainly familiar with Descartes's "systematic doubt." Hence the frequency of the inbuilt disclaimer: When she speaks of *dolor* (sorrow) and her "melting heart," one is ready to take her word for it. Yet would a person so unself-consciously abandoning herself really so self-consciously rejoice in her own strategy ("rhetoric," "intentions")?

As her choice of the restrictive sonnet form attests, Sor Juana, for all her pyrotechnic virtuosity, exemplifies the Baroque ideal of controlled exuberance. All of her poems aspire to a harmony of movement, to a balance of opposites either of which would run wild if it were not restrained by a masterly formal will. Polarity creates tension—male/female, intellect/feeling, sacred/profane—and Sor Juana uses the poetic means of balanced opposition to turn tension into intensity, only to dissolve it into a sleight of hand of grace and wit. Fiction and its illusion-creating devices form the essence of Sor Juana's kind of reality—an open-ended one that ceaselessly mirrors its own mirror images.

While in other poems Sor Juana creates original metaphors—and "Primero Sueño" ("First Dream"), her only noncommissioned and longest poem, is an example of the most esoteric symbolism—here she does something that is perhaps even more sophisticated: She deliberately uses clichés, infusing them with new semantic energy by means of unusual associations, thus triggering new images. The heart becomes a distillery. *Amor* (love) and *dolor* (sorrow) are stripped of their mawkishly sentimental connotations and become *dramatis personae*, helping agents: *Dolor* poured the tears; *amor* came to the "help of my intentions." The supreme ironist "proceeds masked": She knows that the reader is aware that she is not using these naïve clichés naïvely; they are so obviously banal that they warn the reader to stay alert.

Themes and Meanings

This poem is one of the earliest "feminist" texts—a tour de force in seventeenth century New Spain. (In another poem, "Stupid Men Who Accuse . . .," Sor Juana condemns the inconsistency of men who blame women for what they themselves have caused by means of their persuasion: surrender and loss of virtue.) The poem's spirit resembles that of late twentieth century postrevolutionary, conciliatory feminism. It sincerely exalts a woman's love for a man, but does so with a grain of irony: Men are so easily fooled by conventional female weapons, such as tears. Tears are a literary convention too, however—a cliché symbolic of the effusions of that supreme cliché, the heart. A craving for convention and fiction, including crocodile tears, is thus the common characteristic of both amorous males and readers who are more than ready to "suspend disbelief."

In the hands of the superior woman or of the master writer, however, banal material turns into precious substance. The catalyst in this alchemy is emotion combined with intellect—that is, the controlled ecstasy of the Baroque—an apparent contradiction in terms that is familiar to a nun as part of her spiritual training. The amorous strategy of persuasion is conceived—Baroque irony of the second degree—by a nun. Feminism here joins the art of writing in a peculiar synthesis, not in the ordinary antagonistic manner of Virginia Woolf's essay *A Room of One's Own* (1929).

If circularity and authorial self-consciousness are formal markers of the Baroque style, they are also the essential marks of much great writing of any time—such as Miguel de Cervantes' *Don Quixote de la Mancha* (1605, 1615; *Don Quixote of the Mancha*, 1612, 1620) or Johann Wolfgang von Goethe's *Die Lieden des jungen Werther* (1774; *The Sorrows of Young Werther*, 1902). Sor Juana's instinctive knowledge of the illusory nature of all things worldly did not prevent this surprisingly worldly nun from passionately loving the world: She loved it *as* an illusion, which is why the Baroque illusion-creating techniques were her ideal medium.

"This afternoon, my love" may have many intended and unintended "messages," but above all it is about writing. The lover here is the reader, the indirect object of the "rhetoric" who is invited to suspend disbelief. Sor Juana's all-consuming passion, writing, relegates the presented "passion"—the likes of Aldonza-Dulcinea or Lotte—to the rank of mere material; it is nothing but a pretext for creative fantasy.

Christine de Lailhacar

THIS IS JUST TO SAY

Author: William Carlos Williams (1883-1963)
Type of poem: Epistle
First published: 1934, in *Collected Poems, 1921-1931*

The Poem

William Carlos Williams's "This Is Just to Say" contains three stanzas, each composed of four short lines. No line exceeds three words. In the first stanza, the narrator-writer of a memorandum asserts that he has eaten plums that were in the icebox. In the second stanza, the narrator addresses "you" and acknowledges that the reader of the note was probably saving the plums for breakfast. In the first line of the third and last stanza, the narrator-writer asks for forgiveness and then expresses his relish of the plums.

The appearance of the printed poem emphasizes the brevity of the unusually short lines, for white space dominates. Of the twenty-eight words in the entire poem, twenty-one are one-syllable words. Only two words are capitalized. Williams uses no punctuation. The pronouns "I" and "me" designate the narrator-writer, and the pronoun "you" addresses the reader of what appears to be a hastily written note. The brevity, the informality of the writing as exemplified by a complete absence of punctuation, and a partial absence of capitalized words combine with the title, "This Is Just to Say," to create the register of a note or memorandum.

After the sentence "I have eaten/ the plums. . . ." in the first stanza, Williams maintains a focus on plums by using three pronouns placed through the poem to refer to the fruit. In the third line of the first stanza, the relative pronoun "that" stands for plums in the clause "that were in/ the icebox." In the second stanza the relative pronoun "which" stands for plums in the clause "and which/ you were probably/ saving/ for breakfast." In the last stanza the personal pronoun "they" refers to "plums" in the closing independent clause, "they were delicious/ so sweet/ and so cold." Although two humans, the writer and the reader of the note, exist in the poem, the focus remains on the object, the plums.

The poem progresses in a narrative sequence of the narrator-writer eating the plums that had been put in the icebox. Stanza 2 works like a flashback in narration as the narrator surmises that the reader has saved the plums for breakfast. The third stanza has the opening line "Forgive me" with "Forgive" as the only word in the poem, other than the pronoun "I," capitalized. Then the narrator evaluates the taste of the fruit with three adjectives—"delicious," "sweet," and "cold."

Forms and Devices

"This Is Just to Say" appears artless. The poem appears in the form of a note, such as a spouse might write to explain missing plums that had been stored in the refrigerator. Figurative language, usually so plentiful in poetry, is not apparent upon a casual reading of Williams's poem.

Upon careful reading, "This Is Just to Say" yields rich sensory pleasure. The pattern of words that leads the senses to taste include "eaten," "plums," "breakfast," "delicious," "sweet," and "cold." Because poetry must work intensely out of sound, the taste must be linked with the muscular sounds of the words Williams has chosen to suggest taste. The key link occurs between "delicious" and a juicy flow as the word rolls out of the mouth. Sound is joined by the kinetic element as the jaws of the plum-eater feel the flood of juice and then move tongue and lips to hold the juice before it dribbles out of the lips, just as the word "delicious" almost overflows the mouth.

The key noun in the poem—"plums"—also requires a linkage of sound and facial movement. The *p* pushes out the lips and opens the mouth. The *l* brings the tongue up to form a barrier of the tip of the tongue against the upper front teeth. The *u* opens the barrier, and the *m* closes it a second time. The *s* holds the sound and juice in the mouth in a reveling of taste. "Plums," like other onomatopoeic and mimetic words such as "squish," captures both the shape the mouth must take and the juiciness of the plum.

Williams used plums in a second poem, entitled "To a Poor Old Woman," published in a 1935 collection. In both poems, the plums carry succulence, the juicy tang that brims in the mouth. The tang is furthered by the long *e* sounds of "eaten" and "sweet" in "This Is Just to Say." Juiciness is prolonged in the *s* begun in the pluralization of "plums," continued in "delicious," and sustained in the alliteration "so sweet." Again the mimetic links with sound as Williams ends the poem with the assonance created by the *o* in "so cold." The noun phrase of focus, "the plums," the sole words in the second line of the first stanza, and the three adjectives that close the poem, "delicious," "sweet," and "cold," serve the poet in two ways. The words are referential, and they are also mimetic. As a consequence, as readers intellectually follow the narration, they are also physically involved with the act of eating sweet, cold plums.

Rhythm adds to the referential-mimetic correlation. Although Williams was averse to singsong rhythm, he did hold to one pattern used in four strategic positions in the poem. The pattern is one unstressed syllable followed by two stressed syllables. This stable pattern, amid a jumble of other varying meters, creates closure at the ends of the three stanzas. The pattern also appears in the first line of the third stanza: "Forgive me." The first stanza closes with "the icebox," the second closes with "for breakfast," and the third stanza closes with "and so cold."

Each closing line of a stanza ends in a spondee, in which two syllables in a foot are stressed. The metrical pattern then coincides with the stress patterns of ordinary speech, for each noun within the compound nouns is stressed. "Ice" and "box" create a spondee, as does "breakfast." In the third stanza, the intensifier "so" is stressed, as is the adjective "cold." The joining of ordinary speech patterns with the poetic spondee charges the apparently artless memorandum with artful poetic power.

Themes and Meanings

The rhythm of everyday speech, the absence of punctuation, the title, the message of "I have eaten/ the plums," and the brevity of "This Is Just to Say" combine to suggest that the poem poses as a hastily scribbled note. The pose may convey the theme of

Williams's poem. If so, the parallel between this particular poem and a note is a crucial issue.

A note is an interchange between a writer and a reader. In the interchange between the "I" and "you," the plums become the center of attention. In the first stanza the writer admits to eating the plums. In the second stanza, the writer expresses the belief that the reader of the note was saving the plums for breakfast. In the first line of the third stanza, the writer asks for forgiveness. After doing so, he then extols the sensuous pleasure of the forbidden fruit. A tension arises in the third stanza as the first line, "Forgive me," suggests humbleness. In contrast, the closing three lines are exuberant, as the writer revels in the remembered pleasure of eating the plums.

The plums have tempted the writer of the note, who succumbs and asks forgiveness for his weakness. Then the writer re-creates the sensuous temptation through the only adjectives used in the poem. This second reveling in the sensuous pleasure of the plums is possible only through words, liquid adjectives that mimic the muscular facial movements that have occurred during the actual eating of the plums. It is in the last three lines that the poem overtakes the note. The poetic timbre of the last three lines indicates that the prosaic timbre of the title is a guise; the register of the note is a guise. Because poetry is metaphorical rather than literal, poetry readers expect guises, but Williams, in his seemingly artless little "note," has disguised a poem as a memorandum.

Williams's metaphor of poem posing as note suggests several meanings. One is that the human, the writer of the apologetic memo, can transcend mere physical ordinariness through sensuous pleasure taken in physical objects: The senses enable the transcendence. Asking for forgiveness suggests a spiritual transgression. Paradoxically, the human senses that have so enjoyed the fruit have also caused the transgression. "Forgive me" is one brief line that seems not so important as the crescendo of following adjectives that extol the pleasures of the fruit. A second meaning of the metaphor lies in the brevity of the note: These stolen sensory pleasures are brief. A third meaning occurs in the ordinariness of a note. One does not expect transcendence in a note as one does not expect transcendence from the icebox. Williams thus seems to suggest that humans may not need a cathedral for every transcendent experience. The senses may offer transportation into the sublime.

Lana J. White

THIS LIME-TREE BOWER MY PRISON

Author: Samuel Taylor Coleridge (1772-1834)
Type of poem: Lyric
First published: 1800; collected in *Sibylline Leaves*, 1817

The Poem

"This Lime-Tree Bower My Prison" is a moderately long (seventy-six lines) poem divided into three verse paragraphs. Its speaker is clearly the poet himself. The poem is "Addressed to Charles Lamb, of the India House, London," and in line 27 and the final nine lines, the poet openly addresses his friend. Nevertheless, the poem opens as a private meditation and continues in that vein for most of its length; Lamb is addressed only infrequently, and then as an absent friend. Though Samuel Taylor Coleridge termed this a "conversation poem," it may be described as a long lyrical and dramatic meditation.

Coleridge prefaces his poem with a note which sets the scene. In the summer of 1797, he was visited at his cottage by friends. His cottage was at Nether Stowey in Somerset, England; his friends were Lamb as well as William and Dorothy Wordsworth. The poet "met with an accident," which prevented him from walking with his friends. (His wife accidentally spilled boiling milk on his foot; his friends left him to walk in the nearby Quantock Hills to get a view of the Bristol channel.) Coleridge continues: "One evening, when they had left him for a few hours, he composed the following lines in the garden-bower." The reader pictures Coleridge immobilized in his backyard, shaded by large, beautiful lime trees (a species also called lindens).

At first, Coleridge is irritated at being left behind; his garden seems a prison. He resents not being with his friends, who are seeing remarkable sights and responding with intense feelings to them. Not only would these sights and feelings have been good in themselves, but also they would have remained in the poet's memory to cheer him later on, when he is old and even blind. Coleridge childishly complains that he may never see his friends again. With envy he lists the sights he imagines they see: a shady dell, an ash tree, a waterfall, tall weeds, and cliffs.

At the beginning of the second verse paragraph (line 20), he imagines his friends coming out onto open land and seeing fields and the sea. At this point, Coleridge's mood begins to change. He thinks of Lamb, who must spend most of his days in London and who must patiently bear an unnamed "strange calamity." (Lamb was burdened with the care of his sister Mary, who had recently murdered their mother in a fit of madness.) Coleridge now imagines the beauties of the oncoming evening and the colors that the setting sun brings out in the clouds, the sea, and the land. He hopes that at that moment Lamb is feeling what he, Coleridge, has felt at such scenes in the past: the presence of an "Almighty Spirit" in nature.

In the last verse paragraph, Coleridge knows that he is happy for his friends, and his thoughts return with comfort to his own situation in the lime-tree bower. As night approaches, he looks intently around him, especially at the beautiful leaves of the lime and of the walnut and elm trees; he sees a bat and hears the sound of a solitary bee. He concludes that it was a good thing that he could not accompany his friends, for now he is appreciative of the nature he finds in his own garden. He imagines that the bird he sees fly across the face of the risen moon is also seen or heard by his friend Lamb, wherever his walk has taken him.

Forms and Devices

"This Lime-Tree Bower My Prison" is written in blank verse; its verse paragraphs informally divide the speaker's thought processes into three sections of approximately equal length. The progression is dramatic and seems at first to follow the process of association, not the rules of logic. The speaker begins by expressing irritation, then feels sympathy for his friend Lamb, then is both happy that he is enjoying his own situation and hopeful that Lamb can feel what he feels.

That Coleridge classified this as a conversation poem suggests that its language is close to the language of everyday speech. It begins colloquially: "Well, they are gone. . . . " The sentences that follow are like those of conversation: There are no startling inversions; clauses and lists seem to develop informally. The poet is most interested with evoking the scene. Only occasionally does he locate the reader firmly in his sentence by supplying a verb: "wander" (line 8) and "behold" (line 17). This paragraph's most impressive effects derive from its vivid visual images: "The roaring dell, o'erwooded, narrow, deep,/ And only speckled by the mid-day sun," and the "branchless ash,/ Unsunned and damp."

The second paragraph develops the poem's themes more seriously. When the poet gives over feeling sorry for himself and begins to understand his friend's happiness, his language becomes more thoughtful and less colloquial. Clauses are shorter, and even though there are several vivid descriptions, the reader becomes more aware of Coleridge's thought processes, as expressed in precise grammatical relationships. The poet is also more assertive; he not only describes the sun but also commands it to shine and the clouds to burn. Word order is heightened by inversion ("tract magnificent"), and one encounters a more poetic vocabulary ("betwixt," "methinks," "thou," "thy," "ye," "doth"). Toward the end of this paragraph, the poet signals the arrival of an important idea with exclamation points, strong emphases ("yea"), repetitions ("gaze"), intensifiers ("such") and the strong consonance of *s* and *p* sounds.

The poet's thoughts do exhibit a kind of logic. Like a syllogism of the emotions, the poem returns in its third verse paragraph to matters more close to home, more like those of the poem's opening. For the first fifteen lines of the third paragraph, the style once more is conversational and visually evocative. Then at line 59, Coleridge changes to less visual, more abstract, and more philosophical notes; his vocabulary now is somewhat heightened, and he uses an uncommon subjunctive verb ("be but Nature"). In the last eight lines, he ties up the poem's various strands: Now he is related to Lamb in that they may observe the same bird. This bird not only provides a vivid visual image that appeals to the senses, it also carries great significance, quite literally by being the agent that enables the separated friends to be united.

Themes and Meanings

Romantic poets such as Coleridge often protested that the abstractions of earlier times (such as Virtues and Principles) lacked meaning for their age. Accordingly, when they attempted to describe and define great issues and forces, they took great pains to describe those forces in concrete situations, often in the actual situations and places in which the poets themselves learned about them. It is therefore very important in "This Lime-Tree Bower My Prison" that Coleridge sets the scene literally in the backyard of the house he and his wife were renting in Nether Stowey, Somerset. One has no reason to doubt the outlines of the story; in June, 1797, the poet had something like the experience he describes in which his mind moved from irritation, to imagination, to sympathy, to vivid sensations of the backyard in which he was sitting. This is the way a person has such thoughts; this is the way Coleridge (and other contemporaries, such as Wordsworth) believed these ideas should be presented to be most effective.

The poem takes very seriously the importance of friendship. Coleridge is unhappy about being left behind. He is hurt by the thought that he may never see his friends again, but his spirits revive when he thinks of Lamb. Just as important is the poem's insistence on the value of experiencing nature. Coleridge envies his friends' sensations; he remembers the places they will visit, then he looks at the heavens and at the trees in his own bower. Although these sensations are almost exclusively natural and are primarily visual, they are not simply beautiful descriptions of trees and flowers. The reader is shown the unlovely "dark green file of long lank weeds" as well as "the smooth clear blue" of the sea. The images are of a mixed sort—arresting and detailed rather than conventionally beautiful.

Coleridge is interested in the effects of a person's real experiences of nature— unprettified and unsensationalized. In this poem, he illustrates how such experiences (and memories of them) can lead one to intuitions that are beyond nature as one usually thinks of it; the reader may think that Coleridge is vague about these matters. He says at the end of the second verse paragraph that when he gazed at a "wide landscape" it began to seem somewhat insubstantial ("Less gross than bodily") and more and more like the outward manifestation (the "veil") of "the Almighty Spirit." Note that Coleridge sees himself and others like him (perhaps Lamb) as "Spirits" themselves, suggesting that at such moments something in his own soul is responding to the spirit he apprehends in Nature.

After he has rediscovered "the Almighty Spirit," Coleridge returns to his present situation and lovingly responds to its beauty. He is now happy and confident that "Nature"—the veil of the Spirit—"ne'er deserts the wise and pure" no matter where they are. Perhaps moments of spiritual deprivation are the necessary preludes to moments of enlightenment (lines 64 to 67). Certainly, he hopes and imagines that Lamb is having a similar experience at that very moment. (Coleridge's hopes and perhaps the requirements of this poem caused him to misrepresent seriously the actual character of Charles Lamb, who after reading this poem complained that he really preferred London to the country and was not "gentle-hearted.") "This Lime-Tree Bower My Prison" is an informal, selective, versified, and dramatic account of an experience that Coleridge had in 1797. In it he meditates on how the influence of "the Almighty Spirit" works through nature on individuals and how it can provide the basis for a close friendship with another.

George Soule

THIS PAINTED LIE YOU SEE

Author: Sor Juana Inés de la Cruz (Juana Inés de Asbaje y Ramírez de Santillana, 1648-1695)

Type of poem: Sonnet

First published: 1690, as "Este, que ves, engaño colorido," in *Poemas*; English translation collected in *A Sor Juana Anthology*, 1988

The Poem

This poem appears in anthologies under three titles. It is most commonly referred to as "Este, que ves, engaño colorido," or "This painted lie you see," which is the poem's first line. The original title, however, which is sometimes dropped, even in Spanish editions of the poem, is more complex. The purpose of the poem is explained in this title, which Alan Trueblood has translated as "She Disavows the Flattery Visible in a Portrait of Herself, Which She Calls Bias." The poem is sometimes simply called Sonnet 145.

The poem, which focuses on a single painting, is written in a standard Petrarchan sonnet form: its fourteen lines are divided into two quatrains and two tercets. In Spanish, each line is composed of eleven syllables; this is known as a hendeca-syllabic line.

The first four lines, or quatrain, rhyme *abba* in Spanish and function as a complete clause. The poem immediately addresses a person, a "you," who is looking at the painting that is the subject of the poem. The painting, which is a flattering portrait of Sor Juana Inés de la Cruz herself, is nothing more than a "painted lie" or a "cunning deceit of the senses" because the "exquisite beauty of art" functions, in fact, through "false syllogisms of color." The poet seems to be suggesting that art lies.

The second quatrain, following the same rhyme scheme, continues the description of the painting and further explains the poet's philosophical position. This portrait of the poet attempts to "triumph over old age and oblivion" by stopping the progression of time. Sor Juana believes that this type of flattery, which tries to exempt her "from the horrors of old age," is both dangerous and false.

In the final two tercets, which in the original rhyme *cdc*, *dcd*, Sor Juana makes nine different statements about the painting. Each statement further develops the ideas that were begun in the first two quatrains; no violent shifts in perspective disrupt the focus of this poem. The painting, a "vain artifice," is actually a "useless defense against fate." Despite its attempt to preserve the beauty of the poet, the portrait is as powerful as a "delicate flower in winds." Looking closely at the portrait, one can see what lies behind the "foolish effort" to preserve the poet's physical features: The painting records what, in reality, is "corpse, is dust, is shadow, is nothing." The poem ends not with the grandeur of art's devices, but with a sobering thought about human mortality. Looked at long enough, the body reveals what the future holds—not permanence or an escape "from the cruelty of years," but death.

Forms and Devices

Sor Juana draws the reader into this frightening poem by means of a simple direct address: "This colored deception that you see." In Spanish, she uses the familiar form of the word you—*tú*—and personalizes her invitation for the reader to see the world as she sees it. By removing herself from the poem, she convinces her readers that the thoughts in the poem are their own.

Many sonnets, including some by William Shakespeare, use an abrupt shift or turn in meaning, usually in the closing couplet or tercet, to surprise the reader. In Sor Juana's sonnet, the idea of the poem is apparent from the opening quatrain, and it does not change; what alters is the syntax, or sentence construction, in the poem. The first and second quatrains, which are joined in their use of the same rhyme scheme and rhyming syllables, are composed of extremely complicated, almost convoluted clauses that slow the reader down. It is almost as if the reader were being forced to look closely at what lies behind the subtle beauty of the portrait. Once that has taken place, Sor Juana rushes the reader, in the final tercets, which are also joined by the repetition of their rhyming sounds, to the inevitable conclusion of the poem. All of the baroque descriptions culminate in the simplicity of her final line: This portrait of the artist reveals the vanity of worshiping the flesh, since everything ends in and "is dust, is shadow, is nothing."

The syntax employed is joined with another basic technique to emphasize the bald, striking emptiness and horror of the final images. Throughout most of the poem, Sor Juana links each of her nouns with adjectives, usually adjectives that decrease the power of the nouns: "false syllogisms," "delicate flower," "vain artifice," "decrepit zeal," "foolish diligence," and "useless protection." The nouns whose denotations are already negative are allowed to stand alone: "oblivion," "fate," "old age" (one word in Spanish, *vejez*). When the reader arrives at the final line of the poem, the power of the words is emphasized because there are four unadorned nouns in succession—corpse, dust, shadow, and nothing; not even the indefinite article "a," which preceded the five previous nouns, is used here. The language becomes sparse to emphasize the barrenness of the final images; adjectives and articles don't belong in the empty world of death.

The writers of poems that talk about paintings usually create lush and imagistic surfaces in their poems. Sor Juana, in the first thirteen lines of this poem, provides only one image, a delicate flower in the wind, which really serves only as a symbol for the transitory nature of beauty. The rest of her language is extremely abstract: "deception," "syllogism," "oblivion," "artifice," "zeal," and "flattery." Once again, she subverts the reader's expectations in the final line by providing four images: corpse, dust, shadow, and nothing. The flesh, the things of this world, do not really concern Sor Juana; it is the absence of flesh, the abstract realm of ideas, that is her obsession. The irony of the poem lies in the tremendous sensual appeal of the sound of its language; although its theme denies the importance of the senses, its rich, ornate music can have power only in this shadow world of the senses.

Themes and Meanings

Sor Juana, a Mexican nun in the Roman Catholic Order of Saint Jerome, has her eyes on God and the spiritual realm, and she wants to give moral instruction to her readers. Although God and a judgment day are never mentioned in the poem, the poet tries to warn her readers that the world of the flesh is transitory; the most beautiful body is merely a corpse dressed in flimsy clothing. She remembers and recalls for the reader the biblical statement that humankind is dust and shall return to dust.

In many poems of the seventeenth century, especially in Elizabethan England, poets addressed this same theme, but they often found a way to escape death's power: Love helped the memory of someone to endure, or art ensured the immortality of the person who was honored in a poem or painting. As Shakespeare said, "As long as men can breathe or eyes can see,/ So long lives this [the poem] and this gives life to thee." Sor Juana offers no such hope. In fact, the world of art is simply a realm of deception and trickery, a place for syllogistic reasoning. The only truth lies outside the human sphere. In other poems, she makes direct reference to the spiritual realm, but here it is only inferred.

Many critics have pointed out the debt Sor Juana owed to Luis de Góngora y Argote's poem "Mientras por competir con tu cabello" ("While in competition with your hair"), which was written in 1582, more than one hundred years before her poem. There are many similarities: Sor Juana's Sonnet 145 and Góngora's poem both follow the Petrarchan sonnet conventions; they have the same rhyme scheme, *abba, abba, cdc, dcd*; they share the same theme about the inevitability of death; and, most remarkably, Sor Juana imitates (or steals?) the closing phrasing of Góngora's poem: "se vuelva . . ./ en tierra, en humo, en polvo, en sombra, en nada" (it turns into earth, into smoke, into dust, into shadow, into nothing). What makes Sor Juana's poem amazing, however, is not the similarity between her poem and Góngora's, or the fact that the music in her poem is more effective, but the subject and focus of the poem. Góngora addresses a woman and comments on her vanity, her obsessive concern with her beautiful lips, hair, neck, and face; Sor Juana addresses herself and, by implication, the reader. The fact that she is commenting on her own portrait, on her own eventual disintegration into dust, gives her poem tremendous power. She is a greater teacher than Góngora because she faces her own mortality; this gives her greater credibility when she invites the reader to face his or her own demise.

Kevin Boyle

THOMAS AND BEULAH

Author: Rita Dove (1952-   )
Type of poem: Poetic sequence/narrative
First published: 1986

The Poem

Rita Dove won the Pulitzer Prize for Poetry in 1986 for her collection of poems *Thomas and Beulah*. The collection, which is dedicated to the poet's mother, contains poems that are meant to tell two sides of the same story and are meant to be read sequentially. In the back of the collection, a chronology of events in the lives of Thomas and Beulah aids in understanding the events dramatized in the poems.

The collection consists of forty-four poems arranged in two parts, some of which had been published in various places before 1986. The collection is divided into two parts: Part 1, entitled "Mandolin," presents twenty-three poems; part 2, entitled "Canary," consists of the volume's remaining twenty-one poems. The volume has eighty pages including the chronology. An epigraph from Melvin B. Tolson's *Harlem Gallery* (1969) prefaces the first part. The quotation attached to the second part is taken from Anne Spencer's poem "Lines to a Nasturtium." Both authors' passages further elucidate the permanence and depth of Thomas and Beulah's love. Their love becomes the "fire" they pass on to their children and grandchildren. Their union becomes the family's bridge over the "troubled waters" of variance, a "viaduct," as Dove calls it, that spans the differences between their families.

Thomas and Beulah is a volume of narrative verse that presents the saga of Dove's family, depicting the generations that started with her maternal grandparents. Thomas was born in Tennessee, and his wife, Beulah, who was four years younger, was born in Georgia. When Beulah was two years old, her parents moved to Akron, Ohio, Rita Dove's birthplace. Thomas is portrayed as a virile young man when he arrives in Akron, Ohio, in 1921. Three years later, he and Beulah are married, and two years afterward (1926), their first daughter, Rose, is born. The story thus continues to unfold, telling of the birth of all their daughters and the death first of Thomas and then of Beulah.

The first part of the collection tells Thomas's story. The opening poem, "The Event," portrays Thomas as a young man on a riverboat leaving Tennessee. It boasts of his silver falsetto, his good looks, and his mandolin. "Variation on Pain," "Jiving," and "Straw Hat" show Thomas assuaging the pain in his soul with the help of his mandolin; going to Akron, Ohio, in 1921 and his attractiveness to the young women there; and, finally, his meeting with Beulah. Set in the parlor of Beulah's parents, "Courtship" and "Refrain" depict Thomas's growing love for and courtship of Beulah. The mandolin continues to play an important part in his romance because Thomas uses it to serenade his love, Beulah. "Variation on Guilt" is a poem about the birth of their first child and the guilt that Thomas feels because of his disappointment when he learns that he has a daughter rather than a son. In "Nothing Down," Thomas buys a new car and allows Beulah to pick the color. She tries to please him with her choice, and they take their first ride through the countryside. In "Zeppelin Factory," "Under the Viaduct," and "Lightnin' Blues," Dove portrays Thomas's struggles during the Depression, the trials of family life, and racism. "Compendium" tells that Thomas, to his wife's delight, has now become a tenor in the gospel choir; "Definition in the Face of Unnamed Fury," "Aircraft," and "Aurora Borealis" take Thomas from the period of struggling to make a living to the time of his job in an aircraft factory during World War II to the period after the war. His first daughter's marriage is lyrically narrated in "Variation on Gaining a Son." "One Volume Missing," "The Charm," "Gospel," "Roast Possum," and "The Stroke" follow Thomas through his mature years a he finds time to read, reflect on his life, quit the gospel choir, and tell stories to his only grandson, Malcolm. In "Satisfaction Coal Company," Thomas speaks of his part-time job at the company and reflects on the events of his life. After his stroke, he ponders what he should do with his leisure time. The final poem in part 1, "Thomas at the Wheel," relates the death of Thomas. Significantly, his last thoughts are of his wife, Beulah.

After the poem on the death of Thomas, part 2 begins with the aptly titled "Canary in Bloom," for it is Beulah's song. The first poems, "Taking in Wash" and "Magic," narrate events in Beulah's childhood and describe her relationship with her parents and grandparents as well as her youthful hopes and dreams. "Courtship," "Diligence," "Promises," and "Dusting" follow Beulah through her courtship with Thomas, her marriage, and her thoughts as she goes through her household tasks. "A Hill of Beans," "Weathering Out," "Motherhood," and "Anniversary" continue Beulah's life and thoughts through the Depression, when food was scarce and there was no meat for the beans; her first pregnancy, her daughter's birth, and her fear of motherhood; and her twelfth anniversary.

"The House on Bishop Street," "Daystar," and "Obedience" describe the family's move to the house on Bishop Street after the birth of their third child, Liza; Beulah's reaction to the overwhelming tasks confronting her as mother, wife, and housewife; her aging; and her dreams. "The Great Palace at Versailles," "Pomade," "Headdress," and "Sunday Greens" relate the continuing nature of Beulah's life with Thomas. In these poems, Beulah takes her first job, in Charlotte's Dress Shop, and dreams and reads about the courtiers in the palace at Versailles; she relates the death of her very dear friend, Willemma; and she starts to make hats while continuing her household tasks of cooking and cleaning. The poem "Recovery" describes Beulah's reaction to Thomas's stroke and recovery. "Wingfoot Lake" narrates the events of a picnic with Beulah's daughters and grandchildren on Independence Day in 1964. As her daughter tells her they are now Afro-Americans, she reflects on the changing times and the changes in her life since Thomas's death. "Company" recalls Thomas's death and her words to him: "we were good, though we never believed it." The final poem, "Oriental Ballerina," with its evocative images of sun and light, narrates Beulah's death.

Forms and Devices

Rita Dove's concept of poetry is especially influenced by such other twentieth century American poets as Robert Frost, Langston Hughes, Melvin Tolson, and Gwen-
dolyn Brooks. This influence can especially be seen in the rhetorical structure of her
work. Moreover, her poetry is often elliptic and shows the influence of the Imagist
movement in its lyric quality. Dove employs poetic devices such as alliteration and
half-rhyme and is not tied to the conventions of strict verse forms. The narrative technique that she uses in *Thomas and Beulah* tells the story of the courtship, love, and
marriage of her grandparents. It is clear, however, that she is also interested in the
form of poetry for its own sake.

In several crucial poems, she has used the dramatic monologue and compressed
narrative admirably, and her well-disciplined use of rhetoric sets her poetry apart. Her
poetry also demonstrates a keen sense of history; thus, her characters and their voices
move fluidly over the years, and they transcend the biographical, becoming decidedly
universal.

Thomas and Beulah is not the first use of the narrative technique by Dove. Her
chapbook *Mandolin*, published in 1982, also used this poetic technique: Some of the
poems that later appeared in *Thomas and Beulah* also appeared in that chapbook.
Poems used in both of these publications, such as "The Event," "Jiving," "Courtship,"
"Refrain," "Compendium," "Aurora Borealis," and "The Stroke," use the metaphor of
music, musical instruments, and dance as a vehicle for expressing beauty, youth, sexuality, and vitality.

"Mandolin" and "Canary" transcend simple metaphor to serve as the poet's metonymic rendering of two people who chose to create a life in the often-constricted environment of post-World War II America.

The use of music and the musical instrument is depicted in the poems "The Event"
and "Variation on Pain." In fact, the title of part I of *Thomas and Beulah* is "Mandolin." Thomas's musical instrument serves as an enticement to women as well as to
people in general. In his more somber moods, he finds reassurance and comfort in his
instrument, and in "Refrain" Thomas is called "The man inside the mandolin," further
emphasizing his identification with his instrument. The extended metaphor of music
is continued when Thomas joins the gospel choir. Beginning with the first poem, "The
Event," the impact of Thomas's beautiful voice (his silver falsetto) is stressed. His
voice influences his life, his love, and his relationships.

The musical quality is extended to Beulah, who is called "a chirping canary"; her
narrative is entitled "Canary in Bloom," thus further strengthening the importance of
song in the lives of Thomas and Beulah. During their courtship, she listens to
Thomas's mandolin; however, in "Courtship, Diligence" Beulah states that she would
have preferred the music of a pianola to the cigar-box music of the mandolin.

Dove's poetry in *Thomas and Beulah* has been described as poetry that has no un-
necessary matter and as poetry of pure shapes and thrift. In her presentation of her
grandparents' love story, Dove has reached a level of technical perfection that is equal
to that of more experienced and older poets.

Themes and Meanings

The titles of her poems, chapbooks, and books indicate the universality of Dove's work; however, in *Thomas and Beulah*, she is decidedly African American. As early as her first book, Dove's thrifty use of language and the narrative technique reveals her cultural universality. She makes use of a complex and multitextured imagery to relate her themes in this Pulitzer Prize-winning collection. The primary theme of *Thomas and Beulah* is the durability of their love as it is intertwined with history and pride in ancestry. The poem inspires an appreciation of the depth of the love shared by Thomas and Beulah and its influence on their children and grandchildren, who are thereafter enmeshed in the web of their parents' and grandparents' lives and histories. Because Thomas and Beulah have become "one flesh and one spirit," they are able to impart, carefully and lovingly, this wholeness to their children. As a result, their progeny is capable of coping with the pain, guilt, despair, bereavement, and loss of illusion seen in "The Event" and "The Stroke" just as Thomas and Beulah have done.

In "Under the Viaduct," permanence is further depicted as the couple live through the hard years of the Depression and Thomas is looking for work. Moreover, Thomas and Beulah's marriage remains intact in spite of personal disappointments. When Thomas's first daughter is born, he feels shame and guilt because he wanted a son. He muses on what he would have said to a son. Again in "Under the Viaduct," Thomas decides to stay in spite of his disappointments; he eventually even joins the gospel choir. In "Variation on Gaining a Son," when his first daughter marries, he accepts a replacement for his dream of having a son.

Beulah also has dreams that she gives up for the permanence of marriage. "Magic" depicts her childhood dream of going to Paris. Later, after she marries Thomas and becomes a mother, her narrative poem "The Great Palaces of Versailles" tells that she still dreams of Paris. The grand design of Beulah's imagination must thrive amid the confines of the dress shop where she irons for whites. Nevertheless, the theme of permanence and diligence is further emphasized in part 2 in the names of the poems: "Courtship, Diligence," "Promises," "Motherhood," "Anniversary," and "Obedience." Indeed, Beulah's voice only becomes free after the death of Thomas. In her narrative, "Daystar," she herself admits that the duties of mother and wife tie her down, and she longs for a place for herself away from children and husband. Similarly, in "Weathering Out" Beulah explains that she likes the mornings best, when Thomas goes to look for work and she can linger over her coffee. This longing for her own space took place even before her first child was born, even while she was pregnant.

Permanence in spite of Thomas's death occurs when Beulah acknowledges in "Company" that the marriage had been good and in "Wingfoot Lake" when she is at a picnic with her daughters and their families.

Musical symbolism is prevalent in *Thomas and Beulah*. Music evoking the broad spectrum of emotions is used to represent the vitality and sexuality of both characters. The dynamic quality of Thomas's personality is symbolized through his mandolin and his beautiful voice, and Beulah is compared to a chirping canary. In "Company," Beulah concedes that Thomas is dying and that even his music cannot help him. His sexuality, as symbolized by the young woman in red pedal pushers next door, is of no help either. Beulah therefore tells him to "give it up." In addition, the singing canary appears throughout the collection of poems. A singer on the radio is referred to as a canary in "Lightnin' Blues." Thomas becomes a singing canary when he joins the gospel choir in "Compendium," and the symbol of the canary is strongly tied to the character of Beulah; Beulah arranges the canary's cage in "The House on Bishop Street."

Dove uses color symbolism effectively in *Thomas and Beulah*, and the shades used are somber. There is gray cloth in "Dusting," the gray bank of clothes and the black suit and collarbone in "Under the Viaduct," and the white wolf whose white fur seeps red in "Motherhood." Furthermore, in "The Palace at Versailles," the flower colors of the ladies who strolled the palace are contrasted with Beulah's out-of-fashion gray skirt. The somber colors reflect the sobriety and the diligence that characterize the lives of Thomas and Beulah. Thus, while their life is not exciting, it is full of devotion to each other. Dove is not a stereotypical African American writer. Although the theme of African American pride and history is indeed present, it is subject to her larger themes of love, devotion, and permanence.

Betty Taylor-Thompson
Kirkland Jones

THOSE WINTER SUNDAYS

Author: Robert Hayden (1913-1980)
Type of poem: Lyric
First published: 1962, in *A Ballad of Remembrance*

The Poem

"Those Winter Sundays" is a short lyric in which the speaker remembers a moment in his childhood and thinks about the sacrifices his father made for him then. This split or double perspective of the poem provides its power, for the poem's meaning depends upon the differences between what the boy knew then and what the man—a father himself, perhaps—knows now.

The poem begins abruptly. The second word of the first line, "too," in fact, assumes actions that have gone before—that the father got up early on other days as well as Sundays to help his family. In this first stanza the reader learns about the father rising in the cold to heat the house before the rest of his family gets up. The last line of the stanza contains the first hint of one of the poem's central themes: "No one ever thanked him."

In the second stanza, the narrator recalls waking as the cold, like ice, was "splintering, breaking" as a result of his father's having lit a wood fire to warm the house. And "slowly" he would get up and dress—in the stanza's last and the poem's most difficult line—"fearing the chronic angers of that house." At this point the reader can only guess at the source of those angers. The third and final stanza continues the actions of the narrator, who speaks "indifferently" to the father who has worked so early and so hard to heat the house for his family and has "polished my good shoes as well." It is Sunday, and probably the boy and his father (and other unnamed family members) are going to church.

In the concluding couplet of the poem, the adult narrator, who has been implied throughout the poem, suddenly steps forward with his final poignant question, "what did I know/ of love's austere and lonely offices?" If the body of the poem deals with the gap between the father and his son, the poem's focus in the last two lines is clearly on the gap between the boy, so indifferent to the father's sacrifices then, and the adult narrator who in his repetition of the question—almost like some incantatory prayer— reveals the pain this memory holds for him: "What did I know, what did I know . . . ?" I was a child then, the couplet implies, and I did not realize what it means to be a man, a father, and to perform the "austere and lonely" duties that family love demands. I never thanked my father, and I cannot today.

The last stanza, and especially those concluding two lines, hardly resolve the tensions of the poem. Rather, the reader is only now fully aware of the real conflicts the poem has described—not only between the indifferent child and the hard-working father, but between the narrator as a boy and the man he has become, who now knows what he missed as a young child. "Those Winter Sundays" is a poem without resolution, a poem with its pains redoubled rather than resolved. The speaker's final question,"What did I know?" can only elicit the answer "nothing" from the reader. In addition, the mystery of line 9 about the "chronic angers of that house" remains unsolved. Are these the angers of any house with young children? Are they only the angers that result from dragging reluctant children to church? The reader cannot be certain.

Forms and Devices

"Those Winter Sundays" is a fairly direct and accessible short lyric. Its language is clear and precise, its metaphors are those of everyday life, and its metrics present no particular difficulties. The form of the poem fits its content closely, and the poem's power comes from this almost perfect fusion.

One interesting thing about the poem is that it is fourteen lines long; poems of such a length are usually called sonnets, but Hayden's poem—instead of having an octave and a sestet, or three quatrains and a concluding couplet, as most conventional sonnets do—violates the sonnet form by having three almost identical stanzas of five, four, and five lines. Yet the spirit of the sonnet form (which often poses and then tries to answer a question or problem) lies beneath the poem's lines in this three-part structure. The first five lines describe the father's actions, the next seven the boy's response (or lack of response) to those actions, and the concluding two the final agonizing question that the narrator, now grown himself, is left with. Thus the sense, if not the structure, of the sonnet form is replicated in "Those Winter Sundays."

Even more noticeable than the stanzaic form of the poem is its language. Rarely in such a short lyric do readers find such intense imagery. The "blueblack cold" of the second line evokes a picture of ice, which is "splintering, breaking" four lines later. The cold is rendered vividly in such an extended image. Likewise the "cracked hands" of line 3 imply that the father is a laborer of some sort, which makes his work for his family even more difficult: His hands are already roughened by his efforts to support his family; now, every morning, they suffer more from working in the freezing cold. The alliteration of the repeated k sounds in the poem—"blueblack cold," "cracked," "ached," "banked," "thanked," and so on—reinforces the discomfort. (At the same time, the assonance and internal rhyme of the poem soften this harshness somewhat.)

Finally the poem's last line, "offices," reverberates with meaning. An office is a job, a duty, but it also carries the idea of a form or service of religious worship, and that sense clearly exists in the poem. Family love demands "austere and lonely offices" (austere denoting ascetic self-denial), for a family member's actions may never earn any kind of acknowledgment. And yet, as in any religious service, family love also carries a spiritual and transcendent meaning—and it is, after all, Sunday morning when the poem's actions take place.

Themes and Meanings

"Those Winter Sundays" benefits from biographical and historical interpretation. Robert Hayden was a mid-twentieth century African American poet who rarely called attention to racial issues. In fact, he was often criticized in the decades before his death by younger and more political black writers for not using racial themes more overtly.

The themes are there nonetheless. Hayden grew up in Detroit in the 1920's as that city was being transformed by the migrations of hundreds of thousands of blacks moving from the South to the industrial North for work. His neighborhood was changing daily. In addition, his own family life was a difficult and unstable one. His parents abandoned him as a baby, giving him to neighbors to raise. He believed that he had been adopted by the Haydens, but they were only his foster parents. To complicate matters even more, the woman who used to come to stay with the Haydens when he was young, Hayden later learned, was in fact Robert's biological mother. Such a strained family situation undoubtedly created tensions for all involved.

This background gives new meaning to the poem, and especially to line 9 and the unresolved question of the house's "chronic angers." Hayden spent his early years in a home full of family secrets and in a city undergoing its own incredible transformation. The angers may be explained, in part at least, by the complex personal and sociological changes going on within and around the house.

This background can thus provide context for the poem's central meaning, the tension between the child who is so indifferent to the sacrifices, the "offices," his father performs almost invisibly, and the man who recognizes now what they meant. In the poem's present time, it is implied, the speaker is a man; perhaps he is a father himself. He has, in a sense, become his father. Now he knows what family love and devotion mean, and he can appreciate the complex tensions and relationships in any family. He also knows the full story of his painful and complicated family history. The poem suggests that it may be too late, however; apparently the speaker cannot thank his father (or foster father) or tell him what he now feels. As so often happens, the poem suggests, family members miss the opportunity to express their gratitude until those who should be thanked are dead and gone.

Hayden created a poem that describes a universal human situation, but he drew from his own personal history for the texture of the work. The result is a short and powerful lyric that gives its readers a sense of the pain and suffering life often inflicts but only rarely resolves.

David Peck

THE THOUGHT-FOX

Author: Ted Hughes (1930-1998)
Type of poem: Lyric
First published: 1957, in *The Hawk in the Rain*

The Poem

"The Thought-Fox" is a poem of twenty-four lines divided into six stanzas. The title tells the reader that the poet is drawing an analogy between a thought—specifically, in this case, a poetic composition—and a fox.

The poet speaks in the first person and in his own persona. He begins by evoking the silence and mystery of a forest at midnight. An atmosphere of suspense is created as one becomes aware of "something else" that is alive in the imaginary forest outside. The world of the forest is set against the world of the room where the poet is working, characterized only by the presence of a clock and the poet's as yet blank paper.

The second stanza intensifies the suspense. The poet shifts his perspective, taking the reader's awareness outside the room as he looks through the window into the black, starless night. The "something" is approaching, beginning to solidify out of the darkness. The third stanza gives the first tangible sense of the creature in the form of the fox's cold nose investigating the surrounding twigs and leaves.

The poet introduces the fox into the reader's sensory field in parts: a nose, then two eyes, as the fox stealthily moves between the trees of the silent, snowbound forest, then the whole body as it flashes across clearings. The fox in its literal sense as a fox is fully realized by the fifth stanza; it is "Brilliantly, concentratedly,/ Coming about its own business."

The final stanza is a sudden and shocking transition back to the fox as a metaphor for thought. "With a sudden sharp hot stink of fox/ It enters the dark hole of the head." The reader is reminded that, although the poet has presented a vivid picture of a fox, he was all the time comparing it with the creative process. Like the fox in the darkness of the forest, a thought begins in the subconscious mind as a vague sense or movement. As it rises to the conscious level of the mind, it becomes increasingly concrete and definite, until it finally "enters the dark hole of the head" as a conscious, coherent thought.

The reader is brought back to the poet's room with a reference to the window, "starless still." One senses the unbounded, uncreated reality that underlies individualized creation, unchanged and undiminished by the ever-changing manifestations that emerge from it. The ticking of the clock brings one back from the timeless world of the imagination to the world of time and space. "The page is printed" states that the thought has taken its final form—as the very poem that is before the reader. The poet has witnessed the act of his own poetic creation. Thus the poem is reflexive; it is a poem about its own composition.

Forms and Devices

Ted Hughes extends his central metaphor of fox-as-thought with great skill. Although the fox is symbolic of poetic creation, the reader is able to maintain a strong sense of it as a "real" fox. Even when Hughes is conveying abstract ideas, he uses precise detail and concrete sensory images from the natural world.

Hughes often uses strong contrasts to convey his notion of nature as interacting opposites: life and death, light and dark, predator and prey. The main contrast in this poem is between the intense vitality of the imagination (the world of the fox) and the impersonal vacancy of the poet's self and environment. The unidentified "something else" in the forest seems more real, more alive than anything in the room, including the poet. More human feeling is accorded to the clock in its "loneliness" than to the poet. He is defined in negatives, in absent terms. There is a disembodied quality to the image of the blank notepaper "where my fingers move," as if the fingers had a life of their own and were acting independently.

The abstract phenomenon of the creative process is made into a living creature of independent will. "Something more near" than the starless night, yet "deeper within darkness," solidifies out of the blackness. This apparent contradiction, of something being real yet elusive, is descriptive of an idea at its genesis. One is aware of the idea's existence, yet it has not yet gained sufficient definition for one to grasp it. The atmosphere of suspense relaxes into the first concrete sensory images of the fox—the cold touch of its nose, then "two eyes"—as the fox edges cautiously into vision. In the beats of "now,/ And again now, and now," and the three consecutive strong stresses of "sets neat prints," one hears the rhythm of the fox's tentative steps.

Hughes often uses alliteration (repetition of consonants) and assonance (repetition of vowel sounds within words) to add an incantatory quality to his verse and to bring images to life. In the alliteration of "touches twig, leaf," one feels the delicacy of the fox's nose investigating its environment. The strong sounds of "Of a body that is bold to come/ Across clearings," together with the positioning of "Across clearings" at the start of a new stanza, give a sense of sudden energy as the fox emerges into the open.

The most memorable image forms the poem's climax: "With a sudden sharp hot stink of fox/ It enters the dark hole of the head." The fox has realized its symbolic status as metaphor for thought. The thought fills the expectant vacancy that has been the poet's consciousness until now. The image is intensely violent, evoking speed, flavor, temperature, and smell.

Two images introduced at the poem's beginning and repeated at the end reflect its circular journey: from the everyday world, into the imaginative world, then back into the everyday world enriched by the gift of the imagination, the poetic composition. The image of the still-ticking clock, echoing the third line of the poem, recalls one to the world of time and space into which creation manifests. "The window is starless still," also a repeated image, brings one back full circle to the unchanging eternity that preceded the coming of the thought-fox and continues undiminished after the event. "The page is printed"—referring to the page one has read—resolves the central metaphor. The thought-fox has found its fulfillment in the completed poem.

Themes and Meanings

In his essay "Capturing Animals" (*Poetry Is*, 1967), Ted Hughes recalls his boyhood hunting expeditions with his brother. Hughes's job was to retrieve the many different creatures that his brother shot. When he was fifteen, however, his attitude to animals changed. He gave up hunting around the same time that he began to write poems.

It was several years before he realized that "my writing poems might be partly a continuation of my earlier pursuit. Now I have no doubt. The special kind of excitement, the slightly mesmerized and quite involuntary concentration with which you make out the stirrings of a new poem in your mind, then the outline, the mass and color and clear final form of it, the unique living reality of it in the midst of the general lifelessness, all that is too familiar to mistake." It is hunting, he wrote, and the poem is a new type of creature. "The Thought-Fox" was the first of Hughes's many animal poems. He says, "It is about a fox, obviously enough, but a fox that is both a fox and not a fox. . . . It is both a fox and a spirit." The poem is a clear expression of his notion that writing poetry is a kind of hunting, an attempt to capture the unique essence of an experience or an object.

According to Hughes, a poem, like the fox, comes of its own volition. Also like the fox, it comes shyly, "warily," and step by step. The implication is that it could easily be frightened away at any stage. In fact, in his essay "Learning to Think" (also in *Poetry Is*), Hughes describes how his experience of angling taught him to write poetry. His technique to catch fish was to keep perfectly still and allow his mind to settle on the float, which would attract the fish. Similarly, the would-be poet must first learn to still his mind on an object in order to catch the myriad thoughts that gradually attach themselves to it.

"The Thought-Fox" embodies Hughes's vision of poetic creation—that a poem, before it takes on a manifest form on the page, has a life of its own, independent of the individualized self of the poet. The poet's role is impersonal. He only has to stay quiet and alert, to be receptive to the poem. Then he can capture it as it emerges from the depths of uncreated reality and delicately makes its way into conscious awareness.

Hughes shares his vision of the creative process with the English Romantics, who commonly viewed poets as channels through whom inspiration flowed from a transcendent source. Hughes's unique contribution to this tradition is his ability to clothe profound metaphysical truths in simple, precise language and concrete images from nature.

Claire Robinson

A THOUSAND MILES OF STARS

Author: Walter McDonald (1934-   )
Type of poem: Lyric
First published: 1998; collected in *All Occasions*, 2000

The Poem

Walter McDonald's "A Thousand Miles of Stars" consists of four eight-line stanzas written in rhythmic free verse of four to six beats per line. A lyrical reflection, it focuses on the changes in personal values that come with years and experience. The speaker first describes, with comic irony, his youthful, romantic vision of his place and potential in the world. He then contrasts this speculation with the more down-to-earth vision that characterizes his maturity. Although the things he values have changed with age and circumstance, his passion for life and the world in which he lives remains.

The poem begins with the speaker's memory that he thought he would "need a thousand sweethearts" when he became a famous rodeo rider. So great would be his wealth and fame that he would pass his days in "villas in Italy,/ Geneva, Tahiti." Not only humans but also animals would respond to him with love and devotion. "Palominos" would nudge his fist for sugar; dogs would call him master "with their tails"; and even the more exotic creatures of his romantic retreats, "leopards" and "monkeys," would do "amazing tricks" to please him. His toucans would welcome him home with their singing.

Such were the dreams that, after a long day in the saddle, the young cowboy would enjoy in the bunkhouse. The excitement of "straddling a black,/ two-thousand-pound bull" with "a thousand fans cheering" had understandably filled him with youthful arrogance. If his rodeo riding had not done so, his pursuits after the rodeo would have. He enjoyed the affections of his admirers on the barroom dance floor, with their "purple eyes/ and perfumed, tequila breath." His thinking about such relationships went no deeper than the passions and clichés of country songs, "old western words from a jukebox."

The third stanza moves from memory to the narrative present. No longer a young rodeo rider or barroom favorite, the narrator is now "sixty" and "stiff." When he does ride at all, it is on the back of an old, fat gelding. His desire is no longer for rodeo fame or the pleasures of the barroom, but for the simple comforts of family life. The prizes he treasures are not rodeo awards to "stack on the mantle," but his grandchildren. When they visit the ranch, he and his wife hold them close until they leave, and they stand waving goodbye until the children have disappeared down the dirt road.

After the two "hobble" back to the porch in stanza 4, they reflect upon the moments spent, cherishing each child's action, possibly as they once relished the details of the speaker's rodeo performances. Their feelings are not for their grandchildren alone, though: In the dark they "rock and hold each other," enjoying being together on the ranch, listening to the sounds of the night. In the final image, dogs bark, a windmill turns, and the two listen to "the far-off roar of stars." The two seem to be in love not only with each other but also with their place in the universe.

Forms and Devices

The overall structure of this poem hinges on the narrator's shifting focus, since that contrast demonstrates how values and perceptions change with age. The details of the first two stanzas portray the romantic vision of youth with hyperbole and ironic overstatement. The narrator will "need" a thousand sweethearts—a testament not only to his passion for excitement but also to his perceived virility. His lifestyle expectations, too, are wildly exaggerated. In his dreams, he will live among the scenes that real cowboys experience only in travel films or brochures—Italy, Geneva, Tahiti. The creatures that surround him will not be horses and cattle—creatures of real ranch life—but monkeys, leopards, and toucans—creatures of his imagination.

The aural system of the poem, too, supports the ironic tone McDonald is creating. Typically his poems are a richly woven tapestry of sound, and this one is no exception. In the first two stanzas, however, he sacrifices his customary subtlety to engage an aural extravagance that meshes with the young man's romantic dreams and at the same time confirms the speaker's ironic distance. The images of youth are a lavish intertwining of internal rhyme, alliteration, assonance, and consonance. For example, he "thought [he'd] need a thousand sweethearts"; the dogs he envisions would be "wagging, dragging my slippers"; in his imagination "Palominos pranced," then "nudged . . . nibbling my palm"; "monkeys [would do] amazing tricks to please me," and "red and blue toucans . . . cooing" would be "free to fly in and out."

The syntax also enhances the poem's effect. Two rhetorical questions serve as a bridge from the past to the present. In stanza 2 the speaker asks, "What did I know, straddling a black,/ two-thousand-pound bull twisting and bucking,/ a thousand fans cheering the cowboy and the bull?" The implied answer is that he knew nothing or very little. The reader wonders what he knew little about: The contrast presented later in the poem indicates that he knew nothing about what would take on lasting value in his life.

The speaker then asks, "how could I whisper more// than old western words from a jukebox?" As a youth, he valued wealth, fame, and the dance-floor sweethearts they would bring him. He had not, he realizes now, ever considered relationships more deeply than the values expressed in country songs. That his mount of choice is now a "fat gelding" suggests his current opinion of sexual appeal and virility. The bucking bulls of his youth have been exchanged for a castrated horse.

The syntactic patterns also suggest his passion for his grandchildren and for the life that he and his wife share. Beginning in the third stanza, line 1, the narrator reflects upon his grandchildren in a cumulative sentence that continues for six lines, fifty-four words. This is followed by a similarly elongated sentence in which the two remember the actions of their grandchildren, six more lines, fifty-two words. These are followed with the simple sentence, "We rock and hold each other," a phrase that reads all the more emphatically because it creates a sudden jolt after two long, emotion-packed units.

The poem's closing image is a peaceful pastoral scene of the couple sitting on the porch in the deep quiet of the evening. They "listen hard" and hear dogs barking a mile away, the turning of the windmill, and, last, the "far-off roar of stars." The image at first seems homely enough, but the sounds are presented in climactic order based on rarity. The night-time barking of dogs is common; considerably more rare is the sound of turning windmills; rarer still, however, is the experience the speaker communicates through synesthesia (the description of one kind of sensation in terms of another): They listen to "the far-off roar of stars." As they watch the stars, something about their superabundance, as indicated by the poem's title, pushes the speaker to imagine them figuratively as sound as well as sight. The effect is an image more exotic, in its own way, and more full of wonder, than the romantic vision of the young cowboy.

Themes and Meanings

McDonald is well known as a western regionalist. Many of his poems are set in the hardscrabble country of the American West, and his lines are often rich with the details of ranch life. Thus the rodeo and cattle range setting here is a familiar one. Yet McDonald is also a poet of everyday life, and works focusing on family relationships form another significant portion of his canon. In this poem, the two mental regions come together as the cowboy ages, allowing the development of two themes: loving relationships and the apparently rapid passing of time.

The love that the speaker feels for his grandchildren is central to the poem. They are the prizes that have replaced the rewards of the rodeo ring. He and his wife hold them to their chests and only reluctantly let them go. The smallest actions of the children become heroic in their telling: "the toddler" took a fall but climbed back to the porch "giggling." They learned to rope surprisingly quickly. The teenagers made "long-distance calls . . . to boys."

However, the love for the grandchildren is not the only love shown. In stanza 3 the point of view suddenly shifts to the first person plural—the voice becomes the original speaker along with his wife. The implication is that the love that is felt for the grandchildren is a love the couple share together, that it becomes a strand of their love for each other. In essence, they become one, in stark contrast to the speaker's earlier romances on the dance floor. This is highlighted with the emphatic "We rock and hold each other."

The perceived speed with which life passes is also a part of the emotional complex of the poem. The memories of youth are vividly recalled, implying that they seem recent. Change feels sudden: With two rhetorical questions, roughly forty years pass. In the last image, even the windmill is said to be "spinning fast." Finally, if the stars are metaphorically roaring, they are most likely roaring as they whirl through space. Time and change are the natural way of things.

It is worth noting that the speaker feels no shame for a youthful, romantic view of himself. Such feelings seem as natural to him (witness his granddaughters' calls to boys) as the more mature excitements of old age. The narrator's passion for his life is no less, and maybe no less romantic, than that of his earlier self. Now, however, his feelings are precipitated less by his imagination and more by the realities of an everyday existence.

William Jolliff

THREE FLOORS

Author: Stanley Kunitz (1905-   )
Type of poem: Lyric
First published: 1971, in *The Testing-Tree*

The Poem
"Three Floors" is a short formal poem; divided into four rhyming stanzas, it resembles a ballad or hymn. The title suggests the interior of a house and raises the question of what is happening on each floor. The reader is thus led to expect some contrast or tension.

"Three Floors" is written in the past tense, evoking the memories of one specific night. It establishes an immediate emotional context by opening with the word "Mother." The mother, however, is described only in metaphorical terms as "a crack of light/ and a gray eye peeping." Instead of seeing or experiencing the mother, the reader is asked to have the visual experience of a small boy who is lying in bed at night, aware of his mother as a physical presence outside the door. There is a sense of intrusion. The "I" of the poem—the small boy speaking—breathes hard, pretending to be asleep. He refuses to acknowledge her or to respond. He will not allow her to pry into his thoughts.

The second stanza of the poem introduces another "floor," downstairs, beneath the boy's bedroom. This stanza begins with the word "Sister." The house contains, at this point, a family. This stanza further expands the possible relationships, because the sister has a fiancé—a "doughboy," or soldier—who has recently asked her to marry him. The boy listens as she plays the piano, one sound over and over, *Warum*. This might be the title of a popular tune of the time, but it certainly uses the device of onomatopoeia, reproducing the rumble of the piano as the boy might hear it from the floor above. The word means "why" in German.

The third stanza presents the third floor—the attic, which contains a trunk referred to as one "whose lock a boy could pick." Inside are a hat (specifically a "red Masonic hat") and a walking stick. By the end of the stanza, the reader has not been told to whom these items belong, but there is a strong suspicion that it might be the father, who has until now been absent from the poem. This raises the question of why the objects are locked away. The final stanza recalls how the boy, after pretending to be asleep, sits "bolt upright" in bed and sees his father "flying." The final two lines are almost surreal: "the wind was walking on my neck,/ the windowpanes were crying." Obviously, there is a storm, and the boy, with the kind of hallucinatory vision that comes from a combination of darkness and fear and desire, sees everything in a new way. Because wind does not walk and windowpanes do not cry, the reader realizes that the father's flying is also the product of the child's imagination. The reader is left to assume that the father's absence is due to death or desertion and that the boy's need for a father leads him to the moment when, in the midst of the stormy night, he can actively conjure his presence.

In sixteen lines, "Three Floors" has peopled the house with ghosts: The mother is sensed but not seen, the sister is remembered as a scrap of song, and the few vestiges of the father are locked in a trunk. The small boy is literally caught in the middle between the past (his father's loss) and the future (his sister's marriage, his own manhood). The poet re-creates the various claims on his affections as he presents the immediate moment of the poem—the darkness and the visionary sight of his father flying. His private thoughts are depicted as turbulent, guilty, and psychologically necessary. The reader is drawn into the poem's emotional complex in such a way that childhood itself, with all its confusions, is awakened in memory.

Forms and Devices

Stanley Kunitz is a master craftsman, writing both formal and free verse. "Three Floors" is formal in that it has regular four-line, rhymed stanzas and a dominant iambic beat. Rhythm is one of the poem's essential elements—Kunitz's ear is so skillful that the variations in the strict iambic foot become a part of the meaning. In fact, the first line, "Mother was a crack of light," is trochaic, opening the poem with a melancholy tone. It is not until the third line, with its rigidly metrical iambic tetrameter, that the basic rhythm of the poem is established.

From this point on, the poem is a study in variation. Alternating between four- and three-stress lines (with slight differences in syllabic count), each stanza is at once familiar and surprising. There is a contrast between the strong masculine end rhymes of "hand/grand" and "pick/stick" and the haunting feminine rhymes of "peeping/sleeping" and "flying/crying." These variations call attention to themselves and help to establish meaning by forcing the reader to linger over certain words. For example, "whose lock a boy could pick" is iambic trimeter, but the strong beat is muted so that each word must be read in a slower, more measured cadence.

Over the solid warp of the poem—a strict stanzaic and rhythmical structure placed there to support the sweep of memory and imagination—the poem is a sea of shifting images and associations. It moves from bedroom to sitting room to attic, then returns, full circle, to the bedroom. The "characters" shift as well, moving from mother to sister to trunk to father. The sight of the mother behind the open slit of doorway gives way to a kind of wild, visionary experience in which the father is seen to be equally real. Inside and outside become one. All distinctions are blurred, much as the moments before sleep blur reality and dream.

A blend of the literal and the metaphorical, "Three Floors" is filled with specific detail (such as the sound of the sister's playing or the objects in the trunk) as well as the more ephemeral references to each individual parent. The mother becomes a "crack of light" and an "eye," as though her essence could be summed up in those two images. Similarly, the wind and windowpanes are anthropomorphized so that they seem more human than the actual humans who inhabit the poem. Certain words take on collateral meaning: Both "bolt" and "crack" suggest the storm outside as well as the internal circumstances.

The final couplet creates a sense of closure by returning to the strict meter of the poem and, at the same time, by moving into the realm of fantasy. In this way, the make-believe sleep of the first stanza is contrasted with, and equated to, the wide-awake vision of the last. The poem thus feels complete in its metrical package even as it opens up a strange emotional world where nothing is quite what it seems.

Themes and Meanings

"Three Floors" is one of several poems in which Stanley Kunitz mentions his father—or rather the felt absence of his father. The most famous of these are "Father and Son," published in 1944, and "The Portrait," which was collected in *The Testing-Tree* (1971) along with "Three Floors." In the earliest of these poems, Kunitz searches for his drowned father beneath the surface of a pond, but the father turns a blank face to him. In the two later poems, the need for a father figure is contrasted with vivid memories of the mother—a mother who jealously and even angrily denies the child any access to his father.

Loss is at the heart of this poem. The mother is hardly real as she hovers on the other side of the door. The sister is soon to be lost, and the child is all too aware of her impending marriage. The father has never been there at all; he becomes a mystery to be solved. The child picks at the metaphorical lock of the family, hoping to discover his own identity. In the trunk, he finds only a hat that suggests a secret adult male society and a walking stick, with its implications of freedom and mobility. These powerful absences add up to a very real (if imagined) presence.

In the final stanza, the poem itself becomes a vehicle for the imagination, creating a father for the son. The child adds the possessive pronoun and the lowercase ("my father"—he cannot call him "Father") as he wills him into being. The father is "flying," though. Even as he is apprehended, he seems to be leaving. In a frenzy, the child perceives an elemental loss where the external world reflects his own amorphous grief.

Behind loss is a question: *Warum*—why? The sister plays the song, almost absentmindedly, on the piano, thinking of her soldier and the war. The question, along with its rhythm, pervades the poem, establishing a fatal sense that some things have no reason. The father's death, the mother's anger, the child's internalized conflict—nothing makes sense. Without an answer, the child is fated to ask this question throughout his life. The imaginative act, then, is seen as a way of discovering meaning—of making a divided house, however briefly, whole.

Judith Kitchen

THE THREE MAGI

Author: Stanisław Barańczak (1946-   )
Type of poem: Narrative
First published: 1977, as "Trzej Królowie," in *Ja wiem, że to niesluszne: Wiersze z lat 1975-1976*; English translation collected in *The Weight of the Body*, 1989

The Poem

"The Three Magi" is a poem of twenty-four lines of varied length. The title refers to the wise men who visited the infant Jesus with gifts denoting kingship and holiness and whose coming is traditionally celebrated on Epiphany (January 6). "Epiphany" literally means "shining forth" and refers both to the holiday and, more generally, to any moment of profound insight. The title is sardonic, comparing the Magi with the three government agents who appear at the door of the man to whom the poem is addressed; however, the police who come to the door of the "you" of the poem bring only threats and despair rather than gifts. The poem has no epiphany in the usual sense of an important realization, just as there are no gifts. There is also no trace of respect or honor given to the recipient of the agents' visit. The agents of the old Communist government of Poland have come to question the man, evidently an author, perhaps about the book he tries to push under the couch without their noticing it. At the end of the poem, the officers, instead of departing from the author as the wise men departed from Jesus, take the man away for questioning, perhaps never to return (hinted at ominously by the last line, "Wasn't this a vast world").

The poem reflects the difficulty under which many writers found themselves during the days of Soviet domination of Eastern Europe, when writing the "wrong" things could be disastrous and being caught with banned books was a crime. It is noteworthy that although the original collection of poetry in which "The Three Magi" first appeared is in Polish, it was first published in Paris, France. The oppression Stanisław Barańczak describes was so real he could not publish his work in his native country; not only would official censors have prevented the book's publication, but also Barańczak himself would have been subject to arrest and probable imprisonment by the government.

Forms and Devices

Most of the force of the poem comes from contrasting the traditional image of the Adoration of the Magi with the unwelcome visit of the coldly polite but intrusive agents. The Magi are conventionally pictured as coming at night following a star; the officers arrive just as night gives way to morning, jarring the author they have come to interrogate from a sound sleep by banging at his door. The only star these "Magi" have is on an official identification they flash at the door while demanding entry. Like the wise men, whose visit is commemorated in the first week of the year, the police always seem to come shortly after New Year's Day. The Magi (called *Królowie*, or

"Kings," in Polish) are the representatives of the world outside the village of Bethlehem who came to reverence and acknowledge Christ. In a parallel fashion, the government agents, although not kings, come into the writer's home from the large, outside world of Communist bureaucracy as official representatives of the government and its disapproval to acknowledge him as a source of dangerous ideas who must be silenced. While Mary and Joseph are usually pictured as being dazzled by the visit of the wealthy foreigners, the recipient of the agents' visit is dazed and shaken by the abrupt intrusion of the highly paid government officers. Further heightening the satiric comparison, the man is compared to a newborn baby, helpless and unable to think clearly when the agents begin to interrogate him.

The biblical Magi brought three gifts: gold, frankincense (sometimes generically called "incense"), and myrrh. The man, contemplating his visitors, thinks distractedly that they indeed have gold (the expensive watches they wear) and incense (the cigarettes, implicitly foreign and costly, they smoke) but that they have no myrrh. Like many modern readers of the biblical story, he even is unsure what myrrh is and promises himself that he will look it up in a dictionary when he has the time. This promise suggests a sad irony, since the man is unlikely to be able to do so for a long while. Just as Mary and Joseph had to flee to Egypt to escape King Herod's persecution after the Magi left them, the "Magi" visiting the man insist "You'll come/ with us, sir," interrupting his thoughts about myrrh. While Mary and Joseph reached safety by leaving their homeland, the man is taken from his home into custody by his visitors.

The poet also suggests a contrast with the conventional images of the Magi, depicted by artists since the Middle Ages as wearing rich, vibrant colors appropriate to royalty visiting a newborn king. This image, unspecified in the poem but so much part of the conventional image as to be suggested simply by the reference, is contrasted with the colorlessness of the cold January morning on which the well-dressed but mundane agents arrive. The light is gray, and, as the man is led out, he muses first on the whiteness of the snow and then on the blackness of the car into which they load him. Other than the gold of their watches, no other color is mentioned in the poem. Instead, everything is bleak and uninspiring. The bleakness is further emphasized by repeating the same sentence structure three times: "Isn't this a" gray dawn, white snow, or black Fiat. This leads to the final thought, which changes the thrice-repeated wording into the past tense: "Wasn't this a vast world."

Themes and Meanings

"The Three Magi" contrasts a well-loved part of the Christmas story, particularly popular in dominantly Catholic Poland, with the cruelty and fear associated with an oppressive government. The worship and nobility of the Magi are set against the official coldness of the representatives of the dictatorial regime. The exotic, royal presence of the Magi also contrasts with the ordinariness of the men who come on the gloomy morning, emphasized by the man's recognition that one of the visitors is an old schoolmate who has changed little from days gone by but who now treats him without warmth or recognition. What should be, in any normal situation, a joyful reunion is aloof and unfriendly, heightening the quiet brutality of a government that operates by such tactics and making an ordinary man seem less appealing or impressive than commonplace humanity. Although prosperous, the agents lack any trace of the regal qualities usually associated with the true Magi.

A further grim threat to be feared is implied by the aftermath of the Magi's visit in the Bible. The foreign visitors unintentionally awaken Herod's jealousy, causing him to send his soldiers to kill all the boy babies of Bethlehem so he will be sure he has slain the infant king the Magi were seeking. Mary and Joseph barely escape, but there is much suffering in the village of Bethlehem as those who remained mourn their murdered children. This suggests a dark future for the unfortunate detainee, for, in his case, the government representatives did find the person they were sent out to apprehend. Like Herod and his soldiers, the government the agents represent believes any measure, however drastic or callous, is justified if it maintains the existing state of affairs. "The Three Magi" is not entirely harsh, however. The episode of the man wondering about myrrh and resolving to find out more about it provides a lighter touch, for many readers have wondered about the same thing. Similarly, his musing that his old friend might have gained a little weight reminds the reader of normal experience. In the end, though, the softer, almost amusing side of the poem reinforces the overall sense of unfairness as the man with whom the reader has come to sympathize is carried off by his visitors to an uncertain future.

The poem was dedicated to Lech Dymarski, a writer, theatrical figure, and critic of the government of Poland during the middle and late 1970's. The "you" of the poem, the man who is taken away, is in a position in which both Dymarski and Barańczak were fully aware they could have found themselves, for writers were frequently questioned by the government in Poland at that time. The interrogations could end with only minor punishments such as reprimands and fines, but there was always a risk of imprisonment, exile, or worse. It is the threat that men and women such as Barańczak and Dymarski faced that Barańczak commemorates and describes in "The Three Magi."

Paul James Buczkowski

THREE MOMENTS IN PARIS

Author: Mina Loy (1882-1966)
Type of poem: Poetic sequence/satire
First published: 1915; collected in *The Last Lunar Baedeker,* 1982

The Poem

"Three Moments in Paris" is a three-poem sequence in free verse, each poem numbered and titled. "One O'Clock at Night" contains twenty-nine lines, and both "Café du Néant" and "Magasins du Louvre" contain thirty-six. Stanza lengths vary in all three poems. The point of view also varies; Loy uses a first-person voice in the first and third poems, and a third-person voice in the second poem. The shift in voice can best be understood in the light of the title's significance and of developments in art at the beginning of the twentieth century. Cubist painting rendered its subjects as collages of geometric shapes; Futurist painters added dynamic juxtapositions and urban imagery to this approach. Like Gertrude Stein, Loy applied these visual concepts to her writing. In "Three Moments in Paris," she creates a verbal collage that satirically examines modern male-female relationships in the wake of increasing social autonomy for women.

The female speaker in "One O'Clock at Night" is leaning against her lover in the chair they are sharing, and she is falling asleep as he argues about Futurist aesthetics with his brother. She awakens when her lover clears his throat and is able to catch "the thread of the argument." The speaker then claims that its issues—"dynamic composition" and "plastic velocity"—mean little to her, and her waking signals her recognition of the difference between men and women. The focus of the poem is on the nature of that difference. The poem abruptly closes with the words of the male lover, who cites the speaker's exhaustion as a reason to end the argument and go home.

In "Café du Néant" ("Café of Emptiness"), the field of vision shifts from the café as a whole, to a pair of young lovers, to an individual female. A sense of futility permeates the poem. The decadent atmosphere of the café reflects the state of human relationships found there. Communication between the sexes has decayed into lies, silence, and meaningless language. Behaviors fall into predictable roles, in which the male is controlling and the female passively tolerates his control. The female figure who closes the poem presents an image of death in contrast to the modern life outside the café.

"Magasins du Louvre" ("The Shops of the Louvre") returns to a first-person speaker, though the reader is not aware of the speaker's participation in the scene until late in the poem. The opening line, "All the virgin eyes in the world are made of glass," is repeated twice—a third of the way through the poem and at its end. It provides closure, serving as a refrain that draws attention to the poem's emphasis on perception. The poem places readers in a shop where lines of dolls sit throughout the store and hang from the ceiling. Within this surreal atmosphere, the speaker observes two apparently unrelated events. In the first event, a man sets out to flirt with and possibly harass the shop girl. In the second, the speaker observes two cheaply dressed young women who examine the dolls and then exchange knowing glances; they see themselves, like dolls, as commodities to be bought in a sexual marketplace. The poem juxtaposes blind innocence and the perception that comes with experience.

Forms and Devices

Several characteristics associated with free verse give "Three Moments in Paris" a modern look and sound: lack of exact rhyme and end rhyme; lack of consistent line length and meter; lack of punctuation; extra spacing within the line; sentence fragments; and words that are completely capitalized. Assonance, alliteration, and slant rhymes replace exact rhyme, and at times these are found, along with the use of anaphora, at the beginning rather than at the end of the line. Loy's line lengths vary from one word to seventeen. The spacing within the lines, which at times creates the pause normally provided by punctuation, and the use of sentence fragments contribute to the poems' collage effect. Urban settings, characteristic of this sequence and of most of Loy's poems, provide another modernizing touch. Loy renders her scenes with precise description and multisyllabic diction that at times draws on a scientific or intellectual vocabulary.

The paradox in the opening lines of "One O'Clock at Night"—"Though you had never possessed me/ I had belonged to you since the beginning of time"—suggests the irony and satire to come. Although the speaker claims she understands nothing about her lover's Futurist argument, the poem is clearly influenced, in both form and content, by Futurism's precepts, most of which were set down by Loy's one-time lover, Filippo Marinetti. Thus, the poem's literal depiction of a woman intimidated by male intellect is an ironic facade. It is not Futurism the speaker fails to understand, but rather the male tendency to engage in endless intellectual disputes. The poem's subtle satire comes at the expense of the speaker's lover and his brother.

The juxtapositions in "Café du Néant" are central to the poem's irony. In a café where candlelit tables look like coffins and lovers wearing black resemble corpses, Loy collides images of light and darkness; youth and decay; stale values and modern ones; and artistic pretension and everyday living. Finally, life and death become capitalized emblems of the exaggerated, pretentious behavior of the café patrons. Given the bohemian atmosphere, the patrons could be parodies of *fin de siècle* artists and intellectuals who, like the bourgeoisie they reject, rely on conventional role-playing in their courtship.

"Magasins du Louvre," which opens and closes with the same line and is thus an envelope poem, also draws heavily on juxtaposition. The innocence suggested by the dolls provides a striking contrast to the sexually experienced "cocottes" (prostitutes) in the shop and to the lecherous man who pursues the shop girl. This juxtaposition invites comparisons to William Blake's "Songs of Innocence" and "Songs of Experience," though Loy's poem is thoroughly modernized in that it deals with sexuality from a woman's point of view. Here, as in all three of the poems, Loy allows the juxtapositions to offer their significance without providing authorial explanation. Although satire is a didactic form, Loy manages to produce satire in a very nondidactic way.

Themes and Meanings

Like a number of early twentieth century women poets, ranging in style from Dorothy Parker and Edna St. Vincent Millay to H. D. (Hilda Doolittle) and Laura Riding, Mina Loy was concerned with the nature of romantic attachment between men and women. Why, in an age that seemed otherwise so modern, did men remain dominant in relationships while women continued to be overly dependent upon them? This age-old "battle between the sexes" was no longer limited to husbands and wives; it now included lovers outside marriage as well as writers and artists of both sexes positioning themselves on the intellectual landscape. Loy's response to this issue was somewhat complicated by her attraction to Futurism, with its underlying strain of misogyny. Although she would later reject this aspect of Futurism, Loy appears to hold both sexes accountable in "Three Moments in Paris."

An emphasis on vision, through the use of withheld and explicit images, pervades all three poems in the sequence, suggesting that the first step in the transformation from flawed relationships to successful ones is clear perception. The female speaker in "One O'Clock at Night" cannot recognize the differences between men and women until she awakes and has to adapt herself to the male world of intellectual argument. Yet given the poem's irony regarding the speaker's knowledge, even these differences are satirized, since the poem is itself an argument against male posturing.

The lover's eyes in "Café du Néant" are also eyes lined with kohl; their darkness parallels the atmosphere of decay that permeates the café and its patrons. Unable to see themselves clearly, the patrons are doomed to repeat their old patterns of courtship even as modern life, in the form of a cab, moves on outside the café. Both men and women participate in a *fin de siècle* facade that offers little relevance to male-female relationships in the second decade of the century.

Three sets of eyes appear in "Magasins du Louvre." The eyes of the dolls are the "virgin eyes of the world," suggesting not only blindness among the sexually inexperienced but also that there is "nothing" to see "through the human soul." All humans have is what the physical world provides them. Thus, the next two sets of eyes—those of the cocottes and those of the speaker who observes them—are all too human. Embarrassed by the juxtaposition their presence in the doll shop produces, these human eyes become averted and secretive, mirroring the type of communication that typifies and complicates male-female relationships. At the same time, the mutual recognition that both female innocence and female experience via sexuality are salable provides a Joycean epiphany in the poem: What passes for modern love remains strangely tied to old habits.

"Three Moments in Paris" sketches a world of romance as oblique and difficult to understand as any reality of romance one is likely to encounter. Yet Loy's poem functions within the best tradition of satire. Clearly embedded in its images of boredom, decay, and avoidance is a voice that insists on a better, though yet undefined, alternative to love as it is generally understood.

Rhonda Pettit

THRUSHES

Author: Ted Hughes (1930-1998)
Type of poem: Lyric
First published: 1960, collected in *Lupercal*

The Poem

"Thrushes" paints a picture of birds as efficient, instinctive killing machines. The poet is observing some thrushes on his lawn; the observations lead him to contrast them to human beings, such as himself, whose best acts seem produced by the suppression of such energies as the birds display, and at enormous cost.

The poet looks at the thrushes hunting for food, such as worms, slugs, and beetles, in his yard. Normally, thrushes are associated with domesticity or song, certainly with nature tamed. Instead, Hughes sees them, no less than the hawk in his poem "Hawk Roosting" (also in *Lupercal*), as ruthless killers. Each bird is doing its natural thing in its pride of life as it drags "out some writhing thing," which it devours in "a ravening second."

He wonders what motivates this single-minded ruthless purpose. Is it, he asks, the way they are programmed to some point of evolutionary perfection? Have they been taught by equally skillful elders, or is there some survival of the species instinct, driven by "a nestful of brats"? Perhaps it is genius: an almost indefinable term, but one which reminds him of the composer Wolfgang Amadeus Mozart, who seemed to have superhuman ability to produce perfect music apparently without trying.

His questioning thoughts turn on the phrase "automatic/ Purpose" toward the shark. The shark's automatic purpose is to attack the smell of blood, even if it is its own blood pouring from its side. The shark then devours itself. It is "too streamlined for any doubt." In other words, such efficiency is questionable. The same movement is seen in "Hawk Roosting," where the hawk's megalomania is reminiscent of human megalomaniacs such as Adolf Hitler and makes readers withdraw any admiration from the bird.

Here however, Hughes pushes the poem in a different direction, by explicitly contrasting animal with human (presumably, Mozart's genius is somehow seen as inhuman). "With a man it is otherwise," he starkly begins the third and final stanza. Humans are capable of "Heroisms on horseback," in the traditional notion of bravery, where any notion of violence is suppressed. Yet such heroic acts are beyond humanity's usual mode of being, which is bound by daily routine. Such heroisms are, like the carver's patiently working "at a tiny ivory ornament/ For years," in a sense outside of people. Such acts achieve worth or value almost impersonally. They are rare, unlike the animals' daily acts of perfect killing.

In conclusion, the poet sees the typical nature of humankind as a continually frustrated search for personal integration within a civilized context, signaled by such widely divergent markers as art, heroism, and "desk-diary" routine. The search is never-ending as "the distracting devils" of "Orgy and hosannah"—unrestrained lust and unrestrained joy—assail humans from their unconscious as if from hell-fire and "black silent waters" from above, perhaps from the accusations of conscience. This is each person's confusion and yet also his or her nature. Ultimately, the poet leads readers from an apparent admiration of the simplicities of the bird to a cry that is both anguished and celebratory of the complexity of being human.

Forms and Devices

The poem consists of three eight-line unrhymed stanzas. In each stanza, six of the lines are roughly pentameter (five stresses per line), one line is lengthened by one or two extra feet, and the last line is shortened. In stanza 1, line 4 is lengthened to ensure a climax, with "with a start, a bounce, a stab," "bounce and stab" being repeated in line 7 as the typical movement of thrushes. In stanza 2, the lengthened line is the fifth, climaxing on the self-destructive nature of instinct in the shark. In the last stanza, the fifth line is again lengthened. As with the previous stanza, it is not end-stopped but rushes on, climaxing on human inner dividedness and dichotomy, in a patterned contrast to the shark's single-mindedness.

The final lines of the first two stanzas are dimeters and thus have a sound of finality. They are likewise contrasted to the final line of "Of black silent waters weep," where the line is extended to four stresses and significant alliteration, giving a slow and quite unexpected final cadence as the focus closes on the human condition.

As with much modern verse, the effect of the speaking voice is maintained by the large number of unstopped lines, particularly noticeable in stanza 2. The effect is to put the stress on the first syllable of the next line, a slightly explosive effect, running counter to the more rising meter of the last stanza. However, the suppressed energy within humanity is reenacted exactly in the sixth and seventh line of that stanza, as the run-on lines push the stress to the first syllables of the words "Furious" and "Orgy," reversing the rising meter of the other lines. Hughes's sureness of rhythmic effect is nowhere better illustrated.

The more the poem is analyzed, the more "poetic" it appears: Hughes consciously uses poetic devices in a highly developed way. The use of the violent alliteration in "start," "stab," "steel," and "stirrings" of the thrushes is contrasted with the softer alliteration in the words describing humankind: "worships," "what wilderness," "waters weep." In the first stanza, the repetition of "No" and "Nothing" already prefigures the contrast of animal to human with the human "indolent procrastinations" (with Latinate polysyllables) and "yawning stares"—perhaps the poet himself in the act of creating this poem.

The mode of the first stanza is statement; of the second, interrogation; of the third, exclamation. However, the modes are ambiguous: The interrogation of the second stanza resolves itself into statement, but, as has been noted, it is a statement that begins to undermine the certainties of the first stanza. In the third stanza, the exclamatory markers "how" and "what," as in "how loud and above/ what," could be read as a question: Does it have to be like this?

The imagery is striking, also, in the unromantic machine terms of the first two stanzas: "coiled steel," "Triggered," "bullet and automatic," and "streamlined," words that break traditional associations. It is, however, the sheer density of imagery and the un-expectedness of the final stanza that point to Hughes's originality as a poet, an origi-nality exploited in later volumes of verse, as *Wodwo* (1967) and *Crow* (1970, rev. 1972). The alliterative phrase "Heroisms on horseback" is dense with meaning, as is the equally alliterative metonymy "desk-diary at a broad desk," the word "broad" be-ing a note of brilliance, suggesting space, which is then contrasted abruptly with the "tiny ivory ornament" of the next line.

Themes and Meanings

Insofar as the poem is about nature, it must be termed Romantic, but certainly not in the Wordsworthian sense of a creation that inspires through beauty or pathos and wit-nesses to some divine purpose. Rather, it is the "Nature red in tooth and claw" that the Victorian poet Alfred, Lord Tennyson noted—a post-Darwinian nature of the survival of the fittest. In some of Hughes's poems in *Lupercal*, various humans are described as survivors through their animal-like energies or instincts. Here, however, Hughes seems more concerned to divide humanity from nature. As in a previous poem, "The Water-Lily," humans live in two worlds: the suppressed instinctual world, which be-comes for them "distracting devils," and the disciplined, civilized world, symbolized by the "desk-diary at a broad desk." In this Hughes echoes psychoanalyist Sigmund Freud's dictum that the price of civilization is the suppression of sex drives, as well as Carl Jung's awareness of the shadow side of humanity, which, if denied, becomes dia-bolical. More specifically, the man at the desk observing the thrushes becomes the poet himself, whose act of creating a poem is a disciplined act that "worships itself," yet at a psychological cost for him.

The poem echoes not only Tennyson but also D. H. Lawrence, who was similarly fascinated by the instinctive life force in animals, as well as Gerard Manley Hopkins, who celebrated the "thisness," the specificity, of each created thing. However, while Hopkins celebrated the wilderness in its wildness in poems such as "Rannoch by Glencoe," for Hughes, the "wilderness" is within each human. It is "Of black silent waters" that "weep" because they have been denied. In the denial, wilderness be-comes bewilderment. The poem thus explores dualism, dichotomy, and desire, rather than achieved, to-be-celebrated creation.

Like Lawrence and the Irish poet William Butler Yeats, Hughes looks back to the older Romantic tradition but manages to reapply it to the spiritual and emotional bankruptcy of modern Western civilization. The questioning of Freud's dictum on the price of civilization is clearly implicit in many of the poems in *Lupercal*; in this poem, it is explicit. Later volumes of Hughes went on to explore what humanity's latent vi-tality would look like reactively if released, even anarchically so. His final volumes returned to more traditional nature themes in some sort of achieved synthesis. The strength of "Thrushes" is that it already engages these major issues in a focused and powerful way.

David Barratt

THUS I RAN OUT OF THE WORD

Author: Nelly Sachs (1891-1970)
Type of poem: Lyric
First published: 1959, as "So ran ich aus dem Wort," in *Flucht und Verwandlung*; English translation collected in *The Seeker and Other Poems*, 1970

The Poem

"Thus I Ran Out of the Word" was first published in Nelly Sachs's *Flucht und Verwandlung* (1959; "flight and metamorphosis"). The book's central theme is transformation, and this poem, the last in the book, describes one person's transformation becoming complete. The "I" of the poem charts her passage from one world into another toward a "homecoming." The poem could be interpreted as a meditation on one's passage into death.

The first line is an abrupt decree, and it suggests a summing up. In fact, the speaker begins this poem practically in mid-sentence. In the line "Thus I ran out of the word," the reader senses resignation, acceptance, and a readiness to enter the "night/ with arms outspread." "The word" certainly has biblical connotations ("In the beginning was the Word . . . "), but here "word" might refer primarily to the speaker's self—that which she had been trying to create. To run out of words—language, communication, ideas—is essentially to lose one's identity. In this sense, the speaker's transformation begins with giving up ego, or consciousness of self.

The second stanza suggests some sort of preparation for the transformational journey taking place. "A piece of night" indicates partial reckoning with the night (death's representative?), and the "arms outspread" make a welcoming gesture. In another metaphor, however, the outstretched arms are imagined as a scale, the type with a dish on each side for balancing opposing weights. The scale "weigh[s] flights."

The motif of flight (both fleeing and soaring) is a common one in Sachs's poetry, but here "only a scale to weigh flights" is perplexing. This mysterious phrase could suggest that the night, personified, weighs (judges) the hardships of a person's life. Flight as escape is a recurring theme in Sachs's poetry and is possibly evoked here with reference to the many flights from persecution the Jewish people have had to endure. Is the traveler's past being examined to determine the reason for this next departure?

Perhaps to "weigh flights" is to gauge the extent of suffering. The calm voice of this stanza makes the speaker seem willing to accept what arrives with the night, as well as what has been lost, including "the word." Such unquestioning acceptance allows her to consider death—hers or that of others—without the prolonged and purposeless anguish that becomes in the end only frustrating.

In "this star-time/ sunk into dust/ with the fixed tracks," one finds a reference to a painful past. Dust and stars, recurring images in Sachs's poetry, symbolize the past; and the most important past event influencing her work is the Holocaust. Furthermore, the rigidity of "the fixed tracks" indicates an immobile, unchanging past: It cannot be undone, nor can (nor should) its suffering be forgotten. Nevertheless, Sachs's poem seems to suggest that in order to have a loving life and a death that is graceful, one must reconcile oneself with the past—not to forget it, but to absorb it, and thus be delivered from its painful hold.

Given this knowledge, it is right that stanza 2, describing the moment of transition, should lead to a state "without gesture of burden." The lines describe in their quiet tones a peaceful passing between worlds. In fact, the speaker seems fairly to be melting away. Her body disperses: "my shoulders . . ./ sail away." The harmony and balance are so apparent—"The lightness leaves me/ and the heaviness as well"—that this particular "homecoming" seems to be a welcome event, not a death to be feared at all. That it is "deep and dark" seems only to ease the transformation.

The last line feels like a weary traveler's sigh of relief to be home again. "Home," in the end, could be read as death, or perhaps only death of the ego—slipping into a different consciousness; it could even describe one of the simplest and most common transformations we experience: falling asleep. This intensely personal yet haunting poem, spoken in an almost ecstatic voice, attempts to describe a profound change in consciousness. It seems apparent from her poetry that one such moment in Sachs's life must have been when she summoned the strength to forgive death and its engineers for the suffering she witnessed while living through the Holocaust.

The paradox of the poem is that the poet must deal with language to communicate what her imagination has discovered, even after the opening line has announced that "the word" and its power are gone. The poet attempts to do what in the end is impossible: that is, to convey a moment of silence and nothingness by using her only tool, language.

Forms and Devices

In "Thus I Ran Out of the Word," Sachs uses devices common to all of her poetry. One immediately notices the poem's imagery, its intense yet enigmatic metaphors and symbols. The prominent symbol in this poem is night—personified perhaps as death, perhaps simply as a presence that indicates another realm of consciousness.

Present too in the imagery are two of Sachs's recurring images: stars and dust, as well as the "fixed tracks" and the scale—deeply intriguing images which do not easily yield to interpretation. Stars and dust in Sachs's poetic cosmology allude to the past, and perhaps "fixed tracks" does, too: events—history—that are fixed in the past and cannot be undone or denied. This interpretation fits the poem into the central theme of Sachs's canon: the Holocaust and how to deal with memories of it, and that it happened.

In this poem, Sachs tries to achieve a mood and tone that balance precariously between feverish cries and hushed, thoughtful pronouncement. The shortness of the lines helps achieve a feeling of immediacy, as does the absence of punctuation and capital letters. (Only the ends of the stanzas and the first and last lines of the poem are punctuated.) Thus the poem sounds as if it were being delivered almost breathlessly, excitedly, quickly before time runs out. The short lines create an agitated rhythm.

The stanza beginning "Now it is late" provides a good example. The sentences are run together in a rhythm of hurry and amazement. Use of the first person also enhances the feeling of intimacy and immediacy. The speaker is very much present, not withdrawn.

Sachs often uses cyclic forms in her work. "Thus I Ran Out of the Word" is a cyclic poem; it begins and ends with night, suggesting the process rather than the result of transformation. If content determines form, the poet's interest in a circular form makes sense. In her way of thought, neither state—life or death—has an ending; they flow into and out of each other. Life and death inform each other. Therefore, "The color of homecoming is always deep and dark." Homecoming can be repeated.

Themes and Meanings

In *Flucht und Verwandlung*, in which this poem was first published, the poet muses relentlessly about death, attempting to understand and celebrate its ties with and necessity to life. Some other titles (in translation) from the book are "Death," "End," "Far Away," "This Is the Dark Breath," and "What darknesses," which ends "Oh, no arrival/ without death." Sachs is fond of open-ended poems such as this latter one, because they allow one to stop short of violating a mystery (attempting to convey what cannot be conveyed). "Thus I Ran Out of the Word," with its peculiar beginning, which is also an end, seems to come from a previous thought. The poem's insistent energy comes from its effort to describe what one has already admitted cannot be described.

Despite the book's preoccupation with death, the mood of *Flucht und Verwandlung*, like the mood of "Thus I Ran Out of the Word," is not grim. Always thoughtful, and often illuminated by pain, but not fearful, the voice inside these poems is wide-eyed and hopeful. The poetry reaches continually into and through what Hans Magnus Enzensberger called "the speechless horror of the documentary reports [on the Nazi concentration camps]." The poet also wishes to get beyond raw anger and blind sorrow. One must transcend these emotions, however useful they are at first, to learn how to explore the positive side of death. In this poem, Sachs speaks almost ecstatically about acceptance of death.

"Writing is my mute outcry," said Sachs. Thus, despite its urgency, one finds a quietness approaching silence in this poem. Yet "Thus I Ran Out of the Word" also possesses the strong, clear voice of a person in grace who, until her death in 1970, patiently and lovingly continued to "till [her] acre/ behind the back of death" (from "But perhaps," in *Flucht und Verwandlung*).

JoAnn Balingit

THYRSIS

Author: Matthew Arnold (1822-1888)
Type of poem: Elegy
First published: 1866; collected in *New Poems*, 1867

The Poem

Matthew Arnold's "Thyrsis" is a pastoral elegy consisting of twenty-four ten-line stanzas. The stanza form of the poem is adapted from John Keats's "Ode to a Nightingale" (1819) and has the rhyme scheme *abcbcadeed.* In each stanza the lines are iambic pentameter except the sixth, which is iambic trimeter. Following the traditional conventions of the pastoral elegy, "Thyrsis" laments the death of Arnold's close friend and fellow poet Arthur Hugh Clough, who died at age forty-two in 1861. Clough is the "Thyrsis" of the poem, while Arnold refers to himself in the poem as Corydon. Although the poem is mainly concerned with the death of Clough, it also deals significantly with Arnold's love of Oxford, his belief in a spiritual quest for unity and totality, and his preoccupation with the modern Victorian world as a place of dehumanization, confusion, distraction, and futility.

The poem begins with Arnold's description of the landscape around Oxford, which he associates with his own youth and his early friendship with Clough. Returning to this beautiful countryside as an adult, the poet still feels its charm and loveliness, but he is haunted by the many changes he sees in it, and most of all he is haunted by Clough's absence. As Arnold or his persona walks from Oxford out into the surrounding country, he looks for a "signal-elm" that he and Clough as students associated with the wandering, questing figure of the "Scholar-Gipsy," who according to an old legend left Oxford to go in search of mystical powers among the gypsies and who was the subject of Arnold's earlier poem "The Scholar-Gipsy" (1853). For the young Arnold and Clough, as long as the tree stood it was a sign that the Scholar-Gipsy was still questing.

Initially failing to find the tree, Arnold meditates on how Clough and he were both driven to leave the pastoral innocence and idealism of Oxford, Arnold by economic necessity, Clough because of philosophical and moral doubts. Clough as Thyrsis left the "shepherds and the silly sheep," his "piping took a troubled sound," and he died amidst the "storms that rage outside our happy ground." Like a cuckoo despairing because of the passing of spring, Thyrsis flew away from Oxford into modernity and death, leaving Arnold, figured as the pastoral Corydon, alone.

Arnold notes that "when Sicilian shepherds lost a mate" they sang of their loss in pastoral elegies, but he is far from certain that such elegies can be effective still. Nevertheless, he wishes not only to lament the death of Thyrsis, but also to continue the quest that he and Thyrsis and the Scholar-Gipsy once shared.

Arnold recognizes that he and the landscape have changed, that the night is falling, and that life seems baffling and death almost attractive. For a moment he seems about to give up the quest for unity and illumination when, suddenly, he sees the "lone, sky-pointing tree." Although the tree cannot change the fact of Clough's death, it reminds Arnold of his friend's questing spirit and of their shared dream of the Scholar-Gipsy. Thus, it remains for him to resist despair and carry on alone their quest for wholeness in a fragmented world. The poem ends with Arnold's hope that Clough's spirit will remind him of this quest when he must return to London's "harsh, heart-wearying roar."

Forms and Devices

The most obvious of Arnold's technical achievements in "Thyrsis" is his effective use of the classical pastoral elegy. Although the ancient form first used by Theocritus and Moschus had been employed brilliantly by such earlier English poets as John Milton and Percy Bysshe Shelley, a subgenre which depends upon the expression of mourning using shepherds and elaborate pastoral conventions presents obvious problems that few poets have solved since Shelley.

Arnold's triumphant use of the form depends on a number of elements. First, Arnold vitalizes his pastoral elegy by making it, in a sense, modern. The world of pastoral innocence and beauty is throughout the poem contrasted with the distracted, tormented, and confused chaos of modern cities and modern political and religious conflict. Moreover, Arnold shows a kind of modern integrity in refusing to offer his readers the usual pastoral consolation for Clough's death. For Clough or Thyrsis there is no easy rebirth or resurrection; there is only Arnold's stoic determination to carry on the quest in Clough's absence.

Another way in which Arnold enlivens his classical form is through the Keatsian stanza and diction of his poem. The ten-line stanza of "Thyrsis" not only derives from Keats but also has a richness, elaborateness, and gravity of movement that rival Keats and yet are distinctly Arnoldian. So too the diction of the poem is Keatsian in its felicity, lushness, and sensuality. This is particularly evident in the remarkable treatment of flowers in the poem. Thus, Arnold celebrates spring, which brings "whitening hedges, and uncrumpling fern," and "blue-bells trembling by the forest-ways."

The harmonious combination of classical form, Romantic style, and modern philosophical perspective in "Thyrsis" is typical of Arnold's rich layering of textures in the poem. One can see this same quality reflected in his treatment of landscape in "Thyrsis." On one level, the landscape is appropriately and generally pastoral. It is rural, bucolic, and associated with shepherds and traditional country life. On another level, the landscape is concretely and specifically real. That is, it is a remarkably detailed and graphic evocation of actual Oxfordshire. Finally, the landscape is morally and philosophically symbolic. The flowers, hills, stars, night, and weather of the landscape symbolize movements of feeling, moral states of mind, decisions, losses, and victories. Of all of the symbols in Arnold's landscape, the most important is the signal-elm, whose survival symbolizes both the survival of Arnold and Clough's youthful dreams, the mythic figure of the questing Scholar-Gipsy, the quest itself, and Arnold's continued commitment to that quest.

Themes and Meanings

Throughout his poetic career Arnold was a writer of elegies. He wrote more than a dozen actual elegies, and many of his other poems have important elegiac elements. For Arnold, the elegy was the perfect form in which to express his distinctive personal blend of melancholy and stoicism. It also offered him a congenial form in which to lament the tragic realities of what he once referred to as "this strange disease of modern life." Of all of Arnold's elegies, "Thyrsis" is one of the greatest and most complex.

Arnold's theme in "Thyrsis" is not simply the loss of Arthur Hugh Clough. Rather, the poem is a lament for many kinds of loss: the lost paradise of Oxford, the loss of Arnold's youth, his and Clough's lost innocence, and the loss of meaning and direction in the society and culture of his day. Also, given that "Thyrsis" was Arnold's last important poem, it is a kind of elegy for his own career as a poet.

In much of his greatest poetry, "Dover Beach" (1867), "The Buried Life" (1852), "The Scholar-Gipsy" (1853), and "Stanzas from the Grande Chartreuse" (1855), Arnold is deeply concerned with his moment in history, with what he sees as the special problems, anxieties, and crises of modern Victorian life. Indeed, it may be said that Arnold's sense of angst, alienation, and dehumanization mark him as the first significant English poet of modern consciousness.

In "Thyrsis," Arnold's awareness of the conflict, storm, struggle, futility, and care of modernity makes his poem not simply an elegant imitation of the pastoral elegy or a tender tribute to a lost friend, but rather a lament for his entire age and civilization. In this context, Clough in Arnold's poem is treated as a painful and tragic example of just how deadly the soul- and life-destroying strife of the modern world can be. Although Arnold and Clough were close friends, they disagreed significantly about both life and poetry. Clough viewed Arnold and his poetry as in retreat from the demands of his age; Arnold felt that Clough was sacrificing both himself and his poetry to the age. In "Thyrsis," Arnold treats Clough with respect and love, but he underscores the waste of his engaged life.

Arnold's alternative to this engaged life forms another major theme in "Thyrsis," the theme of quest. For Arnold, the lonely, pure, personal quest represented by the Scholar-Gipsy and his signal-elm is the only alternative to the chaos and emptiness of the outer world. The precise object of the quest may seem vague ("A fugitive and gracious light he seeks/ Shy to illumine"), but the very act of spiritual questing offers a unity of purpose and an integrity of life that contrast powerfully with the "heart-wearying" conflict of ordinary life.

Arnold's powerful treatment of his major themes in "Thyrsis," loss, the tragedy of Victorian modernity, and the need for spiritual questing, makes this poem one of the great poetic works of the Victorian period. Along with such poems as Alfred, Lord Tennyson's *In Memoriam* (1850) and Robert Browning's "Childe Roland to the Dark Tower Came" (1855), "Thyrsis" defines a poetic age marked by post-Romantic sadness, a distinctly Victorian spiritual energy, and a philosophical angst which would help define literature for a century after Arnold.

Phillip B. Anderson

TIME AND MUSIC

Author: Janet Lewis (1899-1998)
Type of poem: Lyric
First published: 1929; collected in *Poems, 1924-1944*, 1950

The Poem

In the first of three four-line stanzas, the speaker of "Time and Music" establishes that Time, which medieval scholastic philosophers defined as the measure of motion, both permits music to exist and creates the silence into which it disappears: Thus, although time enables music to exist, every piece of music must come to an end and be overtaken by silence. In an article on Janet Lewis's poetry published in *Southern Review* (1987), Helen Trimpi offers an extended paraphrase of "Time and Music." In the poem, time is said to give being to music, according to Trimpi, even as it provides an end for melody, the ordering principle of music. Unlike a picture, a song is not a static, concrete object but always a temporal and temporary phenomenon.

The second stanza goes on to compare a melody, "riding" upon time, to a boat riding upon the waves; the comparison is continued in a second image of a bird flying through air until it disappears from sight. In the third stanza, the speaker says that "we," like music, also move through time, or else we are lost from it. Being lost from time, the speaker goes on to say, means being "unqualitied," undifferentiated by the "strife" or particularities mentioned in the first stanza as the very character of "motion"—that is, life. To be lost from time is to be lost from life and death, the speaker says, and therefore to permit of no identity or interpretation: Such a condition would be featureless and formless, lacking "design" and "beauty."

The poem's concluding two lines repeat the epigraph with which it begins, "Here, trapped in Time," and then go on to qualify the phrase with a "but." The poet asserts that while time is a kind of trap ("snare"), it is also life ("breath and motion"). The snare or trap of time may be construed, to cite Trimpi again, as consciousness cut off from reality and imprisoned in its own ideality; the mind lives only in a world of ideas, not in the "real" world of things as they are.

Forms and Devices

"Time and Music" follows the sonnet form in that it is composed of fourteen lines; however, the lines are iambic tetrameter rather than the more usual pentameter. The rhyme scheme suggests but does not follow both the Italian pattern of octave and sestet and the Shakespearean scheme of four quatrains and a concluding couplet. The first two stanzas rhyme in couplets. The third stanza has the chiasmic rhyme scheme *abba* characteristic of the octave of the Italian sonnet, and like Shakespeare's sonnets, the poem concludes with a couplet. Rhyme is conventional throughout most of the poem, the only exception being the off-rhyme of "us" and "is" in the concluding couplet. The poet makes extremely sparing but effective use of alliteration. The *m* of "music" in the first line is repeated in "measuring" and "motion" in the second, further emphasizing the heavily marked rhythm of these opening lines. In the penultimate line, the alliteration of the quoted phrase "trapped in Time" is reemphasized in the repetition of the word "Time," opening the speaker's capping rebuttal to the implications in the epigraph.

The handling of meter is unostentatious, a characteristic of Lewis's poems. The first three lines of the poem are headless iambs, meaning that the lines begin with stressed syllables and contain seven rather than the full eight syllables of the usual tetrameter line. The effect is to mark the rhythm heavily, since the stressed syllables at the ends and beginnings of lines occur next to each other; the rhythmic emphasis is in keeping with the subject of the lines, which is the meaning of measure and tempo— literally, time. Beginning with the mention of melody in the poem's fourth line and continuing to the end, the lines are fully iambic, the rhythm less heavily marked, and the effect more subtle and melodic; again, the aural effects are appropriate to the subject as the poet turns to melody in its passage through time.

Like many other of Lewis's poems, "Time and Music" is an example of the plain style identified in Renaissance poets such as Ben Jonson and continuing through the tradition of English poetry down to twentieth century exemplars such as Louise Bogan and Thom Gunn. The style is characterized by controlled emotion—which may nevertheless be extremely intense—by precision of diction, and by the infrequent use of figurative language and rhetorical ornamentation. The poet makes sparing but apt use of similes, beginning in the second stanza, with the comparison of melody to a boat and bird. The boat is a "fisher's" boat: The image suggests not only that melody floats and moves, like a boat, but also that it moves toward some end and actually seeks to capture something, as the fisher does. The implicit image of the fisherman with his line prepares for the metaphor of the snare in the poem's concluding couplet. The second simile, comparing melody to a swallow flying through the air, emphasizes the synesthetic quality of the imagery by comparing a disembodied and invisible melody not to the song of the bird, but to the sight of it. The disappearance of the bird is not a function of its flight but of the ability of the watcher to see, in the same way that the existence and disappearance of melody is dependent on the presence of a listener. This contingent nature of music is also taken up more explicitly in the conclusion, where the poet asserts the contingency of existence in time.

In the third stanza, the poem's third simile compares human life to music, and this comparison forms the major argument of the poem. "We" humans are like music in that our existence, like that of music, is a passage through time. Thus time, like air, is the medium of human existence, even as it is also the process that inexorably brings everyone to the end of life. There is a pun in this stanza on the notion of "keeping" or "losing" time: If one is "lost" to time, the poet says, one becomes undifferentiated, losing character and identity in the same way that the musician who fails to "keep" time loses the contours of a piece—the music disappears into mere undifferentiated noise. The simile is elaborated and brought into focus in the last line of the stanza, which notes that the person, like the melody, "lost to time" has neither form ("design") nor "beauty."

Themes and Meanings

The epigraph of "Time and Music" comes from the last lines of "The Vigil," a poem by Yvor Winters, Janet Lewis's husband. "The Vigil" is an intense and anguished expression of terror in the face of madness and infinity; the speaker expresses willingness to undergo the experience of madness—an unmediated encounter with infinity—in an unsupported expectation that such a leap will permit return to sanity, like a pendulum: "Here. Trapped in Time." This phrase provides both epigraph and counterargument for Lewis's "Time and Music."

As a poet's response to another poet, "Time and Music" resembles poems such as Sir Walter Raleigh's "The Nymph's Reply to the Shepherd," written in answer to Christopher Marlowe's "The Passionate Shepherd to His Love." In such poetic dialogues, the participants further, rebut, modify, or enlarge the discourse initiated by the original poem. Here, Lewis offers an alternative vision of the human predicament of being "trapped in time." Trimpi's reading of the poem suggests that "the figure of time—temporal existence—as a 'trap' or 'snare' suggests the Gnostic symbolism of the world as 'prison' and of the soul as longing to 'escape' the world," and that certain aspects of Gnosticism are juxtaposed with Lewis's perception that "time is, in fact, both 'breath and motion,' i.e., a condition of existence." The Gnostics held that the person's true life resided only in the spirit's existence, and denied value to the body. If "Time and Music" answers Gnosticism, it is by asserting that the body is valuable both in and because of its temporality, as contrasted with the Gnostic exaltation of the eternal life ascribed to the soul. The metaphor of the poem that equates human life with music asserts the value of temporal being: The abstract beauty of music, which is perceived by the spirit (psyche or mind), can be apprehended only by the body, the ear, which alone encounters the finite, ever-vanishing melodic line. Only by means of the temporal body can the everlasting soul confront the divine beauty of form and design in music, as in life.

Helen Jaskoski

TIME AND THE GARDEN

Author: Yvor Winters (1900-1968)
Type of poem: Lyric
First published: 1940, in *Poems*

The Poem

"Time and the Garden" is a didactic lyric written in rhyming couplets of regular iambic pentameter—that is, in heroic couplets. The speaker is the poet himself, meditating on his craft.

The poem consists of three parts. In the first part (lines 1-12), the speaker considers the springtime budding in his garden and the "excitement," the sense of anticipation, that the spectacle arouses in him. In the second part (lines 13 to 20), he realizes that to write great poems, the poet much achieve intellectual maturity and discernment; he then concludes that the great poet's goal and achievement are the same as those of the wise scholar.

As the poet contemplates his garden, he becomes aware of the newly revived hidden bustle in the vegetation, which manifests itself in the "darkening" tints of unfurling leaves and budding fruit. In "vine, bush, and tree," the future is slowly ripening and building what in time will be fruits of different sizes, shapes, and tastes— "Persimmon, walnut, loquat, fig, and grape." They will ripen in gradual stages (they "will advance in their due series"), and this measured growth will create a tranquil, enclosed space that will seem like a peaceful abode.

The poet is excited by this new burgeoning and by what time will bring; he is impatient. He wants to hurry the process of growth; "crowd the little garden"; gather up its harvest in the springtime; and then in a single moment taste the condensed sweetness of all fruits without waiting for the harvest season. He wants the trees to hurry to their great size, trees whose slow but rhythmic growth marks his advancing age. He realizes, however, that his wish goes unheeded: He is slowed down by the determinate march of time.

His impatience to taste the fruits before their appointed time reminds him of another kind of impatience. As a poet, he desires to possess the "greatness" of the "tougher" poets—the five English Renaissance poets George Gascoigne, Ben Jonson, Fulke Greville, Sir Walter Raleigh, and John Donne—before having "fairly earned" the recognition deserved of a mature poet. These poets wrote their poems over a period of many years. Each poetic line was a solid achievement, an enduring statement that few appreciate and bother to think through, but which no one can "retract." The desire to achieve this enduring poetic knowledge is both the birthright ("heritage") of scholars as well as the duty placed on them by a frenetic civilization. From the books they study, scholars gather an "unbroken wisdom," which they compress into a "single look," a fixed attitude or insight that is the culmination of a long season of intellectual inquiry. Scholars dedicate themselves to this task even though this wisdom is final and fixed only in death: Scholars may be dead, but the mind is "immortal." The reasoning powers of the mind and what the mind achieves in its quest for knowledge transcend the individual and are thus beyond time: The final knowledge of the poet and scholar is permanent, available to anyone willing to submit his or her mind to the slow, hard task of seeking it.

Forms and Devices

The opening description of spring arriving in the garden is sparse and, despite the few concrete details, abstract; the reader is thus prepared from the start for the poet's philosophic conclusions. A suggestive simile occurs in line 6, when the growing garden is compared to a spacious, peaceful dwelling place where serenity stands in contrast to the physical excitement that spring arouses in the poet.

In his later poetry (including this poem), Yvor Winters wished to emulate what he called the "plain style" tradition developed by the English Renaissance poets he admired. Of the five poets whom he names, only Donne often wrote in the other Renaissance style—the ornate style—influenced by the Italian poet Petrarch. The "plain style" is characterized by terse, often unadorned, and even platitudinous, statements rather than by exuberant figurative language characteristic of ornate poetry, and hence suited to the poet's goal of distilling the hard kernel of knowledge from experience instead of re-creating it.

The "garden" is a traditional metaphor, but it is not developed and remains a hidden resonance. The image of the spring garden is presented not as a metaphor or symbol, but as a direct analogy that provides a concrete context in the manner of an objective correlative to the abstract statements that follow; the setting makes them precise. The experience of returning spring also reminds the speaker of the poet's and scholar's quest; the final fruit in both cases comes at the end of a measured period of development. The five fruits he lists are examples of what the tree, bush, and vine will bear; but they are seen abstractly as "Degrees and kinds of color, taste, and shape," words that the reader can link to the five great poets and their work.

Winters, by means of this analogy, forces the reader's attention to the levels of meaning that the abstract terms yield within the semantic context created by the spring garden. A key term, for example, is "greatness": It refers to the size, age, solidity, and texture of the trees in the garden. This meaning reflects the meaning of the abstract "greatness" of the poets and the "great" poems they have written—the poets' stature in the world of letters and the density, strength, and endurance of their poems. Another key term is "space": The garden's growth creates a tranquil enclosed dwelling; the spacing of poems over many years also creates an enclosed poetic garden within the poets' minds.

The regular meter and rhyme have the effect of giving Winters's conclusions a tone of firm, unambiguous finality. Nothing is tenuous. The lines move in an iambic meter, which, though regular, is sinuous and subtle, not mechanically rigid; it allows for voiced emphasis at significant points in the poem. Winters achieves this by varying the pauses (caesuras) within the poem, using run-on lines, and placing alternately heavy and light accented syllables in the position of metrical stress, giving the effect of trochee or spondee. In line 18, for example, the stresses on each monosyllabic word are rhythmically so heavy as to almost obliterate the iambic beat: The line is thus given particular emphasis. The last two lines are unambiguously iambic—all but one word being monosyllabic—and provide a confident, magisterial closure.

Themes and Meanings

"Time and the Garden" is about time and growth, a growth that paradoxically leads to death. The speaker, contemplating his garden in early spring, is impatient to seize the season's rich promise in a single sensuous moment. In an analogous way, he desires to possess the greatness that the five poets have achieved, but this he cannot do, for it is the task of a lifetime. As the trees grow and mature slowly, so do tough, unsentimental poets. The task of discerning the wisdom necessary for this creative task is slow, arduous work, as the one emotional outburst in lines 12 and 13 indicates. This growth brings the poet gain, but it also brings the final dissolution of death, just as the ripeness of the garden's fruits is the prelude to decay.

Suspicious of mere inspiration and sheer expressiveness, Winters rejected the romantic notion of poetry as an outpouring of powerful emotions. Poetry was for him, as it had been for the five Renaissance poets he names, a "vision of permanent" truth. This poetic truth, as the summary of the scholar's quest makes clear, is the knowledge—tough, sobering, and skeptical—which undermines the illusory hopes and promises of unlimited possibilities that spring and youth can inspire. Only the greatest poets and minds can discern this truth, and once formulated with precision, it is absolute, unchanging. A poem is a moral act—a responsible, rational evaluation of experience. Such tough wisdom, however, has to be earned: Only growing older in "duress"—in suffering, in the exhausting work of study—brings the necessary clarity of vision for recognizing this knowledge. That is why few are attracted to this kind of poetry: To appreciate it, one must share the poet's hard-earned certitude. It is also a limited certitude, however, for knowledge is complete and perfectly fixed only in death, which is both the starting point and the conclusion of the quest for meaning.

Poet and scholar are trapped in time; only the mind and the limited absolute knowledge it can achieve transcends time and the individual. Yet despite this melancholy awareness, scholar and poet cultivate their minds, as one cultivates a garden, in order to reach a tranquil maturity and gain the meaningful knowledge available to them. As in real gardening, one must cut and prune, subdue and discipline, in order to reap the greatest gain. The "garden" is little, carved out of the vast area that lies beyond and cannot be tamed or known. Working within this manageable space, however, brings order to chaotic nature; cultivating the knowable garden of the mind brings precision and order to the confusing flux of raw experience.

Hans-Peter Breuer

TITHONUS

Author: Alfred, Lord Tennyson (1809-1892)
Type of poem: Dramatic monologue
First published: 1860; collected in *Enoch Arden and Other Poems*, 1864

The Poem

In seven blank-verse paragraphs, Alfred, Lord Tennyson's "Tithonus" reflects upon the strange and tragic fate of its speaker, the doomed lover of Aurora, the goddess of the dawn in Roman mythology. According to legend, the Trojan prince Tithonus received the gift of immortality from the gods at Aurora's request. Because the goddess neglected to obtain for him the gift of eternal youth, however, Tithonus continued to grow old, without "the power to die," until he was turned into a grasshopper. In the poem, Tennyson's ancient Tithonus laments his alienation from human community, provides a requiem for his lost youth and beauty, and vainly implores the goddess to release him from love and life. By using Tithonus as an object lesson, Tennyson suggests that eternal life may be more of a curse than a blessing.

"Tithonus" begins with what appears to be a traditional lament on the transitory nature of life and the inevitability of death. However, the speaker refers to death as an unexpected blessing from which he alone, of all living things, is doomed to be exempt: "Me only cruel immortality/ Consumes." Tithonus also portrays himself as the dawn's emasculated victim, an insubstantial "shadow" of a man who "wither[s] slowly" in the infinite void of its heavenly prison.

In stanza 2, memory heightens Tithonus's sense of physical and sexual loss, as he recalls his "glorious" youth, when the goddess made him her "chosen." Ravaged by time, Tithonus blames his lover for his fate, although he also shows his willingness to accept responsibility for choosing to become immortal. He repents his proud though human desire to transcend earthly limits, telling Aurora to "take back" her poisoned gift.

Tithonus vividly describes the awakening dawn in stanza 3 as an anthropomorphic goddess who brings light and heat to the world in her chariot. He emphasizes that Aurora is as much woman as divinity by depicting her sensual beauty, including her "redden[ing]" cheek and "sweet eyes" that brighten like the rising sun. As Tithonus reveals in stanza 4, their brief communion follows an all-too-familiar pattern, with Aurora refusing to answer him before her departure, leaving behind only her tears on his cheek. After her apparent disappearance, Tithonus gives voice to the dawn's sadness and silence in stanza 5, revealing his own fear of Aurora's powerlessness; as he suggests, "'The Gods themselves cannot recall their gifts.'"

The erotic sixth stanza revisits the speaker's distant past, as Tithonus explains how the dawn's appearance and embrace once inflamed his desires. Then, her love was fresh and new; now, she fails to elicit a sympathetic response but only makes him "cold," as the final stanza shows. Feeling isolated from even his lover, the world-weary Tithonus returns to thoughts of those "happy men" who are mortal or already dead. In the last five lines, Tithonus looks to the future and prays to be released by his omniscient, if not omnipotent, goddess. In death, Tithonus seeks not only forgetfulness but also deliverance from the burden of endless recurrence, as represented by the dawn's cyclical and eternal return.

Forms and Devices

Even among Tennyson's innovative dramatic monologues, "Tithonus" is unusual in many respects, beginning with the implied listener herself. Unlike the human auditors of other monologues, Aurora is a goddess. Surprisingly, Tithonus never calls his lover by name, although he addresses her throughout the poem. She seems to have departed by stanza 6, leaving the speaker entirely alone, thereby making the rest of the poem into a soliloquy. In her presence and absence alike, Aurora's divine silence speaks resoundingly. Whereas the listeners of other dramatic monologues stay silent by convention, Tithonus expects Aurora to answer his prayers, and her speechlessness becomes a reason for him to despair.

Through the poem's extensive use of personification, Tennyson transforms Aurora from a natural phenomenon into a supernatural being. Aurora is, literally speaking, the dawn itself; thus, Tithonus refers to the morning star that precedes sunrise as Aurora's "guide." He also imagines the morning dew as his lover's tears, lending the dawn a personal and emotional aspect that is mirrored by the "weep[ing]" vapors, or storm clouds, of the opening section. Tithonus even describes the dawn's radiant body at length in the third and sixth stanzas, which together form a blazon, or hymn of praise. Tennyson extends the personification of nature to time itself when Tithonus refers to Aurora's "strong Hours" as agents of resentment and revenge.

Tennyson also incorporates the traditional form of the aubade, a morning song which either welcomes the dawn's arrival or denounces it as a nuisance. Like John Donne in "The Sun Rising" (1633), Tennyson depicts his two lovers lying together in bed at daybreak. For Tithonus, his lover and the dawn are one and the same, so his ambivalence about Aurora suggests his divided attitude toward the return of day. In stanza 3, the luminous Aurora rises like the sun itself; the "old mysterious glimmer steals" from her brows and shoulders as she lights up their chamber and then the sky. Morning brings with it the speaker's regret, unlike the days of old described in stanza 6, when Tithonus basked in dawn's warm glow.

In terms of its rhetorical devices and effects, the poem creates a sense of slowness and weightiness through its balanced repetitions and parallelisms, including such lines as "The woods decay, the woods decay and fall" and "Thou wilt renew thy beauty morn by morn,/ I earth in earth forget these empty courts." In addition, Tennyson uses a number of grammatical inversions, as in "a heart renewed" and "cold/ Are all thy lights, and cold my wrinkled feet," to provide a sense of emphasis and elevated expression. He also relies on frequent antithesis and contrasting images of light and dark, heat and cold, and youth and age to reflect the opposite natures of Aurora and Tithonus.

Themes and Meanings

The genesis of "Tithonus" is important to understanding its meaning. Tennyson explained that he originally conceived of the poem as a pendant or companion piece to "Ulysses" (1842), which he wrote soon after the 1833 death of his cherished friend Arthur Hallam. However, the first version of "Tithonus," called "Tithon," underwent extensive revisions before its publication in 1860, more than twenty-five years after it was begun. Because of Tennyson's emotional distance from his personal loss, the final version of "Tithonus" presents a more detached view of death and immortality than its predecessor.

Even though "Tithonus" does not respond in an immediate way to Hallam's death, it can still be read as an extension of and an alternative to "Ulysses." In both poems, Tennyson looks to a classical story for insight into the problem of mortality. His aged and alienated speakers share a similar predicament in their dissatisfaction with a life that has become monotonous, and both pursue death as a means of transcending this sort of existence. Ultimately, though, the two men are distinguished by their very different attitudes toward life. Unlike Ulysses, who clings to life and sets out for more adventures, Tithonus has given up on life and longs for oblivion in the grave.

Consequently, Ulysses is active, defiant, and hopeful, whereas Tithonus is passive, resigned, and despairing. As such, these two speakers represent antithetical aspects of Tennyson's own attitude toward life and death. With its origins in Homer's "Hymn to Aphrodite" (c. 8th century B.C.E.; Eng. trans, 1624) and Horace's *Odes* (23 B.C.E., 13 B.C.E.; Eng. trans., 1621), "Tithonus" further shares its tradition and themes with Tennyson's other classical monologues, "Tiresias" (1885) and "Oenone" (1832), which reflect upon dying and the danger of loving a god, respectively.

As a personal response to mortality, "Tithonus" is also related to Tennyson's elegiac *In Memoriam* (1850), in which the poet addresses Hallam's death explicitly and at length. Like this extended elegy, "Tithonus" considers the relation of humanity to nature and God. As a liminal figure who is neither human nor divine, Tithonus finds himself excluded from the natural order of things, in which "Man comes and tills the fields and lies beneath." As someone who ages without dying, Tithonus is exiled from humanity, caught between "that dark world where [he] was born" and the eternal "halls of morn."

Alienated from even his former self, "once a man," Tithonus seeks to provide himself with a sympathetic companion in either nature or God. In his descriptions of the dawn, he tries to endow the natural world with human warmth and compassion. By attempting to combine sensuous immediacy with permanence in his portrait of Aurora's "immortal youth" and beauty, Tithonus recalls not only "that strange song [he] heard Apollo sing," but also such Romantic odes as John Keats's "Ode to a Nightingale" (1819) and Percy Bysshe Shelley's "To a Skylark," published with the verse drama *Prometheus Unbound: A Lyrical Drama in Four Acts* (pb. 1820).

Despite his efforts to reach out, both nature and divinity seem cold and unresponsive to Tithonus, who experiences a crisis of faith as a result. In showing the apparent indifference of the gods to human destiny, Tennyson suggests that God, like Tithonus's Aurora, is not immanent but transcendent. At the end of the poem, then, a chastened Tithonus comes to accept that his place is not with the gods, but rather with living and dying humanity.

Michael W. Hancock

TITLE DIVINE—IS MINE!

Author: Emily Dickinson (1830-1886)
Type of poem: Meditation
First published: 1924, in *The Complete Poems of Emily Dickinson*

The Poem

"Title divine—is mine!" is a short poem of fifteen lines written in 1862 and first published in *The Complete Poems of Emily Dickinson*. The poem's metrical formula and rhyme scheme are irregular but loosely follow those used in hymnals. The word "divine" in the title has a religious connotation as it calls the reader's attention to a power structure that has been notorious in placing women at the bottom of the social totem pole and suggests the congeneric connection between two social institutions the poem addresses: religion and marriage.

The narrator in the poem is apparently a newlywed. On her wedding day or shortly after, the narrator reflects on her marriage and on women's lives in general. Typical of Emily Dickinson's poems, "Title divine—is mine!" starts with affirmation. The tone in the opening of the poem is almost euphoric. The narrator is overwhelmed. She appears very excited about all the titles and accolades the wedding has bestowed upon her ("Title divine—is mine!/ The Wife—without the Sign!"), and she is thrilled about the new possibilities marriage has promised her ("Acute Degree—conferred on me—/ Empress of Calvary!"). The first part of the poem, however, ends with an ominous note. The word "Calvary" reminds readers of both the place where Jesus Christ was crucified and an experience similar to that of the Crucifixion, an experience of extreme suffering. As the narrator looks beyond all the titles the wedding has brought her, she starts to see something different: She is "Royal—all but the Crown"; she is "Betrothed," regardless of whether she has experienced "the swoon"; and, because of her gender, she is relegated to a group of people who allegedly are only attracted to material possessions, things ranging from "Garnet to Garnet" and from "Gold—to Gold." From birth to marriage and then to death, this pattern would never change.

The next three lines ("Born—Bridalled—Shrouded—/ In a Day—/ Tri Victory") play a pivotal role in the poem: They represent a turning point where the narrator must face how she feels about the wedding and what it portends. In appearance, the wedding day represents a victory for the narrator. As the midpoint between birth and death, marriage is supposed to represent the peak and consummation of a woman's life. However, when the narrator notices the clichéd pattern of a life that a woman is too powerless to change, she starts to question whose victory it really is. It is a life replete with monotonous and pernicious repetitions perpetuated by both the way women are treated by others ("God sends us Women—/ When you—hold—Garnet to Garnet—/ Gold—to Gold—/ Born—Bridalled—Shrouded—/ In a Day—") and the way they treat themselves (" 'My Husband'—women say—/ Stroking the Melody—"). The poem ends with the narrator questioning whether this is "the way."

Forms and Devices

Similar to Dickinson's thematic approach, the predominant form of her poems also epitomizes a paradox. Many of her poems follow, with some variations, the standard hymnbook metrical formula and rhyme scheme. However, unconventional punctuation, unorthodox capitalization, and irregular metrical beat all highlight an effort to break away from the established grammatical and literary conventions. Dickinson frequently uses a dash where a comma should be. In doing so, she is able to control the rhythm and flow of ideas, accentuating those she deems important. In the opening line of "Title divine—is mine!" for instance, the dash not only accentuates the phrase "Title divine" but also reveals the narrator's hesitation and inexperience in dealing with the situation. Similarly, by playing with the capitalization of the key words in her poems, Dickinson invites readers to participate in the process of creating tropes. The word "Calvary," when spelled with a capitalized *C*, refers to the place where Jesus Christ was crucified. When the letter is lowercase, however, it also suggests an experience similar to that of the Crucifixion, an experience of extreme suffering. Since Dickinson capitalizes her nouns almost as whimsically as she accents her lines, the word "Calvary" used in the poem is as much a reference to how the narrator feels she is treated on her wedding day as to what weddings have portended to many women for centuries.

Dickinson's poems celebrate individual spirit, freedom of choice, and social equality. They condemn oppressive social institutions, establishments, and structures. The syntax, punctuation, and capitalization of her poems correspond to her thematic concerns, calling for change and urging people to find ways that can accurately portray, describe, and represent human experiences. The form of Dickinson's poems in general and that of "Title divine—is mine!" in particular, therefore, is the message. The poem's circular movement suggests both emotional and physical confinement. The conflict between the narrator's emotional response to the occasion and her keen observation and rational reflection remains unresolved. The glorious accolades do not conceal the fact that the marriage has contributed to more of the stigmatization that the narrator has been experiencing throughout her life. She is put on a pedestal without being fully understood and appreciated. She must carry signs that are placed on her whether she likes them or not. She must behave the way she is expected to behave by society.

Themes and Meanings

Dickinson's thematic approach in "Title divine—is mine!" is as ironic as it is paradoxical. In appearance, the wedding day is the biggest celebration in the narrator's life. It brings her recognition and titles. It represents a "Tri Victory" connecting the past and the future. However, the narrator gradually realizes that she is a person who has been acted upon rather than one who has acted, a person who has been forced into the role of a passive receiver rather than an active participant. The emotional conflict the narrator reveals in the second half of the poem is, in fact, embedded in the very beginning of the poem: She is given a title by someone who apparently is more powerful than "divine," she is given the sign "Wife" with or without her consent, and she is conferred the "Acute Degree" that makes her the "Empress of Calvary." If the narrator's reading of history is accurate, the end is, indeed, in the beginning.

Thematically, "Title divine—is mine!" is firmly anchored in and representative of a large group of Dickinson's poems that protest against society's discriminatory treatment of women and condemn a system in which people are treated not as individuals but as types. In "They shut me up in Prose," Dickinson portrays a female teenager who, because of her gender, is questioned about her natural poetic talent. In "My Life had stood—a Loaded Gun," the narrator complains about a metaphoric marriage in which her volition, thanks to her social status, has been deprived to the point where although she has "the power to kill," she does not have "the power to die." "Title divine—is mine!" follows the same thematic line, calling the reader's attention to the pernicious impact of a social institution that has physically imprisoned and emotionally tormented women for centuries. All the accolades the narrator has received do not conceal the fact that there is no true mutual understanding and respect between two human beings as long as one of them is judged not by who she really is but by who she is supposed to be. The titles are as nominal and empty as the prejudice against women is strong. They are as misleading as the stereotypes and preconceived ideas that people use to judge other people.

What distinguishes "Title divine—is mine!" from Dickinson's other poems with similar thematic preoccupations is its juxtaposition of religion and marriage. The poem abounds with words with religious connotations such as "divine," "the Sign," and "Calvary." The juxtaposition of two established social institutions challenges oppressive power structures in general. Marriage can function the same way as religion if the power structure is not built on equity and justice. In "Title divine—is mine!" readers are forced to confront a reality that suggests exactly the opposite of what they expect out of both institutions.

Qun Wang

TO A FRIEND: IN MEMORIAM

Author: Joseph Brodsky (1940-1996)
Type of poem: Elegy
First published: 1977, as "Na smert' druga," in *Chast' rechi: Stikhotvoreniya, 1972-1976*; English translation collected in *To Urania*, 1988

The Poem

"To a Friend: In Memoriam" is a twenty-eight-line elegy replete with irony. The poem is a first-person address to the poet's dead friend. The poet's friend is also a poet, the author of "the most smashing ode" and a "word-plyer," and hence is a double to the narrator-poet. Despite the poem's specificity—the anonymity suggests the friend could be anyone—the narrator also addresses the condition of loss. Though the poet is separated from his friend by the grave as well as by geography ("I'm up here and, frankly, apart from this paltry/ talk of slabs, am too distant for you to distinguish a voice"), the poem has the immediacy and intimacy of direct address. The poem's long lines and lack of stanzaic division underscore the immediacy.

The poem begins by establishing the relationship between the poem's narrator and the unnamed "you." It continues, in lines 9 through 16, as a catalog of the friend's qualities: "a word-plyer, a liar, a gulper of bright, measly tears,/ an adorer of Ingres, of clangoring streetcars, of asphodels' slumbers." At line 17, the poem shifts to the poet's wish that his dead friend may "lie, as though wrapped in an Orenburg shawl, in our dry, brownish mud." The poem shifts again at line 20 to an acknowledgment of the pointlessness of death as exemplified by the circumstances of the friend. The final three lines are the poet's farewell.

The poem changes its tone at several points. It opens with a political joke—that the Soviet authorities can, if they so desire, rehabilitate one from beyond the grave: "It's for you whose name's better omitted—since for them it's no arduous task/ to produce you from under the slab." The poem maintains this sense of irreverence as a backdrop, although it moves very assuredly into moments of pathos and anger, comic epithets, and searing commentary. It never lapses into generalities: Every phrase is descriptive of both the poem's subject and of the poet's emotional reaction to the death and the culture that tolerates such conditions of spiritual and material diminishment. This does not shift the poem into a strictly political posture, however. The meaninglessness of death and the diminishment of life throughout Russian history, both Czarist and Soviet, is Joseph Brodsky's theme.

Forms and Devices

Brodsky's poems are richly allusive, often drawing upon Greek mythology and literary history. "To a Friend: In Memoriam," as might be expected in an elegy, mentions "Gloomy Charon," who, in vain, seeks the fare for the soul's passage to the underworld. The poet bids farewell from the shore, but confesses that he cannot distinguish which shore (of Charon's river Lethe) he is on. Such a slight allusion to Charon nevertheless serves several distinct purposes. It interjects a rhetorical seriousness to the poem: The allusion maintains the decorum expected of an elegy. The allusion, and the use of allusions in general, conserves poetic idiom, iconography, and the memory of one's entire being while forestalling sheer transience.

The reference to "the laced Goncharova," the young and frivolous wife of Alexander Pushkin, exemplifies Brodsky's use of literary allusions. At the height of his poetic powers, Pushkin died uselessly in a duel with one of his wife's lovers. As with the death of the poet's friend, Pushkin's death is meaningless; indeed, the culture they all inhabited has an overwhelming fatalism. The "Orenburg shawl," in which the poet wishes his friend wrapped, further emphasizes the sense of oppression and fatalism, for Orenburg was the site of the 1774 suppression of a peasant uprising that resulted in the strengthening of serfdom by Catherine II.

Brodsky, as is typical of Russian poets, brilliantly and, at times, flamboyantly uses rhyme. "To a Friend: In Memoriam" is no exception. Brodsky, an accomplished translator of John Donne, Andrew Marvell, and Czesław Miłosz, translated this poem himself, and it gives a clear indication of the types of rhymes he utilizes: slant rhymes, perfect rhymes, and internal, compound-slant rhymes.

Brodsky's poetry is as highly figurative as it is allusive and well crafted in rhyme and meter. The poem is filled with epithets, such as "Man of sidewalks" and "Gloomy Charon," as well as synecdoche and metonymy, as demonstrated by such phrases as "that homeland of bottle-struck livers" and "the Third Rome's cold-piss-reeking entrance." "To a Friend: In Memoriam" utilizes hyperbole juxtaposed with understatement, which creates an ironic portrait, as in "you . . . the offspring of a widowed conductress, begot/ by the Holy Ghost or by brick courtyard's soot circling all over." The poem also employs allegorical personification as in the line, which, incidentally, demonstrates Brodsky's interest in the English metaphysical poets, "Maybe Nothing has no better gateway indeed than this smelly shortcut." The wide use of tropes, or figurative language, demonstrates Brodsky's virtuosic handling of language.

Lines 9 through 16 present a list of qualities that define the dead friend. This list climaxes with one of Brodsky's more surreal images: "a monogamous heart and a torso of countless bedchambers." Here the synecdoche of "heart" (used as an abstraction) is made physical by the metaphor of "a torso." The combination of the suppressed erotic is refigured but distorted in the image of a classical torso opening into many bedchambers. Such surreality is not uncommon in Brodsky's work. Brodsky's poetry often contains radical juxtapositions of language and image that suggest the inclusiveness of the poetic idiom as well as its potential to surprise. Juxtaposition also occurs between the figurative language and the more formal sensibility of rhyme and meter.

The language is reminiscent of the descriptive, but also ironic, language of novelist Nikolai Gogol. In fact, the twenty-third and twenty-fourth lines ("as you drifted along the dark river in your ancient gray, drab overcoat/ whose few buttons alone were what kept you from disintegration") recall Gogol's stories of poverty and the disintegration of personality. This poem, like Gogol's stories, maintains a grim but redeeming comic realism.

Themes and Meanings

"To a Friend: In Memoriam," like many elegies, describes a life. Implicitly, Brodsky realizes that one's life cannot be exempt from the far-reaching forces of one's cultural history. Brodsky's poems are deeply concerned with betrayal, solitude, suffering, and separation. They also demonstrate his intense belief in poetry as an ethical process linked with life. To Brodsky, poetry is a form of endurance, a means of witnessing survival. "To a Friend: In Memoriam" is a means of memory surviving because the poem survives life and death.

Both the poet and his double exemplify endurance. They greet adversity with ironic humor that is simultaneously self-effacing and fully aware of the ironic circumstances. When confronted with the prospect of eternal nothingness, the poet's double states, "This will do for the duration." This ironic response suggests that although readers are at the mercy of their definitions, through irony or other figurative uses of languages, they may call into question their perceptions or customary ways of understanding the conditions and concepts by which they live.

Such metaphysical wit, however, is tempered by the poet's own realism, which has the last word: "for you now it has no importance." The inclusive "it" absorbs not only the poet's farewell, but the whole of the poem, the record of life. This final phrase demonstrates the poet's unwillingness to elevate his perceptions or to privilege his position. The final phrase also reveals a certain amount of resignation and pain. The poet realizes the extent of his powers, and for his friend these poetic powers are limited severely. The poet may recall for readers this past life, but not even his farewells can be heard by the one being elegized. Hence, the poet's words are silenced; his address fails to reach its intended listener while readers simply overhear this address.

The final phrase reflects the opening of the poem, where the arbitrary nature of the state reflects the arbitrariness of death. The anonymity of the friend draws one's attention to the poet's condition. The poem speaks to the reader's transience, but in a way that is both irreverent (achieved through the poem's juxtapositions and irony) and modest (demonstrated by the poet's almost self-denying stance toward his work). Brodsky, like his mentor, W. H. Auden, is a consummate elegiac poet. "To a Friend: In Memoriam" is perhaps his most bitter and ironic elegy.

James McCorkle

TO A LOCOMOTIVE IN WINTER

Author: Walt Whitman (1819-1892)
Type of poem: Lyric
First published: 1876, in *Two Rivulets*

The Poem

It could be said that Walt Whitman bridged the movements of the Romanticism that preceded him and the modernism that was to follow. In the spirit of Romanticism he wrote in praise of the beauty of nature, as in "O Magnet South," "The Dalliance of the Eagles," and "Germ." He also championed the individual, as "Song of Myself" demonstrates so strikingly. His poetry shunned the classical emphasis on order and balance to the point of creating a style unique in his time. Yet many of Whitman's poems move him some distance from the styles and objects of Romanticism. His abandonment of traditional modes of meter and rhyme makes Whitman the most important precursor of the style of free verse. Furthermore, he foreshadows the early twentieth century movement of modernism.

His style was a self-conscious break with the traditional forms and subject matter of poetry. His use of unrhymed lines in a form without meter was a departure from all who preceded him in poetry. His innovation in subject matter is seen in such poems as "The Beauty of the Ship" and "Sparkles from the Wheel," in which he celebrates the plain and the mundane. Yet nowhere does he do so more conspicuously as in "To a Locomotive in Winter," in which he calls the locomotive a "Type of the modern." Here is a conscious turning away from Romantic content to a very modern theme, the machine, as an object not only of interest but also of the poet's admiration, even his adoration.

The poet calls his work a recitative, a declamatory recital of his praise for all the aspects of this great machine. Whitman was born as the railroad was experiencing its birth in the United States. He grew up during the rapid expansion of the network of steel, crossing and crisscrossing the eastern seaboard and soon the inland areas of the East Coast. "To a Locomotive in Winter" was written as the nation was celebrating and enjoying this new "pulse of the continent"; the transcontinental railroad, which joined East with West, was completed in 1869, only a few years before the poem was first published. Whitman's response to modernization is his poem honoring this steel and steam phenomenon, which romanticizes this very utilitarian invention.

In two verses of twenty-five total lines, the poet recites his description of the locomotive "in action"—in winter, in its many aspects of style and behavior. The style of free verse fits well the unbridled behavior of a machine that cannot be bound by patterns imposed from without. That is the "Fierce-throated beauty" of this object, which not everyone would describe as beautiful. Impressive as the locomotive might be in itself, Whitman finds all that is to be admired in its parts and its motion.

The admiration of the locomotive as a manly creature makes it difficult to ignore the sexual orientation usually attributed to the poet. In spite of his idle boasts of having fathered several children, it is most likely that he had strong homosexual tendencies—although evidence that he acted out these impulses is lacking. Other poems by Whitman, notably "I Saw in Louisiana a Live-Oak Growing," employ symbolism that suggests homosexual themes. There is here, however, no attempt at carrying any such theme to a conclusion. There is in "To a Locomotive in Winter" no story of a sexual encounter, only a description of the wonders of the adored male figure. There is no question of its gender: "No sweetness debonair of tearful harp or glib piano thine." The theme of sexuality is allowed in no way to overwhelm the poem as a whole.

Forms and Devices

Chief among the poetic devices Whitman uses in "To a Locomotive in Winter" is that of personification. He attributes human personality to the locomotive throughout. This is seen from the first word, "Thee." Although the poem can be described as a paean, in the tradition of Greek lyrics of invocation addressed to Apollo, and later to other gods and to deified heroes, this address is not to be thought of as an ascription of divinity. Rather, terms such as "thee" and "thy" seem more human than divine. The terms were reminders of forms of address in the languages of American immigrants, which distinguished between the second person familiar tense and the second person formal. This is personal address. The poet sees himself on personal, familiar terms with the machine. He addresses the locomotive as a friend, dear, even adored, but in no way distant as formal address would suggest.

Whitman attributes numerous human characteristics to the locomotive, as the making of music: "all thy lawless music" and its "madly-whistled laughter." Mainly the overall characterization is of a being that simply runs but also breathes and moves, acting of a volition all its own. It is a "Law of thyself complete."

The appeal to the senses is paramount throughout the poem. The locomotive is seen clad in armor ("panoply"), with a black cylinder of a body, clothed also in brass and steel. The side bars, connecting rods, headlight, springs, valves, wheels, and lamps all create the visual image of the locomotive. Its action, with its "vapor-pennants" and clouds of smoke, can be easily visualized by the reader. The sounds the engine makes are described all through the poem: the throbbing beat, the ringing bell. Descriptions of movement and motion appeal to the sense of touch. The locomotive is described as an earthquake, convulsive, the "emblem of motion and power," rumbling along. The heat of the engine contrasts with the feel of the wind and snow of winter. One can almost smell the "out-belching" produced by the smokestack.

In the poem the author uses alliteration in many places: "silvery steel," "tremulous twinkle," "thy silent signal lamps to swing," "now swift, now slack." There is no particular pattern to the use of the device; it appears almost incidental yet effectively heightens the sound wherever it appears. The power of the poem's imagery reflects the power of the locomotive.

Themes and Meanings

Although it might appear the poem is external to the poet, "To a Locomotive in Winter" is clearly a reflection of Whitman's self-image. Much of what he wrote is an extension of the theme of the poem "Song of Myself." This is not an egotistical pride, but a very honest and open celebration of the self. As the opening inscription of *Leaves of Grass* (1855-1892) declares: "One's-self I sing, a simple separate person." He invites the locomotive to join the poet: "For once come serve the Muse and merge in verse, even as here I see thee." The bold masculine imagery is a reflection of how Whitman thought of himself: manly, strong, capable of whatever was at hand.

Similarly, while the poem shares little of the patriotism exhibited in many of his works, it is about his beloved country. In the brief "To Foreign Lands," he promises in his poetry to "define America, her athletic democracy." His was no naïve chauvinism, but a hearty hope for what America might become. Near the end of *Leaves of Grass* he wrote in "One Song, America, Before I Go":

> As Life and Nature are not great with reference to the Present only,
> But greater still from what is to come,
> Out of that formula for thee I sing.

In "To a Locomotive in Winter" Whitman celebrates a machine that he knows will help make America fulfill that promise of what is to come.

Greater still is the hope and promise of the individual who is manly, capable, and strong. The locomotive's is not an easy solo journey. It has a job to do: lug its "train of cars behind, obedient, merrily following." It does so in the declining hours of a winter day, in the middle of a driving snowstorm. The moments of calm are more than matched by moments of gale, "with buffeting gusts of wind." Through it all struggles the locomotive. To the accompanying sounds of its own echo, it traverses "the prairies wide, across the lakes," and finally attains "the free skies unpent and glad and strong."

Eugene Kenneth Hanson

TO A SKYLARK

Author: Percy Bysshe Shelley (1792-1822)
Type of poem: Ode
First published: 1820, in *Prometheus Unbound: A Lyrical Drama in Four Acts*

The Poem

Like so many of Percy Bysshe Shelley's poems, "To a Skylark" describes a natural phenomenon and then uses that event as a jumping-off point for discussing the power of nature to transform men's lives. Shelley wrote the poem near Leghorn, Italy, in 1820, presumably after experiencing the situation he describes in the opening lines of the poem: The sound of a small European skylark, which sings only when in flight, calls the speaker's attention to the presence of the bird soaring so high that it cannot be seen by the viewer. Trying to spot the bird in the sky leads the narrator to imagine what the bird is actually like, and after running through a series of comparisons, he turns to contrasting the joyful life of the bird with that of men who are bound to earth, with all its cares.

The poem's twenty-one stanzas divide logically into three parts. In the first section, the speaker addresses the bird whose song he hears but that he cannot see high in the sky, where its warbling fills the air with sweet music. The bird seems to be a kind of "unbodied joy" (line 15) whose "shrill delight" (line 20) makes the whole world a happy place.

In the middle section of the poem, the speaker makes a series of comparisons to try to explain what the bird's song is like. Drawing images from the world of men and the world of nature, Shelley likens the bird to a summer shower, a rose, a highborn maiden, a rainbow cloud, even a glowworm. None of these images is sufficient, for none captures the essence of the joy the poet feels in hearing the bird's song. Finally, the speaker asks the bird to share with him the secret of its special joy. The unbridled joy of this creature is unlike that felt by men, who know pleasure only in comparison to the pain and tragedy that are an integral part of human existence. Hence, when possessed of the skylark's secret, the poet will be able to transform the lives of his readers and improve humankind; such, Shelley implies, is the power of poetry when it is suffused with the power of nature.

Forms and Devices

The twenty-one stanzas of "To a Skylark" consist of five lines each, rhyming *ababb*. If one reads the first four lines of any stanza with natural stresses, one can see that these lines generally consist of a first stressed syllable followed by two iambs. The final line in each stanza is an Alexandrine (six iambics), and in all cases Shelley closes his thought in the final line, so that there is no enjambment between stanzas. The effect is to make each five-line grouping a self-contained unit of thought, giving the reader pause for reflection on the idea expressed in the stanza.

Like so many of the Romantics' poems, "To a Skylark" is addressed to a creature of nature as if that creature were capable of discourse with the speaker. The joyful life of the skylark is seen as the object of envy, and the speaker poses as a supplicant seeking from the bird some insight into its natural wisdom and its consummate happiness.

Six stanzas are given over to similes (lines 31-60) in which the poet compares the bird to various animate and inanimate natural objects, each of which gives joy to the viewer or listener: a cloud in the sky after a rain, a poet singing his verses to the world, a maiden playing on her instrument, a glowworm, a rose, even the rain. These comparisons are Shelley's attempt to suggest the power of the skylark to awaken feelings of joy within those who hear the sound of the bird winging far above them; the piercing song of the bird, whose presence is felt by those who hear it, suggests to Shelley that it has discovered the secret of happiness. Each of the stanzas in which these comparisons are drawn forms a kind of miniature word-painting of a natural scene intended to evoke feelings of joy and contentment in the reader.

In addition to the similes in these six stanzas, Shelley includes briefer comparisons throughout the poem to suggest by analogy the skylark's special qualities and the importance of its "secret" for humankind. It is "like a cloud of fire" (line 8) or "a star in Heaven" (line 18); its joy seems to the speaker to be "Better than all measures/ Of delightful sound" (lines 96-97) and "Better than all treasures/ That in books are found" (lines 98-99). The comparisons run the gamut from ethereal to subterrestrial, but the effect is the same: They suggest that the happiness the poet feels in hearing the skylark's song is the distillation of all the natural happiness he can imagine, and he longs to understand not only what the essence of that happiness is, but also how he may create such a feeling in his own life and in the lives of his fellow humans.

Themes and Meanings

Harold Bloom has described "To a Skylark" as Shelley's "farewell to the theme of the power hidden behind nature and the poet's relation to that power" (*The Visionary Company: A Reading of English Romantic Poetry*, 1971). In this ode, Shelley attempts to identify the essence of that powerful force that gives human beings such feelings of joy and excitement when they confront the natural world directly. The unseen bird whose song prompts the poet to engage in a rhapsody of comparison stands as a metaphor for nature, and Shelley's vain attempts to find a way to make the power of the natural world seem intelligible suggest the general inability of humanity to comprehend the forces outside itself. In this sense, the forces of nature can be equated to the imagination, which for the Romantics is a kind of divine power that invests them with special insight.

Easily lost in the extensive list of comparisons in this poem is the central contrast that Shelley makes between the simple, freewheeling joy found in nature and the complex, paradoxical joy that humans feel, a joy bound up with desire and tragedy. Shelley makes this point clear in the eighteenth stanza when he describes the way people seem to view the world: "We look before and after," he observes (line 86), thinking of the human tendency to dwell on the past and the future rather than the present. Humanity's "sincerest laughter" is always "fraught" with some form of pain (lines 88-89), and its "sweetest songs" are those "that tell of saddest thought" (line 90).

Shelley suggests that the suffering humanity undergoes gives it the opportunity to understand the kind of joy the skylark represents. "If we were things born/ Not to shed a tear" he observes, "I know not how thy joy we ever could come near" (lines 93-95). Unlike the bird, humans define their essence—their humanity—through suffering as well as through joy. Nevertheless, being able to comprehend the joy the bird represents is important to the poet, for he believes that, should he be able to translate this joy into words, he would be able to help make life better for those who would read his poetry. Were he to learn "half the gladness" (line 101) that characterizes the skylark's life in nature, "Such harmonious madness/ From my lips would pour" (lines 103-104) that he could transform the world. Such, Shelley believes, is the high calling of the poet.

Laurence W. Mazzeno

TO A WATERFOWL

Author: William Cullen Bryant (1794-1878)
Type of poem: Lyric
First published: 1818; collected in *Poems*, 1821

The Poem

Both lyric and didactic, "To a Waterfowl" creates a natural scene in order to derive a moral lesson from it. The poem consists of eight quatrains, or four-line stanzas. Each stanza is written in pentameter and trimeter verse with an alternating rhyme scheme. The poem subtly blends descriptive scenes with inward reflections on them. The poem's title indicates an unspecified waterfowl, which some critics have suggested must be a goose. By not specifying the waterfowl's species, the poet suggests a more universal image that will help in conveying his theme. The poem opens with a question and the interrogative form is used in both the first and third stanzas.

The whole poem encompasses the flight of the waterfowl from two viewpoints. It appears to the poet at dusk as it gently floats overhead and gradually disappears into the horizon. The poet also projects the journey of the bird over vast territories as it flies from its winter abode to its summer home. The immediate image of the bird has the poet reflect on the bird's destination and the nature of its flight. In his whimsical meditating, the poet addresses the bird directly as though to open up a dialogue between nature's creature and the poet's inner soul. However, it is not until the last stanza that the poet reveals himself and speaks out his message in the first person.

The poem is organized clearly around the scenic images alternating with the poet's reflections. The first three stanzas describe the bird's flight and possible destination, while the fourth meditates on a "Power" that guides the bird's flight. The fifth through seventh stanzas return to the description of the bird's excursion, and the last stanza comes back to the guiding Power and brings out the poem's message. Thus, the poem twice repeats three descriptive stanzas followed by a meditation.

The poem opens at sunset as the sky glows red and evening dew falls. The poet sees a bird flying alone in the distance and muses that it is safe from any would-be hunter who would do it harm. The bird, alone and solitary, is silhouetted across the evening sky. As it floats smoothly by, the poet wonders where it is going. Is it headed for the edge of a lake in an area covered with weeds? Does it seek the margins of a wide river, or is it heading for the oceanside, "chafed" by the constant beat of the surf?

Then, the poet feels that some Power is leading the bird over coastlines that have no path, over a wide aerial expanse. Because this Power guides the bird, it can wander alone without ever getting lost. The bird will be flapping its wings the whole day, far above the earth in the cold, thin atmosphere. The bird may be weary, but it does not land even when night comes on. Nevertheless, the poet realizes that the bird's tiring journey will soon come to an end, and that the bird will be able to rest in its summer home, make noise among the other birds of the flock, and have the reeds cover its nest.

The poet tells the bird that it is gone, that it is "swallowed up" in the heavens. However, the image of the bird leaves a message in the poet's heart. The poet feels that the same Power that guides the bird from one area to another will guide him in the right path in his solitary journey through life.

Forms and Devices

This poem, like most of Bryant's poems, is filled with nature imagery. Bryant felt that the American poet should capture all the wonders of the American landscape and should also bring forth his own personal expression. This poem satisfies both goals. Bryant captures the natural scene of the bird at sunset. He shows how the sky glows with "the last steps of day." This metaphor unites the temporal with the spatial as day is seen in steps. There is also a unifying theme introduced in the poem's very last stanza, which states that the Power that guides the bird will "lead my steps aright." The metaphor of the "last steps of day" combines with images of the "crimson sky" and "rosy depths" to add the color of the natural sunset and to highlight the silhouette of the bird "darkly seen." The imagery and figure of speech help to create a vast and shaded background. However, the movement is graceful as the figure "floats along."

In describing the bird's journey, Bryant again paints a vast American landscape using vivid nature imagery, such as "plashy brink/ of weedy lake," "marge of river wide," and "chafed ocean side." Rivers, lakes, and oceans emerge in an immense vista. The bird becomes a compelling force in the sky that Bryant compares to a "desert" empty and vast; so high is the bird that the coast is "pathless." The bird has "fanned" the air with its wings as it continues on its strenuous journey. Bryant also uses dynamic auditory imagery to show the mood of the bird when its journey is over. When it reaches home, it shall "scream among" its "fellows." The use of "scream," instead of a word such as "cry," accentuates the bird's exhilaration. Moreover, the sibilant alliteration of "scream," "shall," "soon," and "sheltered" adds to the dynamics of the bird's homecoming.

In the final image of the bird, Bryant uses the metaphor of the throat in which the "abyss of heaven/ Hath swallowed up thy form . . ." This disappearance of the bird as a natural image lays the groundwork for the analogy between its flight and the life of the poet. Also, in showing the journey of the bird and comparing it to the life of a person, the poem focuses on a figure that is "Lone wandering, but not lost." "Lost" literally means not being able to find one's way; here, however, it also signifies the damned, those who are morally lost. The imagery and figurative language of the poem show a natural journey and compare it to an inner spiritual journey.

Themes and Meanings

According to one of his biographers, Bryant was inspired to write "To a Waterfowl" when he was a twenty-one-year-old aspiring lawyer on his way to a new town. As he walked through New England hills, sad and concerned about what would happen to him in his new life, he saw a solitary bird flying against a sunset and wondered about its destiny. When he stopped at an inn, he wrote what became the poem's last stanza.

Bryant not only wrote in the tradition of the Romantics, who saw sublime images in nature, but also followed the American Puritans, who saw natural events as signs of spiritual import. Like the Puritans, he read Nature as God's book, which can deliver insightful messages about the spiritual world. His poem depicts the figure of the solitary bird in its natural pattern of migration. He shows how it has no map to lead it across the "pathless coast"; yet it is "not lost." The solitary bird pursues its way tirelessly; even through the night, it does not land to rest. It continues on its way until it reaches its home or shelter. From a moral point of view the poet sees the flight of the bird as a metaphor for his own life. Like the bird, he is alone, a solitary wanderer, unsure of his path through life. Moreover, just as the bird is guided by a Power, the poet is also in the hands of providence, a benign power who would watch him "tread alone" and would "lead" his "steps aright."

Not only does this poem deliver a personal message that life is not aimless or left to chance, but it is also an argument for God or providence by use of design. The argument of design holds that the world and all its parts are so well designed and so well run that there must be some designer who put everything in order and keeps it that way. Because the migratory bird has such a "certain flight" over vast regions, there must be some Power to design and control its flight. The corollary to this argument is that the same power influences humans on their journey through life.

Like much early American literature, this poem also celebrates American individualism. The bird is not flying within a flock, but alone. The poet also is walking his journey alone. Individuals are responsible under the guidance of divine providence to walk their own paths, not to follow the herd. There are no institutions, governments, or social organizations to bolster individuals as they seek their destinies. As well as celebrating the power of divine providence, the poem acknowledges the individual's lonely struggle to discover himself anew. The solitary individual, nature, and divine providence are at the core of Bryant's poem.

Paul Rosefeldt

TO ALL GENTLENESS

Author: William Carlos Williams (1883-1963)
Type of poem: Lyric
First published: 1944, in *The Wedge*

The Poem

Gentleness, even all gentleness, may sound restrictive, but the poem "To All Gentleness" asserts that apparent opposites are akin. The first simile, likening "pink roses bending ragged in the rain" to a plumber's silvered cylindrical tank, posits a relationship between apparent incomparables. The speaker encounters both on a trip through the rain, the cylinder advertising a plumber's shop. Both, the speaker finds, invoke "enduring" gentleness. Surrounded by rain, the roses support a cylinder of raindrops above them, linking them surprisingly but with the clarity of geometry to the plumber's tank. The soft, organic, and vulnerable and the hard, mechanical, and indestructible are thus seen to be related. Indeed, the rose plant itself, to protect its tender flower, produces thorns and is thus a combination of gentle beauty and the threat of violence.

His contemporaries, the speaker reflects, ignore the lessons of nature about survival depending upon complementary contraries, the soft and hard, the gentle and fierce. People foolishly distinguish between high art—opera and the classics—and the everyday, the "anti-poetic." That distinction is, the speaker asserts, "Garbage." Poetry should not divide the world but should, like an old painting of the biblical prophet Isaiah's ideal, the lion and lamb lying down together in peace, cause one to see the unity of what otherwise seems opposed. People aim too narrowly, failing to see relatedness. An archer regards her ability as a route to prizes and a teaching job. Others exercise themselves in law courts to avoid intimate human relationships. Still others engage in business as a wedge that unnaturally divides their heads, creating oppositions within them. They buy nature instead of appreciating and living in it. With World War II raging, the speaker mentions a fighter plane that crashed. Even violent mechanical failure can, if the pilot falls into the sea, result in seawater salving his wounds. Gentleness and fierceness are linked, even as a wave rising and a wave turning into foam are one. That young pilot, a native of Seattle, would be able to return home alive. The speaker asks, Why separate astronomer Copernicus and musician Dmitri Shostakovich from what they accomplished; why separate the "occasion" from them? Such differences are like distinctions between halves of an apple. The wave that lifts and the wave that dashes down, death of one creature and provision of food for another, are parts of a unity. Caught up in only half their lives, people ignore the beauties of nature, "blind to/ the sun and moon, the brilliant/ moonlight leaves."

Military violence and the "packed word," encrusted with acquired connotations that shroud clarity, prevent humans from discovering relationships. They must understand through physical presence at opportune moments, presented in cleansed language. "Strength/ thrust upon weakness, the convulsive ecstasy," images of sexual union, the thrusting male and soft receiving female, should be seen as evidence of the constructive union of apparent opposites, not as violent images of conquest. Neither violence nor gentleness is the "core" of being; both are—even as milkweed and an embankment, a plant "reaching up from sand and rubble" are—elements of a single reality.

The speaker refers to a thin, pregnant woman who is a forewoman at the ship foundry, a valuable worker during wartime. She has had three miscarriages, and her husband married her in order to produce sons. That slender pregnant woman is tough, impervious to pain—gentle enough to be a calming place for violence, to embody the unification of opposites as do the cylinder and thorny rose with which the poem began.

Forms and Devices

Readers do not know specifically whom the poem's speaker is addressing. Perhaps they are simply overhearing a soliloquy, or perhaps the speaker is actively trying to persuade the reader. The poem takes a form appropriate to talk—paragraphs of free verse. The form and diction of much of Williams's poetry, a selection of everyday words in an arrangement free from formal strictures, was sometimes called "anti-poetic," but such a judgment is simplistic and misleading. The poem is shaped by an inner logic. The importance of "enduring," for example, warrants a full line, the space of many words, because endurance is long-lasting, often despite adversity. The form responds to content. The thought of paragraph 1 is not quite done, so the paragraph that follows "enduring" is hemi-stitched to it, a subparagraph picturing the indissoluble union between flowers and a boiler, two objects of the first paragraph. Physical form in this kind of poetry both enhances and depends upon meaning. Significance determines its own formal embodiment. Thus the seemingly "free" verse is shaped by the content it conveys, the significant elements of the whole.

In Williams's poetry, those significant elements are communicated through objects, events, and representations of people's thoughts: wilting roses, a plumber's tank, the misguided thoughts of opinionated people, the ambitions of an archer, the tribulations of a fighter pilot, the penetrating and receiving aspects of love and sexuality. The poems speak through "concrete" references, abiding by Williams's dictum that truths should be sought "in things." This commitment to inherent truth identifies Williams as a modernist. His wedding of truth in things to everyday words, allowing him to address a broad audience, identifies him as an inclusive modernist. His democratic values spring to life in both the content and the forms of his poetry, helping to shape the free, sinewy, and meticulously ordered poems in which he embodies his thoughts.

Themes and Meanings

Williams's commitment to concrete, "embodied" meaning was shared by many of his contemporaries, including the poet Ezra Pound, a fellow student at the University of Pennsylvania, where Williams obtained his medical degree. Pound argued that poems should be a "presentation" rather than a telling, that they should communicate through "images." He and another contemporary, Amy Lowell, were largely responsible for Imagism, an approach to the writing of poetry that entailed communication through concrete language. The novelist Joseph Conrad had a comparable belief that "all art . . . appeals primarily to the senses." The young James Joyce, working to create "epiphanies," moments of sudden insight built up out of mundane events, concurred, and T. S. Eliot wrote of the need for "objective correlatives" that convey through the senses the significant content of a work of art. What lies behind such dedicated attempts to ground truths in physical evidence is the realization that received beliefs are frequently wrong.

Even received words seemed to Williams suspect. He not only preferred everyday words to the presumptuous terminology of intellectuals but also sought to cleanse his words of "packed" connotations, falsifying associations that attach to them over time. "To All Gentleness" is part of a volume he called *The Wedge*, a title he associated with "LangWedge"; language, he thought, if misused, can divide people within themselves, separate them from one another, and keep them from understanding.

On the other hand, precise language provides access to truths, glimpses of what nineteenth century philosopher Immanuel Kant called the numenal world. Those opposite possibilities, both derived from language, help one to see from yet another perspective the essential point of "To All Gentleness": that opposites, properly approached, interpenetrate constructively. As the experience of the pilot thrown into the water from his crashing war plane demonstrates, both death in nature and being sustained and saved by nature are features of existence. Williams himself, the child of parents who combined Basque, Dutch-Jewish, English, and French heritages, was composed of apparently contradictory sets, an American melting pot in microcosm.

The term "anti-poetic," to Williams's chagrin, was used by his friend and contemporary, poet Wallace Stevens, to describe his poems. Stevens, like Williams, functioned in both the practical daily world and the world of art: Williams was a physician; Stevens was an insurance executive. However, Stevens distinguished between the two worlds he occupied, whereas Williams saw them as unified. As this poem demonstrates, a pregnant factory worker is no more or less poetic than a rose, a fighter pilot, or a plumber's tank. The seemingly contradictory elements in the factory worker and in her life actually form a unity, and her sinewy strength has a beauty that poems should aspire to attain. "To All Gentleness" wonderfully presents the paradoxes and urges readers to resolve the contradictions of their own lives in quest of a better world, created and peopled by an accepting and generous humanity.

Albert Wachtel

TO AN ATHLETE DYING YOUNG

Author: A. E. Housman (1859-1936)
Type of poem: Elegy
First published: 1896, in *A Shropshire Lad*

The Poem

"To an Athlete Dying Young" is written in seven quatrains of rhymed iambic tetrameter. Each line, therefore, normally contains eight syllables, with the even-numbered syllables stressed. In each quatrain, the first and third, and second and fourth lines rhyme on the final syllable.

A. E. Housman was an Englishman by birth and a classical scholar (mostly of Roman poetry) by profession. In many of his poems, these two aspects of their author combine to create a paradoxically unchanging world of human vicissitudes. In this poem, for example, there is no clearly defined setting, either in space or time. Having a universal theme, it could take place anywhere at any time, whether in ancient Greece or modern England. Housman, therefore, is not describing a particular situation (or an actual life), but a universal condition of humankind. The "athlete" of the title is entirely fictitious, having been created by Housman to exemplify his unorthodox religious view that humanity has been thrust by someone or something into a world alien to its desires.

The first quatrain recalls an event in the recent past (less than a year before, presumably) when the unnamed young athlete had won a track meet sponsored by competing municipalities. In recognition of his feat, the people of his own town (to whom he had brought this much-desired victory) honored him profusely by parading him through the marketplace to his home in a sedan chair (mounted on poles and carried on the shoulders of either two or four men).

The second quatrain, starkly juxtaposed to the first, similarly describes the young runner's funeral. Once again, he is being carried "shoulder-high," but this time in a coffin rather than a sedan chair. Both are rectangular boxes of approximately the same size and therefore look rather alike. The "home" to which the runner is brought this time, however, is his grave. The "threshold" is the edge of the grave pit, and the "stiller town" is the cemetery. How, when, or why he died the reader does not know.

Quatrains 3 through 7 are the unidentified (but clearly older) narrator's comments on the runner's seemingly tragic death; they represent thematic development rather than narrative. The comments are addressed directly to the dead runner—presumably able to hear them—who is praised for having chosen the right time in life to die. Thus, he will never be around to see how temporary his fame was. Nor will he ever know the agony of being beaten in another running of the same race another year. Among the dead, if not among the living, his fame will endure forever.

Forms and Devices

The form of the poem is deliberately simple, as if chiseled in stone, and appropriate to the generality of its theme. Descriptive elaboration is minimal throughout, so as not to distract the reader from more general considerations or to suggest that the runner's death is merely a tragic incident rather than a universal symbol. Knowing that the runner is fictitious, one then sees that the race is metaphoric. In line 5, specifically, all humans become "runners" in the inevitable race toward death that they are powerless to avoid. Similarly, everyone runs a race to be remembered for one thing or another, competing for the prize of fame, but time destroys whatever reputation a person can build. The course of life, then, leads not only to death but also to oblivion.

"Smart lad," at the beginning of line 9, is deliberately abrupt—*both* syllables are stressed—so as to emphasize the paradoxical nature of the poet's assertion that it is more intelligent to die than to live. "Glory" in the same stanza means both fame and light, the implied sunset being death. Wreaths made of laurel were normally awarded to winning athletes (and poets) in the ancient worlds of Greece and Rome. The laurel in Housman's poem is therefore another reference to fame or recognition. The rose has long been a symbol of beautiful ephemerality; it represents a fine moment that cannot survive the passage of time. In the fourth quatrain, "shady night" invokes not only darkness but also the similarly obscure abode of departed spirits (shades) of Greco-Roman mythology. Housman's references to the afterlife are only poetic devices, however, as he did not actually believe in survival after death of any kind. In the fifth quatrain, "renown" and "name" are personifications.

The "So" of line 21 tells the reader that the last two stanzas together form the conclusion of the poem. Housman's image of fading echoes (derived from footsteps no longer heard) is another reference to the ephemerality of fame. Both the sill and lintel of that quatrain refer to an imagined window between the world of the living and the dead. The narrator urges the dead runner to look back through the window toward the world of the living and to display to it the "still-defended" (because no one will ever beat him) challenge cup that he received for winning the race. On the death side of the window (quatrain 7), other shades will then gaze in wonder and admiration at the runner to find that his seemingly temporary fame is now destined to endure among them for eternity. The "garland" of the last line suggests the one given to the Queen of May in traditional English festivities on the first of that month, when she reigned for that day only.

Themes and Meanings

"To an Athlete Dying Young" is clearly not about a particular teenager or even about athletes in general but about life. In Housman's bitter experience, life is a series of disappointments. (Probably the greatest disappointment in his own life came at the conclusion of his college years when, in part distracted by an unfortunate love affair, he did poorly on terminal examinations and had to struggle in obscurity for years before achieving the recognition as a scholar that he unquestionably deserved.) In other poems in *A Shropshire Lad*, Housman more explicitly rebels against the supposed Maker of this world for having designed a cagelike "home" for humanity that is so inhospitable to human well-being and so unlikely to fulfill human desires. Typically,

Housman advocates a kind of stoic endurance (often fortified with good English ale) in the face of the wretched uncertainties and predictable disappointments that are the lot of all humankind.

The beauty of dying young is that all the disappointments of adult life can be avoided, and the Maker who seemingly (through design or indifference) inflicts them can be thwarted. In this poem, however, Housman finds no one to blame and seemingly accepts the human condition—one falls into oblivion even before death—as if it were the law of gravity. It is surely not in the nature of fame to endure, any more than it is natural for roses to exist forever. Oblivion follows fame as night follows day or silence follows applause. Paradoxically, then, one can perhaps achieve fame, but only at the expense of life—and only by accident, never by design.

Dennis R. Dean

TO AUTUMN

Author: John Keats (1795-1821)
Type of poem: Ode
First published: 1820, in *Lamia, Isabella, The Eve of St. Agnes, and Other Poems*

The Poem

"To Autumn" is an ode divided in three eleven-line stanzas. John Keats employs an elaborate rhyme scheme, setting off with a semicolon the first four lines as a syntactic unit rhyming *abab* from the next seven lines, which rhyme *cdecdde*. An ode is a serious and dignified lyric poem, usually fairly long, written in an elevated style and adhering to a stanzaic form.

In this ode, Keats personifies autumn, attributing human qualities to the season. The first stanza gives a general personification of autumn; in the second and third stanzas, the personification is intensified by apostrophe, a direct address to autumn. Moreover, autumn is personified as a woman whose union with the male sun sets the ripening process in motion: "Close bosom-friend of the maturing sun;/ Conspiring with him how to load and bless/ With fruit the vines that round the thatch-eves run."

In the first stanza, Keats presents the early stages of autumn; the weather is still warm. Late flowers bloom, and the bees think summer will never end, since "Summer has o'er-brimmed their clammy cells." Everything in the stanza comes to repletion: the sun, the vines, the trees, the gourds, the nuts, and the hives are brought into ripeness.

In the second stanza, the ripening process is fulfilled. Autumn, directly addressed as "thou" in line 12, is seen amid her harvested grain or found sleeping on a "half-reap'd furrow," deceived by the late-blooming poppies that lured the bees in the first stanza to the same deception. Awakened, autumn watches the oozing of apples in the cider press "hours by hours," as if in halting the time she can hold off winter's arrival.

The last stanza presents autumn having progressed past ripeness and harvest, heralding the coming of winter. Keats, alluding to spring, admonishes autumn to appreciate her own sounds and her own beauty, exquisitely evoked by the late autumn sun setting on the harvested fields: "While barred clouds bloom the soft-dying day,/ And touch the stubble-plains with rosy hue." The sounds of late autumn are the mournful sounds of natural completeness. The day that had begun so "mellow" in the first stanza is shown "soft-dying" in the last.

Forms and Devices

"To Autumn" is rich in imagery, evoking the perceptions of sight, hearing, smell, taste, and touch. Each stanza highlights one of the senses. The first stanza especially evokes the senses of smell and touch. The sharp smell of the early-morning mist, the mellowness of ripe apples, and the sweet-smelling flowers attracting bees all work together to tempt the reader into believing that summer will never end. Nothing appears static in this stanza; the fruit, the nuts, and the honeycombs swell, bursting into ripeness, spilling out of their shells.

Keats emphasizes the sense of sight in the second stanza by inviting the reader to see autumn as harvester, her hair "soft-lifted by the winnowing wind," checking, cutting, and gleaning the crops. The sights evoke a certain lassitude. Autumn moves slowly amid her stores; she sleeps, "drows'd by the fume of poppies"; idly, she watches the "last oozings hours by hours." The frantic movements so prevalent in the first stanza are slowly replaced by stasis in the second stanza until time seems no longer to move toward winter.

Although visual beauty is evoked by the sun going down on the "stubble-plains," it is the sense of hearing that sets the tone in the last stanza. The reader and autumn are reminded that the songs of spring have been replaced by a different but no less beautiful music. One hears the mourning sound of the gnats, the bleating of the full-grown lambs, the whistling song of the red-breast, and the twittering of the swallows as they gather for their flight toward summer. The sudden chorus of sounds breaks the heavy silence of the second stanza, where in the midday heat of a fall day all sounds were hushed. The music brings autumn to a fitting close; the cycle of nature has been completed, and winter has come with a natural sweetness as the day dies softly to the mournful sound of the gnats.

In addition to the rich imagery, Keats uses an intricate structure and rhythm to bring the day and the season to their "soft-dying" close. The first stanza pictures early morning and pre-harvest ripening: "Seasons of mist," "maturing sun," and "warm days." In the second stanza, it is midday and mid-season. The time is ripe for harvesting; cider presses are in full use, and the afternoon induces sleep. The last stanza pictures the evening and post-harvest sounds as the sun sets over stubbled fields, awakening the mournful sounds of evening.

The first stanza is replete with single-syllable verbs that receive strong primary stress: "load," "bless," "fill," "swell," and "plump." In the second stanza, well-chosen alliteration and assonance induce the hushed appearance of the time of day and of season: "Thy hair soft-lifted by the winnowing wind." Some of the words in the third stanza are onomatopoeic, imitating the natural sounds they portray: "bleat," "wailful," "twitter," and "mourn."

Themes and Meanings

The double progression through the day and the season point to a theme that recurs in many of Keats's poems, the theme of transience. In "Ode on a Grecian Urn" and "Ode to a Nightingale," this theme is treated with anguish and rebellion; in "To Autumn," the theme is treated with serenity and acceptance.

The first stanza tries to prolong summer, yet the sun is qualified by the adjective "maturing," hinting that he matures the harvest as well as grows old himself. The second stanza pictures autumn as a reaper, a harvester of the now-ripened crops; the image of the reaper also calls up death itself. Death, however, is momentarily suspended, found sleeping in a "half-reaped furrow."

In the last stanza, the notion of death, the natural completion of the process begun in the first stanza, gathers strength as gnats are mourning, the sun is setting, and the swallows gather to escape the coming of winter. The idea of rebirth and spring is subsumed in the question "Where are the songs of Spring? Ay, where are they?" Yet the music of autumn, of completion and death, is not only accepted but also enjoyed for having its own fulfilling sounds. Death is not to be shunned or feared but accepted as the natural end of life.

Another theme, closely linked with the theme of transience, is the juxtaposition of melancholy and joy that pervades this and many of Keats's poetic works. Melancholy can be defined as a certain feeling of sadness or depression. The theme that joy can only be appreciated in juxtaposition with sadness is explicitly stated at the close of "Ode on Melancholy": "Ay, in the very temple of delight/ Veiled Melancholy has her sovran shrine."

"To Autumn" implictly illustrates the union between joy and melancholy: life can only be lived to its fullest extent if death is present at its very conception. The beauty and joy experienced in "To Autumn" are heightened by the passage of time and the coming of winter. In "Ode on a Grecian Urn" (1820), spring is frozen in its perfection: "Ah, happy, happy boughs! that cannot shed/ Your leaves, nor ever bid the Spring adieu." Yet this, Keats declares, is a "Cold Pastoral." In "Ode to a Nightingale," the nightingale, "immortal Bird," sings "of summer in full-throated ease"; the singing, however, is "too happy in thine happiness." Yet, in "To Autumn," the beauty and joy of the dying day are reflected in and complemented by images evoking sadness: the sun setting on the stubble fields and the wail of the gnats.

Keats composed this poem on September 19, 1819, after a long walk. He wrote to one of his friends about the contentment that he felt on that autumn afternoon:

How beautiful the season is now—How fine the air. A temperate sharpness about it. Really, without joking, chaste weather—Dian skies—I never lik'd stubble fields as much as now—Aye better than the chilly green of the spring. Somehow a stubble plain looks warm—in the same way that some pictures look warm—this struck me much in my Sunday's walk that I composed upon it.

That contentment, because it directly evokes sadness and implies acceptance of the process toward death beyond grief, is mirrored in Keats's poem.

Koos Daley

TO DISAPPEAR ENHANCES—

Author: Emily Dickinson (1830-1886)
Type of poem: Narrative
First published: 1890, in *Poems*

The Poem

In this twenty-line poem comprising five four-line stanzas, Emily Dickinson deals with the topics that she most frequently addresses in her poetry: death, loneliness, the hope (but never the promise) of immortality. She begins with the observation that the man who runs away, who disappears, is enhanced by his having left, because his memory lingers and perhaps is softened by his absence. He is, in Dickinson's words, "tinctured for an instant/ With Immortality," which is Dickinson's initial hint that the poem will be concerned ultimately with death.

Yesterday's vagrant today resides in memory, where he takes on a "superstitious value" as those who knew him tamper with their memories of him, adjusting those memories to suit their own consciences. In the first two stanzas, Dickinson toys with the notion that distance alters memories. Her capitalization of "Immortality" lends an enhanced importance to the word, often the most significant word in her poems.

The phrase "We tamper with Again'" at the end of the second stanza implies that the man who runs away, the vagrant, is better gone. This leads into the word "Never" in the next line, where the anonymous "we" in the poem cannot cherish the man but can adorn him with memories softened by his departure.

By the beginning of the fourth stanza, it is clear that the poet is talking about more than just a man who runs off, a vagrant who disappears, because in this stanza she introduces "Death," with a capital *D*, prominently in the first line. As soon as readers encounter this word, their minds leap back to the first stanza's "tinctured for an instant/ With Immortality."

As is usual in Dickinson's poems, the poet leads her readers into the poem on a literal level but quickly moves to a more metaphorical level that is related in subtle ways to the initial literalness of the poem. She clinches the metaphorical meaning in the fourth stanza, then she moves on with considerable whimsy to the final stanza, which can be taken in a variety of ways.

The "Fruit perverse to plucking" can be read as a person unready and unwilling to die, but it can also be read more personally on a Freudian level to suggest something about Dickinson's own sexuality. She was the quintessential virgin, the unviolated woman with volcanic passions that, in her time and in her social situation, she dared not expose except in her poetry. Her poetry is redolent with sexual innuendo if one chooses to read it in that way. Certainly the bases for such interpretation exist within many Dickinson poems.

It is clear that this poem is about loss, but the poem does not bemoan the loss. Rather, it accepts the loss as the basis for creating memories that are perhaps more agreeable than the actual presence of the one who disappeared. Proximity does not always breed appreciation. Whereas physical beings frequently act independently of others, when such beings cease to be present, others completely control their own memories of them. Dickinson seems comforted at the thought that such control is possible. In this poem she sets up an interesting dichotomy between reality and memory, between proximity and distance.

Forms and Devices

The short stanzas and overall brevity of this poem typify much of Emily Dickinson's verse. Her longest poem ("I cannot live with You—") consists of a mere fifty lines. Few of her poems exceed twenty-five lines. The economy of words in all of Dickinson's verse is notable. Like most accomplished poets, Dickinson regularly calls upon a single word to do double or triple duty.

This poem is more abstract than some of Dickinson's other poems and as a result has less of the visual imagery that one finds in a poem such as "I taste a liquor never brewed—" or "I like to see it lap the Miles—." "To disappear enhances—" deals essentially with nonvisual things: disappearance, honor, memory, immortality, excellence, delight—things of the mind. Even words that usually evoke visual images, notably "fruit," "man," and "vagrant," as used here are so metaphoric that their visual qualities are diminished, an effect that Dickinson intended.

The rhyming patterns exemplify the various kinds of rhyme with which Dickinson experimented constantly. In the first stanza, she uses imperfect rhyme when she ends line 2 with "away" and line 4 with "Immortality." Dickinson does not stray from perfect rhyme because she is incapable of achieving it. Indeed, her manuscripts, detailed in Thomas H. Johnson's edition, *The Poems of Emily Dickinson, Including Variant Readings Critically Compared with All Known Manuscripts* (published by the Harvard University Press in a three-volume edition in 1955), reveal that she often achieved perfect rhyme only to alter it consciously into imperfect, suspended (saw/now), or so-called eye rhyme (one/lone). In this poem, one finds eye rhyme in the second stanza, where "lain" and "again" look more similar than they sound.

In the third stanza, Dickinson stretches even further when she ends line 2 with "thing" and line 4 with "adorn," where the only auditory link is the *n* sound. In the following stanza, she creates a similar situation, ending line 2 with "discern" and line 4 with "then," again using the *n* sound as the most prominent commonality between the two words.

Dickinson pushed poetry to new limits because she consciously and continuously strove to avoid the conventional, monotonously rhyming poetry that is often the mark of popular but not very accomplished poets. One might call Dickinson a minimalist whose impact is subtle but striking. She likes to select words that will explode in readers' imaginations. The key word in this poem is "tinctured," which evokes visual and olfactory images in many readers, who, upon encountering the word, think immediately of something such as tincture of iodine, with its sharp, characteristic smell and its typically deep orangish color.

Themes and Meanings

It is interesting that in the first stanza, Dickinson, who is a conscious wordsmith of unquestionable competence, refers to "the Man *that* runs away" rather than to "the Man *who* runs away," which would be the more usual relative pronoun to use in this instance. By using "that" rather than "who," Dickinson decreases the humanness of the man in question, making him more of an abstraction than he would be had the more usual pronoun been selected.

On one hand, the theme of this poem is concerned with the loss of a person. On the other hand, it is concerned with control because the "we" in the poem can re-create the lost individual, the vagrant, simply by tampering with their individual memories of him. Whereas Dickinson begins by applying this control to someone who has gone away, she quickly moves toward universalizing it by introducing Death in the fourth stanza, making it clear that subtle overtones of death lurk barely visible even in the first two stanzas. The first two lines of the second stanza seem funereal after one has read the fourth stanza, although they might not strike one that way initially. The term "superstitious value" in the second stanza assumes ghostly tones when read in the light of the fourth stanza.

The "we" in the poem is a collective we, a Greek chorus kind of "we," reflecting the conscience of a community in regard to loss, separation, and ultimately death. The quotation marks around "Again" and "Never" in stanzas 2 and 3 emphasize two opposites, as does Dickinson's idiosyncratic capitalization of these words. Her terminal punctuation—dashes rather than periods, and not even many dashes—undergirds the theme of continuance that the poem suggests by its emphasis on memory, which in this case becomes a virtual synonym for conscience.

The last stanza of "To disappear enhances—" is a curious one. It is infused with sexually charged words, notably "plucking" and "ecstatic." The choice of "perverse" in this context suggests but does not clearly state Dickinson's views on her own sexual restraint and virginity. This suggestion is buttressed by the words "unobtained Delight," used with considerable irony at the poem's end. Dickinson during her lifetime had platonic attachments to several men; it is speculated that she was in love with at least two of them, Thomas Wentworth Higginson and Judge Otis Phillips Lord. This poem can perhaps be read within the context of her unfulfilled love as well as within the context of the imposed sexual restraint of her era and her society.

The final stanza is about as puckish as Emily Dickinson ever becomes, particularly in line 2, where she implies an openness to love and, indeed, to sexual encounter, although one must probe far below the literal surface meaning of the poem to arrive at such an interpretation. In many ways, the last verse of "To disappear enhances—" is a maverick verse, close to but not quite being a free-standing poem unto itself.

R. Baird Shuman

TO EARTHWARD

Author: Robert Frost (1874-1963)
Type of poem: Lyric
First published: 1923; collected in *New Hampshire: A Poem with Notes and Grace Notes*, 1923

The Poem

"To Earthward" is a lyric poem of eight stanzas contrasting the airy pleasures of youth with the more earthy, yet more spiritual and congruent, passions of maturity. Robert Frost wrote the poem in 1914 while he was living at Little Iddens in England. He was not to publish it until nine years later, when he was close to fifty years old.

While the development of a kinesthetic motif is central to the meaning of the poem, Frost makes it clear that human experience necessarily embraces different forms of sensuality and that joy and pain are always mixed. His poem distills a select number of especially vivid images that combine a variety of sensual impressions. For example, the musk and grapevine springs combine taste and smell; the honeysuckle coalesces touch and odor; the lips both taste and feel.

The poem is evenly divided into two sections. The first four stanzas recall the paradisiacal intensity of the sensual pleasures of youth, while the last four describe the attraction of human spirit toward the earth, an attraction which necessarily involves the more holistic experiences of maturity. The first section describes youthful love in exquisitely tactile terms. The touch of love "at the lips" (perhaps a kiss) was as much as the poet could bear. He recalls living on air that teased him with what may have been the scent of musk, and he remembers the confusing swirl and ache from the touch of dew shaken on the knuckle.

In the final four stanzas, Frost describes the experiences of maturity and the mixed nature of passionate love. He now sees a direct relationship between love of the earth and love of another human being. While the first four stanzas appear to lament the passage of an intensely sensitive period of youth, including the poet's awakening to the beauty of the earth, he now descends to a more inclusive description of his longing to feel its weight and strength with his whole body. While his images are still very tactile, he enjambs them with other, peripheral sensations. No feeling is seasoned enough or sufficiently preserved that does not have just a dash of pain.

In the fifth and sixth stanzas, Frost presents a complex, intensely passionate, and even rough inventory of feelings and sensations. He says that he craves not only the pleasures but also the weariness, the imperfections and faults, the sadness and tears, that are an integral part of love and fulfillment. His catalog of sensuality is characterized by "salty" things and a spicy blend of preservatives: bitter cloves, sweet bark, the salt of tears, and the salt on the wounds of life.

The poet describes his spiritual and physical hunger to embrace the hard actualities of life in the last two stanzas. His hand is made stiff and sore and scarred from leaning hard on the grass and sand. His reference to such scars suggests an implicit acceptance of the scars of experience which come with age. His description of the sacredness of his love suggests that he feels a rough, perhaps almost masochistic, pleasure in resisting death and in reviving the senses. Yet there is a direct and very physical connection between the sensation of his hand on grass and sand, his acceptance of death, and his metaphorical and symbolic hunger to embrace the whole earth, a passion which is even more fully described in the last stanza.

In the final stanza, the poem affirms his hunger to move beyond the effects of mere sensation, exquisite as it may be. He attempts to transcend the limits of sensuality by making a connection between the total spectrum of his emotions and his whole body. In his awareness of the onset of old age, he longs for enough weight and strength to feel the hard actualities of life with his whole being and with his whole length.

Forms and Devices

All eight stanzas consist of four lines each which are rhymed *abab*. Each stanza has three lines with three stresses modified by a two-stress fourth line. The poem starts with a trochee (strong accent first), which is followed by an anapest (two unstressed syllables followed by a stressed syllable). This startles the reader and directs attention to the word "lips," with its connection to passion, and it puts a special emphasis on the word "love," the subject of the poem. Generally, however, the poem maintains a relatively constant iambic rhythm (an unstressed syllable followed by a stressed syllable).

The poem has many monosyllabic words. This suggests a need to strip away complications and to simplify to get at fundamental truths. The poem's images can be somewhat confusing, however, because they tend to merge a sense of the fragile and of the strong. Most suggest primary sensations, and there are no strong visual images anywhere. Instead, the poem's imagery depends on the primitive sensations relating to touch, smell, and taste.

Frost once wrote of his hunger to "lean hard on facts, so hard . . . they hurt." In "To Earthward," he sets up a delicate balance of contraries in which images of pain become as much a correlative of fulfillment as pleasure. To the mature poet, pain, the "aftermark of almost too much love," is now a corollary to the airy pleasures of youth. This delicate balance is further developed, not only in the first four stanzas dedicated to the poet's remembrance of his youth and in the four dedicated to his description of maturity, but also in the balance of lips and air, air to earth, earth to his scarred hand (which necessarily pushes the earth away while it presses to the earth), and his hand to his full length, which would be pressed to the earth without resistance, as if they were made one.

Finally, in embracing the earth, the poet may also be reconciling himself to the feminine aspect of his nature. Archetypally, the earth is commonly regarded as a female symbol. The poet thus appears to embrace and become reconciled with the feminine and nurturing facet of his being.

Themes and Meanings

The poem is a lyric meditation on what it means to move and grow toward wholeness and physical and emotional congruity. It is an admission that feelings are not selective and that they do not simply encompass the ecstatic and pleasurable. Pain and pleasure, ecstasy and anguish, sorrow and celebration, life and death are integral with each other and are essential parts of the same range of human emotions. Also, the poem suggests that any honest understanding of maturity will insist that the feelings and experiences of youth be a congruent and integrated part of the adult. The implied pain of love in youth, described in the images of petals, musk, and honeysuckle, is now tacitly acknowledged as not only feeling good but also being almost unbearable in its capacity to give pleasure. As such, it is painful as well as exquisite.

The poem suggests, then, that the process of living and maturing involves a curious totality. Frost was forty when he wrote the poem, and he claimed that the changes he had undergone during his lifetime were a matter "of record" in "To Earthward." The poem suggests that the process of being fully alive and fully mature necessitates a capacity to embrace and compact the full range of human emotions, sensations, and experiences. As one ages, one begins to realize that to understand life, one must understand death and pain; to accept love is to accept the pain of loving, for love must invariably lead to sorrow. The experience of being fully alive and fully human thus insists that a person hope for weight and strength enough to embrace all of life and all the limits of life in its most painful and in its most beautiful complexions. That same experience also requires an implicit understanding of one's own mortality and a willingness to accept death, which is a part of life. In embracing the earth, then, the poet not only seeks to revive and intensify his passion for life, he also admits a longing to return to earth, which is both the mother of life and the grave.

Whereas in youth the poet saw pleasure in terms of parts—in lips and knuckles for example—he now longs to embrace it with his whole being. Passion, then, is not objectified as an isolated or singular experience affecting only one facet of his being. It is all-enveloping, involving the total self with a complex of sensations and emotions that cannot be made selective toward the pleasure end of the spectrum. The poem describes the very essence of maturity. It was probably the change which Frost said was a matter "of record" in the poem, and it is most certainly an elegant testimonial to an unqualified acceptance and love of life.

Matts Djos

TO ELSIE

Author: William Carlos Williams (1883-1963)
Type of poem: Lyric
First published: 1923, in *Spring and All*

The Poem

"To Elsie" is a free-verse poem of sixty-six lines, divided into twenty-two stanzas of three lines each. The title indicates the person to whom the poem is addressed: Elsie, the poet's housekeeper.

Elsie's early life is sketched in a few lines: "reared by the state and/ sent out at fifteen to work in/ some hard-pressed/ house in the suburbs." Not even the first mention of her name, "some Elsie," dispels the aura of obscurity that surrounds her. Moreover, this introduction is delayed until the fourteenth stanza, well into the poem.

Before Elsie herself is acknowledged, the poet implies her benighted conception: Stanzas 3 through 9 report promiscuous encounters between "devil-may-care men" and "young slatterns." Such coupling is brutish and violent in its carelessness: "succumbing without/ emotion/ save numbed terror."

Issuing from such an act, this "desolate" girl expresses "with broken/ brain the truth about us." She embodies the indictment that opens the poem: "The pure products of America/ go crazy." Elsie's body—her "ungainly" hips and "flopping" breasts—represent the perversity of a vulgar, ultimately sterile culture. Her attraction to "cheap/ jewelry" and "rich young men with fine eyes" suggests the roving, lustful acquisitiveness that causes Americans to treat the earth that bears and would nurture them as "excrement." They live as "degraded prisoners/ destined/ to hunger" until they "eat filth."

Although the poet envisions "isolate flecks" in which "something/ is given off"—illumination in glimpses—"No one" is there "to witness/ and adjust"; that is, to interpret the signs and institute reform. The poem concludes with the observation that there is "no one to drive the car." America runs recklessly, devoid of vision or good judgment.

Forms and Devices

An innovator in American poetry, William Carlos Williams promoted Imagism and its metamorphosis into Objectivism. His declaration "No ideas but in things" articulated his emphasis on re-creating objects and events rather than on directly expressing thought and emotion. In this poem, Williams's feelings and convictions about American culture are concentrated in his portrait of the tawdry, crazed Elsie.

Fellow poet Octavio Paz has called Williams "the author of the most *vivid* poems of modern American poetry." The critic Hugh Fox identifies Williams's point of departure as sensation, which, through language, is transformed into things—more precisely, into "verbal objects." The poem—in Fox's words, a "fusion" of the "liveliness of sensation" and "objectivity of things"—itself constitutes a verbal object. Its self-defining, organic form is what Williams meant by free verse.

Rather than adhering to any formal metrical pattern, Williams based his work on the pauses and inflections of idiomatic American speech. He sought a "language modified by our environment, the American environment." The stanzaic structure of "To Elsie"—a short line preceded and followed by longer ones—conveys the groping-for-words spontaneity of colloquial speech.

"To Elsie" evidences Williams's focus on the local and the particular. As if searching out a specific spot on the map, the poem locates the reader in the "ribbed north end of/ Jersey" and finally in the "suburbs." With intense detail, the poet re-creates the geography of the place—"isolate lakes and/ valleys," hedges of "choke-cherry/ or viburnum," "fields of goldenrod in/ the stifling heat of September."

Within this perspective, the human scale diminishes; "deaf-mutes," "thieves," "devil-may-care men," "slatterns," and "degraded prisoners" populate the poem. These oblivious, bewildered souls bathe in and eat "filth" and flaunt "sheer rags." Williams ends the poem with a metaphor for the delusionary and self-destructive narcissism of contemporary America: a driverless car. The poet refers to what popular culture celebrates and advertising exploits: America's obsession with the automobile.

Williams intended his poetry to simulate "the inevitable flux of the seeing eye." The poet shared the aim of the cubist painters he admired: to revolutionize perception. His confounding of background and foreground in the plane of the poem, for example, challenges conventional ways of seeing. Editor Charles Tomlinson notes cubist effects in Williams's use of ellipses, incongruous juxtapositions, and "verbal collages."

Themes and Meanings

"To Elsie" is found in Williams's book *Spring and All* (1923), which critic Jimmy Breslin reads as a reaffirmation of the creative principle, thwarted and repressed as it may be in America. Williams, a practicing physician, diagnoses his culture's disease as rapaciousness, a craving for stolen pleasures and quick, easy wealth. America's history chronicles her rash exploitation of the land. Both adventurers and Puritans pursued a mastery of nature that misprized the earth as a mere dung heap.

In this context, Elsie—her impressionable mind and voluptuous body suffering humiliation and decay—becomes an American Persephone. Stolen away and ravished by Pluto, god of avarice and death, Persephone personifies the virgin American wilderness, despoiled by greed for wealth and conquest. She embodies the buried creative principle, whose resurrection and transfiguration usher in spring and its fulfillment of promise.

D. H. Lawrence credits Williams with having taught him two ways of being American. The "chief" way, by "gutting the great continent in frenzies of mean fear," is the "Puritan way." An alternative, "heroic" way demands contact with America "as she is; dare to touch her!" Williams's concrete, tactile verse—what Anthony Libby called a "mysticism of particulars"—constituted the poet's way of knowing America with the intimacy and candor of touch.

This ready engagement enabled Williams to hear the "inarticulate poems" of his patients. Such responsiveness to the lives of others demonstrates one of the poet's most attractive qualities: his humanity. It helped him to achieve what John Keats termed "negative capability," or the ability to dissolve the boundaries between perceiver and perceived, which is to unify experience.

Amy Adelstein

TO GO TO LVOV

Author: Adam Zagajewski (1945-   )
Type of poem: Lyric
First published: 1985, as *Jechać do Lwowa*; English translation collected in *Tremor: Selected Poems,* 1985

The Poem

"To Go to Lvov" depicts an imaginary journey, a dream journey, to Lvov, the city of poet Adam Zagajewski's birth. Lvov was in a district that was appropriated from Poland by the Soviet Union after World War II; in consequence, Zagajewski's family moved into western Poland where the poet grew up. This poem thus involves looking backward into the lost world of childhood, but it implies that everyone possesses such a landscape that is simultaneously lost and always available in memory. The poem consists of eighty-three lines of free verse in one long stanza. The lines have roughly ten syllables, although many are longer and the last five are noticeably shorter than the rest of the poem. In its translated version, it has no metrical pattern. Instead, its organization rests on its consistent tone and on certain elements that are repeated in the course of its descriptions of Lvov.

The poem begins with the speaker's invitation to the reader to make the journey to Lvov, although from the very beginning it hints that Lvov may not exist at all except in dream. That is why the poem seems uncertain about whether this journey is taking place in September or March and even about which station is the right one "for Lvov." The speaker goes on to describe the natural landscape of Lvov with its poplars and ash trees. In line 18, the speaker introduces an architectural element of the city: the Roman Catholic cathedral "as straight/ as Sunday." It is one part of the city's religious heritage that also includes Russian Orthodox Christians as well as Jews. The details that describe the cathedral are embedded in other pictures of the gardens and botanical life of the city, including weeds, Queen Anne cherries, and forsythia. In line 25, the speaker says that "there was always too much of Lvov," an idea that becomes a sort of refrain in the central part of the poem.

In line 42, the speaker begins to describe memories of his family, his aunts and their family servants, and his philosophical uncle; he also includes fragments that hint at their home life. Once again the speaker asserts that "there was too much/ of Lvov" and that it constantly overflowed every attempt to contain it, but, in line 59, the speaker modifies the refrain: There may have been "too much of Lvov" in the past, but "now/ there isn't any." It has been cut away just as a child cuts out a paper figure, leaving all its inhabitants to bid farewell and to die and leaving its exiles to feel like Jews seeking Jerusalem. However, the speaker asserts at the end that Lvov survives as a place to which one may travel at any time.

Forms and Devices

The logic of childhood memories, like the logic of dreams, is often built on surprising associations. The poet who is attempting to recapture some of the sense of childhood's landscape often uses those associations as an organizational technique. In this poem, the speaker first establishes that the journey being described is not to be taken literally. "Which station/ for Lvov," he wonders and then says one can make the journey "only if Lvov exists,/ if it is to be found within the frontiers and not just/ in my new passport." Such a statement is relevant only if it is possible that the city does not exist. From that point, the poem piles on images in the confused way one's mind might call them up when one remembers a place from one's childhood. The images are interwoven, but they form several strands. One concerns the plant life of the area, another details the religious setting of the city, and a third pictures the speaker's family.

Botanical imagery permeates the poem almost from its beginning. The speaker thinks of the poplars and ash trees that stand like lances and breathe aloud "like Indians"; he thinks of the burdocks and weeds in the city's gardens, the plants that the Jesuits "baptized," and the roses, forsythia, soft ferns, and Queen Anne cherries. The wealth of detail suggests rich growth in a city where there is "always too much." The religious detail forms another strand of imagery. Lvov is the home of a Roman Catholic cathedral and nuns whose cone-shaped headdresses let them sail "like schooners." It is also the home of a Russian Orthodox church with its own silence, different from that of the cathedral. References to Lvov's religious life flicker through the poem as they flicker through the memory of the speaker.

It is the people, however, who form the most vivid of the speaker's recollections. He recalls his aunts who "couldn't have known/ yet that I'd resurrect them" in a poem. He recalls the servants and an uncle who "kept writing a poem entitled *Why,*/ dedicated to the Almighty." He thinks of the small events that formed their lives, recalling a visiting lecturer, a family Bible reading, and someone sleeping "on a sofa beside the Carpathian rug." In the end, the speaker acknowledges that Lvov has been snipped away from reality as neatly as a child might cut out a paper animal, keeping to the dotted lines. The scissors cut away "fiber, tailors, gardeners, censors/ cut the body and the wreaths." The same passion for detail that loaded the town with greenery and relatives now lists a variety of cutting implements, but all of them lead to the same result—the speaker's permanent loss of those who have been sliced away.

Themes and Meanings

On one level, "To Go to Lvov" seems intended to call up a childhood home that is now lost to the speaker. Although it is cast in the form of directions for going to Lvov, the speaker's uncertainty about whether Lvov even exists, along with the dreamlike refrain that asserts the wealth of the city ("too much of Lvov"), seems more intended to invite the reader into the dream than to instruct the reader about going to a real place. The illogicality of dreams allows the speaker to assert things that do not make sense on the literal level. Thus he can say "joy hovered/ everywhere, in hallways and in coffee mills/ . . . in blue/ teapots, in starch." The surreal sense of dreams is particularly active as the poem moves toward its end. The scissors and other sharp implements (penknives and razor blades) that first cut away "too much of Lvov" next seem to cut the very inhabitants away from each other as surely as death.

In line 76, as the speaker pictures Lvov's people saying good-bye to each other, the separation asserts that it is indeed death that does the cutting: "I won't see you anymore, so much death/ awaits you." That death may refer to Lvov's troubled political history, but in a more general way it can easily refer to any childhood home and the deaths of family and friends that inevitably occur as the years pass, separating the one who was once a child in the place from the people and events of childhood. Line 78 links Lvov to Jerusalem: "Why must every city/ become Jerusalem and every man a Jew?" the speaker asks, suggesting that Lvov (and by extension every lost home) is like Jerusalem to the Jews, an object of love and longing, a spiritual home even if the exile has never been there physically.

Throughout the poem, the speaker has directed the reader to pack a suitcase hurriedly and go to Lvov. In the last five lines, just after suggesting that Lvov is as unattainable as Jerusalem, the speaker uses words that recall the poem's opening lines in urging the reader to "go breathless . . . to Lvov, after all/ it exists." On this new level, the uncertainty about Lvov disappears, and the speaker uses one more botanical reference to describe Lvov: "quiet and pure as/ a peach." The last line asserts what the reader has come to assume about Lvov. In saying "It is everywhere," the speaker suggests that the city can take on the character of anyone's childhood home, a place that might be both lost and always present, always approachable through memory that stores the detail that the speaker has offered in this dream journey to Lvov.

Ann D. Garbett

TO MARGUERITE—CONTINUED

Author: Matthew Arnold (1822-1888)
Type of poem: Lyric
First published: 1852, in *Empedocles on Etna and Other Poems*

The Poem

"To Marguerite—Continued" was first published in 1852 under the title "To Marguerite, in Returning a Volume of the Letters of Ortis." In 1853, Arnold gave this poem the simple title "To Marguerite" and included it in a group of poems with the general title of "Switzerland." In 1857, he titled this poem "Isolation," but in 1869 he gave that title to another "Switzerland" poem and assigned to this poem its final title.

Even though neither Marguerite nor Switzerland are mentioned in the poem, Arnold's shufflings of texts and titles makes clear that "To Marguerite—Continued" belongs to his "Switzerland" group. Arnold visited Switzerland in 1848 and 1849. These poems, written mainly between 1847 and 1850, tell a love story of meetings and partings. There have been many theories of who Marguerite was; even though some have doubted her existence, these poems probably had their beginnings in a real—and unfulfilled—love relationship. Other "Switzerland" poems hint that Arnold found his desires thwarted by his inner moral voice, or by differences in the lovers' cultural pasts (Marguerite may have been French), or by her sexual experience, or by Marguerite's fickleness. At the end of the poem that eventually was placed before "To Marguerite—Continued," Arnold abstracts from his experience: Unlike other men who dream that two hearts could become as one, Arnold knows that he is truly alone. As a whole, these poems are both poignant and somewhat juvenile in their tone.

"To Marguerite—Continued" begins with the word "Yes!," as if affirming what has just been said, either by the book being returned or by the preceding poem. The underlying idea of "To Marguerite—Continued" is simple: Every human being lives his or her life in isolation. The first stanza introduces the poem's basic metaphor: Life is a boundless sea; people are all separate islands in it. Humans are conscious of their predicament—"feeling" and "knowing" that something separates them from other persons.

The second stanza takes off from an earlier hint (the straits are "echoing") to describe an element that seems to make the human state more bearable: At certain times each island is filled with beautiful music. What is more, other islands are close enough that the various melodies cross the sea and are heard on these other islands. In short, some communication between the essentially isolated people is possible. However, this realization leads not to joy but to despair. Stanza 3 describes how the partial communication of stanza 2 leads each human being to yearn for total communication. Stanza 4 asks a general question: What power has caused this situation to exist? Arnold answers, "A God."

Forms and Devices

This poem is written in iambic tetrameter, a meter that usually reads quickly. Yet its four stanzas' rhyme scheme of *ababcc* makes each end in a rather emphatic couplet, ensuring that the poem's progress is stately and, even when impassioned, not out of control.

The essential device of "To Marguerite—Continued" is its metaphor comparing human beings to individual islands separated by "the sea of life." What makes this poem remarkable is how this rather simple comparison grows and branches out to say more and more about the human condition. The islands are conscious. Each person feels caught in the clasp of the sea and thereby knows his or her bounds or limits. Stanza 2 further develops the metaphor by emphasizing that each island is near a number of other islands, so near that occasionally songs can be heard from other islands. The season of "spring" implies that these occasions happen mainly when one is young, and songs suggests that the possible communications are lyrical and emotional.

Stanza 3 takes the idea of this island even further: As each island has its "farthest caverns," each individual yearns in the deepest part of his or her being. Moreover, back in geological time the islands could have been "Parts of a single continent!" That is, each human being yearns so hard that he or she envisions a time when these yearnings were satisfied and prays that the islands can meet once again. The last stanza proceeds without a metaphor in its opening lines, then Arnold eloquently brings out what had been only implicit before—the nature of the sea itself, of what isolates human beings.

This metaphor is the poem's most obvious device, but Arnold effectively controls other aspects of language as well. Stanza 1 begins with four very straightforward lines uttered in an assured tone, quite unlike the adolescent whining and posturing of many of the other "Switzerland" poems. Here Arnold forcefully constructs a periodic sentence leading with heavy alliteration ("mortal millions") to the essential word "*alone*," which he italicizes for emphasis. The tone becomes more tender in the concluding couplet as readers are invited to feel what the islands feel. This couplet was set off by an indentation in its first publication.

Stanza 2, describing the lovely night of brief melodic communion, is the poem's most lyric passage. With its moon, hollows, glens, and nightingales, it provides the poem's most extended description of a scene that readers can see and hear in their imaginations. Whereas stanza 1 was declarative (two sentences, three independent clauses), this stanza is not really a sentence at all, but a long evocative dependent clause or string of clauses.

The third stanza hits a strident note as the full flood of yearning surfaces. The poem has five exclamation points, three of which occur in this stanza. Two are in the first sentence, which is a cry for what might have been; the second marks a prayer for what Arnold hopes may be.

In stanza 4 Arnold changes to a less intimate tone. He grandly demands to know who is responsible in the poem's most rhetorically pointed and rhythmically jagged lines: "Who order'd, that their longing's fire/ Should be, as soon as kindled, cool'd?" He answers his question with emphatic repetition and the poem's last exclamation point: "A God, a God their severance ruled!" This line was also emphasized by indentation in its first publication, and its impassioned force then yields to the controlled, eloquent, and perhaps bitter acceptance of the slow and regularly paced final couplet. Here Arnold's diction is particularly resonant. The gulf between humans has unknown depths; perhaps it may be plumbed in the distant future, but for now it is too deep to cross. It is salty: Literally, the ocean is salty, but salt makes wounds even more painful, and salt is the stuff of tears. It is "estranging"—it makes people strangers.

Themes and Meanings

Even though "To Marguerite—Continued" is a lyric poem rooted in its own age, it shows strong influences of the Latin literature that Arnold knew from his studies. The most important verbal parallels are from an ode by Horace; Arnold's word "estranging" probably came from a translation of an ode made by a famous Latin master he knew. The ocean for Horace only divided him from a friend for a time, whereas the estrangement of Arnold's ocean is a permanent feature of life. Similarly, Arnold's isolation is not that of Ortis, a rather Byronic and romantic outlaw figure whose letters are mentioned in the poem's first title.

Some critics have thought the poem reflects Arnold's lifelong criticism of English culture for being isolated from enlightened European thought, but even though this idea is strongly present in "Dover Beach" (1867), Arnold's other major poem about isolation, it is no more than a suggestion here.

The poem is not about simple estrangement, but rather a range of estrangements. Certainly, the poem emphasizes the impossibility of love, including sexual love. Arnold regarded it as one of his "Switzerland" poems, which tell a story of explicitly sexual love that seems to be thwarted by Arnold's hesitations and inhibitions. The bits of communication that are able to occur in stanza 2 consist of nightingales' songs on a conventionally romantic spring night.

Readers probably respond to this poem for its extravagance. It speaks of longings that come from the heart's deepest recesses; it unites sexual yearnings with all hopes for intimate knowledge of other people. The word "divinely" may suggest religious yearnings as well. In all cases, the source of unhappiness is located in the sea, not the islands: If it were not for a power outside the individual, that individual might be free.

Arnold's central metaphor should be contrasted with the famous passage from John Donne's *Devotions upon Emergent Occasions* (1624): "No man is an *Iland*, intire of it selfe; every man is a peece of the *Continent*, a part of the *maine*." Against a background of Anglican ritual, Donne says that all men and women are joined in the human condition and stresses the illusion of self-sufficiency.

Two hundred years later, Arnold was a voice of a new generation. The Church of England had been weakened by dissent and by doubt (in "Dover Beach" the "Sea of Faith" is ebbing). Moreover, such forces as the industrialization of central England and the speed of the passenger train had begun to tear apart the social fabric of the old order. People were becoming more isolated; many Victorian sages noted that fact. Arnold's poem not only is a poem about immature love and human isolation but also is a response to the beginnings of a recognizably modern world. This poem is one of the nineteenth century's most eloquent evocations of this theme.

George Soule

TO MARINA

Author: Kenneth Koch (1925-   )
Type of poem: Meditation
First published: 1979, in *The Burning Mystery of Anna in 1951*

The Poem

"To Marina" is a long autobiographical free-verse poem of approximately four hundred lines devoted to the woman of the title, with whom the poet had an affair twenty-five years before. She also served as the inspiration for many of Koch's best-known early poems, several mentioned by name or alluded to in this poem. The second-person addressee of the poem, the "you," is Marina, and much of the poem recounts events in the long-ago lovers' affair: who said what, when, and how the poet felt, though he cannot know exactly how Marina felt. Since the affair produced many poems by Koch, he has retained evidence of their love and of the creativity to which great love and negotiation of differences may give rise.

The fact that Marina was Russian is introduced early, via comments on her accent (in her speech, "The quiet, dry Z/ Leaped up to the front of the alphabet"), and many of the lovers' differences arise over the question of nationality. Marina is from a nation with more direct experience of the hardships of war, and she is more serious and realistic than the younger, naïve American Koch. For the poet, these differences are exotic and exciting, suggestive of experience and providing a muse, as is indicated in an early section of the poem where Marina points out Kenneth's naïveté, and the poet reponds with desire rendered in lyric imagery: "Oh Kenneth/ You like everything/ To be pleasant. I was burning/ Like an arch/ Made out of trees."

The reader should be aware while reading the poem of a split between two different Kenneths: the younger poet whose experiences with Marina are recounted and the older poet of today who remembers and makes sense of these experiences. While the poet is remembering his lover and speaking to her, he is also remembering himself, remembering youth and inexperience after a life of experiences. Certain moments of the poem act almost as snapshots of earlier moments in life, as when Koch describes a day with Marina in New York a quarter-century earlier in the present tense: "We have walked three blocks. Or four blocks. It is New York/ In nineteen fifty-three. Nothing has as yet happened/ That will ever happen and will mean as much to me. You smile, and turn your head." The event described in this memory is less important than the state of mind the poet remembers being in when it occurred, just as a photograph from one's past may not have meaning for someone else but is deeply meaningful to the one who knows when it was taken and can remember long-since-outgrown feelings it recalls. The remembered smile cannot be called significant, except that it has been recalled for more than two decades and corresponds in the mind of the poet to a time emblematic of his youth and corresponding feelings of potential, possibility, and joy.

Marina represents experience for the young Kenneth; their love is "illicit," Marina already married and having to deal with consequences Kenneth does not after the two have begun their affair. At other junctures of the poem she represents erotic danger (telling him, "Kenneth you are playing with fire") and a love whose pain in ending paradoxically makes the poet feel truly alive. In the end, while he laments, "You were the perfection of my life/ And I couldn't have you," he also realizes that little else remains but poems from this time—"I am over fifty years old and there's no you—/ And no me, either"—a time when experience was fresh and became permanent in the beauty of poetry.

Forms and Devices

The reader is advised to take a look at some of Koch's early lyric love poems, especially those mentioned in the poem, such as "To You," "Spring," and "In Love With You." While the author does not expect every reader to be familiar with every poem he alludes to, some familiarity with his earlier work is assumed and will help the reader comprehend that Marina in this poem is as important as a muse as she is as the poet's former lover—and perhaps more so.

Like other poets of the so-called New York School (such as Frank O'Hara and John Ashbery), Koch frequently writes about what might not seem to be serious poetic subject matter—daily events from his own life. O'Hara called such poems "I do this, I do that" poems, because events frequently follow upon events without the poet explicitly telling the reader what they are supposed to mean. This is meant to mimic formally daily experience, in which the things that happen to one on any given day do not conform to a particular subject heading, but simply happen. In "To Marina," Koch pushes some of this formal experimentation further by varying line lengths, distorting syntax, and employing odd, even surreal, juxtapositions in order to approximate the feelings that the lines are meant to convey. The second stanza begins, "It is wise to be witty. The shirt collar's far away./ Men tramp up and down the city on this windy day." The sing-song rhyme conveys a mood of ebullient, even flippant, joy. Norms of grammar and syntax are deliberately altered: "A clock rang a bird's song rattled into my typewriter." Koch is a firm believer in nonformulaic verse, to the point of adopting all manner of devices even in free-verse lines. He takes great pains to rid himself of anything that would smack of routine. Some stanzas are punctuated according to rules of standard usage; others have little or no punctuation. The attempt is to write a poem that is never lazy, retains fidelity to different aspects of human experience, and conveys that fidelity through forms designed to express different states of mind, settings, and events.

Themes and Meanings

It is interesting that while Marina is older and more experienced than the young Kenneth of the poem, he now realizes that through her he was able to gain access to childish wonder, which transferred itself to poetry. The poem ends with the poet calling his time with Marina his "Renaissance," "when I had you to write to, when I could see you/ And it could change." The suggestion of these lines is one familiar to readers of William Wordsworth and other Romantic poets, that poetry is a function of "child-like" perceptions—that as people grow into adults and become familiar with the world, they lose the magic of youthful sight. "The things which I have seen I now can see no more," wrote Wordsworth in "Ode: Intimations of Immortality from Recollections of Early Childhood." Koch himself devoted two books (*Wishes, Lies, and Dreams*, 1970, and *Rose, Where Did You Get That Red?* 1973) and much of his teaching career to teaching poetry to children. "Renaissance" means, literally, "rebirth." Now, the poet laments, the ability to perceive afresh in verse is no longer second nature to him. That the time is gone when an undefined "it" "could change" indicates that life for the poet has become less surprising, more domesticated and routine, and that consequently to write poetry—the type of poetry Koch once wrote, which called routine its enemy—is now a struggle.

Perhaps this situation helps explain the variety of line lengths, styles, and approaches employed in "To Marina": The poem is perhaps an energetic attempt to recoup some of that which has been lost. Alternatively, if like the years themselves this ability has been lost forever, it may be an attempt to call upon artificial means to reproduce something that once came more naturally. This interpretation adds depth to the pain of reflection upon the poet's lost love: He has lost not only youth, not only the beauty of his beloved, not only the unexpectedness of her character and the insights it gave him, but his very self, his occupation. It can still get him from place to place, but without the same joy and ease, as when normal human locomotion is replaced by movement in a motorized wheelchair.

If this is the state of the despairing mind of the poet at the end of his meditation, it discounts neither the excitement he once felt at love and poetry nor the ways in which "To Marina" succeeds as poetry. It can serve as both an introduction to Koch's work—introducing the reader to themes and devices at work throughout Koch's poems—and, on its own, as a meditation on a poet's lost muse. While writing would seem to be an individualistic occupation, Koch's remembrance of his muse makes clear that no writer ever achieves greatness entirely alone.

Ted Pelton

TO NO ONE IN PARTICULAR

Author: Marvin Bell (1937-   )
Type of poem: Lyric
First published: 1976; collected in *Stars Which See, Stars Which Do Not See*, 1977

The Poem

"To No One in Particular" is a poem in free verse. The title functions much like the "To Whom It May Concern" salutation of a letter that carries a message to anyone that can make use of it. It is written from a first-person perspective with nothing to indicate that the poet is speaking through a persona (a character distinctly different from the poet who functions as the narrator of the poem). Both the voice and the ideas expressed in the poem are consistent with those in many other poems by Marvin Bell, so it seems reasonable to assume that there is no philosophical difference between the "I" of the poem and the poet himself. With no stanza breaks and no extra spacings or peculiar formatting, the poem's fifty-five lines appear on the page like one long, narrow paragraph; however, there are some easily distinguishable sections of the poem.

The first two lines of the poem, "Whether you sing or scream/ the process is the same," prepare the reader, like the thesis statement in an academic essay, for an exploration of "the process" behind human vocalizations. The next eight lines act as an introduction to a comparative analysis of two very different types of human speech— learned and instinctive. They also point out crude aspects of the actual vocal instrument—"spittle and phlegm."

In lines 11 through 22 the poet speculates that if one were to grab someone by the throat and beat him, someone else would almost certainly try to record the event in minute detail, right down to the individual utterances made by the victim. The problem, as the poet explains it, is that the person recording the events would embellish on what he or she had heard and would try to gloss the sounds made by the victim "in one of those languages/ revered for its vowels./ But all the time, it's consonants/ coming from the throat."

In the third section, lines 23 to 35, the poet focuses on the victim, "still gagging out the guttural ch—/ the throat clearing, Yiddish ch—/ and other consonants." He then follows the victim home, where the victim in turn victimizes his wife. Once he has exhausted himself, he falls asleep and snores, and the poet tells the reader that "all the time/ he hasn't said a word we can repeat./ Even though we all speak his language."

In the fourth (the last and longest) section of the poem, Bell returns to the more ecclesiastical voice he uses at the beginning of the poem, questioning even the possibility of understanding humans' most basic sounds. His questions come rapidly: "Who will write down this language?/ Who will do the necessary work?/ Who will gag on a chicken bone/ for observation?" and so on, until he concludes by telling the reader that everything of real importance in his life "occurred in another language."

Forms and Devices

Marvin Bell is well known for creating free verse that has the deceptive appearance of prose broken into lines; however, a keen ear or eye soon recognizes that his work is pure poetry. He uses very few quickly discernable devices in this poem. The most obvious of these are juxtaposition and anaphora. The poem begins with the juxtaposition of two human sounds—singing and screaming. He states that the "process" of creating these two sounds is essentially the same and that both of them use "spittle and phlegm." The difference stems from fear causing the throat to constrict. The juxtaposition of "consonants" and "vowels" is so prevalent that it becomes a theme of the poem.

Anaphora is the practice of repeating the same word or phrase at the beginning of lines, clauses, sentences, or stanzas. Bell makes back-to-back uses of this device in the last half of the poem. Beginning at line 35 he starts three consecutive sentences with "Even though," and immediately begins the next four with "Who will." Probably the single most famous use of anaphora in the English language is the Beatitudes of the Bible, nine statements attributed to Christ, each of which begins with "Blessed are." Although Bell's reasons for using this device may differ from the biblical author's, the effect is essentially the same; it establishes a strong tone of authority, a voice that simply will not be ignored. Unlike the biblical use of the device as an introduction to a sermon, Bell uses it near the end of his poem, providing a dramatic burst of speed and energy.

Most of this poem's imagery centers on the throat. When the throat constricts, "the back of the tongue/ can taste the brain's fear." To give someone a good beating, one should start by grabbing him "by the throat." People try to clear their throats with "the guttural ch—," the "Yiddish ch—." In the morning, we feel "the toast in our throats" and "gag on a chicken bone." The shape of the poem relies more on syntax than on lineation. Many of the line breaks ignore obvious phrasing in favor of limiting either the length of the lines or the number of stresses in particular lines.

"To No One in Particular" ends, as many of Bell's poems end, with a personal memory, real or imagined, and a direct statement to the reader—a statement that carries some mythic or mystic message for human beings in general. "The Self and the Mulberry," "Gradually, It Occurs to Us . . . ," and "The Mystery of Emily Dickinson" are good examples from this same volume by Bell that have this type of ending.

Themes and Meanings

Like any good work of art, this poem has several things to offer, but one in particular is the notion that a common language can be a common problem. Language is a major theme throughout Bell's work, and in this poem he tries to show that humans have two types of language. First, there is natural language, the utterances that humans, as animals, instinctively make—the guttural sounds and consonants that squeeze out of throats. People give no thought as to how or why they make them or to what they mean. These sounds are instinctual, products of evolutionary processes.

The other form of language is synthetic, a system of utterances developed to help communicate more complex and detailed ideas. At its best this type of language is a tool that facilitates cooperation among humans. No matter how far humans think they have evolved, no matter how detailed and protean synthetic language has become, they are still animals. In times of stress, frustration, fear, anger, or any other situation that engenders emotional response, they revert to this first language, a language that is not tied to "an alphabet meant to make sense."

Throughout the poem Bell makes references to instinctive language as guttural, squeezed, or primarily composed of consonants, whereas he depicts the synthetic type of language as musical and "revered for its vowels." Inextricably tied to this theme of two types of language is the notion that humans must never allow—as if it were possible—their tendency to analyze things to replace or destroy their ability to feel things. Analysis is often the practice of "some fool" whose elaborate glosses take people further and further away from what they actually feel.

The great irony here is that synthetic language is the meat and potatoes of every poet. In no way does this fact invalidate this poem, however. In fact, it demonstrates that not even poets can tame that language that sometimes explodes to the surface from deep down inside and exposes, for the moment, who people really are.

Edmund August

TO PENSHURST

Author: Ben Jonson (1573-1637)
Type of poem: Epistle/letter in verse
First published: 1616, in *The Forest*, part of *The Workes of Benjamin Jonson*

The Poem

"To Penshurst" is a 102-line poetic letter written in heroic couplets. It is primarily descriptive and discursive and mimics the pastoral poems of Horace (65-8 B.C.E.) and the invitational poems of Martial (40-103 C.E.). The poem is addressed to Penshurst, the estate home of the Sidney family located in Kent. At the time when the poem was written, Sir Robert Sidney was the head of the Penshurst household; Sir Philip Sidney, the poet and courtier, had died in 1586. While rooted in the physical reality of the actual Penshurst estate, the poem also uses myth and satire.

The poem begins with a negative statement: Penshurst is not, like other country houses, dependent for its reputation upon "polished pillars" or "a roof of gold." It is admired, but the basis for its stature is the natural and social systems it epitomizes, not its physical structure. The poem divides in half at line 46: The first half concentrates on the natural bounty of the Penshurst lands; the second half details the social constructs that revolve around the house.

The details of the grounds that Ben Jonson provides blend the English countryside with classical mythology and the history of the Sidney family. Lovers are fauns and satyrs; a particular tree is remembered because Lady Leicester went into labor under it. Having established a pastoral world, Jonson begins a realistic catalog of the grounds with domestic animals, wild rabbits, and birds. The abundance of animals suggests an Edenic fertility, but it is significant that the animals are all functional: The birds are "willing to be killed" for the table of the house. From the animal world, Jonson moves to the aquatic, and again the emphasis is on fecundity and the willingness of the fish to sacrifice themselves to the fisherman. He ends his catalog of the natural world with a description of the bounty of the garden and orchard.

The walls that surround the garden act as a dividing line between the first and second movements of the poem, and Jonson now addresses the human inhabitants of the lands. The emphasis on bounty, however, remains. The peasants and farmers bring offerings of food to the house to "express their love," and their daughters are as ripe as the plums and pears they carry.

The generosity of nature and man ensures Penshurst of provision. This, in turn, guarantees hospitality, the social bond between host and guest. Jonson revels in the fact that guests at the house receive the same victuals and drink as the lord: No one will count his cups, and he is guaranteed of comfortable lodging. That this generosity is especially laudatory when lavished on a poet is emphasized by the juxtaposition of this passage with a description of an actual visit to the estate by King James I and Prince Henry.

Finally, Jonson moves to the family of the house. He praises the lady for her "housewifery," nobility, fecundity, and chastity. The latter, Jonson emphasizes, is a quality notably missing in other contemporary noble ladies. The children of the house are properly religious and have learned the "mysteries of manners, arms, and arts" through the excellent example of their parents.

The poem ends by returning to the opening contrast between Penshurst and other country houses. Those "ambitious heaps" are built by their lords for show. Penshurst lacks that architectural pretension, but its lord "dwells"; he lives life to the fullest, in harmony with nature and humanity.

Forms and Devices

Although the poem appears to be discursive and anecdotal, it is in fact carefully structured by means of a series of progressions. The poem is organized by the physical movement around Penshurst and by a simultaneous ascending movement from the lowly to the exalted. The poet circles the grounds, moving, in the first half of the poem, from the "lower land" to the "middle grounds" to the "tops," while at the same time moving from the animals on the ground to the fruit in the trees for which one must reach.

In the second half, the poet, like the peasants on the Penshurst land, moves indoors. Once inside, the movement is from guest to king to family, until finally it ends with the lord of Penshurst himself. The poem as a whole, then, spirals in and up to Penshurst and its lord as the defining centers of an ideal, harmonious community.

The poem is also structured by means of time. Jonson implies a measured passing of seasons, especially in his depiction of a garden in which each fruit, from the "early cherry" to the "later plum," ripens in its allotted time. Against this are set broader temporal structures: A tree grown tall was first planted when Sir Philip Sidney was born. Broader yet, the mythological allusions serve to place all of Penshurst in a classical pastoral world. Life on Penshurst is at once timely—everything in its proper season— and timeless. The king's visit was unique, so it is the only historical event that is described at length.

Finally, the poem is structured by means of a framing device. It begins and ends with a direct address to Penshurst itself. As the house defines the limits of the poem, so too does it define its community. Both art and society receive their forms from its example.

The dominant images of the poem are of food and birth. Penshurst is unmistakably Edenic: The abundance of animal and vegetable life, all willing to be sacrificed for the table, implies a prelapsarian world in which man does not have to labor. The descriptions of the peasants' offerings and the guest's dinner emphasize Penshurst's role in sustaining life.

If Penshurst nurtures like a mother, it also breeds, and the poem suggests that Penshurst is a womb. This fecundity is emphasized by the birth images: The birth of a tree on the estate is paralleled with the birth of Sir Philip Sidney. Children reach for fruit and suckle knowledge from their parents. Prince Henry rides the land with his father, the king.

Themes and Meanings

The themes of the poem are largely political. Jonson uses Penshurst as an epitome of proper social order, a social order that relies on harmony and love rather than competition or coercion. This harmony is found, tellingly, in a rural, not an urban, environment and is emphasized by the animals' willingness to be killed for the table and the fact that the pikes do not eat their own kind. The ruthlessness of court life has been left far behind.

Jonson's diagram for an ideal community, and by extension commonwealth, requires a delicate balance of tradition and practicality. Human decency is essential to the social contract, and so it is significant that the walls of Penshurst were "reared with no man's ruin, no man's groan," and no one would see them pulled down. In return for the bounty provided the lord, the lord and his family provided an example to the community.

One of the defining features of Penshurst that is of special interest to Jonson is its relation to the arts and culture. As the home of Sir Philip Sidney, Penshurst is historically aligned with the arts. The classical allusion that dominates the first lines of the poem implies that tradition and learning are an integral part of Penshurst. The form of the poem itself, with its use of Martial and Horace, suggests that Penshurst partakes of a tradition that extends back to antiquity. The juxtaposing of the poet's repast at Penshurst with the king's visit also suggests that culture has found an appropriate patron in Penshurst.

The defining opposite of the Penshurst ideal is implied in the satirical parts of the poem. Approximately one-eighth of the poem is given over to negative contrast. Perhaps the most obvious satire arises from a contrast in the description of the lady of Penshurst. She is chaste, and the lord of the manor knows that his children are indeed his own, "A fortune in this age but rarely known." Besides satirizing the moral laxness of contemporary womanhood, Jonson is attacking the bad example set by the upper classes.

It can be argued that the poem is merely a sycophantic reiteration of Elizabethan social orthodoxy, but there is also in the poem the implication of advice. Jonson may be doing more than describing; he may be prescribing. The lord does not need ostentatious show; his lands provide all that is necessary. The smallness of the estate makes possible the harmony that Jonson celebrates. The poem may be a warning to the lord not to overreach.

Paul Budra

TO RAJA RAO

Author: Czesław Miłosz (1911-   )
Type of poem: Epistle/letter in verse
First published: 1973, in *Selected Poems*

The Poem

Czesław Miłosz composed "To Raja Rao" immediately following a long theological discussion he had in Berkeley in 1969 with the Indian writer and philosopher Raja Rao, a man whose international stature, literary and philosophical interests, theological bent, and (perhaps most important) bicultural background parallel Miłosz's. It soon becomes apparent, however, that "To Raja Rao" deals less with these parallels than with the quite different ways in which the two writers—one a Catholic Pole, the other a Hindu Indian—deal with the "malady" introduced in line 2, but never specifically defined anywhere in the poem. This absence does not mean that the poem is merely or even chiefly confessional. "To Raja Rao" is Miłosz's attempt to understand and explain the nature and cause of this malady, and in this way define and explain his own essential being to an addressee who, whether Rao or some other reader, shares his general predicament, though not necessarily his background or his understanding of what that predicament means and what it entails.

Looking back, Miłosz characterizes his life in self-exile in terms of displacement, unreality, and restless longing, his "hope of moving on." (Miłosz asked for and was granted political asylum by France in 1951; he accepted a teaching position at the University of California at Berkeley in 1960 and became a naturalized citizen of the United States in 1970). Conflating the psychological and the geopolitical, Miłosz positions himself "on the border of schizophrenia," willing neither completely to reject nor completely to accept linkage of his "peculiar case" with "the messianic hope" of his native land, the Poland whose modern history of subjugation and partition has often made it a nation in exile, living on in name (or memory) only.

Because to live on the border is to live simultaneously in two (or more) places and in no one place at all, Miłosz feels "ill at ease" both in a Poland ruled by communist tyranny and in an America of moral lassitude and "aimless bustle." Miłosz eventually does make his separate peace and is able to say (though not with complete conviction), "this is my home." saying so does not assuage the feelings of guilt and shame to which his poem gives eloquent voice. In fact, rather than easing his sense of spiritual discomfort, rather than narrowing the distance between the image of the self he should have been and the mere shadow that he is, Miłosz accentuates the dis-ease and widens the schizophrenic gap. At this point, the only explanation he feels he can possibly offer is the Catholic concept of Original Sin. Anticipating Rao's objection, Miłosz concedes that he is relying on "a ready argument," but he also points out that the phrase itself—Original Sin—does not adequately express the idea Miłosz wishes to convey.

Rejecting Rao's Hindu-Socratic claim "that liberation is possible," Miłosz accepts his own sinful state. Unlike Rao, who emphasizes what man can become, Miłosz emphasizes what man in his "hidden essence" is. Just as he earlier came to question his own optimistic vision of "a permanent polis," he now questions Rao's different but equally hopeful vision. Instead of moving ahead to the realization of either, Miłosz moves back beyond the Poland evoked at the beginning of the poem to the very origin of his dis-ease and spiritual exile, to the Original Sin that is the sign of his weak and divided nature. Against both the vanity of the ego and the visions of human utopias, Miłosz posits the sinful self accepting his agony, struggling with himself, praying "for the Kingdom," and "reading Pascal."

Forms and Devices

Read in the context of Miłosz's other poems, "To Raja Rao" seems at once anomalous and familiar. Of the 181 poems included in *The Collected Poems, 1931-1987* (1988), "To Raja Rao" is the only one originally written in English. It is written, however, in one of Miłosz's favorite forms, the epistolary (though only two such poems appear in *The Collected Poems*). The epistolary form suits "To Raja Rao" particularly well. By addressing, or apostrophizing, Rao and by beginning the poem *in medias res*, as if the poem is continuing their conversation, Miłosz creates a sense of immediacy that the poem's stanzaic structure reinforces. Miłosz divides his fifty-two-line poem into eighteen short stanzas. Eight of the eighteen are just two lines long; four are three lines; and six are four lines, with four of these relatively long stanzas clustered at the very center of the poem. Conventional terminology—couplet, triplet, even the more broadly defined quatrain—simply does not apply here; Miłosz's stanzaic units are too irregular in form for that. On the other hand, the poem is far from structureless. The stanzas are, after all, from two to four lines each; and Miłosz's line length follows a similarly flexible pattern. Lines expand or contract in individual stanzas as need dictates at a particular point in the poem, thus creating a variable but nevertheless rhythmical structure. Just as there is no narrowly defined metrical pattern, there is no rhyme, but the repetition of similar syntactical phrasings, along with the formal devices previously mentioned, impart to the poem its own sense of order and direction. In this way, "To Raja Rao" comes to embody in its very structure and movement Miłosz's conception of poetry as a "search for direct forms" and "the passionate pursuit of the real."

Within the poem's enabling epistolary structure, Miłosz conducts his "search for direct forms" in the language of "simple speech." The artful "simple speech" of "To Raja Rao" contributes not only to the poem's immediacy and accessibility, but to the appearance of the poem as unmediated personal experience. As already noted, however, "To Raja Rao" is not confessional in style and bears little similarity to the works of the American confessional poets Robert Lowell, Sylvia Plath, and Anne Sexton. Although he believes that poetry "comes only from pain, only from personal experience," Miłosz contends that art must never be merely or even chiefly subjective. Poetry, he maintains, is not self-exposure; it is, rather, the "distillation" and "transformation" of life into art via form, or rather the "search for direct forms" previously mentioned.

Themes and Meanings

The overriding and unifying theme of "To Raja Rao" is exile, but exile of a very complex kind. In its simplest form, the exile is personal and cultural. Having lived for two decades in self-imposed exile, first in Paris and then in Berkeley, Miłosz has become something of a displaced person. Contrasting the gregariousness that characterizes his European past with the loneliness of his more recent Western and especially American experience, he feels dispossessed, foreign, and, above all, "other." "Somewhere else," he believes, there exists the "real presence" that his American life lacks.

The personal dimension of Miłosz's exile borders on the political. The unnamed Poland nostalgically evoked in stanzas 2, 3, and 4 gives way to a more pragmatic realization of the Stalinist tyranny that characterizes the modern Poland Miłosz fled in 1951; that, in turn, leads him from nostalgic reverie to futuristic fantasy—the dream of a "permanent polis," perhaps not unrelated to the "messianic hope" which has long been a part of the Polish national identity and so is a part of the poet's own identity as well.

Far from curing him of his "malady," Miłosz's pragmatic accommodation to his new (nominally or at least geographically American) life in fact deepens his predicament as exile, adding psychological and, more importantly, spiritual layers to the cultural and political ones already described. The shame he feels as the result of having failed "to be/ what I should have been" leads Miłosz to image himself in terms of a still deeper schizophrenia. "The image of myself," he writes, "grows gigantic on the wall/ and against it/ my miserable shadow." As this powerful passage, with its echoes of Isaiah and T. S. Eliot, makes clear, the shame derives from the guilt that Miłosz has said is "central" to his poetry. It is this guilt that leads Miłosz to accept the Catholic doctrine of Original Sin from which that same shame and guilt may be said themselves to derive. (The doctrine also connects Miłosz's contemporary predicament with that of the earliest exiles, Adam and Eve.) Thus considered, Miłosz feels homeless because this fallen world is not his home, spiritually speaking. In Miłosz's case, however, the generalized spiritual predicament of all people exists side by side with a decidedly personal sense of Miłosz's own individual guilt—specifically the guilt of the survivor of Nazi and Stalinist tyranny.

Miłosz acknowledges his human unworthiness and his own sinful nature—the monsters that trouble his dreams and show him his essence. His search for home, for an end to exile, parallels his search for direct forms, for a truth in and beyond expression. It is a search for forms that becomes a search for a firm foundation upon which to base human existence. In embracing his exile, his Catholic faith, his Polish-Lithuanian identity, his agony, and his dis-ease, Miłosz offers an assertion and affirmation of "what I am" as an alternative to all forms of "totalitarian terror," however beguiling those visions may be before they turn into the nightmares of history.

Robert A. Morace

TO THE DANDELION

Author: James Russell Lowell (1819-1891)
Type of poem: Lyric
First published: 1845; stanzas 6-8 and 10 omitted from the version collected in *Poems: Second Series*, 1848, and later editions

The Poem

James Russell Lowell's "To the Dandelion" consists of ten nine-line stanzas. The third line of each stanza has six syllables, the seventh has eight, and the rest have ten. Addressing the dandelion, the poet meditates on the riches of ordinary nature, which stimulates his imagination and recalls his childhood. He draws moral lessons and also realizes the joy and consolation such humble gifts bring, even in life's "dreariest days."

The poet opens by addressing the "Dear common flower." Children rejoice in it as though it were a treasure, "An Eldorado in the grass." The flower blooms in early May, but the poet values it more than "all the prouder summer-blooms." The metaphor of gold continues in the second stanza. Unlike the gold that Spanish galleons sought in the New World or that misers hoard, spring scatters this gold lavishly, though most people overlook it. For the poet, the flower transports him in imagination to warmer climes and to a pleasure greater than that of the bee delighting in a summer lily. In the fourth stanza, the dandelion stimulates the poet to imagine a pastoral summer landscape. He recalls his childhood in stanza 5, "When birds and flowers and I were happy peers."

The poet is now led to moral insights. The lowly dandelion is the "type" of the "meek charities," the small kindnesses that often nourish "A starving heart" and give it "Some glimpse of God." The flower's seeds are like the words of poet and sage, borne on the wind to the future, raised into the sky as guiding stars. All the lowly plants would teach this wisdom, could one but read it. Yet earnest faith may cull a few syllables that can soothe life's ache and open heaven's portals, which are near humans in everyday life. By lavishing this flower, at once "gold" and "common," nature teaches the poet to deem every human heart sacred. People could read the heavenly secrets if they read "with a child's undoubting wisdom . . ./ . . . these living pages of God's book."

Yet, whether the poet can learn this wisdom or not, the flower brings back to him the purity of childhood. Even in dreary days, "Nature's first lowly influences" continue to bring "peace and hope."

Forms and Devices

The poet uses a variety of devices to express the extraordinary value that he sees in the dandelion, a common natural object. The first three stanzas present a series of contrasts and metaphors that interlock in complicated ways. The poet calls the flower "harmless gold" by the dusty road and then elaborates the flower's color into a comparison with the precious metal. Into a sentence that states his preference for the dandelion over the "prouder" flowers of summer, he inserts a long subordinate clause, picturing children rejoicing in the golden flowers as a treasure, "An Eldorado in the grass." In the third stanza, the dandelion contrasts with the gold that the Spanish sought and that misers hoard. It is scattered before rich and poor but commonly overlooked. Thus, children, God, and the poet share a perspective that values the dandelion, in contrast to proud or greedy people who neglect or overlook it entirely.

The poet now carries through on the contrast between the dandelion and later summer flowers. The dandelion makes the poet think of warmer climates. This imaginative pleasure is greater than that of a bee enjoying a lily in summer's prime. In the fourth stanza, the poet fills out this imaginative stimulus by describing a complete pastoral summer landscape. In the next stanza the dandelion carries the poet's mind back to childhood and the robin's song. The imaginative engagement with nature leads to recollection of an actual engagement in childhood. Thus the poem proceeds by elaborating real or metaphoric associations to flesh out the basic theme: the value of the dandelion.

These imaginative and remembered pictures lead to moral reflections. Placing the right value on the common dandelion supports placing the right value on common kindnesses. They are "Love's smallest coin," a phrase that carries forward the metaphor of a dandelion blossom as a gold coin. They give the suffering and lonely a "glimpse of God." Both the connection to divinity and the sense that daily life is marked by strife, indifference to wisdom, and dreariness continue through the remaining stanzas.

The flower's seeds are seen as "words of poet and of sage." They are borne on the wind of time to the future and up to the heavens, where they become guiding stars. The use of metaphor continues through the rest of the poem. From all of nature's lowly plants, if people approach them in the right spirit, they can "cull/ Some syllables" of wisdom, "A spell to soothe life's bitterest ache." From nature's prodigality with gifts like the dandelion, people also learn to value "every human heart." People are like "pages of God's book," but to read them one must see "with a child's undoubting wisdom." Thus the motif of the child's perspective returns and leads into the final stanza. The poet may or may not be able to attain these moral insights, but at least he can read the "legends of childhood." To nature's early influence, people owe the "peace and hope" that sustain them in dreary days. The recurrence and elaboration of motifs and metaphors help unify the poem.

The style of the poem is a remarkable fusion of formal complexity with conversational flow. Each stanza is a single long sentence, sometimes punctuated with semicolons, colons, or dashes but giving the effect of a slow-moving rumination. Enjambment often carries the thought over a change in rhyme, again sustaining the winding course of thought. The rhyme scheme begins with five lines of crossed rhyme (*ababa*), assuring forward motion, but each stanza ends with two couplets (*ccdd*), bringing it to a gentle stop. The meter is iambic but with considerable flexibility, so that the stresses reflect the rise and fall of spoken language and avoid stiffness and monotony. The diction and phrasing are rarely "poetic" but for the most part that of ordinary educated speech.

Themes and Meanings

The poem's themes are clearly indebted to William Wordsworth. He first established the pattern of describing a natural scene or object (rock, stream, tree, flower), often interwoven with reminiscences of his own childhood, to lead up to and authorize a moral insight. Wordsworth believed that poems should express genuine feeling in actual—not artificially elevated—language.

Lowell follows Wordsworth's general themes closely. The reader might wonder why the poet values the dandelion so highly. The first answer is its power to liberate his imagination, exhibited in the imagined but still natural, pastoral landscape of stanza 4. If the poem ended here, then the theme would be that of the poet's imagination as both the source of his sensitivity to nature and its reward; ordinary people lose the child's imaginative power, but the poet keeps it alive.

The fifth stanza, however, introduces a fresh theme. The dandelion stimulates poetic imagination, but it also brings memories of earliest childhood. The description of children in the first stanza anticipated this theme, but here it becomes personal. The poet recalls a time of organic unity with nature.

Does this turn lead to the moral reflections that follow, or do they simply intrude? When Lowell published this poem in a book, he printed only the first five and the ninth stanzas. He apparently felt that the moralizing was excessive. In stanza 6, the dandelion suggests the value of commonplace acts of kindness. It also hints that life can be sad and lonely, and this pessimism grows more far-reaching in the following stanzas. The seventh stanza raises a different issue: the indifference of the present age to words of wisdom or beauty, which only a later era will appreciate. The eighth stanza states that all natural objects can convey moral, even divine, wisdom. The ninth stanza turns to all human beings, "the common brethren," whose divine value would be visible if they looked on one another "with a child's undoubting wisdom."

It may be that Lowell thought these sentiments too miscellaneous. Of these four stanzas, he retained only stanza 9, which continued the motif of children and stayed closest to the basic theme—the high, even divine value of what is commonplace. The stanza gives the theme its general form: imaginative interaction with nature (expressed in the form of address to the flower, "thou") teaches the poet ("me") what all people ("we") need to know to value one another properly. The poet is not contrasted with insensitive fellow human beings (as in the first two stanzas) but becomes the agent through whom the wisdom of creation is brought to all.

This gives the shorter printed version a suitable coherence, but the original version ended on a different note: the return of the personal in the form of the poet's childhood, fused together with the theme of consolation in the face of life's troubles. Not just imaginative stimulation, but also moral strength and solace are conferred on the poet by the early influence of nature. The poet offers not so much moral insight—which his fellow human beings need—as what he himself needs to sustain his joy in living. That is a different but not less valid conclusion, and readers may decide for themselves which they prefer.

Donald G. Marshall

TO THE FATES

Author: Friedrich Hölderlin (1770-1843)
Type of poem: Ode
First published: 1800, as "An Die Parzen" in *Sämtliche Werke*, 1846; English transla-
tion collected in *Hölderlin: His Poems Translated by Michael Hamburger with a
Critical Study*, 1952

The Poem

"To the Fates" is an Alcaic ode, its twelve unrhymed lines divided into three four-
line stanzas. The unstressed and stressed syllables of each line are adapted from a
classical Greek pattern; Friedrich Hölderlin was Germany's most accomplished poet
at using these challenging forms. The poem is written in the first person. Its title is a
call to the three Fates—a group of three grotesque old women who spun, measured,
and finally cut the thread of life for each human being, according to myth. Hölderlin
uses the Roman word *Parcae* to refer to them here.

The first stanza consists of two thoughts: First, the poet requests time to bring forth
mature poetry, and second, the poet explains that the seasons that the Fates grant will
make him more accepting of death. He will be sated by the intense sweetness of producing poetry, but he needs the intervention of the Fates to assure himself of sufficient
time for this autumn harvest.

In the second stanza, the poet uses the simple dichotomy between life and death to
say that, if he is not permitted to complete his poetry, then he will find no peace in
death. Using the roman name "Orcus," Hölderlin refers to the underworld, the realm
of the dead in the ancient worldview. Hölderlin believes that writing is both special
and sanctified. Therefore, if his poetry is finished and he has written it well, then he
will welcome death. He says that death is the "still world of the shades" because, in
the ancient classical view, humans became pale, flitting shadows when they died.
Their once-warm bodies are also "cold," and in some English versions, the translator
has generalized this quality of the dead to include the place in which they reside.

At the end of the final stanza, with special emphasis on the word "once," the poet
explains that, even though his stringed instrument will not accompany him into death,
the act of creating poetry will have made his life like that of the gods. This former
glory will compensate for his death; he needs nothing more than the experience of poetic fruition that he has requested from the Fates.

Forms and Devices

An Alcaic ode is a refined type of poem, meant originally for the Greek language,
which has a different set of rhythms from those poems found in English and German.
The reader encounters a complex series of syllables. The first line of a stanza consists
of five alternating unstressed and stressed syllables, a pause, and then a pattern of one
stressed syllable, two unstressed syllables, one stressed, one unstressed, and one

stressed. The second line duplicates the first, and the third line has nine syllables that alternate between unstressed and stressed. The fourth line of a stanza is an elaboration of the last parts of the first and second lines. Its pattern is composed of one stressed syllable, two unstressed syllables, one stressed, two unstressed, one stressed, one unstressed, one stressed, and one unstressed. Each four-line stanza repeats this formula.

The metaphors in Hölderlin's poem are connected to the timeless world of the seasons, death, and immortality. In the first stanza, the most striking comparison is between the ripeness that results from summer and autumn and the poet's development of his craft. These seasons are traditionally the times of fullness of growth, thus the use of the adjective "mellow" to describe the poet's "song." Autumn is also a time for the celebration of harvest, a standard theme in poetry. Michael Hamburger, his translator, states that Hölderlin's "images are extremely obvious, general and elemental, never far-fetched or complex."

References to Orcus and the "cold world of the shades" describe the death of the poet after he completes his work. Both of these metaphors are frightening in the sound of the words (in English and German) and in their connotations of dark emptiness. Furthermore, when these metaphors are contrasted with the positive images of the first verse, with its song, sweetness, and ripeness, they take on an even more forbidding aspect.

The poet uses one more metaphor, that of playing on a stringed instrument, before giving final emphasis to the theme of immortality. Playing on a stringed instrument, (*Saitenspiel*), like references to harvest, the underworld, and shades, is both a classical and a standard poetic image. Because classical figures such as Orpheus, Hermes, and Apollo are associated with stringed instruments, such objects have come to represent poetry composed in imitation of the absolute excellence of Orpheus or Apollo. In "To the Fates," the poet knows that the "music of his strings" will not accompany him on his downward journey. Death means the end of poetry.

The final triumphant pronouncement of the poem is that the poet has been like the gods, or almost a god himself, because he has brought forth perfected art. The reason for his elation is that the poem remains forever perfect, no matter how ephemeral the poet's season of harvest. Karl Viëtor states that most of Hölderlin's odes and elegies are composed of a thesis, an antithesis, and a synthesis which is beyond sadness and conflicting emotions. These elements are seen in the metaphors of harvest, with sweetness (thesis), quiet death (antithesis), and immortality (synthesis).

Themes and Meanings

"To the Fates" is a poem about the fondest hope of the person called to the task of creating poetry—that he may live long enough to finish it. He already possesses the talent, which Hölderlin terms a "god-given right" because it is a gift rather than a craft which is acquired by diligence. The poet's prayer to the powers who control length of life recalls how fragile a hold humans have on the external forces that determine success and failure. Talent alone does not assure success; there must also be time to allow talent to ripen.

The poet suggests that he is willing to barter with the Fates. If they agree to allow him the short seasons that he needs to accomplish his divinely appointed task, then he agrees to go willingly to a death described as grimly in this poem as the ancients viewed the afterlife. The word "once," however, written in italics and reinforcing the repeated "one" and "only" of the first stanza, is the reward that he will reap in the bargain. He has been godlike *once*, he has reached the height of achievement.

The fear of dying before completing the artist's task is a recurring theme in poetry, such as in the poems of the young John Keats. While Hölderlin repeats a familiar theme, however, the force of his feeling and his grace of expression are noteworthy. Hölderlin's years of poetic productivity were briefer than the date of his death may attest because he was plagued by mental illness for the last thirty-eight years of his life. Most critics agree that his last poems of value were produced in 1805. This fact adds poignancy to the request in this poem, a plea which was surely granted, because Hölderlin would write scores of great poems, including "Diotima," "Hyperion's Song of Fate," and "Half of Life," in the next few years.

Ironically, therefore, poets, including Hölderlin himself, are never condemned to "silence" or to be "songless," as the word has sometimes been translated into English. The granting of a season of perfect poetry confers immortality that is almost equal to that of the gods on Hölderlin and, by extension, on every excellent poet. This reward is compensation indeed for a brief but brilliant life, an idea with which the ancients would have agreed. Thus, the classical Alcaic form and the classical themes that are stated simply but passionately in this poem are in consonance with one another. They glorify the brief but creative life.

Erlis Glass

TO THE HOLY SPIRIT

Author: Yvor Winters (1900-1968)
Type of poem: Lyric
First published: 1946; collected in *To the Holy Spirit*, 1947

The Poem

"To the Holy Spirit" is written in rhyming trimeter divided into four stanzas of varying lengths. The expansion of the stanzas—from ten lines in the first, to twelve lines in the second and third, to fourteen in the fourth—reflects the development of the subject of the poem. The title suggests a prayer or a petition to the Holy Spirit. This part of the Holy Trinity traditionally is a source of hope, inspiration, forgiveness, and consolation for humans. The Holy Spirit is the mediator between God and humans. The poem is written in the first person, and the speaker is calling on the Holy Spirit to come to his aid as he tries to believe in God.

The poem's epigraph, "from a deserted graveyard in the Salinas Valley," sets the poem in California. It also allows the speaker the opportunity to meditate on life and death in a serene environment. The graveyard is abandoned, and the speaker of the poem has arrived there in late morning. Once there, the speaker observes how nature and death possess powers that humans cannot easily comprehend. The graveyard setting lends itself to contemplations of the limits of reason and ultimately of human mortality. While the speaker does not seek immortality, he does appeal to the Holy Spirit to guide him in understanding how God and he can coexist in the world.

In the first stanza, the speaker arrives in the graveyard on a hazy, not too warm summer day. He seems to be surprised to have encountered the site on his walk. As the speaker surveys the scene of neglected graves, he contemplates how death is the great equalizer: "the bones/ Beneath are similar:/ Relics of lonely men,/ Brutal and aimless, then,/ As now, irregular."

The speaker recognizes individual dignity ("relics") in these graves and is forced to consider the relationship between life and death that is a part of all humans. The speaker's acknowledged problem in stanza 3 is how to think about the Holy Spirit and God, abstractions in which he feels compelled, irrationally in the presence of death, to believe. In stanza 4, he longs for the blind faith he presumes the dead have. He then concludes the poem by suggesting that whatever his thoughts are on life, death, immortality, and God, they are irrelevant in the face of the reality of mortality. In his own mind, through his meditations, the speaker has established a reason to believe in God. His position is theistic—that is, a belief in the existence of God, who reveals himself to humans.

Forms and Devices

Imagery, language, and meter are carefully chosen to produce the meaning and effect of "To the Holy Spirit." Winters was particularly attracted to the barren ordered beauty of the desert landscape and the open spaces of New Mexico and California. He spent his twenties in New Mexico and later moved to California; he was a college professor at Stanford University for over thirty years. The images of the desert, with its wordplay on "deserted," are created in the first two stanzas of the poem. They yield a sense of limitlessness and some discomfort in the dry heat, dust, and sand. Although the poem has an emphasis on landscape, it is not a Romantic poem. Instead of images of lush, fertile, friendly nature, this landscape is harsh, yet uniquely beautiful; the mood is tense, and the speaker struggles to find reconciliation in nature.

The language is clear and direct. The use of older forms of address in stanza 3, "Thou," "thee," and "thine," lends seriousness to the speaker's reflections. They carry the weight of tradition. The image patterns in the poem move from obscurity to clarity. In the first stanza the haze blocks the speaker's ability to see the vista he suspects is before him. In the second, with the advent of noontime, the haze begins to clear. By the third stanza he sees more clearly in his mind the nature of his problem with belief in God, and in the fourth his physical eyes and his mind's eye see the truth of his situation.

The poem's vocabulary is specific yet rich in connotation. The first two words, "Immeasurable haze," create an image of vastness, a picture of an open landscape marked only by a few paltry trees. They give an immediate sense of the limits of sight but not of imagination. Measurement is a precise activity, and the speaker recognizes the haze as "immeasurable." The haze, which engulfs the speaker and obscures his vision, is not cloud or fog, but particles of water vapor, smoke, or dust; again, natural elements symbolize the speaker's condition and how he has defined himself in nature. A third word that carries precise meaning is "graveyard." While the dictionary shows cemetery and graveyard as synonyms, Winters chose the latter to name the poem's setting. Cemetery's root word, from the Greek, means "to put to sleep," whereas graveyard is an Anglo-Saxon compound noun. It includes the word "grave," which means several things besides a burial place for the body. Of special note are its meanings as an adjective—describing situations or places filled with great importance, filled with danger, or solemn and dignified. In this one word the reader perceives the poem's content as active, not passive, and as serious, not lighthearted or superficial.

The poem is written in the three-foot line known as trimeter, a nice choice as the three-beat line keeps the three-person God in focus. Trimeter was popular with some British Romantic poets as well as with the Irish poet William Butler Yeats (1865-1939). Using trimeter allows Winters to participate in the tradition of writing about nature's role in leading humans to certain understandings of the world.

Each stanza rhymes irregularly. Couplets are used in stanzas 1, 2, and 4. Stanza 3 is the climax of the poem, and here Winters uses alternating rhymes (*ababcdcdefef*) to echo the speaker's indecisiveness. As a formal poet, one who used rhyme and meter, Winters was aware of the value of traditional versification in giving structure to verse. The variations in rhyme combined with the metrical steadiness create a feeling of ambivalence while promising resolution.

Themes and Meanings

"To the Holy Spirit" is concerned with the logical conflict of faith with reason. The speaker, until the last stanza of the poem, is trying to comprehend how he can know an unknowable, and he is uncomfortable in exchanging sensory truths for acts of faith. Yet he feels limited in knowing that the end of life is only death. He settles on the realization that what he thinks will not affect his ability to believe in the power of the Holy Spirit and the existence of God. Only the living are preoccupied with the meaning of death; the dead are experiencing it. Only the living worry about what there is to know, and the speaker appears, at the end of the poem, to be solaced by his awareness that when death comes, he will be rationally and spiritually prepared because he has had God revealed to him in the graveyard. It is important to recall that Winters's speaker accepts the existence of God but makes no claims for the validity or purpose of any particular religion. This speaker is ultimately satisfied with a hierarchical worldview in which he is a rational believer in the existence of a higher power.

"To the Holy Spirit" is acknowledged by critics as among Winters's best poems in both form and content. John Finlay wrote of the poem as "a summary of Winters' entire poetic career, one which began in free verse, imagism, and aesthetic relativism and which ended in traditional meter, classicism, and theistic absolutism." In becoming a critic of his own desire to have faith, the speaker challenges himself to deal with cultural assumptions about the limits of reason and the need to believe in the existence of anything greater than humanity. When he leaves the graveyard, the speaker has driven away the irrational facet of faith and replaced it with a reasonable observation: "And I, alas, am bound/ Pure mind to flesh and bone,/ And flesh and bone to ground."

Beverly Schneller

TO THE LADY

Author: Mitsuye Yamada (1923-   )
Type of poem: Meditation
First published: 1976, in *Camp Notes and Other Poems*

The Poem

The content of Mitsuye Yamada's thirty-six-line poem "To the Lady" is deceptively simple. The speaker ruminates about a gathering—perhaps a lecture or poetry reading—in San Francisco at which an anonymous lady had asked why most Japanese Americans did not resist internment in United States concentration camps during World War II. As the speaker thinks about the question, she "rewrites" her experience in an imaginary dialogue with the lady that ironically refashions a speculative history.

The poem's second stanza enumerates eight courses of action that "I," the speaker as persona of the Japanese Americans in the woman's question, might have taken. The imagined alternatives are ironic, exaggerated, and highly topical in relation to the poem's composition in the early 1970's. The speaker first considers "run[ning] off" to Canada. The immediate topical connection implies those draft resisters who sought asylum in Canada rather than fighting the Vietnamese; the contemporary reference also suggests a historical parallel with slaves from the United States who fled to Canada before the Civil War.

The next alternative, hijacking a plane to Algeria, alludes to airplane hijackings in the 1960's, often connected with anticolonial struggles such as the Algerian war for independence from France; like running to Canada, this alternative suggests escape. The third entry in this brief catalogue conflates the brassiere—a simpleminded icon of the entire feminist movement by referring to a few Dutch women who burned brassieres—with the American slogan of lifting oneself up by one's bootstraps: The speaker envisages lifting herself "from [her]/ bra straps," but the undertone of violence continues in an image of kicking "them" in "the groin."

Next, escalating violence and self-destruction continue with robbing a bank and self-immolation; again, the references are topical. Some bank robberies in the 1960's and 1970's were motivated, according to the perpetrators, not by desire for personal gain but for redistributing wealth in a more equitable society. On the other hand, some American protestors against the Vietnam War burned themselves to death in public to protest the war.

The last three entries are linked to specific incidents. First, the speaker imagines withdrawing into a wooden house and being burned up as television viewers watch the event on the news. This scenario alludes to May of 1974, when members of a counterculture group known as the Symbionese Liberation Army, who had hidden in a small wooden house in Los Angeles, were surrounded by police, who burned the building and its occupants as millions of people watched on the evening news.

The speaker next alludes to a famous photograph that shows a straggling group of Vietnamese villagers fleeing from the bombs destroying their homes; at the center of the picture is a weeping child whose clothes have been burned off her naked body by napalm. Finally, the speaker refers to the death, in the early 1960's, of Kitty Genovese, a young woman in New York City who was assaulted and murdered as dozens of her neighbors listened to her cries for help.

The following stanza consists of the single word "Then," which turns the poem to address "the lady" directly for the first time, with another catalogue of five imagined responses of "the lady" to the speaker's plight. Again, the list of imagined responses melds irony, exaggeration, and topical references. The listener might have rescued the speaker like a knight "in shining armor," the catch phrase commonly referring to escapist fantasies, or she might have laid herself across railroad tracks. The latter image fuses the real protests of individuals, such as poet Allen Ginsberg, who have placed their bodies on railroad tracks to protest the secret transport of toxic war materials with the old serial-film stereotype of the heroine tied to railroad tracks and rescued at the last minute.

A third possibility is that the listener might have marched on Washington, D.C.; here the speaker alludes to the comparative invisibility of injustices against people of color until mass movements, like the celebrated civil rights march on Washington in the 1960's, unite a significant number of the privileged majority with victimized others who seek to exercise their rights.

Next, the listener is reminded that she might have resisted injustice by identifying with the persecuted Jews of Europe through tattooing a "Star of David on [her] arm"; again, the speaker suggests that atrocities such as the Holocaust can occur because narrow self-absorption prevents identifying with oppressed peoples. The last possibility the speaker enumerates is writing "six million enraged letters" to Congress. This suggestion entails mass action rather than individualistic, isolated acts, and it suggests a nonviolent, even banal type of engagement.

In the next stanza the speaker moves from "I" and then "you" to talk as "we." However, the statement is negative: No appropriate action was taken by anyone. A new series emerges with five parallel phrases in which "order" is noted as social, moral, and internal and linked to "law and order." In this series the speaker also anchors the poem's field of reference to the Japanese American internment by naming "Executive Order 9066," President Franklin D. Roosevelt's directive for the uncompensated removal of American citizens and resident aliens of Japanese descent from United States coastal areas to concentration camps.

The poem's brief final stanza contrasts "YOU" and "I" with an abbreviated "them" in the phrases "YOU let'm/ I let'm." Finally, the speaker includes even the blameworthy "them" in the final three-word assessment that "All are punished." That is, allowing evil to happen hurts everyone, not just those being persecuted.

Forms and Devices

Like most of Yamada's work, "To the Lady" is a straightforward statement with little literary embellishment. As noted, the text relies on exaggeration, irony, and topical allusion. The poem's framework combines the device of catalogue and the rhetorical form of dialectic within the tradition of meditative poetry. Typical of meditative poetry, the entire statement is understood as taking place within the speaker's mind; furthermore, the statement moves from a problem or question to a resolution and new insight. The resolution comes about through a dialectic that first postulates an initial impetus (imprisonment without due process of law), then a reaction (what the speaker says she might have done), which is followed by responses to the reaction (what "the lady" might have done).

Following the dialectical exchange, the speaker turns away from speculation and inserts unadorned facts of history: Executive Order 9066, which reminds the reader of the failure of every American of any ethnic group to set boundaries against injustice. Out of this recognition of failure comes the insight that in a society where injustice is unopposed both persecutors and persecuted are punished.

The free-verse rhythm, short lines, and austere language emphasize the poem's irony. In the first stanza the speaker's insistent repetition of "should've" prepares for the clipped, almost tight-lipped accusation-reminder in the last three lines, in which the perpetrators of injustice are reduced to a single letter for "them" in "YOU let'm/ I let'm." Exaggeration pervades the catalogue addressed to a capitalized "YOU," reminding the reader of the egotism of this privileged lady in the audience who assumes the right to advise the speaker on what should have been done. In another subtle irony the speaker through this device reinforces the parallel between the speaker's "I" and the lady, addressed both times in capital letters as "YOU," and suggests the possibility of an emphatic, "uppercase" collaboration more visible and potentially powerful than the minimized "them" now collapsed to a mere lowercase letter "m."

Themes and Meanings

The brief, austere statement of this poem offers little incentive to search for obscure or hidden meaning. Content and theme are the same: Injustice hurts everyone, perpetrator and victim alike. However, the irony and exaggeration in the speaker's literal interpretation of "the lady's" question—in the satirical picture of an individual responding personally as if she were an entire group—address the dangerous and finally antagonistic premise of "the lady's" question. To ask the Japanese Americans "Why did [they] let/ the government" imprison them implies that the persecuted are responsible for their persecution: Victims are to blame for their mistreatment.

The speaker initially retorts to the woman as "other," as the uninvolved outsider who would be the "you" that watches the speaker's immolation on the evening news, or the "you" assaulted by the picture of the abused little girl. The first capitalized "YOU" emphasizes the distance between speaker and listener. However, the poem's dialectic leads ultimately to collaboration and cooperation of the "I" and the "you" against the persecuting "them." While historically both the speaker (representing all those unjustly interned) and the listener (representing all well-meaning people who do nothing) are united negatively in their failure to act, even this negative assessment implies potential for positive, and therefore effective, collaboration. Contrasting the analogy of Kitty Genovese, emblem of all those abandoned by their neighbors, the allusions in the poem to the march on Washington and to millions of letters sent to lawmakers are examples of such mass action. These references reflect the author's philosophy as expressed consistently in the body of her writings and in her lifelong activism as a pacifist and as an officer of organizations promoting peace and justice.

Helen Jaskoski

TO THE MEMORY OF MR. OLDHAM

Author: John Dryden (1631-1700)
Type of poem: Elegy
First published: 1684, in *Remains of Mr. John Oldham in Verse and Prose*

The Poem

John Dryden's elegy "To the Memory of Mr. Oldham" presents a tribute in verse to the poetic achievement of John Oldham (1653-1683), whom Dryden knew as a younger contemporary. Although he produced a variety of poems and translations, Oldham gained fame through his highly topical *Satyrs upon the Jesuits* (1681). In twenty-five lines of heroic couplets, an unusual verse form for an elegy, Dryden laments Oldham's premature death and assesses his literary merit.

In the first of the poem's three sections (lines 1-10), Dryden follows established elegiac convention by announcing the loss and, speaking in the first person, identifying himself with the younger poet. Their souls were allied through their mutual devotion to study and art as well as their mutual dislike of knaves and fools. Yet Oldham, as Dryden admits, achieved poetic fame earlier in life than Dryden had, a condition comparable to the race narrated by Vergil in the *Aeneid* (c. 29-19 B.C.E.), book 5, involving Nisus and Euryalus. The older Nisus, leading in a foot race, falls down but manages to trip the nearest competitor. As a result, he has the pleasure of seeing his young friend, Euryalus, become the victor. This classical allusion foreshadows another less optimistic Vergilian reference and concludes the poem's introductory section.

In the second section (lines 11-21), Dryden assesses Oldham's literary achievement, remarking on the poet's youthful display of genius. Yet he points out that Oldham's verses lack smoothness and polish, an indication that his art is defective. To place the defect in a more generous context, Dryden suggests that satire really does not need as much polish as other poetic forms and that, after all, Oldham's creative ability is evident from the verses he wrote. Dryden thus recognizes that Oldham's satires brought him recognition and fame despite their rough meter and somewhat unskillful poetic tone. The elegy suggests that Oldham's genius overpowered his art while affirming that genius lasts despite the aesthetic limitations of its forms of expression.

The concluding section (lines 22-25) returns to the balanced and subdued tone of the beginning, with the classical formula, "hail and farewell." An allusion to Marcellus—whom the Romans had viewed enthusiastically as the successor to Augustus Caesar, but who died before his emperor—serves to enforce the theme of premature loss. The poem concludes by emphasizing the incongruity of early achievement combined with early death through the symbolism of traditional classical crowns made of leaves. Crowned with ivy for youth and freshness and laurel for achievement, Oldham was overpowered by "fate and gloomy night."

Forms and Devices

Normally the heroic couplet, Dryden's most commonly employed verse form, is viewed as more suitable for epigrammatic wit and reasoned argument than for elegy. Yet in "To the Memory of Mr. Oldham," Dryden admirably demonstrates that the couplet possesses a range of tones adequate for its use in an elegy. By relying throughout on schemes of repetition, carefully chosen sound effects, and classical allusions, Dryden creates a tone of moderate and measured grief.

Among the schemes, balance and antithesis in the poem's first section establish a tone of restraint at the outset. The initial line includes the balanced construction, "too little and too lately," balance being reinforced by double alliteration on the "i" and "t" consonants. An abundance of open vowels and sonorants serves to lengthen the lines, adding weight and somberness to the tone. Balance continues through "think and call" and "knaves and fools," reaching an emphatic and artful balance and double antithesis in line 8, "the last set out the soonest did arrive." Like many of Dryden's verses, this one creates the pressure of poetic expression simply through the schemes without reliance on metaphor or other figures of speech.

In the poem's second section, balance and antithesis give way to carefully constructed sound effects, as Dryden evaluates Oldham's poetic achievement through the traditional neoclassical polarity, nature (genius) and art. At this point in his career, Dryden had assimilated the neoclassical principle that sounds, even when not onomatopoeic, should echo or complement a poem's meaning. Lines 15-16 are made to echo the harsh metrics of Oldham's verses, while asserting strongly that harshness does not obscure his genius: "wit will shine/ Thro' the harsh cadence of a rugged line." Later Dryden introduces a triplet, with its slow conclusion in a hexameter, to suggest that artistic perfection in itself may suggest dullness, a concession that blunts his criticism of Oldham's art. Although maturing time brings mastery in art, it "but mellows what we write to the dull sweets of rhyme." Arguably, few verses in English poetry match Dryden's sound effects in this hexameter in creating a dull, mellow tone.

The final section returns to the subdued tone established through balance, employing the classical elegiac formula "hail and farewell" in its initial line and sustaining it till the end with balanced phrases and nouns: "with ivy and with laurels" and "fate and gloomy night."

The two classical allusions to Vergilian characters further enhance and sharpen the polarities inherent in the poem, for both imply a contrast between youth and age and both express the theme of early distinction. They may also reflect Dryden's inclination to use the monarchical metaphor, using the concept of rulers and successors, not only in the state but also in the kingdom of letters. The Nisus-Euryalus allusion serves to call attention to Oldham's early achievement, though, ironically, unlike the early victor Euryalus, Oldham died shortly after his success. The Augustus-Marcellus reference focuses on failed succession and early death. Both allusions place Oldham's achievements against the honored background of Latin classical literature.

Themes and Meanings

"To the Memory of Mr. Oldham" is an occasional poem dealing with the poignancy of early death and a concomitant loss of literary promise. Little is known about Dryden's relationship with Oldham, who died at age thirty and was twenty-two years Dryden's junior. Since Dryden acknowledges in the poem that he and Oldham were too little and lately known, one gathers that they were not close friends. Apart from the wording of the poem, only anecdotal evidence to the effect that they first met in 1682, barely a year before Oldham's death, serves to link them. Notably, the poem reflects little personal grief; it is rather a reflection of Dryden's tendency, as the chief literary figure of his time, to pay tribute to younger contemporaries. Assuredly, whatever the personal relationship, Dryden would have known Oldham's poetry; the elegy suggests that he took a keen interest in Oldham's satires, which appeared in print only a few months before Dryden's satiric masterpiece *Absalom and Achitophel* (1681).

Dryden's intellect often combines the tendency toward polarities with a second toward hierarchical thought. The hierarchical pairings of Nisus-Euryalus, Augustus-Marcellus, and Dryden-Oldham place the younger poet's life within a classical context and suggest succession—that Oldham might have continued the satiric tradition that the two poets shared. Yet they also complement one another in a duality that is a hallmark of Dryden's criticism: the distinction between nature (genius) and art. One should note that in this dichotomy, Dryden consistently gives greater weight to genius.

When he assesses the value of Oldham's poetry, Dryden follows the lead of Ben Jonson, who praised William Shakespeare's genius but found his art defective. Dryden well knew that Oldham's poetry was often harsh and irregular. His acknowledgment that satire does not require polish indicates his awareness that earlier English satirists, such as John Donne, John Cleveland, and Samuel Butler, wrote rugged and sometimes crude lines. Even Dryden's contemporaries such as John Wilmot, earl of Rochester, and Charles Sackville, earl of Dorset, took little pain to achieve smoothly flowing lines in satire. English poetic tradition had accepted the view that satire was normally rough and irregular. That this view changed was primarily because of the effort and example of Dryden, who in his own satires sought to achieve not only the wit but also the smoothness and polish of Horace. Dryden reversed the dominant trend in satiric style by making the genre a demanding form of poetic expression, replacing rough meters with keen iambics and invective with rational expression fraught with irony. In the neoclassic canons that prescribe both originality and excellence in expression, he finds Oldham excelling in genius but deficient in art. Although he states that art is no requisite for satire, his own practice demonstrates otherwise.

Stanley Archer

TO THE MEMORY OF MY BELOVED MASTER
WILLIAM SHAKESPEARE

Author: Ben Jonson (1573-1637)
Type of poem: Lyric
First published: 1623, in *Mr. William Shakespeares Comedies, Histories, and Tragedies*

The Poem

In 1616, "rare Ben Jonson," the unofficial poet laureate under James I, published his collected works, the first time an English author had done so. In 1623, William Shakespeare's plays were collected in the first folio, which contained this prefatory tribute to Shakespeare by Jonson, who was determined to give his contemporary his due as a universal literary genius.

The title conveys Jonson's high estimation of Shakespeare as his beloved master, his superior whom he admires and loves to the point of idolatry. Shakespeare died in 1616; seven years later, Jonson is evaluating what Shakespeare has bequeathed to him and to his audiences, then and in the future.

The poem consists of eighty lines, divided into four parts and written in heroic couplets—rhymed five-beat lines containing ten syllables each. Jonson spends the first fifteen lines describing the wrong kinds of tributes usually paid to famous authors. By contrast, he will not praise Shakespeare out of envy, ignorance, blind affection, or hidden malice.

The second section starts with line 17, in which Jonson begins his eulogy of Shakespeare as the "Soul of the age!"—the spirit of the time, the delightful essence of creative expression. There is no need to make a place for Shakespeare in the conventional burial place of England's great poets, Westminster Abbey, because he transcends place, being a "monument without a tomb" who still lives in his plays, which will always be read and praised. Similarly, Jonson declares that he will not compare Shakespeare to other Elizabethan dramatists, such as John Lyly, Thomas Kyd, and Christopher Marlowe, whom he so far outshines that such a comparison would be insulting. Despite Shakespeare's meager classical training, he is also superior to the thundering tragedians of ancient Greece and Rome.

The third section begins on line 43, with Jonson's claim that Shakespeare transcends time through the universality of his creativity. By means of his native genius, Shakespeare was able to create natural works that will last for all time, unlike the Roman writers Plautus and Terence, who have become outdated. Shakespeare is not only an exuberant natural force, he is also a diligent craftsman. To achieve the laurel crown, the poet must revise, "must sweat,/ . . . and strike the second heat/ Upon the muses' anvil."

Jonson begins the final section (lines 71 through 80) by calling Shakespeare the "Sweet swan of Avon," an exclamation that contains important allusions to Shakespeare's life and art. First, Jonson depicts Shakespeare as a royal swan in the River Thames, revered by the two monarchs for whom he wrote, Queen Elizabeth and King James I. Second, Jonson recalls Shakespeare's birth in Stratford, on the Avon River, and depicts him as the dying swan who has left us his beautiful plays as his legacy. Finally, he declares that Shakespeare has ascended into the sky as Cygnus, the swan constellation, a glorification befitting classical demigods and heroes who were exalted after death with a heavenly apotheosis. From this lofty position, the "Star of poets" continues to shed the light of his inspiration on the "drooping stage."

Forms and Devices

The poem is written in heroic couplets, both closed and open. The closed couplet comes to a full stop at the end of two lines, while the flow of the open couplet continues into succeeding lines. Jonson alternates these types of couplets throughout the poem to create a distinctive rhythm of two-line and larger units.

Ironically, Jonson begins the poem with an ambiguous couplet that can be read as closed, but that also can be linked with the next two lines to create a four-line unit. In the first couplet, Jonson declares that he does not intend to make Shakespeare the object of envy through excessive praise, although, as he states in the next couplet, it is impossible to praise Shakespeare too highly. After this masterful use of ambiguity and hyperbole, Jonson continues with six closed couplets that epigrammatically dismiss the false types of praise he will avoid.

In the second part of the poem (lines 31 through 40), in which Jonson compares Shakespeare to his classical predecessors, he employs five open couplets to depict the superior power of Shakespeare's creativity. Sometimes Jonson varies the alternation between open and closed couplets with an intervening, short, unrhymed line that adds a succinct decisiveness to his pronouncements. For example, after using four open couplets to describe how a "good poet's made as well as born," Jonson inserts the terse "And such wert thou!"

Jonson's major rhetorical device is the use of negation to praise Shakespeare. Usually, one thinks of praise as being positive, but Jonson cleverly uses varieties of negation to increase the superlative qualities of Shakespeare's achievement. Jonson declares "he was not of an age, but for all time!" when he compares Shakespeare to other writers, he uses the negative to diminish them and to enlarge him:

> I will not lodge thee by
> Chaucer or Spenser, or bid Beaumont lie
> A little further to make thee a room:
> Thou art a monument without a tomb.

Jonson uses the metaphor of lineage to indicate that Shakespeare has made us all his heirs through the universality of his genius. This metaphor is suggested in the last part of the poem's full title, "and what he hath left us," and is developed in the third section. Jonson first compares Shakespeare to a sweating blacksmith hammering out his lines on the anvil, and then depicts him as the father of his "lines," which are the exact expression of their progenitor's mind and manners. These lines represent the words he has written in his plays; the succeeding generations of writers that he has inspired to attempt to emulate his creativity; the audiences that will always enjoy his work; and, finally, the military troops of intelligence he has dispatched to "shake a lance" at ignorance.

Themes and Meanings

The theme of this poem concerns the nature of the praise that can be given a great writer by a contemporary of almost equal stature. Jonson has the task of devising a strategy that will enable him to praise Shakespeare without sounding foolish, sycophantic, envious, or uninformed. He has to create a poem that will give a universal genius his due. This is no easy matter, and he has to do this in such a way as to prove his own credentials as a poet.

The major theme of the poem is that Shakespeare transcends time and place, and belongs to the ages. For Jonson to perceive this and to state it with such grace is a magnanimous and outstanding achievement. At the outset, he declares his competence to evaluate such greatness by saying that he will not draw envy on Shakespeare with excessive praise, although he confesses that it is impossible to praise him too highly. This craftily qualified opening is followed by a series of dismissals of ignorant, blindly affectionate, and deceptively malicious praise. Shakespeare is "Above . . . the need" for such tribute; the word "Above" is important because it expresses the theme that Shakespeare has ascended into the empyrean, where he outshines the achievements of his classical predecessors and contemporaries.

Jonson applies the transcendent, or spiritual, term to Shakespeare to indicate that, although he is physically dead, he is still present through his creative genius. He is the "Soul of the age," "a monument without a tomb," an enduring influence who does not need to be buried next to other great authors to display his greatness. His work is enough to grant him immortality: "And art alive still while thy book doth live,/ And we have wits to read and praise to give."

At the beginning of the third section, Jonson goes beyond his earlier praise of Shakespeare as the "Soul of the age" by saying that he is "not of an age, but for all time." Shakespeare was born in a time when the muses were in their prime, and he is at one with them and nature; as a result, his lines are both natural and carefully formed: "Shakespeare's mind . . . brightly shines/ In his well-turned and true-filed lines."

In the last section, Jonson brings Shakespeare to his final ascendance when he depicts him as the "Sweet swan of Avon." Since his death, he has ascended to the heavens as a constellation that still influences the earthly stage. Shakespeare continues to shine forth as the "star of poets," whose volume, his magnitude as expressed in the First Folio, lightens, that is, brightens and lifts, "the drooping stage."

Frank Ardolino

TO THE READER

Author: Charles Baudelaire (1821-1867)
Type of poem: Dramatic monologue
First published: 1855, as "Au lecteur"; in *Les Fleurs du mal*, 1857; English translation
   collected in *Flowers of Evil*, 1931

The Poem

As the title suggests, "To the Reader" was written by Charles Baudelaire as a preface to his collection of poems *Flowers of Evil*. It is a poem of forty lines, organized into ten quatrains, which presents a pessimistic account of the poet's view of the human condition along with his explanation of its causes and origins. Baudelaire, assuming the ironic stance of a sardonic religious orator, chastises the reader for his sins and subsequent insincere repentence. He proposes the devil himself as the major force controlling humankind's life and behavior, and unveils a personification of Boredom (*Ennui*), overwhelming and all-pervasive, as the most pernicious of all vices, for it threatens to suffocate humankind's aspirations toward virtue and goodness with indifference and apathy. The tone of *Flowers of Evil* is established in this opening piece, which also announces the principal themes of the poems to follow.

The first two quatrains of the poem can be taken together: In the first quatrain, the speaker chastises his readers for their energetic pursuit of vice and sin (folly, error, and greed are mentioned), and for sustaining their sins as beggars nourish their lice; in the second, he accuses them of repenting insincerely, for, though they willingly offer their tears and vows, they are soon enticed to return, through weakness, to their old sinful ways. The next five quatrains, filled with many similes and metaphors, reveal Satan to be the dominating power in human life. The power of the thrice-great Satan is compared to that of an alchemist, then to that of a puppeteer manipulating human beings; the sinners are compared to a dissolute pauper embracing an aged prostitute, then their brains are described as filled with carousing demons who riot while death flows into their lungs. The seventh quatrain lists some violent sins (rape, arson, murder) which most people dare not commit, and points a transition to the final part of the poem, where the speaker introduces the personification of Boredom.

The eighth quatrain heralds the appearance of this disgusting figure, the most detestable vice of all, surrounded by seven hellish animals who cohabit the menagerie of sin; the ninth tells of the inactivity of this sleepy monster, too listless to do more than yawn. The final quatrain pictures Boredom indifferently smoking his hookah while shedding dispassionate tears for those who die for their crimes. Presenting this symbol of depraved inaction to his readers, the speaker insists that they must recognize in him their brother, and acknowledge their share in the hypocrisy with which they attempt to hide their intimate relationships with evil.

Forms and Devices

Baudelaire selected for this poem the frequently used verse form of Alexandrine quatrains, rhymed *abab*, one not particularly difficult to imitate in English iambic pentameter, with no striking enjambments or peculiarities of rhyme or rhythm. The theme of the poem is neither surprising nor original, for it consists basically of the conventional Christian view that the effects of Original Sin doom humankind to an inclination toward evil which is extremely difficult to resist. This apparently straightforward poem, however, conceals a poetic conception of exceptional brilliance and power, attributable primarily to the poet's tone, his diction, and to the unusual images he devised to enliven his poetic expression.

Believing that the language of the Romanticists had grown stale and lifeless, Baudelaire hoped to restore vitality and energy to poetic art by deriving images from the sights and sounds of Paris, a city he knew and loved. Elements from street scenes—glimpses of the lives and habits of the poor and aged, alcoholics and prostitutes, criminal types—these offered him fresh sources of material with new and unusual poetic possibilities. This kind of imagery prevails in "To the Reader," controlling the emotional force of the similes and metaphors which are the basic rhetorical figures used in the poem.

Baudelaire's similes are classical in conception but boldly innovative in their terms. People feed their remorse "as beggars nourish lice"; demons are squeezed tightly together "like a million worms"; people steal secret pleasure "like a poor degenerate who kisses and mouths the battered breast of an old whore." This last image, one of the most famous in modern French verse, is further extended: People squeeze their secret pleasure "hard, like an old orange" to extract a few drops of juice, causing the reader to relate the battered breast and the old orange to each other. Baudelaire uses a similar technique when forming metaphors: Satan "lulls" or "rocks" people's souls, implying that he is their mother, but he is also an alchemist who makes them defenseless as he "vaporizes the rich metal of our will." He is the puppeteer "who holds the strings by which we're moved." As they breathe, death, the "invisible river," enters their lungs.

At the end of the poem, Boredom appears surrounded by a "vicious menagerie" of vices in the shapes of various repulsive animals—jackals, panthers, hound bitches, monkeys, scorpions, vultures, and snakes—who are creating a din: screeching, roaring, snarling, and crawling. Boredom, uglier, wickeder, and filthier than they, smokes his water pipe calmly, shedding involuntary tears as he dreams of violent executions. The seven kinds of creatures suggest the seven deadly sins, but they also represent the banal offenses people commonly commit, for, though threatening, they are more disgusting than deadly. The picture Baudelaire creates here, not unlike a medieval manuscript illumination or a grotesque view by Hieronymus Bosch, may shock or offend sensitive tastes, but it was to become a hallmark of Baudelaire's verse as his art developed.

Themes and Meanings

Most of Baudelaire's important themes are stated or suggested in "To the Reader." The inner conflict experienced by one who perceives the divine but embraces the foul provides the substance for many of the poems found in *Flowers of Evil*. This preface presents an ironic view of the human situation as Baudelaire sees it: Human beings long for good but yield easily to the temptations placed in their path by Satan because of the weakness inherent in their wills. People can feel remorse, but know full well, even while repenting, that they will sin again: "And to the muddy path we gaily return,/ Believing that vile tears will wash away our sins." Baudelaire once wrote that he felt drawn simultaneously in opposite directions: A spiritual force caused him to desire to mount upward toward God, while an animal force drew him joyfully down to Satan. The diction of the poem reinforces this conflict of opposites: Nourishing "our sweet remorse," and "By all revolting objects lured," people are descending into hell "without horror."

From the outset, Baudelaire insists on the similarity of the poet and the reader by using forms of "we" and "our" rather than "you" and "I," implying that all share in the condition he describes. "Our sins are stubborn, our repentance lax," and "The Devil holds the strings by which we're worked," reflect a common culpability, while "Each day toward Hell we descend another step" unites the readers with the poet in damnation. The tone is both sarcastic and pathetic, since the speaker includes himself with his readers in his accusations. The poem is then both a confession and an indictment implicating all humankind. All are guilty; none can escape humankind's shameful heritage of original sin with its attendant inclinations to crime, degradation, and vice. This theme of universal guilt is maintained throughout the poem and will recur often in later poems.

Baudelaire ends his poem by revealing an image of Boredom, the "delicate monster" *Ennui*, resting apart from his menagerie of vices, "His eyes filled with involuntary tears,/ He dreams of scaffolds while smoking his hookah" and would gladly "swallow up the world with a yawn." This monster is dangerous because those who fall under his sway feel nothing and are helpless to act in any purposeful way. They are driven to seek relief in any sort of activity, provided that it alleviates their intolerable condition. Human beings seek any alternative to gray depression, deadness of soul, and a sense of meaninglessness in life. A character in Albert Camus's novel *La Chute* (1956; *The Fall*, 1957) remarks: "Something must happen—and that explains most human commitments. Something must happen, even loveless slavery, even war or death. Hurray then for funerals!" This character understands that Boredom "would lay waste the earth quite willingly" in order to establish a commitment to something that might invigorate an otherwise routine existence. The final line of the poem (quoted by T. S. Eliot in *The Waste Land*, 1922) compels the reader to see his own image reflected in the monster-mirror figure and acknowledge his own hypocrisy: "Hypocrite reader,—my likeness,—my brother!" This pessimistic view was difficult for many readers to accept in the nineteenth century and remains disturbing to some yet today, but it is Baudelaire's insistence upon intellectual honesty which causes him to be viewed by many as the first truly modern poet.

Raymond M. Archer

TO THE VIRGINS, TO MAKE MUCH OF TIME

Author: Robert Herrick (1591-1674)
Type of poem: Lyric
First published: 1648, in *Hesperides: Or, The Works Both Humane and Divine by Robert Herrick, Esq.*

The Poem

"To the Virgins, to Make Much of Time" is a short lyric poem that at first reading seems to be simply a call to young women to enjoy life, particularly its physical pleasures, while they are young.

Robert Herrick is considered one of the circle of poets (sometimes called the "sons of Ben") that gathered around poet and playwright Ben Jonson in London in the early seventeenth century. Herrick became a country pastor in 1629, but when upon the advent of the English Civil War he remained loyal to his king, he was ousted from his post by the Puritans, who closed the theaters and taverns—and eventually executed the king. This political exile deprived Herrick of his living and cut him off from the possibility of returning to London. It is hard to tell when Herrick poems such as "Delight in Disorder," "Upon Julia's Clothes," and this one were actually written, but since they were published together in 1648, only a year after Herrick was removed from his post, they may constitute a kind of challenge to Puritan strictures.

The title of the poem begins the address to the virgins. To "make much of time" is both to make something happen while time is passing and to pay attention to its passage. In the first stanza, one use to be made of time is to collect flowers before they are yet in full bloom, because time passes so quickly that soon new flowers will be withered on the vine.

The idea of the passage of time is given a new image as the second stanza describes the movement of the sun. By casting its circuit through the sky in terms of a "race," the sense of how quickly time passes is emphasized; in the same way that the passing away of the "smile" of the flower is inherent in its bud, the setting of the sun is implicit in its rising. The combination of the idea of gathering in the first stanza and the reference to the sun in the second seems to echo the well-known injunction to "make hay while the sun shines."

In the third stanza, the idea of the passage of time is cast in human terms: The "first" or young age is "best," "warmer," more active. Just as heat is expended by the sun, however, the heat that makes youth warm is also "spent" and diminishes from "best" to "worse" to "worst." The passage from youth to age in this stanza is parallel to the progression of bud to bloom to death of the flowers in the first.

The shift to human terms in the third stanza anticipates the return in the fourth to direct address to the virgins. They are admonished not to be "coy," which means "to shrink from familiarity," in two senses: in modesty or flirtatiousness. So what this request calls for is that the virgins not, in either innocent ignorance or in proud folly, forget how quickly time passes. They are further instructed to marry while they can, with the warning that once they have lost whatever it takes to get a husband, once the time to do so has passed, they may "tarry," wait, or procrastinate, forever.

Forms and Devices

The four stanzas of this poem are quatrains (each has four lines). These are "hymn" or "common" stanzas, since they take the form most often found in traditional hymns: a metrical pattern of four iambic feet in the first and third lines and three in the second and fourth lines, and the regular rhyme scheme of *abab*. It is likely that it was intentional on Herrick's part to adapt a church form to his very secular theme.

The stanzaic form is given a sense of lushness and superfluity by the hypermetrical syllable at the end of each second and fourth line. The final syllable is not part of the three feet of the line, but seems to pack it with sound; it is also probably not an accident that these syllables have in each case what is called a "feminine" rhyme.

The iambic pentameter is nearly perfect, although the strength of the stressed syllables varies enough for the poem not to be monotonous. Two variations are worth noting. Both syllables of "gather," the first word of line one and the first foot of the metrical pattern, have nearly the same stress value, which establishes a sense of the imperative from the outset. The fifth line contains two implied elisions: "glorious" metrically must be "glor'ous" and "heaven," "heav'n." Leaving extra syllables that require contraction in the line generates the sense that the sun's passage is both unusually lengthy and unaccountably shortened.

The punctuation of the sentences is consistent with the ends of lines and stanzas throughout most of the poem, which gives it a calm and measured pace. The caesura that occurs with the comma in the middle of the eleventh line causes a break in the poem, increasing the sense of abrupt finality that comes when youth is "spent." The only enjambment of the poem follows immediately after, in lines 11 and 12, so that the "worse and worst/ times" that come after youth is spent seem to drag on. The later caesuras in lines 13 and 14 are milder and seem to echo only the first, so that within the advice being given, the threat of that break, that expenditure, is repeating itself.

This poem is part of a tradition of persuasion poems. In *Englands Helicon*, a miscellany of mostly pastoral poems published in 1600, a poem of Christopher Marlowe's "The Passionate Shepherd to His Love" expresses the same kind of plea by begging, "Come live with me and be my love," and promising all kinds of sensory delights. It is answered by a poem written by Sir Walter Ralegh, "The Nymph's Reply to the Shepherd." The nymph recites the changes that will be brought about by the passage of time, and asks whether love will "still breed" after them. A few decades after Herrick's poem, Andrew Marvell published "To His Coy Mistress" (*Miscellaneous Poems*, 1681), which even repeats the stock images of flowers and the sun used by Herrick.

Themes and Meanings

The reading that has been given the poem thus far can be summed up by the Latin phrase *carpe diem*, which means "seize the day." In this sense, virginity is not literal, but is merely a metaphor for a kind of innocence combined with receptivity that should be exercised as much as possible before it is lost, which with experience it will be.

The sexual theme is obvious but not simple. It can be understood very differently, depending on what one takes to be the sex of the reader. The gathering of rosebuds can be a metaphor for defloration; the rising of the sun, a metaphor for male erection, and "spend," a term for ejaculation. This reading is not merely sensual; it is also sexually threatening. Defloration is rape—that is, taking the flower of virginity from an unwilling victim. The reference to the personified sun is a reference to Apollo, famous for his attempts at ravishment. In a certain sense, then, the phrase "To the Virgins" could be understood to be a call to attack, such as Henry the Fifth's cry of "into the breach!" in William Shakespeare's *Henry V* (1600). In this sense, the "ye" addressed would be male, and the loss with which the poem is concerned is that of male potency: Women will be old before pleasure can be taken of them, the "sun" will set too soon, the energy of youth will pass, and sexual drive with it. As "Old Time" also appears personified, it is important to remember that Chronos, the god of time, seized power by castrating his rival.

If, on the other hand, one reads the poem as addressed to female virgins, then to gather rosebuds, in a sense, is to retain the flower of virginity, to gather it to oneself. The twin of the sun god, Apollo, is the moon goddess, Artemis, who is also the goddess of virginity (Ben Jonson calls her "Queen and huntress, chaste and fair" in "Hymn to Diana" from *Cynthia's Revels*, 1600-1601). With the setting of the force of male dominance, the twin force of female celibacy rises. In this sense, it is virginity, one of the few forms of currency a woman had, that is to be hoarded, not lost or "spent."

When marriage is promoted in the fourth stanza, Herrick is not making a moral distinction between fornication and sex within the sanctity of wedlock. Instead, marriage is proposed as an alternative to both sexual violence and sexual withholding, both of which are asocial and nonproductive. The injunction to "go marry" instead of to "tarry" in this sense has to do with not getting caught up in a vicious circle of mutually exclusive possibilities, but to move and grow into something that is beyond either of them.

Thus the poem is expressing a concern about the state of society. This concern also surfaces in the third stanza if one reads "age" and "times" to refer not to an individual's years but to the eras of humankind. Read this way, the lines suggest that only in the first age, the youth of a civilization, is it at its best; what follows is only a decline. It is here that one gets a sense of Herrick's lament for his own times and what he thinks has been lost.

Laurie Glover

TO URANIA

Author: Joseph Brodsky (1940-1996)
Type of poem: Lyric
First published: 1987, as "Uraniia," in *Uraniia*; English translation collected in *To Urania*, 1988

The Poem

"To Urania" is the title poem of *To Urania*, a collection of Joseph Brodsky's poetry in English and translations from his Russian poetry. Like most of the Russian poems in the collection, "To Urania" was translated by Brodsky himself.

The title of the poem leads one to expect that it is an invocation to the Muse, an apostrophe, or direct address, to a personified source of inspiration. Urania is one of the nine muses of classical mythology, the daughters of Zeus and Mnemosyne, or Memory. She is the muse of astronomy, the science which, for the ancients, offered a way of reading the pattern of human destiny in the mysterious symbolic language of the heavens. Consequently, many Renaissance writers considered her to be the muse of poetry. She is invoked by John Milton at a crucial juncture in *Paradise Lost* (1667).

"To Urania" contradicts the expectations raised by its title. It is really an interior monologue, directed at no one in particular. The "you" referred to at certain points is as impersonal as other pronouns used in the poem, such as "one" or "a man." Brodsky never speaks directly to the Muse here. Note the following apostrophe to Urania from Brodsky's "Lithuanian Nocturne" (1988): "Muse! from the heights where you/ dwell, beyond any creed's stratosphere . . ./ look, I pray you." In place of the formal, elevated mood of such passages, "To Urania" gives the impression of a man talking to himself. There is a pervasive note of gentle self-mockery. The poem moves back and forth disconnectedly between an impersonal, intellectual tone and a casual, ironic one, devoting itself now to concrete imagery, now to abstract statement.

The emotional keynote of the poem's opening is a sense of loneliness and confinement, the loneliness that "cubes a man at random." Yet this condition of sad helplessness is not unconditioned by hope for, as the poet tells the reader, even the sorrow he feels has a limit. The idea of limits is linked to the image of a leaf trapped on a grate and the windowpane that "stalls a stare." This sense of stalled movement is projected onto these spare details and, one comes to realize, flows out of the poet's own situation. The comical image of the fifth line, the camel that "sniffs at the rail with a resentful nostril," evokes, in a single stroke, a remote provincial railway station, the boredom of waiting for a slow, inefficient train.

These hints, which suggest that the poem records the thoughts of a melancholy traveler, are confirmed and elaborated by the imagery of the poem's final lines. The traveler is leaving behind the miserable towns where he was once well known, "in whose soggy phone books/ you are starring no longer. . . . " He has made a sudden imaginative leap which carries him out of the frustration of the present moment. As he paces back and forth, waiting for the train, he envisions himself traveling through the Soviet Union and the rest of Asia and into the vast ocean beyond.

The point at which Urania is compared to her younger sister Clio, the muse of history, is the crux of the traveler's leap from the frustration of the here and now into a vision of the journey completed. The mythological story helps the traveler get past the sense of limits that his philosophical musings impose. It helps him to imagine a world whose "pate," or head, is "free of any bio," or biography. The poet looks to a world in which the history of his former life can be left behind.

In the closing lines, the growing sense of rapid movement and open space conveyed by the unimpeded rhythm of successive images leads to the end of the emotional journey mapped out by the poem. In his imaginative flight, the traveler seems to move beyond the limits of his present sorrow toward the "clime where the traveller's journey is done," as William Blake writes in "Ah! Sun-flower." He imagines a sublime expanse that "grows blue like lace underwear." With this simile, however, the poem ends on a puzzling note. The image of the "lace underwear" undermines the sense of the sublime grandeur of the ocean to which it is compared. In the end, the desired destination is placed on a par with the object of a mundane sexual fantasy.

Forms and Devices

In "To Urania," philosophical statements about time and space, fate and freedom seem to be reconciled only partially with descriptive images drawn from the immediate surroundings. The use of comical imagery and word choices, as well as peculiar partial rhymes ("Clio" and "bio," for example), creates a deceptively casual tone which heightens this contrast.

The way in which the statement flows into and is connected with the imagery has two aspects. The first is logical and demonstrative. The poet uses the images of the window and the leaf in the second and third lines to illustrate and confirm the statement with which he opens the poem. In the next two lines, he places himself alongside these inanimate objects, conveying how he sees himself as part of the scheme of powerless, limited things.

Similarly, the long series of images that conclude the poem logically support the poet's sudden insight into the difference between Urania and Clio. The simple things that the poem places before the reader's eyes are pointed to, verbally, as verifying this insight. "There they are, blueberry-laden forests" the poet declares, as if to say, "These are the things that Clio hides and Urania reveals." This kind of verbal pointing is called *deixis*.

The shift from philosophical to mythological statement, likewise, is presented as a logical connection. The traveler suddenly realizes, "That's why Urania's older than sister Clio!" as if all the foregoing led quite rationally to this conclusion. The free flow of images that follow serves, again, to illustrate this conclusion. The formal order of the poem is that of the enthymeme, a type of logical syllogism in which some links in the chain of reasoning are left implicit. Everything seems to follow logically from the general principle announced in the first line.

Statement and image tend to work together to flesh out the picture of the scene. Though he has made only barest mention of the railway, for example, one can imagine, from the thoughts that the traveler has about them, how the rails lead away from the station and disappear over the horizon, a line drawn across an austere desert landscape. In this way, images and ideas complement and complete each other, while retaining their own distinct forms of expression. Perhaps this is why there is very little figurative language in "To Urania" until the odd simile of the final line. Poets often use figures such as metaphors and similes to convey abstract meanings by means of concrete images. In this way, an image and the ideas or feelings aroused by it can be combined and expressed simultaneously, or the meanings and associations of one thing can be enriched by those of another. Brodsky, however, uses the final simile to create not a sense of harmonious resemblance between the two things compared but rather a sense of discord. This kind of discord, termed "irony," is the main device of "To Urania." The other discords in the poem are between imagery and statement, between casual and philosophical tones of voice, and especially between the expectation aroused by the title of the poem and what the poem actually describes.

Themes and Meanings

"To Urania" deliberately moves, as the old saying goes, "from the ridiculous to the sublime." The idea of the "sublime" in philosophy and art traditionally refers to the transcending of physical and intellectual limitations toward a vision of higher reality. Dante ascending into Paradise is a classic example. The image of the limitless ocean evoked in the final lines of this poem is, in fact, a conventional symbol of the sublime in the writings of philosophers such as Edmund Burke and Immanuel Kant.

The sublime also often implies losing one's sense of identity when confronted with something that overwhelms the power to influence or comprehend it. In "To Urania," the motivation of the journey, the desire to abandon a burdensome former identity, is very much in keeping with the quest for such an experience. In this way, the search for the sublime comes into contact with the experience of exile. Exile is a theme of great personal significance to Brodsky, a Russian émigré.

In contrast with the sublime, the "ridiculous" expresses what it is like to be subject to the limitations of circumstance and the foibles of human nature. Therefore, in the end, as the stranded, frustrated traveler seems to transcend his limitations, his imagination takes a comic turn. The mundane desires symbolized by lacy underwear are juxtaposed with the limitless expanses of the ocean. The poem's last image injects a note of comic anticlimax, or bathos, the very opposite of the sublime.

Finally, "To Urania" is an important poem because its ironies encompass a tension crucial to much of Brodsky's poetry, an unresolved conflict between classicism and modernism, between the past, as reflected in poetic tradition, and the present. This tension is evoked by the poet's myth of the rivalry between the sisters, Urania and Clio. As the muse of history, Clio represents the disorderly flux of human affairs, confined to time and space. Urania represents a transcendent, unchanging reality. As the traveler turns from Clio toward Urania, then, he moves toward a moment in which this implicit idea of transcendent reality turns out to be nothing more than a reflection of mundane desire. If everything has its limit, as the poet says at the outset, perhaps the only unchanging truth about the human condition affirmed by "To Urania" is that there is no escape from Clio, no escape from the time-bound, desire-bound self.

Colin Brayton

TOADS

Author: Philip Larkin (1922-1985)
Type of poem: Lyric
First published: 1955, in *The Less Deceived*

The Poem

"Toads" is based on an extended analogy and presents a common complaint: In order to afford the enjoyments of life, people spend so much time working that the labor often overshadows and ultimately spoils their enjoyment. Philip Larkin, who compares work to a toad, takes the complaint one step further by confessing that although he is envious of those who have conquered work, he cannot break free from the expectations of the system because "something sufficiently toad-like/ Squats in me, too" (lines 25-26). It is this final, greater toad that prevents Larkin from ever fulfilling the romantic dream of getting "The fame and the girl and the money/ All at one sitting" (lines 30-32). "Toads" is thematically divided into four sections. The first section, stanzas 1 and 2, sets up the problem and introduces a toad as a metaphor for work. The toad "*work*" squats on life, soiling six days out of seven, a disproportionate percentage, but "wit" or cleverness seems to be a solution to the despair it causes. Stanzas 3 through 5 look at the people who have banished the toad. Such people include "lecturers, lispers, loblolly-men and louts" as well as the outcasts of society. The speaker is amazed that although these people have shunned the "accepted" way, no one is a pauper and "No one actually *starves*" (line 20).

In the third section, the narrator tries to visualize himself as someone who could make a similar leap past the socially accepted and expected, but he finds himself unequal to the task. He cannot muster the courage to shout out a defiant "*Stuff your pension!*" (line 22). This could only be accomplished in his wildest dream. The second toad, introduced in stanza 7, is the reason that he cannot make the jump. This toad is passivity, and its hunkering inside the narrator is as ruinous to positive action as the toad work's squatting is to the better part of the week.

The final section of the poem is the last stanza, which brings the two toads together. The narrator says that having one toad does not necessitate having the other. In other words, working does not necessarily mean that one has a passive nature, and being passive does not mean that one can avoid the burden of work. The narrator points out, however, that it is difficult to overcome either the fear of nonaction or the depression caused by work if both amphibians are acting simultaneously.

Larkin's own responsibilities as a university librarian could well have caused personal frustration and prevented a more complete dedication to his writing, but he seems to recognize that such "work" is necessary for him as well. At times, it even provided inspiration and motivation for his poetry. In an order almost like a formula, Larkin seems to confess that he is torn between irreconcilable differences. Though he wrestles with the problem, there is no quick solution, and the conclusion suggests that an insoluable problem will remain.

Forms and Devices

The major and most obvious poetic device that Larkin employs is the extended metaphor of a toad, first representing work and then a sense of conformity or a reluctance to oppose the majority. Larkin's toad work "squats" on life, impeding action and poisoning the workweek while the second toad impedes any attempt at rebellion against socially accepted norms. Ironically, when one thinks of toads, verbs such as leap and jump come to mind. Larkin's toads, however, neither leap nor jump but remain sluggishly inactive, "heavy as hard luck,/ And cold as snow" (lines 27-28). These two similes indicate why the narrator of the poem is unable to make the leap out of the restraining mold of his present life into a new one: He chooses to remain motionless like the toads, constantly appearing ready to move but resisting the urge.

The choice of the toad as a symbol is also significant because of the English slang word "toadie," which suggests an individual who caters to others' ideas and complies with society's demands. Larkin also uses irony, however, when he depicts those who have escaped the toad work as less than stellar examples of what humanity can become. Several are described as worthless or contemptible, yet another connotation of the word toad.

Another technique utilized by Larkin is the interjection of humor into a potentially depressing poem. Through near rhyme (for example, other/either, truth/both in the final stanza), he establishes a playful *abab* pattern that does not mesh with a tragic message. The lively *l* alliteration of stanzas 3 and 4 also balances out the sinister *s* sounds of stanza 2 and the heavy *h* sound in stanza 7. The diction chosen also defies the reader to interpret the poem too seriously. Characteristically, Larkin also opts for British colloquialisms such as "loblolly-men" and "nippers" and selects lower-class speech when the narrator is motivated to rebel by shouting *"Stuff your pension!"* (line 22).

Larkin also relies on dual meanings provided by words that can function as either nouns or verbs. Thus lines 33 and 34 may be read as "one bodies the other one's spiritual truth" or as "one body [is] the other one's spiritual truth." This is also true of the word "hunkers" in line 27, which can mean either "to squat" or "haunches." In either reading, the heaviness of the body or the squatting suggests the difficulty faced by the narrator who wishes to leap but finds an immovable force preventing him. Dual meaning is also suggested in the verb "Stuff" (line 22) and the noun "stuff" (line 24).

Themes and Meanings

Larkin's "Toads" can be seen as a humorous criticism of the illusion produced when one believes in romantic ideals. Striving to get the "fame and the girl and the money" (line 31), one works six of the seven days of the week. Rather than the glorious result one had hoped for, there is only enough money for "paying a few bills" (line 7).

Worse than the general tragedy of being forced to work is the inability to stand up to the system and leave, to assert that one's own choices are more important than the approval of society. The second toad in the poem, passivity, is even more tragic because it is an inner rather than an outward force. In the final stanza, the lack of individual choice becomes more than the problem of a single person. It is not only the narrator who cannot make the leap; all humankind is affected. All human beings squat in their own little lives, unable to move, unhappy to stay.

In a way, then, "Toads" is more than a poem about the unfair proportions of work and play; instead, it is a poem about taking a chance. What is it that keeps one from following one's dreams? Is it the way society is structured (toad 1) or, instead, something inside each individual, some action-freezing fear of the unknown and untried (toad 2)? Although he refuses to assert a definite relationship between the two toads, Larkin speculates that perhaps "one bodies the other's spiritual truth" (lines 33-34). Perhaps the system represented by society was invented for and built to support humankind's own inner fears; perhaps work is only a physical representation of insecurity.

The possibility also exists that there is no escape from this dilemma. If one body [is] the other's spiritual truth, perhaps it is impossible to escape. Those who do escape the toad work, for example, become "toads" of another sort: worthless, flawed individuals. Yet "Toads" does not seem intended as a depressing piece of existentialism. Perhaps, rather than bemoaning the tragedy of humanity, "Toads" pokes fun at humankind's romantic idealism and shows the reader once again that "the grass is always greener on the other side of the fence." The author describes fulfillment of his dream as "blarney my way," suggesting jovial flattery as the answer to success. This spurt of fun runs throughout the poem, culminating in *"Stuff your pension!"*—hardly the conscientious shunning of the problems of contemporary society.

Thus the humor in "Toads" seems to suggest Larkin's mock seriousness or his paradoxical merging of the serious with an attitude of playfulness. The dilemma is real, but so is the ambivalence of the author. Work is a "brute," but it is also a vital necessity; passivity is harmful, but it does keep the world rolling smoothly. Larkin advocates recognizing these facts, but he does not deny the inevitability that both will remain to trouble him.

Michael J. Meyer

TOAST

Author: Stéphane Mallarmé (1842-1898)
Type of poem: Sonnet
First published: 1893, as "Salut"; in *Les Poésies de Stéphane Mallarmé*, second edition, 1899; English translation collected in *Poems by Mallarmé*, 1936

The Poem

"Toast" is a sonnet whose fourteen lines are broken into two groups of four lines and two groups of three lines. Stéphane Mallarmé delivered this "toast" at a banquet on February 9, 1893, to encourage his companions to drink in celebration of the magazine *La Plume*. The poem has a festive, optimistic tone befitting the purpose of its original composition. The poem's French title, "Salut," conveys the double and perhaps triple meaning that Mallarmé intended better than does the more static English translation, "Toast." *Salut* is the word used to describe a speech one delivers as a prelude to drinking, but *salut* is often also an imperative part of that speech, in which the speaker encourages his companions to raise their glasses with this word, as one might say in English, "Cheers!" or "Bottoms Up!"

"Toast" is both a representation of the toast that Mallarmé gave and an encouragement to the reader to "drink," to enjoy the feelings that the poem evokes. In effect, the poem itself (and the other poems in Mallarmé's collection *Les Poésies de Stéphane Mallarmé*, 1899) becomes the intoxicating liquor for the reader, inviting him or her to take in their essences. This mixture of the sensory impressions associated with drinking and poetic creation was a favorite Symbolist technique. Since Mallarmé chose this poem to open the last collection of works that he assembled before his death in 1898, the poem finally serves as an encouragement to the reader to "drink" in the poems that follow in the collection.

"Toast" does not provide a strong narrative pattern, nor does it seek to establish (as a sonnet often does) a problematic situation followed by a resolution; instead, it seeks to establish an image of life as a journey—one that can be aided by the power of poetic composition. The poem does not comment on the success of such a journey, only on the fact that it does exist and that everyone should feel joy in following such a path.

Forms and Devices

The principal set of metaphors in "Toast" concerns the comparison of the microcosmic world of the tossing foam in the speaker's champagne glass with the macrocosmic world of the ocean, or life, on which the speaker and his listeners are journeying. The speaker suggests that like Homer's Odysseus and his crew, he and his drinking companions are traveling through the foam of the sea, passing "a troop/ Of many Sirens upside down." Furthermore, like the Odysseus of Alfred, Lord Tennyson's "Ulysses," this speaker himself is somewhat older than his companions, for he notes, "We are navigating, my diverse/ Friends! I already on the poop/ You the splendid prow which cuts/ The main of thunders and of winters." In the original toast to his drinking companions, Mallarmé was referring to his age with respect to his companions: They were the ones who were breaking the new waves of poetic creation, while he surveyed their developments from a position in the rear (the rear deck, or the poop, of a ship). Taken as the opening poem in his book, one may realize that Mallarmé is speaking to the poem itself, after having created it for a toast, for placement at the head, or prow, of his collection of poems. In this respect, Mallarmé and his poetic crew (his earlier written and published poems, now being arranged into an edition of complete works) look to this little poem "Toast" as the "splendid prow" which cleaves the waters of the public's reception, preparing the way for the rest of the collection.

Mallarmé also emphasizes the evanescence or insubstantiality of poetic creation in this short poem. The opening lines, with their repetition of the concept of absence in "Nothing!" and "nought," indicate Mallarmé's fascination with the idea of "nothingness." To understand this difficult concept, one must return to the basic situation of the poem. The speaker delivers a toast, while holding his champagne glass; the occasion is relaxed and happy, not one where deep analysis of spoken or written speech is usual. Yet Mallarmé is delivering more than a happy prelude to drinking; he is also linking the idea of poetic creation with the travels of an Odysseus figure. The foam is both the champagne froth and the waves on the sea where Odysseus travels. Mallarmé specifically seems to deny that one can make such a comparison by noting that the foam and his "virgin verse" (unspoken before the toast and, in 1893, unpublished at the time of its delivery) refer to nothing other than the cup. Yet he immediately continues the comparison by noting the presence of "Sirens upside down."

Mallarmé justifies this apparent contradiction again without leaving the central metaphor of the poem. A toast such as this is not only the prelude to drinking but frequently is also one of a series of toasts given throughout an evening. The speaker indicates that he is, in fact, already a bit drunk, "A fine ebriety [*ivresse*] calls me/ Without fear of its rolling/ To carry, upright, this toast." (*Ivresse* can also be translated simply as "drunkenness.") Here Mallarmé blends the drinking party with the voyage again. The speaker, as a result of his drunkenness, rolls a little as he stands to deliver the toast, yet he is without fear of spilling his glass. Some form of control allows him to maintain his upright posture, even while he sees "Sirens upside down" beckoning him to spill his glass and forget his toast. Therefore, although the speaker is not, perhaps, tremendously coherent (he seems to contradict himself in what the poem or the toast should refer to), he is able to convey something of his self-control or self-discipline as he reminds his companions why they have set out on such a voyage, toward "Solitude, reef, star/ To whatever it was that was worth/ Our sail's white solicitude." That self-control lies in the desire to pursue goals beyond the ordinary, but the pursuit is undertaken happily.

Themes and Meanings

"Toast" upholds well the Symbolist dictum that truth should be hinted at indirectly or evoked through a succession of sensory, rather than rational, clues. The poem indicates the identity that Mallarmé believed exists between poetic creation and making sense of one's journey through life. In poetic creation, as in life, the proper attitude, according to the speaker of Mallarmé's poem, is one of celebration, of joyous acceptance of "whatever it was that was worth" having set out in the first place. Paradoxically, however, when that "whatever it was" [*A n'importe ce qui*] is examined in the light of rationality, it disappears into evanescent foam, or the distorted remembrances of a slightly drunken man offering a toast to equally inebriated companions. This is the essence of the Symbolist technique: to allude as provocatively as possible to a concept that motivates living or the writing of poetry but to stop short of exactly naming that concept, allowing the *ivresse* of the reader following in the mood the poet has created to discover the meaning himself or herself.

"Toast" also provides a demonstration of the method of palimpsest, or the simultaneous layering of multiple levels of meaning. That is, the poem was originally composed to encourage a group of drinkers to contemplate the relationship between poetry and the voyage of life. The ship and journey referred to indicated the lives of the poets listening to Mallarmé's toast. Later, and now inextricably, the poem serves as an invitation to the reader to participate in the evocation of moods throughout the collection of Mallarmé's poetry in *Les Poésies de Stéphane Mallarmé*. Therefore, the poem serves as the symbol of the toast itself; it also serves as the symbol of how Mallarmé would have those poets present approach their lives and careers. In its position as the lead poem in Mallarmé's book, it encourages the reader to adopt the joy of the 1893 poets while reading the following collection. Finally, the poem itself is the object that opens the collection; it is the prow that precedes. "Toast" is a perfect definition of what a "symbol" was to the Symbolists: a poetic object that simultaneously calls attention to itself and to something beyond itself as equally valid sources of meaning, but that refuses to name that "something beyond" concretely.

Peter D. Olson

THE TOMB OF CHARLES BAUDELAIRE

Author: Stéphane Mallarmé (1842-1898)
Type of poem: Sonnet
First published: 1895, as "Le Tombeau de Charles Baudelaire"; English translation collected in *An Anthology of French Poetry from Nerval to Valéry in English Translation with French Originals*, 1958

The Poem

In the early period of his poetic career, Stéphane Mallarmé derived much of his use of imagery from the example of Charles Baudelaire's verse. His homage to Baudelaire, however, written near the end of Mallarmé's life, while still retaining the sonnet form and a few images that may have been found in the earlier style, attains a complexity of expression much beyond it.

The traditional Petrarchan sonnet is part of a loosely related sequence of poems honoring, also, Edgar Allan Poe, Paul Verlaine, and Richard Wagner. Each sonnet uses the image of a tombstone or other object that, along with the sonnet itself, will form an enduring monument to the man it honors.

In "The Tomb of Charles Baudelaire," the initial image is not that of the tomb but of the dead poet himself. The "buried temple" must be that of Baudelaire's body, which, though already buried in the Montparnasse cemetery, still has mud and rubies issuing from its mouth, a reference to both the filth and the beauty contained in Baudelaire's poetic utterances. The analogy with the "idol Anubis" further underlines the theme of burial in that the Egyptian jackal-god was said to preside over tombs.

In the second quatrain, the imagery changes entirely. Multiple details suggest the presence of a prostitute in the street, although the woman is never specifically named in the poem. This technique of suggestion, common in Mallarmé's work, evokes the woman through elements of her anatomy—the "lock of hair" and "pubis"—emblems of her beauty and her sexuality.

Yet *la mèche* may refer either to a lock of hair or to the wick of a lamp. The ambiguity remains in the line in which the word immediately follows "the gas," an apparent allusion to a street lamp by the light of which one might see the prostitute. Whether *mèche* refers to hair or wick, the adjective *louche* remains applicable, with its own multiple meanings of "ambiguous" or "suspicious." The lamplight flickers on the dubious activities of the woman. Similarly, the verb "twists" might refer to the twisting of either the wick or the lock of hair. This exploitation of the dual meanings of words, frequent in Mallarmé's work, reflects his belief that words related by sound might be related in meaning.

In the sestet, Mallarmé finally reaches the image of Baudelaire's tomb, "the marble," against the background of which the other images of these lines appear. Initially ambiguous, the phrase "come elle se rasseoir" would be easy to read as an image of the prostitute sitting on the marble tomb. Yet, just as the images of the two quatrains are separated by a discontinuity, those of the sestet form a coherent unit. If one looks ahead for a feminine noun, "Celle son Ombre" identifies this presence as that of Baudelaire's ghost, appropriately remaining at his tomb.

The emptiness of death appears in the image of the dry branch that alone will serve as a votive, or object symbolic of devotion, to the soul of the poet. The poem also portrays death as an ambiguous state, in which the soul seems present within "the veil that surrounds it" but is at the same time "absent."

Forms and Devices

While in this later poem Mallarmé's structures are no longer derived from Charles Baudelaire, many of the themes and images link him to the poet of *Les Fleurs du mal* (1857; *Flowers of Evil*, 1931). From the initial reference to "mud and rubies," Mallarmé recalls both the moral dualism of Baudelaire's work, in which beauty could be seen as derived from what was evil or unbeautiful, and the images of gemstones Baudelaire used in many of his poems.

The section of the poem closest to Baudelaire, however, is probably the second quatrain, with its motif of the prostitute. Baudelaire, who spent much of his life among the desperately poor people of Paris who would turn to prostitution or any other means for survival, frequently wrote with great compassion of their lives. Thus it seems appropriate that the only person near his tomb is a prostitute. She is there to ply her trade in an out-of-the-way place, and she is united by a spiritual link with the poet.

In addition, the prostitute echoes Baudelaire's portrayal of women. The moral dualism of *Flowers of Evil* involves the poet's quest for a visionary ideal. The woman, in whose eyes he believes at first he sees a reflection of heavenly light, becomes, as he soon realizes, a distraction and an impediment to his quest. Thus, the prostitute in Mallarmé's poem, "the one who will wipe away the shames he has undergone," corresponds to the woman who, for a time, allowed the poet to forget his separation from the ideal.

The "immortal pubis" may bring more than only a reference to an age-old profession, however; Baudelaire, like many other poets, attempted to immortalize woman's beauty in his verse. In his sonnet "Beauty," he describes female beauty as "eternal and mute," like the stone of statues; in "Hymn to Beauty," it could make "the universe less hideous and time less heavy."

Baudelaire embraced the consoling presence of women, but ultimately believed this was to his loss. In the final poem of *Flowers of Evil*, "The Voyage," the traveler looks back over a long life and says that his experiences have shown him only "the boring spectacle of immortal sin." Sin, like the prostitute's profession, may be immortal, but it does not have the same sort of immortality as poetry or as the human soul.

In this context, the last line of Mallarmé's quatrain, "whose flight moves according to the streetlamp," contains a sinister suggestion. This may refer merely to the flickering light of the gas lamp, which would cause shadows of those in the street to move. If, however, the "flight," or experience inspired by the woman's sexuality moves (in a way linked to a bed by the choice of the verb *découche*) according to the lamplight, it will not, in this wavering light, produce durable vision. The ephemeral form of these moving shadows anticipates the idea of death that closes the sestet. The poet will truly die if all that remains of his life is this fleeting image.

Themes and Meanings

The source of a poet's immortality, and the reason for Baudelaire's special importance to Mallarmé, lies in the durable impact of his verse. When Mallarmé begins by calling Baudelaire's body a "temple," a place containing something that is holy, he draws on an idea common to the Romantic poets and to Baudelaire: that the poet, born with a special capacity for visionary insight, had a duty to use this talent to enlighten those around him. In saying that Baudelaire's mouth "divulges" mud and rubies, Mallarmé adds to the idea that these are a hint at some form of revelation.

The image of the fierce Egyptian jackal-god, Anubis, combines a reference to the supernatural importance of the poet's mission with an indication of the violence that is linked to it, as the mud was linked to the rubies. The cry of Anubis's "flaming muzzle" is a "fierce bark." By barking, he adopts the manner of an animal, but a bark is nonetheless an utterance. A poet's speech, no matter how unintelligible, should be taken seriously. It was surely a serious matter to Mallarmé, who documents his own striving for poetic expression as he confronts his still-white page.

The poet's message often shocks the public, as Baudelaire's did when the first edition of *Flowers of Evil* was condemned for immorality, not only because of its violence but also because it chose as its subject aspects of life others would prefer not to see. Baudelaire's verse documented the "cities without evening" where the setting sun saw the streets fill with prostitutes and where the street lamps created an artificially extended day.

Yet, while it may have been shocking, the poet's message remains sacred. Thus, Mallarmé senses the need in the sestet for some votive offering to "bless" Baudelaire's ghost. The presence at the tomb, however, is called not a "ghost" but a "Shadow," the capitalization attesting its importance, recalling the imagined shadows projected by the gas light in the second quatrain. Like a shadow, it has a form of presence in absence, just as Baudelaire's influence has survived his physical body.

The shadow may also be a ghost in the sense that, for Mallarmé, it becomes a haunting presence. To him, Baudelaire had brought "a tutelary poison." The image is one Baudelaire himself had used, but in his poem, "Poison," he defines it as "the poison that flows/ From your eyes." Addressed to a woman, these lines attest her intoxicating influence. Both poets may have defined "poison" as an emblem of some temptation, but while Baudelaire desired the woman, Mallarmé desired to write. The poison for him was "tutelary" in that it drew him to imitate Baudelaire's poetic productivity.

The poetic enterprise tempts Mallarmé. He must "breathe" its poisoned air, but poison necessarily brings the threat of death. The poet fears not the inevitable death of the body, but the intellectual death that may result from the failure of his poetic creation. A key word in the last tercet, "if," posits the tenuousness of this exercise. Still, Mallarmé, grouped together with Baudelaire in the "we" of the last line, must take up this challenge despite its dangers.

Dorothy M. Betz

THE TOMB OF EDGAR POE

Author: Stéphane Mallarmé (1842-1898)
Type of poem: Sonnet
First published: 1877, as "Le Tombeau d'Edgar Poe," in *Edgar Allan Poe: A Memorial Volume*; revised in *Les Poésies de Stéphane Mallarmé*, 1887; collected in *An Anthology of French Poetry from Nerval to Valéry in English Translation with French Originals*, 1958

The Poem

Fifty years after the death of Edgar Allan Poe, American admirers of Poe planned a memorial volume, and the organizer of the volume, Sara Sigourney Rice, began to spread the news of the project. The French poet Stéphane Mallarmé, who had fervently admired Poe most of his life, offered to contribute to the volume. His poem "The Tomb of Edgar Poe" appeared in the volume; it was later revised for appearance in Mallarmé's own works.

The poem is a sonnet. The octave, the first eight lines, outlines the career of Poe; the last six lines, the sestet, expresses Mallarmé's indignation at the treatment of Poe at the hands of his contemporaries and concludes with a prediction of the future of Poe's reputation. In the first quatrain, Mallarmé declares that Poe frightened his century because of the presence of death in his voice.

The first line, "Such as into himself eternity changed him," suggests that death has purged Poe of all accidental and neutral features and has left only the essential Poe. The following three lines say that Poe, like all great creators, actually forced his civilization into existence, as with a naked sword. The century, however, limited and uncreative, remained terrified of the voice that created it, since that strange voice was filled with death. The next four lines describe Poe's contemporaries as recoiling from the poet ("the angel") like a Hydra, a mythical monster with many heads. They try to slander Poe by spreading the rumor that his work was nothing but the product of an alcoholic and a drug addict.

The countrymen of Poe are then called enemies of solidity and of symbolic suggestivity—both sources of poetic power. Mallarmé here expresses the hope that, even if this poem cannot recover the reputation of Poe, the tombstone of Poe (here regarded as a meteorite) may act as a milestone or terminus to the commentary of the envious, frightened, petty people of this world on the poetry that gives them their civilization and their ways of thought. That is, "blasphemy" against poets and thinkers should never go farther than the attack on Poe has gone. Mallarmé in his notes referred to Poe as an *aèrolithe*, a meteorite, that in its descent to earth burned out all of its nonessential elements and came down to humankind in a state of purity that they cannot understand.

Forms and Devices

The poem is a Petrarchan sonnet, rhyming *abbaabba*, *ccd*, *ede*, and in many ways it is in traditional form. Like most of the mature poetry of Mallarmé, this poem is highly concentrated. The meaning must be extracted carefully from the packed lines, and from the sometimes unorthodox syntax. Part of the problem in reading Mallarmé is that he keeps throwing metaphors at his subject; in this poem, almost every line contains a new metaphor, and many of them have no connection with one another.

There is a general opposition of hard versus soft in the poem, however; the hard granite and stony permanence of the creations of Poe are contrasted with the soft sliminess and ugly amorphous gestures of Poe's enemies, who naturally think of evil liquids in connection with the poet. Therefore, the tombstone of Poe is also a "solid" metaphor expressive of the life and power of the poet. The identification of Poe with his tombstone, of the tombstone with a meteorite, and of the meteorite with a milestone provides the poem with a thematic backbone.

Another source of "solidity" is to be found in the use of perfect participles in the poem, as in *épouvanté*, *bu*, *chu*, and *épars* (which is an adjective derived from a verb). Perfect participles represent completed action, and therefore they convey the idea of "frozen" activity, which is the ideal form for Symbolist poets such as Poe and Mallarmé himself.

Otherwise it is a fairly orthodox French sonnet in Petrarchan form, employing feminine and masculine rhymes in a traditional fashion. It is part of French poetic form to have a certain number of rhymes with weak endings mingling with some strong endings. In the octave of the sonnet, therefore, one finds the feminine rhymes (silent *e* is not silent in French) *change* and *étrange*, and *ange* and *mélange*, and the masculine rhymes *nu* with *connu* and *tribu* with *bu*.

Themes and Meanings

Once the lines are deciphered, the poem's meanings emerge without too much difficulty. The poem was written for an occasion and fulfills its function—to defend Poe against his attackers and against Philistines generally. After Poe's death, a "friend" of his named Rufus Griswold produced a biography of the poet which emphasized his faults and his lifelong struggle with alcohol. Since the world often seems ready to believe the worst about poets, and about creators in general, Griswold's account of the life of Poe did him considerable harm. It took several decades, and the devoted work of many of Poe's admirers, before Poe's true stature—the first American writer of originality, and a creator of world importance—became apparent.

The French, especially, came to Poe's defense. Charles Baudelaire, who felt very close to Poe in personality and aesthetic principles, translated many of Poe's stories and poems, and Mallarmé himself worked for many years to introduce Poe to the French literary scene. The life of Poe, filled with poverty and suffering, seemed to the French exactly what the life of a creator in a Philistine society would be. The French poet Paul Verlaine, who also admired Poe, invented the phrase *les poètes maudits*, the accursed poets, to describe the fate of poetic creators in the modern world. Of these, Poe was held to be one of the most *maudit*. Therefore, when Mallarmé flew to the defense of Poe, he was fighting for all poets against the petty and mean jealousy of the world.

Edmund L. Epstein

TONY WENT TO THE BODEGA BUT
HE DIDN'T BUY ANYTHING

Author: Martín Espada (1957-   )
Type of poem: Narrative
First published: 1987, in *Trumpets from the Islands of Their Eviction*

The Poem

Martín Espada's poem "Tony Went to the Bodega but He Didn't Buy Anything" is composed of forty-four lines of free verse. The lines are divided into stanzas of varying lengths, from only four lines in the final stanza to the longest, eleven lines, in stanza 2. The poem describes Tony's maturation from elementary school to law school. Each verse encapsulates some feature of Tony's development as he seeks his place in the world.

The opening five lines introduce a fatherless Puerto Rican boy trying to survive the "Long Island city projects." He takes a job at a local bodega (grocery and liquor store) and learns how to be polite to the *abuelas* (grandmothers) who are regular patrons and how to grin at the customers in imitation of the shop owner Makengo, who knows how to charm his clientele. Each successive stanza recounts another point in Tony's education. He receives a scholarship to law school away from New York but feels out of place. The academic environment of graduate school and the upwardly mobile condominium communities seem inhospitable to the young man. He searches for a sense of belonging and finds it in a Hispanic neighborhood on Tremont Street. Tony finds refuge in a Boston bodega where people speak Spanish and are as "island brown as him."

The inclusion of Spanish words and phrases shows the blend of English and Spanish that comprise Tony's world. The vocabulary of the poem is accessible; the language of common people, while the diction is suggestive and imagistic. The work possesses a contemporary sensibility with its references to New York, Boston, Long Island, and Tremont Street. The irony of the poem is that Tony has the ability and opportunity to escape the Long Island projects, but as an adult he returns to a similar neighborhood because that is where he feels at home. Espada suggests that true success for Tony means returning to his Hispanic roots, where the language and people are familiar—where he finds a sense of belonging that he does not find in academic or professional communities. He returns to the bodega, but he no longer needs to buy or sell anything.

Forms and Devices

Espada has been described as an Imagist poet. The term "imagist" derived from a literary movement between 1909 and 1918 in which poets such as Ezra Pound and H. D. set forth a poetic style using a specific mode of image, diction, and rhyme. In her work *Tendencies in Modern American Poetry* (1917), poet Amy Lowell asserted, among other things, that imagists use the language of common speech, but "employ the exact word—not the nearly exact." They avoid clichés, create new rhythms, explore any subject, and "suggest rather than offer complete statements." Espada's "Tony Went to the Bodega but He Didn't Buy Anything" reflects elements derived from the Imagist movement.

The poet mixes Spanish and English terms easily in the colloquial speech of the narrator. There is the "puertorriqueño boy" who works for "Makengo the Cuban" at the bodega, in the second stanza. Tony finds the "primavera" (spring season) in Boston cold and uninviting, as described in stanza 3. Only stanza 4 contains no Spanish terms. Those lines describe Tony's sense of alienation as he "walked without a map/ through the city,/ a landscape of hostile condominiums." The turning point occurs in stanza 5, when Tony discovers the Boston projects and visits the local bodega:

> he sat by the doorway satisfied
> to watch la gente (people
> island-brown as him)
> crowd in and out,
> hablando espanol.

Espada's narrator uses the vernacular; the people Tony meets in the bodega are as "brown as him." Nonstandard construction replaces the standard grammatical pronoun usage, which would be "as brown as he is." Espada depicts the conglomerate language of the inner city; his portrait of Tony's dilemma is subtle yet clear.

The verses are both rhythmic and conversational even though the poem contains no fixed metric pattern. The lines vary in length from three to thirteen syllables. The word "Tony" begins three of the stanzas, and the phrase "So Tony" begins the fourth. It is his story, and the rhythm of his name creates a strong trochaic pulse in the opening lines, with an accented syllable followed by an unaccented one. However, the driving accents of those lines are tempered by predominate iambic or anapestic feet in other lines such as "above the bodega" and "the cooking of his neighbors," in which accented syllables are preceded by one or two unaccented syllables.

Alliteration also contributes to the rhythmic quality of the verse, illustrated in the lines "Tony's father left the family," "the dry-mop mambo," and "walked without a map." Stanzas 3-6 are moved along by the fluid *s* sound in the phrases "spoke Spanish," "sidewalk-searcher," and "success story."

Paradox is employed throughout the work as well. In stanza 2, the young boy learns shop keeping from Makengo. He emulates the sly smile that Makengo gives his customers; however, when Makengo grins, he shows his "bad yellow teeth." The portrait of Makengo's expression provokes an image that is both charming and revolting. Tony's success described in stanza 3 is also bittersweet. Tony leaves the projects "with a scholarship for law school," but Boston is not home to him. Spring often denotes a season of rebirth or renewal, but Tony curses the "cold" Massachusetts spring. He becomes a "sidewalk-searcher lost" in the "darkness of white faces." The Puerto Rican boy feels isolated, perhaps even alienated, when he leaves the Long Island projects even though a professional education can provide him with a lucrative future. The poem does not say that Tony finishes school and becomes a lawyer on his way to supposed material success, yet Espada asserts in the closing lines that "today Tony lives on Tremont Street,/ above the bodega."

Themes and Meanings

A political poet, Espada sings of the urban poor and other disenfranchised members of society. A Puerto Rican activist from Brooklyn, Espada has worked as a tenant lawyer and advocate for socially liberal causes. His poetry often describes the struggle of immigrant Americans striving to overcome economic disadvantage, discrimination, or political corruption. In "Tony Went to the Bodega but He Didn't Buy Anything" Espada portrays the struggle some Latinos encounter in bridging two cultural spheres.

The poem suggests more than it tells about Tony's life story, which is consistent with Lowell's description of the tendencies of the imagist poet. Each of the six stanzas presents a snapshot of the boy's experience as an inner-city immigrant lad. The poet elicits the readers' sympathies with his vignette of the nine-year-old "puertorriqueño boy." Tony is "mongrel-skinny" and "had to find work" even though he is just a child. The scene in the bodega shows how Tony learns from experience. He takes lessons from Makengo the Cuban to learn how to do business. Stanza 3 reveals that Tony is an intelligent youth. He is able to leave the projects and attend law school. However, the opportunity does not offer Tony a better life as might be expected. Tony misses Spanish speakers and the smell of cooking in his neighborhood hallways. Divorced from his roots, Tony is lost in a hostile landscape of "white faces." In these stanzas, Espada is reminding his readers that success and education should not depend on one having to abandon his or her cultural identity.

The bridge for Tony is represented in stanza 5: "Tony went to the bodega/ but he didn't buy anything." What the bodega offers the adult, educated Tony is not merchandise but a sense of belonging. The Boston projects remind him of his native Long Island. He is satisfied to listen to the customers speaking Spanish, and he grins from enjoyment, not from a need to charm customers. The people look familiar. They, too, are "island-brown." Espada concludes in stanza 6 that Tony's story is a "rice and beans/ success story." The description is an artful play on words—the rice and beans of Spanish speakers in a Boston baked bean environment. At the close of the poem, Tony is no longer poor; he has risen in society; hence, he lives above the bodega. His sense of belonging is firmly rooted in the society he knew as a child. He cannot turn his back on his roots.

In an interview for the *Milwaukee Journal Sentinel*, Espada recalled that being the only Puerto Rican in town while growing up in Long Island was difficult. His response was poetry: "I needed a way to respond. I think poetry is a great way to assert your humanity." Thus Espada's poem about Tony reflects not only his own experience as a lawyer-poet but also the struggles of those who find themselves isolated or disenfranchised, seeking to reconcile different cultural, educational, or social realms.

Paula M. Miller

TOUCH ME

Author: Stanley Kunitz (1905-   )
Type of poem: Meditation
First published: 1995, in *Passing Through: The Later Poems, New and Selected*

The Poem

"Touch Me" is the final poem of *Passing Through: The Later Poems, New and Selected* (1995), published on the occasion of Stanley Kunitz's ninetieth birthday. Kunitz, who among his many honors has received the Pulitzer Prize and the Bollingen Award, had a long and distinguished career as poet and teacher. Unlike many of his earlier poems, "Touch Me" does not have a particular stanzaic form; instead it moves down the page in thirty short, tightly controlled lines of free verse. The poem begins with the words *"Summer is late, my heart,"* from one of his earlier poems, "As Flowers Are," written in 1958. The speaker remembers the feelings that sparked the earlier poem when he was younger and "wild with love." Now, nearly forty years later, he finds that it is his "heart" that is late, that he has already had his "season." He has spent the afternoon gardening, listening (almost as when he was a boy) to the sound of the crickets, marvelling at their very existence, questioning the nature of creation. So now, in the present-tense voice of the poem, lying in bed listening to the wind and rain, he goes back over the afternoon, reaching for the man he used to be.

When asked about his recent poems, Kunitz replied, "What is there left to confront but the great simplicities? . . . I dream of an art so transparent that you can look through and see the world." "Touch Me" represents just such an art; the poet's desire to fix the moment in memory means that the reader is asked to see every detail through a shaping eye. Haunted by wind and rain, by the branches thrashing against the windowpanes, the poet sees through to the heart of things. The poem is meditative, however, not visionary. Turning to direct address, the poet speaks to his wife—"Darling, do you remember/ the man you married?" The line break is crucial. If she remembers, then he has identity; if she remembers, she connects with the person who was "wild with love"; if she remembers, she is the link between the old man, his younger self, the child, the cricket, and the very earth in which he has been gardening all afternoon.

The title is interesting in that, instead of opting for the more universal concept of "touch," Kunitz has particularized it—"Touch Me." The "me" functions in several ways. It limits the act, both temporally and spatially. Following his directive, his wife can reach across the bed and touch him to "remind" him not only of his former self but also of the power of love. With great honesty and vulnerability he admits to a need for another to restore him fully to a sense of himself, a self rooted firmly in the present tense: "who I am." Again, the "me" (as recipient) resonates with the persistent questions of who he is and where he fits in the larger "garden." The underlying question of identity rests on the simple question of being.

Forms and Devices

The first thing one notices in "Touch Me" is its extreme simplicity. Its monosyllabic lines—"when I was wild with love" and "It is my heart that's late,/ it is my song that's flown"—are comparable to those of Robert Frost. At the same time, these lines reveal an underlying iambic rhythm that is characteristic of Kunitz. The churning question—"What makes the engine go?"—is more effective because of its regular stresses, and the answer to the question is reinforced through repetition of meter as well as of the word itself: "Desire, desire, desire." The procreative force has been reproduced not only in the cricket's song but also in the sounds on the page.

At the same time, Kunitz sometimes cuts across his regular cadences, using trochaic or spondaic rhythms to undercut the essential optimism of the poem: "scatter like leaves" and "under a gunmetal sky." The old longing for the dance (echoed in the rhythms of the poem) is mitigated by the poem's one broken line: "One season only,/ and it's done."

The tone of "Touch Me" is informal; it is filled with contractions that suggest a spoken voice. Still, it is an internal voice, one overheard and internalized by the reader. Although informal, however, "Touch Me" has a tight structure. The reader learns early that it is a night of "whistling wind and rain" and so is not surprised when the poet returns from reverie to the present weather of the poem. This pattern of memory and memory recollected allows the poet to become "like a child again," to look at everything through fresh eyes. This looking produces a circular movement, from recent past to present to remembered past, which is broken by the phrase "and it's done." Only then can the poet fully enter the present, breaking out of his own meditation to speak to his companion.

"Touch Me" displays an intricate network of rhymes—more a crocheted pattern than a woven one. The slant rhymes create a pattern like the fluid course of a soccer ball as the players move it down the field: rain/flown/afternoon/down, and, later, again/machine/done, or the initial "air" echoed in clear/pour/desire. Then, as in a reprise, "air" is caught up again in "remember"—the operative word of the poem.

Themes and Meanings

"As one who was not predestined, either by nature or by art, to become a prolific poet, I must admit it pleases me that, thanks to longevity, the body of my work is beginning to acquire a bit of heft." This sentence, from the author's note to *The Poems of Stanley Kunitz, 1928-1978*, was written nearly twenty years before the publication of "Touch Me." By his ninetieth birthday his longevity had led to an even more substantial body of work, of which "Touch Me" is perhaps emblematic.

"Touch Me" gives the reader, above all, a sensibility. It is an old man's poem, a poem of looking back, of putting a lifetime in perspective. Yet it is also a poem of continued renewal, very much of the present. The ending is not elevated; it does not try to make language fill the void. The poet falters at the edge of the visionary, where the song has "flown," pulling back from the urge to fabricate in favor of the urge to resuscitate. At the exact moment when Kunitz's earlier poems would have made a transformative leap, this poem settles back. The poet forgoes rhyme and rhythm in favor of statement, a deflated kind of poetry that makes the ending both terrifying and poignant. Moving quickly from contemplation to a moment of action, or implied action, the poet connects to his past and his future simultaneously. The emotional moment has already been completed, and the poem is recapitulation. "Remind me," he says, not "tell," or "show." The act (the touch), if it comes, will remind him of what has already been fulfilled.

In some ways, "Touch Me" is about poetry itself and its regenerative, life-giving powers: "The longing for the dance/ stirs in the buried life." The "buried life" of the garden is echoed in the poet's buried past, brought to life through memory. His need to give and receive love has been reactivated through coincidence—the intersection of memory and geography that gives rise to the poem. There is, however, some implied equivocation: Poetry can only do so much. Thus "Touch Me" is a poem of completion and incompletion; it makes the link for the poet (as in his memory of his earlier line), but that is not sufficient. His wife can reconnect him to his life through touch, the physical act no poem can reproduce. The gesture of poetry is superseded by one of human contact.

Speaking of poetry as a form of blessing, Kunitz tells readers (in an introduction to *Passing Through* that he called "Instead of a Foreword") that "it would be healthier if we could locate ourselves in the thick of life, at every intersection where values and meanings cross, caught in the dangerous traffic between self and universe." In "Touch Me," Kunitz has located himself at that intersection. If he is the equivalent of the "battered old willow," then he is also the man who can turn to his wife with an endearment and rekindle love. If the speaker is merely "passing through," as the title of the entire collection suggests, then what is the meaning of an individual life? Stalled in the memory of youthful emotion, Kunitz admits vulnerability. Yet the title of the poem is reciprocal. In asking her to touch him, he touches others through his poem. In its very uncertainty, "Touch Me" is affirmative; as the poet finds himself asking all the old questions, he sees through them to where, although life has "one season only," he is happily and healthily still in the thick of it.

Judith Kitchen

THE TOWER

Author: William Butler Yeats (1865-1939)
Type of poem: Lyric
First published: 1927; collected in *The Tower*, 1928

The Poem

"The Tower" is a lyric of 195 lines, divided into three parts. The title refers to an ancient stone tower in western Ireland, called Thoor Ballylee, which William Butler Yeats purchased in 1915. It provides the setting for the speaker, the poet, who refers to his movements through the tower to its top, whence he looks across the landscape to contemplate life and history.

Section 1 begins with the poet asking how to deal with old age. Perhaps he will give up poetry and turn to Platonic philosophy to tame his imagination of its wild desire for sensation. If he does not do something, imagination will mock his helpless old age.

In Section 2, the poet has climbed to the top of his tower, where he views the landscape. In evening twilight, he ponders the history and folklore of this region. He imagines the life of Mrs. French, who once lived nearby, whose servant brought her the ears of a farmer who had insulted her. More remarkable is the story of a beautiful woman who also lived nearby, and whose beauty was the subject of a popular song. Some men went looking for the woman of the song and one of them drowned in a bog. The man who made that song was blind, like Homer; neither saw the women whose beauty they celebrated. The poet wishes he could make poems with the power to drive men mad.

The poet recalls a figure of his own creation, Hanrahan, the hero of stories Yeats published in earlier years. Hanrahan was tricked into giving up his search for his fiancée; while playing cards, Hanrahan thought the cards turned into hounds chasing a rabbit. He pursued the hounds toward something the poet cannot remember. Instead, the poet thinks of the bankrupt man who once owned this tower, and then of earlier centuries when medieval men climbed the stairs in their armor.

The poet would like to ask each of these persons, including Hanrahan and Mrs. French, whether they also complained about growing old. He sees the answer in their eyes. He dismisses all except Hanrahan, a lecher pursuing love even beyond life. Driven by passion never satisfied, Hanrahan may know secrets to help the poet deal with his own passionate imagination. The great question is whether imagination is driven more by thinking of the woman lost or by contemplating the woman finally won. The poet cries out that Hanrahan turned away from the one chance he had to win his woman; therefore, if he has been driven by the woman lost, it is his own fault.

The third section turns away from the terrible confrontation with Hanrahan. The poet writes his will, accepting mortality. His heirs are men who can climb mountains to fish at dawn. His bequest is his Anglo-Irish pride: a tradition of tolerance, moderation, and generosity, which he inherited from men such as Edmund Burke (1729-

1797) and Henry Grattan (1746-1829). It is also a natural pride, generous like morning light and spring showers. It is a pride of accomplishment, like the song of the dying swan.

The poet affirms his faith in life and imagination. He dismisses Platonic ideals and defies the threat of death, declaring that all reality, including death, is the product of the human power to imagine. He feels at peace with such an affirmative view, acquired through study of Italian culture and Greek art, poetry and love, history and dreams. Abruptly he turns his attention to some birds building nests in his tower. They drop twigs one at a time until a warm hollow is made for the female to brood over her eggs. To this natural process the poet compares his own life's work of making peace.

To the young men he leaves faith as well as pride. Like them he once climbed mountains to fish in early morning dawn. Now he will discipline his soul to study, take it past the wreck of his body to recognize, in the decay of flesh and death of friends, the signs of transition. Decay and death are little more than clouds that dissipate with the fading day, cries of birds in darkening shadows of evening.

Forms and Devices

"The Tower" is a medley of tones played through a variety of rhythms. The first section is an arrangement of quatrains, so well made that the rhymes are barely noticeable. This creates a tone of controlled anxiety: The speaker worries about growing old, but the rhyming verse suggests the worry is under control. The second section is more formal, using a stanza (like ottava rima) borrowed from Abraham Cowley (1618-1667). Here the tone is solemn and meditative, searching history, folklore, and personal experience.

Section 3 drops the discipline of the middle and turns with abandonment to shorter verse with irregular rhyme, tending toward regularity as the poem draws to its conclusion. Here the tone is quietly firm, personally declarative; it balances the anxious interrogative tone that opens the poem, and it overrides the hesitant solemnity of the middle section with confident singularity.

The tower itself, sun and moon, and animals (especially birds) are major sources of imagery. Climbing the tower, pacing back and forth on its battlements, and pausing to notice birds are rhetorical moves governed by the speaker's relationship to the tower. Climbing mountains, recalled from the poet's youth, is paralleled with climbing Thoor Ballylee, both images suggesting the "climbing" of life itself.

The landscape around the tower lends images of streams and trees, but more important, it is the poem's setting of evening twilight, when sun yields to moon. From this, the poet draws metaphors of light, which he develops to describe the effects of imagination on perception. This leads him to hope that mixing sun and moon will be the effect of his own poetry. This same metaphorical mix of lights, possible in evening as well as through art, provides symbolic functions of bird images in the poem.

First is the conventional notion that a swan sings once only, just before it dies. Evening twilight is a traditional emblem for old age, both for swan and human being. This identifies poet with swan, poem with swan's song. "The Tower" modifies this conventional emblem, however, with a more personal and more delicate one in describing daws building their nest. The poet compares the process of his own life's work to the birds building their nest, a domain for new life. Thus the poem concludes affirmatively, reversing bird images in the last section.

Themes and Meanings

The controlling theme of "The Tower" is concern for growing old. This is complicated by the contradictory experience of imaginative vitality in a failing body. Conflict between mind and body is a contest between philosophies of idealism and materialism. It is also expressed as the humiliation of the mind, degraded by loss of control over the flesh. The poem begins with a question about managing this crisis of confidence, and moves to transcend personal anxiety to reach a realm of universal meaning in which life is affirmed in all its variety.

To reach an affirmative conclusion celebrating pride, faith, and peace, the poet draws upon history, myth, and poetic imagination. Fear of failing bodily powers is overcome through historical imagination, initiated by signs in the landscape surrounding the tower. History shows that people have always contended with physical failure by drawing upon spiritual resources. Misused, abused, and sometimes dissipated, those resources are still there for everyone to try.

Mythic imagination is so strong it can confuse the senses. Thus one may mistake moonlight for sunlight, fancy for reality, and that mistake can lead to disaster. Sensation is not master of the mind; quite the contrary. Neither is mind only abstract intellect. Full identity is mastery of matter by imagination. Thus may a blind person stimulate the vision of others, because vision is a power of imagination, not a product of sensation. Finally, beneath history and myth runs the shaping power of human vision. Pride displaces humiliation when the poet rediscovers the sources of his identity in imagination, faith overcomes anxiety when the power of imagination is found in desire, and peace settles over all as the pieces of life are made into a whole pattern by visionary imagination.

The tower is not itself a symbol of life, and neither is the labor of birds sufficient to represent the wholeness of human life. The tower as art and the birds as nature combine to express the meaning of human life in general, of creative purpose in the life of this individual speaker, a poet confronting the end and ends of being.

Richard D. McGhee

TRANSFER

Author: Sterling Brown (1901-1988)
Type of poem: Ballad
First published: 1975, in *The Last Ride of Wild Bill and Eleven Narrative Poems*

The Poem

"Transfer," a poem of nine balladic quatrain stanzas rhyming *abcb*, employs the African American folk tradition that characterizes all the poetry of Sterling A. Brown. The poem is divided into two parts: Part I re-creates the event that caused a black man to be imprisoned, and part II narrates the circumstances and consequences of his escape from prison. More significantly, part II concludes with the hero's folk wisdom concerning the directions and goals of the African American life.

The title of the poem alludes to the last stanza, in which the former convict realizes that he needs to "transfer" from one line of thought and direction in his life to another. He senses that the direction of his life heretofore has been the wrong one for black people to follow in the United States. The term "transfer" also literally refers to the transfer (a piece of paper) that one receives when changing from one bus line to another.

"Transfer" is written in the standard third-person point of view of the ballad form, and the poet acts as the narrator who relates to the reader the poignant story of the unnamed black convict. In the first four stanzas, the poet reveals the circumstances that lead the black man to the conclusions he reaches in the final stanza. The first stanza relates that in a fit of possible absentmindedness, the young man forgets to say "sir" to a white man during the "Jim Crow" era in the South. As a result of his negligence, he is beaten with a crank by the motorman and clubbed by the conductor. Nevertheless, he survives and is sentenced to four years on the prison farm by a supposedly "merciful" judge for "bruising white knuckles" and inciting a riot on the Atlanta Peachtree line. In the third stanza, the poet states that the hero has been beaten so severely that his jawbone is displaced; he is deemed harmless and made a prison farm "trusty."

The second part of the poem begins with the fifth stanza. The hero mounts a horse and flees from prison to Atlanta, where he is taken in by the "folks" and fed, clothed, and hidden. He comes out only at night in the black neighborhood, because all the white policeman disappear from that part of town after dusk. The seventh stanza reveals that he begins preaching at the car stop. The eight and ninth stanzas relate the basic theme of the sermon he always preaches: The convict had thought that if he stayed in "his place" (followed all the laws of segregation and Jim Crow), he would be allowed to live in peace with his white overlords; now, however, he has come to the conclusion that he was on the wrong "line" (referring to bus line), and that he needs to change directions because African Americans can no longer obey the old laws that afford them neither safety nor freedom.

Forms and Devices

"Transfer" is a literary poem written in the style of the folk ballad. Sterling A. Brown was especially adept at and fond of adapting traditional folk forms such as the work song, folk song, ballad, and the blues in his poetry. These forms were especially expressive of the southern African American culture and ethos that Brown wished to evoke.

The poem consists of nine stanzas rhyming in the traditional ballad form of *abcb*. It is an adaptation of the traditional English ballad form, which is written in four-line stanzas with lines 1 and 3 having four beats and lines 2 and 4 rhyming, with three beats.

The traditional folk ballad tells an exciting story of the tragic and strange. Brown's adaption in "Transfer" follows this tradition in both form and content. The poet purposely divides the poem into two distinct sections with Roman numerals I and II separating the time sequence. Part I tells how and why the hero is imprisoned, while part II tells the story of his escape and epiphany. The symbol of the hero's spiritual revelation is a transfer comparable to the one used for transferring from one public transit line to another.

In order to relate the narrative and the poem to African American folk life and demonstrate the folk wisdom of the hero whose intelligence prevails despite his lack of formal education, the ballad uses the language of the common man. Words and phrases used to depict theme and setting appropriately express implicit and explicit folk meanings; terms such as "daft with the heat," "brained with his crank," "skittish," "Darktown," "daffy," and "figgered" are used throughout the poem. In addition, words that refer to transportation abound in the text. The poem begins at a bus line. The hero escapes from prison after becoming a trusty by simply riding away on a mare, and his final sermon takes place at the car-stop.

The last two stanzas of the poem further demonstrate Brown's skillful use of the nuances of folk speech as a poetic device. He closes the stanzas with a proverb; "I stayed in my place, and my place stayed wid me." The poem employs narrative devices characteristic of the ballad form. When the poet attempts to render the essence of the hero's actual sermon at the car stop, however, Brown uses dialectal spellings such as "doan," "wid," "git," "stan," and "ma" to imitate folk speech.

"Transfer" exhibits Brown's superlative gift for adapting traditional forms to African American folk material as well as his genius in the creative use of language. "Transfer" stands out as an example of Brown's characteristic ability to transcend folk material and language to express universal truths about injustice and human suffering. In addition, the poem explains African Americans' ability to survive in a hostile universe while retaining and manifesting keen folk wisdom and intelligence.

Themes and Meanings

The theme of the poem is the racial injustice meted out to African Americans no matter how "well they behave." Since one of the usual topics of a ballad is an event of historical importance to a nation or a people, the theme of Brown's ballad is apropos—the discrimination, suffering, and violence inflicted upon African Americans in the Southern states. The folk hero in the poem is the convict who, after escaping, comes to the realization that African Americans have been on the wrong track in adapting to the restrictions of a segregated and discriminatory society, and who now finds it necessary to change directions—that is, to transfer to a new train of thought.

Since the convict represents a black "Everyman" and his situation is one that was common to the life of the Southern African American, the poet uses the ballad to condemn the general injustices suffered by blacks. Violence is a secondary theme in the poem, for in part I of the ballad, the hero is brained, clubbed, and beaten until he is senseless and his jawbone is broken. It is ironic that only when the black man is beaten senseless can he become a trusty, and only if he is "skittish" can the whites be sure that he is harmless.

Nevertheless, the hero is permanently neither senseless nor skittish, and his mind returns completely as a result of a long day in the hot sun. Clearly, the sun represents the light that kindles the hero's intelligence and allows him to have the presence of mind to ride away. In the city of Atlanta, he is hidden away in "Darktown," a name that symbolizes not only the race of its inhabitants but also their condition. Moreover, the hero cannot afford to come out during the daylight because he will be seen by the white policemen, who only feel safe in Darktown during the day. Hence, Darktown has an inverse symbolic meaning. Instead of being safe in the light, as would be common in European color symbolism, the hero of "Transfer" is safe only in the dark, the darkness of the color of his skin and the skin of the residents who ensure his safety by feeding, clothing, and hiding him.

Another prominent symbol used by the poet is transportation. Throughout the poem, the prominent events all occur in places where one can get on and ride (go) somewhere. The hero is beaten at the bus stop by the motorman, rides away on a mare from the prison farm, and relates the wisdom of his epiphany at a car-stop. The final words of the hero express his understanding that African Americans have been riding on the wrong route, one that has failed to get them anywhere in American society. Therefore, the hero concludes that African Americans need a transfer to a new direction, not in place but in thought. It is interesting to note that Brown published "Transfer" in his 1975 *The Last Ride of Wild Bill and Eleven Narrative Poems*. By this date, African Americans had truly transferred to a new line of thought that led them in the direction of the Civil Rights movement.

Brown is skillful in his use of the ordinary man as hero in this poem. The hero of "Transfer" is a common man without sophisticated education or skills; however, he has a folk wisdom that allows him to deliver a sermon that demonstrates a practical wisdom garnered from living and surviving in a harsh and brutal environment. Thus, when Brown speaks of the tragedy of the hero's life in this poem, he also speaks of his triumph.

Betty Taylor-Thompson

TRANSLATIONS

Author: Wing Tek Lum (1946-   )
Type of poem: Lyric
First published: 1987, in *Expounding the Doubtful Points*

The Poem

"Translations" is a poem in three parts that considers the ways in which provocatively descriptive language influences and reflects attitudes toward cultural communities located outside of conventional representations of life in the United States. Speaking with the thoughtful, reflective voice that is characteristic of his work, Wing Tek Lum begins the poem with the word "Ghosts," a focal point for an exploration of the manner in which the terminology chosen by a people to describe themselves may differ significantly from the words used by outsiders to refer to them. The first lines of the poem recall the innocent pleasure of a child's delight in the thrill of the supernatural, a series of images evoking the harmless fun of "running around in/ old bedsheets," enjoying the reassuring comic-book fantasy of the friendly Caspar, and then "marveling at/ the trick/ camerawork" in a television show about Cosmo G. Topper. These familiar, pleasant vignettes from popular culture are placed in sharp contrast with Lum's adult perspective on ghosts as the second section of part 1 begins with the word *Gwái*, a Chinese term for "demon" or "devil." The transition to a term loaded with negative connotations introduces a darker, more sinister element to the poem, which Lum amplifies by references to "Shaw Brothers horror/ films" and "rites of exorcism" before concluding the section with a cryptic comment about "Old Demons who wear/ white skin/ and make believe/ they behave/ like men."

The second part of "Translations" moves away from Lum's closely personal account of his changing perspective on the word for "ghost" and toward an omniscient position in which the poet proceeds as the voice of communal experience. Summarizing decades of cross-cultural confusion and intrasocietal clashes, Lum states that "The Chinaman" (a stereotype) gave "the Demon" (another stereotype) "what/ the former thought/ the latter thought/ were things/ Chinese." This mutual misconception resulted in "a comedy/ of errors" that Lum, maintaining a degree of distance from the humiliation involved, describes as "part fawning, part/ deception and contempt" for both groups. He concludes part 2 with a mordant observation, pointing out that "There is no/ word for/ fortune cookie in Cantonese," a statement that effectively undercuts one of the most prominent assumptions about Chinese life held by many non-Chinese.

In the third part of "Translations," Lum somewhat ruefully recalls the name that Chinese Americans gave to their home: *Tòhng Yàhn Gāai* ("China-People-Street"). As an indication of the pressures placed on an ethnic minority by a dominant culture indifferent to the nuances of their lives, Lum says that Chinese Americans eventually "mimicked/ Demon talk" and began to use the term *Wàh Fauh* for their address. This is the predominant descriptor in many American cities, the "China-Town" that is regarded primarily as an exotic tourist destination. In conclusion, Lum explains that the difference in names is obvious. "The people" (that is, the soul and spirit of the community) have "disappeared," or, in a unifying trope that reaches back to the first word of the poem, they have become ghosts.

Forms and Devices

"I have always been slow in my verbal skills," Lum commented while discussing his processes of composition. "Since the fourth grade I have resigned myself to plodding along with the written word," but then he realized that "by nature poets choose their words carefully" and that what seemed like a limitation could be an aspect of his strength as a writer. Rather than the "razzle-dazzle of the flow of words," Lum's poems often provide what he calls "epiphanies of passion, of something deeply-felt" that he deems "important to share." Consequently, Lum has emphasized "the clarity of the image" so that in a poem such as "Translations" the political element that he has always recognized in his work emerges from the juxtaposition of the images that he presents.

The controlling image of "Translations" is that of ghosts rendered first in terms of a child's delight with features of a magical cosmos then darkened by the adult's realization that there is a component of psychic danger in horror films and exorcism rites. The establishment of the twofold nature of the ghost phenomenon enables Lum to begin to examine the ramifications of the ghost/*Gwái* polarity, a division in which the demon's "white skin" is a disguise camouflaging its nonhuman behavior or attributes, an inversion of the friendly nature of Caspar, whose white ghost form covers a humane disposition. This doubling of the human/devil image expresses Lum's opinion that white people have sometimes acted with demonic malice and ignorance in transcultural matters.

The clarity of the ghost imagery permits Lum to place a conundrum at the core of the poem. The intricate reversal and inward reflection of his assertion that "The Chinaman gave/ the Demon what/ the former thought/ the latter thought/ were things/ Chinese" is a tightly wrapped enigma that demands close attention but that contains a kernel of meaning that becomes accessible in accordance with the previous presentation of imagery. Even as the general idea becomes comprehensible, however, it remains elusive, which is part of Lum's point: The thinking of both groups is muddled and biased, and the "things Chinese" are subject to misinterpretation and misconception. Lum's designation of this as a comedy of errors somewhat softens the force of the language he uses to describe the postures of the participants in the play (their "fawning," "deception," and "contempt" are not conducive to any kind of admirable human interaction), while his matter-of-fact observation about the absence of a word for "fortune cookie" in Cantonese epitomizes his exasperation at assumptions that avoid any comprehension of a complex reality.

The poem concludes with a fusion of word and image that is reminiscent of the characters used in the Chinese written language. Lum's recollection of the original name for his neighborhood, *Tòhng Yàhn Gāai*, is translated into English as "China-People-Street," as if each word is also an image representing its meaning. Then, as he and his neighbors accede to "Demon talk" and write only *Wàh Fauh*, the alteration and the absence of the key word for "people" has literally changed the appearance of the place, both in written language and in the way in which language shapes perception.

Themes and Meanings

In the special dedications for the poems in *Expounding the Doubtful Points*, Lum says that "Translations" is "for Jeffrey Paul Chan in appreciation of his letter to the editor, *New York Review of Books*, April 28, 1977." Chan's letter was written as an explanatory corrective to a review (significantly entitled "Ghosts") by Diane Johnson in which Johnson discussed Maxine Hong Kingston's *Woman Warrior: Memoirs of a Girlhood Among Ghosts* (1976). The thrust of his critique is that Johnson "knows nothing about Chinese-American society" (which he demonstrates with considerable historical support) and that her contention that "Chinese-Americans are a notably unassimilated culture" is nonsense. Contrary to her claim that "generations go nameless," Chan explains that to comply with immigration regulations many Chinese American families give their children both an American and a Chinese name in a subversion of the "white Christian missionary invention of the double name system to break down the hold of Chinese language and culture on converts." In other words, the question of identity is contested on linguistic grounds since the entire history and heritage of a people is threatened with extinction if ancestors become amorphous, ghostlike entities.

Lum's goal in "Translations" is to explore the complex nature of the assimilation process in terms of his understanding of his "ethnic self" as "first neither Chinese nor American." He is determined to resist all of the stereotypes perpetrated by opportunists and exploiters from both cultures, the fawning by phonies pretending to appreciate each other's exotic characteristics, which disguises the contempt they actually feel for anything differing from their own world. The "Chinaman" and the "Old Demon" who scuttle around trying to anticipate each other's preconceptions are Lum's figures for fools locked in a dance (thus the circular arrangement of part 2) of deception so that the people behind the caricatures have essentially disappeared. As Lum has eloquently put it in an essay on Asian Americans, "Denial and deceit are some of the hallmarks of the self-hatred which so often is the survival response" in the face of insidious stereotypes.

Lum's efforts in "Translations" and many other poems to overcome the "self-hatred" he deplores and to support what he calls "an ethnic identification, an understanding that there is a group of individuals who share . . . common sensibility, culture and tradition" is based on his conviction that he cannot let the people of "China-People-Street" disappear. His method stems from what he calls "an honest acceptance of who we really are." In "Translations," this means a return to the poem's opening in which a significant part of a Chinese American childhood is recalled in terms that most people would regard as entirely separate from the Asian experience that is supposed to be its defining frame. Just as he marveled at the trick camera work of mysterious ghost stories, Lum would like his readers to look with fascination rather than fear at the unfamiliar facets of a community whose strangeness does not imply hostility.

Leon Lewis